THOUGHT & THE GLORY OF THINKING

BY

TORKOM

SARAYDARIAN

T.S.G.
PUBLISHING FOUNDATION

Thought and the Glory of Thinking

© 1996 The Creative Trust

ISBN: 0-929874-27-7 (Softcover)
ISBN: 0-929874-28-5 (Hardcover)

Library of Congress Catalog Card Number 92-61034

Printed in the United States of America

Cover Design: *Tim Fisher*
                    Phoenix, Arizona

Printed by: *Data Reproductions*
                    Rochester Hills, MI 48307

Published by: **T.S.G. Publishing Foundation, Inc.**
                    P.O. Box 7068
                    Cave Creek, AZ 85331-7068
                    United States of America

Note: Meditations and visualizations are given as guidelines. They should be used with discretion and after receiving professional advice.

Dedicated to a great Teacher

Morya Sahib

Table of Contents

Diagrams

Preface

Within all manifested Universes there is one Thinker, a Kosmic Thinker. But as evolution proceeds, each kingdom develops its own way of thinking until in the human kingdom each individual develops his own way of thinking.

So, there are two kinds of *thinkers* — a Universal or Kosmic Thinker, and small thinkers. Small thinkers in the mineral, vegetable, and animal kingdoms are swayed by the thinking of the Kosmic Thinker. In the human kingdom the thinking becomes individual.

Thinkers living in certain forms think the way the Great Thinker thinks, and there is no friction between these thinkers and the Great Thinker. The only difference is that the interests of the small thinkers are mostly limited to their own individual interests. The Great Thinker thinks for the interest of all that exists.

Similarity of thinking between the Great Thinker and others occurs in those who did not yet develop their own creative thinking and in those who, because of their supreme mental achievements, are synchronized with the Supreme Thinker.

Those individuals in the human kingdom who do not think in harmony with the Great Thinker are divided into three groups:

1. Those who are insensitive to the currents of the thoughts of the Supreme Thinker because of their bad karma

2. Those who rebel against the Supreme Thinker and use their mind to distort the Laws and Principles of the Supreme Thinker to try to stop His Plans

3. Those whose mental machine is damaged and cannot operate accurately

Gradually however, thinkers in all groups approximate their thoughts to the Great Thinker after great cycles of pain and suffering. The thoughts of that Great Thinker are everywhere and in everything through an electrical substance which permeates everything. In Sanskrit it is called *mahat*, the mind stuff. The ancient Greeks used to call that which permeates all that exists *nous*.

Thinking is a complicated action. In a human being there exists a thinker who thinks on various levels. For long ages a person's thinking is limited to providing the necessities of his physical body and serving the needs of the body.

Then for a long time his thinking is limited to protecting his physical body and supplying the needs of his emotional body.

Again for long ages his thinking is limited to providing all those elements which will secure the survival of the individual human being, his clan, his group, or his nation against the interests of others.

The thinker in human form eventually makes all his bodies think harmoniously with his thinking. This is how integration is achieved. The thinker in man cannot make a breakthrough to a higher level of thinking unless he emancipates himself from the dominance of the thinking of his vehicles and their individual interests.

After his emancipation and freedom from the pressures of his vehicles, he tries to align their interests with his interests and bring about what is called *an integrated personality.*

Some thinkers can bridge the gap existing between their form and the form of others.

Each thinker must put his own mechanism in order throughout ages, releasing in his mechanism the sensitivity to a higher guidance. If such a sensitivity develops in a certain number of people, they attract each other and we now have what is called *a group.*

On each level the thinking of the vehicles synchronizes with the ruling Thinker in each man.

It sometimes happens that this Thinker prematurely stimulates the small thinkers and they come together and form an integrated entity. Instead of seeing the goal of the real Thinker, they become an independent entity with a goal separate from the goal of the Thinker. This is how a conflict starts between the prematurely integrated personality and the Thinker who has not yet sufficient power to redirect and control the sum total of the thinkers which we call the vehicles of the personality. Such a conflict often continues throughout many lives and creates those personalities who have strong integrity but are without a vision and are firmly cemented in egoism, from which proceed all inhuman actions that lead to suffering, separatism, and pain.

In a higher stage, the real Thinker makes a breakthrough, sheds light into the heart of the personality, and gains final cooperation for his goals. The Thinker uses the thoughts of the little thinkers to navigate the course of his life in many circumstances and conditions.

The real Thinker never imposes himself on the little thinkers but helps them have their own original, pure thoughts as much as possible. Through such thoughts, the Thinker prepares his symphony of life, as the conductor prepares his own orchestra.

All forms of life in Nature and in man *think.* Under ideal conditions, the whole existence thinks in harmony with the Supreme Thinker. But this ideal condition is achieved gradually over millenniums. As in man, so in Nature.

Progress is accomplished through certain crises. Sometimes the Thinker and the small thinkers cannot get along, and each works for its separate ends. It is in such a state that chaos starts in the entire form, and the thinkers act against each other's interest without realizing that a common interest will be the road to their own survival.

Chaos leads to disintegration. Mother Nature dissolves all those forms that cannot reach their destination and builds new forms to carry on Her plan. Disintegration can be seen first in the quality of the thoughts of the little thinkers. Then it spreads to their mechanisms, no matter what they are — a cell, an organ, a man, a nation, a planet, a solar system, or a galaxy.

Man is in a stage of consciousness in which he can realize that he is only a symbol to explain the mystery of the *One Thinker*. There is only One Thinker above all forms, manifested or unmanifested, tangible or intangible. It is this Thinker Who thinks through each atom, each cell, and each form in any magnitude.

In the past, people created a term: "inanimate matter." Upon such an erroneous concept we built a whole civilization of materialism. In the future, we will understand that there is no inanimate matter, but *all* lives, feels, and thinks. Upon such a concept, the new civilization will be built — a civilization of conscious livingness.

Thinking goes wrong in little thinkers because of a factor that is given by the Great Thinker to each atom, cell, form, and entity. This factor is called "choice." It is this factor of choice which *chooses*, first naturally, then mechanically, then consciously.

Natural choice is always in harmony with the Thinker in Nature, but it has no individual merit. Mechanical choice is the critical point in which a right or wrong choice is made according to the accumulated right or wrong data in the form. Conscious choice is always in harmony with the Thinker in Nature.

The difference between natural choice and conscious choice is that in natural choice there is no independent thinker, while in conscious choice there is an independent thinker who is fully coordinated and harmonized with the One Thinker. The living form which uses natural choice is like the wheel of a big car; the living entity which uses conscious choice is like the driver of the car. One is closer to attaining global, solar, or Cosmic responsibilities. The other is still a little seed dreaming about a great vision.

The human soul, the real thinker, thinks mechanically and becomes an automaton when he is lost in the thinking of the physical, astral, and mental atoms or centers and has no thought of his own. He begins to think only when he becomes aware of the thinking of the personality and develops his own thinking to provide better conditions for his personality.

The thinker in man must develop his own thinking, independent from his physical, emotional, and even mental thinking. He must also develop his thinking independent from other individuals' thinking and mass thinking. Independent thinking is an effort to think in harmony with the Thinker in Nature.

The Great Thinker, to coordinate the process of thinking in Nature, provides various means to awaken the power of thinking and even provides great

Individualities to teach the science of thinking. These Individualities have different names in the history of humanity. For example, they are called Great Beings, Great Lives, Archangels, Avatars, Saviors, Leaders, and Solar Angels. They cyclically appear and indwell in humanity, and even in man, and teach the science of thinking.

So man is composed of vehicles which we call physical, emotional, and mental bodies. Each body has its own form of thinking. The unit of consciousness in man has a great job to integrate these lower forms of thinking, to make them work harmoniously with his advanced thinking, to synchronize them, and to create a thinking that meets the needs of all the vehicles and the thinking unit.

When this is achieved, then his joy is to make himself sensitive to higher Thinkers, to planetary, solar, and Kosmic Thinkers, gradually forming a part of greater and more advanced groups.

The human soul is an ever progressive light. Innately he is in harmony with Kosmic thinking, but as he evolves he develops his own thinking as does every living form, every entity in the Universe on the path of its unfoldment.

Often the human soul's thinking is unconsciously different from the Kosmic Thinker's. These moments of difference are the moments of crises, learning, adjustment, pain, and suffering, leading finally into harmony. The thinking of each unit of consciousness is conditioned by its needs and by the needs of the Great Thinkers in whose body he is a cell or organ.

Each unit of consciousness has also a tremendous urge to follow his independent thinking, which finally leads to harmony with the Kosmic Thinker.

The science of thinking gives man the keys to open all the mysteries of Creation. As man creates integrity within himself, enabling his nature to think harmoniously, in the same way must the nucleus of a nation or of humanity create integrity until all men and women in the nation think in harmony with each other for a supreme goal, for each and for all.

As such, the process of integration is the effort and duty of each human being and each nation in relation to global humanity; so also is the process going on in each solar system and galaxy and in all manifestation. All that is manifested eventually will form a symphony, and the great Composer will eventually achieve the great Consummation.

Of course, this process of orchestration of a man, a nation, a solar system, or a galaxy will pass through constructive and destructive crises until the Composer achieves His vision.

Thinking is the process of orchestration of Nature as a whole. Man can be a co-worker with that great Thinker or great Composer by gradually merging his thoughts with the thoughts of the Kosmic Thinker.

In summary, man is composed of vehicles which we call physical, emotional, and mental bodies. Each body has its own form of thinking. The unit of consciousness in man has a great job to integrate these lower forms of thinking to work harmoniously with his advanced thinking, to synchronize them and create a thinking that meets the needs of all the vehicles and the thinking unit.

When this is achieved then his joy is to make himself sensitive to higher Thinkers, to planetary, solar, and Kosmic Thinkers, gradually forming a part of greater and advanced groups.

The human soul is an ever progressive light. Innately he is in harmony with Kosmic thinking, but as he evolves he develops his own thinking as does every living form, every entity in the Universe, on the path of its unfoldment.

Often the human soul's thinking is unconsciously different from the Kosmic Thinker. These moments of difference are the moments of crises, learning, adjustment, pain, and suffering leading finally into harmony. The thinking of each unit of consciousness is conditioned by its needs, and by the needs of great Thinkers in whose body he is a cell or organ.

Each unit of consciousness has also a tremendous urge to follow his independent thinking, which finally leads to harmony with the Kosmic Thinker.

This book is an effort to inspire such a vision and create enthusiasm for that goal.

Introduction
Thought and Responsibility

What is thought? What does thought do? How can we use thought for our advantage? How can we exploit the mysteries of thought and be responsible for our thoughts?

The Living Ethics says,

> *One more misconception: often, because of ignorance and self-justification, people think that their thought is insignificant and can reach nowhere, whereas the potentiality of thought is great, and for thought there exists neither space nor time. But those who think chaotically are, like those who wave their hands in the dark, unaware of the object they hit. Moreover, thought accumulates in space. One can conceive of a mighty choir of harmonious thoughts, but one can also imagine a flock of chattering black jackdaws. Such congregations also fill space and disturb the higher worlds. Dear thinkers, jackdaws, you are also responsible for the quality of your thoughts. Thus, even you create your future.*[1]

"One more misconception." What is the misconception? "Often, because of ignorance and self-justification, people think that their thought is insignificant." People think that when they think here, there, and everywhere, about this thing, about that thing, their thoughts are insignificant. Being insignificant means that thought does not create a result, does not influence people, does not create problems, or does not create creative activities. But the Great Sage says that thought is a very powerful energy, an electromagnetic energy which we release every time we think, and this thought goes and sticks to chairs, to people, to walls, to tables, in space, in people's minds, and everywhere. It is something that

---

1. Agni Yoga Society, *Hierarchy*, para. 172.

we must be careful about because every minute we are releasing thoughts. Every minute we are thinking and we are releasing thoughts. Either those thoughts are going to build something beautiful or something destructive.

The first line says, "one more misconception." Actually, if we think about the Teaching and think about how to define the Teaching, we can define the Teaching as something which disperses the illusions, the unreality, the misconceptions, the misunderstandings, and establishes reality. This is a very, very nice definition. If somebody asks you what the Teaching is, say that the Teaching is like a light which eradicates misconceptions, illusions, and misunderstandings.

What are misconceptions, illusions, and misunderstandings? They are some kind of form in our mental body which eats the reality and does not let our brain, our body, our mind, our hands, our feet to work through reality. Whenever you do not work with reality, in reality, you are in danger because you are deceiving yourself. You do not have the right tools in your hands. You do not have right understanding about the problems, about the need, and now you are in chaos.

What does the Teaching do? The Teaching takes your mind and puts it into reality. That is the greatest power of the Teaching. When your mind is not in reality, you are always in the wrong direction. You are not successful, you are not healthy, and you do not have right human relations with other people because all your thoughts are based on unreality. The greatest power of the Teaching is to clear your mind of misconceptions.

One misconception is that you think your thoughts are insignificant. The Sage says that there are two reasons that you think this. First, there is self-justification. You say, "These thoughts are nothing. I can think about them, play with them." You justify yourself to do these things. Second, you are ignorant about the effects of thoughts. Because you are ignorant, you use your thoughts destructively and in such a way that in the future you will see that every thought that you created became an obstacle on your future path.

The first thing to learn from this verse is that we must think that everything we are thinking is very important. It is important because it affects our health, our relationships, our moods, our destiny, our future, the destiny of people, their relationships, their health, right human relations. Also it goes beyond to space and it destroys if it is a bad thought the rhythm, the harmony of the Universe. We think it is a little thought, but thoughts travel through space and time whether they are good or bad thoughts.

The other day I was talking with someone. I said, "There are no big things and no small things. Everything is equal to each other." A microbe is a giant. A giant is a microbe. A little virus enters into a man, and that powerful man is destroyed in ten days. An elephant hits a man, and the man goes to the hospital and recovers or dies. There are no big and small. There is only one measure. If you analyze this thought, you will find that people are wrong in thinking that there are things bigger and things smaller. There are no small and big things. They are all the same size but because of their relation to other things, they seem bigger or they seem smaller. So when you are thinking, check your thoughts — small thoughts, big thoughts, square thoughts, triangular thoughts. Check them. What kind of thoughts are they?

Thoughts also are not big or small, but their quality is important. What is the quality of your thoughts — constructive or destructive? Lofty thoughts are constructive, creative, uplifting, purifying thoughts. Destructive thoughts are criminal, polluting, and confusing thoughts.

"People think that their thought is insignificant and can reach nowhere." But the reality is that insignificant thoughts can reach everywhere, and there is no space and time for them. That is very interesting. For thoughts there is no time and space. The Teacher says that every thought is an electromagnetic wave which when it enters into space, which is an ocean of electromagnetism, does so instantaneous. What happens? You think here about a crime. That thought immediately is gone. It has gone maybe to China, and some people pick up that thought and commit a crime. You are responsible in the universal computer for committing that crime because you originated that thought. That thought went and was absorbed by one who had the same frequency or was very susceptible or very weak, or the thought was strengthened by an entity and carried over to that man to make him a slave of that thought. These things are so beautiful to know about because later you can guide your mind.

An interesting thing is that no matter what your social position and educational position, it does not matter. Always you can err in thinking — whether you are high or low, whether you are fat or lean, whether you are rich or poor. That power is given to you to create thoughts, to think.

Some people create fantastic thoughtforms. For example, this Temple is a thoughtform. Do you see how beautiful it is? Somebody thought about this and things came together and here we have a Temple. If that man was a thousand years ahead, the Temple would be different because the thought would be different.

Thought not only creates the outer things that you want to create with your thought, but also it creates your whole body. One day scientists will be able to find some devices and apparatuses to know how your voice and thought create the corresponding chemistry which builds your body, your emotions, your mind, your spirit.

Thought is the creator of chemistry. All of you are surrounded with thoughts. Wherever you live, you are surrounded with the thoughts that were created by those who were living there. The Great Sage says that a thought needs sometimes two thousand years to leave a place.

We are told that in olden times people built new palaces for new kings so that they were not contaminated or polluted or conditioned by the accumulated, old thoughtforms in the old palaces. In Akbar's kingdom they always tried to destroy the old palaces or do activities in them which were opposite to the activities done before. In this way they destroyed the thoughtforms, and the new king could think without being conditioned by the previous thoughts existing there. That is why it is sometimes nice to build a new house and dwell in it, instead of renting, instead of buying. But of course there are methods with which you can purify them. More or less you can purify them.

The important thing is that thoughts are there, and subconsciously or consciously they are influencing you. Slowly, slowly they are making you think in the way the thoughtforms were organized in that house.

There was a friend of mine who bought a house in which two insane people used to live. The family remodeled and changed everything, painted, used lots of incense, and so on. Eventually, ten years later, they noticed that their minds were flipping out of control. Thoughts slowly, slowly, gradually but eventually ate them up. Science will laugh at this, but they have lots of proof that the thoughts of others are influencing them.

Thoughts are energies, and they have a kind of energy that sticks to your walls. If you invite a guest and you see that he is very obnoxious, is thinking very wildly, very crudely, very incoherently, remember that eventually these thoughtforms, like little entities, will stick to your walls. For a while they do not resonate. But immediately you start thinking, talking about something similar to them, they say, "Hi, we are here," and start influencing your mind. People think this is superstition. How come radio waves are affecting us from here to China? And the mind is the best radio station.

"Moreover thought accumulates in space." There is a chapter about this in *A Treatise on Cosmic Fire*.[2] All the little thoughts from little people, little groups, little men, little nations go and collect themselves according to their frequencies in space. That is very beautiful to think about. There is order and rule and law in Nature. Imagine that the whole of Nature is a computer, and we are in that computer as computer chips, acting and doing the same things voluntarily and involuntarily, consciously and unconsciously. We are in that big computer. Thoughts go and accumulate according to their frequencies. For example, there are thoughts of beauty, thoughts of heroism, thoughts of friendship, thoughts of love, thoughts of sacrifice, thoughts of goodness, joy, freedom. These thoughts accumulate in certain spaces of the Universe.

Evil thoughts accumulate in other places. For example there are thoughts of war, thoughts of crime, horror, violence. Imagine how many are accumulating! Every day our radios and televisions are filling space with tons of violence, tons of ugliness, tons of crimes. They are accumulating.

All people are antennas. You are little antennas. You see, the old fashioned teaching is finished! You are all antennas receiving these things. Both kinds of thoughts you are receiving. You are receiving both because sometimes you are beautiful and sometimes you are ugly. You are catching everything and creating inner turmoil, inner friction, inner destruction. You don't know which thought is good.

---

2.   Alice A. Bailey, *A Treatise on Cosmic Fire*.

If your discrimination is strong, if your character is strong, you slowly, slowly cut yourself from this antenna and focus yourself in that antenna where there are beautiful thoughts. Once you are hooked into beautiful thoughts, your life changes. Your life becomes beautiful because the reservoir of the whole energy is there. According to your striving, wishes, and desires, this energy is coming to you, impressions are coming to you, higher creativity is coming to you.

First you will experience health, happiness, joy, freedom. Second, you will have high aspirations. You will say, "I wish every man in the world would have food to eat and a place to live, that all these crimes would stop, that my body transforms and that I become like the angels to help people, to be everywhere." This is aspiration.

Then, mentally tremendous ideas come to your mind, but you must hook them. That is the meaning of meditation.

What is meditation? Meditation is schooling to teach you how to think good thoughts. That is it . . . . Every day you sit for five, ten, fifteen minutes and create beautiful thoughts.

Let us say your seed thought is *beauty*. "I want to be beautiful in my dressing, in my expressions, in my face, in my hair, in my relationships, in my words, in my thoughts, in my aspirations, in my letters, in my books, in my creative functions." In that fifteen minute meditation you are training your mind to think only good thoughts. If you do it for three months, three years, thirty years, your mind will learn to think in the right way. Then immediately when an ugly thought comes, the mind rejects it because the mind itself forms a mechanism that rejects ugly thoughts. From that moment you can see that your life is becoming rich, your family life is becoming rich, your friendship is becoming rich. Many people do not have good friends, a good environment. You create a good condition by becoming a container of a superiorly beautiful water that comes from space. You fill yourself, and you share that fullness, that water, that creativity.

The Great Sage says that thoughts recognize neither time nor space. They are instantaneous. If I think something good here, it went already into your mind. Look how responsible I am to think right thoughts! Later I will be sorry if I know that my thoughts really misled you.

The Teaching, the meaning of the Teaching, the work of the Teaching is to create reality so that you do not walk in the mist, in the fog, in the hallucination, in the phenomena. Wherever you stop you know that it is real — something you are seeing is real, something you are hearing is real, something you are doing is real, something they are doing is real. Your life slowly, slowly goes "from the unreal to the real."

"One can conceive of a mighty choir of harmonious thoughts, but one can also imagine a flock of chattering black jackdaws." When I meditated on this and thought about this, I found out that He is saying that thoughts have *sound*. I have had that experience. One day someone was thinking something about me.

I *heard* what he was thinking. Then I realized that thought can turn into sound in my ear. What a complicated mechanism!

We know from the movie industry, for example, the shadows on the film go through a mechanism and become music or talk. We have already found it and we know about it. Why will it be impossible to hear your thoughts? But that can be a very unfortunate thing. When everyone can hear everyone's thoughts, they will the next day be crazy. It signifies something. Our thoughts are still not on the level of constructiveness and beauty. Do you see how interesting this is? Eventually, we are going to be clairaudient to our thoughts.

Some people hear voices. I examined, I worked through the years to find out from where these voices are coming. It is their thoughts they are listening to, plus other thoughts, of course, but first you listen to your thoughts.

All these things mean that *you are going slowly to develop a little attention, a little control and mastery over your thoughts.* When you are thinking ask, "Is it real or unreal?" "It is real." Then the second question, "Is it beautiful or ugly?" "It is ugly." Do not have anything to do with it because to occupy yourself with those ugly thoughts means to put your finger into the hornet's nest.

"Dear thinkers, jackdaws, you are also responsible for the quality of your thoughts. Thus, even you create your future." This is very significant. Whatever you are thinking, that is what you are going to become. First time in the life Buddha said, "Everything is created by thoughts." Everything? What about me? You are created by your own thoughts. Little, little thoughts, over centuries, over millions of years create what you are — a Logos or a trash.

The future is created by you. The physical future is collected in the physical permanent atom. Whatever you are speaking, thinking, the atom is registering; and according to the registration of the atom will be the creativity of the atom which is building your physical body.

It is so interesting. We think very chaotically. For ten minutes we think about beautiful things. For another ten minutes we think about ugly things. Now we have two kinds of chemistry building our body. Half is sickness, destruction, disintegration; half is very beautiful. That is our life. How to minimize the thoughts that are chaotic, ugly, criminal, unpurposeful, contradictory and replace them with thoughts that are creative, beautiful, future oriented, harmless, inclusive . . . especially inclusive!

Inclusive thoughts create the healthiest body. Inclusive thoughts create the healthiest group, the healthiest nation. Look at the nations that are suffering. In Europe they are suffering. Millions of people are in agony. It is because of destructive, separative thought — my religion, your religion, my country, your country. What are we saying? Fifty years later, people will laugh at us.

Our future is built by our own thoughts. Not only our physical body but also our future activities, our future positions, our future talents, our future victories and achievements — all are built in the little, little thoughts that have been accumulated throughout the ages. They become huge and influential, and eventually they show us that whatever we thought, that is what we are going to see with our eyes.

Again we come back to the idea that if we want to have a beautiful life in this world, in other worlds, because other worlds are the continuation of this world, we must have good thoughts. It is a circle. You come here for seventy years, go to the astral plane, go to the mental plane, and come down again and become a baby, then go again. That is the computer of the world.

Q&A

Question: *How do we protect ourselves from ugly thoughtforms? How do we keep them out?*

Answer: Increasing your meditation and good thoughts keeps ugly thoughtforms out. Let us say you are in the middle of the ocean. You make concentric waves that go out, and other waves do not come in. Increase your meditation, increase your good thoughts, increase your reading. Immediately when you find out that somewhere you flipped, catch it and repair it. For example, when you are talking about a friend you said, "That son of a gun." Correct it. Say, "I am sorry. I did not mean that. He is a very good man." Now you have started to be a conscious disciple. You are taking your life in your hands consciously, and you are leading that life into future glory. That is what you need to do.

Now there was a lady who came and said, "I have migraine headaches." Of course the medical profession has ten, fifteen reasons why people get migraine headaches. For me there is only one reason — mixed, chaotic thinking. Electrical waves hit your cells right and left, good and bad, let's do, let's not do, let's go, let's not go. It is chaotic. There is no purpose, there is no relationship between thoughts. That creates migraine headaches. But then you say, "Migraine headaches are associated with certain chemicals." But where did these chemicals come from? The source of chemicals is your thinking.

The source of chemicals is your thinking. Think about love and analyze your saliva. Think about a crime and analyze your saliva. Both are different. How can that be? Thought is chemical. This science is going to come. Search for this science.

Question: *Do the thoughts that come from the television or the radio stick to the walls the same way? When the news is on, you don't know what they are going to say next.*

Answer: Yes. That is what our calamity is. We are unprotected and are slaves. When a man comes and says, "I will kill you," it is going to your bones, and that event is linking you to an ugly accumulation of thoughts. They do not know what they are doing to the nation, to humanity, but one day they will pay for it. The five senses register everything immediately and even more than you think. Sometimes consciously you cannot see a few things, but unconsciously you can see the motives even, the vibration. Whatever is registered is a part of your experience. You experience it. It means there are some recordings in your computer. That computer, who knows when, by what laws and rules, will reactivate it again. We do not know yet, but we are slowly seeing that it is a very complicated thing.

Yesterday I was reading that a scientist was cutting the brain of a salamander and flipping it over and putting it on the other side. The salamander could still think, and move. The scientist does not know where the memory is. If he wants to know where the memory is, he must read about the writings of the Great Teachers.

Question: What is the relationship between silence and thought?

Answer: Thought is always silence until it becomes sound. The impressions that are coming from the tower to your television have no picture. The picture is created at the right moment when it hits the mechanism of your television.

Question: What is the difference between a thought and a thought that is spoken?

Answer: Thoughts that are spoken are sometimes more powerful, and sometimes very distorted. Speech can distort the real thoughts. Sometimes it amplifies. Sometimes it distorts. For example, if you have a good thought and you cannot really formulate that thought, your thought is dead or paralyzed or half dead. But if you can formulate it exactly as it is, then your thought is amplified.

Question: Why is a silent OM more powerful than an OM that is sounded?

Answer: That is very interesting. In sounding the OM you sometime put your personality into it, your wishes, your desires, your ego, your vanity. There was a man who would shout the OM. He was putting his personality into it. Wherever there is personality, it is weaker than the soul. In the silent OM you do not have vanity, ego, you do not have interest, self-interest, and really you go into the OM. But a personality OM is an outside phenomena. It is not real.

Question: *How do you tell the difference between the thoughts you have created and thoughts you are receiving?*

Answer: For a long time you cannot. That is my experience, not that I am making any order. For me, for a long time I could not find which were my thoughts, the thoughts of the Solar Angel, the thoughts of great Thinkers, the thoughts of space, the thoughts of the Solar Logos, and beyond. I could not find the difference. But eventually I found it, and it is in this book.

It is not easy to find where the thoughts are coming from. Imagine, thoughts are coming from all televisions and radios, from all people everywhere, from all initiates up to Hierarchy, from all great Initiates higher than Hierarchy, from all centers of galaxies. These thoughts are all here, but they all have their own frequencies. They do not mix. When you raise your frequency, you tap into them and receive them. That is the beauty.

Eventually you must start experimenting with these kinds of things. Eventually you are going to say, "Today I received a thought from my father," or "some thoughts from a creative thoughtform of space." What is the difference? The first time the difference does not make any difference, but eventually you get used to it. You can learn it and discriminate it. When you discriminate it, it means you have raised your level to tap into another higher level of origin of thoughts.

Question: *Can the thoughts from a great Thinker cancel and annihilate the ugly thoughts of masses of people at a lower level?*

Answer: They do sometimes. But, this is a very controversial discussion. For example, a great Avatar sends light to a nation and disperses its bad thoughts for a hundred years. After two hundred years their condition becomes worse than before because they did not reach that height by their own hands and feet.

Sometimes, when you have disciples, you can see these things. You have a disciple and you tell him everything, everything. Then he becomes the most obnoxious man. You leave him, and he goes down to the place he came from. Everything that you are becoming must be the result of your striving and labor. Nobody can make you somebody. You must make yourself somebody. That is the right way to go.

Question: *How do thoughts transform substance?*

Answer: Do you know what you are asking? Thought is matter. Lower mind is matter. Higher mind is matter plus substance. The Intuitional Plane is totally substance. What is substance? It stands under matter. It is the prototype, the archetype of the matter.

Question: *Would the results of one's negative thought be linked to persons serving time in prison? Are they spending time in prison for an act they committed that really is the result of imported thoughts to them to commit that act? Are they really guilty, or is it the person who originated the thought?*

Answer: Always it is possible to overcome yourself and change things. This is a Universe in which not everything stands as it is. You can change things by higher fire, by higher dedication, by higher energy and power. In the future most of you are going to write pamphlets to prisoners, saying that in the past you were a criminal. It does not matter. Now what can you do to be an angel in the future? The prison time — ten or fifty years — is nothing in comparison to eternity! You have eternity in front of you.

Nobody does this. It is, "Sit in the electric chair and die." Judge them. Sentence them. Destroy them. They have already been destroyed five hundred times in the trial. It was easier for them if they were killed immediately. Do you understand?

You must do something! You must tell your neighbors, "You are thinking wrong." How to think right? How to have right movies, right theaters? Write articles and teach people. The greatest thing now is to write such kinds of beautiful articles in the way that you can pass through the doors of the prisons and teach them how to think about the future.

Poor people, they must not die hopeless. They did something, so what! Who did not do anything? The Bible says something that I like, "Every man is guilty." There is no "innocent man," or else you will not be here on this planet. You are here. It is proof that you were obnoxious. So, give hope to them.

We must send lots of the books to prisoners. Prisons need lots and lots of help, especially prison guards.

Question: *How does jackdaws' chattering affect our life?*

Answer: The chattering of jackdaws creates the urge to fight. It leads to depression, sickness, and argumentative behavior. It encourages us not to think and to be satisfied with the mechanical thinking of others. It creates static in our brain, confusion, greed, and great tension. Concentration becomes difficult if those near you are "jackdaws."

Question: *Can you talk about accumulation of thoughts?*

Answer: As we said, thought accumulates in space, on the walls of our homes, on the furniture, and in the objects we use or touch. Your pencil has many thoughts stuck to it. That is why in olden days people used to keep the pens or pencils of great people as a source of inspiration. Stronger and more elevated thoughts dissolve or transmute the weaker thoughts.

As the thoughts of a man affect his life through his health, planning, and direction, so do the saturated thoughts of a nation, of humanity, of the planetary life. This is why it is so imperative that the science of thinking be the most important science taught to humanity.

Thought creates the chemistry of glands, the chemistry of organs, the chemistry of man's dense and subtle bodies. Thought creates the chemistry of relationships of groups, nations, humanity. All events in the world are the result of ideas and thoughts.

If we learn how to create and use thoughts according to Cosmic laws and principles, we can create the most productive conditions in the world to succor the happiness of humanity and the graduation of humanity from the school of this planetary life.

Question: What is chaotic thinking?

Answer: Chaotic thinking is

- purposeless thinking

- thinking without a plan

- contradictory thinking

- thinking without a goal

- harmful thinking

- mechanical thinking

- unconscious thinking

- uncontrolled thinking

- limited thinking

- selfish thinking

- uninspired thinking

- thinking without vision

These forms of thinking harm our body and relationships and lead us to ultimate failure.

Chaotic thinking disturbs the Higher Worlds and creates barriers between Higher Worlds and our earth, cutting the source of supply of inspiration and guidance both in man and in the Universe. We become cut from the world of beauty and follow ugliness. Any disturbance causes crime, war, ugliness, chaos, totalitarianism, and interference.

Chaotic thought prevents concentration and continuity. Creativity becomes impossible.

Question: Is thought affected by time and space?

Answer: Thought has no obstacles. Thoughts penetrate every home on the planet and affect every man and living being, regardless of time and space. Thought even accumulates on objects. People give gifts which are flooded with their thoughts. Houses, the furniture we use are charged with our thoughts. Accumulations of thoughts in space become thought currents which either inspire you, depress you, or mislead you. Discrimination of thought currents is very important.

Thoughts can go through various processes:

1. Originator of thought

2. Creative formation of thought

3. Distortion of thought

4. Reflectors of thought

5. Merchants of thought

6. Manipulation of thought

7. Customers of thought

The originators of thought are thinkers who are impressed by powerful ethical impressions. They are the Cosmic, Solar, and Planetary Souls, the Initiates, the Solar Angels, and the human souls. What happens after that depends on the response or reaction of the recipient.

The future depends on your thought. Good, high thoughts lead to health, prosperity, peace, harmony, joy. Ugly, evil thoughts lead to disease, crime, anarchy, death.

Chaotic thinking disturbs the Higher Worlds — the Higher Worlds in the planet, the Higher Worlds within you.

The future depends on your thoughts because thoughts are the soul of your future.

Meditation trains your mind to manufacture high and lofty thoughts. It builds your bright future.

Question: What about books?

Answer: Books carry an enormous amount of thoughtforms. The author is responsible for the thoughts he spreads throughout his book. It will be possible to measure the power of books through some electrical machine.

The most practical books are those that speak about future joy, light, love, and virtues and contain pure knowledge.

Every book has a duplicate form in the Subtle World. Both affect the consciousness of humanity.

Sometimes the book in the Subtle Worlds is the originator of the tangible book. Those who read a book broadcast the thoughtforms attached to it and make the subtle book active in spreading its influence in the Subtle Worlds.

Some entities communicate through such books. The *I Ching* is one of them. The *Bhagavad Gita* and the *New Testament* are others.

My father used to concentrate for a moment and ask a question in his mind, then open the book, put his finger on a page, and there was his answer. The answer was from the Subtle World. It put his finger on the spot where the answer was. Of course, these answers are not straight answers. One must think for a moment to understand the subtle answer which meets the question.

When someone distorts and changes the book, its subtle counterpart sends a distorted frequency which affects very negatively the person who made the changes in the actual book. Sometimes the changes are so vicious that the book is severed from the subtle one.

There are some books in the Kalachakra series which are strongly protected by thoughtforms. If they are read by an uninitiated one, very negative events occur in their life, even sometimes they die or contract terrible diseases. The thoughtform, like an electrical sphere, protects the book from those who are not worthy to read it.

> ***Question:*** *How can we protect ourselves from the attacks of ugly thoughts?*

Answer: Thoughts are not necessarily aggressive unless you invoke or evoke them through your own thoughts or behavior. The ideal attitude in the world of thought is to have a mind that is devoted to great achievement. Such a mind will gradually tap the sources of creative thought in himself or in the Universe.

A man also must be careful that when he contacts a current of higher thought he tries to keep its purity and tries to translate it in the simplest ways.

Sometimes a creative current of thought assumes manifold translations. Sometimes the translations even contradict each other because the receiving agent did not have the needed purity of mind and was either polluted by vanity and ego or was confused or self-interested. Pure thought needs a pure receiver.

1

Sources of Thoughts

Thoughts are electrical waves with different frequencies and voltages emanating from minds.

People move constantly within the presence of thoughts. Thoughts exist in space, and they have their life cycles. Some live long years and influence people's minds and Nature as a whole. Some live a short life, and some fade away right after they are born.

Human minds radiate thoughtwaves constantly. They create them or reflect them. They amplify them or weaken them. Thoughtwaves always keep the human mind and human life busy.

You can accept thoughts or reject them. You can see the effects of your thoughts on others and on yourself. Also, you can see the effects of the thoughts of others on life in general. You can produce thoughts that are beautiful and that help you and others enjoy life and progress on the path of perfection.

Thoughts as objects can be known and brought under your control through

1. observation
2. concentration
3. discrimination

These three steps will enable you to master your thought life and use your thoughts creatively.

Through observation you can find out how thoughts are produced, their quality, the sources of various thoughts, and how and by what centers they are registered.

Some people do not know that they have thoughts. They do not know that thoughts exist as separate objects. In some cases they are identified with their thoughts.

There are mainly eight sources of thoughts:

1. Thoughts are produced by lower level human beings. These beings are mostly focused in the centers below the diaphragm. Eighty percent of all thoughtforms are generated by such beings. They are mostly thoughtforms of

desires such as sex, food, objects, anger, fear, and greed. Although these thoughts live a short life, like flies they multiply at a high speed and affect the human mind to a great extent.

With observation, concentration, and discrimination you will be able to find the source of these thoughts, how and through what center you registered them, and how to take right action toward them.

People are of the opinion that thoughts are registered only by the brain. This is not true. You can register thoughts with your whole aura. Thoughts affect the centers in your etheric, emotional, and mental bodies by synchronizing or tuning in with them. It is important to find out where the thoughts are registered and how they create independent reactions from your centers or conscious responses from your mind.

2. Thoughts are projected or emanated from lower entities trapped in etheric or astral spheres. They have a powerful urge to come in contact with living beings to satisfy physical cravings that have been taken away from them. These thoughts are related to various crimes dealing with narcotics, alcohol, sex, etc., and they create serious pollution once they find a person or group to broadcast them. Often they build a contact with a person's mind. If they are accepted, they slowly obsess and possess him and lead him to those experiences through which they satisfy their cravings, urges, and drives.

Most of the thoughts of an average man are influenced by such thoughts, and, because he is not aware of the source, he thinks these thoughts are his own thoughts and he tries to actualize them.

Through observation, concentration, and discrimination a person can stop such kinds of thoughts before they become rooted in his mind. Like a watchful guard he says, "Wait a minute. Who are you?" And in some cases he may reject them.

If such thoughts are not checked with discrimination, and if they have a chance to penetrate your mind, you become their victim because you feel that they are your own thoughts and your body and emotions obey your thoughts. Ninety percent of the people do not have guards on their mental door. They do not have fences, and thoughts of a lower order ceaselessly penetrate their mental territory.

Through observation, concentration, and discrimination, one finds the sources of thoughts.

We must remember that lower thoughts enslave us; higher thoughts liberate us from our limitations.

3. Thoughts are produced by the Fiery World. These are higher thoughts. The Fiery World is the mental plane and higher planes. In those planes there are many entities who know how to think and project creative thoughts. Also, the

Fiery World is the world in which living human beings can create their thoughts, if they are advanced enough on the Path.

These thoughts are projected directly or indirectly, and received voluntarily or involuntarily. They impress our aura and influence our life. These thoughts are not our own thoughts, but we identify with them and think they are our own thoughts. Actually, we are not thinking, but thoughts are reaching our mind and creating mental responses.

These thoughts are mostly on the line of creativity. They are thoughts that meet the problems of our life, thoughts that inspire us to make progress. They carry great ideas and visions.

It is important to know that lower entities or undeveloped human beings do not think, but they reflect thoughts after coloring them with their glamors, maya, vices, and blind urges and drives. The most dangerous thought is a thought which has a high origin but is colored by the desires, glamors, and blind urges and drives of a lower entity or person and projected into space.

You will be able to discriminate among thoughts through their results or effects. There are thoughts which urge you to take a certain action, but you feel resistance from your inner being. You do not like such thoughts, but eventually they may weaken your resistance and make you obey.

When you learn to observe the mechanisms of thoughts, you can eventually discriminate among them and either protect yourself from them, take action to rechannel them, or even destroy them.

One must experiment in the field of thoughts because they are the main force center making life move in a destructive or constructive direction. Learning about thoughts is the first step. Experimenting in the field of thoughts and gathering realistic experiences will lead you into greater creativity and success.

Through observation you will one day suddenly see that you are able to detect the sources of your thoughts and the centers which are welcoming them. It is after such an experience that you begin to take action to prevent the thoughts that are not in line with your plan and purpose.

You will see that there are thoughts that are like thieves; they sneak in in mysterious ways and try to control your life. Once you raise yourself above the mental plane, it will be a game and a joy for you to deal with these thieves and learn the mechanics of thought.

If human beings do not learn the mechanics of thought and how to discriminate among various thoughts, they will soon be invaded by the thoughts of lower entities and lower human beings and our civilization once more will sink to its barbaric level. We see the evidence of such degeneration in the increasing crime, increasing violence, exploitations, and vanities of the leaders of nations.

Lower thoughts have a high-voltage magnetism due to their astral or emotional content, and they are very contagious once they capture the lower centers of man.

Thoughts that come from the Fiery World have, in fact, a fiery nature. You can sense their fiery nature through your heart, throat, and head centers. You feel these thoughts throughout your aura and on the spine. You feel the fire in your enthusiasm, joy, and aspiration. This fire creates great colors and flames in your aura. The Fiery World is not a symbolic expression but an expression of reality.[1]

Fiery thoughts create action, striving, renunciation, patience, sacrifice, and the urge to create. Through fiery thoughts you burn and melt many hindrances. It is very important that you develop sensitivity to fiery thoughts because they give you guidance and open you to infinite values. They guide you when you are stuck in problems. But if you cannot register various thoughts and discriminate among them, they cannot help you because you will follow your habitual path instead of registering the thoughts of guidance from the Higher World.

In order to be able to register fiery thoughts, one must elevate his consciousness. Unless one elevates his consciousness, the thoughts that are projected from the Fiery World will be mixed with his lower thoughts and glamors and eventually will create reverse effects.

When the fiery thoughts reach your aura and you are not able to record them and use them, they will be used as food for your base thoughts and will create great complications in your life.

Those who contact the Fiery World without being ready for it prepare their own destruction.

4. There are still other sources from which great currents of thought reach us. One of them is the domain of the *Plan*, and another source is from the world of *Purpose*. The Plan radiates streams of thoughts and ideas. They are very creative and powerful, and they are related to the culture and civilization of humanity. Thoughts from the Plan are related to the seven fields of human endeavor, and they help us create changes and bring new vision into those seven fields. Thoughts coming from the Plan create cooperation, harmony, understanding, and service.

Thoughts coming from the Purpose are dynamic, electrical, and revelatory. They operate like lightning and give you a sudden realization of facts which reveal the Path and the destination of the Path. Thoughts coming from the Purpose create willpower, direction, consistency, stability, endurance, solemnity, striving, and inclusiveness.

By observing the thoughts you eventually learn to discriminate between them.

---

1. For more information on the Fiery World, see *Other Worlds*. Also see *New Dimensions in Healing* for information on centers.

5. Thoughts come from your Solar Angel. These thoughts are very uplifting, inspiring, and encouraging, and they awaken in you a spirit of striving and achievement. The thoughts of the Solar Angel are sources of wisdom and are like seeds for your garden of creativity. The thoughts of the Solar Angel inspire you by giving you endurance and equilibrium during the dark nights of your life.

When a man is in the process of paying great amounts of karmic debt, the thoughts of the Solar Angel make him pay them joyfully, willingly, silently, and without complaint.

Another very peculiar characteristic of the thoughts coming from the Solar Angel is righteousness. You see clearly that all that is happening to you is righteous. This gives you a great release, and you prepare yourself to pay your karma in joy and in patience.

Observation is the characteristic of a man who wants to advance. Those who do not want to advance are called "gophers." A gopher is a man who does not observe. He lives underground and is happy there.

Observation is the road to progress. Observe your actions and reactions. Try to find the origin of your actions. Try to recognize and discriminate among your thoughts, and you will be a wise man.

6. Another source of thoughts is the human soul. As the human soul advances, he changes the source of his thoughts; he tries to receive thoughts from higher and higher sources, and a time comes when he becomes a "thinker."

First he discriminates between thoughts. Then he receives impressions and clothes them with his own thoughts. Eventually he senses the impressions coming from his own Core. It is at this moment that the human soul starts to think in line with the Plan and Purpose of the Supreme Thinker.

In each human being a Divine genius is hidden, and it manifests through the creative thought of the human soul. There are very few souls who know how to think or how to express the electrical energies and directions coming from their own Core. Meditation and contemplation are techniques to contact the Core and release It.

When the human soul is in the process of making greater and greater contact with his own Core, he becomes more and more sensitive to the impressions coming from higher sources and from archetypal thoughts. The most creative period of the human soul is the period in which he can observe, discriminate, and use the thoughts reaching him from his essential Core.

7. There are thoughts that come into existence when impressions streaming from higher sources contact the human soul. Impressions are not thoughts. They are radiations of great Lives, great Entities. These impressions change into thoughtforms when the human soul contacts them and tries to translate them according to his needs and according to the conditions of life in general.

We translate impressions according to where we are, what we are. They radiate Beauty, Goodness, and Righteousness, and we can translate them into objects of beauty, actions of goodness, and expressions of truth.

8. Thoughts come to our mind from the archetypal planes. Archetypes are Divine thoughts. When the Solar Lords meditate and think, They create Archetypes in the Cosmic Mental Plane. These Archetypes slowly come down and impress our mind, and we try to create according to them. But our creativity is like the drawings of a three year old child in comparison to the art of a Leonardo da Vinci.

Such thoughts are faint echoes of the Divine thoughts, but in those faint echoes the seed of the vision of the Archetypes is present. Such kinds of thoughts open the path of steady progress in all fields of human endeavor. These Archetypes are Divine thoughts which are in the process of manifestation or objectification.

When one contacts such thoughts, he builds a thread of contact through which he gradually penetrates deeper into the Divine Mind.

Every form in the Universe is the shadow of an Archetype. Man cannot create a form whose Archetype does not exist in higher planes. The creativity of man depends on his ability to surpass progressively the forms that he produced through his labor and on his ability to find the higher correspondence of the forms he created. As he advances in perfecting his creativity, he penetrates deeper into the Divine Mind. Each perfected form leads him closer to still higher perfections.

Any manifestation is a faint echo of the thought of the Solar Lord. Our responsibility is to build our life on the line of the Archetype's perfection. Reality is the Archetype. Unreality is partial manifestation of the Archetype. When a manifestation is the perfect image of the Archetype, you have the real, the reality. This is why the mantram says:

Lead us, O Lord. . .

From the unreal to the Real

which means, "Lead us, O Lord, from all shadows, reflections, echoes, and illusions toward the Archetypes."

We are told that there are pure thoughts and impure thoughts. Pure thoughts are those thoughts which come from the Fiery World[2] and higher sources. They are not polluted by our glamors, illusions, maya, and vanities. Pure thoughts always lead us toward Beauty, Goodness, and Righteousness.

Thoughts are electrical waves, and those who have advanced receivers register them in their pure state. It is also known that there are centers of distortion

---

2.   For information on the Fiery World, please see *Other Worlds*.

which try to create static in our station and make it difficult for us to receive the broadcast in its purity and entirety. This brings us to the subject of the Rainbow Bridge, or the antenna of the human soul. If this antenna is built, the reception from higher sources will be possible. If not, the human soul will wander long ages in the darkness of materialism, pain, and suffering.

The source of the thought is more important than the form of the thought. It has been observed that some entities project good-looking thoughts that are easily accepted by people. But later they find out that those good-looking thoughts had evil intentions. Dark forces can play with thoughts, but they cannot hide their motives permanently when human beings begin to think.

The disciples on the Path must learn to discriminate the source of their thoughts. They must know that the fragrance of a rose cannot emanate from a skunk. But how can we know the source of thoughts?

The only way to know the source is to find out in what centers [3] that thought is registered. If it is registered by lower centers, it has a doubtful origin and one must be careful, no matter how colorful or idealistic the thought sounds.

You can learn something from people who advertise cigarettes, alcohol, gambling, and even prostitution. Despite their most colorful expressions and very good-looking thoughts, you know that their intention is to make money at the expense of your health, morality, and sanity. One must develop discrimination through observation so that he also does not yield mechanically to the influences which try to pour messages through automatic writing, through hypnotism, or through hypnotic mediumship.

Once Christ said that there are wolves who will approach you with their sheepskins.

One must not only discriminate among the thoughts that he receives or contacts, but most urgently he must discriminate among his *own* thoughts. Animal man became a man when he started to think, but somewhere along the path he lost his ability to think in harmony with the Purpose of life. When he lost his ability to think in harmony with the Purpose, he became trapped by his animal nature. In general, all that man now thinks is within the boundaries of the trap. The more he thinks, the more he is trapped.

Can't we see this trap in our modern life? Why, with all our thinking, are we almost ready to end life on this planet? Why, with all our thinking, do we pollute our air, oceans, rivers, and earth? What kind of thinking is this! Why do we create communications, televisions, and satellites and use them against our own survival? We are in a trap of depression, in traps of economic, political, and educational chaos, and we call all these blind efforts in the trap our "experiments."

Man will never learn right thinking until he liberates himself from the trap of his separatism, selfishness, materialism, competition, exploitation, greed, and

---

3. For information on centers, please see *New Dimensions in Healing*.

crimes. These are the bars of his trap, and right thinking is only possible outside of these bars.

Before a man learns how to think or how to utilize the creative thoughts, he must develop his heart and his compassion and live a life of virtue. The possibility of right and clear thinking is always there, but the willingness is absent.

When people continuously yield to their animal nature, they live for the thoughts of others and others manipulate them.

Once a dictator said, "I do not want my people to learn how to think, and the best way to prevent their thinking is to open wide the doors for their animal nature to manifest. Thus we can control them." Every pure thought is a great danger for those who are in the trap and want to protect their interests in the trap.

Thus when one is the slave of his animal habits or animal nature, he does not want to think, though he can if he really wants to. This is why Mother Nature creates opportunities for her trapped children to think when, through natural catastrophes, she destroys the accumulated vanities of ages and tries to bring her children to their senses. The difficulties of life challenge us to observe, to concentrate, and to discriminate.

Observation is the ability to see things as they are.

Concentration is the ability to relate yourself to objects you see.

Discrimination is the ability to choose between the objects according to your goals and intentions.

It is really interesting to see how people are trapped. One of the greatest traps is our glamors. Once we think that our glamors are what we want and need, we are stuck in them. We do not look for anything else. Watch a man who is using drugs. Tell him, "Mr. So-and-So, the drugs are not good for you, for your health, happiness, and success."

"I know."

"Then why are you using them?"

"I can't help it. I want them."

You warn him and say, "Do not use them." He promises, but he uses them again.

In this same way we are trapped in our traditions, fanaticism, vanities, and illusions. We know they are obsolete, but we cannot help ourselves, especially if we are surrounded by people who are in fanaticism, in separatism, and in illusion.

For example, whatever you say to a religious or political fanatic increases his fanaticism. He is trapped, and he thinks his trap is the whole world. The only way to come out of the trap is through pain and suffering, which karma brings to his life.

People are also trapped in certain strata in the Cosmic ladder in a very interesting way. This needs a little explanation.

When a man is ready to depart from the physical life, a mysterious thing happens. In the last few minutes, his life-film passes in front of his eyes, and he is given a chance to have certain realizations. For example, in the light of the moment of passing he can see the futility of greed, fanaticism, exploitation, hatred, possessiveness, and so on; and in those few moments he can renounce those things and purify his consciousness and his future directions. Thus, in a sense, he leaves behind all those things that may tie him to the earthly sphere.

This chance is not given to those who are subjected to sudden, unexpected death. For example, a bomb explodes and wipes away thousands of people instantly. They did not have the chance to renounce their own lives and gather wisdom. It is these people who are trapped in their earthly cravings, glamors, fanaticism, superstitions, greed, separatism; and they constantly broadcast them to humanity or bring them back to earth when they reincarnate.[4]

There are also people who are trapped in their habits and want to obsess people to satisfy these habits. They emanate low thoughts and influence the lives of millions. That is why wars do not solve problems and are the most fertile sources to produce and multiply problems, thereby increasing the suffering of humanity.

People are born with their past hang-ups, and they continue their life where they left off previously.

Is it possible to change the life of the planet in view of the above facts? Some people think it is an impossibility. Others think it is a possibility. Both are right. If something seems impossible for a man, it becomes impossible for him. If something seems possible for him, it becomes possible for him. Also, something that is possible for me can be impossible for you for a while. This is why one cannot say that something is possible or impossible. It can be one or the other.

A disciple is a man who makes impossible things possible and possible things impossible.

An Initiate is a self-made soul.

---

4. See also *Other Worlds* for additional information on this subject.

2

Thought and the Teaching

When the physical body is nourished by wrong food and led into wrong conditions, it degenerates and becomes an obstacle on our path. The same thing happens to our mental body if the mental body is nourished by wrong food: by lies, by illusions, by hatred, by destructive thoughts. With this wrong food we attract low-level atoms to our mental sphere. This eventually makes a dull, lazy, and stagnant mental body in which many germs of crime live and lead us into destructive actions.

The lower level atoms often accumulate in such a density that they form a dark wall around the mental sphere. This wall cuts off the Indweller from those impressions which come from higher sources, or it distorts those visions which are projected by the Inner Guide.

In the past, crimes were committed by the physical bodies, but in this age crimes are committed by thoughts. We must be very careful with our thoughts and cultivate extreme caution in manifesting our thoughts. Our thoughts can lead us into crimes, into confusion, and into darkness if the mental body is not in a healthy condition.

In the past, people tried to conquer others through their physical strength. They also used extreme emotions to reach their goals. In the present, it is the mind that conquers. It is the mind that causes failures. The greatest strength and power belong to a man whose mind is enlightened and controlled by his True Self.

In the future, it is the light of the Intuition that will carry the victory of the human soul. The light of the Intuition will closely work with the mental body.

Thought is the child of an idea within the mental body. When we think, we express an idea or a vision, we translate an impression coming through the senses or from higher realms.

A thoughtform is an organized and densified thought. It is like a seed which grows into a fruit or a tree. Thoughts are causes. Thoughtforms are effects, and they can exist independently after they are built in the mental sphere. They can even travel over great distances and carry the message of the thought to others. Thought is the meaning, and the thoughtform is the letter carrying the thought.

We know that thought changes the world. And the changes caused by the greater Thinker in Nature create new changes in our thoughts. Thus two Thinkers, the Thinker in man and the Thinker in Nature, can cooperate with each other if the human mind is developed, cultivated, purified, and disciplined.

We can change politics if we elect those people who are on a higher level of awareness. When we elect people on the same level, they do not help us solve our problems even though they present the problems with different viewpoints and promises. Problems are solved only when a higher level person is selected for an office.

Changes in our life must come through the changes in our consciousness. Those who want to improve their life, work on improving their thinking. They try to purify and focus their thinking, and the outer life follows the change.

Changing the world of forms or the personnel helps for a short while, but the real help comes when the thinking of people is changed and expanded.

In the Teaching we read, "*. . . not everything can be immediately assimilated. But if you will assimilate or even memorize certain formulae, you will simplify a number of things; also, you will develop an alertness and vivacity of thinking that is most essential. Never forget that* **we conquer by thought**."[1]

Assimilation is a slow process and it is done through meditation. If we memorize certain wise sayings and meditate on them at certain times, we will assimilate them faster and make the Teaching a part of our being.

Thinking about the Teaching or "formulas" will eventually raise our consciousness to the level on which the Teaching was given and put us in contact with the Mind that conceived the thoughts and formulated them into words.

As food is digested in the physical mechanism, so does the mental body assimilate ideas, thoughts, and the Teaching. Assimilation nourishes the mental body and makes it grow and expand.

Knowledge is mental food. Reading or listening to great ideas nourishes the body if one meditates on them, mentally understands them, and tries to live them. We are told that the assimilation of great ideas is possible only when we try to make them a part of our life or try to live them.

Through assimilation we change the polarization of the atoms of our mental body. The polarization of the mental body manifests itself through our interests. We begin to be interested in the higher values of life, with the deeper meaning of life if the polarization of mental atoms is oriented toward the higher planes. If the atoms are polarized toward the lower planes, the mind is used for physical and emotional urges, drives, and pleasures. Polarization changes as we assimilate higher thoughts, visions, and ideas.

Assimilation creates radioactivity and puts into action the higher spirals of each atom. We are told that each atom has seven spirals. Not all of the spirals are unfolded and active. As assimilation goes on, the spirals slowly unfold and gradually release more light from their central core. This eventually leads to a state of unfoldment which is called Transfiguration or Enlightenment.

---

1.   Agni Yoga Society, *Letters of Helena Roerich*, Vol. 1, p. 93.

In memorizing the Teaching one builds receivers in his mental body. These receivers attract the ideas related to the Teaching and open in his mind new avenues of contact. Memorization of a part of the Teaching also builds a bridge between the thoughtform in the mind and the source of the ideas or thought. It is through such a bridge that new inspirations come into a person's system and slowly penetrate the deepest layer of the memorized Teaching.

For example, the Great Sage says, "Blessed be the obstacles through which we grow." Let us say that one memorized this but did not really penetrate into the deeper layers of it. In memorizing it, he first built a thoughtform within the mental body which acts as a receiver, and as he meditates upon it, new light streams forth into the mind, and eventually the person sees the real meaning which was in the mind of that Great One when He formulated it. Thus is established a relation with the source of the Teaching, and this relation opens new ways of inspiration and vision.

Any time one meets an obstacle, if he repeats that formula, he will immediately feel a new energy circulating in his system and he will have more power to face the obstacle and emerge from it triumphant.

Memorization has two levels. It can be done with the higher mind or with the lower mind. When it is done without meditation, one receives a little help. But if it is memorized and meditated upon, the formula of the Teaching brings great inspiration.

"*Alertness and vivacity of thinking*" can be achieved if an idea is assimilated and the mind is connected to a higher level of inspiration.

Thinking becomes dull and dead if there is no inspiration and no self-actualization or realization. Realization starts when the thoughts produce deeds.

"Never forget that *we conquer by thought*."

The word "conquer" means the ability to climb the summit within oneself, step by step conquering his nature and becoming the True Self. Who cares if a man gains the world but is unable to conquer his lower nature and meet himself? The greatest failure in life is the moment when a person chooses to be conquered by his own wealth, blind urges and drives, and his successes and failures.

In true victory one conquers his physical, emotional, and mental bodies and reaches the realization that he owns these bodies and can use them according to his own and their eternal goal.

In gaining the world, a person is the same level man. In conquering his nature, a higher being is emerging from him. One is havingness or doingness, and the other is beingness and transformation.

There was a very wealthy man who realized his misery was being caused by his wealth. So he went and gave it away to learn at the feet of a great Teacher the wisdom and mystery of life.

The person who gains the world lives a short life as a man of success. But those who conquer their human nature are conquerors of all the ages. Such are the men: Hermes, Krishna, Buddha, Jesus, Mohammed, and others.

Those who are slaves of matter make life a darker prison, and those who are caught by it run after their own tails.

Conquerors of spirit penetrate into the greater laws and principles of Creation and through them try to meet their essential Divinity. Great creative people conquer the hearts and minds of humanity without guns and bombs and encourage them to strive forward toward their spiritual goal.

Thus the word "conquer" has a different meaning, and one can be a conqueror only when he achieves victory over his vices, lies, weaknesses, inertia, depression, glamors, illusions, greed, vanities, separative thoughts, and selfishness.

A king had many slaves, and when a Sage showed him that he was the slave of his own selfishness and greed, the king let them go free and made them his co-workers. Conquering oneself leads to freedom. Conquering others leads to slavery.

"We conquer by thought" because in thinking we find the right way to use the laws of Nature and the energies of Nature. In right thinking we cooperate with Nature. In wrong thinking we create friction between us and Nature. Friction creates pain, suffering, and delay on the path of our evolution.

One day in the morning a good friend of mine was waiting for his girlfriend, but she did not come. He waited calmly until 9:00 p.m. and then he blessed her and concentrated his mind on a great Teaching. After a while he went to bed and said, "Goodnight, God. I want to sleep. You take care of it, if there was some problem in her heart." And he went to sleep. This really impressed me. He was rejected, but he never developed any anger or emotions. He conquered the voices of his lower self and slept peacefully.

One day a teenager came to talk with me, and she was very depressed. She looked as if she had been crying.

"Come on," I said. "Think of something beautiful."

"What?"

"Something that would make you happy."

"Nothing can make me happy."

"What about the boy whom you love? Let's say he comes in suddenly and hugs you."

"I would like it."

"Then stand up. Imagine he is coming close to you. Approach him and hug him."

She did. Then she sat down with a big smile.

"Okay," I said. "What do you want to talk to me about?"

"I guess everything is okay. I was feeling very lonely."

If we learn how to handle our thoughts, every minute we can win a victory over our personality.

A great Sage said, "Our thoughts are with you."

Thought travels faster than light. If we learn how to think, how to build our thoughtforms, how to direct them to certain persons, we can be a great help to many people we know and to many others we do not know.

Imagine a dark room in which one is trying to find something lost. Suddenly a beam of light streams into the room, enabling that person to see and to find the object. A similar thing happens to a man who suddenly receives a beneficent thought-beam from a friend. His mind rejoices in the thought, and in it he finds certain solutions to his problems. This is how help is attained with thought, sending to friends beams of loving thoughts, enlightening thoughts, encouraging thoughts, elevating thoughts, and joyful thoughts. Such thoughts are as precious as the beam of light in a dark room.

One day I was feeling angry, depressed, and revengeful toward a certain man. In that darkness the words came to my mind, "Our thoughts are with you." I felt a Great One looking at me, and in His presence I could not remain in the same state of emotions. My thoughts turned to Him. I thought, it is better for me to send loving thoughts to that man. I felt he was wrong, but maybe factors beyond his control had affected his behavior. A few minutes later, as I was coming back into my happy and forgiving state of consciousness, the telephone rang.

"Hello."

"T?"

"Yes."

"Do you know who I am?"

"Yes, I know."

"Are you still angry? Look, I am sorry. I know I hurt you. Will you forgive me? I have great respect for you. May I come and see you?"

I was surprised at how thought works.

"Our thoughts are with you" reminds us that the Great Ones think about us, about our unfoldment and blooming, as gardeners do who visualize the flowers as they put the seeds into the ground. They see us as blooming flowers. Their thoughts create those conditions in which we grow. It is in Their thoughts that we take refuge.

"Be courageous. I conquered the world." What an immense power is hidden within these words. It is possible for us to conquer our weaknesses, the causes of our failures, and eventually live a life of joy, freedom, and service. . .if we do not defeat ourselves with our thoughts but receive strength in the thoughts of those who stand on our path as our future visions. The most important thing in keeping our contact with the higher sources of thought is "to destroy the germs of base thoughts, which are more infectious than all diseases. One should be careful not so much about uttered words as about thoughts."[2]

---

2. Agni Yoga Society, *Leaves of Morya's Garden*, Vol. II, p. 80.

Our thoughts are with you, and we know that all will come about safely unless we ourselves sever the silver cord by our selfishness, sluggardliness, and superficial attitude toward the Advices.[3]

The silver cord mentioned here refers to a communication line between the Teacher and the student. This line can be blocked by our actions, feelings, and thoughts if they are based on selfish motives, hypocrisy, and inertia. This line of communication is always kept open if the aspirant hears the "Advices" and puts them into action.

The "Advices" come from higher principles such as Goodness, Beauty, and Righteousness, and one must accept them if he wants to keep the communication line clear between higher values, higher centers, and himself.

The silver cord is severed and the energy current is cut when we are selfish or when we fall into sluggardliness and superficiality. A selfish person uses the help and wisdom of his Teacher for his own ends.

Sluggardliness is laziness. A lazy person wastes the precious wisdom given to him by not using it for the welfare of others.

A superficial person presents the Advice or Wisdom coming from higher sources in a very shallow, non-solemn way or ridicules it. These attitudes toward the Teaching or Advice sever the "silver cord" between the Great One and a person. The Advice or the Teaching is given only to transform the life, to spiritualize the life.

We read in the Teaching,

I rejoice to see how the lightning flashes of foresight regarding the people's welfare sparkle amidst your thoughts. These thoughts have to be launched into space. If you could daily spare half an hour for the future! Verily, the bonfire of your thoughts would receive Our welcome.[4]

Isn't it beautiful to know that when a thought is aflame regarding the welfare of people, that thought flashes like lightning? But if a thought is contaminated with base thoughts, it is more infectious than all diseases. Base thoughts are selfish, criminal, hateful thoughts which spread faster than any germ and cause moral sicknesses everywhere.

How can we know the difference between base thoughts and good thoughts? The answer is very simple. Good thoughts are based on Beauty, Goodness,

---

3.   Agni Yoga Society, *Letters of Helena Roerich*, Vol. I, p. 105.
4.   Agni Yoga Society, *Leaves of Morya's Garden*, Vol. II, p. 181.

Righteousness, Joy, and Freedom. Base thoughts are based on slavery, ugliness, separativeness, selfishness, and hatred.

When a person thinks, he should ask himself, "Is my thought leading to beauty, to unity, to freedom, to wholeness?" If the answer is yes, he should continue his way of thinking. If the answer is no, he should stop and change his thinking.

It is very important to know that our thoughts are not kept within our head. Immediately when we think, our thoughts become the property of space. We may plant beautiful flowers in space or throw germs and pollution into space through our thoughts.

Base thoughts will be absorbed by those people in the world who have corresponding thoughts in their minds, and they will be forced into destructive actions. In a sense, most of us are responsible for the crimes in the world because of our base thoughts thrown into space. *If you could daily spare half an hour for the future!*

One day a child asked a great Sage, "What am I going to be ten years from now?"

"A teenager."

"Twenty years later?"

"A man."

"Two thousand years later?"

"Maybe a great artist, statesman, an Initiate, or a Master."

"Is that the end?"

"No. You will face a challenge to expand your consciousness and talents to work in the solar system, in our galaxy, in Kosmos."

"I like that."

"Then you must work for it."

For half an hour think about a bright future in which you bloom in all your beauty, in which all plans to serve others come into reality, in which you surpass yourself continuously toward Infinity. What a healing energy is contained in such a thought.

After traveling the path of human evolution, one will sit at the shore of our solar system and strive toward a greater Space.

The future is an ever-expanding unity with the existing Whole.

3

The Nature of Mind

There are two main parts of the mind:

1. The abstract mind

2. The concrete mind

The abstract mind deals with ideas, visions, virtues, and abstract subjects like beauty, purity, love, and so on. The concrete mind deals with daily problems and subjects which are related to the physical, emotional, and lower mental materials. The concrete mind is a bridge between the abstract mind and daily human life. These two minds function separately and, if the lower mind is evolved, in unison.

Some people think that the mind always fabricates and one must pass beyond it. It is good to pass beyond the mind, but if the mind is not totally transmuted, it is impossible to pass beyond the mind. The mind only fabricates when it is not enlightened or not healthy. The mind is as important as your car which carries out your will in your journey.

When you pass to the buddhic or intuitional level of awareness, you need to keep your communication with the world. How can you do that if your mental body is not trained in right motive and purified? The consciousness of Buddha passed through His mind, and He never fabricated but gave His ideas in clear definitions because of His purified mind. Without His mind we would not have His Teaching.

A person who prematurely tries to pass to the intuitional level leaves behind him, if by any chance he succeeds, a big danger. He turns into a source of illusions if he tries to communicate his ideas to others. The intuitional level of awareness is best entered after the mind is purified of any materials that hinder the light of Intuition from manifesting.

Psychic energy emanates from the Lotus. This energy is the energy of the human soul and of the Solar Angel fused together. As time goes on and the petals are more open, this energy increases. At the Fourth Initiation when the Solar Angel departs, the psychic energy charges the mind with extremely powerful currents, and man becomes an Arhat. For a long time still, the energy of his Solar Angel abides with him, and toward the Fifth Initiation the psychic energy streams forth from the Spiritual Triad and the Monad. We are told that the Solar Angels are related to the Solar Logos and that They serve in the Council of the Solar Logos. Man, when he is perfected, serves in the Council of the Planetary Logos. This is the difference. Solar Angels are many cycles ahead of human beings.

Also we are told that "the work of the solar Pitris [Solar Angels] *from their point of view*, is not primarily the evolution of man, but is the process of their own development within the plan of the solar Logos."[1]

The Tibetan Master often uses the word "Thinker" to refer to the human soul. Man cannot think by himself until the human soul comes into being. Before that all thinking is carried on by the Solar Angel and is used by the personality according to the level of its evolution or the soul's evolution. Thus the Light, Love, and Willpower pass through the Intuitional Plane and through the higher mind to be formulated by the lower mind.

In the higher mind this formulation of energies is carried on by the Chalice. The Chalice is the center through which these energies pass and form the prototypes of thought formulation that will be done by the lower mind.

There is the Solar Angel and the human soul. In the process of evolution the Solar Angel takes the lead, but when Soul-infusion starts, the human soul begins to think. The thinking of the Solar Angel or human soul passes to the mechanism of the higher mind when the correspondence of formulation of the lower mind takes place. Upon this formulation and according to the purity of the lower mind thoughtforms are made.

The mind is an extremely important mechanism which must evolve to the degree that it can register the energies coming from higher sources, ideas, pure thoughts, and thoughtforms. This is why all Great Ones speak about the importance of the mind and give various methods to coordinate it. Of course, along with the mental body, care must be taken to have a healthy and evolved brain.

Various Levels of the Mind

We are told that the mind is divided into three main sections: the lower mind, which includes the four lower levels of mind; the higher mind, which includes the three higher levels of mind; and the Chalice. We are told that when thoughts originate from the center of the Chalice, a spark flashes out and goes into the higher mind like an explosion of fireworks or a rainbow of fire. Then it takes a form in the lower mind.[2]

If outer thoughts from confusing sources are attracted to the lower mind, the higher mind does not show any resonance, and no flash comes out of the Chalice. Every genuine thought from the Higher Worlds creates a fiery conflagration in the higher mental plane and descends to the lower mental plane to take a form.

---

1.   Alice A. Bailey, *A Treatise on Cosmic Fire*, p. 843.
2.   See *The Subconscious Mind and the Chalice*.

But the impression of the thought on the lower mental plane takes place only by the electrical charge emanating from the Chalice.

Thus these three sections of the mind work as an electrical unit. The electrical flash emanating from the Chalice is the act of affirmation and amplification of the thought attracted by the higher mind from higher sources. No flash emanates from the Chalice if the thought in the lower mind is not in accord with the principles in the Chalice.

Thus, accumulations of low-level and impure thoughts create disturbances in the mental body, but the accumulation of higher thoughts organizes and integrates the mental body, as if the instrument and the music have been fused within each other.

We are told that the Chalice is the body of the Inner Guide. This is true, but as man, or the human soul, advances, the Inner Guide withdraws from the Chalice into Its real habitat, which is the Spiritual Triad. Actually Its body is formed of higher mental, intuitional, and atmic substances. As the Solar Angel gradually withdraws into the Spiritual Triad, the human soul unfolds in the Chalice and develops more knowledge, more love, and more sacrifice. We are told that at the Fourth Initiation his fire is so intense that it burns the petals of the Chalice and from the "ashes" of the petals a new son of God emerges.

At this stage, the Solar Angel leaves Its higher vestures to the human soul and departs for "home." The human soul has reached a high degree of maturity and is now able to *think*. He is an Arhat now. All his thoughts are fiery and charged with the fiery will energy, the Purpose, and the Plan.

A thoughtform embodying a genuine idea is the result of the participation of various mental mechanisms working as a unit. Centers found on the mental plane put into action the corresponding centers on lower planes through the instrumentality of the mental unit.[3] Here we must notice that many sublime impressions or ideas or thoughtwaves of a higher nature are lost or degenerated due to unhealthy conditions in the mental plane. The mirror, the tubes, the condensers, the transmitters, and the receivers must all be in good condition to produce clear pictures on the screen of the mind and the brain.

Meditation in its early stages puts these mechanisms in order, cleanses, coordinates, integrates them, and eventually aligns them together in such a way that the mental mechanism as a whole is ready to be highly creative and cooperative with the greater Thinker on higher planes.

The act of using the mind is not thinking. The mind can be used by different factors and in different ways. For example, we can dramatize our emotions and pains through creating an image. If there is fear, it can use all the images that are in the lower mind in an associative manner and create a complex dramatization, wasting the energy and the substance of the mind.[4]

---

3. For more detail, see *New Dimensions in Healing,* especially, pp. 105-145.
4. See also *The Subconscious Mind and the Chalice,* Part I.

Pains can use the mind by bringing together all the negative memories in it and creating a fearful picture. These images further control the mind, pushing away all beautiful pictures created through the higher mind. These are mechanical ways of using the mind.

We can also use the mind through memory arrangement. For example, we have a geometry problem to solve. To solve this problem we need to remember various formulas. By bringing the needed formulas together, we can solve the problem. This is a more advanced way of using the mind, but it is still not creative thinking.

Creative thinking starts when, through meditation, we learn to translate great ideas and impressions coming from the Transpersonal Self, the Solar Angel, and then express them in terms of the need of the time and in terms of future unfoldments.

There are differences between the functions of memory arrangement and creative thinking. In the first case the lower mechanism of the mind is used: the mental unit, the four levels of mind, the centers, the etheric brain, and the brain. In creative thinking all of the above mechanisms are used, plus the Chalice, the higher mind, and the Mental Permanent Atom. The first one is mechanical, and the second one is creative. Only in the creative use of the mind is the link kept between the lower and higher mind and the bridge built for the advancement of the human soul.

Actually, the actors in the thinking process are the Inner Dweller, also known as the Thinker or the Solar Angel, and the unfolding human soul. The unfolding human soul is our Real Self in the process of unfoldment and mastery. He is like a little child who is nourished by the Thinker; the Thinker gives him ideas or thoughts that inspire him on the path of his evolution. The Thinker holds the plan and knowledge for the child; and as Its child grows, the Thinker imparts to him greater knowledge, greater thoughts, and greater ideas. Through such a communication the human being, whom we call the unfolding human soul, awakens and eventually communicates more closely with his Inner Master. This communication is called *thinking* when it is related to the transient personality life and *meditation* when it is related to the life of spiritual progress.

Thinking and meditation are the forms of communication with the Inner Teacher. There is no difference in technique between thinking and meditation, but there are differences in motive and dimension. For example, you can think to find easier ways or means to hurt someone. But if you are meditating, or thinking in the light of the Inner Teacher, your motive is *only* to help, to uplift, to save, to free, to protect, to guide, and to be an example.

In the first instance you receive light from the Inner Lord and use it for your own advantage. In the second case you receive the light of wisdom and use it for the benefit of all, including yourself. Thus the thinking process is an electrical exchange between the point of light called man and the shining light of the Inner Teacher.

I intend to be a bestower of bliss, of beauty + of Light.
this is my intention.

Meditation starts at that moment of our life when we begin to feel that this life has a purpose and we want to know that purpose and live accordingly. Meditation eventually eliminates all our personality interests and makes us a bestower of bliss, of beauty, and of light.

It will be helpful if we study the mind as it is considered in esoteric terms. The mind is built of billions of fiery atoms which form a magnetic field around the head above the shoulders. It is at first chaotic and colors are not distinct in it. Later it slowly develops seven scintillations with the hues of yellow and orange. Eventually a greater light focalizes itself at the center and emanates seven rays of great beauty, in the midst of which man observes a lotus shaped formation with many petals of different colors.

The developing human soul, on the path of his evolution, travels up from the physical to the emotional nature and eventually locates himself in the lower mind. The lower mind is the first four levels of the mind. There a concretion of ideas takes place. The higher mind is the next three levels, which are called the formless levels of mind. They are used to attract great impressions from various sources of abstract thoughts.

These seven levels of mind usually express themselves in five stages of consciousness:

1. The physical stage

2. The emotional stage

3. The lower mental stage

4. The higher mental stage

5. The stage in which the developing human soul controls and uses all these stages to reveal Divine beauties and help the evolution of life

When we say *consciousness*, we mean an area of light in the mental body by which and through which the unfolding human soul acts, lives, sees, subjectively knows, and understands. At first this lighted area is very small and foggy. Eventually it gets bigger and clearer. This is what is meant by the *expansion of consciousness*. The light that creates this field of consciousness comes first from the Inner Teacher, until the light of the unfolding human soul develops and he releases his own light to enlighten the field of the mind. This so-called beam of light is the *beam of intelligence*.

As the field of the mind is purified, the beam of intelligence increases. Eventually these two beams crisscross each other and fuse within each other, creating the state called Soul-infusion.

Before a man enters into the path of true meditation, he passes through six stages of consciousness:

a. The butterfly stage

b. The stage of confusion

c. The stage of preoccupation

d. The stage of expansion

e. The stage of one-pointedness

f. The stage of self-control

Upon the path of his evolution, man passes through these stages until he reaches the stage of self-control where he is free from the control of his physical, emotional, and even mental natures and uses them to further the Plan of evolution on the planet and become a revealer of the Divine Purpose. In this stage he is a man of meditation, which means that he is one who has heard the call of his Inner Teacher and is ready to put his life under the inspiration of his Inner Lord for humanity. His meditation gradually changes into contemplation, which leads into illumination, inspiration, and identification with his true core of being, his Self.

Meditation has long been done through a special technique which may be called *The Technique of Four Viewpoints.*[5] This was given by the great Patanjali many thousands of years ago in his famous sutras. He said,

> *The consciousness of an object is attained by concentration on the fourfold nature: the form, through examination; the quality, through discriminative participation; the purpose, through inspiration (or bliss); and the Soul, through identification.*[6]

Let us take the stages of the mind. The first one is called the *stage of the butterfly mind.* If you have observed how a butterfly acts when it is in a garden of flowers and trees, you have seen how it flies from one flower to another, from one branch to another, and never sits on any spot for a long time. Its interest changes constantly. This is symbolically referring to those infant minds who go from one subject to another without spending time for study, analysis, and assimilation. Their interest changes constantly, and they do not have any plan, any aim, but are drawn to the object that stimulates their senses and gives them pleasure. People who are in this stage are controlled by their physical senses, and their emotional and mental natures serve to fulfill their changing interests.

---

5. Additional information on meditation is found in *The Psyche and Psychism, The Science of Meditation,* and *The Ageless Wisdom.*
6. Alice A. Bailey, *The Light of the Soul,* p.33.

There is a parable which states that when you frequently change the location of a tree it cannot spread roots and it eventually dies. For a long time man wanders from one object to another trying to satisfy his senses, but the day comes when the evolving human soul gets tired of this wandering and wants to spread roots and deepen his experiences. Yet he cannot locate the object of his desire; he cannot choose; he cannot discriminate.

Next starts the *stage of confusion*. The person is tired of going from one object to another. He cannot find one object which is worthwhile. Life has no aim, no plan. All is silly. Where to go? What to do?

This stage lasts a long time and creates many psychosomatic disorders. It leads to chaotic actions such as crimes and suicides if the daily labor, the daily needs of life, do not force him to live at least as an automaton.

In this stage the emotional nature, or solar plexus, rules over the physical and mental bodies, using them for its ends. The evolving human soul is in the depths of such confusion and despair that he searches for a point of certainty on which to rest his whirling mind. He then finds at least one object of interest: money, an idea, love, ambition, position, an organization, a teacher, religion, or philosophy. He sticks to it to the end, and he is possessed by his chosen object. All his interest revolves around the axis of his object. All other interests are inhibited, rejected, and attacked to protect the one he has chosen. This is the *stage of the preoccupied mind*, the obsessed mind.

It is very interesting to note that at this point the man may be either an extremely well-intentioned man, a saint, a martyr or a criminal, a maniac possessed by a special idea or by the spirit of crime. All fanatics are generally in this stage of mind, and their fanaticism turns into violence once they feel they are in danger of losing their object of interest. This is the stage in which the lower mind rules the emotions and physical senses and uses them for its ends.

In the history of humanity such a state of mind has often been created by some leaders and used for various ends. We see them mostly in the religious and political fields when, for the sake of an idea, all is sacrificed to the point of death. This stage of mind continues for longer periods of time than the previous stages.

Eventually the unfolding human soul, life after life, develops the power of concentration, the power of control over his physical and emotional natures, and he makes himself ready to penetrate into the next stage of mind. This stage is called the *stage of expansion*, the stage of inclusiveness, discrimination, and control of the idea which previously controlled him.

This happens in a curious way. In one incarnation he is possessed by a certain idea and rejects any idea which is diametrically opposite to his chosen idea. Because of this strong refusal and rejection of the new idea, the man develops closer contact with it. He studies it more deeply and becomes aware of any movement concerning that idea. Because of these close and reverse relationships in which a great deal of emotion and karma is involved, the man, in one of his next incarnations, is attracted to the field which is focused entirely on the idea which he rejected previously. Here he grows, with special training, and reaches the same stage of fanaticism as in his previous incarnation, but this time in another field.

In esoteric literature we are given examples of those who hated certain nations and certain doctrines. Subsequently they incarnated in countries or environments where they exemplified a greater fanaticism in that which they had formerly condemned. They often committed genocide and widespread crimes upon those still adhering to their former ideology.

This is why fanaticism is heavily condemned in all esoteric schools of the world. This chain of fanaticism, or the preoccupation stage, slowly cools down, incarnation after incarnation, when man eventually starts to see beauty in other ideologies and trends of activities.

The next stage he passes into is called the stage of control of the idea or ideology, or the *stage of one-pointedness*. One-pointedness is evidenced by his steady and firm striving toward perfection, toward fusion with his True Self. He is now free of the ideology which was like a chain or a prison for him. Because of this freedom, he can now see the relative importance of his ideology and the beauties in all others. Thus he can use the best part of his ideology to appropriate his life and create cooperation, harmony, and coexistence. It is in this stage that man totally dominates his ideas, or ideologies, and even discards them as obsolete tools not fit for the developing life around him.

When he reaches this point he enters into the sixth stage, which is called the *stage of the self-controlled man*. He is a man of tolerance; he does not favor anything or anyone but sees beauty in all and can synthesize to create greater cooperation and creativity. In this stage he controls his body, his emotional nature, and his mental realms and is not affected by any restimulation or automatic reaction in or from his lower nature or environment.

It is here that occult meditation starts. The man has cleaned his house and exhausted his physical, emotional, and mental urges and drives. Now his water and air are calm and under control. He can penetrate into the depth of his Real Self to become a revealer of the Purpose of life and to bring harmony, beauty, and creativity to the world.

It is the true knowledge that increases the receptivity of the light of the mental atoms and thus expands the field of consciousness. True knowledge is rare. It is the knowledge of the laws of Nature and the ways in which they function on all planes. True knowledge is the knowledge of the causes and significance of the phenomenal world, and it can be achieved by study, meditation, and experience. Only experience and realization can expand the field of consciousness and make knowledge one's own.

4

Mental States

There are nine mental stages which characterize stages of our development. They are

1. Dullness

2. Agitation

3. Mechanical reflection

4. Concern

5. Engagement in problems

6. Thinking

7. Deeper thinking

8. Higher thinking

9. Creativity

These nine stages of mind gradually develop in us through our striving. They are characterized by

1. Dullness, inertia, involvement in maya, carelessness, apathy, depression, indifference

2. Agitation of the senses which demand pleasure, satisfaction, food, dress, shelter, transportation

3. Mechanical reflection, following instincts, following orders, commands, thoughts, or desires of others, following the ideas and opinions of the masses

4. Concern about business, life, wife, husband, children, future

5. Engagement in problems such as food, health, money, housing, war, pain, suffering

6. Starting to think on our own, trying to solve our own problems, trying to protect our body, family, future, and finding the ways and means to do it

7. Deeper thinking, seeing the causes of many events, trying to find the laws controlling life in general, trying to prevent destruction, transmuting energies to higher centers

8. Higher thinking, coming closer to the Hierarchical Plan, cooperating with the Law of Hierarchy, finding the laws controlling the astral and mental worlds, receiving impressions from higher sources and formulating them to meet the needs of life

9. Creative thinking, bringing into existence those forms which will allow people to surpass their difficulties and their present level, come in contact with beauty, energy, love, light, and joy, and find their way toward superhuman evolution

We can prepare for higher mental states by exercising

1. Discrimination

2. Dispassion

3. Self-control

4. Desire for liberation

Discrimination is thinking in relation to the Plan or the Purpose, or in the light of the Plan and Purpose. Discrimination is not only knowing but also choosing the factors that are in harmony with the Plan and Purpose.

Dispassion is the ability to insulate oneself from the influence of self-interest, the influence of objects and persons, and think in the clear light of the consciousness.

Self-control is the ability to control your personality and life with the purpose of your divine Self.

Desire for liberation is the urge to stand above your physical, emotional, and mental worlds and act by the intuitional light.

5

How Thought
Affects Our Lives

Thinking, in most cases, is a mental effort to discover the things you are looking for and to find the answers to your questions.

Thought is the conclusion of your thinking, of your discovery.

A thoughtform is the formulation or formation of your intention, based on your discovery and conclusion.

Thinking generates energy. Thought accumulates and focuses it. The thoughtform carries it to its destination.

Thought builds a pattern in your aura, and the pattern and quality of its substance affect your body through the aura. A pattern is a form of a thought. Whenever you think, you build a pattern. The substance of the thought is drawn from the vehicle to which the thought is related.

Thoughts are like clouds which accumulate within our aura. People have a huge number of clouds following them day and night like their own shadow. Each of our thoughts leaves a trace. They accumulate through the years. They are like seeds in our aura, like causes which affect our system.

Thoughts carry energy from various centers within our aura. Thoughts of Beauty, Goodness, and Righteousness bring in energy from Soul levels and from the higher mind. Thoughts of fear, hatred, anger, greed, and jealousy bring in force currents from the solar plexus and sacral centers, mixed with the energy of the base of spine center.

Thoughts of sacrificial service, heroism, and nobility bring in energy from the Spiritual Triad. Compassion brings in energy from the heart center. All these centers are related to their corresponding glands and organs.

It is very interesting to know that when an energy is used it increases and nourishes the corresponding center, gland, and organ. When force is used, the center or gland is spent or wasted.

According to the substance that we bring into our aura, we influence our life and the lives of others. Once we learn how to control our thinking and keep it in the right direction, we enter the road of prosperity, health, beauty, wisdom, and nobility.

In the future, physicians will check the trend of the thoughts of their patients. They will diagnose a man through his thoughts, and they will advise him to purify and transform his thoughts before they take care of his body.

Healing must start with the changing of the thought process. If one is dumping poison into his aura through his thoughts, he will never recover totally from his physical sickness. It is possible to cure a man by physical means, but if his mind is not pure, the sickness will repeat itself in different forms.[1]

Our thoughts and thoughtforms are magnetically held within our aura. They follow us as our shadows do. Thoughts of crime, hatred, greed, jealousy, fear, and anger follow us like smog coming out of an exhaust pipe. Like a big tail this smog follows us, not only in our physical incarnation but also in the subjective worlds, making our life sad and miserable.

People complain about many kinds of pollution. There is the pollution of poisonous gases, the pollution of noise, the pollution of water and land; but the strongest pollution is the pollution of thought. Negative, poisonous, destructive, and criminal thoughts fill space and form dark clouds in the air. It is these clouds that mislead and distort the minds of many generations through their electromagnetic nature. These thought accumulations create epidemics, earthquakes, and other natural calamities because they disturb the energy system of the globe.

There are important points which must be considered if you want to use your thoughts constructively and without creating bad karma. When you talk about someone or when you think about someone, have good thoughts and speak good words about him. This is important because any time you think and talk, you build a thoughtform and the thoughtform goes and sticks to the aura of the one about whom you are talking or thinking. If your thought-picture is of high quality, it creates sublimation in his aura and urges him to transform his life. If the thought-picture is ugly, it creates disturbances in the aura of the subject, and if this is continuous, it pollutes his life and forces him to think and live through the ugly ways imposed on him.

Great Sages advise us to think about the good qualities that people have, to build good pictures about them in our mind, because the pictures built in our mind will affect them and will affect us.

Even if a man is really ugly, do not think about or dwell on the image of his ugliness. Try to see the causes of it, and try to eliminate them if you can. Instead of blaming and cursing, analyze his problem and find a way that you can help him.

People often act on and within the pattern projected on them by their parents, friends, and associates. If your mother says you are an idiot, sooner or later you act like an idiot. If she forced her thoughtform on you, your mind will keep itself busy bringing that thoughtform into manifestation. But if your mother, father,

---

1.   See also *New Dimensions in Healing*.

friend, husband, or wife cultivates beautiful thoughts about you, you will feel a challenge and you will strive to reach the standard of beauty built for you.

A man often lives among those people whom he created with his own thoughts. The people surrounding him reflect his thoughts.

Our thoughts directly affect the lives of others. Very often our thoughts are amplified in movies, in television programs, in books, in cartoons, and they carry their destructive or constructive effects into the psyches of people everywhere. Thus our thoughts build the society.

Ugliness is very malignant, and those who have only developed their lower mind mechanically imitate the ugliness of others and enjoy doing it.

Good thoughts are not easy to contact and register once your mind is blocked with distortions and ugliness. Good thoughts need cleansed or highly developed minds to register them. That is why ugliness and evil have more of a chance to impose themselves on others and to have a greater influence on the events of life.

I once lived with a friend who had the habit of looking at my eyes every morning and saying, "You look weird. Are you sick?"

No matter how joyfully I acted, he repeated this day after day. One day I told him I would prove his words if he continued. The next morning he said it again. I gave his face a slap and said, "This is the proof that I am weird. Now do it again!"

"Man," he said, "I was joking."

"Couldn't you find something beautiful to joke about?"

"You cannot joke about beauty."

"Then you don't need to joke if you are hurting my feelings."

He never did it again. For a long time his words were still echoing in my mind — "You look weird."

One day I told him I was going to leave and go to another city.

"What's the matter?" he asked.

"Well," I said, "I am weird. You made me weird."

"I am sorry. Can I do something good?"

"Yes, you must tell me every morning and every night how beautiful and good-looking I am, and maybe I will stay."

"How many days do I have to do that?"

"As long as I am living in the same house with you."

The next morning he came to my room and knocked on the door.

"Good morning."

"Good morning."

"Well, you are really beautiful. You look healthy and rested."

"Thank you. Make some tea and let us drink it together."

After a few months, his and my attitude toward life began to change. We were more positive, joyful, understanding, and respectful toward each other and toward our friends. I was sorry that he needed a hard manner by which to learn his lesson.

People do not realize how much effect they have on other people, not only with their manners and words but also with their thoughts.

One day a man came to me and said that his son was not doing well in school. Then he added, "He is intelligent and does not use any drugs. He is not interested in cheap music. . .but I don't know why he is not successful."

Because I knew the man very well, I said, "I want to talk with you frankly, if you don't mind."

"Of course, go on!"

"Well, you insulted him many times in front of me, calling him stupid, an idiot, and you could never find any reason to justify your words. But this is not what I want to tell you. I want to ask you something, and I need your sincere answer."

"Ask me!"

"Do you often think that he is going to fail and be a bum in the future? Do you think he is good-for-nothing?"

"As a matter of fact, I do not need to think about it. It seems to me that he is not going to make it in school and even in life."

I said, "Do you know that you are committing a crime? You do not have any reason to 'know' that he is going to fail or that he is going to be a bum. Do you know that your thoughts are molding his life? Do you know that your thoughtforms are creating great obstacles in his efforts to be successful? Once you stop thinking about him in the way you are thinking now, you will see how he will improve and be successful in school and in life. Just think positively and see him in your creative imagination as a successful, beautiful man."

He tried very hard, and to his amazement his son became brighter and brighter and graduated from high school with honors. It was at the graduation ceremony that his father said the most beautiful words about his son to me.

"Today is happening exactly the way I imagined it. I imagined him graduating with honors, and here he is. He made it!"

"Thoughts are energy currents. They build or destroy. You helped your son build his life."

In the Ageless Wisdom it is said that energy follows thought. Once we control our thoughts, we will develop a great power over our thoughts. This power will enable us to use our thoughts constructively for the advancement of life. Once a man develops control of his thoughts, he will be able to see clearly the consequences of his thoughts.

Negative thoughts will lead him into self-defeat. Positive thoughts will lead him to the path of beauty, to the path of survival, to the path of joy and success. Positive thoughts will reveal his True Self. Negative thoughts will block the manifestation and actualization of his Self. Positive thoughts will pave his way to the higher dimensions of existence. Negative thoughts will chain him to the earthly path, to pain, suffering, and failure.

It is possible to receive poisonous thought-arrows from others and become weaker and weaker. But if you shield yourself with thoughts of Beauty,

Goodness, and Righteousness, the arrows either will fall outside the shield or fly back and hit their source.

Protection is essential if a man intends to climb higher ladders of spiritual awareness. Protection is possible if a person stands in the light of his Soul, in the light of his divine Teacher, and shields his life with the energy of his good motives and sacrificial deeds.

Thought energy not only affects the minds and thoughts of other people, but it also affects the atmosphere, the elements found in the atmosphere, and the energy currents active there. This means that the composition of the elements of the air changes due to human thoughts.

Thought affects the cloud formation and the ionization of the air. It affects magnetic polarization, lightning, thunder, and rain. It causes earthquakes or creates stabilization. It causes epidemics and natural calamities if it is massive and negative.[2]

Thought charges the vibrations of the objects we use. It charges the elements of a living room. It is a powerful energy. The greatest victory of a human being is his ability to control his thoughts and direct them toward a great beauty, a great vision, a great sacrificial service.

Many crimes in the world are committed by men and women through thoughts imposed upon them. Many beautiful acts, services, and heroic deeds are performed by men and women through the inspiration of higher thoughtwaves.

Our thoughts can carry great currents of beauty, lofty images of heroism and nobility, and strong waves of healing energy into space. These thoughts are drawn in by creative people, by people of pure heart and goodwill, and used by them to change themselves and their environment and bring in a better life on this planet. Every human being can add his share to this accumulation of good thoughts and serve the Common Good.

Negative and ugly thoughts prepare your future enemies. You increase the number and power of your enemies with your ugly thoughts. Your present enemies are those people whom you poisoned or polluted in the past with your criminal and ugly thoughts.

It is possible also to create enemies because of your beauty, nobility, and achievements. But such enemies do not weaken you. On the contrary, they are the ones who help you become stronger, more successful, and more powerful.

Your real enemies are those people whom you damaged in the past with your ugly thoughts, and they are here now to make you pay for the damage you caused them. Such enemies do not help your growth and progress. You are indebted to them, and often you slow down your own progress in paying them.

Self-created enemies cannot gain power over you because of your beauty and achievement. Through their own acts they spread your influence all over the

---

2. See also *Earthquakes and Disasters, What the Ageless Wisdom Tells Us.*

world. But when you create enemies or criminals through your ugly and criminal thoughts, you are preparing your own defeat and digging your own grave.

Gossip and destructive criticism are ways and means to develop ugly thoughtforms and send them to your victims. You will spare yourself from such a crime by sending people your blessings and constructive thoughts.

Benevolent thoughts give us the right to enter the higher realms of existence. No one can advance toward higher realms unless he proves that he is worthy of it. His worthiness is based upon the service he rendered to humanity with his benevolent and beautiful thoughts.

Beautiful thoughts increase the magnetism in a person's aura. This magnetism becomes the path of contact with higher forces.

Thoughts travel through mental currents in space toward various destinations, or they float in space, affecting many kinds of transmissions from higher or from human sources.

Thoughts are released into space or directed to certain objects through our words, lectures, singing, or music.

Thoughts are carried out through our writings, letters, and signatures. They are charged with our constructive or destructive emanations. Thoughts create certain changes within those who read our books and especially our letters. Handwriting directly transmits our thought energy.

Our thoughts are carried out through our imagination, visualization, and daydreaming. Such actions carry out our thoughts either for constructive or destructive purposes.

Concentration and meditation are powerful methods to spread our thoughts. Meditation spreads the fragrance of higher thought into space.

The objects that we use and the clothes that we wear are charged with our thoughtwaves. Thoughts are carried away through our gifts and objects sent to other fellow beings. Money carries away many of our thoughts and psychic forces. Through sounding the sacred word, the OM, we can transmit our thoughts or broadcast them into space.

Telepathy is a direct method for the transference of thought.

Objects which pass through many hands collect lots of polluting thoughts. These objects are carriers of such thoughts to our homes. It is possible to purify these objects and get rid of polluting thought formations by using the following methods:

1. Make the sign of the cross on any object before you take it into your home and say, "In the name of power, love, and light, let this object or money be purified and used for good purposes."
Repeat this three times.

2. Before eating, purify the food, saying, "In the Name of the Almighty Power, let this food be purified and blessed by the holy presence of divine energy." Make the sign of the cross upon the food.

3. The Great Invocation must be used any time you ride a bus, airplane, or walk in public parks. The Great Invocation builds a protective net around you.[3]

4. You must bless water before you drink it. Say, "Gratitude to You, Lord, for this water. Let it be purified with Your holy presence."

5. You can purify places from dark and negative thoughts by saying the Great Invocation seven times, by burning sandalwood incense, by spreading bay leaves, or by using bay or pine oil.

6. Rose oil is a great disinfectant of thought currents and a repeller of psychic attacks.

7. Men and women can bless each other daily to protect each other from attacks of dark thoughts. One must stand and the other must kneel. The standing one must put his two hands upon the head of the kneeling one and say, "The Lord of fire, through Your fiery essence, purify (name) and charge him (or her) with Your light, love, and power."

These words must be spoken very slowly and with great concentration. After this, the blessing one kneels and the blessed one does the same thing. Then they both stand and hug each other. This can be done daily, every evening. This can also be done with children. Such a ceremony brings great joy and a cooperative spirit to the home.

8. If someone suggests negative, destructive thoughts, immediately build the opposing thoughtform in your mind. For example, if someone says, "You are ugly," imagine you are really beautiful. Even tell him that you are a rare beauty. Do not let people direct their negativity toward you and weaken you.

9. Every day you can say this mantram a few times:

> *More radiant than the sun,*
> *purer than the snow,*
> *subtler than the ether*
> *is the Self,*
> *the Spirit within my heart.*
> *I am that Self;*
> *that Self am I.*

---

3. See *Triangles of Fire* and *Five Great Mantrams of the New Age.*

This will help you to think as the Self and repel destructive and belittling suggestions.

Exercise severe discipline in your thoughts and words. It is only through such a discipline that you develop a natural immunity toward dark attacks of destructive thoughts or thoughtforms.

Thoughts are words, and they are amplified and magnified in space. Most of the time they are audible to devas and advanced beings on the mental plane.

When thoughts are put into words or into speech, they are audible to etheric and astral entities. That is why in the Teaching people are advised to learn to keep silent on mental, astral, and physical levels.

As you can think on the physical plane but not speak your thoughts, similarly you can think on the mental plane but not speak your thoughts. This happens if you are aware of things, but you do not formulate them into thoughts.

One must know that not every thought can penetrate Higher Worlds. When a mixed thought is released into space, the fire of Space burns it, as ore is burned in a furnace; and if a part of the thought remains, it is allowed to pass toward Higher Worlds.

Many ashes of thoughts float in the lower mental world, and many thoughts form a network of darkness near the surface of the earth. After passing into the Higher World, thoughts of high quality glow in greater beauty. It is such thoughts that transmit higher vision to those who can key in to them through their expanding consciousness. This is how higher spheres are protected.

People cannot penetrate into Higher Worlds if their thoughts are of low order. When a man forces himself to penetrate into Higher Worlds, his low-order thoughts create conflagration, and this burns some fuses in his brain and affects his health.

When evil thoughts enter the Fiery World, they gain strength and their influence grows in space. Also, they attract each other according to their frequency and form a cloud of evil which often is used by the members of the dark path to destroy people and to prepare their followers before they take a new incarnation.

The members of the Hierarchy fight against such formations and often They destroy them. This wastes Their time and energy and fills the space for a long time with the "ashes" of evil thoughts.

The accumulation of evil thoughts does not protect the originators. It is they who come under attack first. This attack manifests as mental disturbances, increasing emotional and physical pressures, irritation, and diseases. Sometimes the clouds of evil thoughts hang over originators for many lives, leading them to miserable and dark corridors of life.

Accumulations of evil also turn into a menace for innocent ones, leading them to moral and spiritual destruction. That is why the Teaching warns us not to pollute or infect space with evil thoughts but to beautify it with the flowers of loving and enlightening thoughts.

A creative thinker in any location is like a fountain of fresh water or a flower of rare fragrance. A creative thinker protects the location where he lives from the invasion of evil thoughts and establishes equilibrium and balance in the energies of Nature. That is why the presence of an Initiate is a service for life.

We are told that man often forgets his evil thoughts, but his thoughts do not forget him. If by any chance they do not return to him while he is living, they find him in the subjective world and attack him and obscure his path toward the Higher Worlds. Sometimes such thoughts are called man-eating vultures which follow the soul and cause him great suffering for many years or ages in the subjective world. Such vultures are created by fear, hatred, anger, greed, and jealousy.

Good and creative thoughts follow their originators with their fragrance and beauty and encourage them to strive higher and higher on their Path.

Legends say that beautiful thoughts are like rose petals flying around the king entering the palace, or like angels accompanying him throughout his journey in the subjective world. This is why we are advised by great Sages to keep our thoughts pure, beautiful, and in line with Beauty, Goodness, Righteousness, Joy, and Freedom.

When pure thoughts penetrate into the Fiery Worlds, they build a communication line between man and higher spheres. It is through such a communication line that a steady flow of creative inspiration passes from the higher spheres into the consciousness of man. The steady flow of inspiration makes the man a source of Beauty, Goodness, Righteousness, Joy, solemnity, and creativity.

We are told that thoughts run faster than light, but after they enter into the sphere of fire of higher planes, they bounce back if they cannot continue to exist in the fiery spheres.

Evil thoughts act like boomerangs. Lofty thoughts are like communication cables between worlds.

Our thoughts are heard in higher spheres if they are really built by the pure fire of the heart. Otherwise, our thoughts create lots of noise in lower strata and attract unwholesome guests.

As action exists on the physical plane, thought is action on the mental plane. As there are stupid, non-goal-fitting, destructive, criminal, faulty, evil actions on the physical plane, similarly there are stupid, non-goal-fitting, destructive, criminal, faulty, and evil thoughts on the mental plane. As discrimination and solemnity are needed in our actions, similarly discrimination and solemnity are needed in our thoughts.

Often our actions are not controlled by our own thoughts but by our disturbed emotions. Often our high and beautiful thoughts cannot turn into action. The reasons for these conditions are as follows:

1. Often our actions are not controlled by our thoughts when our actions are controlled by our habits, by the thoughts of others, by posthypnotic suggestions, or even by obsessions.

2. Our disturbed or low-level thoughts can easily control our actions if the personality is not refined and easily responds to the low vibrations of low thoughts.

3. Our high-level thoughts cannot turn into actions on the physical plane if the personality is not refined and is full of karmic complexities.

The ideal situation is when our higher thoughts synchronize themselves with the personality and manifest as constructive and creative actions. This is how the integration of the physical brain and the mind takes place.

For the *resurrection* of the human soul, one needs to build ladders and bridges. Integration and alignment are other names for ladders and bridges. Things above must manifest below.

The Western world puts extreme emphasis upon the human mind without balancing the development of the mind with a similar development of the heart. When the mind is unduly developed, it slays the real purpose of life. It works against itself and creates separatism, antagonism, pollution, crimes, and wars.[4]

But if the heart is developed, it can balance the mind and lead the mind toward actualizing the visions and the revelations of the heart. The heart is in contact with the source of Cosmic principles, and it is the only guidance in our life. The mind at its best is the servant of the heart.

The Great Sage says,

> It was said long ago of the holy man — "He walked before the Lord." That means he did not violate the Hierarchy, and thus purified his heart. Through the slightest purification of the human heart, one can manifest a waterfall of Benefaction.[5]

Thinking is powerful when it is charged with the Intuition of the heart.

The distance between compressed thoughts can be filled by unfolding the main thoughts. This must be done rhythmically, and after each explanation, a stronger thought must be released.

It is better to use more inclusive and more penetrative thoughts at the end of conversations or writing. Mild thoughts must be released first; then gradually they must be synchronized with heavier and more charged thoughts. The

---

4. See also *The Flame of the Heart*.
5. Agni Yoga Society, *Heart*, para. 13.

conclusion must be reached with a very condensed thought which will synthesize the spirit of the talk or writing or open a new vision.

Thought must be given in a compressed way. The distance between thoughts must be short. They must hit the target rhythmically, one after another.

The wording must be focused, clear, and impressive. Diffused wording originates from confused thoughts. Unclear wording means that one does not understand his subject. If the thought is not impressive, there is no psychic energy, faith, or enthusiasm behind it.

Clear thinking is like a battle against ignorance, against corruption, against slander and malice. Clear thinking exposes vanity and reveals values, reality, and quality.

The impact of thought is stronger if unnecessary words are not used.

Sometimes it is necessary to put thoughts in direct wordings. Sometimes it is necessary to be allegorical and use parables, hints, and suggestions.

Crystallizations are easily loosened when one starts with hints and parables; and to prevent the reorganization of the pieces of crystallization, it is necessary to use direct thoughts as if they were commands.

In the process of expressing your thoughts, you sometimes need to give people time to digest, to rest in order to grasp your thoughts easily, and to avoid the mood of rejection or apathy. To eliminate this danger you must create intervals and fill them with joy, laughter, and humor which will allow the people to come alive, to come to attention, or to recharge their minds for new receptions.

Every audience is an entity. It has its cycles of ebb and flow. The thinker intuitively must discover these cycles and use his intervals accordingly.

Your thoughts must not create confusion, indigestion, or antagonism. People love to cooperate if you find the right way to present your thoughts.

People do not realize that the deepest urge of an aggressive enemy is to surrender himself. But people reject the enemy by using all those techniques which keep the animosity alive and the urge to surrender asleep. Thoughts must be put in those forms that facilitate the surrender of the enemy, without hurting his pride.

As a basic rule one must understand that thoughts cannot conquer unless they are based upon and charged with Beauty, Goodness, Righteousness, Joy, and Freedom. Any wrong motive weakens thoughts and produces reverse effects.

Thoughts originating from evil intentions, separatism, and greed eventually organize those forces which put an end to the source of the thoughts. This sometimes takes centuries, but it never fails.

Obsession of thought is a fact, but people sometimes wonder about the origin of such thoughts.

Our astral body is sometimes hit by a subtle current or emanation coming from astral entities. They deliberately or accidentally project their desires. Such desires or emanations create imagination in our astral body.

Imagination is a method of our astral elemental to translate such an impact from the astral world. After the imagination is formed, the mind reacts and creates corresponding thoughts. The elemental thus takes form in the astral body and increases in potency through imagination and thoughts.

This astral form builds itself further as it attracts similar thoughtforms and turns into a problem in the astral body. It not only affects the emotions and imagination of man, but to a great extent it also controls the thinking of man. This form is especially restimulated when man acts, reads, or finds himself in situations which key in with the form. Such an obsession is not easy to destroy.

Most of our sex drives originate from such formations. People are often victims of their formations.

To start the fight against such formations, one must first of all know that the excitement does not originate from his real nature, but it is the effect of an intrusive element in the aura. One must be firmly convinced that the thoughts about the urge do not belong, or do not originate, with him.

The second step is to stop the imagination whenever it appears because it is the imagination that evokes thoughts to enter the path of actualization.

The third step is to avoid any literature or imagery related to the urge.

The fourth step is consciously to decide not to satisfy the urge for certain intervals, no matter how difficult it seems. For example, if one feels forced to have sexual relations every day, he can decide firmly to have them only twice or once a week, or once a month.

With these four steps it is possible to weaken the obsessive formation because thought nourishes such formations and keeps them alive for a long time.

The fifth step is a mental exercise.

For instance, if the formation is a sexual one, the person must visualize an image of the object of desire and in his imagination burn it. Inch by inch, he must turn it into ashes and blow it into space. During such a process one feels he is cutting something from his body, and he feels attached to it. But no matter what he feels, he should continue burning the formation.

Burning not only affects or stops the course of imagination taking place through the power of formation, but it also creates a disintegration in the formation.

It is possible that elementals from the subtle or astral world do not reach a person directly but through a contact with someone who is obsessed by them. Remember that the emotional plane is liquidic and things travel quite easily in it from one body to another. This is why things are more contagious in the astral than in the physical plane.

An obsession in the astral plane can be transferred to one who is fusing his astral body in sex with another person.

Those who have a close relationship with the astral world, through mediumistic activities or because of their psychic nature, are very prone to astral attacks. Things in the astral plane stick. One must avoid such contacts as much as possible so as not to become contaminated by many kinds of emanations.

Mediums are mostly carriers of such emanations. A great many problems can be brought in through contacts with mediums or through those who are astrally oriented. The problems of a victim increase if he or she lives in a place where such obsessive formations have almost materialized.

Obsessive formations sometimes act like entities or ghosts within many dwellings. Such ghosts are those obsessive formations which have grown to such a degree that they can have an independent existence and still be tied to the original person.

Of course, one must understand that such obsessions are not only related to sex but also to greed, hatred, jealousy, fear, depression, treason, malice, etc.

Certain people have loads of these vices during their departure from the earth, and many parts of such loads fall on the highway of life — so to say — and people pick them up due to the influential pressures of those who are already contaminated by them.

When we talk about purity, we have also in mind a way of life which is not contaminated by such astral elements.

6

The Mechanism of the Mind

We were told that Socrates was once invited to a wedding party. The wedding was going to be held in a neighborhood village. Socrates took his servant with him and set off for the village. It was evening when they were going through a mountain pass. Socrates slowed his pace and sat down on a rock. The servant, thinking that Socrates was taking a little rest, waited a few feet away. After resting a few minutes, Socrates told his servant to proceed to the wedding. He was going to sit on the rock for a while and think.

The servant left him, once in a while looking back to see if his master was proceeding. Eventually Socrates was alone in the darkness of night. The wedding party lasted until morning, but Socrates was absent. The servant hurried back early in the morning by the same path. As he came near the rock, he saw Socrates still sitting, like a statue, in deep contemplation.

The servant sat by the rock and waited. As the sun rose above the horizon, Socrates opened his eyes, smiled, stood up, and said, "Let us give thanks to the Source of Light, and let us go home."

Without such a life of meditation and contemplation, Socrates would not have been able to carry the torch of wisdom throughout the ages, influencing creative minds all over the world, opening for them the path of Goodness, Truth, Beauty, and immortality.

It is very probable that Socrates had some questions in his mind, and he wanted to find the answers to these questions. For him the wedding party was not as important as the wedding ceremony within his mind between the question and the answer.

A life of continuous meditation eventually releases the innermost creative fire in the human being. It is this release that produces all the beauties of the world. Talents are the result of a life of meditation. A genius is an unfolding talent expressing the creative fire to a greater degree.

As a man progresses on his path of evolution, his dedication toward the search for answers increases. He uses his mind more and more, until one day his mind reaches enlightenment.

Once an enemy soldier approached Archimedes, who was trying to solve a geometrical problem in the sand. The soldier's intention was to kill him. Looking at the soldier, Archimedes said, "Don't kill me until I solve this problem."

But the soldier pushed his dagger into the chest of that great man. As Archimedes was about to die, he said, "Yes, you took my body, but I am taking my mind with me."

In all centuries great thinkers emphasized the need for using the mind in right directions. No human being will improve his conditions or his environment without learning how to use his mind.

I had a religious friend who used every occasion to remind me that the mind is the source of all our troubles. One day we were about to travel. When we purchased our airline tickets, I looked at him very seriously and said, "You know, I think we must not travel by air. We must walk."

"Are you crazy? We have five thousand miles to go."

"But," I said, "the airplane was produced by the human mind. If we did not have such thinkers, we would have to walk."

He looked at me with a strange smile and said, "Let us *think* in the airplane. You are right."

Every moment in our life we are forced to use our minds; but the mind is a complicated mechanism, and only those who learn how to use it and how to protect it can raise themselves above average humanity and enter into their Divine heritage.

In Western psychology we do not have clear information about the mind. In the esoteric Teaching we are told that the thinking process uses the following mechanisms:

1. brain

2. etheric brain

3. pineal gland, pituitary body, and carotid gland at the base of the skull

4. mental body

5. Thinker

6. unfolding human soul

7. mental unit and Mental Permanent Atom

1. The **brain** is formed by billions of electrochemical nerve cells. It is a network of tangible electrochemical energy which is in ceaseless activity. Nature worked millions of years to produce such a mechanism, which is used by the human being as a receiving and transmitting mechanism.

In the brain we have three glands:

— pineal gland

— pituitary body

— carotid gland

The brain has three main functions:

a. To inform the etheric brain of the impressions coming through the five senses

b. To transfer messages to the five senses and put them into action according to the command formulated in the mind

c. To transmit forces coming from etheric, astral, and mental planes to the physical system

2. The **etheric brain** is an electromagnetic prototype of the physical brain, penetrating and surrounding the brain and the spinal column. It acts in two ways:

a. It receives impressions from the emotional and mental bodies and transfers them to the brain.

b. It receives the impressions from the brain and transfers them to the mental body.

The etheric brain also acts as an electronic anchorage tube when the man is not functioning in his body but is functioning within one of his higher vehicles while asleep or in a trance. Impressions from these vehicles contact the etheric brain and are transferred to the brain via etheric magnetic lines. This transference process is done properly and in the best way when the brain is in good condition, which means

— nourished and in a healthy state

— not tired

— not intoxicated

— not agitated by violent emotions, worries, fears, etc.

— not registering pain

— not ill-formed or ill-developed

This transference is also done in the best way if the etheric brain is developed and has good connections with the mental centers.

It happens sometimes that because of inner disturbances, the fusion of the etheric brain with the physical brain is not complete, and there exist gaps between the connecting links. Inner disturbances are caused by psychic attacks, obsessions, possessions, or by directed ill-thought currents. Dislocation of the etheric brain can also be caused by identifications, as in the case of mystics or highly devotional or fanatical people.

3. The **pineal gland,** the **pituitary body,** and the **carotid gland at the base of the skull** form one mechanism in the brain as a triangle of energy. These glands are the objective manifestation of the three centers in the head. These three centers are

head center — pineal gland

ajna center — pituitary body

alta major center — carotid gland

The head center channels the will energy to the personality through a triple thread which is called the Antahkarana. [1] In the thinking process this center brings the light of the Purpose and galvanizes thoughtforms with "electric fire." We are told that this center becomes fully active at the Third Initiation. It is related to the mind through the etheric brain and through the pineal gland.

The ajna center is formed in the etheric body, immediately above the two eyes. It brings the light of intelligence into the brain through the pituitary body. It is this light which is used to create thoughtforms and appropriate them to the inner conditions of the mind and to the outer conditions of life. Through the ajna center, man materializes and puts into action the thoughtforms which he was building. It functions after the Third Initiation.

Also, the ajna center acts as a spokesman of the personality, transmitting the aspirations of the personality to the mental body. The part of the Antahkarana, which is called the creative thread, carries the messages from the ajna center into the three vehicles of the personality. When a close connection is established between the ajna center and the throat center, the creative ideas pour down from the mind via the ajna center and find creative expression through the throat center.

The pituitary body acts as the recipient of lower mental, astral, and etheric forces and grounds them in the brain. These forces reach the pituitary body via the life thread. It is interesting to know that when the heart center becomes fully active, the pituitary body starts to function. [2]

---

1. For further information see Ch. 45, "The Antahkarana," and Chs. 46-47 in *The Psyche and Psychism.*
2. For further information see *The Psyche and Psychism,* Ch. 45.

The alta major center has a very important role in our meditation. It relates the thought energy to the spinal cord and controls the organs of the body. It is a physical center and closely related to the base of the spine. Actually the fire of kundalini is transmitted to the head center through the alta major center. It is the development of the throat center which puts the alta major center into action.

The alta major center is built by the lowest ether. The throat center is built by the substance of the third ether. The heart center is built by the substance of the second ether, and the head center is built by the substance of the first ether.

The pineal gland draws energy from the head center, and the energy of purpose or goal or aim is available for the thoughtform-building process. This energy sets the destination of the form, as a motivating power in the core of the thought.

The pituitary body brings in a kind of energy which may be called form-building, desire energy. This energy binds the substance of the mind together and brings in the form.

The alta major center is like the bow which releases the arrow, the thoughtform. The energy which it brings in is nerve energy, which is closely connected with the energy of the etheric body and the nadis, or etheric nerve channels.[3]

It is in dedicated service and through right meditation that these centers are related magnetically and used for their specific tasks to produce those thoughtforms by which light, love, power, plan, and purpose are broadcast into space and into the minds of men.

This does not mean that thoughtforms can only be created with the combined actions of these three centers. In most human beings these centers are not awake at the same time; one or two are in the process of stimulation.

Most thoughtforms are built by the power of desire. Often such thoughtforms disintegrate in a short time and create pollution in the aura. That is why we are urged to "guard our thoughts."

The higher thoughtform-building process starts when the unfolding human soul has a contact with the Inner Lord and sees, in a flash, some part of the Plan or some light shed on a problem.

Thoughtforms become really influential or effective when the above-mentioned three centers are in an active condition. It is at this stage that the disciple becomes a White Magician, a creative power for his environment, and a Path "through which men may achieve."

To think well means to be able to be impressed by the Plan. To think deeper means to be impressed by the Purpose and be able to adapt the impressions coming from the Purpose to the needs of humanity.

_____

3.   See Ch. 4, *Cosmos in Man.*

A talented man is a man who has access to the Chalice. A genius is a man who has contact with his Monadic Core and builds his thoughtforms with the three centers and three glands mentioned above.

4. The **mental body** is the next mechanism of the thinking process. The base of spine center in the mental body corresponds to the base of spine in the physical body. Before the base of spine begins to be active, this center in the mental body must awaken and build a bridge through its radioactivity toward the sacrifice petals of the Lotus. The mental body must be so pure that the fire coming from the sacrifice petals reaches, in its purity, this center in the mental body and then, via the astral base of spine center, reaches the base of spine in etheric matter. Only through such a process is the kundalini fire stimulated and raised safely to the head center via the bridge — the alta major center.[4]

The base of spine center in the head is used by the Thinker to control the creative fires of the body and the etheric body. The base of spine center controls the adrenal glands and their functions. These glands play a major part in the chemistry of the human body. Because the center is directly related to the mental plane, it is easy to see that our thoughts have a great effect on these glands and on the chemistry of our physical body. Most of the imbalance in the chemistry of the body is due to thoughts that are not in accord with the main note of life within us.

The generative organs center in the mental body controls the generative functions of the male or female. Our sexual problems can be totally solved when a man purifies the atmosphere of this center in his mind. This center acts as a switch for the generative organs in the astral plane and then in the physical plane, turning them on and off according to the thoughts affecting them.

Sometimes a great deal of congestion exists in the mental sphere when great amounts of thoughtforms play as stimulants for sexual activity. This center is also connected to the throat center, through which thoughtforms create the splendid arts of the world — literary works, poetry, music, sculpture, and so on.

The solar plexus center on the mental plane corresponds to the solar plexus center in the astral and physical-etheric planes. This center is connected with the love petals of the Lotus, and in the mental plane it fuses all the centers below the diaphragm. Thoughts which are not in harmony with the life of the Spirit hit many organs that this center controls. It fuses thoughts with emotions. Through the solar plexus, emotional force flows into the etheric body and physical body.

In an advanced aspirant it is this center that contributes the fire of emotion to thoughts and thoughtforms and makes them dramatic, fantastic, and emotionally magnetic. Great writers, poets, musicians, and painters use emotions with ideas and thoughts in their creative work.

---

4.   See also Ch. 12, "The Kundalini Fire," in *New Dimensions in Healing.*

The physical manifestation of the solar plexus is the pancreas and the stomach. It is also related to the liver. This makes us feel the importance of clear, pure thinking. No wonder the Master says, "Friends, I repeat — hold your thoughts pure, this is the best disinfectant and the foremost tonic expedient."[5] And, "It is time to recognize the fact that thought is born in the fiery centers."[6]

Fiery centers are all those centers that exist in the mental body: the Lotus, the four centers, the mental unit, and the Mental Permanent Atom.[7] All these centers relate to parts of the physical body, and this is why the mental sphere must be pure and not polluted with ill-thoughts, illusions, blind and dark commands, and hypnotic suggestions.

The solar plexus in the mental body, as well as in the astral and etheric bodies, has two parts. The lower part of the center is the door to lower psychism and astralism. The higher part of the center is connected to the head center in the etheric body and the love petals in the Chalice. The higher part of this center in the head awakens and functions as the person changes his desires into aspiration, then into spiritual striving. Advanced psychics use this center in the mental body, and they demonstrate great gifts of spiritual life. Healing work is done also with the higher part of this center.

5. After the mental body, we have the **Thinker**. Only in esoteric tradition do we find information about the Thinker. It is very strange but true that man does not think most of the time. There is some Presence within him Who thinks. The Thinker is a very advanced Soul Who plays the role of a Guardian Angel within man. It is not the man. It is a separate Being, and Its duty is to lead the human being to a degree of advancement where he can think by himself and can handle his own life consciously according to the Purpose of life.[8]

Through thinking the human soul first sees the laws of Creation and the immediate plan for his individual life; and second, he appropriates these laws and the course of his life in such a way that the Plan works out through him and the Purpose is fulfilled.

To do this, the human soul must put himself in contact with the higher planes, the Higher Worlds.

On a higher spiral the Thinker does the same thing. It comes in contact with the Hierarchy, where the Plan is formulated, and with Shamballa, where the Purpose of God is known. In deep meditation It tries to impress part of that knowledge upon the unfolding human soul so that the human soul adjusts his life accordingly and secures his own progress on the Path. For a long time the

---

5. Agni Yoga Society, *Community*, para. 23.
6. Agni Yoga Society, *Fiery World*, Vol. II, para. 234.
7. For additional information on the centers of the three bodies, please refer to *New Dimensions in Healing*.
8. See also *The Solar Angel* and *Other Worlds*, Ch. 59.

human soul cannot do this, but he instinctively follows some of the communications from the Solar Angel.

After a long time of suffering and hardship, the human soul tries to raise himself to the mental plane. This is a very difficult phase in which the person tries to detach himself from the identifications of physical and emotional life and focus himself on the mental plane. A time comes in which he begins to educate himself and exercise his mental body. Eventually he engages himself in occult meditation in which he learns the laws and the science of thinking. At this stage in his meditation, he tries to touch the thoughts of the Soul or Solar Angel, analyze them, and live accordingly.

For a long time the progress of the human being is based on such an inner communication with the Soul. Finally, a time comes when he learns to use his mind and has flashes of thinking. We are told that eventually the man is able to communicate with Higher Sources and start thinking. After the human soul learns how to think, the Solar Angel gradually withdraws and departs.

6. The **unfolding human soul** is the Spark within the human form, the Real Man Himself, the Monad on the Path of return. This Spark, throughout ages, first tries to control and use the physical body to such an extent that he identifies with it; he assumes that he is the physical body and that with the destruction of that body he is annihilated.

In the next stage he passes into the emotional vehicle, then the lower mental vehicle — each time through identification and detachment. Eventually he succeeds in knowing himself as an independent being who is other than his vehicles of manifestation.

The longest period of struggle is in the lower mental plane where, around the mental unit, are accumulated all the fears, prejudices, superstitions, suppressed urges and drives, racial inclinations, symbols, and traditions of ages. These are so strongly rooted there that the human soul has a very difficult time coming out of such a jungle and acting in free space. Thus for long ages man cannot break through and remains a slave to his past. He lives in the past, thinks in the past, and any progressive idea creates violent reactions in him.

Sometimes even advanced disciples fall back into their former shallow waters within the lower mind, especially in old age and loneliness. They seek refuge in past memories, religious or racial customs, ceremonies, and traditions. Old patterns of thinking, if not totally wiped away, come back and with full force dominate the consciousness of the man.

7. The **Mental Permanent Atom** is the future. It is the seed of the next mental body in which are accumulated the best micro-records of the thoughts of the past, thoughts that are related to the three higher levels of the mind. The human soul travels from the lower mind to the higher mind, and eventually reaches the Mental Permanent Atom.

This permanent atom is surrounded by the highest mental substance, and it is a center of force which controls the formation of the mental body for the next incarnation. It is also a point of highest communication in the mental body with the Intuitional and Atmic Planes. The Mental Permanent Atom carries the charge of that energy which we call the Monadic Ray. It is in a sense the physical sun of the personality, through which energies and forces are distributed to all cells and atoms of the threefold personality.

The nucleus of the Mental Permanent Atom is a Monadic essence, the Monadic fire. This is also true of all permanent atoms. It is this essence that unfolds through the spirillae.

The mental unit has only four spirillae. Each of these spirillae is formed by a different group of lives which have specific functions of their own, whereas the Mental Permanent Atom and the physical and astral permanent atoms each have seven spirillae.

In the creative thought process, the Mental Permanent Atom and the mental unit are very closely involved. A continuous stream of sparks flows from one to the other. The Mental Permanent Atom sends charges, and the light is seen on the fourth mental plane through the mental unit. Then it penetrates the etheric brain and into a force field created by the pineal gland, the pituitary body, and the alta major center. It then passes to the cells of the brain. When the creative activity is of a very high order, the unfolded petals of the Lotus participate in the evaluation of impressions and ideas coming down from Higher Sources.

The mental unit registers our experiences in the waking state of mind. It controls the impressions coming from the five senses and takes conscious actions, as far as its unfoldment permits.

Posthypnotic suggestions cannot penetrate into the mental unit. They go into the physical and emotional permanent atoms and to the three lower levels of mind, which we call the subconscious mind, where they turn into irresistible commands.[9]

The Mental Permanent Atom registers all events, whether we are conscious or unconscious. It also registers impressions coming from Higher Sources and transmits them to the mental unit as impulses. It registers all conscious and unconscious experiences, but it does not react to posthypnotic suggestions. Its contents can be used after a man builds the bridge between the mental unit and the Mental Permanent Atom. However, when a man is hypnotized, the mental unit carries out the commands registered by the physical-etheric and astral permanent atoms. In such a course of action, it tries to rationalize its actions without really having a support within itself. As hypnotic suggestions continue to flow into the other permanent atoms, the mental unit enters into a state of

_____

9.   See also *The Subconscious Mind and the Chalice.*

"confusion," and a time comes when it no longer can discriminate "reality" from "unreality."[10]

It is through the mental unit that de-hypnotizing starts, if the Mental Permanent Atom or an external agent helps the person through the process of observation, logic, common sense, and dramatic action. But total de-hypnotizing is achieved when the consciousness shifts itself from the mental unit to the Mental Permanent Atom where things are seen as they are.

In the educational process these two atoms (the mental unit and the Mental Permanent Atom) must be related, and man must register his subjective and objective impressions in both of them simultaneously. When we bypass the mental unit, or the so-called conscious mind, and work on the permanent atoms and on the subconscious mind, we plant within ourselves the seeds of grave trouble for the future. The integration, alignment, and fusion of the mechanism is the goal of education. Only a unified and synchronized mechanism can bring higher results.

Education is an effort to grasp the laws and principles of the Universe and put them into application. Only an integrated, aligned, synchronized, and fused mechanism can be impressed without distortion and receive and translate impressions without changing their implications. Only a unified, integrated, synchronized, and fused mechanism can register the events of life without alteration, gaps, and distortion.

Progress in life is only possible if the human soul has the right data received from subjective and objective worlds. Without right information and right data, the human soul resembles a commander who gives wrong orders because his messenger brings him distorted or wrong information.

It is also possible that the mental unit is forced into action by the pressure of the permanent atom involved. Such actions are responsible for the strange behavior you express on certain occasions. For example, sometimes you hate someone without an apparent reason. Let us assume that in the past you had a bad experience with a person. Years later you meet a man who has some resemblance to the person with whom you had the bad experience. You do not recall your past experience, but you feel that you must keep away from the present person because, without your awareness, he reminds you of the former person.

Your attitude toward that person becomes aggressive, and you try to attack him if he does the slightest thing that hurts you. That slightest thing releases the memory in you of that previous experience.

Memories and experiences are all registered in the permanent atoms and in the etheric brain. Those experiences which bypass the mental unit and are impressed in the two lower permanent atoms release themselves at the time any These restimulated impressions exercise a great pressure on your nervous system

---

10.   For further information on hypnotism, please see *New Dimensions in Healing* and *The Subconscious Mind and the Chalice*.

to make you act according to their nature and direction, but the mental unit cannot understand their demand because it has no record of them. This is how tension is created on the mental plane and eventually is expressed in various disorders and sicknesses of the emotional and physical bodies.

The hypnotist bypasses the mental unit and tries to release these memories or experiences, or plant new suggestions in the man. But when the man returns to his normal consciousness, the mental unit discovers that the person is acting in a strange way, the cause of which is not known to the mental unit. This time it tries to block the flow of the impression. This creates a great tension and causes many troubles in trying to block an activated flow of hypnotic suggestions on the road of expression.

For example, a man has a habit of scratching his head every time he meets a girl. There are various causes for such an action of which the mental unit is not aware. The man acts that way because of the force released from his permanent atoms, or from the subconscious mind.

After hypnotizing the person, the hypnotist suggests to him that he must not scratch his head. Since the man is unconscious, the mental unit is not aware of it. When the man stops scratching his head, the mental unit is bewildered about this new behavior. It tries to restore the former behavior but meets the resistance of the permanent atoms. This is how conflict starts. The permanent atoms, being the owners of the impressions, continue to act as they were ordered to do. Since the mental unit cannot prevent the permanent atoms from acting as they do, it tries to block the action, changing the direction of the flow. This creates complications in the direction of the flow, as the flow is forced to express itself through organs which are not used to it.

The only way to release the unwanted impressions from the permanent atoms is via the mental unit. This is why it is imperative to build the Antahkarana,[11] make the mental unit aware of all that is registered in the three personality permanent atoms, and then release the unwanted impressions consciously.

The mental unit operates all involuntary actions of the body such as circulation, secretions, the repair work going on all the time, the actions of various glands, elimination, etc. This is why it is very dangerous to aggravate the mental unit in any way. Any aggravation causes disorders in the autonomic nervous system, and because the mental unit also controls all conscious actions, you see similar disorders in the actions of man which are carried on consciously.

The disturbances occur in the following way. The mental unit has set ways to run its machine, the human body, and it also has the ability to respond, act, or react to all impressions coming to it from the five senses. If the mental unit is bypassed and the permanent atoms are impressed with certain actions or directions, a conflict will occur between them.

_____

11. See also *The Psyche and Psychism*, Chs. 45-47.

Any conflict between the permanent atoms and the mental unit will end with the submission of the mental unit. Actually, any submission of the mental unit causes a distortion in its mechanisms, and it immediately affects the autonomic nervous system with physical or health consequences.

There are specific differences between the permanent atoms and the subconscious mind:

1. Permanent atoms record all that man experiences in his conscious and unconscious moments. The subconscious mind only records during unconscious moments.

2. The recordings of the permanent atoms are copies of facts. The recordings of the subconscious mind are a mix of facts and fantasies.

3. The recordings of the permanent atoms do not change. The recordings of the subconscious mind change and reorganize continuously.

4. The recordings of the permanent atoms condition the nature of our future bodies. The recordings of the subconscious mind affect our future only by creating karma — when controlling the actions of man.

5. The recordings of the permanent atoms do not interfere directly in our daily thinking, feelings, and actions. The recordings of the subconscious mind interfere in our thoughts, emotions, and actions when restimulated.

The nature of our future genes is the collective result of the recordings of our three lower permanent atoms. The exception is the mental unit, which does not record when man is unconscious.

Any impression accumulated through the five senses within the three lower permanent atoms — physical, emotional, and mental — without *the awareness* of the mental unit is a hypnotic suggestion. And any hypnotic suggestion creates inner conflict, inner chaos.

Those who are very involved in their emotional nature and have not cultivated their mind through education and meditation are subject to astral hypnotic suggestions, which are given by dark forces or their agents in the astral plane.

At the time of sleep the mental unit does not register any impression occurring on the astral plane unless a part of the Antahkarana has been built.

Impressions received from higher senses found on Intuitional and higher Planes do not produce hypnotic suggestions if continuity of consciousness is a fact and if the Antahkarana, or the bridge of consciousness, has been built. If the bridge is not built and if higher impressions are registered by the higher planes, they create either noble and creative urges or low and destructive urges in man, depending on the conditions of the etheric centers.

The first bridge of consciousness is built between the mental unit and the Mental Permanent Atom. When this is accomplished, the man on the personality plane is aware of the Soul's activities and of the complicated records of the Mental Permanent Atom. Thus the subjective life and the objective life, or the idealistic life and the practical life, meet each other.

Close to the Fourth Initiation the Mental Permanent Atom supersedes the mental unit, and the unfolding human soul, mostly working within the boundary of the mental unit, escapes and functions in the higher mind.

The mental unit is "the spark of mind" that the second wave of Solar Angels kindled in the fourth level of the mental plane. It is the sixth sense. When the mental unit was formed in the mental plane, the polarization of man came down from the astral consciousness to the brain-waking state of consciousness.[12]

The mental unit is closely connected with the mental body, with the physical body, and with the etheric head center. If it is in any way blocked or misused, its condition reflects on the mental body, the physical body, and the head center with dire consequences.

We are told also that "being of mental matter, devachan might be regarded as a centre, or heart of peace, within the periphery of the sphere of influence of the mental unit. The four spirillae form four protecting streams of force."[13]

The mental unit plays a great role for the reincarnating soul.

Also, when a *mayavirupa* is going to be built, it is the mental unit that, with the astral and physical permanent atoms, creates the body which is composed of the highest substance of the etheric, astral, and lower mental planes.

For a long time it is the mental unit that functions in the mental plane, until slowly the Mental Permanent Atom makes its influence felt.

The devas who function on the lower mental plane are related to man through the mental unit. These devas are related to the great fiery Lives Who live on the Cosmic Mental Plane, and They come in contact with humanity through the mental unit.

In addition, the mental unit is closely related to the Ray of the Monad, and subjectively it makes the conditioning influence of the Ray permeate throughout the life expression of the man when he enters the path of initiation.

On the path of initiation, the mental unit is superseded also by the Atmic Permanent Atom, and the whole field of the mind is irradiated by the atmic light and atmic power. Actually, the mental unit is like a door through which the human soul passes beyond the lower mental web and enters into causal awareness.

On various occasions, an association restimulates the records of the permanent atoms. Restimulated records release a current of force into the field of operation of the permanent atoms. This force turns into a drive or an urge. The mental unit, being the commander of conscious actions of the body, does not

---

12. See also *The Legend of Shamballa* and *The Solar Angel.*
13. Alice A. Bailey, *A Treatise on Cosmic Fire*, p. 1109.

understand the nature of the blind drives and urges, but because of their innate force it lets them pass into action. The mental unit cannot understand their nature because they were registered in the permanent atoms when the mental unit was practically absent, due to pain or moments of unconsciousness.

The mental unit uses the method of rationalization as it gives permission to the urges and drives to pass into action. Other times the mental unit acts as common sense. For example, while you are eating an apple, you feel something different in your mouth and you identify it as a worm. Such an experience is immediately recorded by one of your permanent atoms and by the mental unit. Later it happens that while you are eating a sandwich, you experience a similar feeling to having a worm in your mouth. At this time, even though it is not a worm, this similar feeling reawakened in one of your permanent atoms the old memory, an experience which you hated at that time. However, this time the mental unit informs you that it is a piece of vegetable and suggests to you to take it out of your mouth and see it for yourself, but you still hate the feeling.

This is an example of conflict between two recordings: the recording of the permanent atom and the recording of the mental unit. If the recording of the permanent atom is very strong or if more than one atom is involved, then the mental unit compromises and finds a way to tell you that "even though it is not a worm, because you hate the feeling, let us throw the sandwich away and never eat any more sandwiches." This is how certain attitudes are justified without reason.

At the time of suffering and intense pain (except in rare cases), the mental unit shuts itself off. This is our escape mechanism. But when it shuts off from all that is happening, things are registered in the permanent atoms as posthypnotic suggestions. This is why we say that man is mostly a machine working through push-buttons.

When such recordings are abundant, a split personality is the result, and there is obsession or possession. There is no organic disorder, but the conflicting waves of the permanent atoms and the rational mind, the mental unit, create the turmoil.

Suffering and pain do not produce the same effect when the consciousness of man works on higher planes such as the third, second, or first mental subplane. In this case the mental unit has progressed to higher planes, and the man can see the causes of the sufferings and tries to eliminate them or counteract them.

Many great souls enter the field of suffering after they raise their consciousness to higher subplanes of the mental plane in order to help awaken sufferers from their posthypnotically controlled lives. They are conscious sufferers, though this term is inaccurate because conscious suffering is a way of intense spiritual joy.

7

What is Thinking?

Thinking is the process to

> a. search and discover
>
> b. translate
>
> c. relate
>
> d. transmit energy
>
> e. create
>
> f. direct energy
>
> g. destroy
>
> h. analyze
>
> i. solve problems
>
> j. put things into application
>
> k. synthesize

These are the eleven main qualities of a mind that is in the process of thinking.

a. The mind *searches* for causes and for their possible effects. It learns how the causes produce effects. It sees how effects in their turn become causes to produce further effects. If we develop our minds, we will be able to avoid creating causes which will lead us to destruction, and we will know how effects can be annihilated by creating new causes.

b. The mind also *translates* the impressions coming from the five senses. It also translates impressions, ideas, inspirations, and visions coming from higher sources and formulates them for application. It is only through right translation that the mind communicates the source of the "message" and takes right action.

c. The mind *relates*. Thinking is a process of building relationships. Through thinking man learns that life can exist only on the foundation of right relationship. Thinking means to relate things to each other in right ways. It is just like writing a paragraph: each word must be related in the right way to express a meaning. If the words are related improperly, there will be no meaning but only chaos. The mind tries to relate to give manifestation to an idea.

d. The mind *transmits energy*. If the mind is not in order, the physical body does not receive the proper amounts of energy. We are told that prana is digested only when the mind is in high order.
The mind is the transmitter of energy into the nervous system. The slightest conflict or agitation in the mind weakens the nervous system, the glandular system, and their corresponding organs.
As the mind develops and refines, it transmits higher energy to the body. A period even comes in the life of the individual in which the mind not only transmits energy but also regenerates, heals, and transforms the body.

e. The mind *creates*. Thinking is a creative process. The creative process is an effort to translate and manifest an idea in a form that was not in existence before.
On every level, in every age, we have different needs. The mind tries to meet our needs by constructing forms that can be used, forms which give intense joy, forms which lead us toward higher achievements.
True creativity is a process of actualizing an idea. If the idea is not in the created form, it is a failure.

f. The mind *directs energy* through thoughts, through thoughtforms, through concentration, and through vision.
As the human being develops, he will be able to energize seeds, plants, trees, and human beings through his thought power. Through thought power man will put his physical, etheric, emotional, and mental mechanisms in order and eliminate factors that are not in harmony with health, joy, and freedom. It will even be possible to use the mind to eliminate and destroy hindrances in the seven fields of human endeavor.

g. Thinking can also *destroy*. In one sense it destroys superstitions, prejudices, illusions, vanities, and ignorance. In another sense it destroys cultures, civilizations, spiritual values, and those who are carriers of values. For a long time thinking can go in both directions unless the heart sheds its light upon it. Once the light of the heart is felt in the mind, thoughts only destroy those elements that hinder the path of humanity toward freedom, unity, and synthesis.

h. The mind *analyzes*. Thinking is a process of analysis. In analysis we try to see the individual parts that form the whole. The concept of wholeness cannot be achieved until the analyzer realizes that the parts only have a value in the wholeness. Once the relationship is seen between the parts and the whole, the analyzer finds out how to condition the parts to make them have right relationship with the whole.

i. The mind *solves problems*. Thinking is a problem-solving labor. Those who do not know how to think create problems. Those who know how to think solve problems.

So far, the human mind has solved many problems created by those who did not know how to think. If human thought is guided by higher principles, the planet will survive. If not, through wrong thinking, selfish thinking, dark thinking, we will end all that we created on this planet since the Atlantean disaster. The sinking of Atlantis proved that Atlanteans did not know how to think. Do we?

j. The mind *puts things into application*. This is thinking. If you cannot think, you cannot use all that exists around you. You may misuse things, which means you do not use things for the purpose for which they were created; you use things not for your and others' best interests but for creating chaos.

Thinking is the art through which you apply things in right ways and receive maximum results.

k. The mind *synthesizes*. Thinking is a process of orchestration of many laws, principles, objects, memories, formulas, plans, and goals. Each thought is a synthesis, and real thinking has the power to synthesize.

To synthesize means to relate things in such a way that all parts benefit, dedicating themselves for the Common Good, for the whole. The greater the power of synthesis, the greater the mind. One can keep his balance and harmony with the energies of the Universe only through surfing on the summits of synthesis.

Furthermore, thinking has three levels. On the first level the evolving human soul penetrates the peripheries of the light of the Inner Guide and through that light solves his basic problems.

On the second level the evolving human soul penetrates deeper into the light of the Inner Guide, and a kindling process takes place within his Core. It is through increasing the light within himself that the human soul tries to meet his problems.

On the third level the evolving human soul fuses his light with the light of the Inner Guide, and with this blended light he meets his problems. At this stage he has the viewpoint and strength of the light of the Inner Guide, which not only illuminates his mind but also inspires and reveals higher visions.

Thought is creative when it is the manifestation of an inner Plan and Purpose and causes transformation in others, leading them toward a purposeful life.

There are thoughts that are not inspired by the Plan and Purpose, and they often stay and stagnate in the aura. They are caught in the aura and they die there, polluting your aura. That is why you must have living thoughts which can go out and vitalize the world.

Every weak, selfish, and separative thought either dies in the aura or oozes out into the aura of others, causing much damage to them.

The Inner Guide gives direction when you ask for it. Most of our thinking is not to ask for direction but to ask for knowledge of how to acquire objects. Curiously enough, almost everyone knows in his heart his own direction, and he knows, too, whether his direction is right or wrong. You must find your own *direction*. That is where your value is.

Direction comes from your Inner Guide or from your Inner Core.

Wrong thinking is not really thinking but wrong application of thoughtforms existing around you due to interferences of your glamors, illusions, and blind urges and drives.

Motive is not related to thoughts or thinking but is controlled by the level where your interest is focused. Often your motive is your fear, hatred, posthypnotic suggestions, past impressions, and many other things.

You discover your level in the process of the application of thought. It is your motive that conditions the direction of your application. In the application of your thought you see what you are, where you are.

People also confuse the mind and the mental body. The mind is intelligent electricity in the mental body. When this intelligent electricity is in operation in the mental body, we say man has mind.

When the electricity flows into the light bulb, you have light; you have mind. When the electricity is not on, you have a mental body but not mind.

Consciousness comes into existence when the beam of intelligent electricity illuminates an area in the mental body, sublimating a certain amount of mental atoms. This field of light expands slowly as the man applies the light in his life.

One may ask, is Intuition a process of thinking? The answer is no. Intuition is awareness, not consciousness, not thinking. But Intuition needs to manifest through thinking, thought, and thoughtforms.

The manifestation differs due to the various stages of the mental mechanism through which mental electricity manifests. It sometimes happens that when the mind is mixed up, the incoming impressions create chaos in the mind and develop illusions.

The progress of a human being does not totally lie in his ability to think. The ability to think is of extreme importance, but the progress of a human being also depends upon his motivation.

Motivation is the door which leads a person to higher spheres or locks him within his own prison with all his wealth of thinking. When thinking is not applied correctly, it multiplies the world problems.

Thought is the conclusion and result of our thinking.

A thoughtform is a form that we build to put our thought into action. A thoughtform is conditioned by our Rays, education, and background. It is the thoughtform that translates our thoughts, and it is our thoughts that conclude the process of our thinking.

When one is able to be impressed by the currents of energy of the Inner Guide, charged with meaning and significance, we say that man is thinking.

Meditation is a step ahead of thinking. Meditation is thinking to know the Plan and Purpose and an effort to use this discovery for the advancement of life. In other words, meditation is purposeful, goal-fitting thinking, or thinking to manifest the Divine Plan and Purpose of this Earth.

We can see that the crucial point in the process of thinking is the *motive*. Motive is the power which controls the formation and direction of a thought or an action. This power is generated when the human soul contacts a portion of the Plan and uses it as the spring board for his thinking and action. That is why man is not equal to his thinking, but he is equal to his motive.

Great Ones choose Their disciples by their motives. If their motive is grounded in the interests of the three personality levels, They do not extend Their call to them. But if the motive is in harmony with the light of the Inner Guide and in harmony with Its Plan, They trust them and call them for higher service and discipline.

The Inner Guide does not interfere with our motives. No matter what motive we have, It answers our questions if we can grasp them. But of course, when we misuse the knowledge given by our Inner Guide, our receiving mechanism eventually decays and we no longer receive the answers to our questions. We lock our own door.

Motives are not necessarily the product of conscious thinking, but they often come into existence by emotional, physical, or mental desires. A motive may come into existence as a reaction or a response to a situation or person. It may be the result of a decision taken in higher states of consciousness or the result of a posthypnotic suggestion. One must find the originating source of motives.

Right motives are built by conscious thinking. Conscious thinking is thinking in the light of the Soul. Such motives are all-inclusive, progressive, and serve the Plan. Conscious thinking cannot produce wrong motives, as where there is light, darkness disappears.

A right motive is in harmony with the spiritual interests of all the vehicles and with the laws of progress. In creating a right motive, the light of the soul evokes agreement from all vehicles. This is why an imposed motive — imposed through hypnotic methods — creates disharmony between the vehicles and the human soul.

Motives built by reaction and response are also partial and belong only to one body. A consciously created motive integrates the vehicles and produces energy in them. This is why those who have lofty motives are invincible.

The difference between intention, goal, and motive must be clear in our understanding. When a motive begins to be in action, it creates tension. Intention is the expression of the motive in the mental plane. The goal is the projected image, or the future contemplated result of the motive.

Right motives cannot be artificially built in people. They are the result of hard labor, experience, transformation, and contact with the Intuitional Plane.

The light of the soul, or the consciousness, is absolutely impartial, non-separative, and all-inclusive. It works in harmony with the laws of the Universe. It sees things as they are, with their short-range and long-range effects and results.

The light of the soul is found in gradient magnitudes and different intensities, but the difference in intensity and magnitude does not affect the ability to see things as they are. However, if the light is less, it limits the field of operation and the expression of the ability to see things as they are. The greater the light of the consciousness, the greater the ability to cause changes in greater fields through that light.

8

Unfolding Consciousness

There are fourteen major steps through which we can develop our mind and expand our consciousness.

The mind cannot be developed by pushing into it endless information and data. Sometimes we can even paralyze our mind with excessive information which is not useful for our daily life, relationships, and creative efforts.

Humanity will be able to survive if its mind is developed and cultivated so that it is able to solve the problems of life.

If we want to define the mind, we can say that it is a problem-solving computer. Man has survived up to now because he was able to solve the problems that Nature and the environment presented to him. Life is not going to reduce the problems, and man at the present is living in a condition in which his man-made problems will multiply as the years go by.

These fourteen steps to develop the mind are actually fourteen steps of discipline and contact, and they are the path to expand the consciousness.

1. Aspiration

2. Observation

3. Concentration

4. Increasing the viewpoints

5. Meditation

6. Sincerity

7. Contemplation

8. Recognizing the principle of Hierarchy

9. Developing an impersonal outlook and renunciation

10. Illumination

11. Rejecting imposition

12. Inspiration

13. Creating a balance between abstract and concrete realms

14. At-one-ment

1. **Aspiration** is an intense focus of the emotional nature upon an object of beauty, an idea, or a person who manifests greatness, goodness, beauty, and truth.

In the process of aspiration, the subject makes great efforts to sacrifice all limiting walls in his nature to reach the object of desire. This develops his will and organizes his life along certain lines. He tries to know more, to have more, to be more. He is the one who has left behind the life of pleasures and now searches for reality. He senses some beauty, some reality; he sees deeper meaning in life, and he tries to collect all his powers and focus on the object, trying to sublimate and transform himself through raising his heart or emotions to the object of his aspiration.

It is on this level that the aspiring human soul transcends his nature to reach the object of his desire. These changes are made sometimes through various techniques which are called renunciation, penance, and detachment. Through these techniques the man throws away all obstacles that prevent him from reaching the object of his aspiration. Esoterically, aspiration is the result of a deeper feeling that you are not that which you think you are. You feel that a greater beauty is ready to manifest within you, leading you into greater joy and greater freedom. Every time you aspire to a greater beauty, the petals of your nature unfold and literally bloom.

Aspiration eventually leads to observation.

2. **Observation** is a very necessary step to develop a seeing eye. There are many exercises you can do to develop observation, but a good one is as follows:

Every day think about a different person and try to remember the shape of his nose, the color of his eyes, the design or color of his clothes, his shoes, etc., and a unique quality that makes him different from others. Do this for three months. Then observe people's emotional behavior for one month. Then for another month try to see their mental patterns, their mental behavior. Then for another month observe the man as a whole and his relation with the spiritual Path.

Observation is believed to be related only to the eyes, but real observation involves all the senses. To start with, we must observe with our eyes, ears, and nose — with our seeing, hearing, and smelling. Then we can go to the other senses, slowly developing observation, which means we are in close contact with the object of observation. We are alert, full of attention, and, because of our alertness and observation, things are impressed clearly in our minds.

Most of our senses are used while we are absent-minded. Try to use your senses as if you were in your senses. Actually, senses are parts of your Real Self, manifested as organs.

Observation means to be in your senses. When you are looking, be in your eyes. When you are touching, be in your touch. When you are hearing, be in your ears.

Observe through all your senses and try to retain the memory. Observation and memory are closely related — the keener your observation, the clearer is your recording or memory.

Can you remember what kind of handshake you had with that man? Soft, warm, cold, bony, fat, sneaky, relaxed, nervous, etc? Just observe, and you will notice how much you will increase your knowledge and develop your mind.

To develop the mind needs observation, knowledge, and memory. When the senses are used in their optimum capacity, the mind blooms because it acts in the right way, with less confusion and less wrong data.

Daily you can observe through your ears the voices around you, the music, the noises, etc. and eventually reach the conclusion that observation increases the supply of your energy in the three levels of the personality.

3. **Concentration** is the stage of one-pointedness, the stage when all of our mental and emotional energy is focused on an idea, vision, or service from which no force can distract us. Through aspiration we touch the object of our desire. Through concentration we assimilate the vision, the idea, or the beauty and make it our own. This is done by using not only the focus of our emotional powers but also of our mental powers.

We are told in the *Bhagavad Gita* that it is as difficult to control the mind as it is to control the wind. Throughout the ages we have been given all those rules and techniques through which we can master the mind and focus it on any line of action or on any idea, vision, or object. The stage of concentration is an advanced stage in which the willpower is quite active on the mental plane and is able to hold the substance of the mental plane in a certain direction without letting it be diffused or scattered in any other direction. A concentrated mind not only does not waver but also rejects any influence coming from the outside world in the form of impressions.

Man stays a fairly long time in this stage until he proves that he can hold an object in his mind and focus all of his mental energies upon it, and in the meantime live a life that is solely run in a certain preconceived direction. He then graduates to the step of meditation.

Concentration and meditation are exercises on how to stop the mechanical fluctuations of the mental sphere. The mental substance, with all its thoughtforms and thought patterns, is in ceaseless movement due to external impressions and internal urges and drives. Until these fluctuations and mechanical responses are conquered, the human soul has little chance of learning how to think.

Concentration and meditation are methods of carrying on a conscious and controlled activity in the mental sphere, an activity which coordinates and arranges many unrelated thoughtforms into a related whole.

Concentration is mental observation, or an endurance and perseverance in your plan and purpose. Concentration is like a magnet attracting to you all that you need. Concentration strengthens the muscles of your mind and does not let its energy be wasted.

Concentration integrates your physical, emotional, mental, and spiritual realms and enables your mind to direct forces and energies without dispersion or leakage. Concentration evokes latent greater powers in your mind and renders them active.

A concentrated mind develops integrity among all its parts: the brain, the three glands in the brain, the etheric brain, the Chalice, and the mind.

Once you learn how to concentrate on physical, emotional, and mental objects, you increase your power of control over these planes. Concentration creates a direct relationship between your consciousness and the object on a given plane.

Inspiration, impressions, and telepathic communications require intense concentration of consciousness. Concentration creates an etheric and mental tube which isolates the consciousness from various interferences and enables the consciousness to have direct and uninterrupted communication with the source of inspiration, impression, or telepathy.

The slightest deviation of mind or agitation of consciousness creates gaps in reception and distorts the message directed to you. If the message, impression, or inspiration is received in a disturbed and distorted state, it creates complicated mental problems not only in the receiver but also in those who are in contact with the receiver.

Thus, many communicators damage their instruments because of lack of concentration and create social disturbances with their false or distorted presentations.

The continuous exercise of concentration and meditation is needed before one attempts to come in contact with broadcasting stations on the mental plane and the Intuitional Plane. There are many receivers whose mechanisms distort the message because of a lack of training in concentration.

In creative moments one can observe the value of concentration. A momentary short in the current of concentration brings in

a. The influence of the object of interference

b. A possible shift of direction by dark forces

c. A mixing of the creative flow with weak and unnecessary elements

d. Damage to the mechanism of creativity

Of course, one can eventually create artificial tubes to filter outer and inner interferences, but the most powerful insulation is the power of concentration itself.

There are many interferences and much static in space which can be avoided by intense concentration. For example:

a. Thoughtwaves which are antagonistic to your work or have some affinity with it, but, because of their quality, weaken or distort your creativity

b. Thought currents specially directed by dark forces to disturb your communication and your communication system

c. Electric storms in the atmosphere

d. Disturbances in globes and stars

e. Accumulated noise in space

f. Certain memories and recordings which come to the surface of your consciousness from your etheric brain, disturb your creativity, and mix it with unnecessary or polluting elements

It is also possible that, because of certain weaknesses in your nature, the mechanism of reception in you short-circuits itself when it can no longer absorb high-voltage energies of inspiration, impressions, or telepathic messages.

The answer to these problems is a developing and advancing, intense concentration. Concentration is like building a pipe toward a mountain lake. Once it reaches the lake, you have all the inspiration you need.

All our failures and all our victories and achievements depend upon the degree of our concentration. Concentration is active communication.

4. The fourth step to develop your mind and expand your consciousness is to **increase your viewpoints** as much as you can, without losing the focus of observation.

Increase your viewpoints about things under your observation. Also, try to see from various viewpoints the things presented to you. Do not accept things as they are presented until you are convinced that you want to accept them. But this acceptance must be the result of your observation from as many viewpoints as possible. By increasing your viewpoints, you make a breakthrough into the sphere of Intuition.

Whenever some news is presented to you, try to find other, even opposite, sources to check it. This will give your mind flexibility and expansion. Whenever we do not increase our viewpoints, we fall victim to those who have developed the techniques of exploitation.

See things from the individual, group, national, and international viewpoint; even try to see from the global, solar, galactic, and Cosmic viewpoint. See things as if you were in another form, as if you were a spirit or living in another dimension. See things from the viewpoint of politics, education, communication, art, science, religion, and economy.

Whenever your mind is stuck, give it a new viewpoint, and it will start again and run well.

5. **Meditation**. It is important to emphasize that meditation is not effective and beneficial if the mind is not trained in concentration. If one notes any failure of concentration while performing meditation, he must put aside his meditation and start his exercises on concentration.[1]

Meditation is a process of opening the mind to the light of the Inner Thinker. Meditation is an effort to come in contact with that Inner Dweller and tune in with Its thoughts, visions, and revelations.

Meditation eventually leads us to increase our light, knowledge, and ability to penetrate into the treasure house of our past experiences and use them in the light of our present needs.

Meditation will help us eventually to be a thinker. People have the impression that most everyone knows how to think. The fact is that thinkers are very rare. For example, a few thinkers created the automobile or the airplane, but millions and millions of people work on these to assemble them, use them, and repair them. All these people are using their minds to reflect the thoughts of the real thinkers. Of course, one must use his mind in order to use the engine or repair it, but his thought in doing these things is a mere reflection of the thought of the originators.

After being a mechanic for many long years, one who has cultivated his mind finds errors in the engineering and creates a new part for the engine. Or, he may even create a new engine that works better. Such a man is on the way to becoming a thinker if he is using new principles in engineering.

A meditator passes through similar stages. First he tries to understand the meaning of an object or seed thought. Then he tries to live according to the higher meaning and principles of life. Then he becomes a self-actualized man, one who creates a new personality.

Our physical, emotional, and mental natures are shaped by our reactions and responses to life in general. When we consciously respond and reach a greater awareness level, then we will be able to create a body that fits our purpose, to create a new emotional vehicle through new responses and reactions, and to build a new mental body through new mental responses. The whole personality is

---

1. See Ch. 6 in *The Science of Meditation*.

changed when a man becomes his own master and starts to think. Through meditation we learn how to control forces and direct energies and how to cause transmutation in the nature of those with whom we come in contact.

Meditation creates rhythm within your mental body in harmony with the Cosmic Rhythm. It is the manifestation of the Cosmic Rhythm that makes you really creative. Every living form rhythmically pulsates in response to the rhythm of the Cosmic Magnet. There are physical plane rhythms and emotional, mental, and spiritual rhythms. The Cosmic Magnet expresses a symphony in which many rhythms harmoniously complement each other. This symphony has the rhythm of the Seven Cosmic Planes. All creation is in this symphony, and as one expands his consciousness from physical to spiritual levels, he submits himself to higher and higher rhythms.

Rhythm is the moment of contact with higher sources of energy. Through rhythm the higher will conducts the lower will, and thus harmony is created in the rhythm of various forms.

Meditation creates heroes. A hero is one who thinks as a Spirit, an immortal soul, free from the limitations of the physical, emotional, and mental interests and concerns. As long as one is attached to his personality interests and concerns, he cannot be a hero. Heroism is the moment of liberation from limitations. A hero does not negotiate with his lower self; he gives an order and expects obedience.

A hero is fearless but not stupid. He knows that he can do it. He finds his way in darkness by the light of his dedication. No force can resist a hero. A hero lives in the light of the Divine Plan and Divine Purpose.

Advanced meditation schools produce great heroes, especially through occult meditation. Occult meditation is scientific meditation in which you know what steps you are taking and the reasons you are taking those steps. The goal of occult meditation is to meet your True Self and, through your Self, the One Self.

With scientific steps you are going to handle your progress, knowing the causes and effects of energies and forces playing upon your own progress, handling them in the right way to reach your goal — which is to be one with the Self of the Universe through your own Innermost Self.

Life is a graded path of learning. It is similar to our educational system. There is the nursery, the kindergarten, elementary school, high school, then college, then the Life. The sad point on the spiritual path is that the teachers at each grade pretend they can give their students the final graduation, instead of passing them to the next grade's teacher who has greater qualifications for more advanced work.

In the future the spiritual work will be organized in such a way that through a clear network of communication the teachers will lead the students to those groups or Ashrams which better fit their needs and stage of evolution.

For a reason one student must not meditate but must do physical labor and listen to short instructions. For a different reason another student must abstain from certain things, and he must be placed in a group that fits him. All these arrangements can be made if spiritual teachers have their *Light Center*[2] where they are trained, from which they are graduated and ordained, and where they go for higher learning and more spiritual discipline.

At this time, kindergarten students visit universities and slowly reject all teachings presented to them. . .because the things that we do not understand, we reject. On the other hand, those who are ready for the university go to high school and feel bored. It is true that some of them eventually find their right place, but the majority waste their time and energy doing things that they are not supposed to do. A trained Teacher in the Light Center can be a great help to them.

Liberated persons are those who are able to detach themselves from the past and build a new mind by the light of the future, by the vision of the future. The mind is renewed in working for a vision and in planning to reach that vision.

When a man is on the physical plane, his vision is translated in physical terms — in physical fitness, beauty, strength, etc. When he is focused on the astral plane, his vision is translated in terms of emotions, joy, enthusiasm, and so on. When he is found on the mental plane, his vision is translated as intelligent activity and creativity.

When the human soul is fused with the Solar Angel, he thinks that he is the vision itself toward which he was going. This is the stage where the great Renunciation or Crucifixion starts. As he advances, his Solar Angel leaves, and the man thinks everything is lost because a part of himself has disappeared. But real progress starts from that moment, and man tries to find his Self. It is the first time on the path of his journey that the man stands on his own feet because there is no one else on which to depend except himself.

People must pay more attention to their spiritual evolution than to their material satisfaction. Your spiritual progress is even more important than your physical well-being. Your physical well-being will last, for instance, only sixty to seventy years, but your spiritual well-being will travel an endless path.

Christ once said, "Lay up for yourselves a treasure in heaven, where neither rust nor moth destroy, and where thieves do not break through and steal."[3]

The spiritual treasure in heaven is your spiritual achievements, your transformed, transfigured being, and the "rust" and "moths" and "thieves" cannot approach there. But if your treasure is your body, eventually the "rust" will destroy it, the "moths" will destroy it, and the "thieves" will break through.

One of the important things about meditation is that through meditation we learn to think clearly and holistically and develop the power to use the fire of thought for construction and benevolent destruction.

It is very important to know how to think in our daily life because right thinking is the only compass for right direction.

---

2.   Also known as their Ashram.
3.   Matt. 6:20

The power and benefit of thinking is not limited to this physical world only, but its usefulness is a thousand times more in the subjective world. The only tool we can take into the subjective world is thought. Through thought things are created, things are destroyed, things are arranged and built; and it is through thought that communications are established with higher forces and with those who need help in lower spheres.

Right and clear thinking paves the way for future evolution and progress through the Higher Worlds, and it also prepares the conditions in which future incarnations will be taken.

No matter how elevated a soul is, he needs the power of thought and the art of thinking.

In the future, the whole healing process will be performed through thinking. Thought communication will replace all other worldly communications, and it will even replace all worldly transportation systems. Such a glory is waiting for those who learn how to think.

Through meditation we learn to be impressed by the great wisdom coming from various sources: from our Soul, from our Master, from the Hierarchy, from the Shamballa, from the Sun, and even from Cosmic Sources. We not only register these impressions in greater and greater clarity and beauty, but we also learn how to formulate them and use them for the needs of the world.

Meditation is a creative process, and when it is carried on upon abstract mental planes, it has seven steps through which the consciousness penetrates into the world of meaning:

          a. analysis

          b. synthesis

          c. creativity

          d. purification

          e. communication

          f. recognition

          g. revelation

a. *Analysis*. With this step we concentrate on an object, word, sentence, idea, or thought and try to analyze it. We try to look at that subject from different viewpoints, from different angles. For example, we look at the subject from the viewpoints of present, past, and future. We may look upon the subject from the viewpoints of life, death, or as a whole, or as a positive or negative factor. This is like a man who separates an engine into its various parts, checking and examining each one to learn its true function and its individual role in the engine as a whole. After such an analysis, he puts the parts together and looks at them as a whole. He studies the form of each part, then the quality of each part, then the purpose of the whole, and then the cause of the parts and the whole.[4]

Such an activity is a scientific process, and, if carried on continuously, it stimulates many dormant cells in the brain and many centers in the head, enormously expanding the consciousness into the heart of the objects or events under consideration.

The object of meditation may be almost anything. For example, I can choose a flower, a complicated social or political problem, a doctrine, or a movement and submit it to the analyzing light of my mind. Whatever the object, it can be handled through the seven steps and will lead toward greater revelations.

In general, ninety percent of our social conflicts would disappear if our leaders would, instead of creating excitement, submit their problems and conflicts to the light of their meditating minds and analyze them with pure and selfless motives.

It is very important that any subject be approached from various angles, even from the angle of one's enemies. This will help to raise the problem out of the emotional domain, out of the field of personal interests, and put it under the clear light of his mental analysis.

Complicated social problems are generally abundant in those countries where there is pressure, slavery, or exploitation. All these problems need to be resolved in such a manner that the harmonious unfoldment of society and the enjoyment of life are not deteriorated. Whenever there is social conflict, there is proof that the conflicting sides were not able to solve the conflict through selfless attitudes. They were not able to reach a conclusion based on clear and inclusive thinking.

Only a free mind and a free person can reach an independent conclusion. Those who are under the influence of any doctrine, power, or pressure cannot observe problems with clear eyes. They cannot reach an independent conclusion and exercise their divine right of seeing things as they are.

Our outer life is the mirror of our inner life.

b. *Synthesis.* The second step of meditation is the effort to synthesize. The ability to synthesize is one of the wonderful powers of the mind.

In essence, to synthesize means to find the principles and fundamental laws behind the subject. It is the process of observing various phenomena through the light of the discovered laws and principles.

When one analyzes different problems from several levels to reach the fundamental axis, principle, or law which controls them, he finds different ways to the same goal. It is here that apparently conflicting lines of effort, movement,

---

4. For more information on the parts of meditation, see *The Ageless Wisdom*, Ch. 26, *The Science of Meditation*, and *The Psyche and Psychism.*

or problems find harmony with each other. Instead of weakening each other, they strengthen each other.

In the process of synthesis, the negative emotional urges fall down and disappear, and the mind achieves freedom to think clearly and without self-interest.

The effort to synthesize brings joy. Joy is a state of a higher, elevated consciousness. Such a state exists when the mind is integrated in harmony and balance and is whole.

Divine spiritual energies and inspirations can produce problems, complications, and diseases if they meet agitated, polluted, and cracked mental states or conflicting waves of thoughts and thoughtforms on their path of manifestation. Harmony always produces health, prosperity, and progress. Harmony is the path of synthesis. Synthesis is not produced by any psychological or physical means. We only restore it. Synthesis is the essence of man. It is synthesis which must manifest and impose itself on the vehicles and on conditions created by the vehicles.

Synthesis may be observed from another angle. In meditation the mind slowly penetrates through the four viewpoints into the seed thought and reaches the soul of the object, event, or problem. However, it does not stop there. A moment comes when the mind becomes super-sensitive; the strings of the mind reach the supreme stage of fusion. The mind as a whole contacts the thoughts and thoughtforms found in space and draws the waves of thought which have special relation to the object of meditation. Thus the meditator reaches a multi-visioned state of mind and new horizons open in his mind. New possibilities emerge and sources inspire him in such a way that when he is meditating, writing, or speaking, many new and inspiring thoughts flow into his mind and he has immediate contact with his subject. Thus he remembers words, books, persons, experiences, and events and relates them in such a way that his expression is rich, balanced, and whole. One of the greatest gifts of meditation is that it puts the mind in contact with the mental atmosphere of space and gives the mind selective and discriminative power.

In many cycles man uses his mind and thought about the subjects that are presently under consideration. The mental waves of these thinkers are already part of the mental atmosphere of space.

Often when we think seriously about a subject but for a time cannot reach a solution, one day, suddenly, the solution reveals itself to us. It may take time, but, like a computer, the thought mechanism works, selecting all those minute points which in their totality form the answer and impressing them on the mental plane at the right moment.

In meditation we also contact the Universal Mind, which is the source of all prototypes, blueprints, knowledge, and wisdom. It often happens that the answer cannot be found in the mind or in the thought atmosphere of the world, but only in the Mind of the Universe.

When we think about a subject, it may take days, years, or even lives to get the answer, but one day the answer will reveal itself. All questions directed to the Universal Mind have their answers, but it takes time for the brain to register them. Meditation increases the sensitivity of the brain.

All human aspirations, prayers, and mental strivings evoke answers from the Universal Mind. It takes time for people to tune themselves to these answers and draw them into their mind and into the world of human relations. If the antennas of the thinkers are not immediately ready to absorb them, the released answers lose their intensity and power on the path of their descent.

Even when some thinkers are able to catch the answers, it takes a long time to assimilate, formulate, and pass them to humanity. In this process, again, much of the beauty of the original answer is lost. But always we must remember that each answer has a hidden key in itself to open the doors of greater possibilities and lead to the originating source of the answer. Through meditation we not only come in contact with the light of the human intellect, but we also communicate with the answers that are projected from the higher levels of Nature.

This is how a genius works. He is aware of the question or the need. He is aware of the answers given through the ages by highly developed intelligent beings, and above all he is aware of those answers which emerge from the Universal Mind.

The synthesizing labor is a wonderful labor, and man can do it only through meditation. In deep meditation, all pairs of opposites agree with each other, and all contradictory waves build themselves into a new construction around one principle. Whenever one raises his consciousness and touches the essential ideas and causal energies, it becomes easy for him to clean distortions and unify different manifestations in a coherent, functioning expression. Thus, many apparently unconnected subjects give birth to a new idea and to a new form.

All complicated mechanisms and all complicated architectural buildings are the result of the synthesizing quality of the human soul. In all these forms, individually unconnected objects become connected and are harmonized with each other in the idea that stands as the cause of the construction.

c. *Creativity.* The object or the problem put under the light of meditation is simplified slowly, and through the act of synthesis it is turned into a subtle form which projects its roots into the world of ideas and into the world of needs and practical life. When this form reaches a certain degree of power and beauty, it feels the urge to manifest itself as a way of living, as a creative work of literature, music, sculpture, as a direction for leadership, as an enthusiastic and inspiring life, or as a great striving.

Thus man, in the depth of his meditation, unites himself with the vision he created, and day after day his life becomes more coordinated and a multicolored beauty. The way of his speech changes, and his personal, family, and group life take a more constructive form. His creative energies increase, and he becomes able to give birth to the visions, dreams, ideas, and light which he receives in the hours of meditation.

If an artist does not reach such a degree in his meditation and life expressions, his works will not carry the seal of Divine power, supernatural influence, and great magnetism. One hears music which brings great upliftment to the emotional nature. One reads poetry which brings Divine impressions to the soul. One reads works of great literature which open a new world. True art, true culture always has a transforming effect because the music, the word, the voice, or the painting is charged by the energy pouring down from an electrified, Divine level from within.

Such creative impressions bring a stupendous energy and charge the manifestation of the art object. Whoever comes in contact with it may be uplifted almost to the level where it originated. Thus the consciousness is exalted and ecstasy is registered. Every time one contacts a higher level, he transforms his nature and builds a channel between higher and lower worlds. It is in these moments of ecstasy that great decisions are taken to make one's life more real and to be more the Higher Self. It is not strange that in these moments of upliftment, people sometimes have great moments of repentance and contrition.

In the sphere of true creative art, one feels that he is in an electromagnetic field where all his cells become radioactive. Within his vision a new and higher world opens.

d. *Purification* is the process of transfiguring the vehicles of the soul through meditation. When the mind continuously comes in contact with higher ideas, energies, and thoughtforms, it regularly submits itself to higher vibrations and rhythms. Then gradually the three vehicles, under the influence of these higher vibrations, undergo a process of transmutation to such a degree that the substance of the physical, emotional, and mental world is refined and purified and becomes radioactive.

Observe a man when he is in a labor of creative action. He radiates a powerful stream of energy. He is in contact with his source of inspiration which floods his aura with a new energy, color, and rhythm. Within such a sphere the physical, emotional, and mental bodies undergo changes. The cells and atoms show a higher sensitivity while some of the sleeping cells in the brain slowly awaken. The glands function harmoniously. The higher etheric centers, especially the heart, throat, and head centers, become more active, and a fiery shield forms around the body which can repel or burn many waves of negative emotions and thought currents coming from the outer world.

In the presence of such people one sometimes feels that his conscience bothers him because of a past deed or thought. Then he has a feeling of peace. He notices something changing in himself. The influence of that creative person penetrates into his sphere and changes his physical, emotional, and mental worlds.

At this stage of meditation, a person builds his future vision of perfection and slowly identifies with that vision in his inner being. This identification causes further purification in his vehicles, changing their rhythm to a higher level. Unless a man reaches this stage of purification, he cannot undergo the long-lasting pressures of mental activities, creative labor, and fiery inspirations. A man should not do advanced forms of meditation until purification is an accomplished fact in the three personality vehicles. Through meditation fiery energies are evoked, and they can burn the unready and spread destruction around him.

Djwhal Khul, a great Sage, once wrote:

> . . . *Meditation is dangerous and unprofitable to the man who enters upon it without the basis of a good character and of clean living. Meditation then becomes only a medium for the bringing in of energies which but serve to stimulate the undesirable aspects of his life, just as the fertilizing of a garden full of weeds will produce a stupendous crop of them, and so crush out the weak and tiny flowers. Meditation is dangerous where there is wrong motive, such as desire for personal growth and for spiritual powers, for it produces, under these conditions only a strengthening of the shadows in the vale of illusion and brings to full growth the serpent of pride, lurking in the valley of selfish desire. Meditation is dangerous when the desire to serve is lacking.*[5]

The process of purification avoids all these dangers and opens the way for mysteries and initiations.

One of the occult laws of the Ageless Wisdom is "Energy follows thought." Wherever there is thinking and thought, there is energy because every thoughtform creates a magnetic field into which waves of energy are attracted. Thought emanating from higher levels of the mental plane or from Great Ones creates polarity in space and causes circulation of energy. Sometimes such thoughtforms create a great energy whirlpool which charges and tremendously stimulates all those who come in contact with it. If the thoughtforms are negative, they eventually cause deterioration in the vehicles of all those who communicate with them. If they are creative, they cause unfoldment, refinement, and they release their energy in the vehicles of those who come in contact with them.

Before a man undertakes esoteric or occult meditation, he must purify and sanctify his three personality vehicles. Through the techniques of observation, detachment, concentration, and through putting his life in order, the aspirant

---

5.   Alice A. Bailey, *A Treatise on White Magic*, pp. 204-205.

eventually reaches the instructions of advanced occult meditation in which begins the true path of sacrificial life. Such meditation slowly brings out all dead material from the nature of man and expels it or transmutes it into new forces.

Throughout ages man has collected many experiences, glamors, and illusions. All these elements slowly come to the surface and melt away in the fire of true meditation. Actually, true occult meditation is a great healer on all levels. Through such purificatory processes, the whole nature of man becomes radioactive, and within his field spiritual electricity circulates freely, spreading waves of peace, healing, illumination, and bliss.

e. *Communication.* The fifth point in occult meditation is communication. After purification man can engage in advanced meditation and come in contact with his Inner Dweller. He learns gradually to enter into the light of his Soul and hear the Voice of Silence. Thus, stage by stage, he withdraws his being from the lower vehicles, contacts higher planes, and absorbs the life, the energy, and the magnetic power of these planes. The life of the Soul pours into him, flooding him with true love, wisdom, and the spirit of sacrifice. The light of the Soul enlightens him, and in that light he feels the Presence Who leads him from darkness to light. From this point he enters into the sixth stage of meditation, which is called the stage of recognition.

f. *Recognition.* At this stage man for the first time meets his Soul, and in the light of his Soul he recognizes himself as an immortal being, full of creative powers and possibilities of infinite unfoldment. Meditation not only leads him to light, wisdom, purity, and power but also into the presence of his Soul.

After such an experience of Soul-realization, man passes to the seventh stage of meditation, which is called the stage of revelation.

g. *Revelation.* It is at this stage that the path leading to the Father is revealed in deep meditation. Here the person sees the path leading him to his Self and sees the path which he will travel age after age to change the shadow into Reality.

6. The next step to expand your consciousness and unfold your mind is to develop **sincerity**. You can never really develop your mind if you have the habit of lying, of being a hypocrite, or of being insincere. If you are not sincere with yourself, you create conflict within the forces and mechanisms of your mind. No matter how many diplomas you put on your walls, you will remain on the same level if you are a hypocrite, if you are insincere, or if you have the tendency to fabricate lies.

The development of the mind causes changes in your level, expands your consciousness, and enables you to manifest your Inner Glory through your deeds, words, and thoughts.

Hypocrisy, insincerity, and lies build a false personality around your soul, and you need ages to get rid of that shell. We are even told that the forces of that false personality follow you into the subjective worlds.

Sincerity is the way to meet yourself and then your true, eternal Self. Continuously contradicting your Real Self will bring you a hard labor to destroy your pseudo-self and find your True Self. The mind needs a pure atmosphere in order to grow. It cannot grow when you or others are continuously projecting images on it which are built of hypocrisy, insincerity, and lies.

Sincerity is the ability to clear your calculator before you start to engage yourself in something real and serious. When one occupies his mind with false images, the mind will wear out or will be distorted.

Sincerity will be cultivated within your own self, within your heart, within your relationships. Nature does not open new gates to us until we are worthy of them.

In our universities almost all subjects one can imagine are taught, but sincerity has no class or professor and sincerity is the foundation of knowledge.

A legend says that there was a village where people were taught how to lie and be hypocrites. When all were graduated from the course, they saw that it was impossible to deal with each other and to have certainty, trust, or peace. Eventually they decided to start a new course on how to eliminate hypocrisy!

There is no survival or success on the path of hypocrisy and selfish interests. Hypocrisy has its roots in separative self-interest. The flower of the mind will never grow to its full beauty in a polluted aura. This is the reason why, in spite of increasing M.A.'s and Ph.D.'s, governments are not able to stop increasing crime rates.

Sincerity is the sign of culture, the sign that man has in his nature the most essential foundation of life.

7. When meditation is used as a tool and its goals are achieved, the disciple uses a higher technique to contact greater reality. This technique is called **contemplation**. In the first step, contemplation is nothing else but the process of watching the Divine Plan and communicating with It in the light of the Soul. The Ageless Wisdom says that beyond the higher mental plane there exists the Intuitional Plane which inspires the creative souls. In the process of meditation, man functions on the higher mental plane. In the case of contemplation, he works between the higher mind and the Intuitional Plane. It is here that he sees the prototypes, their origination, and their expression. He deals not with the objects and forms but with ideas, blueprints, prototypes, principles, and energies.

In the process of meditation, man had under his hand the known measures, scales, symbols, and signs by which he could approach the "unmeasurable" and make it familiar to his mind. He could formulate them with the measures of his mental and emotional natures.

In contemplation, thought transcends all familiar measures. Man cannot express the mysterious experiences on these levels through common language or other ways and means. In contemplation any phenomenon is observed within its absolute reality and relativity. In contemplation words lose their familiar meaning and turn into symbols. Understanding or recognition is not through words or numbers but through straight knowledge.

An occultist is one who has succeeded in building a bridge between the Intuitional Plane and the personality. In necessity, he can bring down all contacted light and formless energies and beauties to the physical plane and express them as laws, arts, meaning, direction, and inspiration.

The mystic is one who, by the power of his purity and dedication, can penetrate these planes of Intuition and express his impressions as joy and energy. The occultist, who has disciplined his mind and cultivated it to the highest degree, not only is awake on these high levels but also is able to impress his brain with their beauties.

The average man cannot easily penetrate into the occultist's formulated expressions, but he feels the tremendous magnetism and the power of one who contemplates. Ones who contemplate are sources of energy and power. Their presence can cause you to strive to your highest and do your best.

On the stage of contemplation man is fused with his Soul, and as a Soul he directs his eyes toward

a. The world of spiritual realities — will and Purpose

b. The world of souls, love, and Plan

c. The physical and emotional worlds

and he fuses them with his own energy and power.

In the second degree of contemplation, all functions of the mind cease, and silence reigns. In silence and peace the Soul-infused man reaches an electrified state of expectancy. This state is sometimes called "immersion into the ocean of God." This stage expands the consciousness to such a degree that it fuses with the awareness of the Intuitional Plane, and man factually experiences that he is other than his body, his emotions, and his mind and thoughts.

In these sacred moments of fusion, enlightenment, and transfiguration, all the forces found within the personality enter into a higher process of sublimation. The lower forces rise up, and those elements that are against the light of love burn off and disappear. All thoughtforms within the mental sphere align and form a rhythmic flow. The roots of blind urges and drives totally disappear, and within this electrified state of expectancy the man sees his star shining above his head and passes into the third stage of contemplation.

In this stage he contacts the sphere of Divine energies within which he touches the Divine Purpose and the Divine Will. Those who reach such a degree in contemplation can stay on this stage for days, experiencing the bliss of Infinity and beauty in which the Divine Purpose slowly unveils itself. Now man is an

Initiate of a high degree, and he descends from his mountaintop to the valley of human life to bring Beauty, Goodness, Righteousness, Joy, and Freedom.

8. The next step is an abstract step, but without it the mind cannot develop in the right way and eventually will contradict itself. This step is the **recognition of the principle of the Hierarchy**. This principle shows that progress travels on an infinite Path and the souls are on various levels, higher and higher. Those who are in the same plane or sphere are called Hierarchies. All Hierarchies are related to each other, but they are engaged in different tasks in the field of Cosmos.[6]

The principle of Hierarchy opens great horizons of possibilities to the mind, and the mind grows and blooms within this principle. Those who deny the principle of Hierarchy cannot create in the harmony of the Cosmic Will, and very often their creations become their own obstacles. The mind can grow only within the principle of the Hierarchy.

Whenever the mind conceives the idea of a dead-end path, it dries up or works against the Common Good. A mind in harmony with the principle of Hierarchy has ever-expanding horizons and ever-deepening humility, two very important factors for true growth.

When a man of logic or of science rejects thinking about immortality and the spheres in which immortal souls live, when he denies and refuses the reality of such a condition, he will have a terrible time in the astral plane. He will find himself in a world that he never imagined. He will find himself alive there. All his mental crystallizations will suffer under the terrible pressure of reality, which he will try to refuse by all logical means. He will try to disprove himself as an immortal being. He will work against truth, against facts, and he will create a great distortion in his mind and an attack from the forces of Nature.[7]

This is a great disaster which descends upon such a man. It takes thousands of years to find out that all his scientific logic was incorrect and that he must resign totally from his former deductions related to immortality to find a true path.

It is known that if such people do not solve their dilemma in the Subtle Worlds, they come back as enemies of human progress or as mentally lost human beings. At best, they put away the mind and enjoy life as a physical body only. Such people show a great fear when they hear about the subjective world, immortality, and Infinity.

The greatest confusion in the mind occurs when all that you try to prove, disproves itself. This means real conflict and chaos in your mind and consequent suffering and pain. Such a condition will be very frightening because the real life

---

6. For further information on Hierarchies, see Ch. 8, "The Twelve Creative Hierarchies," in *The Psyche and Psychism*.
7. For further information on the astral plane, please see *Other Worlds*.

of the subjective world will be considered a dream, a nightmare from which you cannot escape by any way or logic.

Imagine a man who is caught in a dream in which he lives exactly the life which he either rejected or believed in. He cannot awaken, and he has to face the reality which in reality is hallucination. And he cannot figure out how he became caught in that hallucination.

When we enter into the subjective world, we carry with us all our mental measures and gauges, and we cannot understand why our measures are all useless.

The greatest help that a human being receives in his life is not from all that he learns, but it is from the information that is given to him about the subjective world, about superhuman evolution, about immortality and Infinity. Without such information, all other information will block his progress on the path of his evolution.

Man lives with all that he learns for a few decades, but the science of life, immortality, and Infinity will lead him thousands of years on the path of progress and greater service for the future.

Daily think about your immortal Self, and see that that Self lives in many dimensions. Then your knowledge and life will have meaning.

9. The next step is to have an **impersonal outlook and renunciation** or right relationship with things and people.

A personality-bound mind is a one-track mind. It grows to a certain degree, then stops and uses its development against the person's own survival if he does not develop his mind further.

It is really important to grasp this point. If the mind does not develop progressively and continuously, it turns against itself and crystallizes in its former achievements, while the life challenges the person to new achievements to meet new requirements and handle new energies.

People are spiritually and morally bankrupt if they continuously see things and handle things from their own separative outlook. They always say, "me, me, me . . . mine, mine, mine . . . from my angle, from my interest, from my sex, from my stomach, from my dollar, from my savings. . . ." Such people will never go forward in their mental evolution.

Mental evolution starts when one begins to consider things from the viewpoint of the interests of others.

10. **Illumination** has many stages. In the first stage the light of consciousness fuses with the whole mental plane.

In the second stage the light of Intuition pours into the mental plane, revealing the Plan.

In the third stage the Third Cosmic Etheric Plane fuses with the mind and reveals the part of the Purpose "which the Masters know and serve."

There is another stupendous illumination in the Fifth Initiation, and a greater one in the Seventh Initiation, when the Cosmic Will dawns in the heart of the Initiate.

The pilgrim of Infinity does not stop on the mountain of this achievement. He slowly surrenders his will and fuses it with the Divine Will. He becomes able to express that Will in all of his actions, feelings, and thoughts. Then a moment comes in which the veil of his individual existence falls down, and he reaches the stage of a great renunciation, the stage of a sacrificial life. Now the pilgrim is focused in the plane of Intuition and Light. The reality after which he was running gradually approaches him, and in a sacred moment the reflection sees his Essence. Thus, the reflection of the sun floating throughout ages in the sea of matter and substance identifies itself with its Essence and Reality, and from that moment on all glamors, illusions, vanities, and chains of matter fall down and disappear. He is now an Arhat: a man Who has reached pure freedom, a man Who is one with His own Essence.

In this stage he is an Intuitive. He does not need to use His former ways and mind to know. He sees and He knows the things that He wants to see and know. His vision encompasses the past, the present, the future, the cause, the process, and the effect. It is from this stage of achievement that all Seers, Knowers, and true Leaders of humanity emerge. All seven senses reach their highest unfoldment. The eye sees the forms of all planes. The ear hears the sounds of all planes. All other senses reach their sevenfold activity, putting the man in contact with seven planes of the Universe. Now the man is a light within the Sun of Reality.

11. The eleventh step to develop our mind is to **reject those who impose their will, doctrine, or religion upon us**. As long as one is forced to accept things without his free will and understanding, his mind will not develop. The mind develops when it is left free — but inspired, challenged, and guided.

12. **Inspiration**. Inspiration, esoterically considered, has three degrees:

— Inhalation

— Rest (when the Divine breath is held within)

— Exhalation

In the first degree, the Enlightened One spiritually "inhales" energies from His own spiritual and monadic sources and from planetary and extra-planetary centers. He inhales them with His highest centers. These energies are charged with the universal Purpose and Plan and with Divine ideas. They are the sources from which new cultures and new civilizations emerge.

In the second stage, these "inhaled" energies undergo an inner transmutation and appropriation process. According to his duties, responsibilities, and talents, the man adapts these energies to the needs of the environment, time, and achievement level of the people concerned. When this process of transmutation and adaptation is complete, the creative Adept exhales these energies upon His environment.

In the third stage of inspiration, the process of exhalation, manifestation, and practical expression of these energies begins. The Leader, the Knower, the Teacher "exhales" these energies as great works of supreme art, new formulas in science, new ideologies, new leadership, and through various acts of heroic living in many fields.

Energies and impressions from higher sources penetrate into the mental, emotional, and physical worlds and bring out new cultures and new civilizations. Here we can see the importance of purification before inspiration.

When purification has not done its work, dark spots, disturbances, and impediments exist in our physical, emotional, and mental worlds. Here the energy of inspiration can create great complications on the planes through which it passes. For example, when there are illusions on the mental plane, they grow, due to the incoming energy, and eventually control the whole human being and his environment and cause various destructive activities.

If there are glamors on the astral plane, they grow, collect strength, and make the man like a boat lost upon a stormy sea. If these weaknesses or hindrances exist on the physical plane as blind urges and drives or as physical weaknesses, the energies of inspiration produce various diseases.

It also happens that these energies of inspiration do not meet any hindrances in the nature of man but do meet them in his environment. This is how conflict starts within his environment. And, if the incoming energy is strong and is using many individuals as channels of expression, the conflict extends into the nation as a whole. Eventually it flows into humanity, spreading its light and causing purification, destruction, revelations, or wars. Sometimes it happens that the channels of these energies disappear cyclically, and the inspiration turns into a dogma or a doctrine and is compromised, as is the case now in Christianity and other religions.

13. The thirteenth step to develop the mind is to try to **create balance between abstract ideas and concrete realms of manifestation**. If you read something abstract, try to explain it with concrete examples. Then take any event and try to find its abstract cause or significance so that you build a bridge between the lower and higher mind.

The mind grows like a plant: abstract branches, leaves, and flowers and concrete roots deep into the earth. If the mind wanders in space, it is not useful. If it is stuck in matter, it is purposeless.

You may think about abstract ideas and try to visualize concrete symbols for them, or translate them into parables or stories without mentioning the name of the idea or concept. You can do the reverse: take a concrete experience and think about its echo in abstract realms. You can try to relate the finite to Infinity. This is a very potent way to develop your mind in the right direction.

A balanced human being is the one who finds a point of equilibrium between the abstract and the concrete, between Infinity and the finite, between the whole and the individual.

Creativity is the result of the union between the abstract and the concrete. An artist develops his mind because through his creative process his mind is challenged to use all of its resources and relationships with the higher sources of inspiration and the concrete spheres of manifestation.

Creativity exposes the mind to new visions and to new ideas. It makes the mind grasp them, assimilate them, and express them in creative activities. Your efforts for creativity slowly call forth the currents of inspiration from higher sources. Inspiration evokes striving from the mind, and through striving the mind creates.

14. **At-one-ment**. The fourteenth step is identification or at-one-ment. The man who reaches this stage is not an individual, a part, or a portion; he is a whole, a One. As the great Lord said, "The Father and I are One." The reflection is not only identified with the Inner Divinity, but he is also in tune with the Life of the Cosmos.

These realizations can last minutes, hours, days, or they can be a lasting experience. Once a man has such an experience, his measures and scale of values change. Christ explained this state of identification when He said: "Let all be one, as You, my Father, are in Me, and I am in You, that they also be one within Us."

All Great Ones Who gave true meaning to life are Those Who passed through these fourteen steps. Their experiences resulted in all the beauties that are on earth. They represent the spirit of striving through which man achieves new heights on the path of his infinite journey.

Mental and spiritual development give us a spirit of optimism, and we begin to have faith that humanity will eventually reach such higher states of awareness and beingness. The path of this infinite journey starts from the moment we decide to turn our face toward the Sun, toward the Fountain of Light within.

9

Signs of Development and Progress

The mind can develop in two directions: the right direction or the wrong direction.

When it is developing in the right direction, it works for the survival of Nature and humanity as a whole. When it is developing in the wrong direction, it works for the destruction of Nature, for the destruction of the soul, for the destruction of society.

Right development of the mind leads toward cooperation and synthesis. Wrong development of the mind leads to separatism and destructive conflict.

How does one know that his mind is developing in the right direction? There are five signs to measure the development of the mind.

1. As your mind develops you become more creative.

To be creative means to arrange your information in such a way that you solve your problems, or to arrange your information in such a way that a higher beauty is contacted and manifested.

A creative mind always finds new ways to relate to people and Nature, and all his relations are based upon Beauty, Goodness, and Truth.

2. The second sign of an unfolding mind is an increasing ability to see causes of happenings, events, and objects.

If your mind is not developing, you are satisfied with effects. You accept events as they are, and eventually you become a follower, a sheep. A developing mind tries to find the causes, the roots of events.

Have you seen growing children; they ask questions continuously. If they stop asking questions, that is a sign that they are taking a rest in their mental development. A developing mind asks questions, either to those who can answer or directly to himself, and he tries to dig for an answer.

A scientist, a philosopher, an educator is the result of a questioning mind. Those who have a greater influence upon human life are those who had more questions than others and received more answers than others.

3. The third sign of a man who is developing his mind is his ability to conduct his life and the life of society according to the vision of the future.

A developing mind thinks about the future. There are two futures for him. The first concerns the effect in the future of what we do and what we are now. The second concerns the kind of future we want, irrespective of what we are now.

In thinking about a great future, the developing mind directs its energies under the inspiration of the future and thus offsets to some degree the negative consequences of past actions.

A developing mind has a great future vision. The greater a man's vision, the greater the mind he has.

A developing mind not only thinks about the future of man but also about the future of the family, nation, and humanity. As the mind develops, it breathes more in the future.

4. The next sign of a developing mind is that it acts, talks, and thinks in terms of survival.

A developing mind tries more and more to conduct a life that helps the energy of life bring greater beauty, greater success, and greater prosperity.

When the mind does not develop, it begins to think in terms of receiving rather than giving. It thinks in terms of crime instead of helping people. It thinks how to reduce the life potentials in others. Because it cannot run, it tries to stop others.

A developing mind creates an urge to cooperate and harmonize increasingly in higher and more inclusive dimensions.

5. The next sign of a developing mind is independence.

Those who are developing their mind begin to think in new ways, from new viewpoints. They use new approaches. They build new forms and charge them with new ideas.

A developing mind does not like to repeat. It always has a new light, a greater horizon, a deeper insight. A developing mind tries to remain independent from the forms it created in the past. It has no grooves. It does not run in the same circle.

A non-developing mind gradually becomes a slave of the minds of others; it becomes a sheep, a follower.

A developing mind respects the independence of other minds because an independent mind offers him a new viewpoint, a new challenge. Fanaticism is the sign of a drying mind, of a rusty mind, when the machine no longer can take the spark and run.

The whole of Nature is built in such a manner that it produces independence and synthesis. No synthesis can be achieved without independent units, and no independence is lost in a true symphony. The kingdoms of Nature follow the same route. The living forms of Nature go from states of dependency to states of relative independence. This is achieved only through the developing mind. Retarded minds hinder the process of synthesis.

An individuality is the greatest achievement of Nature because through each individuality Nature will compose Its symphony. Each individual is the flower of the efforts to be independent, with its own color and beauty, with its own form, quality, purpose, and destiny.

Compare a man's freedom and independence with the independence of a plant or of an animal. The factor of independence is the mind developing in the right direction. Whenever the mind does not develop, it becomes its own exterminator.

Independence has its own gradations in the human kingdom: physical independence, emotional and mental independence, personal, national, global independence, . . .and spiritual independence, which is the door to symphony.

Once a man said to me, "I started to develop my mind."

"Really? How are you doing it?"

"Well, by reading, studying, and working for higher grades."

"How long have you been doing that?"

"Almost seven years."

"I do not see any development in your mind," I said, "because I can't see any change in you. Your selfishness has increased; your fanaticism has increased; your separatism is more professional. You are not creating a better future. You are not independent. You are not working to build the symphony."

"Well," he said, "I am not a musician, and, by the way, I am making more money."

Thus, the mind cannot be developed until your life changes. To make more money is sometimes the sign of decay if that money will not help you to render a greater service to others. Very often, behind the urge to make more money sit desire, vanity, and ambition. The developing mind transcends such motivation; it becomes more service-oriented, more giving, and more creative.

As your mind develops, it evokes greater potential latent in your soul. It works for the survival of humanity, and it makes you a greater leader and a more successful benefactor for humanity.

The mind is related to the heart and to the Intuition. If this relationship is established, you are on the path of success and development. Your mind must work in the light of the Intuition with the guidance of your heart. If your heart is not open, your mind will be cruel. If your mind is not related to the Intuition, it may have much knowledge but will always drive in the wrong direction.

The mind develops if there is the light of love. The mind develops if there is the rain of Intuition.

Let us now take things that hinder the progress of the evolution of the mind.

1. An easy, luxurious life is the greatest danger to our development.

Once I read that when God loves someone He gives him troubles. It is the difficulties of life that sustain our progress. Great Sages avoided comfort and luxury, and they rejected an easy life. The human mind must be challenged every moment if we want it to bloom.

We must labor physically, emotionally, mentally, and spiritually. A Sage says, "Luxury is the grave of the soul."

2. The second hindrance is uncontrolled worries.

Worries block and stupefy your mind. My grandmother used to say to the young children, "Do not worry too much. Go give your worries to Christ, and He will dissolve them. He wanted us to put our burdens on His shoulders. Do it and you will have a nice sleep."

It is in sleep that we continue to grow mentally. If we clear our minds of worries, we can sleep well and grow well. Of course, this is difficult advice, but the mind cannot run in higher channels if we continuously dump worries into it.

One of my Teachers used to say, "Before daybreak many things can change." Faith, trust, and right decision can knock out many deep-seated worries in the mind and clear it for right action. Stay in your beauty, goodness, righteousness, and purity, and do not worry any more because the karmic laws are watchful forces in the Universe.

3. The next hindrance of the mind is fear.

Fear paralyzes the mind, and the posthypnotic suggestions hidden in the lower layers of the mind take control of it. When a crisis of fear has passed, the mind pays for the damage done by the posthypnotic suggestions. The worst condition of the mind is that state in which the man loses control of it due to posthypnotic suggestions.

Once King Akbar said, "When it is dark, I put my hand in the hand of the Almighty One, and darkness turns into light for me."

4. The next hindrance is irritation.

Irritation eats the mind like a termite. Continuous irritation creates poison in your whole system. The poison of irritation evaporates like a venomous gas into the mental body from the brain and slowly blows out all the finer fuses that were keeping it striving toward the higher spheres.[1]

5. The next hindrance is fanaticism.

The mind of a fanatic never grows, though it can accumulate much knowledge to build its own prison. Fanaticism eventually destroys the mechanism through which it acts.

Fanaticism leads to intellectual blindness and closes all opportunities for mental development. Imagine what would happen if science were fanatical. We

1.   See Ch. 27, "Irritation — The Destructive Fire," in *The Psyche and Psychism.*

would never have had any progress in the world. Actually, one of the definitions of science can be the antidote to fanaticism.

Be careful of those who fanatically impose their ideas and ways on you. Cooperate with those who have open minds and are ready to accept any fact that is approved by their reasoning and Intuition.

Remember the words of Christ, "Seek the truth and the truth will make you free." A fanatical person does not search for the truth. He thinks he has all the truth, and, worse, he thinks all must accept his truth.

6. Prejudice is the next hindrance to the development of the mind.

Prejudice is like telling the mind to see and think the way it has been conditioned. You can take a child and tell him, "You must think that the earth is flat and the sun is turning around the earth." And the child says, "Yes, sir." This is the state of mind of a man in prejudice.

7. The next hindrance is indifference.

Indifference is a lack of interest and a sickness of inertia and mental apathy.

People progress due to their interest. There are many kinds of interests. There are worldly interests and superhuman interests. Every interest presents a challenge to move forward and bring the latent potential into manifestation.

An indifferent man isolates himself from a progressing and synthesizing world.

Indifference is a state of inertia in which the fires of the centers are locked up by past serious crimes, misfortunes, or mental paralysis. Mental paralysis occurs not only due to psychic attacks but also due to prematurely opening oneself to strong currents.

The mind cannot develop in the right way, if at all, if indifference is not removed from the heart and mind of man. An interest is the first hope toward development.

8. The next hindrance is karma.

You must have a certain merit to have a chance to develop your mind. This merit is the result of your service and dedication to others. If you have served in the past, you gain the right to develop your mind further. If you intend to serve greater causes, you put your mind in the right condition to develop. If you misuse your mind, you weaken its powers and eventually lead it to apathy and inertia. No matter how learned you are, you do not have a cultivated mind if you did not do good things for humanity.

It is your dedication and service to greater and greater causes that cultivates your mind. When you serve, the Higher Self plants the best flowers in your mind — which can only be used for the universal good of humanity.

We are told that all expansion and development are gifts to us. Advancement into greater light is an honor given to us by Nature because of our selfless service. As we sincerely serve, we drop our vanities, glamors, and indifference and make our light shine out. Light increases in us when we are free of self-interest.

Karma is an important factor. When people gain knowledge by various means but do not serve, their knowledge is eventually used as their trap.

9. The next hindrance to the development of the mind is hypocrisy and lies.

Hypocrisy and lies create a double personality in you and a severe conflict between your personality and Soul. This conflict results in various sicknesses, but no one thinks that they come from the inner conflict. The mind cannot be cultivated if false images are continuously printed on its page.

Eventually the liar and hypocrite loses his own certainty, like a ship that loses it anchorage.

In cultivating our mind, we try to bring into manifestation the best that we have within us. Lies and hypocrisy are the reverse process. We hide ourself. The real man is eventually imprisoned within us and has no chance to actualize.

10. The next hindrance is posthypnotic suggestions.

A hypnotized mind loses its own identity. It works as a tool for others. Its freedom is taken away from it, and other people are ruling its destiny. If you do not have a free mind, you do not have a mind, and how can you develop something you do not have?

There are other hindrances that you can avoid if you really want to develop your mind:

11. You must not eat sugar or hot or cooked honey.

12. Use as little salt as possible.

13. Do not eat meat. Eating meat delays the evolution of man.

14. Do not use tobacco or marijuana.

15. Do not use hallucinogenic drugs. They are called killers of the mind.

16. Do not use alcohol. It damages your brain and mental mechanism.

17. Masturbation is very bad for the mind, though I know many doctors will not agree with this.

Masturbation wastes the precious energy of your etheric centers. Continuous masturbation creates a bum.

18. Excessive sex and sexual impurity damage the brain and pollute the mind.

Moderation and purity in sex help the brain and the mind be more active and creative.

Oral sex is disastrous for the mind. The sex center slows and obliterates the etheric throat center, which eventually reflects on the mind. Those who are victims of oral sex will eventually see that their higher gears are no longer in operation. The more advanced the man, the worse the damage done to his mind.

19. The next hindrance is bad music such as acid rock, disco, jazz, and rock and roll.

Such music dislocates the etheric centers in the head and eventually closes the opportunity to work on higher mental levels or at higher intellectual tasks. If you take such music out of your children's hands, you will see how they will bring home higher grades and behave better with their friends and family.

There are, of course, other hindrances, but one must find them through his own experiences.

The right development of the mind allows a man to be in harmony with Nature and with the steady progress of the Mind in Nature. The development of the mind makes a man see virtues and be able to actualize them.

The development of the mind makes a man see the real values, the real issues, and navigate wisely between the rocks of life.

The development of the mind enables the brain to be impressed by higher inspirations.

The development of the mind allows a man to live in harmony with the laws of the Universe.

The development of the mind leads a man to right human relations, to goodwill, and to universal synthesis.

It will be a blessing for the child if the pregnant mother occupies her mind with lofty thoughts; checks her motives; is careful about her conversations; keeps herself in the line of Beauty, Goodness, Truth, and joy; is careful about her emotions and relationships; avoids watching television programs full of violence and crimes and, instead, relaxes and enjoys herself in Nature or with inspirational music, books, and creative activity; and, finally, keeps company with loving and joyful people. Mothers will be surprised to see great beauty and integrity in their children when they start them in the right way and then watch the steps of their children.

Mental development starts from pregnancy, and it is possible to have heroes and geniuses if the above points are carefully taken into consideration.[2]

There are two ways to progress. The first way is through knowledge, or knowingness, and through application of your knowledge. The second way is through beingness.

People advance by accumulating knowledge in the seven fields of human endeavor — politics, education, philosophy, arts, science, religion, and economy.

---

2. For more information on healthy children, please see *Woman, Torch of the Future*, and *Sex, Family and the Woman in Society*.

There is one very important point on the path of knowledge. Man can be trapped in his own knowledge and use his knowledge for selfish or separative ends. At that moment his progress stops and he becomes an obstacle on the path of progress of humanity. He must follow at the same time the next path, which is progress through beingness.

Beingness means actualization of your Innermost Self through all that you do, speak, feel, and think.

Beingness means the ability to use knowledge to touch your Self, to unfold your talents, to manifest Beauty, Goodness, and Truth, with all the virtues necessary to make these three fundamentals unfold.

Beingness is not only what you know but also what you are.

Beingness is progressive spiritualization, refinement, purification, control over knowledge, feeling, and action, and transformation and transfiguration of your nature. Only through beingness can your knowledge be used for the survival of natural life and for the manifestation of the Divine Plan.

Knowledge often takes us away from our Self. Beingness brings us closer to our essence and to the essence of Nature.

Knowledge cannot satisfy a human being because knowledge is based on duality. There is a knower and the knowledge, along with the object of knowledge. In beingness, plurality disappears and oneness emerges.

Knowledge, being based on duality, can be used against human interest. The curious part is that knowledge is available even to those who are really planning to make this planet a prison for slaves. And if those people have enough knowledge and position, human evolution will be retarded for millions of years.

Beingness is open only to those who follow the path of Beauty, Goodness, and Truth and are basically self-sacrificial and inclusive.

Every person is essentially a being. He exists. He is a nucleus of light, love, and power, a creative center in the Universe. To actualize this potentiality is the process of beingness through which man becomes his True Self instead of being the slave of his physical, emotional, and mental elementals.

Beingness is achieved when our thoughts transmit higher ideas, higher visions, and higher substance into our vehicles and eventually reveal to us our True Self.

Real thinking is a process through which we become that which we are essentially.

It is said that knowledge is power. Those who have knowledge have power, either for constructive use or for destructive use.

As we increase our knowledge, our power increases. The reason for this is that this Universe is run by a network of thought energy. This network is produced by the thinking process of the Cosmic Mind. All energies and forces run through this network of thought and act according to the directions of thought.

It is from this network of thought that we draw our knowledge through meditation, thinking, study, or Intuition. Any real knowledge is a portion of this network, and once it enters into our mental sphere it connects us with the entire network of thought.

This connection is relative. There are good and firm connections. There are temporary and loose connections. The connection is firm and good when the mental body is not clouded by prejudices, superstition, illusions, crystallized thoughtforms, and fanaticism. The connection is firm and good if the brain is healthy and not polluted.

The connection is firm and good if the agent lives a life of virtue and sacrificial service, ever striving toward greater achievements.

Thus knowledge with spiritual actualization produces a channel for the great energy sources in space.

Birth of New Ideas

A time comes in the life of an advancing person when he begins to create new thoughtforms, creative thoughtforms which serve as the bodies of great visions and ideas to be actualized.

There are many visions and ideas which wait in the space to be born. They need vehicles, and creative people provide such vehicles through their refined, futuristic thoughtforms, which attract these ideas and visions and become their vehicles of manifestation.

Thus great ideas and visions are put in action through thoughtforms and bring changes in human consciousness and human life.

Every advanced thoughtform clears the way for new inspired energies. "Energy follows thought." And new energies are brought down from space to regenerate the life of the planet.

The bridge between abstract ideas and life in general is a well organized, inspired thoughtform.

Sometimes people call futuristic writings *fiction*. Nothing is wrong with a work of fiction if it is the vehicle of our visions, inspirations, ideas, and energies.

Life will proceed onward only through new challenges, and new challenges are given to people with new, inspiring thoughtforms.

10

The Mysterious Power of Conclusion

There is a very mysterious function in the mind. It can be called the power of *conclusion* or *synthesis*.

When a man thinks, experiences, and learns, certain patterns are formed in his mind. They are like sentences or symbols which serve the needs of the man at that time. However, the mind does not cast them out when they no longer serve his current objectives. Instead, it works on them and collects many apparently unassociated sentences or symbols and creates a paragraph or a combination of symbols. In due time it represents to the human consciousness a new idea, a new vision, and a new plan when the man needs them.

The activity of the mind does not stop with this presentation. Paragraphs form parts of chapters. Chapters form parts of a book. Books become parts of an encyclopedia. This is how great symphonies and great movements originate. Such an activity of the mind reflects in the affairs of the world.

The collective mind of humanity does exactly the same thing not only in education, arts, and sciences but also in politics, philosophy, religion, and economics.

There are ever-progressive conclusions of the mind. One conclusion or synthesis expands and becomes a part of a greater conclusion or a greater synthesis. How different the world would be if a human being, or humanity, did not resist the manifestation of such a law but cooperated with it, living a life oriented toward synthesis!

I once saw a boulevard which was filled with small flowers of different colors and kinds. All these flowers were arranged in such a way that one could see a garden and a big lotus in a lake, all made from flowers. That is how ideas are manifested and life is led toward synthesis.

The progressive achievements of the individual and collective minds are not a conscious activity; they are very subjective, selective, and slow due to many obstacles. But one can perceive such achievements on those certain occasions when the mind is producing a new "table," an idea with "lumber" not previously used for the building of various rooms and buildings.

It is very important to know that thinking is also related to the senses. As the senses function more clearly, they register the impressions more accurately. This gives the human soul a greater opportunity to think in a higher quality.

We are referring not only to the physical senses but also to the senses found on higher planes. As the senses gradually unfold plane after plane, the quality of thinking improves and becomes higher, clearer, more accurate, more universal, and more inclusive.

The senses are information lines of the Monad, as if different rays were emanating from the Monad and bringing back information to make the Monad respond to the world around It. Senses exist in the mineral, vegetable, and animal kingdoms, too.

Often animals function more through the astral counterpart of the senses than through their physical senses. This is what gives them extreme sensitivity to smell, color, sound, and movements. Many insects, birds, and fish are highly equipped with very sensitive senses. Their senses function faster than our physical senses because they use the astral counterpart of the senses.

As the human being materializes more and more and involves himself with the physical world, in the majority of cases the higher counterparts of the physical senses disappear. This is so that the physical senses become fully developed and a total coordination and integration, controlled by the consciousness of man, is reached between the senses and the brain.

Man is superior in that he can consciously use his senses and translate impressions through his unfolding consciousness. In lower kingdoms, the usage is mostly mechanical.

Thus the human being — or the Self — slowly renounced his subtle senses during his journey through various kingdoms to develop his physical-level senses, his brain, his mind, and his consciousness.

It is after a healthy development of the senses on the physical plane that man will begin to unfold his senses on higher planes, step by step taking them under his conscious control.

When we develop our senses on higher levels and control their functions consciously, we will be able to hear on all levels, touch, or see on all levels. . . . This is how a man becomes a higher psychic, transcends his limitations, and enters a higher kingdom.[1]

Thinking is often a conclusion. We reach better conclusions when the sources of our information are multi-dimensional. Thus, the quality of thought improves as the senses unfold upon higher planes.

---

1. Refer also to the chapters on the senses in *The Psyche and Psychism*, Vol. I.

11

Defeat or Victory

There are circuits in our mind which act as programmings and control our actions, words, and even thoughts. Some of these circuits are success-oriented. When they begin to be active due to certain causes, man enters the path of success and even attracts those individuals, events, and objects which guarantee his success.

There are also failure circuits, which unexpectedly begin acting in the midst of our path of success and slowly break our speed and introduce into our life failure factors in our speech, relationships, actions, feelings, and thoughts. Once these circuits begin to work, we feel a setback; things become complicated; problems increase; and we arrive at a state where two circuits in us carry on a strong conflict.

If a failure circuit is fed by failure impressions, we will fail. If both circuits are fed equally, we will struggle and go through a time of distress, conflict, and dissatisfaction. Usually, if the failure circuit reaches forty-five percent, failure is inevitable except if some positive interference takes place.

These failure circuits are formed by witnessing, hearing, listening to, or reading about failure events, by having affairs with those who failed in their lives, or by accepting the attacks of dark forces, which usually try to impress failure images in our minds.

Positive circuits are formed in our auras because of success images, reading about successful people, relating with successful people, or using our creative imagination and visualization to create successful images and thoughtforms.

It is very important to reject any suggestions, stories, or thoughts of failure images. Seeds are very small forms, but soon they grow into big plants or trees.

There are several effective ways to fight against failure circuits:

1. Observe your thoughts, words, feelings, and actions and stop them if they are feeding the failure circuits. It is probable that such thoughts, words, and feelings sneak in through expressions such as

— I was right.

— He insulted me.

— It is his habit.

— I want to correct him.

— It doesn't matter.

— I can sometimes take it easy.

— I don't want to be under such pressure.

— It is too much.

— I need relaxation.

The worst attacks are those which use your self-justification and latent weaknesses or your jealousy or ego.

2. The second way to fight against failure circuits is to use your creative imagination and visualization and daily build thoughtforms of success, even using your temporary failures as moments of opportunity to put yourself on the path of success.

3. The third way is to develop a "habit" of gratitude and joy for each of your successes.

In using these methods, you will repulse most of your failure images and prevent the failure circuits from starting to function.

The same is true for our health. The cause of most of our health problems is the activation of negative circuits built over many lives. There are health circuits which are amazingly strong if they are fed by positive suggestions, trust, and hope.

Exercises for Success and Victory

Victory starts in your mind. If you can conquer in your mind, you can conquer the outside. Create obstacles in your imagination and conquer them. Very soon you will see that the difficulties of life will vanish. You can pave your way first inside of you, and the outside will follow like a shadow.

Great conquerors were first victors in their minds.

The first exercise is related to land, earthquakes, stones and rocks, quicksand, accidents, etc.

I.   *Exercise*

Imagine a high hill and see a big rock at the foot of the hill.

Try to roll it to the top of the hill, with all the labor and difficulty and danger of it rolling back. Feel your muscles, feel your heartbeat, sweat, the strain of your muscles, but do not give up. Push it up, up, to the top. If it slips away, start from the beginning. You can even have obstacles such as earthquakes that you overcome.

II.   *Exercise*

This exercise is related to water.

— Visualize a lake and see yourself sitting high on a cliff fifty feet above the lake.

— Prepare to jump. Count one, two, three. . .and jump. Make it as real as possible.

— Swim and come back and sit on the cliff.

— Look down. Visualize the lake.

— Prepare to jump again. Count one, two, three. . .and jump.

Do this seven times. Make it very real. First prepare yourself. Then count one, two, three. . . . Feel exactly how you would feel if you really jumped.

Then swim a little. Feel the water. Get out. Feel the air, and prepare yourself for the next jump.

III.   *Exercise*

This is a fire test for purification, which means destruction of limitations existing in your physical, emotional, and mental nature.
When your limitations are conquered on these levels, you are purified, and to be purified means to be closer to your Self.

Close your eyes.

You are sitting in a garden. You see ten to fifteen people gathering dry branches of trees and bushes and stacking them into a pile. They are pouring some kerosene on it, and a boy comes and lights the pile.

Take off all your clothes and suddenly run into the fire. Stay until your body is totally burned.

Burn to ashes all your flesh. Then walk out of the fire as a skeleton. Then go into the fire again and burn completely to ashes, but see your True Self as a silvery figure which is nonflammable and indestructible.

Burn slowly, outside, inside. Burn your organs, pancreas, liver, stomach, heart, kidneys, lungs, bowels; and now come out of the fire as a spirit, more radiant than the Sun.

Inhale three deep breaths and exhale with OM.

Let the first breath and OM build a new mental body.

Let the second breath and OM build a new astral body.

Let the third breath and OM build the physical-etheric body. See your body as healthy as possible and shining with a golden light.

* * *

To whatever degree you do these exercises, to that degree they will be beneficial. With these exercises a new energy will circulate throughout your vehicles. Through these exercises you get closer to your Real Self. With these exercises many obstacles will come to the surface, and you will wipe them away in a short time.

Do not forget that all victories are won in the subjective levels before they are won on the objective level. Healing starts in the subjective levels and gradually comes and manifests on the physical plane. Be beautiful inside; then you will be beautiful outside.

For years I ran a private high school. One day the mother of one of the girls came and complained about her daughter, saying that she was a very untidy girl. She added, "She is Miss Chaos," and invited me one day for dinner to see the girl's room.

I could not believe my eyes — shirts, belts, shoes, slippers everywhere, books scattered . . .just chaos.

I pretended I did not see. A few days later I called her to my office and said, "I am trying to build a bedroom, and I need your advice. You must write a paper for me, telling me how to build the best bedroom — the bed, the closets, the drawers — an ideal bedroom. After you write the paper, I will ask you to explain every detail of it. Then work on my kitchen. You will be my decorator and my engineer."

She was surprised, but she was happy for my attention and trust in her.

A week later she brought a paper about an ideal bedroom, and she explained about the colors, drapes, furniture, and how to keep it tidy and clean and why. I tried to ask as many questions as possible.

The next week she worked on the kitchen. When she brought the paper, I was surprised. It had all the details and facilities for an ideal kitchen. After I finished my questions, she said, "Now what?"

"Two weeks later I will see you."

Before she went home, I called her mother and asked how her daughter was doing.

"You know," she said, "miracles are happening. I do not believe my eyes. She is acting like a crazy person. She is cleaning everything. She is not acting normal."

"What is happening?"

"Well, the bedroom is changed and the kitchen is going through fundamental changes. She told me how untidy I am. I am acting as if it were no surprise for me and following her suggestions. Today she cleaned my bedroom and warned me to be neat."

Then after a pause, she asked, "What did you do, did you hypnotize her?"

"No," I said. "Later I will talk to you."

This is a good method to change the outer life. . .through inner changes.

I have seen people attacking each other and criticizing each other. For me, especially a husband, a teacher, a close friend must never do that. For example, you must never, never criticize your husband or wife. You must find ways and means to subtly suggest the change to expect — by stories, parables, even by using movies and dramas or plays.

For example, a woman likes indirectness. She has a complicated mechanism, and you cannot hammer it with direct criticism. Once she is hurt, her love slowly fades and a monster starts to build; or at best you create an indifferent woman who "cooks" you alive!

You can do the exercises mentioned like a real drama. Add many factors to them; be creative, and you will see the change. The secret of these exercises is that you are controlling your body, time, space, and matter through your conscious action. When this victory is won inside, you can win the victory outside because all outside phenomena are the shadow of inner causes.

You can also use your visualization in healing. Once a woman came to me with a bad stomach. I said, "I am not a physician, but I can give you an exercise which may help."

"Visualize," I said, "your sick stomach. Detach it from your body. Take it to Christ and ask Him to cure it and repair it. And as He puts His hands on your stomach and transmits healing energy, try to see your stomach totally healthy and transformed into a new stomach."

She did it for a week. Then to the surprise of her doctor, she said to him, "My stomach is excellent now."

"What did you do?" And she explained what she had done.

"Yes," said the doctor, "sometimes crazy people can cure themselves."

When she was telling this story, she was in tears, laughing.

The secret is that *all is thought.* If you know how to visualize, you can move mountains. Do not forget what the Lord said, "He who believes in Me shall do the works which I do, and even greater than these things he shall do."[1]

IV.   *Exercise*

This exercise deals with the air, which corresponds to the higher mental and even intuitional levels.

— Close your eyes and imagine you are jumping from one mountain to another one.

— Then try to go to the moon as if you were flying by yourself. See all the rocks, rivers, oceans, mountains, and the earth getting smaller and smaller.

— Then go to the stars, the galaxies. Do not jump. Take your time and fly, faster and faster, faster than light.

— Every time you rest on a new star during the course of your flight, turn back and look at the planet earth and see how it appears to you.

— Then eventually come back to the planet and to the room from which you departed.

*   *   *

Do these exercises once a week, maybe Saturday or Sunday, and watch the reactions or responses of your physical, astral, and mental bodies.

Through these exercises and through the observation techniques, you will be able to detach yourself from your mechanism and master the worlds to which they are related.

Once you feel and see the sunrise of your Self, you are on the Cosmic Path to freedom, and you can be a co-worker of creative energies in the Universe.

_____

1.   John 14:12

12

How to Cultivate
Higher Thinking

To make this subject simple, let us study the following diagram about the mind:

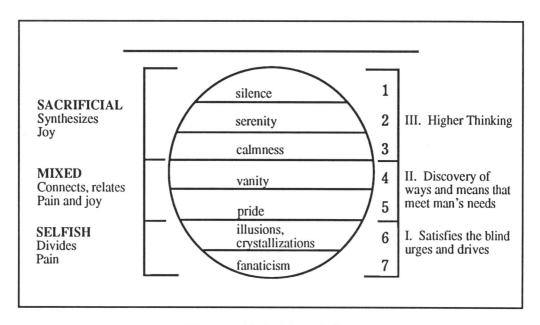

Diagram 12-1   Mental Plane

The mental plane is divided into seven levels which are actually seven frequencies penetrating into each other but keeping their individual frequencies. Layers seven and six can be called layers of primitive thinking. Using these layers, the human soul tries to discover the ways and means to protect his body and his belongings and satisfy his blind urges and drives.

Using levels five and four, he tries to discover all those ways through which he can meet his physical, emotional, and mental needs.

Using levels three, two, and one, the human soul tries to discover those laws and principles in Nature through which he can use the energies and forces in Nature for his infinite progress and for the progress of all life-forms in Nature. On levels three, two, and one, the human soul carries on higher thinking.

Higher thinking does not exclude the utilization of the lower levels but handles them in such a way that they are all synthesized in the effort of higher thinking. Higher thinking is inclusive, oriented toward Infinity and Space, and is occupied with the science of energies, laws, and principles in the Universe. Such thinking tries to cooperate with the goal and purpose of all Nature and secure steady evolution, expansion of consciousness, and mastery of life.

Higher thinking is the ability to contact transcendental values and to formulate them in such a way that they build a progressive ladder for higher and higher revelations and actualizations.

Levels seven and six are used for selfish thinking. Levels five and four are used for mixed thinking. Levels three, two, and one are used for selfless thinking. Levels three, two, and one are levels of rhythm. Levels four and five are motion; levels six and seven are levels of inertia.

Higher thinking is more inclusive thinking. In higher thinking the interests of the personality are transcended but not ignored. In higher thinking the mind is occupied with the interests of humanity, with those laws, principles, and energies of Nature which will help humanity recognize its Cosmic destiny and live accordingly.

In higher thinking the mind strives to formulate the impressions coming from intuitional sources and discover the sources or causes of these impressions to increase its receptivity and expand its awareness of higher realms. The recorded impressions are slowly translated into formulas to be used in the fields of human endeavor.

Factors for Higher Thinking

Higher thinking requires five factors:

1. *Intuitive impressions.* Impressions are formed in our mind by those energy currents which come from the Intuitional Plane or higher and touch the sphere of our mental body. The Intuitional Plane is higher than the mental plane, and it is the sphere of ideas, guidance, energies, and directions.

When energy currents and ideas reach the mind, the mind tries to translate them according to its nature, education, background, and a person's Rays, and builds a communication line between the mental plane and the Intuitional Plane. Thus the man comes in contact with the higher spheres of light and operates his mental mechanism with loftier visions.

Impressions, guidance, ideas, and directions can reach our mind from the Intuitional Plane, from the Ashrams of Wisdom, from our Inner Guide, and from the Spiritual Triad. Through the practice of meditation, eventually we can discriminate between the sources and put the impressions to their proper use.

Impressions coming from the Intuitional Plane enrich the sphere of the mind with currents of synthesis, universality, and inclusiveness. These currents help the mind use thoughts not only in the limited field of the personality but also in relation to Cosmic visions.

Higher thinking synthesizes. Lower thinking separates. Intermediate thinking relates. A mind operates better when all three types of thinking cooperate.

In lower thinking man is interested only in his own personal desires. His religion is "the only way to fly" to satisfy his personal needs.

In intermediate thinking one cares for others as long as they serve his interests. He tolerates other religions, but his is the best.

In higher thinking one forgets about his personal interests and works for the interests of the whole life. He respects all approaches to the Supreme Life because he sees one direction in all spiritual movements.

To be able to receive and register impressions coming from intuitional sources, one must purify his mental mechanism and put it in order through meditation, service, and spiritual striving. Purity, calmness, and serenity increase the receptivity of the mind to higher ideas. A sacrificial life, a selfless life, and a clean life make the registration of higher ideas possible.

Love of beauty, joy, and a spirit of gratitude and harmlessness make the mind creative. Thus impressions are registered and put into practical application.

2. The second factor for higher thinking is *willpower*. Willpower on the mental plane acts as a lens to focus impressions for such a length of time that the sensitive substance of the mental body is impressed adequately. The moment of such a focusing process is a moment of deep silence which one experiences at the time of registration of impressions.

Without willpower the impressions are diffused. Willpower creates focus, concentration, and keeps the keynotes of the impressions in line with the higher Will. It is after focus and registration that the mind begins to formulate the impressions to meet the needs of humanity, the needs of life.

3. The third factor is *visualization*. Visualization is the ability to translate the registered impressions. It is your video tape machine which translates the impressions on the film into color, sound, and form.

Without visualization there is no true creativity. Creativity is actualization of subtle intuitive impressions through the act of visualization.

The clear formulation of ideas depends on clear visualization. It is possible to receive the impact of impressions. Such moments are moments of joy and ecstasy. But they are short moments and do not last, until the impressions are focused by the willpower, visualized, and put into formulation.

Visualization works in the mental body and awakens the sleeping parts of the brain into coordinated activity with the mind. It is possible to have an active mind but a sleeping brain, or an active brain with a sleeping mind. Visualization synchronizes these activities.

4. The fourth factor in higher thinking is *the ability to sustain your consciousness on the frequency of the registered impression.* Many people can receive impressions, can have a momentary focus and visualization, but their consciousness fails to keep the frequency of the impressions alive and pure for any length of time. It is the ability to sustain the consciousness on the higher frequency that offers the opportunity for actualization or realization.

Psychological digestion and assimilation cannot take place unless the consciousness sustains, for a sufficient time, the higher voltage of the impressions so that the lower vehicles are given the chance to absorb them and transform their nature. Without transformation of our nature, actualization cannot take place and our contacts remain in the domain of dreams.

The third level of the mind holds the tensity of calmness. The second level holds the tensity of serenity. The first level holds the tensity of silence. When these three levels sustain their creative tension, actualization is the result.

The agitation and the ever-changing nature of the mind is the greatest obstacle to actualization. Stability is a state of sustained tension. Agitated rivers cannot reflect the beauty found on their banks.

You can test your sustaining power by watching how long you can concentrate your attention on a lecture, music, or a painting and absorb it with all your aspiration and powers of translation. Some people cannot sustain higher-voltage ideas more than a second. The transformation of your nature is carried on within the furnace of your sustaining power or tensity.

Higher thinking is carried on in the tension of the higher mind, in levels three, two, and one. The tensity of the higher mind repels the four most destructive elements growing in the lower mind. They are called vanity, pride, illusion, and fanaticism. These hindrances must be eliminated from our mind in order to give birth to higher visions without distortion.

5. The fifth factor for higher thinking is *the ability to transmit and create.* The manifestation of impressions and ideas is carried on through creative transmission. Creativity is a process of registration, translation, formulation, and actualization of impressions. Creativity is the process of making impressions tangible to our senses.

Creativity is carried out within all the fields of human endeavor. The purpose of creativity is to raise the level of human life and synchronize it with higher and more inclusive frequencies.

If our mind is impressed by the idea of synthesis, we try to actualize that idea through our creativity. Maybe we create a new political system based on the idea of synthesis. Maybe we change our whole educational system and introduce the keynote of synthesis. Maybe we create a philosophy based on the idea of synthesis. Maybe we create various art objects to translate the spirit of synthesis.

We may also make scientific discoveries to prove and utilize the principle of synthesis, create a new approach to the Great Unknown based on the principle of synthesis, create rituals and ceremonies to dramatize the mystery of synthesis, or create a new economic system based on the principle of synthesis.

Creativity is the ability to contact the white light of impressions and radiate it out through the colors of the rainbow.

Impressions are condensed durations. Time is condensed in them. It needs sometimes two to five hundred years or more to manifest an impression that hits our higher mind for one second — in our time concept.

Creativity is a continuous process. If one cannot carry the torch of beauty or the torch of actualization in his marathon race, others will pick up the flaming torch and run toward the destination. Sometimes the success of a creative artist is found in his ability to pass the torch to the next runner on the path of creativity.

The higher mind is often called the Fiery World. The fiery impressions tempered in the mind must be expressed objectively through the creative process. Congestion of creative thoughts produces many complications in the mind. Any conceived beauty must grow and manifest.

Fiery energies can burn our system if they are not directed into proper channels of creative living and expression.

Hindrances to Higher Thinking

There are five major hindrances to higher thinking:

1. Imagination controlled and carried on by selfish, separative, and earthbound desires. This is the first hindrance, and those who have it will seldom be able to penetrate the third, second, and first levels of the mind, or they will misuse the energies leaked from the higher mind. Unless we eliminate this obstacle, we will be unable to function within the higher mind and manifest higher thinking.

Imagination based on selfish interests causes complicated distortions within received impressions. It is through imagination based on selfish and separative interests that a man loses his magnetism and charm.

Higher thinking makes a man continuously radioactive and magnetic.

A Sage once advised his students to keep their eyes pure in the joy of beauty to be able to protect themselves from the danger of degenerative imagination. Imagination based on selfish, separative interests and earthly desires is flooding our television programs, our publications, and our music with various expressions. Those who are saturated with such fruits of imagination will seldom have the chance to function within the higher mind.

The higher mind is the contact point for higher direction. Survival and continuity of creativity are only guaranteed by the ability to function in the higher mind.

2. The second hindrance to higher thinking is pollution found in the brain and the nervous system. This means it is almost impossible to exercise higher thinking when our brain is polluted with hallucinogenic drugs, alcohol, tobacco, and meat and abused by the misuse of our generative organs.

The various gases and pollution in the atmosphere make it extremely difficult to contact higher currents of creative energies. Some Sages even advise us not to meditate when the atmospheric pollution is intense. The channels or transmitters must be clear and pure to render communication possible between higher forces and receivers.

3. The third hindrance to higher thinking is a mind in which is found crystallized thoughtforms, vanity, pride, illusions, and fanaticism. Such a mind is a great danger for society if by chance it contacts higher impressions or ideas.

When the above obstacles are present in the mind, all impressions will be molded by vanity, fanaticism, and illusions. There exist minds which are full of crystallized blocks of energy, like a lake full of blocks of ice. In such a condition the lower mind is paralyzed and cannot transmit any beauty it receives through the higher mind.

4. The next hindrance is composed of the glamors found in our emotional sphere. Glamors distort the rays of impression and make higher thinking almost impossible. Glamors are the images in our aura of those objects with which we emotionally identify ourselves. Such images consume the energy of higher impressions and grow like weeds in our aura.

Elimination of glamors helps the mind think in higher gears. The increase of glamors eventually blocks the receptivity of the mind.

There are many minds which become the slaves of glamors. This is very common. People serve their glamors without even knowing about it. It is only in the moment of a painful trapping that man realizes the power of his glamors.

5. The fifth hindrance is lack of concentration. When a person has developed power over his threefold vehicles, he may have the ability to concentrate his mind and his life in any chosen direction or on any chosen object. Willpower comes into action as the person develops mastery over his mental body.

Purification of the mental body and continuous mental discipline eventually bring the mind under the control of the human soul. Higher thinking cannot be carried on in the mental plane until the mental body is controlled and purified.

Fluctuations of the emotional body and changing physical moods are dangerous signs that higher thinking cannot be exercised. Thought control is of prime importance. Those who can control their thoughts can control their emotional states and physical moods. It is after such control that the human soul can exercise higher thinking.

Concentration is the ability to sustain the voltage of increasing energies and direct them into proper channels without losing the voltage and the intent of the energies.

Characteristics of Higher Thinking

There are seven characteristics of higher thinking by which one can easily know whether higher thinking is being exercised or is not in manifestation or expression:

- Inclusiveness

- Balance

- Purposefulness

- Inspiration

- Simplicity

- Magnetism

- Powerfulness, fieriness

Inclusiveness. In higher thinking a person deals with almost any subject but always in relation to the whole existence.

In any such expression, higher thinking reflects the interests of all. Any subjective expression contains the objective counterpart of it. Any individual manifestation contains the group counterpart of it. Higher thinking can be translated on any plane without losing its beauty, meaning, and guidance.

Higher thinking is never separative. It relates, synthesizes, and unites. It always chooses the common subjective frequency of apparently different objects.

Balance. Higher thinking is not lost in the parts. It is not one-sided. It does not emphasize one side of a subject at the expense of the other sides. It is not suspended in abstract ideas or totally identified with the form side of an object. It uses higher ideas to transform life and tries to transform life to establish the flow of greater ideas. In higher thinking, higher visions meet the smallest needs, and the smallest needs evoke the highest visions.

Balanced thinking is not thinking in extremes. You need two wings to fly. You cannot fly with one wing.

In higher thinking there is balance between the objective and subjective approach, between meaning and expression, between wisdom and actualization.

The art manifested through balanced, high-level thinking brings equilibrium to your heart and mind. In such art you sense the opposing colors, but you also see how they help each other and increase the beauty of the whole painting. Music created by higher thinking brings balance in your nature because its every expression builds a bridge within your psychological system.

Higher thinking creates balance between the unit and the whole and eventually enables man to find the point of equilibrium between the moving and changing equations of the higher and lower, of spirit and matter. Balance leads toward stabilization of spirit in the continuum of manifestation.

Purposefulness. Higher thinking is in harmony with the Purpose behind the manifestation. Higher thinking is naturally synchronized with the *Will* behind the Purpose. It always leads toward synthesis, toward resurrection, toward continuity of consciousness and immortality. In higher thinking the direction of the Cosmic Will shines. Behind the words, colors, sounds, movements, and forms, a silent Purpose radiates out. It is this silent and unseen Purpose that charges any expression with power and makes it a masterpiece.

Inspiration. Higher thinking inspires people, gives hope and future to them, encourages and strengthens them, and opens new doors and new paths in their souls.

Higher thinking brings into your life the fire of enthusiasm, the divine fire, and all your expressions glow with that fire.

Higher thinking puts your system into action through inspiration. You feel challenged and you dare to expand, express, and be.

Simplicity. Higher thinking is not confused thinking. It is clear, correct, and to the point. You can see the great simplicity in the words of Buddha and Christ. Simplicity does not mean a lack of richness of meaning, a shallowness, but a depth which you can see because of its clarity.

Simplicity is directness. It is the ability to present a great beauty, a great truth without confusion.

In simplicity the words or forms of expression do not hinder the light of the manifesting idea, vision, or spirit. They do not curtail it. They do not pretend that they are the spirit. That is why we are told that "the letter kills the spirit," or any form of expression weakens or even kills the spirit when it pretends to *be* the spirit.

In simplicity the expression is the lamp that holds the light and makes it manifest as it is. In simplicity the form disappears in the light of the spirit, in the light of ideas, meaning, and purpose.

In simplicity there is soul-to-soul communication. In simplicity the words are silent to make the spirit sing.

Magnetism. Higher thinking attracts higher forces and higher beings into our environment. These beings and forces bring greater blessings to us.

Higher thinking attracts those who sacrifice, devote, and dedicate their lives to the service of humanity for the expression and distribution of great ideas and visions.

Higher thinking evokes soul or spiritual response. It is possible to convince a man, but it is difficult to make him commit himself to a higher cause. Higher thinking makes people commit themselves because it reaches their soul, their spirit.

Higher thinking resonates in Space and attracts those currents of energy which function under the Cosmic Magnet. Thus, higher thinking enriches itself with Cosmic gifts.

Powerfulness or **fieriness** is another characteristic of higher thinking. It breaks and wipes away all crystallizations which are unworthy on the path of perfection.

Higher thinking rules your life, controls your own physical, emotional, and mental bodies, and leads them to purposeful activity.

Higher thinking never violates the will and freedom of others. Violation of the freedom or will of others is the clearest sign of weakness and baseness of thought.

The power of thought operates in freedom. Actually, true power is the gift of freedom. No one has true power if he is not free. People try to have power without first being free. Such a power is self-destructive.

Freedom is mastery over our own personality and the ability to stand in the pure light of our True Self. Higher thought leads us into freedom, and freedom gives us power. Higher thinking penetrates into the souls of men and evokes recognition, reverence, and decision to strive toward freedom.

Objects of Importance to Higher Thinking

Higher thinking has nine objects of importance:

1. Higher thinking discovers the One Self in all forms of life and occupies itself in creating ways and means to be one with that Self, not in theory but in actuality. You can see this in the *Upanishads* and in the *Bhagavad Gita* very clearly.

2. The second object of higher thinking is Cosmic relationship, or relationship between man and stars and between all forms of life. In higher thinking, one considers the interests of all that exists before he takes action.

Co-measurement is a strange word, but very appropriate, to explain the operation of higher thinking. Higher thinking *measures* and *weighs* the possible effects of events, actions, words, and thoughts upon all that exists. That is why higher thinking follows the path of extreme caution.

Scientific thinking is not higher thinking if it lacks co-measurement. Scientific thinking can test an atomic bomb, but if it does not consider the effects of the bomb and radioactivity upon the life-forms, upon the energy network of the planet and solar system, upon the elements of the three spheres — physical, emotional, and mental — it is neither scientific thinking, nor high-level thinking. High-level thinking is *considerate* thinking. High-level thinking considers the effects of its words and actions before it expresses them.

3. The third object of higher thinking is immortality. There is no higher thinking if the thinking ends in a dead-end street.

Higher thinking is thinking in the *future*, within the future. Higher thinking has the ability to sense, to see, and then to experience continuity of consciousness from plane to plane. For higher thinking, things do not start and end. Higher thinking is a *continuum* in Infinity, with greater and greater fields of awareness.

Higher thinking tries to create all those conditions in which the survival of humanity will be possible, the higher evolution of humanity will be possible, the revelation of the Inner Divinity will be possible.

Higher thinking has visions, has experiences. This is very important to know. Higher thinking is not speculation, dreaming, or formulating hypotheses; *it is experience*. Higher thinking is an act of *experiencing*, not an act of experimentation.

Higher thinking allows the human soul to have experiences that are not limited to the senses of the body. Often it is such experiences that challenge him to step beyond the interests of the common life and penetrate into other dimensions of life. As one penetrates into subjective realities, joy descends to his heart and gratitude blooms in his soul. Gratitude is an intuitive awareness of the imperishability of the human Spark.

Lack of gratitude creates a condition which people call depression. Depression is a sign that the person is cutting himself off from his Inner Guide, rebelling against the plan of his Soul, rejecting his karma, and denying the blessings given to him in his life.

Gratitude cures all these conditions. Ingratitude gradually produces depression. First, it manifests as indifference, vanity, sanctimoniousness; then as remorse, grief, inertia, and finally depression.

Gratitude is appreciation of life, cooperation with the laws of life, and trust in the sunrise of the future.

4. The next object of higher thinking is the Subtle Worlds. As one's thinking refines, he penetrates more and more into higher strata of existence. He sees that life is not limited to the physical plane only but goes beyond to more subtle, electrical, fiery, and ethereal spheres where the experience of life is different, where the measures are different but are continuations of each other.

Higher thinking is an expedition into the higher, Subtle Worlds.[1]

5. The fifth object of higher thinking is the creative process in man and in Nature. Nature is an ever-creative process. It has the inner tension, plan, and purpose to create. The same tension is found in a human being. Higher thinking investigates the creative process and utilizes it to bring life more abundantly into expression.

6. The sixth object of higher thinking is the Plan. Higher thinking develops insight. Insight enables man to see a design, a plan behind the life which is slowly manifesting itself in Nature, in culture, and in many civilizations. Higher thinking tries to know and to cooperate with this Plan to eliminate friction, pain, and suffering. Higher thinking sees that joy is the right of the human being, and joy is established through cooperation with the Plan.

Higher thinking evokes contact with the Custodians of the Plan and experiences telepathic currents, psychic revelations released from the Custodians of the Plan. Higher thinking fuses with joy as the Plan reveals Itself, as the Custodians of the Plan make closer contact with the soul who is exercising higher thinking.

7. The seventh object of higher thinking is the Purpose behind all creation. Is there a Purpose in life for all life-forms, for a human being, for planets, stars, and galaxies? Higher thinking senses an existing Purpose for all creation. Higher thinking knows that the Innermost Core of the forms of life is a condensed Purpose, a microfilm of Purpose, which will reveal itself on the path of Infinity in greater and greater glory.

Higher thinking tries to know the Purpose behind any event, any expression, any manifestation. Those who find the Purpose find their own True Self.

8. The eighth object of higher thinking is initiations. Higher thinking does research on the progressive advancement of the life units. An initiation is a progressive ascent toward higher and higher dimensions of awareness and an expanding contact with all creation.

Higher thinking sees the man as the traveler on the path of Infinity in greater and greater glory and greater bliss.

On the lower levels of the mind — levels seven, six, and five — pain, imprisonment, war, suffering, and disease are experienced. On the fourth level, darkness and light fight; union and separation conflict; joy and suffering wrestle with each other.

On levels three, two, and one, pure joy, serenity, and bliss are experienced.

---

1. For more information, see *Other Worlds*.

Initiation is progressive advancement into bliss.

9. The ninth object of higher thinking is cosmogenesis. The thinker turns his face to the stars and galaxies, contemplates Them, and penetrates into Their secrets.

Cosmogenesis is the delight of higher thinking. Higher thinking fades away if its eye is not permanently turned to the mystery of the stars. It is possible to develop a dialogue with the stars, and that is what higher thinking does. Higher thinking is a dialogue with the stars.

Virtues for Higher Thinking

There are eight main virtues that are needed to cultivate higher thinking:

1. Equilibrium

2. Control

3. Freedom

4. Economy

5. Endurance

6. Divine indifference

7. Joy and solemnity

8. Gratitude

1. Equilibrium means to find an expanding point of balance between the highest and lowest and to stabilize yourself in that expanding point.

2. Control is the ability to direct forces and energies purposefully and create events and manifestations which will produce freedom, survival impulses, and creative expansion.

3. Freedom is freedom from the entanglements of your physical urges and drives, emotional glamors, and mental illusions. It is freedom from your karmic debts. As long as karma is holding your tail in its hand, you will have a hard time climbing to higher altitudes of thinking. Karma holds you in the lower strata of thinking until you pay your debts.

4. Economy is the ability to use energy and matter purposefully and with higher results. Waste of energy and matter holds you as a slave in the lower strata of the mind.

5. Endurance is the fruit of a long practice of patience. Patience builds your vehicles and makes them durable, creates in them strong resistance, adaptability, and the ability to continue advancement in increasing tension.

6. Divine indifference is the ability to stay in the Divine Self and watch all that is going on around you without losing your inner joy, enthusiasm, and urge to serve.

7. Joy and solemnity are two polarities of one magnet. Those who stand in their Divine Self radiate joy in the glory of solemnity.

8. Gratitude is the ability to enjoy and appreciate the life in all its phenomena, and the ability to see the hand of love leading all unity of life to greater and greater beauty.

How to Cultivate Higher Thinking

There are five major means through which you can develop higher thinking:

> — Scientific, occult meditation[2]

> — Daily remembering the fact of your Inner Divinity

> — Evening review[3]

> — Esoteric study

> — Keen interest in life and events on the planet

Through these five means you can slowly change your focus of consciousness from lower to higher levels of the mental plane.

Higher thinking is the path which leads man to his divine destiny. The Great Sage states:

_____

2. See especially *The Science of Meditation.*
3. See *The Psyche and Psychism*, Ch. 80.

The Teaching is given in endless succession, for the purpose of affirmation of fiery revelations and the carrying out of highest laws, and, following the same principle as that governing magnetic poles, can be given only to a fiery spirit that has been aligned with Hierarchy for thousands of years. The intensified fiery action extends for thousands of years. The fusion of consciousness is forged over a span of thousands of years. The united path is carved and paved in thousands of years. Hearts are merged in one Great Service in thousands of years. Immutable is the Cosmic Law, and it should be understood that the succession of the Teaching is affirmed through millenniums. There are many who attempt to infringe upon this great right, but a Cosmic Right is given to a creator in the Fiery World. Therefore humanity must purify consciousness for the understanding of the great Right of succession.[4]

---

4.   Agni Yoga Society, *Fiery World*, Vol. III, para. 21.

13

Various Orders
of Thoughts

Thoughts are of various orders. One of these orders is composed of the thoughts which are related to the welfare of others, to the future well-being of others. Suppose a person sits and thinks about how to help certain people meet their needs, enlighten them, lead them into Beauty, Goodness, and Truth, or help them solve their problems. Such thoughts are full of light and colorful beauty, and they stay in space like the formations of various fireworks.

Such thoughts carry the higher mental, intuitional, and heart energy, and they live a long life in the three worlds of human endeavor — the physical, emotional, and mental planes.

Thoughts created for the well-being of others enrich your own aura, nourish it with fiery colors, and urge you to live a life of sacrificial service for others, leading them toward Beauty, Goodness, Truth, and Joy. Such thoughts, we are told, shine like a bonfire in space and attract the attention of Great Ones. This is how one can build a contact with the Higher World.

Each beneficent thought built for the welfare of others rotates around the globe like a satellite which broadcasts healing impressions to those who tune in to it.

Increasing thoughts for the welfare of others brings greater hope for humanity and evokes greater striving to make life more beautiful for everyone in the world. Good thoughts increase in volume every time a person thinks about the welfare of others. His thoughts fly and join the main thoughtform. Such thoughts eventually become a rain cloud of beneficent thoughts which precipitates impressions of Beauty, Goodness, Truth, and Joy all around the globe. It is such thought formations that keep our world running.

The absence of such thoughts would lead us into barbarism and final destruction. It is through such thoughts that the Great Ones, or Their higher impressions, reach us and guide us on the path of life.

Humanity is learning that the world cannot be changed by military force nor by the force of law. The world changes through great ideas and thoughts and through great stations of beneficent thoughts in space from which the energies of transformation reach humanity and thus change life on the planet. This means that every human being can contribute to the transformation of the world with his thoughts created for the welfare of others.

These thoughts are not only spread into space, but they also fill the objects with which they come in contact. If a holy man full of beneficent thoughts sits under a tree or in a room, that tree or that room will no longer be the same tree or the same room. It will have a new psychic content, and sensitive people will feel the transforming and energizing power left on the tree or in the room.

Thought is part of psychic energy, and through our beneficent thoughts we help the world transform itself. Throughout the ages the Teachers of humanity wanted us to master our thoughts and use them in creative ways so that all thoughts would be beneficial and creative.

We all know that it is very difficult to master our thoughts, but it is not impossible. You can master your thoughts through **persistent efforts**, **continuous watchfulness**, and **by striving toward the future**. These are three very important steps to mastering your mind.

Persistent efforts means to direct your mind again and again to produce good thoughts, constructive thoughts, thoughts built in the spirit of Beauty, Goodness, Truth, and Joy. This is not easy, but, once you are successful, the reward is so great that you will find nothing comparable to it.

Continuous watchfulness means do not be mechanical, do not act unconsciously. Before you think, try to discern your motive. As soon as you become aware of an unworthy thought, stop it, change it, and create a beautiful one.

Striving toward the future means making efforts — physically, emotionally, and mentally — to improve your life, to reach spiritual maturity, to unfold latent potentials within your soul. The future of man is a glorious human being. What the acorn is to the huge oak tree, the man is to his future. His future is the actualization of the glorious image found within his soul.

The future is your highest vision, your highest dream, the highest possible achievement. You are going to strive toward the future by shaping and improving your life every hour of every day.

Thought is a powerful energy within your reach, and you must use it in the right way to achieve your destiny.

Through these three methods you are going to launch great thoughts, great thoughtforms in space and within your aura, thus rendering a great service on the Path of evolving humanity. You are going to launch beneficent thoughts daily through your regular meditation, through your prayers, blessings, creative imagination, best wishes, and your creative thinking. At the time of your meditation, think about the future, about a magnificent future for humanity. Try to see humanity in Beauty, in Goodness, in Truth, in Joy, and in creative achievement. Then think what things you can do to help humanity achieve such a goal.

For example, think what you want to be to make the world achieve its future. Maybe you want to be a physician, a lawyer, a diplomat, a writer, a scientist, an artist . . . anything you want. Choose a goal for one purpose only: to help humanity have a great future. Then try to prepare yourself to reach your goal so that you serve efficiently and with all your heart. Only through such an attitude and labor can you master your thoughts and control your mental body.

Dark and polluted thoughts based on fear, hatred, anger, greed, revenge, jealousy, and malice are signs of a deterioration of your thought world and of your mental body. They are an indication that you are losing control of your mental body. We lose control of our vehicles when they are not healthy. A healthy mental body always thinks in terms of Beauty, Goodness, Truth, Joy, unity, and synthesis. These are signs of mental health.

When you build your goal, your future image of yourself, your thoughts, feelings, words, and actions will slowly harmonize themselves with that image, and eventually all your being will become more polarized toward it. This will bring mental health and sanity to your life and protect you from all that will hinder your future achievements.

Your goal directs your thoughts and actions. For example, you really want to be a pianist, but you do not have a piano, nor the money to buy a piano. Well, go to work, make money, buy a piano, find a teacher, and sit and practice your lessons. . . . This is how the goal guides you in the right direction.

Once I was sitting in a forest. A wind came and took many leaves away and scattered them. I thought that most people are like leaves. The winds of life take them here, there, and move them until they are lost.

One must have a lofty goal, a future in his vision, to have a direction. Without vision one is like a dry leaf. Our thoughts must have direction. The direction is the future. Thoughts can be controlled only by directing them toward the future.

The Role of Meditation in Thinking

One of the means to purify your thoughts and gain mastery over your thoughts is meditation. Meditation is the art of thinking, which must be mastered if a person wants to proceed on the path of his conscious evolution.

Meditation is practiced to purify the consciousness and discipline the mind to such a degree that it can formulate higher impressions and inspirations coming from the Intuitional Plane or from planetary, solar, and galactic centers.

Meditation is the science of right and clear thinking. Our life corresponds to our thinking. Thinking in the mental plane is action on the physical plane. Every action is the result of thinking.

Thinking is conscious, unconscious, and mechanical.

Conscious thinking is like a man who takes some lumber and builds a chair or a table. In conscious thinking there is a *plan, knowledge of the ways and means to reach the plan*, and *motive power* to put the man in action for the fulfillment of the plan.

Unconscious thinking occurs when a higher source or center, or an entity takes over your mechanism and thinks through your mechanism and uses your body for certain activities. The limited mind of man is not conscious of the plan and the goal of the one who operates the mechanism of man. The man sometimes witnesses the operation but remains as an observer and not a conscious collaborator. He witnesses the operation as if he were in a dream. He has no control over the operation even if he wants to.

Unconscious thinking is of two kinds:

1. When one is possessed or obsessed by an entity or by a formation of accumulated thoughts

2. When one is overshadowed, guided, and inspired by one who wants to bring greater light and beauty to the world through him

People sometimes do things without being conscious of their acts. For example, a man feels the urge to go to the garden and five minutes later an earthquake destroys his house. On the other hand, another man feels the urge to take a gun and shoot a man. . . . Both are unconscious actions. One is inspiration. The other is called insanity or obsession.

If the source of control works for the Common Good, then the man does right things. But if the source of control is a servant of darkness, the man commits crimes. In both cases the man in unconscious.

If a man transmits the constructive, compassionate will of a higher source, it means he was worthy of it and karmically ready to render a service for higher forces. If a man transmits the destructive and evil intentions of an entity or of the accumulation of a collective thought, he is guilty because he is the one who, through his unhealthy living, attracted the obsessor.

Mechanical thinking. Your mind is thinking mechanically if the thoughts existing in space are keying in with your mind and operating it and your body, giving you the impression that you are acting on your own.

You are also thinking mechanically if your posthypnotic suggestions and subconscious urges, drives, and memories are controlling your actions. In mechanical thinking you may perform good actions or bad actions according to the content of your subconscious mind.

Meditation is a process to make you conscious of the process of your thinking. It helps you master your mental mechanism and use it as a creative source to spread Beauty, Goodness, and Truth and build a life that reflects Beauty, Goodness, and Truth.

Meditation is also a process to reach out and contact those higher sources which were trying to operate your mental equipment without your conscious cooperation. Through meditation you find the sources of inspiration and impressions which were trying to contact life through your mental mechanism.

Through meditation these sources are revealed, cooperation is established, and the flow of inspiration and impressions is consciously transmitted to the world.

Through meditation the mechanical function of the mind is gradually eliminated. The fleas of the thoughts floating in space are rejected, a sphere of intense insulation is built around the mind, and the art of thinking is practiced.

Through meditation one increases his light, or the light in the world, to such a degree that the existence of darkness becomes an impossibility. This light exposes the crimes, exposes the areas of darkness, and makes it impossible for them to grow and act. Thus, without violence the light disperses the darkness.

Meditation puts the man in harmony with the creative and progressive forces of Nature. Meditation develops *harmlessness*. In no possible way does the man hinder the progress, the development, or the service of another human being or another living form.

When harmlessness is achieved through meditation, it increases willpower and compassion and enlightens the mind. The person equips himself with those forces which bring transformation in his environment, which dissolve certain accumulations of the thoughtforms of crime, and which gradually weaken the attacks of the dark forces.

It is true that great crimes have been committed against pure souls and against sacrificial servers of the race. But such crimes gained victory only over the physical bodies of the Great Ones and gave greater freedom to their souls and ideas to defeat the sources of crime age after age.

It is through refinement and purification of thought that great formulas of life are received from higher sources. But these formulas often are not used for the Common Good, due to human greed. Some are even refused as impractical dreams. It is through such refusals and the use of these formulas with mixed motives that destructive forces take control and affect our life.

Durable Thoughts

There are certain kinds of thoughts which do not originate from our mental plane or from the mental plane of other human beings, but they originate from the Higher Realms. We call them *durable thoughts*.

Durable thoughts are those thoughts which are evoked by a vision, charged by willpower, directed by a decision, enlightened by wisdom, and applied by knowledge.

Vision gives the inspiration.

Willpower concentrates, focuses, and charges the thoughts.

Decision gives them direction.

Wisdom enriches them with beauty, goodness, and joy.

Knowledge makes them applicable in our daily relationships.

Such thoughts spread blessings in space and bring harmony and rhythm wherever they touch. Human progress is the result of such thoughts.

Durable thoughts build bridges between the human sphere and the supermundane world, and they transmit energy and inspiration from higher spheres and higher centers of wisdom.

As a man tries to make his garden beautiful with flowers and trees, he must try to make the *space* beautiful, clean, and full of magnificent thoughts which bloom like flowers and bear fruits of health, happiness, and progress.

In the very near future people will not only forbid you to step in their homes with your shoes on, but they will also warn you about any ugly thought that you might leave in their home which pollutes their space. Very soon people will realize that ugly and contaminated thoughts attract real germs; they attract dark forces and entities and bring misfortune, illness, and disintegration to their family, business, and home.

Thus the Sages have given the advice: Do not bring into your home your invisible dark ghosts, neither by your presence, nor through your radio, telephone, television, and publications.

Higher thoughts emanate from the Spiritual Triad or from the Self. Because of their intensity and speed, they do not touch the network of the mental body and are not channeled through reason and logic or memory banks, but they manifest directly in the aura with splendid colors, magnetism, and radioactivity.

The person, is this case, is not aware of these thoughts in his mental plane. The mental consciousness does not register them, but later the sparks in the aura are slowly absorbed by the mental body, causing expansion in consciousness and revealing new visions and new challenges for the mind. As these sparks increase in the aura, they create the best shield for the mental body. This shield protects the mind from attacks of low and unworthy thought currents and allows the mind to grow between the pressure of light from above, the Self, and from below, the sparks in the aura.

Thoughts which emanate from the Higher Realms in man follow the natural order of compensation to reward the man for his past deeds when the time is due. This kind of thought emerges when the Self makes a contact with "the center where the Will of God is known." Such a contact precipitates sparks from the Self on higher planes, which then fill the aura. The glory of the aura shines out and allows the consciousness of man to expand and register on the mental plane the greater mysteries of life.

In esoteric schools these sparks are called "diamond drops" or "pearls of beauty from the Seat of Grace."

On the path of his progress, the human soul works on many planes simultaneously. Often the function of the human soul is not registered by the mental body if the human soul does not have an anchorage in that body. Thus the man in the lower personality is not aware of many functions of the human soul.

In rare cases the human soul acts on higher planes and contacts higher forces. This contact produces higher thoughts which precipitate into the aura. Also, in rare cases, the human soul detaches himself from his images and identifies himself with his Essence, thus releasing a great amount of light into his aura. These thoughts, these particles of light, are virgin seeds in the aura.

Thoughts created in the mental body are most of the time conditioned by the memories registered in the mental body and by the thoughts existing in the mental sphere. Thoughts coming from higher sources and bypassing the mental body carry their originality down to the aura without distortion and distraction. Of course the mental body eventually assimilates them with a purer acceptance. Such an acceptance occurs during the moments of contemplative meditation, ecstasy, and joy.

Pure auras can nourish such diamond seeds. That is why great Teachers stress the necessity of having a pure aura.

When the sparks of higher thought penetrate the aura, a new polarization sets in within the cells and atoms of the human vehicles and etheric spheres. Sometimes such a polarization causes reorganization and rearrangement, and sometimes painful frictions with crystallized elements.

Thoughts, words, feelings, and deeds are immediately impressed on the aura. The purification of the aura cannot be carried on without the purification of our thoughts, words, feelings, and deeds. The traveler on the path of Infinity increasingly realizes the importance of the purity of the aura because he understands that the aura is the garden where his flowers and trees must grow and bloom.

Practical Thoughts

Practical thoughts are those thoughts which can be immediately applied in our life to bring changes or better conditions. Practical thoughts come into being in two ways:

1. As a response to an immediate need

2. As the extension of the Plan

The first one can meet the need, but in the long run it creates problems and blocks the expression of the Plan.

The second one can be slow in manifesting but works according to the Plan and brings lasting changes in the world conditions. These kinds of practical thoughts are created to adapt or harmonize the life of the planet to the Plan, rather than adapt the Plan to the contemporary conditions of life.

Actually, in the first case, practical thoughts have no vision of the Plan. Instead, they are mechanical responses to the immediate needs of life.

Short-range practical thoughts are mostly based on separative interests. Long-range practical thoughts are based on the interests not only of humanity but of all kingdoms. Long-range practical thoughts do not create setbacks, short-circuits, or failure on the path of evolution, but short-range practical thoughts can produce long lasting distortions and complications on the path of our evolution.

Short-range practical thoughts are manufactured in the lower mind. Long-range practical thoughts originate in the higher mind and emerge in the lower mind without losing their purity, intention, and direction.

Similarly, the need of the world is considered in two sections of the mind. In regard to short-range practical thoughts, the need of the world is considered and analyzed within the lower mind without considering the responses of the higher mind.

In the case of long-range practical thoughts, the need is considered and analyzed within the higher mind, the reactions and responsibilities of the lower mind are taken carefully into consideration, and all available help is utilized to bring abstract thoughts into practical manifestation.

The lower mind is full of practical thoughts. If the user of the thoughts is not focused in the higher mind, they are used for selfish and separative interests and for short-range benefits. In this case the thoughts are used not in synchronization with the tuning of the corresponding thoughts found in the higher mind but as a response to the immediate need.

It is important to know about the nature of needs. There are two kinds of needs:

1. Those needs which are for temporary, transient satisfaction of urges and drives, glamors and illusions.

2. Those needs which are demands of life-forms to proceed on the path of unfoldment, transformation, and advancement. These are real needs.

The practical thoughts of the higher mind respond to the real needs. The practical thoughts of the lower mind respond to the temporary and blind needs.

Meditation is inclusive thinking in an effort to control the practical thoughts of the lower mind and synchronize them with the thoughts of the higher mind. It is an effort to use the lower practical thoughts as a vehicle of manifestation for higher practical thoughts.

There is a continuous fight between the lower and higher practical thoughts, or between those who present short-range practical thoughts and those who present long-range practical thoughts. Long-range practical thoughts remain unused and ineffective without the synchronization of the lower practical thoughts. And the short-range, lower practical thoughts are always self-destructive without the guidance of long-range, higher practical thoughts.

Thus a great idealist cannot create changes or improvement until his ideas and thoughts are put to practical use. And a great practical man cannot keep the results of his labor too long in existence if his labor is not inspired by higher idealism.

The synchronizing factor in the mental body is called the *Antahkarana*,[1] an electrical flow between the mental unit and the Mental Permanent Atom. When this flow is established, the human soul has access to both minds simultaneously and is capable of using thought in the direction of the Plan.

One can assist in the construction of the electrical flow which unites the two sections of the mind by trying to use his thoughts with *insight*, or in the light of idealistic thoughts, or in the light of the Plan.

Another method to build the bridging electrical flow is to meditate on certain symbols or build symbols on certain abstract ideas. Dramatization of ideas can also be a good method to establish a relationship between the two sections of the mind.[2]

---

1. See Chs. 45 and 46 of *The Psyche and Psychism.*
2. For more information see *The Science of Becoming Oneself*, Ch. 18.

14

Thoughts and Our Life

Thoughts have their special colors and formations of flow. They can be long-lasting or short-lived thoughts. Those which last long, shine with very pleasant hues. If one has many related beautiful thoughts, they form a symphony of colors of rare beauty in which the colors flow and form various configurations. This symphony comes into being when the human spirit creates thoughts on the level of high achievements with great vision, revelation, striving, and purity.

There are certain energy currents near higher strata which burn and annihilate unworthy thoughts and thoughtforms and prevent them from infiltrating sacred spheres of light.

Unworthy thoughts built on the foundations of ugliness, separatism, hypocrisy, and lies contaminate space. They are not immediately destroyed; as a matter of fact, they come back and hit their sources and bounce back again into space.

Pure thoughts not only manifest the most translucent colors, but in higher strata they turn into sound and form a real symphony of sound. Thus in higher strata there is continuous music of color and sound. This music functions as a network of communication between higher and lower worlds and transmits spiritual impressions and inspirations to humanity, as far as humanity can register them. But pure thoughts are rare.

In the future it will be possible to learn a technique through which one can destroy base thought formations in space and bring in purification. Specially trained groups in the future will engage in such a task, and unitedly they will create a certain flow of energy through which they will burn base thoughts around the earth and save humanity from self-destructive actions. Meditation is a practice which eventually may lead a man to such a lofty task.

Polluted thoughts contaminate space, which in its turn contaminates the minds of people, creating mass insanity.

In the Teaching we are told to build the bridge between our world and the Fiery World. There are two very important steps which, if taken, can help to build the bridge. One is to fill our actions with beauty. The second is to harmonize the currents of the Spirit and the heart. The aspirations, the desires, and the striving of the heart must be in harmony with the vision of the Spirit.

The Spirit is always focused in the Will or Purpose of the great Cosmic Fire. The currents of Spirit are directed to that Central Magnet. Thus the Spirit is in contact with the Will of the Central Magnet.

The currents of the heart may flow in every possible direction. If these currents are shifted and polarized toward the direction of the currents of Spirit and harmonized with them, the communication with the Higher Worlds starts and the heart begins to sense the beauty of the higher spheres.

As the harmonization proceeds, the clear awareness of the Higher Worlds dawns upon the heart. It is this increasing awareness of the heart that gradually passes into the sphere of intellect and mind, and there the awareness is translated into precious knowledge and information.

Thus the heart and the mind work together to understand the contact with the higher spheres.

Filling all our actions with beauty also means to bridge our physical, emotional, and mental worlds with the world of beauty. Each beauty is a thread between two worlds. Each beauty is a messenger from the Fiery World, and when we try to fill our actions with beauty, we literally extend lines of contact between the Fiery World and our personal reality.

The Fiery World is the world of beauty. Every current in the Fiery World is a symphony of colors, sounds, and movements.

Take a beautiful rose and think, "What would this rose be like if it were one million times more beautiful?" This will give you a hint about the beauty found in the Fiery World.

As one tries, bit by bit, to fill his actions with beauty, the currents of the Fiery World begin to charge all his actions and manifest through them. This is how fire from the Higher Realms is brought down to earth.

Fiery people are distributors of fiery currents of beauty. Thus fire and beauty build communication lines through which the higher direction and wisdom of the Spirit guide the lives of those who love beauty.

Fiery thoughts must be used to purify space. As the astronauts have witnessed from space, there is a thick sphere of various chemical elements around the earth, thrown into space by factories created by modern science. The accumulation of such elements will decide the future of humanity.

Parallel to this poisonous sphere is the dark sphere of human base thoughts, which has a decisive influence on the events of the world.

The chemical sphere will stay a long time and eventually will alter the nature of the rays of the Sun, causing unexpected changes in living forms. This sphere can only be removed by electrical storms, if the accumulated sphere of base human thoughts is washed away. Electrical storms will make the dark sphere of the elements melt away, but only if fiery thoughts evoke the electrical storms.

Each fiery thought can penetrate into the strata of dark thoughts and, like a beam of light, disperse a certain amount of dark accumulations and draw an electrical charge from higher spheres. If groups and masses of people release lofty thoughts, eventually it will be possible to disperse the dark sphere of ugly thoughts and evoke an electrical storm which may disperse all chemical accumulations around the earth.

Actually, the dark accumulations and the creative, fiery, and beautiful thoughts are fighting. The outcome will be either the destruction of the planetary life or the liberation of the planetary life. People cannot see such a fact yet, but the fight between these two forces is almost touching the earthly shores. If humanity is still alive, it is because of the lofty thoughts of millions of people who worry about the future of humanity and daily send beneficent thoughts through prayers, meditation, teaching, and creativity in various forms. Daily, millions of rays of good thoughts destroy a great amount of precipitation from the dark clouds of base thoughts and thus prevent the destruction of humanity.

It is urgent and imperative to learn how to create lofty thoughts. Through no other means can this planet be saved. Lofty thoughts create alignment and synthesis between the worlds, and this greater vision brings harmony within all spheres.

Creative efforts are very favorable for expanding our consciousness. Creative efforts must be carried on in every phase of our life, not only in writing, painting, composing music, and so on but also in cooking, building, repairing, cleaning, gardening, sewing, knitting, etc.

Creativity starts when one does not have all the means in his possession to accomplish his labor, and he strives to create new means or to adapt himself to new conditions. The efforts to create new means and adapt oneself to new conditions create a certain spiritual pressure and physical, emotional, and mental tension through which the expansion of consciousness becomes possible.

Those children who have everything and every means to satisfy their wishes eventually show signs of retardation. Those children who create their own toys, who create new means to play, to build, and to enjoy life are those who will be more successful in life than those who live in luxury.

Children and adults periodically must be taken away from the life patterns in which they live and be led into conditions where they have to use their creative talents to survive or to pursue a constructive life without having all their past means in their possession.

We are told that luxury is the grave of the soul, the grave of the consciousness.

I knew a man who used to do carpentry at his home. One day I saw him using an ax for a hammer and a handsaw instead of an electric saw to build a cabinet. Surprised, I asked, "You have many kinds of hammers and an electric saw to serve your needs best. Why don't you use them?"

"My dear," he said, "my intention is not to produce things but to expand my consciousness. For me it is easy now to use these sophisticated tools, but it is not easy to build a cabinet with these primitive tools. I need to use my creativity to achieve the same results. Having all the means in your hand, you dull your consciousness. This is how the zombies of our civilization are created."

Nature knows this and periodically deprives us of our usual means so that we can expand our consciousness through creative efforts. Nothing is important except the expansion of consciousness.

The majority of people are spoiled because of the sophisticated mechanical means they have in their possession.

In the field of spiritual leadership, those who are not born as leaders complain when they lack people and means to actualize their visions. They say, "If I had ten men who knew how to do these things, if I had twenty girls who could do these things, I could accomplish my dreams."

This is exactly the way which leads to failure. The way to success is to use all that you now have, with your creative consciousness, to build in the people around you the spirit of creativity. You do not need ready-made "tools." You must create them. You must build things out of nothing. And this is how to proceed on the path of perfection.

But all these arguments sound as if we were minimizing the value of all the creative efforts which have given us our tools, machines, and all the means to make our life comfortable. The point is that if we are flooded with the creativity of other people and possess their inventions to satisfy our life, we fall below the level of their consciousness and become the victim of their creativity.

Learning to use machines is not creativity but a kind of slavery.

If you develop your consciousness to such a degree that their tools become primitive means for you, you will make greater efforts to meet your visions through higher creativity. Either you are periodically going to reject all "tools" created by others and expand your consciousness through your own creativity, or you are going to create new visions in front of which their "tools" become primitive or obsolete and you are challenged to create new "tools."

Never try to forget yourself in your luxury and comforts. Satisfaction is the termite of the consciousness.

One of the reasons why mass consciousness is so slow in its development is the mechanical inventions of our modern technology. If this continues as it is going now, the average man will be a button pusher and nothing else.

Expansion of consciousness takes place when man is under pressure to create new means to achieve his goal.

15

Thoughts and Chemistry

In the atmosphere there are many chemical elements, but one must not be surprised to learn that thought brings other chemical ingredients into the atmosphere. Each thought emanates a special kind of chemical element or affects the existing chemical elements and changes them into a new kind of chemical element. These new elements are the products of thought. Some of them are very beneficial elements. Some of them are extremely destructive. Both kinds of elements stay a long time in the atmosphere or create various influences upon all life-forms.

Thoughts directed to the Common Good, toward perfection and progressive unfoldments; thoughts dedicated to bringing man closer to the source of beauty emanate those chemical elements which heal, enlighten, and strengthen the human being. Those thoughts which are charged with separatism, exploitation, and hatred emanate poisonous fumes.

Thought is like a fountain or a spring which brings elements from the inner layers through which it passes.

There are thoughts which bring into the atmosphere elements X, Y, and Z, for example. X is an element of the higher mind. Y is an element of Intuition. Z is an element of Will. These elements are not parts of the chemical combinations of our earth's atmosphere. It is the thought currents coming from higher sources which bring these elements into our atmosphere and enrich it with very rare and precious elements which serve as magnetic waves and transmitters of higher energies into our sphere. Light, wisdom, and higher impressions and inspirations travel along the lines of these elements scattered in the atmosphere of the earth.

Thus higher thoughts form a transmitting channel for the forces of life, light, and guidance for humanity and for lower kingdoms. Such chemical elements are called pearls or gems in space, and only an elevated consciousness can discover and use them for the benefit of humanity.

The chemical emanations of our lofty thoughts stay with our pens, pencils, typewriters, books, and many other objects we use. They stay for a long time and cause improvement in the chemistry of the objects and in the chemistry of those who touch them and use them. The chemistry of thoughts stays within the building we lived in and affects the chemistry of the auras of those who visit us or who live there after us.

This is why the Teaching strongly advises us to emanate fragrance and beauty through our thoughts, rather than poisonous fumes and ugliness through them.

Those locations which are charged with the emanations of lofty thoughts eventually become centers from which emanate the life-giving waves of the Cosmic Magnet. It is good to increase such places on earth because the salvation of humanity will come through such centers.

People will soon realize that the elements created by their pure thoughts condition the equilibrium of the forces of Nature. All dark thoughts distort the equilibrium and attract fiery currents which burn and destroy not only certain parts of the etheric network of the earth but also the etheric network of the human organisms and other living forms. These fires are not fires of wood or charcoal but fires of energies which disintegrate the mechanism, if the balancing force of the element of pure thought is absent.

Every pure thought increases the resistance of the body against destructive fires and germs. Immediately when the element produced by pure thought decreases, the destructive fire takes over.

The element of pure thought strengthens the senses and increases their sensitivity; it builds the bridge between the subtle and concrete worlds and provides the needed substance in the aura which registers impressions coming from higher sources.

When emanations of dark thoughts are combined with radio waves carrying destructive and earthbound elements, it creates the worst poison in the air. This poison is responsible for the increase in violence, crime, and insanity. Emanations of dark thoughts combined with noise cause serious brain damage.

The destructive power of the elements of dark thoughts increases when they are combined with the poisonous gases emanating from the earth. Thus the equilibrium of the earth can only be sustained by the elements of pure thoughts which, when combined with the currents of the Centers of love and power, build the bridge of ascent.

The effect of the emanations from pure thought can be seen on plants and animals. These elements make plants grow and remain healthy, and they make animals joyful and playful.

The emanations of dark thoughts weaken plants and animals. They even sap people's auras and exhaust their resources. But these elements of dark thoughts cannot be seen easily. They travel long distances and, like a vampire, attack their victims.

To protect oneself from such attacks, one must charge his aura with the fire of the elements of pure thoughts.

Thoughts are in various levels and intensities. There are thoughts which are inspired by physical interests, by the body and its urges, drives, and needs. Then there are thoughts inspired by the heart, which have greater depth and are related to the improvement of feelings and relationships.

There are also thoughts inspired by intuitive perception. They are mostly related to sacrificial service, renunciation of self, and dedication to the Common

Good. There are higher thoughts which radiate a tremendous amount of psychic energy and willpower. These thoughts are related to the Plan of the Hierarchy and to the Purpose of Shamballa.

People often think that thoughts can be created only on the mental plane and that beyond the mental plane thought does not exist. The reality is that the thinker is the human soul, and he can build his thoughts with etheric, astral, and mental matter and even with intuitional, atmic, monadic, and divine substances.

Thought is an organized energy with a special intensity, frequency, and purpose. This organized energy can be built of the substance of any plane.

Average humanity builds its thoughts with astral and lower mental energy. Initiates build their thoughts with higher mental matter or intuitional substance. Arhats build Their thoughts with the substance of the Intuition. Chohans build Their thoughts with the higher Cosmic ethers, namely with atmic, monadic, and divine substances.

Thoughtforms are always lower-mental, astral, etheric, and physical in substance. Thoughts are built of higher mental, intuitional, and higher substances. Thus, the thoughts of Great Ones are more fiery than the thoughts of an undeveloped man.

It is a wonderful exercise to observe one's own thoughts and know how they are built, from what level, and with what kind of substance.

Thoughts change. The level of thoughts and their substance can change. But the light of consciousness stays the same, though its substance changes. The higher the substance of consciousness, the greater the light of the consciousness.

It is the expanding light of the consciousness that can receive, assimilate, and retranslate thoughts coming from higher or Cosmic sources. This is why we are told in the Teaching that a man can contact higher spheres, higher centers, and Higher Worlds through his thoughts if these thoughts are built of higher substance.

The magnetic power and the power of assimilation and translation of the consciousness improve to a great extent when the human soul functions on higher planes. The day will come when a man will be able to communicate with higher spheres consciously and by his free will and thus eliminate the gaps existing between the worlds.

It is so important to improve the quality of our thoughts, to make them more universal and more beautiful, and to use them for the upliftment and welfare of humanity.

16

Contradictory and Involuntary Thoughts

In the Teaching we are told that a man must not have contradictory thoughts. This is not an easy task. One must make an effort to have pure thoughts and not pollute his mind by having mixed or contradictory thoughts.

Every thought has its own frequency and its own sound in space, but if the mind sends conflicting thoughts or words into space, the person creates dissonance in space and serious disturbances in his aura.

It is important that thoughts be beneficial and created for the good of others. If, after sending such thoughts, one pollutes space with destructive or malevolent thoughts, he creates disturbances which attract to his aura various destructive fires.

Doubt in thought is a factor which disintegrates the thought and makes it fail before it reaches its destination. This is why we are told that our thoughts must be made of pure light and not mixed with any other elements which can weaken the thought.

Double thinking not only creates chaos in space but also gradually distorts the brain and the mental body.

People continuously use double standards about people. All attitudes and expressions are the result of thought. When thought is used to create double standards, man loses his equilibrium and integrity and eventually falls into chaos. This is why sincerity was emphasized by the Ancients. In sincerity there are no double standards but a straight and pure expression of motives and thoughts.

Thoughts can be charged with fire when they are based on our basic convictions, when they are expressions of our trust, optimism, and gratitude.

Those people who fluctuate between darkness and light, between unity and separatism, between construction and destruction eventually ruin their mental bodies and brains. Every duality in thought weakens the man and eventually makes him a servant of darkness.

When thinking about the future, about our Teacher, about our friends, our thoughts must manifest pure unity without shadows of doubt, suspicion, and fear. Any thought mixed with these elements disintegrates and invites suffering to the originating source.

Dual thoughts serve the dark forces. A dark thought often is less dangerous to others than a dual thought. It is easy to reject a dark thought, but it is often difficult to reject a dual thought because a dual thought enters our consciousness through its bright side and then pulls in its dark side.

This is why the servants of darkness no longer attack the sacred Teaching directly but create every possible way to distort it.

An inexperienced man will look at two different groups and say, "They teach the same thing. They read the same books. They have the same teachers." This may be true on the surface. Both may do this. But, one group puts a little distortion in the Teaching every time, and throughout the years the man becomes used to the distortion because things are presented to him on the plates he likes, or with the formulas he loves. Eventually they increase the dosage of distortion in the Teaching and destroy the foundation.

This technique is also very close to the technique of confusion.

Thus doubt, confusion, and distortion create chaos in the mental world, and one loses his path in the deserts of life.

We are told that if the thought is charged by the fire of spirit, it loses all duplicity and keeps its purity. Pure thoughts are the ones that achieve victory over the hindering elements of life.

It is necessary to exercise thinking with concentration and toward a lofty goal. This is how one can learn to keep the purity of thought.

People think that purity of thought prevents one from approaching an object from various viewpoints. One can observe an object from various viewpoints but keep the unity of his thought. Viewpoints are not different kinds of thoughts but supplementary elements for one thought.

You can even see the destructive and constructive sides of a person without developing double thoughts. You see why the conflicting characters exist in him, but you do not think of him as a bad or good man but a man of double character, as an object which is painted black and white.

Pure thoughts can be developed when people do not exercise judgment but use observation. This is not easy to achieve because each observation evokes a judgment from weak minds. Advanced minds see things as they are and do not fall into the habit of dual thinking and judgment.

Judgment is the process of measuring people with certain standards. Through observation you know what the other person is, but, instead of judging him, you understand him. Understanding evokes pure and benevolent thoughts.

The Ancients used to say that an arrow must not be made of different types of wood. It must be made of one type of wood because every kind of wood reacts differently to the currents of air, to pressure, to the electricity of the atmosphere, and to the psychic energy of the person. Also, the disintegration of the arrow occurs if the parts are not welded perfectly. This is how the Ancients referred to pure thoughts.

Along with conflicting and contradictory thoughts, we also have some very dangerous thoughts which are called *involuntary thoughts*. The majority of these involuntary thoughts come from outside of us, and we must master them if we want to see the potency of the energy of pure thoughts.

Involuntary thoughts invade our mind in a high percentage. They create confusion, inertia, unreasonable decisions and hazards, and weaken the mechanism of the mind. The mastery of the human mind will be the greatest blessing of the human being. When the mental body is mastered, no involuntary thought will be able to put the machine into action. The human soul will be able to admit only those thoughts with which he wants to deal.

Involuntary thoughts are the arrows of dark forces or dark accumulations from space. They are even automatic reactions of the mind to hidden memories. When the mind operates with such thoughts, the presence of the lofty thought will be very uncomfortable in the mind. Besides, the mind cannot operate under the direction of the human soul when the mind is busy with involuntary thoughts.

One of the ways to stop involuntary thoughts is to raise the level of the mind through fixing the attention on lofty subjects. Reading sacred writings, keeping the mind busy with fiery creativity, labor, and service done in devotion and dedication — all can cut the major lines of involuntary thoughts.

We are told that if the mind is open to every kind of thought, it turns into a sponge full of dirty water. Involuntary thoughts waste the precious psychic energy because they are concerned with failure, depression, fear, crimes, sensuality, lower desires, and greed — but mostly fear.

As a man advances in age or weakens in body, involuntary thoughts of fear accumulate around him and sap his energy. Most people die not because of sickness but because of fear. Fear also cuts off the supply of psychic energy.

Most of our involuntary thoughts are imported through imagination, or our thoughts create dramatizations and we busy ourselves in our own dramatizations. Sometimes our mind runs day and night within the vicious circle of our imagination, which is orchestrated by our involuntary thoughts.

The conquest of the mind is not easy, but if this conquest is achieved man will be the king of his life.

It is through voluntary thoughts that all can be changed around us. Through our voluntary thoughts we can control outer circumstances because things control us through our negative reactions or responses. When we change the mode of our response, we will be able to annihilate the effect of the outer control.

Outer control attacks us through our involuntary thoughts. When they are accepted, their control on us is final. But if they are not nourished by our attention or response, their control loses its power and even serves our success.

In most cases, attacks are successful when we make them successful through our reactions of fear, confusion, and cooperation with the attacks. We cooperate with attacks when we concentrate our thoughts on our failures instead of concentrating our mind on our future victories.

We must not cooperate with the logic of attackers, but we must use the attacks to withdraw ourselves from the image of failure they try to impress upon us. Our failure belongs to our enemies, but our future belongs to us.

17

Thoughts and Speed

Thoughts have their various speeds. Some of them are slower than others. Thoughts do not even travel in the same way. Some of them slide, and some of them jump. Some of them go zigzag. Some of them slow down in certain spots. Some of them turn back, make a circle, then go forward. Many geometrical formations occur as thought travels.

For example, we have arrow thoughts which travel right to the target. We have feather thoughts which fluctuate with every influence or force. One cannot expect such thoughts to reach their destination. We also have loaded thoughts which are slow and often are eaten by the load they carry.

Arrow thoughts are pure, victorious thoughts related to the general good for humanity. They are progressive, selfless, full of faith, beautiful, joyful, and accurate.

Feather thoughts lack faith. They have confusing, contradictory elements and lack enthusiasm. They are directed to undecided targets.

Loaded thoughts carry selfish elements and expectations. They look for results. They are separative; they have side motives. Even though such thoughts have a strong directive force, they generally fluctuate and slow down as they travel through purer spheres; and they often disintegrate if they force their speed.

Space is full of traffic of various kinds. Thoughts are airplanes or rockets. Emotions are like boats. Actions are like cars or carriages. All of these have to move. Some of them have a destination; some of them do not. Some of them are wanderers, thieves, and guards with their self-made responsibilities.

There are definite relationships between thoughts, emotions, and actions, and often they synchronize their speed, inspired by each other. It is a sad phenomenon when a thought cannot reflect in an emotion or in an action, and all these three take different routes to find a destination.

Success is the coordination of these three elements with psychic energy. The thoughts that carry the reflection of the emotions and actions running parallel and in synchronized speed have great strength and speed to reach their destination.

Each synchronized lofty thought, emotion, and action draws the fuel of psychic energy from space and spreads benevolent beauty in space.[1]

Slow thoughts make space limited. Faster thoughts understand the Infinity of space. As we unfold our senses on higher and higher planes, space for us expands into Infinity. As we keep our senses unevolved, we limit our space and shorten our life.

Victorious souls always have the vision of Infinity in their hearts. This vision evokes striving to unfold and to be. Beingness is an ever-progressive and conscious fusion with the Cosmic Self.

New races and new groups are put together by the quality of their thoughts. New standards in Cosmos magnetically attract and assemble those individuals who respond to the standards by their thoughts. Our thoughts decide the grouping in which we will find ourselves in the future.

The unification of humanity will be the result of the harmonization of the thoughts of the individuals and groups forming humanity. It is possible to imagine a synthesis of human thought in which there is diversity but unity. The unity of a group is kept by the synchronization of thought energy.

Those individuals who are in tune with Cosmic principles spread those thoughts which serve as links to unite people and lead them to higher and higher spheres of synthesis and unification. Each step taken toward synthesis evokes new and higher unfoldment in the individual.

---

1.   See also A Commentary on Psychic Energy.

18

Thoughts and Regeneration

Thought puts the human soul into action, or the human soul creates thought to engage himself in action. Thought is created when the human soul contacts the spatial currents, which flow along the directions of the Cosmic Magnet. Spatial currents are fiery rivers of ideas, directions, and revelations of the mysteries of the Cosmic Existence. When the human soul comes in contact with these fiery streams, his response produces thoughts. The depth of each thought depends upon the intensity of the response of the human soul and upon the stage of his development.

When the response of the human soul is translated by the mind, thought is created. Actually, thinking is an effort to translate this response to the fiery spatial currents or to give meaning and significance to the response.

Each thought is the formulation of the fiery currents. Each thought is a flame, is a torch, is an arrow of fire charged with the energy of the fiery currents.

Each pure thought is drawn to the Cosmic Magnet. Each pure thought carries the life toward the Cosmic Magnet. Fiery spatial thoughts originate from the Cosmic Magnet, and on their way into Space they charge Cosmic Existences and continue their flow into the Infinite Space.

These fiery currents purify, create, and regenerate the whole manifestation. Each pure thought carries within itself the power of these currents.

Purification and regeneration of life can only be attained by pure thoughts. Creativity in all of Cosmic Space is carried by spatial currents. In each creative act the spatial fire is in manifestation. The spatial fire is a continuous process of unfoldment of the Cosmic Mystery. This is what creativity is. In creativity the Cosmic Magnet manifests its beauty through the spatial fires.

Each pure thought is a manifestation of Cosmic Beauty.

The rays emanating from the Cosmic Magnet or from the fiery spatial currents penetrate into each seed, into the Core of each form, and awaken and intensify the power of the spirit latent in it. The awakening spirit responds to the spatial currents, and each response becomes an act of creativity.

Thus an atom is related to the Cosmic Magnet. Between an atom and the Cosmic Magnet, the spatial currents weave the fabric of manifestation.

Those thoughts that are not directed to the Cosmic Magnet, or do not carry the message or the charge of the Cosmic Magnet, become hindrances on the path of the circulating fiery currents. Such hindrances create friction, and friction manifests as natural cataclysms.

Each globe moves upon the circulating fiery currents. When these currents are interrupted in certain locations of the globe, the harmony and the equilibrium of the globe suffer, and this manifests as natural disasters.

It is only through fiery thoughts that the equilibrium of the globe can be restored, as each fiery thought or each accumulation of fiery thoughts disperses dark clouds of hindrances and lets the spatial currents follow their destined path around the globe. This is why we are told to learn how to think and how to meditate. It is in the depth of meditation that the human soul comes in contact with the spatial currents and conceives pure thoughts.

We are told that there are many zones of light in Space. These zones are created by the pure thoughts of Great Souls. We call these zones of light the powerhouses of energies which restore the equilibrium of life. Wherever these zones are found in Space, the corresponding locations on earth manifest great culture, beauty, and creativity, but often they are blocked by earthbound thoughts. The absence of these zones of light brings disturbances in the forces of Nature.

Each time a man or a group or a nation shifts its direction and turns from darkness to light, a great joy appears in Space. All these shiftings are the result of response to the spatial currents or to the fiery currents of the Cosmic Magnet. From such responses pure thoughts come into being, and they further pave the way for creative striving toward the Cosmic Magnet.

Those who choose the Path toward the Cosmic Magnet are continuously under the pressure of the Cosmic Magnet. Those who have such an experience sometimes tell us that they wear a shirt of fire all the time. Fiery currents emanate from them continuously, bringing much purification in the life of the planet and new breakthroughs.

Each fiery thought is a candle lit on the path of Infinity.

Creative thoughts originate from Cosmic awareness and reveal the power of dignity within you. Dignity is nothing else but the awareness of your own Divinity.

Any time you feel ashamed of yourself, think — Who is the one ashamed, and who is the one I am ashamed of? You can see that in dignity you stand in the presence of your own Divinity and conduct your life accordingly.

When you have dignity you live by the standards of your Inner Self, by the standards of beauty. When dignity is lost, the contact of Inner Divinity is lost and man now starts to live in the lower spheres of thoughts.

People can be lead toward higher consciousness if one can awaken their dignity. Dignity is the result of the memory that once upon a time you were a divine Spark. It is only by living in the awareness of the divine Spark that your thoughts fill space and bloom like multicolored flowers. This is how you make of space a garden of beauty.

There is now a widespread concern to take trash away from our homes and cities, and people do not tolerate their neighbor's trash in their yard. This is a faint beginning of a future great caution. In coming ages people will be concerned about the thoughts of their neighbors, the thoughts of all individuals, the thoughts of their nation because they will realize that polluted thoughts are a thousand times more dangerous and germ-producing than the neighbor's trash thrown in their yard.

The polluted thoughts of our neighbors are sometimes the cause of our diseases or stagnated state of mind. The Ancients advised us to move away from such neighborhoods and regain our physical and spiritual health.

On the other hand, a close friend, a teacher, or a neighbor can be a treasury for us, a powerhouse for us to increase our wisdom, elevate our thoughts, and live a creative life. In a good neighborhood one feels in contact with higher values, and striving toward them seems easier and more joyful.

There is a close connection between thought and energies coming from luminaries. Lower thoughts change the chemistry of the inpouring energies and make them dangerous for the life on the planet.

Low thoughts weaken the mental body of human beings all over the world and make it vulnerable to the rays from luminaries. As the low and criminal thoughts increase, people will witness mass insanity and mass madness.

The only hope for this planet is pure thought, is an aura full of radiating thought, is an environment full of creative thought.

Real thought is the formulation of Beauty, Goodness, Truth, Plan, and Purpose. Such a thought process is a river of light, a creative magnetic current which brings into our life health, harmony, rhythm, and joy.

Everything which is in harmony with Beauty, Goodness, Truth, Plan, and Purpose evokes joy from the deepest corners of our being. These five principles guide the path of true thinkers. When our mind is geared to these five principles, we have real thoughts in our mind. Our thoughts are guiding lights for humanity or ladders for humanity to climb toward the heights of culture and civilizations.

Right and real thinking not only is a light on our path, but it also makes us conquerors on the astral plane. We traverse the astral plane and do not fall into its traps only through right thinking. Right thinking will enable us not only to pass through the astral plane of glamors and traps ourselves but also to help those who have been for centuries slumbering in the astral plane.

Our meditation here on the physical plane sheds a great beam of light into the astral world. All the glamors that we built in the astral plane begin to shatter and dissolve before we go there. And when this process is complete, we will not waste time in the astral world but pass into the mental plane within a very short time, or completely bypass the astral plane.

Real thinking will enable us also to pass very quickly through the lower mental planes. In the lower mental planes we have the manifestation of our illusions. These illusions can keep us there for ages.

Right meditation or real thinking enables us to escape the traps of illusion, enjoy the beauty of the higher mental plane, and see there the causes of all that transpired on the path of our earthly life.

19

Spatial Thoughts

There are three major kinds of spatial thoughts:

1. Thoughts accumulated from the planetary inhabitants

2. Thoughts accumulated from the Hierarchy and higher Centers

3. Thoughts accumulated from Those Avatars Who have solar or galactic origins

Spatial thoughts have their individual characteristics.

Human thoughts are related to the Plan of how to liberate humanity from the hindrances of life and guide humanity on the path of evolution.

Thoughts emanating from the Tower are related to the Solar Purpose.

Thoughts of great Avatars are the real spatial thoughts which carry the secrets of Cosmic Paths. They inspire the spirit and reveal Cosmic horizons. Once a person contacts such thoughts, he is no longer limited by earthly hindrances and obstacles.

These thoughts are accessible to those who have Triadal contacts, which means those whose awareness functions in the sphere of the Spiritual Triad — the sphere of pure Light, Love, and Divine Will.

They are also accessible to those aspirants, disciples, and leaders who have intense aspiration and dedication and live sacrificial lives, despite many obstacles and difficulties.

These three kinds of accumulations have certain relationships. Avataric thoughts are a symphony of colors dominated by pearl white. Hierarchical and Shamballic thoughts are a symphony of all colors dominated by blue and red. Planetary thoughts are in layers, starting from dark brown up to pure white.

As the lightning reflects momentarily in dark forests, caves, and buildings, so the scintillating thoughts of higher Centers and the thoughts of Avatars often reflect in lower formations. Sometimes reflections open many opportunities for progress and expansion. Sometimes reflections are immediately engulfed by dark waves of lower strata.

There are humans whose thoughts penetrate into spatial thought formations like beams of light and transmit many blessings to earth.

When we receive spatial thoughts or thoughts from higher sources, the moment of contact appears as if a bonfire arises on the surface of the mind. This is a phenomenon in which the high-voltage new thoughts are welcomed and assimilated in creative response.

We are told that other phenomena appear when a new thought is received. For example, the chakras are charged with additional electricity and color; the aura appears richer than before and radiates greater joy and healing forces. We also feel "special" vibrations which start from various centers and spread into other centers.

It is very important to have these experiences on record in our diary and discover how we can increase the number of opportunities to receive lofty thoughts. All progress toward higher achievement is based on communication with higher thoughts.

Higher thoughts sometimes create pain and burning sensations in the body if there is a certain resistance to the new thoughts. Sometimes these pains indicate destruction of crystallizations, sometimes heavy oppositions, sometimes a real battle between old thoughtforms and new thoughtforms.

Our aura and our body react to every thought current. We can consciously record them if we develop the power of observation and vigilance. Man is so occupied with the outer world that he does not notice subtle reactions from his body until they accumulate and manifest as pains and joys.

Real thoughts have special destinations, duties, and responsibilities. When the destination of the thought is reached, the friction creates a pure fire called the fire of the Intuitional Plane. The thought melts away and becomes energy as soon as it enters the Intuitional Plane.

When energy takes a specific direction to fulfill a purpose, it becomes a thought. Certain thoughts hang in Space for millions of years and cyclically precipitate great inspirations, visions, and revelations to receptive minds. Until their destination is fulfilled, they continue to exist. When the destination is reached, the whole thoughtform melts away in the sphere of pure fire, once again to be used for future creative labors.

Dark accumulations go through a hard and painful recycling process. Dark accumulations mostly stay in the etheric, astral, and lower mental spheres, and as they dissolve they create pollution in these spheres.

The purification of these spheres is a Herculean task. The rubbish accumulated in lower spheres is a great problem which humanity has not worried about yet. But it is this rubbish that contaminates the possibility of right human relations, our morals, our sense of justice, respect and love, and the spirit of cooperation. It also fosters crime and violence in the world.

This pollution tragically destroys evolving minds, if by the power of their karma people do not overcome the pollution. This pollution makes people use every gift of science and human reasoning for retrogression and degeneration. Cleaning the pollution of these etheric, astral, and lower mental spheres will be the labor of those who contributed to it for ages.

The thoughts of advanced souls, with much sacrifice and suffering, can individually and collectively help to transmute the debris. Group prayers, group aspiration, group progress and enlightenment, and organized group thoughtforms penetrate like beams of light into such dark spheres and cause certain transmutations.

Chemical pollution extending many miles thick into the space around the earth would not exist without the debris of human minds. And, as this chemical pollution or sphere of pollution endangers life on the earth, similarly the pollution in the etheric, astral, and lower mental planes endangers the life-forms of these planes. If this pollution continues, we will duplicate the destiny of the moon.

Expressions of Thought

A thought sent to a person can take various forms of expression. It can manifest as

1. Words in the mind

2. Sound or music in the mind

3. Visible words or symbolic forms and colors

4. Sensations on the spine, over the head, or in various places of the body

5. Fragrance or odors

6. Wind or a breeze

7. Peace, serenity, or agitation

8. Heat or coolness on the body

9. Deep silence around the head

10. Pain in certain places of the body

11. Expansion of consciousness or a sudden realization of certain facts

12. A feeling of connection with higher dimensions

The difference in manifestation is related to the conditions of the atmosphere, aura, centers, and intentions. Sometimes the effect of a thought takes a long time to manifest; sometimes it is instantaneous.

Words are considered the general manifestation of thoughts, but usually they are limiting forms of manifestation. Lofty and highly charged thoughts meet great difficulties in narrowing themselves into words.

If one receives words, he must know that certain words are loaded with many-dimensional messages, and he must ponder on them.

Some thoughts have more subtle manifestations. They create direction, polarization, aspiration, and striving. Some of them light the fire of enthusiasm. Some of them create a decision to be noble and solemn. Some of them turn into a window to Infinity.

The great Gautama Buddha was correct when He said that all is the manifestation of thought.

Thought energy is not limited to human relationships. It has a greater function and destiny. The communication between man and the stars is based on thought.

Thought is not limited to the planetary sphere. One can send his thoughts to the farthest stars and be sure that they reach there and come back. The highest form of communication in space is thought. A man is as great as his contacts. It is thought energy that leads to omniscience and omnipresence.

Through thought energy we must break all limitations of our consciousness. Only an expanding consciousness will have the possibility to raise the standards of understanding and create a new life. Only an expanding consciousness will see the limitations of the past and find new ways of synthesis.

A progressing and expanding consciousness can easily stand above its limitations and see them as hindrances. To reach such an achievement one must break his vanities and personal interests, which are thought manifestations to assist man in certain moments of his life to overcome personal failures.

One must cultivate by all possible means a holistic approach to life and try to see the highest good of all that exists.

It is very important to see that thoughts based on separative interests are misleading and self-defeating mechanisms. Problems seen only from holistic viewpoints may create noble thoughts which help us build better ways to proceed toward our destination, toward perfection.

It is necessary to understand the energy of thought and its manifold manifestations and use them to help Nature transcend Itself.

Real thought starts in our soul. One can hold the thought in the soul and examine it before sending it into the mental, astral, and etheric planes for manifestation.

People think that it is the mind that *thinks*, whereas the mind only gives the mental robe to the pure thought. Once the thought descends into the mental plane, it becomes the property of all mental beings.

Secret formulas and plans are always kept in the Treasury of the soul. Advanced Initiates create or receive thoughts and study them in the sanctuary of Their soul.

There is a higher correspondence of silence in which man keeps total silence about the thought he has in his soul and does not speak it out through the thinking process.

The soul has his sphere through which no one can penetrate. Astral and mental entities cannot sneak in. Every one of us has his sacred tower.

On the path of preparation, the disciple learns the value and the importance of silence. Silence learned on the physical plane becomes a power in the mental plane. Initiates have a private garden of thoughts where they pass their time in organizing the age of beauty.

Meditation, study, observation, and silence eventually lead one to the soul. The true way to say this would be that *one awakens to the reality of his soul.* Unless one is thus awakened, it will be difficult for him to control the mind, and the owner of an uncontrolled mind is in real danger.

In conquering thought man accumulates a great amount of energy within himself which transmits the willpower of the human Core. Through the willpower one can create the shield of the rainbow and turn into a path of light and achievement for others.

It is through such a fiery energy of the will that the path for telepathy and impression is built and that communication is established between selected people and between man and higher planetary Centers.

One must be able to control the movements of the mental body, as one controls the movements of his dense physical body. This must be achieved in the field of daily living and daily relationships.

Mental silence is a reality, and one can keep mental silence after a long period of training and discipline. Through such an achievement man accumulates the fiery energy of the will, and through that energy he can dispel many obstacles on the path of evolution.

After one learns mental silence, he must try to formulate his thoughts in his heart. When our thoughts are submitted to the light of the heart, the thoughts go through a process of transmutation and refinement.

The first effect of such thoughts is stability. Stability is a state of consciousness in which things can be seen in their true light, their true value; in which the vision is seen in its clarity; in which important decisions can be made and important plans can be constructed for distant future goals.

Man works very hard physically to achieve a goal. He works harder emotionally through his incessant imagination and desires to reach a certain goal. He works even harder to reach his goal using his thought energy. But once a man reaches the level where he can conquer his thought, he can discount all these former methods to achieve his goal because, through the fiery power of the will, he can reach *any* noble goal he wants. In reality, Nature and Its forces work for him.

On many occasions our physical, emotional, and mental efforts to achieve a goal work against us. The emanations of such activities repel the desired goal. Only after conquering our thoughts can we have the chance to be a fiery thinker, one who can direct the mighty forces of the Fiery World with his power of will.

Mastery of thought begins in directing our eyes toward Infinity, the future, toward the all-inclusive Self. Unless we direct our thoughts to these values, we cannot control the thought world and the chaos of the thought world.

The second step is continuous vigilance over visiting thoughts, over thoughts evoked by our physical condition, urges and drives, emotions and desires, and by our selfish interests.

The third step is actual practice to keep mental silence for each unworthy thought. Mental silence means not to talk mentally and also not to talk through your behaviors. In real mental silence the mind is silent, as if it did not exist.

Through these three steps man can accumulate a great deal of true information about himself and his mechanism and live a conscious life.

Those who achieve control over their thoughts can travel in the Subtle World, the astral plane, like pillars of light.

The astral world has three main spheres. In the coarsest sphere are found those who live and act like sleepwalkers. The next sphere is the domain of hallucinators, or prisoners of desires and fantasy. The third sphere is for those who try to reconstruct their lamps to travel upward to the Fiery World.[1]

Those who achieve victory over their thoughts do not need to stay longer than a few days or a few hours in the astral world. They are the transients who pass in luminous glory through the astral plane and shed great light and inspire striving in trapped souls.

Components of Thought

Thought has three components:

1. electrical energy

2. form

3. meaning

Electrical energy is the self-propelling and speed-producing energy through which a thought travels faster than light.

The form of the thought is the language of the thought. Our thoughts mostly speak the language through which we think.

The third component is the meaning, which carries the heart energy. What you really mean by any expression is the meaning of that expression, and it comes from your heart.

When one transmits his thought to another person who does not know the language of the sender of the thought, he "hears" the thought of the sender in his own language. This is a very interesting phenomenon for those who think scientifically. The meaning of the thought is received in spite of the difference in the language.

---

1. See also *Other Worlds*.

Does this mean that the receiver is tuned to the heart impulse of the sender, or that he has a translating mechanism within his system, or that the thought current is equipped with such a sensitivity that it changes its language to the language of the receiver before it reaches there?

These mysteries will be revealed to those who conquer their thoughts.

After one conquers his thoughts, he slowly becomes aware of a beam of thought projected from the Higher Worlds to lead his steps from the world of chaos to the world of beauty.

Some people believe that when one passes away, he either leaves all his troubles behind and enters into the peace of paradise or he enters into an everlasting suffering. Such an assumption is not in accord with reality. Man leaves his physical body, but he still has his astral and mental bodies, plus all his memories of many lives if he is advanced.

Our astral body is sometimes the cause of all suffering tasted through our physical body. And very often it is the mental body and our thoughts that lead our physical existence into paths of suffering, pain, and karmic involvements and complications. The physical life reflects all that exists in the subtle planes, but, if the reflecting agent is taken away, it does not mean that the originating source of the reflection does not still exist. We carry with us all our troubles into the Subtle World; or, it is even better to say, we become aware of them in the Subtle World.

Thus a thought, an emotion, or an action expressed on the physical plane is not only the property of the physical plane, but it is also the property of the emotional and mental planes. Of course, the shape or the form of the "property" changes on each plane, but the essence stays the same.

Thus we can say that death is not an escape, as if all your bills are paid, all your problems are solved, and suddenly you enter into the Subtle World as a new being. It is human imagination that created the concept of beginning and end. There is only one reality, which can be termed *continuity*.[2]

One thought, one emotion, one act travels through space and scatters seeds of flowers or weeds in the places and planes about which we have no concept. After these seeds fulfill their cycles of growth, the Cosmic Wind scatters them further into space. This is the eternal domain in which man for a long time meets his former self.

Good deeds on the physical plane create a garden of flowers on the astral plane. Emotions originating from love and compassion on the physical plane create a symphony on the mental plane. Thoughts charged by the vision of Infinity, future, synthesis, and unity on the physical plane create the bridge between the mundane and supermundane worlds.

All is for eternity.

_____

2. See *The Purpose of Life*, Ch. 27.

Karma is considered to be active only in the physical dimension, whereas it has a three-dimensional manifestation or activity. The causes and effects are not limited to the physical plane or dimension only, but they extend into emotional and mental dimensions, too, and there they are as real and active as they were on the physical plane.

The concept of planes is misunderstood. In reality it is the human consciousness that created such a concept to make it easier to understand certain laws and manifestations. In reality, there is only One Existence.

In thinking about the planes, levels, and multiplicity of creation, we must not put aside the fact that all is one whole, interrelated in detail. It is only our growing consciousness that divides things and sees the parts instead of the whole. The growing consciousness eventually will become aware that anything that is done is done forever and for the whole. After such an awareness, a man realizes the depth of his responsibility toward his future and toward all who are involved in his relationships.[3]

In the past, people emphasized responsibility for our actions. Now the emphasis is put on responsibility for our feelings and thoughts as well. In the future, Teachers will develop within us the sense of responsibility toward the future in the Subtle and Fiery Worlds, a responsibility carried with us in more subtle planes of our journey toward Infinity.

People living in subtle spheres hold us responsible for destructive things or disturbances on subtle planes. They want us to realize that we must be aware of the responsibility we have for our ugly and impure thoughts, emotions, and deeds, for the moral and chemical pollution we have created all over the world because all of these affect the life in subtle spheres.

In the Subtle Worlds we find all that we planted here. We also find all that we corrected here. Man lives in one sphere of existence.

---

3.   See also *The Sense of Responsibility in Society.*

20

Thought Amplification

It is observed that one can think better, more deeply, and more creativity if he first has a sympathetic audience, an audience who thinks on the same lines, toward the same purpose; and second, if his thoughts attract those entities who love and enjoy his thoughts. Between these two groups the thoughts of the thinker burn brightly and become amplified by these two currents of energy.

Between these two currents the thinker forms a whirlpool of energy which receives new currents from the entities present and releases a current toward the audience. The quality and depth of the thought increases as the thinker creates a purer resonance between these two groups.

It is known that new layers of thought open in the mind during a conversation or a lecture. The speaker has a foundation, but he finds himself gradually elevated as the synchronization of these elements proceeds.

Ancient philosophers used to say that one must find a good listener, or a group of good listeners, if he wants the resources of light to pour down from his Soul. Ancient prayers used to invoke higher powers to come and help during the process of speech-making.

Thus, for higher thinking, invisible helpers and an audience are necessary. But this audience need not always be present while the thinker thinks. Once the audience is created through lectures and literature, the sympathetic lines are already established with the thinker, and these lines continuously evoke new waves of thought from the thinker. In response to these new demands and evocations, the thinker exerts himself to answer them. He goes deeper into himself, and thus the quality of his thoughts deepens.

When the thinker starts to open his sails on the sea of thought, he immediately feels the wind filling his sails and pushing his boat toward the sea. This is the experience of many thinkers. The wind is the energy and inspiration which one receives from the invisible world when he makes himself *ready* for thinking.

The thinker must express his gratitude to these two elements which help him deepen his thinking into greater layers of Cosmic light.

The quality of thinking increases still more when the members of the audience begin to gear their minds with the thinker and try to penetrate into the deeper layers of the thought presented by the thinker. In time each member of the audience becomes a thinker with his special line of approach, but in harmony with the keynote of the thinker.

Such a development of thinkers provides a tremendous opportunity for Great Ones to inspire the thinkers along the lines of Cosmic constructiveness.

We are told that "Brotherhood is primarily a school of thought,"[1] and it exercises a powerful influence over the globe for purification and advancement of the art of thinking. It is possible to tune to the currents of thought of the Brotherhood and push the boat of humanity toward a new sunrise.

---

1.   Agni Yoga Society, *Brotherhood*, para. 512.

21

Advanced Exercises
for Thought

Thought, being a fiery substance, affects the object upon which it is focused. This effect can be beneficial or harmful.

For example, our clothes, pencils, papers, books, furniture, and cars must be looked upon as our friends, and we must relate to them with loving thoughts. Our food must always be blessed. Before drinking our water, it must be flooded by the thoughts of gratitude. Before we use any clothing, it must be blessed. The vitamins we take especially must be charged with our loving thoughts and gratitude, and they will help us more.

Through our best thoughts our psychic energy must charge everything around us and create an electrical shield over them to protect them from destructive influences and elements.

This is not a superstition but is based on scientific thinking. Thought is energy. It can be directed and charged by our psychic energy and can heal, purify, shield, and transform all objects around us.

One must exercise his muscles. One must also exercise his thoughts. Through the exercise of thought, one can see how the power of thought increases. But along with the power of thought, one must equally increase his compassion. Without compassion, thought power works like a strong current which draws to it those who misuse thought energy personally and collectively.

The discipline of thought starts with the exercises of attention, concentration, focus, meditation, alertness, and vigilance. Such exercises organize the aura, open the consciousness, and make the thinker tense, sensitive, and electrified.

In olden times the devotees of higher wisdom and those who used to keep their contact firm with higher forces lived in vigilance and even had special months or days for vigil.

We are told that the Hierarchy keeps continuous vigil.

Vigilance is a state of consciousness, a state of the aura which is highly sensitive to higher commands or impressions and highly equipped to smash and destroy the darts of darkness in any form. Vigilance, in which thoughts work like laser beams, is one of the signs of an Initiate.

Transmutation of elements will be carried out through the rays of thought. Thought is a mighty power, once it is possessed by an enlightened and vigilant heart.

In the future, groups will be trained to use the power of thought. Throughout many ages this was tried by leaders of the races, but often it ended in massive destruction due to a lack of the element of the fire of love. Schools have been found in which the ancients practiced the power of thought, but mostly this power was used for separative purposes and for the gratification of the pleasures of the body and the cravings of the emotions.

It is hoped that in the future the thought power will be used for synthesis, brotherhood, unity, and for the revelation of the mysteries of life. If this power is misused, it will work against itself, and man once more will commit global suicide.

The right use of thought energy is to have a moment of vigil to hear the silent voice of the heart and be impressed by the Purpose of all creation.

People think that man cannot be impressed by the Purpose of all creation. It is possible to be impressed by the Purpose of all creation in a moment of Beauty, Goodness, Righteousness, Joy, and Freedom. The impression can be like a flash, but it can carry the whole message to which a man dedicates his entire life just to reveal a few layers of such a condensed and packed impression.

The continuous creativity, the sacrifice, and the service of heroic souls are inspired by that moment of impression of the Purpose of life.

It is important to realize that vigilance cannot be obtained without continuous, systematic, and planned exercise and discipline. Exercise is related to the moment when the power of thought is deliberately used. Discipline is related to the rest of the time when the power of thought achieved through the moment of exercise is maintained throughout life.

Exercises

Before you begin the exercises, make the following pledge:

Almighty Power of the Universe, I am a Spark from Your infinite fire, ready to cooperate with Your creative forces active in the whole Universe. Grant me Your protection to begin my conscious transformation.

I solemnly promise not to use my mental powers for my selfish ends, not to violate the free will of human beings, not to interfere with their karma but instead to stand vigilant and do my best to provide that wisdom, those conditions, and those examples through which the liberation of the human soul becomes possible.

Almighty Power of the Universe, I pledge myself to charge all my thoughts with Beauty, Goodness, Righteousness, Joy, and Freedom. As the power of thought increases in me, I promise to keep my humility and never fall into the waves of vanity.

I realize that no matter how powerful I can be, Your lightning can strike from me in one second all my powers if I violate my promise.

The Great Presence in the Universe, bless me at the threshold of my labor.

OM. OM. OM. OM. OM. OM. OM.

This is the pledge which must be taken by those who are ready for the great adventure.

A note of caution:

Those who have used any hallucinogenic drugs or marijuana or who were hospitalized for mental problems or depression must not do these exercises.

These exercises can be performed individually in solitude or in group formation.

The following exercises are specifically designed to make us develop our thinking. One must proceed slowly, carefully, and with perseverance.

Exercise One

1. Build a form in your imagination, then destroy it by changing the object from solid to liquid, to fiery, and reverse.

2. Let the object move and increase its speed. Stop it, then let it melt away. For three weeks, do this every day for fifteen minutes.

Exercise Two

1. Step out of the body.

2. Do various things such as jumping, running, swimming, etc.

3. Use the seven senses while out of the body.

4. Do this for three weeks, every day for fifteen minutes.

Exercise Three

1. Step out of the body.

2. Write a letter while out of the body.

3. Play music and sing.

4. Do this for three weeks, every day for fifteen minutes.

Exercise Four

1. Step out of the body.

2. Visit distant places.

3. Slowly go farther and each time come back to the body.

4. Do this for three weeks, every day for fifteen minutes.

Exercise Five

1. Enter into the Subtle World.

2. Enter into the Fiery World.

3. Visualize your physical body lying down and you as a spiritual entity.

4. Look down at the body and heal it with a violet light coming from your palms and eyes.

5. Change the body to any position you want and let your light penetrate the places you need to purify. Use red flames for purification, then violet light for healing.

6. Do this for three weeks, every day for fifteen minutes.

Exercise Six

Do the same exercise as above with your astral and mental bodies. Do this for three weeks, every day for fifteen minutes.

Exercise Seven

1. Visualize the seven colors of the prism.

2. Build circles, triangles, and squares with each color.

3. Do this for three weeks, every day for fifteen minutes.

Exercise Eight

1. In your visualization try to read a few words on a blackboard.

2. Try to write a letter.

3. Try to open a book and read a few lines. This is not easy, but it is possible if you work on it.

4. Do this for three weeks, every day for fifteen minutes.

Exercise Nine

1. Try to observe a statue from all sides.

2. Do this for three weeks, every day for fifteen minutes.

Exercise Ten

1. Light a real candle and try literally to move the flame with your thoughts.

2. Do the same with incense.

3. Do this for three weeks, every day for fifteen minutes.

Exercise Eleven

Visualize a wheel three feet in diameter in front of your face. Make it turn clockwise as fast as possible, gradually expanding in size and penetrating through your head from front to back as it rotates. This wheel is a wheel built of electric fire.

Then visualize the electrical wheel above your head turning horizontally and passing through your body from head to toes, inch by inch, in very fast rotation. This must be done five times back and forth. Do this for three weeks, every day for fifteen minutes.

Exercise Twelve

Visualize your physical body; then visualize your emotional body apart from the physical body but around your physical body. Continue by visualizing your mental body, your intuitional body, and your atmic, monadic, and divine bodies as if they were living garments ready for you to put on, layer after layer.

Starting from the physical body, see each in greater and greater beauty and in greater and greater glory. Do this for three weeks, every day for fifteen minutes.

Exercise Thirteen

If you want to correct or heal any part of your body, go to the corresponding part on the next higher body until you feel intuitively the source of your body's trouble. With your thought power cleanse, purify, and heal the source. See the reflecting influences of healing in the lower bodies until you feel that the process of healing is complete.

With their glory and beauty, the higher bodies can harmonize and purify the lower bodies if the thought power interrelates with them properly.

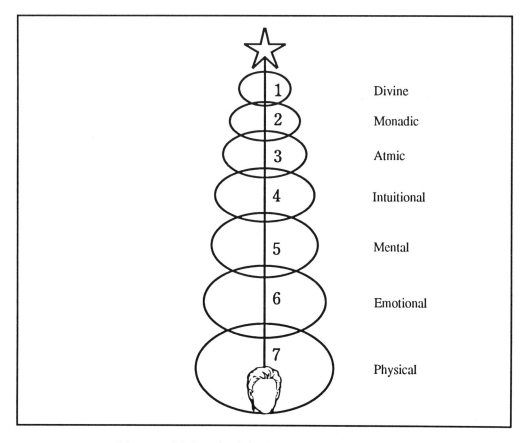

Diagram 21-1   Thought Current and Seven Bodies

Numbers 1 through 7 are the bodies. The star is the Spark, the Self, "more radiant than the Sun." The human form is the reflected image of the form that exists on each plane as its gradient blueprint is impressed on all planes. The line connecting all the numbers of spirals is your thought current.

Visualize your seven bodies, the star, and your thought current penetrating them all. Do this exercise for three weeks, every day for fifteen minutes.

Exercise Fourteen

1. Visualize someone and see him or her

— being joyful

— being beautiful

— being noble

2. Day after day, watch to see any differences in the person's actions. Do this for three weeks, every day for fifteen minutes.

Exercise Fifteen

In your visualization, have a short but beautiful conversation with someone you love or respect.

Such sendings and conversations must not be based on personal dealings because this would create reactions and complications. Remember your pledge. Do this for three weeks, every day for fifteen minutes.

Exercise Sixteen

Think about the Sun and help the rays of the Sun to penetrate all of your bodies, bringing solar beauty, strength, and joy. Do this for three weeks, every day for fifteen minutes.

Exercise Seventeen

Repeat mentally the seven notes of the scale, starting from middle C, and visualize each body one by one, starting with the physical.

Sound the notes with the following vowels:

MUSICAL NOTES		VOWELS
C	=	a, as in *arm*
D	=	a, as in *at*
E	=	e, as in *eat*
F	=	u, as in *fuse*
G	=	u, as in *put*
A	=	uh, as in *hut*
B	=	o, as in *oak*

"O" will be the synthesizing sound for all bodies.

Direct each note to the Core of the body and visualize a flash of light released from the Core for each sound.

Do this exercise for three weeks, every day for fifteen minutes.

Each body has its color:

Physical	gold-violet
Emotional	silver blue
Mental	yellow or green
Intuitional	blue
Atmic	orange-gold
Monadic	indigo (yellow-orange)
Divine	red (fiery orange-gold)

Each of our vehicles has its original color, like the colors of the rainbow or the spectrum. But the corresponding vehicles of many human beings are not of the same hue or shade. There are many kinds of red, orange, yellow, etc. Also, some vehicles have totally different colors due to the mixture with other bodies.

For example, if the etheric body is totally flooded with the emotional body, or if the emotional body is absorbed by the mental body, you have different color combinations. Also, some people do not even have exact colors because their bodies are in formation or obsessed by different entities or thoughtforms.

Exercise Eighteen

Visualize your thought as a beam of light with magnetic properties. Let this beam of light go into Space, deep into Infinity, and attract the precious fires of psychic energy and then transmit them to the treasury of your Chalice.

Psychic energy may be used for healing, illumination, strength, vitality, success, achievement, victory, and contact with higher forces.[1]

It will not be easy to keep this beam of thought straight, as many currents will try to bend it, dissolve it, or make it flicker. But continue your exercise and you will succeed.

Psychic energy within us acts as the most impressive element of higher messages and communications. Unless we have such a fiery element in our Chalice, communication with Higher Worlds will be impossible and impressions will not be recorded in our consciousness.

Do this for three weeks, every day for fifteen minutes.

In mental training one must consider five elements which are important for the success of the thinker.

Thinking is like archery, one must exercise and train himself in using the bow, the arrow, in using the right amount of strength, and in directing the arrow toward the destination. One must even learn the right body positions.

It must be remembered that in the formation of thoughtforms we use various factors. We need mental substance, concentration, thought, psychic energy, and a destination.

Mental substance is not always available, and, if available, it is not always suitable for building thoughtforms. A certain kind of mental substance is like sand: one cannot build a form and throw it to space without making it disintegrate. Thoughtforms built from such substance do not last long in space.

Concentration is the will energy which brings the mental substance together and keeps the constructed form together. Many thoughtforms are dispersed in space by attaching to other fuzzy thoughtforms through association.

Thought is the dynamic meaning and energy, the nucleus, and the life in the thoughtform.

Psychic energy is the fiery aura around the thoughtform which keeps the thoughtform protected from attacks and deformation. It gives wings to the thoughtform and annihilates the chemical, electrical, and magnetic hindrances on its path.

Destination is very important. Without destination there is no motion in the thoughtform. Destination conditions the motion of the thoughtform and its speed.

Destination acts like a magnet and creates a magnetic line between the thoughtform and the target.

---

1.   For more information, read *A Commentary on Psychic Energy* and *New Dimensions in Healing*.

You need corresponding elements to send the arrow to its destination.

Space is full of disintegrated thoughtforms, or mental dust. When the cohesiveness of the mental substance is exhausted, it cannot be used to build thoughtforms. The cohesive element in mental substance is psychic energy. When psychic energy is wasted, the mental atoms lose their cohesiveness. Psychic energy makes it possible to build imagery through visualization. The power of visualization weakens when psychic energy withdraws itself or is wasted through a life lived in harmful activities.

Exercise Nineteen

Practice "thinking and ecstasy over beauty." Thinking is exercised in scientific, occult meditation. Ecstasy over beauty increases your psychic energy. Your target must be a beauty. Ecstasy is the moment when you feel your arrow is ready to hit the target and be one with it.

The Great Sage says, "People have only two real joys — thinking and the ecstasy over beauty."[2]

Every day one must experience ecstasy over beauty. Beauty can be presented as music, painting, poetry, singing, Nature, etc. Ecstasy is a moment of fusion with beauty. Without ecstasy the joy of thinking will be incomplete. In the process of the building of right thoughtforms, these two elements are necessary — thinking and ecstasy. Thinking transforms the mental body. Ecstasy brings in psychic energy.

Do this for three weeks, every day for fifteen minutes.

Exercise Twenty

Think about the future. Think about 2,000 years ahead, 3,000, 50,000, two million years ahead of now. Do not daydream; keep the gears of your mind, your logic, and your creative imagination in action.[3]

Think about the planet: what shape might it take five million years from now. Conclude: what kind of transportation might man have; what kind of development might the senses have, etc.

This is the chronological future.

_____

2. Agni Yoga Society, *Brotherhood*, para. 85.
3. A good guidance for the future is found in *Olympus World Report — The Year 3000* and *The Year 2000 and After*.

Now visualize your spiritual future. Where can the evolution of your senses, of the physical, emotional, mental, and higher planes lead you? What would you be if steadily, time after time, you unfold and bloom and gain total communication with the Universe?

Such exercises will have far-reaching effects on your consciousness and in the expressions of your life.

This exercise must not be done every day but periodically and only for fifteen minutes so that you still remain grounded while you make greater breakthroughs into the space of the future. After working for a long time on this exercise, you will be ready for the next exercise.

Exercise Twenty-one

This exercise of thought is called thinking about Infinity. You must let your thought expand into the Infinite Space, into timelessness, limitlessness; into endlessness and beginning-lessness. When you begin to do this exercise, for the first time in your life you will see how you can silence your mind and fuse it with Space. You will notice how, to a great extent, your creativity increases, your direction becomes clearer, and your steps become more precise. Your sense of co-measurement will be accurate. All your actions, feelings, and thoughts will be open ways to Infinity.

Contemplation can be understood when you carry on this exercise for a year or two for fifteen minutes daily.

Thinking about Infinity slowly and gradually will loosen all crystallizations in your etheric and other subtle bodies. No artificial or forced tension will remain within your system, and you will develop a way of communication with the Infinity within you.

Be slow and gradual. Do not hurry and force your mind.

Exercise Twenty-two

This is an exercise of the discipline of silence. It is known that thought develops and gains mastery over adverse elements in silence. This is why we are advised to exercise the discipline of silence whenever and wherever we can.

It is very beneficial to have periods of regular silence, say, one day per week, one to two hours daily, or one week or one month in a year. It is extremely important to observe such a discipline to gain more mastery over your mental mechanism and over the mysteries of thought.

Partial fasting is recommended, but it is suggested that one must not be in the company of others during the periods of long silence.

Exercise Twenty-three

After observing periodic silence for a few years, one must practice the discipline of keeping emotional and mental silence, as far as they are related to personal life. Aspiration, deep meditation, and contemplation are considered periods of active silence. When these are learned, one must start short periods of total emotional and mental silence. This is accomplished after one learns how to withdraw oneself from the lower bodies and related interests.

Exercise Twenty-four

This exercise is for purification of consciousness. Daily sit for fifteen to twenty minutes and try to think about and communicate with the Hierarchy. Think about the seven main and the forty-nine secondary Ashrams.

Think about the Ashrams as the busiest Centers of labor carried on twenty-four hours daily.

Think about the entire Hierarchy as the bridge between the Earth and the Father's Home.

Visualize the Hierarchy as a network of multicolored light trying to purify and uplift the consciousness of the world.

With these exercises you will discipline your mental body, shape your thoughts, and create a deep aspiration to transcend your consciousness and life and use your existence to serve humanity.

22

Visualizations to Expand Space

Visualize a circle in the center of your head and try to expand it out into space, keeping the center in your head. Expand it into space, stage by stage, without losing the clarity. Remember that it is not a disk or a sphere but a circle.

It may be helpful if you visualize it in different colors when you meet difficulty in expanding it. Start with blue, and see what color helps you to expand.

It is suggested that you do not do the expansion all at once but gradually, day after day, each day for ten minutes. Today expand the circle over your town. The next day expand it over your state . . . the next day over a few states . . . the next day over your country . . . the next day over the world, the solar system, the galaxy . . . Space.

Remember that no matter how much you expand, you must bring the circle back to the center in your head and visualize it as a diamond of light and feel that your whole body is flooded with that light.

During the exercise be very calm, patient, joyful, and totally relaxed. Keep your spine straight and have your hands on your knees.

Exercise Two

When you feel you can do the first exercise, start this one:

Visualize the same circle and let its expansion be accompanied by some musical note which is heard around the whole circle. Visualize the note creating power in the circle and making the circle expand.

You can use the musical scale, giving to each individual note the same duration as the circle slowly expands. Be careful that you keep the circle as a circle, expanding it from all sides of your head.

You do not need to limit yourself to sitting on the chair. You can imagine yourself on a mountaintop or in Space, according to how much your circle needs to expand.

Try not to repeat the same sound. Change it, but try to keep it as part of a chord if you are not using the scale. As in the previous exercise, do not hurry. Build the foundation, which means establish a clear beginning so that your circle is not diffused as it expands.

As you withdraw the circle, again do it through sounding the note silently, and at the center of your head let it merge into silence. Then for a few seconds try to observe the silence.

It seems to us that our consciousness is limited by the size and form of our body, and it seldom tries to break that limitation and expand itself beyond the body limitation. The consciousness assumes that it is tied to the body. You are going to teach it that it can exist beyond the body. . .and even without the body.

Exercise Three

Visualize yourself as a flame on a mountain at night, and see how far your light goes. Expand your light all over the earth and then toward Space as a sphere of light. Let your light gradually expand from one mountain to another mountain. . .until you are able to visualize that your light can envelope the earth, the solar system, and the galaxy.

Again, use the gradient scale, step by step, and, if needed, repeat this step for several days until it is clear. If the mountaintop is limiting you, visualize that you are like a diamond light within the Sun. . .within the Heart of the Galaxy. . . .

Our consciousness must learn to free itself from various limitations imposed upon it by our thoughts.

Let us repeat that these exercises must be done with great patience, with clarity, and in a gradient scale because for centuries we built limiting walls around our consciousness, and our consciousness has become a slave of our personal interests. In reality, our consciousness is the light of our Self, the soul. We are souls, and the consciousness is light.

Exercise Four

Visualize that you are again on the top of a mountain as a sphere of light. This time, feel that *you are the light* and *you* are expanding in space. For the first few days, expand only three or four feet, then gradually more. Always keep in mind that it is not your light that is expanding, but it is *you* who is expanding.

Try to register all that your light is contacting. Start with your room and expand into Space. It is possible that you will contact many things, but keep expanding because contact is not your goal — expansion is.

As you expand, objects of former levels will seem more distinct to you, and you will understand them more clearly. Your understanding will be based in awareness rather than in logic and knowledge.

A day will come when your light will fuse with the Light of the Universe. Here will start your journey toward omniscience.

Exercise Five

This is a meditation called *looking at you with the eyes of your Angel*:

1. Relax and visualize your Angel looking at your body and healing it, repairing it, and strengthening it.

2. See It looking at your emotional nature and cleansing it of many negative elements which you know well, pouring into it purity and love.

3. See It looking at your mental nature and revealing all wrong motives, negative intentions, vanities, and fears, one by one, pouring into it Its light and Its wisdom.

4. See It looking at you as a human soul and showing you the vision of victory, creativity, immortality, and Infinity.

5. See It taking you to the feet of Christ, Who is blessing you and initiating you into His Army of light, love, and beauty.

6. Sound seven OMs.

7. Say "Om Mani Padme Hum"[1] three times.

This meditation may be done fifteen to twenty minutes daily. After the meditation, relax and keep silent for five minutes.

---

1.   Salutations to the Jewel in you.

23

The Effects of Thought

We are told that the effect of thought cannot immediately be seen on the physical plane. It takes time until it substantiates. This time factor is relative to the tension and energy put into the thought.

In the emotional and mental worlds, the effect is more immediate. In the mental world the thought creates its immediate effect. In the Subtle World, thought creates certain waves which gradually turn into effects.

Advanced souls in the subtle planes use thoughts as we use our tools, machines, hands and feet, or our weapons on earth. Thus, Great Ones teach that it is imperative for us to learn the art of thinking to be able to function in the subtle planes.

There is a great difference between the discoveries of certain secrets of Nature through thinking and the ability to control or master our thoughts. It is possible that, after our discoveries, we turn into the slaves of our discoveries or misuse them against our own evolution and survival. But when one reaches the mastery of thought energy, he is already in the light and he never dares to fight the light.

In higher realms the wrong use of thought energy is like putting a knife into one's own body, or cutting one's own throat, or destroying the most precious things one has built. It is a very good exercise to visualize the consequences of one's own thoughts on various levels simultaneously, in terms of the speed of the manifesting effects, colors, and sounds. Through such a visualization, one can learn caution in using thought energy.

Thoughts about five great diamonds, namely Beauty, Goodness, Righteousness, Joy, and Freedom, increase our psychic energy and bring more light into our mind.

In the physical world the effects of our thoughts can be measured in meters or kilometers. In the Subtle World the effects of our thoughts spread over the globe. In the Fiery World the effects of our thoughts spread in Solar Space. This means we have under our possession a power that can create and also destroy on many levels.

It is a great exercise to take the five diamonds and think, for example, how this beautiful flower or person will appear in the Subtle World, in the Fiery World, and in the world of Intuition. What will be goodness in the astral, mental, and higher planes? How will righteousness appear in the subtle planes? How will one feel a great joy experienced in the subtle planes? How will one feel freedom on higher planes?

By having such thoughts, one can expand his consciousness and live in harmony with the symphony going on within the three worlds simultaneously, in greater and greater beauty.

There is an exercise which is called *washing the clothes*. One can visualize his mental body in the mental world and "wash" it with the supreme power of Divine Light; then wash his emotional body with the power of the electricity of Love; then wash the physical body with the light of the inner Jewel. Such an exercise can lead to Transfiguration, if one succeeds in keeping his vehicles pure and immaculate.

One can start this exercise by reminding himself of this mantram:

> *More radiant that the Sun,*
>
> *purer than the snow,*
>
> *subtler than the ether*
>
> *is the Self,*
>
> *the Spirit within my heart.*
>
> *I am that Self;*
>
> *that Self am I.*

One must know that higher thoughts gradually substantiate and become objective on the physical plane. Thus, the effects of thoughts take time to appear on the dense plane, but their effects on the subtle planes are almost immediate.

In doing the exercise given above, you learn that the visualization must be carried out in a state of complete faith and trust. Any doubt or flickering induces disturbances in the subtle formations and brings harm to the physical body. You must do such an exercise with all your heart and might.

When you cross a wide river on a one foot wide hanging bridge, you had better charge your steps with the conviction that soon the other shore will be reached. In every step forward, feel the joy of the other shore. Thus, courage is active joy, and it inspires trust.

There is another exercise which is called *cleaning space of all trash thrown into it from physical pollution, emotional debris, and mental contamination.* This exercise must be undertaken by a group of advanced persons who know how to use the mental energies. The group will visualize locations in space which need purification. Many locations in space are polluted with heavy layers of crime, hatred, revenge, glamors, lies, and illusions, and they create great hindrances to communication between the subtle and physical worlds. Groups trained in the art of thinking and thought can burn away such spheres of pollution, re-establish closer contact with Higher Worlds, and annihilate centers of evil through which dark forces attack humanity.

The procedure is as follows:

1. Have the group sit in a circle.

2. Relax.

3. Raise the consciousness of the group as high as possible to fuse with the group soul and with spiritual realities.

4. Invoke the assistance of higher forces through the following mantram:

    May the forces of light and love and power
    assist us in our service to the Lord of the World
    of clearing and purifying certain places in Space
    around our planet.

    May the fiery angels help us do our service.
    We are grateful to have this opportunity to serve.

5. The group now visualizes certain locations on the planet where there is excessive crime, obsession, insanity, lust, materialism, slavery, confusion, and bloodshed. They focus the group thought two to three miles in space above these locations and feel the accumulated cloud of base thoughts of crime, hatred, malice, etc.

6. The group visualizes a big hose which pours streams of fire into the formation. The group does this until it feels that the work is done and the cloud is totally destroyed.

7. After the cloud is burned away, the group plants the seeds of Beauty, Goodness, Righteousness, Joy, and Freedom in that space.

8. Say the Great Invocation.

    From the point of Light within the Mind of God
    Let light stream forth into the minds of men.
    Let Light descend on Earth.

    From the point of Love within the Heart of God
    Let love stream forth into the hearts of men.
    May Christ return to Earth.

From the centre where the Will of God is known
Let purpose guide the little wills of men —
The purpose which the Masters know and serve.

From the centre which we call the race of men
Let the Plan of Love and Light work out.
And may it seal the door where evil dwells.

Let Light and Love and Power
Restore the Plan on Earth.

9. Sound seven OMs, visualizing Christ radiating light and love toward the earth.

24

Thought and Pollution

Meditation and concentration must not be stressed during times of air pollution. Air pollution poisons the cells of the brain and even affects the etheric body. Higher thoughts will create undue tension on the nervous system.

Pure air is conductive to thoughts coming from Higher Realms. In pure air, the reception is natural. In polluted air, there will be distortion and strain on the brain.

Those who are regular in their meditation practice must choose less polluted areas and live there. If they cannot make a move, then, instead of meditation, they can read and try to understand the pages they are reading; but if they feel tired, even the reading must be stopped.

Many children living in polluted air will show signs of severe mental retardation and strong inclinations toward crime.

Pollution not only affects the health but also weakens the will. A man who has a weak will or no will is like a ship in the ocean without power or rudder. Every wave will move the ship in its own direction.

Weakening of the will leads a man into vices and crimes. As the will weakens, glamors, illusions, and materialism take over the mechanism of man.

The will not only operates the mechanism of man but also gives it direction, a direction which is in harmony with the direction of the Cosmic Intent.

On the emotional plane, the will energy sustains, inspires, and supports positive and constructive emotions. When the will fades away, negative emotions take over.

On the mental plane, the will energy is the structure upon which the thoughtform is built in a goal-fitting manner. Also, for the projection of constructive thoughts, the willpower acts as a bow.

When the willpower weakens, good thoughts disintegrate like clouds and the arrow of a thought disperses in the air like a ball of dust.

The power of evil thoughts and the power that stands behind the stream of evil thoughts is not willpower but etheric, astral, and mental force — integrated and directed by the magnet of the target. The greater the resistance of the target, the greater the power of the evil thought. This is why the Great Ones suggest that we not resist evil. Non-resistance to evil cuts the power line to evil. By non-resistance we mean emotional and mental indifference. This philosophy is madness for contemporary politics, but once the holocaust of atomic war begins, the only places where people will survive will be those places that did not create a resistance and did not become a target.

Pollution leads to war, to destruction, to crime. Statistics show that wherever the pollution of the earth, water, air, and noise is greater, the crime rate is also greater.

It is disastrous to let our politicians live in polluted cities and decide the destiny of a nation and the world.

It is impossible to build a glorious future for humanity by increasing the pollution on the planet.

Humanity is guided by the beams of light coming from the far-off worlds. Pollution deflects these rays, strips them of their wisdom, direction, and spiritually nourishing elements, and lets only the power pass to living beings, which stimulates etheric maya, astral glamors, and mental illusions. Great energy is wasted by spiritual thinkers to keep their mind in harmony with Divine direction and produce creative thoughts.

The rays coming from far-off worlds will help our gardens bloom on all planes, if we ourselves do not pollute the pool or sphere in which we are living.

Many civilizations on this planet committed suicide by letting the poison increase in the sphere in which they kept dancing in their madness. Historians and scientists fool themselves when they talk about the present civilization as starting from a stone age. Not only the stone age but many atomic and super-atomic ages were seen by this planet, and the bones of the previous scientists were melted in the fiery convulsion of the earth.

Man has not learned that the planet is like a tightly sealed room in which one cannot survive when polluting the space of the room. Such a simple fact has escaped the attention of scientists and politicians.

It is still possible to avoid the total destruction of the planet if the leaders of the world gather together in a relatively unpolluted spot in the world and think and meditate for the future of this planet, for the future of this humanity.

If a caricaturist survives in the future, he will illustrate the human life as a carriage driven by a winged Satan, and in the carriage people are busy with sex, doping, drinking, and money-making while the carriage is approaching a precipice, the depth of which cannot be measured.

We are told that AUM is the power of Grace coming from the Heart of Cosmos. In all conditions it is only this mighty thought energy that penetrates all spheres, and nothing can hinder its circulation. But low level thoughts and emotional, moral, and chemical pollution prevent us or make it extremely difficult for us to assimilate this thought energy of AUM and use it creatively.

Thus we can affirm that this mighty thought energy is always available if we tune to it.

The transmission of various thoughts by various sources and levels is received by different centers. In the Teaching we are told to try to discern their sources. These thoughts may come from

1. human beings, good or evil

2. the astral world

3. the mental world

4. still higher spheres

Each of these thoughts creates different reactions or responses and is received by different centers. For example, thoughts from human beings are mostly received by the solar plexus or throat centers. Good thoughts create a pleasant response in the throat center or solar plexus center, but evil thoughts create a painful, uncomfortable reaction in the lower solar plexus or even in the sacral center.

Thoughts received from the astral world usually create certain forms of palpitations in the heart. These palpitations can be painful, straining, and tense, especially when one connects himself to the astral world. He may receive many thoughts whose influence lasts one second or for days.

Similar things happen when one receives thoughts mixed with heavy emotions from the surrounding world.

If these thoughts coming from the astral world or from the emotional realms of people are charged with fear, terror, and anger, they create a very disturbing palpitation in the heart and are sometimes accompanied with pain.

Thoughts coming from the lower mental world create irritation if the thoughts are from the realms of self-interest. These thoughts are mostly related to separative interests and are based on material objects. Such thoughts are usually received by the section of the mental aura near the ears and at the back of the head and shoulders.

Thoughts coming from the higher mental plane are sensed through the head center. We are told that such thoughts sometimes appear with beautiful colors and sounds. If the thoughts are of a very high quality, they manifest as flames or fire. They expand our consciousness and often make us feel free and peaceful.

There are also thoughts which come from higher spheres such as from the Intuitional, Atmic, and Monadic Planes. We are told that these thoughts appear as lightning. Such thoughts are called fiery comets or messengers of fire.

Only highly evolved human beings can contact such messengers, and every time they contact them a new wave of culture, beauty, and wisdom spreads all over the world and lasts for centuries. These messengers are received by our full-bloomed heart center in the head.

In the Teaching we are advised to develop sensitivity to thought currents, to discern between thoughts, and to try to handle them consciously and creatively.

In the midst of our occupations or conversations, sometimes we notice the sparks of some precious thoughts penetrating our consciousness. Usually we do not pay attention to them, and they disappear. Sometimes they wander through our mind and insist on making their presence known, and if we are not preoccupied we turn our attention to them.

Thoughts that come from Higher Sources are called messages. These messages usually try to help us when we are ready to make a serious decision. They are not based on emotions or on the calculations of the lower mind, but they are in the nature of pure light. Because their visit is of short duration, we seldom analyze them, but they are very real. The Ancients used to call them "diamond gifts." Such gifts are mentioned in the fairy tales of many nations.

In moments of contemplation, when the consciousness is magnetically tense, one can have an opportunity to observe the visitations of such thoughts and accustom himself to observe, analyze, and use them.

It is interesting that they can come to us in very unexpected moments. Though they act under law, we do not immediately see their successive steps. They are related to certain frequencies, certain conditions. Our level of consciousness, our thoughts, our needs, our heartfelt aspirations may attract them. Sometimes our decisions and goals can invite them. Sometimes the role we are going to play in the future can bring them to us.

We often do not know our true role in the future. But for advanced beings our direction is as clear as to a man standing on a tower watching the traveler going toward an unexpected swamp or following the right path to the tower.

These sparks of thought often come from the One Who is watching us. In this case they are really private. In other cases these sparks are sent for certain groups of people living all over the world in order to invigorate and water their gardens. Sometimes the sparks are so-called "accidental" ones, and people pick them up in moments of synchronization.

It is very important to distinguish these kinds of thoughts from others which, like worms, swim in our lower mind.

Higher sparks have a very enlightening, inspiring, and creative character, but one must be watchful enough to catch them. They usually melt in our consciousness very quickly if we do not immediately concentrate on them and densify them through our attention.

It is a good idea always to have paper and pen ready to note them down. In this way we perpetuate them to some degree in our consciousness, and later we can analyze them in detail.

Sometimes these sparks are condensations of a volume, of a symphony, of an invention, or of an entire movement in any great field. Like an acorn, sometimes we kick them with our feet, not considering that in them exists a huge oak tree.

Visitations of such sparks become more frequent if our net of consciousness begins to catch them. The presence of their high substance within our consciousness acts as a magnet to draw more of them from Space. Our increasing ability to contain and accept them evokes a greater amount of sendings from the original sources.

It is through such contacts that the communication line between the subjective and objective world can firmly be established.

Progress is made only through establishing links with higher levels of existence. With each link our horizon is expanded.

Each spark of thought carries with it a great amount of substance which causes transmutation in our vehicles if assimilated properly. Thus the traveler on the path of perfection penetrates deeper into the sphere of greater values with an ever-transforming beingness.

Besides these precious sendings, there is also another kind of thought which we call the dark visitors. They bring doubt, fear, and confusion into the sphere of our thoughts. These visitors also obey certain laws which must be investigated to know exactly how they come, how they operate, and to what degree they affect our life. They have many sources. They emanate from our former or past failures. They are hypnotic suggestions received in our subconscious or semi-unconscious state of mind. They are projected by those who dislike us for any reason. They are projected by those who want to create weakness within us and thus retard our progress. They have many other sources which a man can find.

Teachers advise us to dwell on the sparks, on the benevolent visitors, and try to assimilate their message, but they warn us about dwelling on dark visitors.

Dark visitors become malignant when they are kept longer in our mental sphere. We must be careful not even to touch them mentally because they are contagious. They can be handled in many ways. We can

1. Ignore them

2. Cast them out by concentrating our mind on something very positive and beautiful

3. Destroy them with the sword of intuitive light

4. Raise our consciousness to a higher level

5. Create an opposing thought and fix our attention on it

Of course, to do the above things needs a disciplined mind which can be used with exactitude. A disciplined mind will not have difficulty getting rid of dark visitors.

There is a special kind of dark visitor which can be dispelled only by prayer, or by linking oneself with the Hierarchy. When people talk about disciplining their mind, they usually think about certain mental exercises and disciplines. This is preparatory. A better discipline of thought is achieved by developing the virtues.[1]

Various exercises can sharpen the mind, but they do not necessarily transform the mind.

Correct interpretation of the sparkling thoughts is so important. There is the possibility that we receive them, witness them, but misinterpret them. This happens when our mental sphere is not pure and in it the ghost of self-intent still wanders.

Interpretation is not a manufacturing or programming process, but it is a clear understanding of the message. Of course, it is very desirable that the interpretation of the message be put into practical manifestation. But there will be no uniformity in manufacturing or programming due to the different kinds of preparations of the mental mechanism of the receivers, the field of their service, and their Ray characteristics.

But it is the type and clear interpretation that conditions the right direction of the current of the spark through many kinds of manifestations.

Control over forces and dark visitors is achieved only through transformation. It is not an organized mechanism that achieves control but the one that uses the mechanism from a higher level of attainment. This attainment is the result of transformation through living the virtues.

Virtues even build the electrical wall through which a dark visitor seldom sneaks but is caught and burned almost immediately.

It is very important also to realize what kinds of thoughts we leave behind. Are our thoughts emanating from us like fumes from the exhaust pipe of our car? Or are they diamonds falling from our royal garments? Are they seeds of rare flowers scattered by our hands?

By realizing the nature of the thoughts we leave behind, we can have a better chance to watch our mental mechanism more carefully, minimize our pollution, and increase our gifts to Space.

Space has many strata. There are many precious thoughts accumulated in certain strata. Also, there are many destructive and dark thoughts existing in the lower strata where they disintegrate and rebuild themselves continually, creating the worst source of pollution of human consciousness.

It is important to know that emanations of our dark thoughts will condition our future and the future of other human beings. Similarly, our lofty thoughts will bring to us and to others blessings, joy, and beauty.

One must consciously guard his thoughts.

We are told that it is easy to create a thought, but it is not easy to get free from a created thought. You can create a thought in a second, but you cannot free yourself from the existence and influence of the thought for years.

---

1. See especially *The Psyche and Psychism*, Ch. 90, *The Flame of the Heart*, Ch. 3, and *New Dimensions in Healing*, Chs. 69-71.

Thoughts, once created, become substantial in your mental plane. They exist just as your furniture or any kind of article exists.

In the mental plane you need a higher energy than mental energy to disperse the unworthy thoughts in your mental sphere. This higher energy is called the energy of the Intuition or psychic energy, and not many people know about it or can use such an energy. Therefore they remain the slaves of their own thoughts.

Imagine a room where you can create furniture but cannot destroy it. Eventually you imprison yourself and make yourself useless.

It is very interesting to know that higher thoughts do not occupy space, though they have validity in space.

Lower thoughts occupy space, but they do not have validity. They are like lies which occupy space and have various effects on people but do not have validity or a true existence.

To dispel these lies is very difficult once they manage to have a corner in our mind. Though they have no validity, they mold mental matter and create crystallizations in it.

It is very important to confront an ugly thought within us before it spreads roots in our mind or in the minds of many people. Confrontation is a very subtle task in this case. One ugly thought can spread roots in the minds of thousands and form a gigantic tree in space. Ordinary human efforts cannot destroy such formations, and such a tree spreads its bad influence over many thousands of people.

This is why an ugly thought must not have the chance to live. One must not attack an ugly thought. He must expand his own consciousness and inspire himself by the light of a higher thought or of an intuitive perception.

Ugly thoughts can be destroyed more safely if the originator himself destroys it. Outer attacks may strengthen the ugly thoughts and make them a great danger for humanity.

Such formations in space are as destructive as within the human life.

Thoughts of revenge, hatred, and suspicion emanate in space as poisonous mist and pollute space, making it difficult for the waves of light to reach us. Besides this they attack those to whom they are directed.

One can register such thoughts in forms of fearful dreams, in forms of certain irritations, loss of energy, temporary blankness of mind, or in forms of certain sicknesses.

One can advance to the Higher Worlds by learning how to annihilate his unworthy thoughts. Through the process of elimination, one puts a higher energy into action and clears away the jungle which he created by his every unworthy thought.

In the Fiery World one can create explosions if he has no control over his thought and if he creates thoughts not fitting to the higher frequencies.

Human beings must start to learn the power of thought, the power of speech or words. It is important to watch our words. An unfit word is a burden on the aura, but an unfit thought is an inflammable gas.

It is possible to assist oneself by keeping the mind always busy with something worthy. If the machine of the mind is left idling, it runs on the thoughts surrounding our body. The Ancients advised that if one has nothing to think about, he must slowly repeat holy names or the names of virtues to repel the attack of low thoughts.

The purpose of the human being is to penetrate into the higher mental planes, to be in contact with higher realities, and to find the thought direction toward the Cosmic Magnet. This cannot be done without developing mastery over our thoughts.

In the astral and the mental worlds, one can combat evil intentions and dark attacks only through fiery thoughts. Once they are defeated in the Subtle World, their effects on the physical plane are annihilated.

The Ancients thought that if one dreams of an attack and awakens, he must combat it with all his fiery thoughts and in his imagination destroy the image of attack and visualize an image of victory before trying to sleep again.

Many attacks on the physical plane are prevented from taking effect through such a technique, but one must be able to think fiery thoughts.

It is highly effective if a group of people, disciplined in the art of thought, organize an attack on unworthy efforts of dark plans before they are put into action, but they must have the sense of registration of such plans highly developed.

In the future, when the disciples of Great Ones organize more properly, they will be able to prevent and destroy the nests of evil thoughts before they contaminate the life of humanity in the form of wars, chaos, and the depletion of morals and trust.

Fighting on the physical plane against evil is a fight against the germs that a factory produces. No permanent victory can be reached if the factory itself is not destroyed by the power of thought. But there is a great difference between the weapons used by both parties. The dark ones use hatred, malice, fear, and revenge and try to destroy those who walk in the light.

The disciples cannot use such weapons, but in their combat they use the vision of the future, the highest good of everyone concerned, fearlessness, compassion, courage, daring, light, nobility, detachment, and the lightning of willpower. Their thoughts as well as their expressions are highly controlled and are in line with the steps of evolution.

The Ancients told us not to combat evil by using the same weapons. This was great advice not yet understood by those who try to fight evil in the name of Beauty, Goodness, Freedom, and human rights but who use the same weapons as the enemy. This is how one fails in the combat with evil.

Even if the battle is apparently won, the fighter finds himself contaminated by the evil forces which he used to combat evil.

The Ancients also reminded us not to carry on the fight on the same level with the enemy. But, remember, one cannot fight on a higher level if he did not penetrate into that higher level.

25

The Thought World

Thought is a current of energy charged with an idea, vision, intention, and purpose.

Thinking is an endeavor to produce, channel, or direct the thought current.

Thought is not a thoughtform until it is dramatized by visualization, imagination, adaptation, and speech.

A thoughtform is a translation of an impression or inspiration. Thoughtforms are built when the thought stream is condensed by many higher substances or by mental matter into specific shapes in relation to the experiences of the physical, emotional, and mental worlds. Thoughtforms float in the mental body as well as in space beyond the sphere of man.

Thoughts are electrical in nature. Their speed transcends the speed of light and sound. Their charge varies according to the level of the willpower and enthusiasm of the human soul.

Electrical currents and storms in space affect the thought currents if they are not directed by a strong will.

Everything that exists on our planet or elsewhere is the condensation of a thought of a *thinker*, whether it is a solar, planetary, or human thinker.

Thought power not only creates but also transforms or destroys. The mastery of the Universe is achieved only through thought, but it is only through thought created by the heart that the mastery of the Universe brings joy and blessings for the victor.

Thought creates light. As our thought energy is refined and purified, it radiates more light until eventually our mental body becomes a shining light.

Initiates build lines of communication between their brain and higher spheres, between their brain and Higher Worlds. It is through these lines that they communicate with each other and with their disciples. Each initiate has his wireless receiver in the center of his head and his transmitter above his forehead.

People are already building machines through which they can control the thinking and behavior of people. People are also learning the secrets of how to control, manipulate, and even kill other people through their thoughts.

We are living in a very dangerous time of human history. To be able to survive, we must learn how to use our own thought energy on higher and higher planes and create a shield of higher frequency in our own aura. This is the only way by which we can escape attack and survive in the coming age.

We are told that in the Subtle World man fights and protects himself through thought. Those who do not know how to develop and use thought energy will have a very hard time in the Subtle World. Almost everything in the Subtle World is done by thought. All progress and expansion is done through thought. Obstacles and hindrances are annihilated by thought, and the breakthrough into the Higher Worlds is made by thought.

A thoughtless person is a person who does not know how to talk in the Subtle World. A thoughtless person is one who will not understand the language of the denizens of the Subtle World.

All communication is based on thought, and thought transmission is almost instantaneous. Great learning is conducted by the power and direction of thought. It is through the power of thought that the departed ones will be able to contact those on earth who can *hear* and *see* thought.

It is also possible that, as one refines his thoughts and passes from one sphere to a higher one, he establishes contact with those who live in higher spheres. Departed ones hate to come into the worldly spheres, although they like to come in contact with us. They use their thought power, but people here on earth cannot register their thoughts.

As one creates higher and higher thoughts, he penetrates into the sphere of the spirits living on the mental plane and instructs them, or receives instruction from them. Usually, those who are on the mental plane have their meetings, studies, and groups. It is possible to be with them through our thoughts.

The Fire of Space nourishes the fiery thoughts and transmits them instantaneously toward their destination.

There are good thoughts and bad thoughts due to the anchorage of the human soul or due to the condition of the centers behind the thought. It is possible that good thoughts and bad thoughts do not reach their destination but are attracted by someone else. It is possible that a mental body charged with goodness attracts the good thought and a mental body charged with evil intentions draws the bad thought. Evil and good thus decrease or increase and affect our life on this planet.

It is also possible that in certain conditions, when bombarded by evil thoughts, a mental body dedicated to good weakens. The reverse is also true. Good thoughts can weaken evil thoughts if they are consciously built for such a duty.

There are thoughts that carry knowledge. There are thoughts that carry goodwill. Thoughts of knowledge can be used by a mind oriented toward evil. But the thoughts of goodwill weaken the mind oriented toward evil.

The Great Ones work with thought energy. They supply thoughts of beauty, goodwill, and understanding. They send or transmit thoughts of knowledge only to those who can be of service to humanity. But many of these thoughts can be stolen by dark forces from those who receive them. This happens when the receiver goes through moments of vanity and hostility.

In times of emergency, Great Ones pass certain thoughts of knowledge, knowing that part of them may be stolen and used by the enemy; but this does not discourage Them. They know that every energy released into space will be lost in some quantity and serve the dark ones, but also it will reveal the dark ones and their motives. The Great Ones know that the Sun must shine on evil and good alike, and both will forge their own destiny.

It is possible to imagine that a continuous battle is going on upon the mental plane in space. One can imagine that good and bad thoughts are driven like jets by good and bad spirits. We are told that this thought battle manifests itself on the battlefields of the earth in the form of wars and revolutions.

In the future, those who conquer in the mental or thought space will conquer in the earthly space. Those who possess the earthly space but cannot master the thought space will eventually lose their earthly space. Thought space is only won by the arrows of good thought, thought charged with goodwill, universalism, inclusiveness, freedom, and synthesis.

The source of good thoughts is inexhaustible. It is the source of Creation. The source of evil is like a black cloud. It has no foundation, no permanent source. This is why good is always victorious. It is true that evil marks moments of victory, but the history of humanity shows that when evil rises higher, its fall is more destructive. Evil gains only to destroy itself. Evil fights against itself. It is a self-destructive battle.

Those who become the victims of the arrows of evil were those who somewhere, in some degree, served evil in the past or fought against evil for selfish interests.

Pure thoughts emanate a high-pitched *sound* which is audible only by an ear located on the highest mental plane. Such a sound builds links with the high notes of similar pure thoughts and forms a symphonic beauty. Some of the music on earth is a reflection of such symphonic beauties.

On various levels in space pure thought radiates symphonic colors, like those which we see at the North Pole. Many great painters transmit such symphonies on their canvas and thus build a bridge between earth and the source of beauty. These sounds and colors in space work like antennas to bring higher radiations and waves of potent energies from various constellations and galaxies. Thus an artist can become a high priest fused with the Source of beauty and bliss.

Every person who links himself with the frequency of good and pure thoughts eventually steps onto the path of Transfiguration and Resurrection.

One can penetrate deeper and deeper layers of thinking and find potent formulas and new ways of thinking if he uses his thought power for unity and synthesis. But if he uses his thought power for selfish reasons, for destruction and totalitarianism, eventually his thought power leads him into situations in which he destroys himself. This is what happens not only to individuals but to entire civilizations.

Man is the result of his thought.

Seven Mental Spheres

There are seven mental spheres around our planet which condition the direction and influence of incoming energies and the life of the planet as a whole.

As you move your consciousness outward in the spheres, the light increases into an impenetrable light. The seventh sphere is dark and muddy. The sixth one is foggy. Fog is a little brighter light, but the fifth and fourth are greater light. As we go to the first we reach total, impenetrable light.

— The seventh sphere is called the chaotic sphere.

— The sixth one is the muddy or crystallizing sphere.

— The fifth one is the ever-agitating sphere.

— The fourth one is the rhythmic sphere — joy.

— The third one is the sphere of harmony.

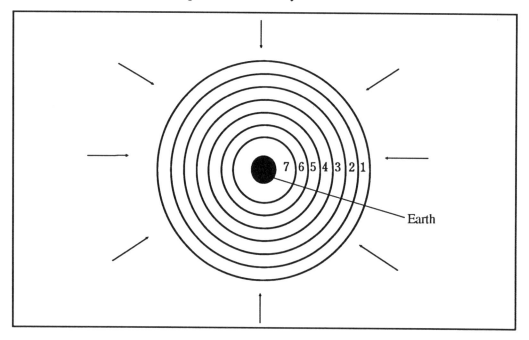

Diagram 25-1   Mental Spheres Around the Earth

— The second one is the sphere of serenity.

— The first one is the sphere of silence.

The third sphere is the accumulation of the thoughts of Nirmanakayas, great Chohans, and the Lord of the World. This is the sphere of Purpose, of Direction. This is the sphere of great Avatars.

The fourth sphere is the accumulation of thoughts of Great Ones and Arhats, or high degree Initiates. This is the sphere where the Purpose, contacted in higher spheres, is formulated into the Plan. This is the sphere of geniuses and heroes.

The fifth sphere is the accumulation of the thoughts of those servers who take the Plan and do the programming. This is the sphere of talents.

The sixth and seventh spheres are loaded with decaying and muddy thoughts.

Each sphere has an effect on human life. The seventh sphere is the plane of criminal thoughts. The sixth sphere provides the thoughts of exploitation of many kinds. The fifth sphere is the sphere of personal and selfish interests. The fourth sphere is the source of creative thought according to the Plan. The third sphere is the source of thoughts of higher creativity, in harmony with the Purpose of life as a whole.

Creative people can increase their productivity as they go deeper into the third and fourth spheres, which are the spheres of joy and beauty.

The seventh sphere is the sphere of fireflies. This means the sphere of short-lived truth. There is some truth in this sphere, but it is short-lived truth. For example, because one is excited he says to you, "I love you," but a few hours later he hates you. One tells you a story in which there is one percent of truth. Usually truth is used in this sphere to cheat people.

Crystallization exists in the sixth sphere. Crystallization is a phenomenon in which a thoughtform is condensed to such a degree by the will of groups of people that the mental sphere faces a hard time to dissolve it or recycle it. Such crystallizations serve as blocking barriers for the incoming creative energies.

Fanaticism feeds itself from the forces of the sixth sphere. Those who enter into this sphere without protection turn into the slaves of crystallized thoughtforms. These are not necessarily bad thoughts, but they are obsolete and they prevent mental and spiritual growth.

The thought world includes all these spheres around our planet.

In these spheres are accumulated all human thought, and they form layers according to their frequency, intensity, and accuracy. These spheres are in an ever-changing, ever-rearranging condition, decay, and growth. The lower parts of the spheres close to earth are in continuous decomposition; the higher parts are in increasing tensity and increasing brilliance. Between these two extremes exist many layers in continuous rearrangement and change.

Every thought that is conceived in our mind is instantaneously registered in these spheres. In a sense, these spheres are the filing system of Nature for human thoughts.

Thoughts are of different qualities:

1. We have particles of decaying thoughts.

2. We have transient thoughts.

3. We have short-lived thoughts.

4. We have long-living thoughts.

5. We have everlasting thoughts.

1. **Decaying thoughts** create momentary reactions. They are thoughts of sex, food, killing, crimes, money, possessions, etc.

2. **Transient thoughts** are reflections of the personality thoughts of others. They are related to physical or emotional interests. They change according to the moods and durations of one's needs.

3. **Short-lived thoughts** are thoughts which have little truth or fact; they are largely imagination or fabrication.

4. **Long-living thoughts** are those thoughts which are related to the welfare of humanity, have a strong charge of love and factuality in them, and are related to the Plan of the Hierarchy.

5. **Everlasting thoughts** are those thoughts which are related to the Purpose and embody the Will of the Life behind our solar system.

Every human being has an antenna. The antenna is the sensitivity of the mental body which eventually becomes a line, a bridge, a rainbow penetrating the mental sphere.

Whenever we think, we are in contact with one of these layers. If our antenna extends only to the seventh layer, we are victims of the seventh layer. We continuously channel these decaying, criminal thoughts which create malice, slander, lies, and hypocrisy.

Decaying thoughts carry infection, disease, disorders, and confusion. They do not have principles. Decaying thoughts are the cause of our many sicknesses, wars, and crimes. Anyone engaged in this layer becomes the slave of this sphere.

When our antenna extends more, it penetrates into the sphere of transient thoughts. Transient thoughts are like billions of light-bubbles which sparkle and pass away. They create short-lived urges and drives and actions.

Short-lived thoughts form a sphere where live those entities who did not develop their thinking power but began to think under the pressure of pain, suffering, and need. The thoughts from this sphere help us very little because they only satisfy us for a short while and then escape our attention.

Average humanity is in contact with this sphere, which is the second largest of the spheres.

Long-living thoughts are the thoughts of thinkers, philosophers, artists, and scientists. If our antenna penetrates to this sphere, we come in contact with strong currents of thought according to our frequency.

Many entities who live in the subjective world channel such kinds of thoughts to their relatives and friends to help them. We also can draw them to ourselves if we create enough magnetism by thinking similar thoughts. With one thought we can key in and draw unending thoughts from this layer because this layer has continuity and integrity and is systematized properly. This layer reflects the Hierarchical Plan for humanity, and those who think in relation to the Hierarchical Plan contribute to this layer, enrich it, and make it a better reference library, useful for a long time.

Everlasting thoughts originate from Solar Sources. They last one scheme of evolution, or throughout seven chains.

Arhats and Manus carry and utilize such thoughts. Sometimes They are called "Lights from Infinity." They are related to the seven Races, the seven globes, and the seven chains.[1]

Everlasting thoughts are very difficult to reach. They form a sphere of impenetrable light, and only fiery arrows can penetrate and bring back the jewels of wisdom and beauty. They are the pure thoughts.

Here you have the thoughts of Masters, Chohans, and Nirmanakayas. Once you penetrate into this sphere, you are an unending source of creativity. You can work your way to the highest sphere if you learn how to meditate, study, and serve.

As our consciousness nourishes itself from lower spheres, we perpetuate war, hatred, greed, jealousy, fear, and anger. As we live in lower spheres, we contaminate our bodies and create various disorders in them. Our friendships are not stable. Lies and hypocrisy rule. Exploitation and totalitarianism rule.

The seventh, sixth, and fifth spheres are called the spheres of ever-changing fluctuations because people in these three spheres go back and forth hundreds of times daily. People who can function mentally only within these three spheres are fluctuating lights which jump up and down in one of these spheres, controlled by outer circumstances.

It is possible to start building a path of consciousness, the Golden Bridge, which can extend from the center of the brain toward the fifth sphere and beyond. In such a case man can be on all spheres, but he stays focused in the higher spheres. He can bring greater purpose and greater plan toward the lower planes and open certain opportunities for people to come out of their dark and misty corners and enter into greater light.

This bridge is built by all our efforts and striving toward the future.

In the Ageless Wisdom the subtle bodies are called "robes," and we are told that people with unclean robes or contaminated robes cannot enter into the Subtle

---

1. For more information, see *Cosmos in Man*, Ch.1, and *Other Worlds*, Ch.59.

Worlds. For example, if one wants to attend meetings held on the higher mental plane, one must have a clean mental body, a healthy and radiating mental body.

Our mental body can be clean and healthy if it is not contaminated by separatism, illusions, lies, hypocrisy, and wrong motives but is nourished by Beauty, Goodness, Truth, and right, selfless motives.

We are told that in subjective flights we suffer deeply if we have defective bodies. Every vice is a wound in the subtle body. The purer the bodies, the higher they can fly in the subjective world.

Many mental, emotional, and etheric sicknesses occur when we force ourselves to visit areas or spheres which are fiery without having pure and clean bodies. If a boat has holes in its hull, it will be in danger in the ocean. If an airplane has a defect, it will be disastrous to fly with it. Similarly, if your subtle bodies are not up-to-date, they remain tied or parked on the shore.

There are many dangers in the Subtle World. Usually for a long time a Guide takes us through fiery spheres, protecting us with his aura.

There are dangers from electric storms and violent attacks by dark forces. There are streams of powerful energies, and one must know how to navigate in such conditions. The pure mental body is equipped with its power to protect itself and with its compass to find its own way.

It is the thought that molds the life of the modern man. If his thoughts are earthly, his life will be earthbound. If his thoughts are spiritual, his life will be sky-bound. There is also a state which fluctuates between these two directions.

Our urges and drives, our feelings, desires, and aspirations attract the substance we want and build our lives, but thought is the most effective builder. Thought can correct past mistakes and transform a life dedicated to corruption. It can build a new structure worthy for evolution. It is thought that can keep pace with the motion of evolution.

The thoughts found in the third, fourth, and fifth spheres are the three kinds of *actual* thought:

1. There are thoughts created as a reaction or response to the demands of life. These thoughts originate from the lower mind and are short-lived.

2. There are long-living thoughts. These thoughts are created by the higher mind as the response to the evolutionary waves in the Universe. These are the abstract thoughts which can come into objectivity through the lower mind. These are called higher thoughts.

3. There are everlasting thoughts. These thoughts are created by the heart. These thoughts are in harmony with the Cosmic Heart. They are charged with the fire of Intuition and reflect the vision of Cosmic directives. These are called pure thoughts.

These three kinds of thoughts exist in the mental sphere, making it either a dark cloud or a translucent sphere of color and beauty.

In forming our life, our culture, and our civilization, we use these thoughts. If our life, culture, and civilization are built of lower thoughts, the waves of space cyclically wipe them away. If they are built of higher thoughts, they last for thousands of years, and man can continuously introduce new changes in them without destruction, pain, and suffering. If our life, culture, and civilization are built of thoughts from the heart, they last for great cycles and are used as a collective path to lead us toward spiritual achievements and unfoldments.

Our life, culture, and civilization as a whole is a mixture of all these currents of thoughts. This is why we have simultaneous destruction, construction, and creativity.

Things built of lower thoughts must be destroyed. Things built of higher thoughts must be remodeled and reconstructed. Things built of thoughts from the heart will manifest as a perpetual source of creativity.

Lower thoughts

1. are earthbound

2. are discriminative

3. are separative

4. are selfish

5. create attachments and identification

6. are repulsive

7. are fanatical

8. are conservative

9. are self-destructive

10. are aggressive

11. are full of vanity and showing-off

12. are past-oriented

These are the seeds which eventually serve to destroy the things built by the lower thoughts.

Higher thoughts

1. are sky-bound

2. are analytical and deductive

    3. build relationships

    4. are group conscious

    5. create detachment and freedom

    6. are attractive and magnetic

    7. are tolerant

    8. are progressive

    9. are self-actualizing

   10. are challenging

   11. are full of joy and the spirit of sharing

   12. alternate between past and future

Thoughts of the heart

    1. are Cosmos-bound

    2. are synthesizing

    3. are holistic

    4. are compassionate

    5. are liberating

    6. are electrical

    7. are all-understanding

    8. are ever-expanding

    9. are self-creative

   10. are enlightening

   11. are full of bliss, serenity, and beauty

   12. see the vision of the future in any moment of life

If we want a new life, a new culture, a new civilization, we have to change the way we think. Unless we change our thinking we cannot change our life. It is only the thought that can create a better future for us. Our future incarnations are our present thoughts.

Through our present thoughts, inspired by a future vision, we can build our physical, emotional, and mental life on a new foundation. It is very important that we deal with our thoughts scientifically and build our future on a plan, with a purpose, in such a way that in our future incarnations we have greater opportunities to enjoy life and have greater penetration into the Cosmic Life.

It is possible that with right, honest thoughts we can change our physical body in a few years. We can change our emotional equipment in a few years, and we can change the whole construction of our mental mechanism in a few years, adapting it to more inclusive, creative ideas and visions.

One must know that he can think differently. This is the key. You have power over your creative thought. Use it! Exercise that power without falling into the grooves of the past in which the wheels of your thoughts used to spin.

Make people think in new ways that are more time-saving, health-saving, and pain-saving. Teach them how to observe and see. Teach them how to study. Teach them how to strive toward the future, toward higher states of awareness and beingness.

As you learn how to think in your heart, you begin to learn also how to control the mechanicalness of your body, emotions, and mind.

If you do not think, your mechanism begins to control you. There is no worse situation than the situation in which man is controlled by his mechanism.

Your etheric, astral, and mental centers are automatic response apparatuses. They are impressed every moment, and they react every moment. People are learning how to control your life by controlling your etheric, astral, and mental centers. To avoid such a danger you must learn about your thoughts; you must know how to think. It is through right thinking that eventually you take under your control these ever-sensitive centers and switch them off or on as required by you.

When these centers are under your control, you have under your control your physical life and the urges and drives of your body. You have under your control your emotional life and the desires, glamors, and aspirations of your astral body. You have under your control your mental life and its illusions, directions, and thought-building power.

Uncontrolled centers continuously leak and waste energy — etheric, astral, and mental energy. Leakage over the years makes the bodies vulnerable, and sickness and diseases build their nests within the three bodies. The Ancients used to say that a castle must always be under watch so as not to allow intruders to enter.

One must learn in a practical way how to stop the mechanical functioning of the centers. This is done by pure thinking. Pure thinking can immediately turn the direction of the centers and redirect them for goal-fitting action.

For example, if the body wants a bottle of whiskey, the mind must be able to stop that craving which is the result of a center which runs by itself under the impact of outer stimuli.

In another example, suppose you go to bed and are starting to fall asleep when suddenly you hear a young boy or girl laughing or singing outside of your home. If the certain center of your emotional or etheric body is not under control, through the law of association you begin to imagine the girl or her body. Then a romance starts, and eventually you find yourself imaginatively involved with the person.

A pure thought can immediately stop such an engagement of gears and direct your attention to higher realms.

Your physical, emotional, and mental automatic reactions can be controlled through planning, creative imagination, and visualization. These are three tools of the mind by which thought controls the lower man.

These three methods are very important: planning, creative imagination, and visualization. Pure thought can use these three techniques to master the physical life, the emotional life, and the mental life.

Planning stops the leakage on the physical-etheric plane. Creative imagination stops the leakage on the astral plane. Visualization stops the leakage on the mental plane.

These three techniques are used by pure thought to transform the overall man in manifestation. Pure thought rearranges things, purifies accumulations of a negative kind, and burns the hindrances and obstacles within the centers.

Many people may be surprised when they realize that thought is higher than the mind. We usually say that the mind thinks and thoughts come into being, whereas there is a different story. The mind provides quality and substance to thoughts. Thoughts are radiations of the human soul or of the Transpersonal Self.

The mind cannot think; the mind reflects the thoughts and contains the thoughts, but it is not the originator of thoughts.

The Thinker is the Transpersonal Self within us until the human soul learns how to think. This does not mean that before the human soul learns how to think our personality thoughts are of higher order. The personality mostly operates by adapting, reacting, or responding to the thoughts of the environment or to the thoughts imparted by education, tradition, and through other ways of communication. The Transpersonal Self's thoughts are Its radiations, and only in rare cases do these radiations penetrate into the personality.

When the human soul starts to emancipate himself from the domination of the personality, he begins to think. When the human soul projects energy to the mental body, energy takes form. That is what thought is.

For a long period of time, the human soul increasingly thinks within the thoughts of the Transpersonal Self until he realizes that the thoughts of his Transpersonal Self and his thoughts must be in harmony and in fusion. After such a fusion, the human soul begins to think his own thoughts according to the path he chooses to take. Of course, after the human soul begins to think, his thoughts are then influenced by the dynamic thoughts of the Hierarchy, later by the thoughts of Shamballa, and later by the thoughts of higher and higher Centers.

As his thinking rises higher, he becomes a more potent source of creativity, a more potent source of reconstructiveness, and thus he prepares himself to be a co-worker with the forces of the Universe.

In these three different dimensions, the human soul can harvest different fruits and find different ways to use thoughts. Thus when he acts as the personality, he helps the personality to grow and he himself learns how to operate in the personality with soul thoughts. When he acts as a soul, he learns how and when to transmit vision, inspiration, and ideas to the personality to have better results. When he acts as the eternal Self, he conditions himself to be open for future development and progress.

It is possible that the human soul observes the created thoughts through three dimensions. For example, the human soul projects energy, visions, and ideas into the mind, and the mind begins to operate and build formations to reflect these visions and ideas. After such a formation the human soul can study and use them

1. as if he were the personality

2. as if he were the soul

3. as if he were the eternal Self

There is a yoga which is called Agni Yoga, or union through fire. This yoga has three stages.

The first stage is achieved when one really masters his thoughts, his mental vehicle, and his mind. The second stage is achieved when he penetrates into the Spiritual Triad, which is an intense sphere of fire. The third stage is achieved when he enters into the flame. Such a man is called a true Agni Yogi.

As the yogi goes through one fire to a higher one, he establishes greater fusion with the Fire of Space. The Fire of Space is an all-healing, all-purifying fire, and it is the fire which connects man with higher sources. Thus the yogi becomes the messenger of the Higher Worlds, of the future.

One must not forget that Space, especially the higher strata, is the treasury of thoughts. In these thoughts are condensed great formulas of light, love, and leadership. In these thoughts are condensed great creative ideas for the liberation of humanity. In these thoughts are condensed the future bridges toward Higher Worlds.

It is not only possible to tune in to these thoughts but also to absorb them into our mental sphere during our fiery flights. Thus during sleep or deep meditation one can enrich his wisdom and improve the life of the planet. But higher spheres are not easy to penetrate due to the condensed layers of evil thoughts accumulated in the lower strata. They build thick walls between man and the treasury of wisdom.

The earth is surrounded with this strata of evil thought which repel the rays emanating from higher spheres. It is these rays that bring inspiration and direction toward the future and Infinity and keep the planet in balance.

The strata of dark thoughts can be dispersed with the thoughts of Beauty, Goodness, and Truth which let the rays penetrate into the earth. When the rays are reflected back by the strata of dark thoughts, the subterranean fires rush to the surface and disturb the balance of the earth, causing various forms of natural calamities.

You can rebuild yourself practically by polarizing your thoughts toward the direction of your future.

If you want to be healthy, do not do things against the laws of health. This is such a simple statement. Observe the laws of health on physical, emotional, and mental levels.

Momentary, short-range happiness and good feelings do not mean health. You can be healthy for one day but sick for months. You can be healthy for a year but sick for the rest of your life. You can be healthy for one life but sick for many, many lives. The seeds of sickness germinate in different lives, in different climates and conditions, so do not be happy that you have escaped pain and suffering in living a life against the laws of health.

One must be guided from childhood to observe the laws of health, and one must know that the laws of health, when observed, help you forever in eternity. One must make the world beautiful to enjoy it in the next life, as one makes his home beautiful to enjoy it in this life.

We are told that thought is the key to all locks. Christ spoke the same language when He said, "Search and you will find, knock and it will be opened for you, ask and it will be given to you."

This means that nothing is impossible for a man if he learns how to live, how to think, how to will. So if one thinks accurately, clearly, spiritually, and in harmony with the thought currents of Cosmic creativity, he will be able to contact higher realms of possibilities and manifest these possibilities in the objective world.

High-order thought is selfless, ever-progressive, universal, all-embracing, and for the Common Good. When one strives along these lines, deeper layers of the thought world open for him. But if his thoughts become separative, selfish, and serve only the body, its urges and drives, glamors, vanities, and illusions, he closes his path of progress with his own hands.

You are equal to your creation. The higher your creativity, the higher you are. Man cannot create a condition that is higher than that of which he is worthy. The life we have is our own creation, the result of our own reactions and responses to the world around us. To change the life we need to change our beingness, our thoughts, and our actions.

As one penetrates higher spheres he becomes healthier, more radiant, creative, and dependable. As one goes down to lower spheres he becomes weaker and full of diseases.

Those who are wasting their time wandering in lower spheres are building for themselves such a barrier, such a crystallization in their aura and in their nature that they will need many thousands of years to make a breakthrough to get out of the muddy spheres. The goal of a human being is to ascend higher and higher and then transcend the mental sphere and penetrate into the greater light of the world of Intuition.

In the world of Intuition there is no consciousness but only awareness. Thus, illumination is a steady penetration into higher spheres of light, during which the human soul manifests greater radioactivity.

The survival of humanity depends upon the expansion of the higher spheres around our planet and the contraction of the inner spheres. If number seven is expanding and covering more space than the third, second, or first one, our civilization is in danger.

We are told that in Atlantean times the seventh (lowest) sphere grew and expanded so much that the other spheres became almost non-existent, and almost the entire continent of Atlantis sank into the ocean.

In the lowest sphere there are crime, syphilis, gonorrhea, and all other sicknesses. Of course, one needs love, but why make love in a trash can and not in a palace?

One must know from where his inspiration reaches him. He must know the controlling sources of his life. If you nourish yourself from higher spheres, you will be healthier.

If anyone wants to change the quality of his life, he must change the quality of his thought. If one wants to change the level of his life, he must change the level of his thoughts.

This must be done practically in our daily life. Every day we have opportunities to redirect our deeds, actions, emotions, and thoughts. For example, when planning to do something, first think. If it does not increase Beauty, Goodness, Truth, Joy, and health, plan something else.

If you are feeling a certain way, try to redirect that feeling with good aspirations and goodwill. If you are thinking negatively or destructively, stop it and try to think constructively, selflessly, and inclusively.

Our greatest victory is won through daily battles and daily achievements. Once we learn to control our thoughts, we are on the royal path to our throne.

Remember that thoughts are everywhere. Every time you identify with your own thought as if no higher thoughts can be found, every time you make your thought your own standard, you imprison yourself within your thought and then the thought uses you instead of you using the thought.

My father once said that we drink from rivers but not from lakes. Stagnated minds cannot vitalize our system; we need ever-flowing rivers of striving thoughts, every wave of which brings health, happiness, unity, joy, and enlightenment.

You can also recycle your thoughts. For example, if you find yourself thinking silly, negative, or criminal thoughts, immediately close your eyes and imagine three hundred people in front of you and try to give them a lecture on Beauty, Goodness, Truth, Joy, gratitude, courage, striving, etc. You will see how it is possible to recycle the dirty waters of your mind and produce the clear water of creative energy.

A great Sage suggests that we can transcend ourselves by directing our thought-eyes toward Cosmos.

Cosmos is organized manifestation. It is integration, a system, an organism; it is not chaos, which means disorderliness, anarchy, decay. Cosmos is a growing symphony. Cosmos has rhythm and harmony. In each part of the Cosmos one feels the pulsation of the Cosmic Heart.

It is very interesting to realize that Cosmos does not exist if that Cosmos cannot be reflected in the mirror of your awareness. Cosmos exists only if you can register it with understanding. The greater your awareness, the greater is Cosmos for you. A limited consciousness cannot sense the Cosmos because it is busy with its own separative self and interests. Cosmos exists only within a Cosmos. Cosmos exists only when you are aware of it and when you deepen your awareness of Cosmos in your heart, when you tune your heart with the Heart of Cosmos.

Thus, when your consciousness expands, when your awareness expands, when your communication and contact with the existence expand, when your Self-actualization expands, you have an expanding Cosmos. But if your consciousness or awareness is contracting, then you have finally come to a state of consciousness where everything is chaos for you and your life becomes chaotic.

We have three stages of registering the Cosmos:

1. Through our consciousness

2. Through our awareness

3. Through our identification

Consciousness only registers things through the mental plane. Awareness is registration through the Intuitional and Atmic Planes. Identification is not registration but fusion, unification, and beingness. It is in this last level that the Cosmos is understood in its highest beauty.

Thoughts can be on the level of consciousness, on the level of awareness, and on the level of identification.

As we direct our thoughts toward the Cosmos, we expand our consciousness in gradually contacting more of the Cosmos; we expand our awareness in contacting subtle layers of Cosmos, and eventually when we identify ourselves with the Cosmos, we become Cosmic.

The area which your consciousness covers is your Cosmos. Through being the area which your awareness covers, you expand your beingness. Through identifying your True Self with the Cosmic Whole, you transcend your existence and become a conscious part of Cosmos.

Try to expand your beingness over the area of which you are aware, and try to be that with which you are identified.

Note that awareness is related to your higher planes.

Once a man asked where the door to Cosmos is. The door to Cosmos is the ability to see in all human eyes the existence of Cosmos. One cannot be allowed to penetrate into the beauty of Cosmos until he begins to recognize the Cosmic Self existing in each human being. This is the only door. If you live according to the realization, according to the awareness that the Cosmic Self exists in each human being and in you, you can open the door toward Cosmos.

You are that *key* and others are the *door*. In each door you must see the Cosmos, and each door can be opened by the realization of Cosmos within you.

The realization of Cosmos is the realization of your True Self. The realization of Cosmos is the realization of your True Self existing in other Selves. This is how the doors of the Cosmos are opened.

This realization should not be a theory or wishful thinking but a practical manifestation in all your relationships, plans, and decisions.

There are three stages in which your thoughts must function:

1. I am a Self.

2. I am one with the Self of the other human beings.

3. I am one with the Infinite Self of Cosmos.

The first stage is not enough and actually does not exist without the realization of the second stage, but the first and second stage must culminate in the third stage if Cosmic realization is to be achieved.

Cosmic realization is the birth of the spirit, and it is only fiery thoughts that can express such a state through symbols and inspirations.

26

Thought Upliftment

People who have a strong imagination can create a sphere of agony for themselves when fear controls their imagination. Once the imagination is built, the thoughtforms of fear accumulate in it through association.

Thoughtforms of fear are created within our aura every time we do something doubtful and feel insecure or when we see something wrong in others and identify with it. These thoughtforms stand inactive for a time because of the neutralizing effects of certain logic. They can become active all together when an imagination starts to form under the influence of an event or attack. It is possible that this imagination even attracts the similar fears that certain people have and turns them into a huge thoughtform.

To smash such a thoughtform and release the mind for its proper function to solve problems, you can use the following methods:

1. Visualize events of beauty, victory, and joy. Such thoughtforms have the capacity to destroy accumulated thoughtforms of imagination.

2. Evoke your Inner Guide and ask It to release Its radiation and disperse your fear. You can visualize the Inner Guide as a sphere of blue light with shades of violet which you enter and find refuge.

Sometimes it is possible that through inheritance we have an aura sensitive to fear. If our mother passed through cycles of fear during the time of pregnancy, this fear penetrates into our genes and affects our sensitivity to fears of similar quality.

3. Invoke the help of a great Being, your Master, or Christ. This is the third method to overcome fear. This kind of help can be evoked in the spirit of renunciation by making a solemn pledge to stand and live in light and for the progress and upliftment of humanity. This can be done through prayers, invocations, and pilgrimages to holy places with a firm decision to leave the past behind.

4. Fear is also dispelled by helping others overcome their fears and receiving the waves of their gratitude and joy.

5. Another method to weaken fear is to face it and find the real power it has over you. See that it is related to time and cannot be permanent. Two years later it may not even exist; in ten years no trace of it will be left.

Fear exists in time and is related mostly to our body, ego, and possessions. Fear helps us confront the factuality of these three factors and release ourselves from their domination.

Freedom from fear can be achieved when, through battle against fear, we gain victory over it. In such cases the accumulated clouds of fear turn into a precipitation of wisdom and vanish.

6. The sixth method is to be careful not to use our knowledge and power without compassion. Every time we use our knowledge and power without compassion, we absorb the fear waves of others which we create in them. Such imported fear can stick in our aura for a long time and may grow and multiply, preparing a strong attack on our body and mind.

Fear created in others spreads roots in our being. Fearlessness develops in us as we try to eliminate any action which causes fear in others. The fear we create in others may associate with us when we are trapped in similar fears.

7. Reading the Teaching of Great Ones creates a magnetic field in our aura. This is not mysticism but science. When our thoughts are electrically fused with the thoughts, visions, and revelations of a Great One, a current of energy from the sphere of His thought is created and accumulated in our aura, purifying, transforming, and sublimating it, and expanding the field of its radiation.

It does not matter when His words were pronounced. Higher thoughts of the Great Ones are like an electrical network which persists for ages around the globe. One can tune in or key in with such an electrical sphere just by reading Their words with concentration, with faith, and with heart. As one focuses his whole being in greater concentration within the ideas of the words, greater becomes the flow of energy into his aura.

8. During the inner and outer conflict and battle, you can also raise yourself up above the clouds by reading the life stories of great leaders, their words, and philosophies. In reading about their lives and words, you evoke the rays of courage, fearlessness, and daring hidden or imprisoned in you. Once these rays are released, they attract victorious thoughts from space that strengthen the aura and gradually break the thoughtforms of fear and failure. They also dispel the dark plans floating around the heads of adversaries.

9. The next method to overcome fear is to develop "divine indifference," a psychology of "so what," by affirming to ourselves that our Inner Core cannot be destroyed by any event, and that time after time it will gain its victory over all conditions which breed fear.

Sometimes imaginative fear is a method of self-punishment through which your inner conscience tries to clear the polluted atmosphere by letting you feel and know the possible effects of your actions.

When you are able to stand above even your faults and keep your consciousness in divine indifference, the clouds of fear do their job and then vanish.

The following mantram is a powerful means to release you from fear, if you sound it with all the concentration of your heart:

> *May the Sun*
> *within my heart*
> *dispel all my fears,*
> *and may I radiate*
> *love, beauty, and joy.*

27

The Enlightened Mind

It is interesting that once the mind is enlightened by the light of Intuition it cannot contain any thoughtforms which are against the principles that enlightenment reveals. Any thoughtform that does not fit in the harmony of an enlightened mind is rejected automatically and without any effort.

A purified or enlightened mind is like a clear day in which the sun shines. This is just like a musician who detects any wrong note in his music and corrects it, or who immediately knows if his piano is out of tune. In the same manner, a purified mind rejects any false, misleading, or degenerated idea or thought and keeps itself in light.

If our mental plane or mental body is not enlightened by the light of the Inner Guide or by the light of Intuition, it can turn into a reservoir of illusions and pollute all our thoughtforms or creative works with these illusions and impurities.

The mental body reaches enlightenment if its substance is transmuted, transformed, and transfigured through observation, detachment, discrimination, discipline, and silence. A purified mind enables the owner of the body, emotions, and mind to have control of his mechanism. It is interesting to note that, in most cases, it is not we who control our life but other factors.

For example, it may be a fear that is controlling us during most of our actions, emotions, and thoughts all the day. It may be excitement, expectation, an interest, or a little pain in our body. It may be hatred, vanity, or pride, or it may be a memory of a loss.

You are going to find out what controls you. It may be a great vision, a great service, a great love, an idea, a plan. When your mind is really purified, you will not even be controlled by all the above things but you will control them. You will be your own master and say, "This idea is good. This vision is good, but I do not want it to obsess me, possess me, and make me a slave of it."

Fanaticism can also be a phenomenon of an obsession with good ideas or good visions. No matter how high your ideas and visions are, you still hurt people and create rejection because of your fanaticism. One thing sane people do not like is to be the slaves of anything. Slavery creates rejection.

You can ask yourself, "What controlled me today and what caused me to be active, to have certain feelings and to produce certain thoughts?" It is interesting that you often see that *you*, the most important factor in the game of life, were absent, and outer and inner factors were controlling your mechanism without your approval.

Our intention is to reach a certain degree of control and mastery over our nature, and the road to reach it is purification and illumination of the mind. Once the mind is purified and enlightened, you can drive your own car. You can use the mind and make it drive you wherever you want to go. But it is very interesting to note that we are pulled by a Cosmic Magnet to walk on the path of perfection. We can see this in all our actions for improvement.

Life is set in a way that you cannot enjoy life and be successful unless you improve yourself, and there is no end to improvement. Improvement takes you to the road of perfection, where you consciously choose the most essential goal and proceed toward that goal.

On the road to your goal you may decide to change your goal. This is possible. Also, you change your goal when you reach it and find out that it does not satisfy you. Actually, even if you are working for an unworthy goal, when you reach that goal you will be so developed that suddenly you will see the unworthiness of it and choose a new one. This is why many hotheaded people, blinded by their ideology, turn against their destination when they reach it and live a new life. One of the historic examples was Saul, who became Paul after he saw the futility of his goal.

We can see this in our daily pursuits. After we have things we want, they do not interest us anymore, or we even reject them.

The pursuit of any goal develops a man. It does not mean that he does not commit mistakes and involve people on the path to his unworthy goal; but when he reaches his goal, he very often realizes that it was not what he expected. This seldom happens if his mind is aberrated and enslaved by illusions and blinded by selfish motives, but all separative endeavors eventually lead into unity. If you see this principle working in the history of humanity, you will feel a little more optimistic for the future of humanity.

Reaching a goal not only sharpens your discrimination to choose a new and higher goal, but it also enriches your consciousness and improves your style of action, which means you do a better job in your new goal.

It is we who form our destination or goal. Our goal or destination is the result of our response to that great magnetic pull toward perfection. Our response is based upon and relative to our level, purity, and energy.

On any level we can have a goal. It can be physical, emotional, mental, spiritual, individual, racial, national, or global. Whatever it is, wherever it is, it is a moment of response to that magnetic pull of perfection that creates a goal or a destination in our life. Even our decisions are our goals.

If a mind is aberrated, which means that the mechanism is distorted to some degree on some level, this magnetic pull creates rejection instead of attraction, and the man works against the path of perfection or against the benefit of humanity and has negative decisions and negative goals.

This is why a healthy mind, a purified and enlightened mind, was the goal of great servers, great educators and leaders. Polarization toward the Will of the Almighty Power is possible only when the negative charge is eliminated from the mind.

This magnetic pull is registered first on the instinctual level, then slowly on conscious levels, and eventually on the intuitional level. As we register it on higher and higher levels, our response to it is firmer, more sacrificial, more conscious, more inclusive, and more selfless. Our path is more direct, with the least waste of energy and time and matter.

Our striving toward a worthy goal develops our centers and senses and unfolds dormant potentials of our soul. All cultures and civilizations are the result of collective strivings and achieved goals. However, all our past achievements must not lead us to passive satisfaction. It is only through dissatisfaction that we surpass our achievements and choose new goals. Dissatisfaction is a feeling which comes into being when we begin to respond to a higher pull of a deeper awareness of new values.

We eat our food, or reach our goal on the surface or lower planes, and then we look for our food on higher levels. To survive we eventually make our neck longer, like giraffes, so that we can eat in the trees. If we search long enough for higher food, higher goals, we will never again be tempted by the surface food, the lower goals.

Even if we do not achieve our goals, our striving prevents us from falling into a lower level of life; and the fiery aspiration with which we are striving burns in us many obstacles and causes a great deal of transmutation in our vehicles.

Our stage of achievement and spiritual realization must be proven by the quality of the service we render to humanity. This is our certificate and diploma on the path of perfection. Man is as great as his service.

Our seven centers in our etheric body are related to our seven ductless glands and to seven states of consciousness. Wherever a complication exists in our consciousness, it reflects in the corresponding center, in the corresponding gland, and in the corresponding organ in our body. Thus, some of our organs do not receive a direct charge from our Soul because of distortions or complications in our consciousness. Lower complications are the result of the complications coming from the next higher level. Often we cannot see this, but even in the case of an accident it is because of a higher cause or subjective cause.

If we have a physical problem, it is coming from astral or mental levels. If it is on the mental plane, the cause is from a higher plane which, because of the distortion in the mind, is creating problems. This is why even some pure Teaching, a great vision, or a revelation may drive a man into the asylum. The distortion pre-existed in his consciousness or mind.

Immortality is the result of the alignment, integration, and harmony of our personality vehicles with the source of fiery life which is our True Self.

We are dying because we have aberrations in our personality vehicles. Death is not a natural process, as people think. It is the most unnatural thing ever expected to exist in the Universe. I am not referring here to the physical vehicles. One does not need to hang on to his body to be immortal. Immortality is the continuity of consciousness through a series of incarnations and disincarnations.

True immortality is transmutation of the vehicles to such a degree that they can serve in any frequency or in any tension. This is called the process of spiritualization of matter, or the transmutation of matter into energy. We are told that Christ and a few of His great disciples achieved such a perfection and became immortal.

Our planetary Hierarchy is formed of such Immortals Who, age after age, appeared and disappeared, leaving a great culture behind Them.

The first human races were immortal. We broke a great law in the Universe and were turned into mortals. We will never reach immortality through all our medical help and hospitals or religious teachers but only through aligning ourselves with the Source of Life within us and within the solar system and through living a life of true virtue, love, and sacrifice.

For example, we break the Law of Unity or Love. How many millions of times do we break this law with our hatreds, jealousies, lies, exploitations, wars, distortions, separative thinking and action, criticism, and intolerance? These violations of the Law of Love are creating greater and greater obstacles to achieving our natural state of immortality. Any violation of the Law of Love makes it more difficult for us to tune to the Source of Life within us and in Nature.

All our violations of the Law of Love are accumulating in space or in the electromagnetic force field of Nature. These accumulations manifest as explosions which create dire effects on the planet and on the living cells of our vehicles, making it difficult for them to receive life energy and grow in life. Our transgressions accumulate in our higher sphere and create tensions and complications which eventually manifest as mental, emotional, and physical disorders or diseases.

People think that because in essence we are indestructible, we are immortal in every way. This is not correct. Immortality is continuity of consciousness. If a man becomes unconscious every time he takes off his jacket and does not remember what he did during the time he was not wearing the jacket, he does not have continuity of consciousness and is not yet immortal. Immortality is awareness of our continuity.

We must remember that life is progressing continuously, but if we are not progressing at the same pace we are creating friction and complications.

Suppose we are tied to a carriage and the carriage is going fifteen miles per hour, but we can only go ten miles per hour. In this case we are pulling the car backward and it is pulling us forward until we get exhausted. This is the case with our solar system. If the Solar Life is progressing faster than we are, then we are going to have unending and increasing problems. If we synchronize our speed with the speed of that great Life, we will have no friction or complications but only a steady flight toward greater achievement to catch another train faster than the previous one.

To synchronize our speed with the speed of life, we must increase our inclusiveness, purity, wisdom, and service, master the vehicles, and be the Self. This is the Path: to reach the Self, the True Self, actualization. Learning is not enough if there is no realization. Learning and knowledge can even be great obstacles which cannot be surmounted in a given cycle of time.

Each cycle has its own requirement. Physical development was the major concern in previous ages; then the major interest was emotional purification; then mental development. Now it is the intuitional cycle, but still many millions of people are sex-bound, solar plexus-bound, or totally occupied with their emotions or traditions or ideologies. All these delays will create great problems because a delay is the result of a wrong action, and a wrong action is the increase of your debts which sooner or later you must pay.

When a group or nation is a few cycles behind, it becomes a problem for those who are far ahead and almost in harmony with the speed of evolution. The speed of evolution is demonstrated to us in every age by those Great Ones who proved it with Their great achievements. In every age a Great One sounds the keynote and stands in front of humanity as an example of the achievement of the future in that age. This is why a disciple of Christ emphasized that we "become perfect men according to the measure of the statue of the fullness of Christ."[1]

In each age the achievement will be higher because the vision will be higher. Those who are not responding to or maintaining the right speed to manifest the standard of achievement of the age will create problems for the rest. That is why the progress of advanced ones is based on their sacrifice and service for those who are left behind in their understanding, labor, and striving.

Those who are not responding to the keynote of the new cycle will have greater difficulties with their physical, emotional, and mental natures and provide great tests for those who are ahead of them.

One day a psychiatrist, who was a friend of mine, came to see me with a confession. He said he had enough money to last a few lives, a very charming wife and beautiful children, social position, and the respect of many, but there was no joy in his heart and he often wanted to commit suicide. He was very sincere and serious.

I said, "Maybe your patients drained you and caused depression in you. What about if you take a quiet, beautiful vacation on some island?"

"I did, but there is something deeper."

I thought maybe he had some hidden guilt complex, but there was nothing of that sort. Then he enlightened me about his situation with a question, "Why are you so happy under the pressures you are passing?"

His problem dawned in my mind.

"You know," I said, "you are suffering from malnutrition."

"What do you mean?"

_____

1. Ephesians 4:13

"I mean that you need better food, stronger vitamins. . . ."

"Don't joke with me, please," he said. "I am serious."

"I am, too."

"But I am eating the best food possible. What do you mean?"

"I am not referring to your physical food. I am referring to your spiritual food. You are feeding only one part of your nature; the other part is starving."

"Which part are you talking about?"

"Your soul is starving. . . ."

Then I went to my library and brought the *Bhagavad Gita* and said, "Eat this."

"You're crazy," he said.

"Eat it."

And he laughed and laughed, in spite of my seriousness.

He took the book and went away. One week later, he called me and said, "Do you have other food?"

"Did you eat it?"

"Not totally yet, but I am so happy. Something in my nature is increasing in joy and bliss, and I started to meditate."

Our knowledge is not enough. Our occupation is not enough. We must feed our higher bodies with greater visions, inspirations, and future.

Most of our psychological and psychosomatic diseases will evaporate when we reach our higher nature with lofty ideas and with the vision of the future because thus we will synchronize our steps with the speed of evolution and tune in with the life principle within Nature.

This is done through the technique of transmutation.

28

Thought Webs

Thoughts have a great effect on the sense organs, for example, hearing, sight, and others. When one is engaged in thought, he can insulate himself totally from the registration of the impressions from the outer world. One can also register them with one part of his mind and continue his thought with the other part of his mind.

Thus the mastery of thought can be cultivated and exercised. Later, one must extend the mastery to emotions and mechanical thoughts.

It is the time to study thought, not in philosophy and the humanities but in physics and chemistry. We must have scientific research on thought.

Thought currents are similar to electrical currents. They create colorful flashes when they clash or fuse. They travel through objects and accumulate in objects. They not only deliver messages, but in the meantime they also carry messages. This double activity is not rare.

Thoughts are considered to be forms, but they are actually rays or currents. They flow out from the source but do not separate from the source. Thus man lives in the area which his thoughts cover; man lives within the network of the thoughts he expresses.

The spider is a good example: Man lives in the webs he produces. All these webs carry his intentions out to space, but each thread also contacts other webs and carries messages to the central Core of man. Often these incoming currents are not consciously registered, but they are there.

Thinking is sometimes a process of tuning consciously to the incoming currents, and a process of translating them to make them fit the needs of life in general.

The webs that man creates become the patterns of his thoughts. He thinks within the borderlines of these webs.

Some people have a small web in their kitchen, bedroom, or office. Some people create their webs in outer space. Some webs are strong and tight; some are loose. Every web is a sensitive mechanism to communicate with spatial thought currents, and each has its own capacity for reception, according to the level of the source.

The webs of thought must continuously expand if a man does not want to be trapped by his own thoughts and if he wants to build webs of many dimensions, extended not only in the physical dimension but also in Higher Worlds. Only many-dimensional webs can give man the possibility of going beyond himself, of going beyond the patterns of his limited thinking.

In the thinking process there is a fact which is called "abandoning the former web." At some stage of our evolution we no longer allow ourselves to live within the borders of our tiny web. We cannot build upon it because it does not provide the possibilities for our vision. Hence we leave the web behind and begin to build a new web, with better engineering, with higher substance, and with greater insight and foresight to make it serviceable for our future adventures.

Our webs are sometimes used by other "spiders." Sometimes spatial electricity wipes them out. Sometimes they form a part of a thoughtform in space which is connected to millions of people.

Making a new web is sometimes like a new birth for a soul who chooses to renounce his former ways of thinking and live in higher and more inclusive dimensions. These webs are built just as, for example, our transportation system has been built from the stone age to the space age. They are gradually refined to meet the greater needs of man.

But just as the motive behind the mechanical system of transportation can be of various kinds, so it is with the formation of thought webs. It is the motive of the builder of the web that makes the web either a network of light, love, beauty, joy, and freedom or a network of crime, separatism, and destruction.

Higher webs scintillate with luminous colors and penetrate into the spheres of the auras of higher Beings. Dark webs stay around the globe and slowly build an iron chain around it.

The two main characteristics of webs are slavery and freedom.

Slavery is limitation of the possibility of expansion and freedom. Freedom is limitation of slavery; it is the process of continuous expansion toward higher dimensions.

Slavery is contraction into our selfish interests. Freedom is the process of sharing all that is light, love, and beauty with a gradually increasing number of people.

We must also remember that when the spider builds its web, it spends the substance contained in itself, and it needs to refill itself with new substance in order to continue to expand its web or build new ones. It is during the moments of "emptiness," when it is in a state of recharging itself or waiting for nourishment from its web, that dark forces can attack the "spider."

The more the "spider" thinks, the more he spends thought energy. Many thinkers feel moments of "vacuum" or "emptiness" and experience attacks of opposing forces. But we are told that immediately when the attack approaches the electrical field of the aura, the aura discharges a high voltage of fire, destroys the opposing current, and fills the reservoir of the "spider" with a new supply of psychic energy.

Sometimes man can see the flashes of thought like diamonds of various colors, like sparks of blue, orange, violet, and red. Sometimes the web appears in a flash. Such appearances pour a great amount of energy into our aura. Sometimes they clear our vision and expand its capacity to see more. These flashes are the moments of fusion with greater currents of energy, or the moments of destruction of a black thread woven in the network.

The many webs that a man creates in the various stages of his evolution are scattered in space. It is these webs that condition his future manifestation, his future personalities. Sometimes a giant is trapped by a web built ages ago. From higher planes one can see the network of conditions in which he must live. . . with the additional gained wisdom.

The recycling process is known in the thought world. It is possible to withdraw the network of our web and recycle it in the furnace of our new vision. But we must remember that it is not possible to control the influence of our thought web left on life in general.

Before one formulates his thoughts, he must think about the consequences of his thoughts. Ask, "What consequences can my thought produce? Can these consequences karmically limit my expansion into great usefulness now or in the future?"

It is known that even Great Ones still pay taxes for Their former thoughts. . . .

It is through our thoughts that we grow. . .or we decay. Wise Ones build Their thought webs between the shining stars and hear the melody of the Cosmic Winds.

29

Inclusive Thinking

It is important to know that meditation is the accumulation of fire. It is this fire that is used for creative action. Fire created through meditation not only causes transformation in the physical and astral bodies, but it also orchestrates the mental vehicle to such a degree that this vehicle becomes capable of traveling through the Fiery World in majestic beauty.

Those who build their mental vehicle with fiery elements can enjoy the entire creativity of the Fiery World, relating to it through the seven mental senses.

There are many inhabitants of the Fiery World who, like some inhabitants of the earth, do not have full ability to communicate with the life of the Fiery World. They exist and care for their existence only, without being capable of exposing themselves to the symphony of life in the Fiery World.

Each meditation, each creative thought, is a preparation for the future. One must grow physically to realize the existence of earth. One must also grow mentally to be fully conscious in the mental sphere. There are many steps for such a preparation.

One must develop his thoughts about the life of the physical plane. Then he must develop thinking in relation to the astral plane. Then he must develop thoughts about the mental sphere.

We must discriminate between thoughts that are physical, thoughts that are astral, and thoughts that are mental. Higher thoughts must lead the way.

Most of the thoughts of humanity are like horses serving the baboons of earthly and emotional interests. This must be reversed, joyfully or painfully. The lower planes are built to serve the higher planes, but the perversion and insanity of human beings created a reverse procedure. Whenever the king begins to satisfy the vices of average people, the kingdom falls. Whenever thought is prostituted to lower urges and drives and used to satisfy them, the entire structure of evolution cracks, and degeneration begins.

People have the notion that man is advanced because he can create spaceships. The real value of thought is not in the form it creates. *The real value of thought is in how and for what purpose that created form is used.* Such an understanding will give us a standard measure to see how advanced are our contemporary thinkers.

Thought can also create impenetrable walls and castles around the spheres of the physical, astral, and mental planes by emphasizing the importance of each sphere and creating a life in each sphere which has no relation to the other spheres. Thus we now have a physical world organized entirely for the physical life, in which one cannot find any door or window leading to higher interests. Thought created such a life and imprisoned millions of souls in such a materialistic sphere of life.

The same is true for the emotional world. Thought created a world of emotions which is only interested in emotional satisfaction, using all kinds of methods to create pleasures and happiness, or to live in an emotional nightmare.

The same is true for the mental world. Thought created the masses of so-called intellects who live and work in a world of measures, weights, discoveries, inventions, and productivity; but all this is done in a separated sphere of thought formations. Their productivity is used by people who have doubtful interests, glamors, illusions, and vanities. The intellectual sphere has no communication line with the lower world to give guidance, nor with the Higher World for a purposeful creativity.

Their creativity is a response to their own sphere. Thought is not used to pave the way for Higher Worlds, to pave the way for spiritual perfection. This is the reason why science has not been able to create a life of right human relations, goodwill, peace, understanding, and abundance but instead gave us poisonous gases, radioactive waste, fumes, and weapons for destruction.

With such insanity and power it is not difficult to know where the world will go.

The only way to escape such a catastrophe is to polarize these spheres beyond the physical, astral, and mental interests to the Plan and to the Purpose of life. Then the spheres will coordinate and communicate with each other and manifest the highest Purpose in all spheres of existence.

The planetary Life is exactly similar to the life of a man. If He is totally occupied with His physical pleasures only, or with His emotional life only, or with His mental life only, He is a person living in His own prison. But if He integrates His three spheres of activity and directs them to a spiritual goal, to a spiritual purpose, He enters the path of perfection and harmony.

Those who live only for the material life will be stuck in the etheric or physical plane for long ages until they make a breakthrough. Those who live only for the emotional life will be stuck in the astral plane for long ages until they make a breakthrough. Those who are stuck to their mental life, and live in their philosophy, science, and politics only, will be stuck in the mental world like prisoners until they make a breakthrough into the sphere of integration and harmony.

It is as bad to be a prisoner in the mental or astral sphere as it is to be a physical plane prisoner. Most intellectuals live in the caves of the lower strata of the mental plane, chained with their dogmas, doctrines, scientific formulas, political viewpoints, and religious fanaticism. They do not even enjoy the summits of the

Himalayas and the splendid colors and sacred symphonies of the higher mental plane.

One of them came to me and said, "I invented this and that and made lots of money, but I feel I have failed in my life. I am frustrated and depressed, and I can't even see any meaning in these intellectual games. . . ."

We call such intellects "trapped fools."

Mental traps are more difficult to destroy than any other traps. So-called theology and religious fanaticism are nothing else but mental traps. Christ warned His followers and advised them to exercise love and tolerance, but the intellectual trap, with the claws of pride, got them.

For those who are able to make the breakthrough into spiritual freedom, the mental sphere, the astral sphere, and the physical sphere will be like fields of service into which they will penetrate and spread greater light and stand on the path of freedom.

It is possible to live in all these three spheres simultaneously but have the ray of purpose beyond these three worlds. When such a ray is contacted, we say that the Path is seen. When one is able to walk in the light of that ray, we say that man lives goal-fittingly.

When the ray is absorbed into our being, we say that the Antahkarana, the golden bridge, is built.

When the man disappears in the ray, we say he became the Path itself.

Thoughts are messengers of freedom. They must not be enslaved and used for our interests in the three worlds. Thoughts are messages bringing us the hope of Infinity, beauty, joy, and freedom. We must follow them to their originating source, and within the light of thought we must discover the purpose of our True Self.

It is through such a discovery that we prepare our vehicles for the journey toward the Higher Worlds.

Right action prepares our future physical body. Right aspiration, dedication, devotion, and joy prepare our future astral body. Right thinking prepares our future mental body. The registration of right thought enables us to live in these three worlds but stand free in the light of spiritual reality.

Thought is the messenger and the bridge of liberation. A Great Sage said,

> "*. . . a single strong striving attunes, as it were, the entire chord.*" [1]

---

1.   Agni Yoga Society, *Fiery World*, Vol. I, para. 248.

30

Archetypes

There are four words that must be defined clearly if we want to understand this subject:

1. Archetypes

2. Prototypes

3. Patterns

4. Blueprints

1. **Archetypes** are those archetypal thoughtforms created by the Divine Mind operating in the Cosmic Mental Plane. The Cosmic Mental Plane is fiery electricity in which exists what we call beauty. The Divine Mind contemplated and created these Archetypes which are saturated with harmony, symphony, and unimaginable beauty. Thus the Great Architect visualizes and builds the Archetype of a man, and then He projects that image into Space.

The image passes through many planes and meets many forces and elements and eventually becomes a "monkey-like" man. But in that "monkey-man" the seed of the Archetype exists. And he goes back "home," age after age, until he becomes exactly that which the Great Architect visualized for him.

We are told that the most exalted beauty on the earthly plane is a muddy shadow of an Archetype.

2. **Prototypes** are the reflections of Archetypes on the mental plane of the Cosmic Physical Plane. It is easy to contact the prototypes of everything that exists on the physical plane. Actually on our level, creativity is the process of bringing the prototypes into physical manifestation.

3. **Patterns** are the reflections of the prototypes in the mental body of a man.

4. **Blueprints** are patterns adapted to the conditions of life.

Everything in our Universe originates from the Archetypes, becomes a prototype, a pattern, and a blueprint, and takes incarnation through Nature or by the labor of a human being. Thus the conception of a constellation takes place in the currents and forces of the Archetype, gradually organizes itself on the mental plane of the Cosmic Physical Plane, and eventually becomes visible in space. But it never freezes, and age after age it strives to become like its Archetype.

Archetypes are powerful spatial magnets which evoke the seed in each form to strive toward perfection. In the real sense, perfection is achieved when the son becomes the Father, or when the acorn becomes the oak tree, the Archetype. It is this magnetic pull between the Archetype and the seed that is the force and law behind evolution.

Each Archetype of a solar system or galaxy is immensely complicated and rich. It is not only the source or the frame of a galaxy, but it also contains the Archetypes of all that will exist on the globe, of all kingdoms and lives that will evolve in that galaxy, with all that these lives need for evolution.

Archetypes are the wombs of all that will exist. In this Cosmic Womb numberless energy currents are orchestrated to make the birth, or sprouting, of the Archetype possible.

The Cosmic Mind is the great Artist. It conceives, It formulates, and eventually brings into existence the Archetype of a galaxy or a flower. Man, on his level, does the same thing. He creates the blueprint and then builds the form. If he builds a blueprint which is very similar to the pattern and prototype, he creates beauty. He creates those forms which will establish harmony between our world and the Higher Worlds. Thus a creator is a bridge builder or a builder of communication lines between worlds.

One must contemplate that in every seed, in every core of any form, the Archetype is impressed. You have a seed in your hand, but you do not know what that seed is going to be. When the seed becomes a flower or a tree, you realize that the whole flower or the whole tree was in the seed, and it is this "Archetype" that unfolded, grew, and *became itself*, to a certain degree.

In every seed there exists the future of the seed. The seed strives toward its future, toward its Archetype. The whole evolutionary process is like the progressive development of a seed which is buried in the earth and tries to make a breakthrough to greet the Sun and to greet its unfolding beauty.

But the unfoldment of this form is not limited to the physical plane. It unfolds simultaneously on the astral and mental planes. The form on the physical plane tries to reflect the beauty of the form found on the astral plane, and the form on the astral plane tries to grow in the likeness of the form on the mental plane — until the seed finds itself bloomed in the Archetype.

Every seed, every core, tries to be that which is impressed in its own heart. The same thing applies to a human being.

We have heard that God created man in His image. This is a mysterious statement. The reality is that the Cosmic Mind created man in the image of the Archetype. This image is in the human being, and the human being will never be satisfied on the pathway of his achievements and becomingness until he reaches the measure of his Archetype, the measure of his future. The perfect man in heaven is the man who became like his Archetype or became his Self on the Cosmic Mental Plane.

On the path to our Archetype are found all gradations of beings. Every seed, every form is in a spiral, racing forward. All are striving toward their Spatial Magnet. This is how Great Ones, Chohans, Angels, Archangels, and even Superior Beings come into existence. On this path one can rejoice knowing that he has a future.

On the path of development, we go through successes and failures. Sometimes our failures provide help for our future successes, and sometimes our successes lead us to our future failures. But no matter what happens on the path, one must feel and sense that there is the Archetype and there is the magnetic Presence of the Archetype in the seed, or in our hearts.

This is why man proceeds with *hope*. Hope is the response in our heart to the magnetic pull of the Archetype.

Imagine how man evolved. Millions of years ago we were not even human, and millions of years later we will say that millions of years ago we never acted like humans. As we evolve, our concepts change. As we get closer to the Archetypal man, we see how far we are from it. But no matter how far or close we are, we are going toward our destination, toward a state of Cosmic beauty. If we hold such a vision, we create a tremendous amount of courage within us and nothing in our life can stop our progressive victory and achievements.

We speak about our goals and purposes. A goal is a sensed prototype. A purpose is the conscious response to an Archetype. Those who have goals and purpose in their life are those who have found the Path. Those who do not have goals or purpose are still in their sleep, and they need to be awakened not by force but by creating in them a sensitivity to the pull of the prototype.

People advance by forming their patterns and striving toward their prototype. Worship and devotion are a response to the magnetic energies of the prototype. Service and sacrifice and a heroic life are the proof that man responds to the magnetic energies of his Archetype. Creativity is the ability to understand and translate the beauty of the Archetype.

There are practical steps which can be taken on this path of great beauty.

1. Every human being must try to find in his heart the reflection of his true Archetype.

Once I asked a man who was the son of a millionaire but used to dope himself and follow the path of crime, "What do you really want to be?"

"I really don't know."

"Just think. Maybe you want to be something you like."

"Well. . . ."

He wanted to be a fisherman, or a president of a nation, a musician, etc. Every time he wanted to be something, I asked very seriously, "Is that all?"

Eventually he came to a conclusion. He said, "I want to be a beauty."

"Well," I asked, "how must you live to be beautiful?"

He suddenly awakened and began to cry.

"I see my misery."

He was very beautiful because his heart sensed that there was no other goal than beauty.

Beauty is the Archetype, and one must strive continuously to overcome all the ugliness that one has on each plane. One can be beautiful on the physical plane but not beautiful in his feelings, emotions, and thoughts. Thus in striving toward beauty one continuously improves his life and makes it a radioactive source of creativity.

But the path of beauty is a hard path. On that path we fall thousands of times and make our nose, knees, and toes bleed. We pass through pain, suffering, joy, and ecstasy. We fall again to the bottom and try to climb to the top, but in this struggle one thing increases within us: We begin to understand that no force can hinder us on the path to our perfection.

2. We must know that our future is guaranteed.

Man is predestined to reach his perfection. Man has a future, even if he is buried in mud. The idea of a future is a source of healing energy, a source of inspiration without which one can hardly advance. If you have the concept of future, you will be victorious, sooner or later.

3. Every day you must make an effort to find out where you stand in relation to your Archetype, to your future. Thus you will conceive your Archetype and slowly shape your life upon it.

4. The path leading to the Archetype is the path of beauty.

By improving in beauty one becomes reality. Reality is the Archetype. You see your face in the mirror, but then you see yourself "face-to-face," as you are. The mirror is the plane or the level on which the Archetype is reflected. When you become yourself, you do not need a mirror; you are the origin of what you were.

5. Improvement in every field, in every thought, word, or action brings us closer to the Archetype.

Seven Major Fields of Archetypes

1. Archetypes of ideal politics and political philosophies. Every political system has its roots in a political Archetype. This means it is highly divine in its origin and essence, but it may be distorted or changed to serve individual interests and selfish or destructive ends.

2. There is the Archetype of education, and this is the reason why education can improve in all its aspects. As the human mind unfolds, it becomes more sensitive to the Archetype. The Archetype is sensed not just in one country but in many countries, according to the development, need, and character of the people.

3. There is the Archetype of communication. We started with the language of movement and reached the sophisticated methods of contemporary communication, but they are not yet perfect. Communication will increase and expand in such a way that the One Self will be in contact with all separated selves in a practical way. You will not be able to hide what you are; anyone will be able to know you as you are. Communication will develop with Spatial Beings, with the Inner Guide, with Guides of the planet and constellations; and as communication expands, human consciousness will expand and will be able to bring the Archetypal communication into greater actualization.

4. We have the Archetypes of beauty and art. More and more artists will contact a higher beauty and will be able to express it as other unfolding fields provide more vehicles for manifestation of a greater art.

Beauty is reality in the Cosmic Mental Plane. Its rays penetrate into our spheres, but one must develop an expanding sensitivity to catch these rays and bring beauties which have never been experienced before.

These beauties are contacted through the techniques of ecstasy, contemplation, and Intuition. This is why if an artist wants to contact greater beauty, he must train himself appropriately in meditation and keep himself pure so as not to distort the impressions received from the Archetypes.

5. In the scientific field the same procedure is followed. Every discovery is part of that great Archetype. Every discovery advances and turns into a multidimensional form to serve the increasing demands of the developing human being.

It is interesting to remember that when scientists have deeper contact with the Archetypes, things will be much simpler. Simplicity is one of the characteristics of Archetypes. The complicated mechanisms of today will be replaced with much simpler mechanisms. Instead of a complicated spaceship, one will be able to use his little carpet to fly, as the Ancients used to do.

Healing will be much simpler because it will not have to do with the body but with the energy adjustments of the subtle bodies.[1] Complication is the fabrication of the mind. Simplicity is the result of deeper understanding and beingness.

_____

1. See also *New Dimensions in Healing*.

Let us remember that Archetypes are sensed not only in brain consciousness but also in astral and mental consciousness. This is why we sometimes have conflict between our physical manifestation and our "dreams" or "aspirations," or between our dreams and our mental impressions or inspirations.

The successful creativity or discovery is the combined registration of the Archetypes on these three levels and its unaltered manifestation on the physical plane.

6. In religion there is the supreme Archetype in higher planes from which we draw and build our own faith. Great Ones are the transmitters of the Archetype of religion, but the human mind distorts it and uses it as a means to his selfish interests.

Religion is one of the ways of coming in contact with the Great Architect and of growing toward the Architect. Religion is one of the ways to witness the God in all creation, in all living forms. Religion is one way to understand progressive inclusiveness.

Religion is one way to prepare oneself for the future states of human consciousness and beingness.

Religion is the expression of a divine Archetype which is set to make the human soul proceed continuously from one plane to another plane, developing all senses of awareness on those planes.

7. Then we have the Archetype of finance, and we see how economics and finance have developed all over the world. One of the characteristics of the Archetype of finance is sharing or givingness, something not practiced sufficiently yet. Loaning is a start, but it is often based on interest and exploitation.

All these seven Archetypes have one original Archetype. This keynote is the synthesizing energy in all of them. This is why all branches of the seven human endeavors will gradually come closer to each other as they unfold, and eventually the symphony of the Divine Archetype will manifest through all of them.

Pure thoughts are the translations and adaptations of Archetypes within our daily life. It is through refining our thoughts that we can understand and actualize the Archetypes in our life.

Thought carries a great charge of energy from Archetypes and prototypes because each pure thought is an extension of either an Archetype or a prototype. Thus pure thinking is the path of all achievements.

31

Future Events

We are told that three conditions are necessary to foresee future events:

1. Astrological conditions

2. Conditions of higher forces

3. Conditions of refined human thoughts

Events originate from many causes. Astrological conditions orchestrate different types of energies, involve different planes, and evoke different responses from galaxies, stars, solar systems, planets, and living forms. Such changing influences of astrological conditions produce changing events in the Universe, which echo many forms in Space.[1]

Events can be beneficial or destructive according to the response or the reaction of the registering forms. The influence of events can be modified or amplified by preparation if the event is foreseen.

Events also come into being from the reactions or responses of living forms to these astrological energies.

Human life and thought create events on the planet which echo in far-off Space.

The striving of great Initiates creates events.

The Hierarchical Plan and the Will behind it are a great source of events.

All these events can be foreseen by a sensitive one who uses the three conditions.

1. **Astrological conditions**. This refers to the utilization of esoteric astrology, the energy formations of the galaxies, zodiacal signs, individual stars, and planets. Through knowledge of the patterns of energies and the particular chemistry formed by the combinations of energies, the initiate can foresee the formation of an event on earth.

---

1. For additional information see *Esoteric Astrology* by Alice A. Bailey and *Symphony of the Zodiac*.

This is the Cosmic counterpart of meteorology. As the weatherman can foresee changes in weather, the initiate can see coming events by studying the astrological conditions.

Sometimes human beings feel frustration in front of Cosmic energy-plays. But Great Ones tell us that it is possible to modify or amplify the effects of energies emanating from certain configurations by applying our thought energy and creating certain spiritual attitudes.

In the future, esoteric astrology will be one of the great subjects in universities. Esoteric astrology is the science of energies and the science of the relationship between luminaries and all that exists.

2. **Higher forces**. Space is full of rays, electrical storms, magnetic currents, mighty thought waves, and powerful etheric flows between planets, solar systems, and galaxies. These forces control the manifestations of future events on earth. They not only affect the life of the kingdoms of Nature, but they also affect human thought, emotions, aspirations, and relationships. They affect our weather and the equilibrium of the planet.

Future events can be known if one is able to see the conditions of such higher forces. Higher, developed psychics are called prophets because they can sense or see the conditions of such forces and the possible reactions and responses and thus forecast the future.

All is controlled or arranged by energy waves. There are moments when the energy waves can produce the best events. There are moments in which these waves, because of their different intensity and course, produce a crisis. One who is aware of such configurations of energies can see the future events.

3. The third factor is **refined human thoughts**. When thoughts are refined, they can sense future events. Refined thoughts can not only sense but also reflect many conditions in Space. Every thought can turn into a mirror which, because of the distance it penetrates, brings to man the conditions of Higher Realms, which are the main originators of world events.

Thoughts not only reflect, but because of their electrical nature they also bring changes within the energies and forces conditioning world events. A strong and fiery thought can destroy the formation of a future tornado. It can disperse accumulating clouds of crimes, war, or revolutions.

Those who are aware of the power of thought can see the future events. There is no mystery in this; it is all an interrelation of energy, cause, and effect.

The human soul engages himself in action by creating thoughts. Without thought the human soul remains inactive. Thought is created when the human soul contacts spatial currents which follow the direction of the Cosmic Magnet.

Spatial currents are fiery rivers of ideas, revelations, visions, and directions of the Great Lives in the Higher Worlds. When the human soul comes in contact with these fiery currents, his response produces thoughts. Each thought is an effort to translate the fiery currents, an effort to transmit energy, and an effort to bring changes in the manifested world.

Behind each thought or within each thought exists the spiritual power of the human soul. Without this power the thought is dead. This power is the spirit of the thought which propels it to its destination and makes it alive and fiery. It is electrical energy.

In each thought the human soul is present through his spirit.

Man creates his thoughts according to the level of his consciousness. If the level of consciousness is low, or if the consciousness is contaminated by evil, then the human soul cannot respond to spatial currents but instead attracts degenerated thoughtforms from space.

The pollution of consciousness is the result of the accumulated lifeless thoughts or thoughtforms wandering in space. Sometimes our consciousness absorbs them like a sponge. The karma of those people who distribute such polluted thoughts will be very heavy. Thought pollution is a thousand times more dangerous than any other kind of pollution. As a matter of fact, all outer pollution is the result of mental pollution. Pollution starts with the mind, then spreads to the astral and physical planes.

Similarly, the degeneration of a human being starts in his mind, then spreads to his emotional and physical natures. After the mental and emotional pollution accumulates upon the physical plane in chemical forms, it multiplies itself, and like a reversing wave it begins to carry a heavier pollution to the Subtle World. This is how a vicious circle is created.

Purification must start from the mental plane and descend to the physical plane. No pollution can be removed from the earth if the pollution is not first cleansed from the consciousness of man.

The human consciousness must come in contact with impressions pouring down from Cosmic sources. Such a contact expands the field of consciousness, and the creation of higher thoughts becomes possible.

Behind all thoughts must stand the fire of the spirit of man because only this fire can keep the thoughts in harmony with the directions of the energies of the Cosmic Magnet. A real thought is actually a messenger of spirit and a traveler toward the Cosmic Magnet.

There are many spatial currents, but they are included in seven main streams which in the Ageless Wisdom are called the Seven Cosmic Rays.[2] Each Ray comes from a mighty Cosmic Being and with millions of threads radiates the vision, the Purpose, and the Plan of that Cosmic Being. The human soul, according to his unfoldment, contacts to a certain degree the network of these Cosmic Rays.

_____

2. See especially the video *The Seven Rays Interpreted.*

All creativity is the result of such contact. The higher and deeper the contact, the higher, deeper, and more glorious is the creativity of the human soul. The creativity of the human soul is, in fact, the effort to translate the impressions received from these Rays into thoughts and into forms for human understanding and for the progress of life.

Thus the human soul creates by coming in contact with the higher sources of inspiration, and he himself becomes a higher source for those lives who are on the Path of their evolution.

Every thought coming from higher sources is creative. Every thought coming from higher sources is a treasure, is a path toward Infinity, is a light on the dark paths of humanity.

People must learn how to make their minds fertile with the seeds of spatial thoughts. As the spring rains bring with them all greenery, flowers, and bushes, so does the precipitation of thoughts from higher sources; life turns into a garden after such a precipitation.

Every lofty thought which is charged by striving spreads beauty in space. Creativity in space is the result of lofty thoughts. Many thoughts cannot materialize in the world, but they create in space. Such creativity becomes the source of inspiration for many. Space is full of creative forms and creative waves. It is possible to come in contact with such creativity through our lofty thoughts.

We can increase the beauty in space through our striving thoughts. A striving thought becomes the co-worker of the current of evolution.

Thought has different charges of energies. There are physically charged thoughts, emotionally charged thoughts, and mentally charged thoughts. There are also psychic thoughts. Psychic thoughts are those thoughts which emanate from the Core of the human soul and are charged by the flames of higher psychic centers. Psychic centers are the astral, mental, intuitional, and higher senses whose contacts with Higher Worlds bring a new charge to the forming thought.

Psychic thoughts carry with them the vibration of all achievements of the human soul.

Psychic thoughts are very sensitive to the pull of the Tower, Shamballa, because the Tower is the highest psychic Center on the planet. Attraction toward the Tower imposes fiery purification upon the nature of man. Thus psychic thoughts direct the man toward greater creativity and achievement.

As the higher senses develop, one can use the thought energy more wisely and intelligently. Also the network of the senses on different planes is used as a magic mirror to reflect the image of the creative thought in motion in space. This network is also used to synthesize the scattered thoughts in space.

Thus an advanced psychic has a greater field of contact, and his thoughts are charged with the fires of higher centers and senses.

The entire mechanism of the reception and projection of thought will be handled in accurate measures. Not a single wave of thought must be wasted or misused. All will be used for creativity and for precise targets and goals.

An organized psychic mechanism turns into a great transformer and transmitter of the Cosmic waves of thought.

The consciousness expands and grows when the higher thoughts are put into application by the consciousness. The application of thought is a process of assimilation of higher substance by the consciousness and also an act of building bridges between the source of thoughts, the thought, the consciousness, and the field where the thought is applied.

Thus the creative fire of thought builds the bridges.

Transmutation of consciousness is imperative if one is going to serve the Hierarchy. Without transmutation of consciousness, man puts himself in grave danger, especially if he pretends that he is serving the Hierarchy.

Transmutation of consciousness begins when the Teaching is understood and lived in all our relationships.

Consciousness does not expand or transform through knowledge, through education, or through increasing information. Consciousness expands and is transmuted when the person lives the Teaching as it is given to him. He not only lives the Teaching but also knows why the Teaching must be lived. As the Teaching is assimilated, understood, and lived, the consciousness expands and becomes fiery.

Only through a fiery consciousness can one receive the impressions released from Great Ones. These impressions inspire him to great sacrificial service. Through a fiery consciousness he observes the requirements of time, obeys the higher law, and destroys all obstacles on the path of service.

A fiery consciousness is a great magnet which attracts visible and invisible co-workers. It is known that a fiery consciousness often creates transmutation, and our enemies become our friends. Indifferent ones become interested in our visions and labors.

Without a transmuted and fiery consciousness, everything runs artificially and there is no taste to anything. Even the gains of a service done without fiery consciousness turn into a burden upon our shoulders.

There are three steps which must be taken to make our consciousness fiery:

1. Purification

2. Transmutation

3. Expansion

Purification is achieved when we master our physical, emotional, vocal, and mental habits.

Physical habits are habits of food, sex, sleep, and drink.

Emotional habits include depression, worry, fear, love, and hatred.

Vocal habits include criticism, negativity, gossip, nosiness, idle speech, and mechanical speech.

Mental habits are addictions to certain interests to the degree that they obsess us — fanaticism, superstition, prejudice, vanities.

These four kinds of habits must be slowly conquered if we want to purify our consciousness.

In addition to conquering our habits, we must also

1. Cultivate control of our body, emotions, mouth, and mind

2. Perform service and labor

3. Cultivate high aspirations

4. Meditate and think about the Hierarchy

Transmutation takes place when one tries to be always in the light of *beauty*, *honesty*, and *nobility*.

Expansion takes place when at certain moments one contacts higher impressions or inspirations coming from Great Ones. Every contact with a Great One expands your consciousness. But let us remember that a contact is not valid if you do not have a purified consciousness and a transmuted consciousness. Any contact with higher energies brings deterioration into your system unless your consciousness is purified and transmuted.

Purification is the annihilation of crystallizations and the destruction of the forms for which higher counterparts do not exist. We call such forms, fabrications.

Transmutation is replacement of the atoms of consciousness with the fiery atoms of the higher levels of the mental plane.[3] Transmutation is a dawning of the light in the field of consciousness.

---

3.   See also *New Dimensions in Healing*, Chs. 46-48, for additional information on Transmutation.

32

Thought Energy

There is an ancient prayer which says, "Enlighten my thoughts, O Lord, so that I choose the right path."

What is thought? To know what thought is we must define

1. brain

2. mind, mental body

3. thought

4. thoughtform

5. human soul

The **brain** is a computer. It registers impressions coming from the five senses and also impressions coming from the Higher Worlds.

There are one thousand and one centers in the brain, but in the average man only twenty-five centers are working, which are related to five centers. As one develops the centers increase, coordination between the centers takes place, and man becomes a talent, a genius, a Master, an Avatar, and so on.

In every initiation new centers function in the brain. At the Fifth Initiation one thousand centers are functioning. At the Sixth Initiation one is added.

The **mental body** is divided into seven layers or spheres, three lower and three higher. The middle one is called the level of choice. The lower mind is called the concrete mind or the form-building mind. The higher mind is called the abstract mind.

Average man is in the lower mind. Advanced man is in the lower and higher mind, but he is focused in the higher mind.

The abstract mind receives directions and impulses from the Soul or from the Intuition, and when the mind responds to these impulses or impressions or directions, **thoughts** come into being.

A thought is the response of the abstract mind to any impression, idea, or direction that comes from higher sources. The lower mind takes the thought and builds it into a **thoughtform**. For example, you have a thought to visit a person.

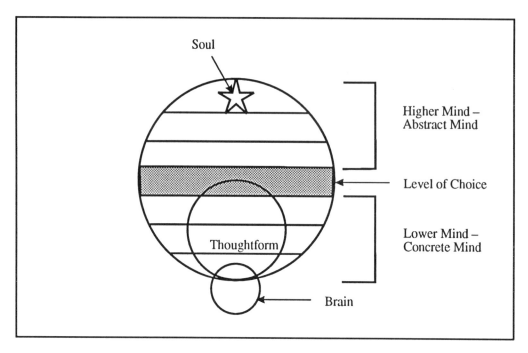

Diagram 32-1   Mental Body

This thought goes to the lower mind and becomes a form. Your lower mind presents to you the possibilities of driving a car, taking a gift, going to a movie together. . . . All this is a thoughtform built around the core of the thought.

The three higher levels of the mind only receive impressions, ideas, and directions which are beautiful, good, and full of truth. The middle one receives from various sources, good and bad, higher or lower, from Masters or from astral entities which masquerade as the Master. Until the fourth level is passed, man is in danger and cannot be depended upon. Once he passes the fourth level, he never turns back any more to the lower life.

33

Thought Energy and Stigmata

We know that it is thought that creates. But thought can act simply as thought energy or as thought and spirit energy fused.

Thought energy is creative energy, but if it is not fused with spirit energy it becomes

destructive

selfish

separative

ugly

totalitarian

materialistic

Thought energy becomes spiritual if it is guided by the light of the Solar Angel.[1]

Later, thought energy will be mixed with the vibration of the emancipated human soul or with the vibration of the Spiritual Triad. Without the light of such sources, the thought energy will be deadly.

This is why when people learn how to think they become dangerous factors in their environment. But they turn into creative agents when their thinking process is guided by the light of higher principles or by the wisdom of the Solar Angel, the human soul, the Spiritual Triad, or even by still higher sources.

Creativity is the result of thought energy acting upon emotional, etheric, and physical matter **to make the glory of the Self to manifest**. Thought energy can use matter and create new forms with it. It can impress on matter various images

---

1. See also *The Solar Angel.*

and guide the matter to various activities or relate it to various sources of influence.

If the consciousness of the person is enlightened, all the powers of thought are used to lead the life toward perfection.

Thought can create those forms which evolving souls use to advance on the path of their perfection. These forms can be mental, emotional, etheric, or tangible forms.

If the thought is not enlightened, it is used as a clever servant by the physical and astral elementals to provide nourishment for their blind urges and drives, glamors, desires, and negative emotions.

An enlightened thought has two currents of energy in it: the energy of mind and the energy of spirit. The energy of spirit is light or electrical energy which comes from the Solar Angel, the emancipated human soul, the Spiritual Triad, or from still higher sources. As the currents of energy from these sources increase and fuse with each other, the thought energy becomes more creative, more inclusive, and more spiritual.

There is a third kind of energy which works through the thought energy. That energy is called psychic energy or the Light of the Holy Spirit. If psychic energy utilizes or uses the thought energy, it makes it highly creative and in harmony with the Plan and Purpose of life.

These three energies — thought, spiritual, and psychic — are creative agents specifically on the Cosmic Physical Plane. A thinking process charged with these three energies provides all those ways and means through which evolving souls find their way Home.

Thought substance is used also to impress mental, emotional, etheric, and physical bodies. For example, if you think about a form, that form starts to be impressed on your mental body. You can also impress your astral, or emotional, body or even your etheric body. An impression on the etheric body automatically passes to the physical body.

Thus, thought energy can be used to heal your bodies and to introduce changes in them.

If one wants to change things in his mental body, then he must use mental concentration or aspiration.

If one wants to change things in his emotional nature, then he must use mental concentration and intense aspiration.

If one wants to change things in his etheric body, he must use mental concentration, intense aspiration, and the energy of willpower.

Most of the changes observed in our physical, emotional, and mental natures are the results of our thinking. These changes can be categorized as desirable or undesirable. Every minute our mind creates an image which, if not controlled by psychic energy and the human soul, can have devastating effects in our life in the future.

As a result of thought impressions, our mental body or emotional and physical bodies are full of marks which play a big role in our way of thinking, feeling, acting, in our relationships, and especially in our health problems. These marks may appear as stigmata.[2]

Stigmata are wounds which are caused through our thought energy, through the energy of intense desire, aspiration, and identification. These impressions are forced upon us, and sometimes they are the result of our conscious and creative thinking.

There are two kinds of stigmata. One is the result of intense identification through aspiration. The other is intense identification through fear or hatred.

Those people who actually duplicate the wounds of Christ through intense concentration and identification prove that our physical body can be directly affected though our thinking, imagination, creative imagination, and visualization. But the physical body is only the shadow of the etheric body, and we have emotional and mental bodies. These bodies are also affected by our thought, concentration, and identification with the wounds of Jesus on the cross.

Stigmata can be caused also by people sending mental or emotional imagery which is painful, destructive, or negative to others. These thoughtforms are built by the forces of hatred, jealousy, and revenge.

There is a difference in effect between a thought that has a painful image and a thought that has joy in it and is full of goodness and beauty. The positive or beneficent thoughtform does not create stigmata but charges our vehicles with energy and distributes it throughout our aura.

Dark thoughts create local stigmata in the form of wounds. On the mental body a clairvoyant can see such wounds or dark spots which do not let the fire of the mental body circulate. The mental results of such wounds are incoherent thinking, over-sensitivity, lack of creativity, dullness, plus paralysis of the mental body. On the emotional plane such wounds manifest as irritability, negativity, sadness, and depression associated with various vices such as hatred, malice, and treason. On the physical plane they create ulcers, tumors, and cancerous manifestations in the organs and skin. Stigmata are those wounds which manifest in the physical body.

Is it dangerous to cause stigmata in our body? The answer is yes, if the intention is to create the wounds only. But some people go deeper and not only communicate with the wounds of Christ but also with Christ Himself. Intense identification through aspiration creates a link with Christ and turns into a path of communication between the person and Christ. The Image of Christ built by intense aspiration and concentration becomes a source not only of transformation and purification but also of creativity, power, energy, and various other gifts — if the person is ready.

The Image of Christ's suffering turns into a satellite which transmits to the person the most precious energy of sacrifice. This energy of sacrifice manifests itself as a life of intense service, leadership, and creativity.

---

2.   See also *New Dimensions in Healing*, Ch. 13.

Stigmata do not always manifest in the physical body, but they manifest on the emotional or mental body with unpleasant effects and even sometimes with painful and destructive effects.

A stigma starts when the mind focuses itself or concentrates itself upon a painful image, upon a painful event, word, or expression. The painful image is impressed on the corresponding location on the body. For example, if one sees a man using a dagger and pushing it into the breast of another person, through concentration the event impresses itself on his own breast, and this is the beginning of a stigma.

Sometimes the emotional and mental vehicles as a whole are affected, not only a small location. We often experience nightmares when this occurs.

Psychic attacks from dark sources and human beings can affect our emotional and mental bodies and create many stigmata. Also, there exist stigmata or "wounds" caused by the movies we see or from our actual life and experiences. These stigmata slowly absorb the energy that circulates in that particular body and disturb the even flow of the currents of electromagnetic feelings or thoughts. Eventually gaps and cleavages come into being on the same body or between the bodies with corresponding stigmata.

These stigmata may remain for a long time or forever. Sometimes they increase in depth; sometimes they decrease. It is the memory and intensity of the impression that conditions their life period. It is very difficult to erase them because as long as the memory exists they draw energy from the memory in our inner resources. Often for certain reasons the memory fades, but a restimulated wound regenerates the memory or visa versa.

Those who are occupied in the healing fields have to consider the stigmata. For example, stigmata control people's allergic reactions, and if the source of the stigmata is always around them, their stigmata are continuously restimulated and cause endless health problems.

Sometimes human thinking and imagination bring these stigmata into physical manifestation in various forms of sickness. This happens when a person tries to interpret some inner sensations of the stigmata as signs of particular sicknesses. Thoughts and imagination allow the energy trapped in stigmata to release and manifest on the physical plane in the form created by the person's thoughts and imaginations.

Many stigmata are the source of skin diseases, bruises, pains in various locations of our body, or even of our various organic diseases. Medicine does not yet know about the facts and influence of stigmata and tries to heal the leaves instead of the roots.

In the process of building stigmata, fear plays the main role. It is mostly in a condition of fear that stigmata are formed in our subtle bodies. Fear is not only a poisonous substance that paralyzes our etheric, astral, and mental bodies, but also it is a conductor of painful images. It builds a bridge between various planes and transports the stigmata from one to another, thus spreading them into various bodies. Fear also nourishes stigmata and makes them more effective.

In the beginning these stigmata do not cause pain; they are like impressions of painful events on the surface of the vehicles. But when fear restimulates them, they slowly turn into wounds, and often into malignant wounds, which spread in the same vehicles or are carried into other vehicles.

The cure for stigmata is psychic energy fused with the energy of bliss. Often the psychic energy of your Teacher and His blessing must be used to fight the initial resistance of fear and wounds.

I often heard my mother say to me, "Be gentle in your words to others and to yourself because the wound caused by a knife is more easily cured than the wound caused by your words." Wounds are direct results of our words charged with anger, hate, malice, and revenge.

Stigmata may be the result of our feelings and thoughts about painful events. Stigmata turn into wounds when hurtful words and expressions overstimulate them. We carry stigmata from life to life, and mainly it is these stigmata that build the mechanism of our reactions and responses toward all life events and objects.

Psychic energy and bliss must always be invoked to carry on the job of healing within our subtle bodies. Thus we must have periods of joy, enthusiasm, and ecstasy to evoke our Teacher's psychic energy and blessings more abundantly.

Stigmata are also transferable or contagious. One can be contaminated by the stigmata of others that resulted through fear or hatred by developing an intense fear or hatred toward a person. The currents of fear and hatred build the needed channels for transportation of stigmata from one person to another.

Subtle stigmata are transported from one person to another during sleep or during moments of intense hatred and fear. The inception of stigmata of this kind is gradual, and they make their existence apparent through the way a person thinks, feels, and acts, after which physical symptoms manifest.

Stigmata formed by intense aspiration, love, devotion, and concentration are not transferable. They need the same labor to be impressed upon our vehicles.

Such subtle or physical stigmata caused by intense devotion and aspiration are like communication points between a person and a Great One, such as Jesus, from Whom the person builds his stigmata.

It is interesting to realize that such stigmata serve as healing centers in the vehicles, whereas the stigmata formed through hatred and fear are centers of increasing problems.

Stigmata are also found at group levels and even national levels. Some nations have powerful stigmata of fear and hatred which last many generations or forever. Others have holy stigmata such as those national majorities who are devoted to Great Ones and try to live according to the impressions collected from Them.

Evidently the higher the stigmata, the more powerful the influence they have over stigmata collected through hate and fear. Such individuals, groups, and nations have a natural resistance against the pollution of lower stigmata.

Natural resistance expresses itself as a strong immune system on the physical plane and on the emotional and mental planes as divine indifference against those factors or persons who try to bring infection into the system.

The higher forms of stigmata continuously attack and erase the lower stigmata and restore the health of a person, group, or nation. The survival potential of an individual, group, or nation depends upon the stigmata received through aspiration, devotion, and ecstasy. The relationships between people and nations are highly controlled by these two kinds of stigmata.

Higher stigmata often are translated in creative arts. Great art mostly uses the treasury of higher stigmata.

Arts loaded with violence, crime, and murder are inspired by lower stigmata. To release themselves from such painful stigmata, people try to express them through "artistic" expressions of violence, crime, murder, and ugliness. It helps them ease their condition for a while, but these expressions cause psychic complications in their system and lead them to insanity. Such artworks in movies, television programs, books, articles, and paintings have degenerative effects on the morality of people and lead people toward anti-survival ways of living.

Our newspapers, radios, and television are also instrumental in spreading sources of stigmata, providing painful events which are impressed in people by association, fear, and hatred.

Stigmata last for a long time. Sometimes we carry them with us life after life, even in Subtle Worlds. Sometimes they increase or decrease.

The emancipation of a person depends upon how clean are his bodies from painful and interfering stigmata.

It is only after the Third Initiation that we fully use the psychic energy to transfigure our personality vehicles.

Stigmata occur not only in our waking state of consciousness but also while we are asleep and in the Subtle World. During our sleep many hostile arrows are thrown at us. These arrows, which cause tension and distress in our subtle bodies, are the ugly and criminal thoughts of our enemies. Often we can fight against them, but in general they impress our physical body.

There are also entities who want to stop our progress on the Path or to stop our service for humanity. They also organize and attack us through their ugly thoughtforms or currents of energy charged with ill will while we are out of our physical body.

Our Guardian Angel often can dispel them if they are mere attacks, but if they are karmic consequences the Guardian Angel lets us fight against them if we can.

These stigmata are received mostly on our etheric and astral bodies, but in due time they appear on our physical body in the form of disorders, swellings, rashes, or pain.

Often we awaken tired and exhausted. The reason for this is the dark attacks upon us, or, if we are advanced enough, the reason is our own activities carried on in subtle planes to protect people from dark attacks.

In our waking consciousness, we are able in general to fight against evil currents of feelings and thoughts, but while asleep we cannot fight due to the unorganized condition of our subtle bodies.

If the attacks are strong and they are aimed at our mental body, stigmata occur on our mental body. If repeated, they turn into wounds.

Most of the insanity experienced today in various parts of the world is the result of such attacks in the mental bodies.

Protection against such attacks is not easy because some of them are reactions to our karmic debts. The best protection is to increase the relationship between the human soul and the Guardian Angel through living a life of virtues, harmlessness, and sacrificial service. Such a life builds not only a closer communication between the Guardian Angel and the human soul, but it also builds the fiery shield around the subtle bodies which often makes the attacks useless.

It is also possible that we receive stigmata in relating sexually in our dream state with someone who is loaded with them.

In physical intercourse the bodies fuse with each other physically, etherically, and astrally. The mental bodies are fused in rare cases if the love is intense and if there are no thoughts of conflict, regret, or confusion.

If both parties are not in tune with each other in joy and happiness, both in the objective and subjective worlds, then when children are conceived on the physical plane, they show signs of cleavages in their nature. This is the result of partial intercourse.

It is also possible to transport stigmata from one person to another at a distance. This is mostly done through mental telepathy. The medium in this case can be in intense hatred or in intense sympathy with the people involved.

People can make each other miserable through their jealousy, revengeful thoughts, and hatred, telepathically transporting their mental stigmata to their victims.

Some of the stigmata on the mental plane create a retardation in clear thinking, confusion, illogical decisions, and conflicting goals until they slowly turn into wounds and manifest in various degrees of mental disease.

Some of the stigmata on the astral plane or in the emotional body create instability of moods, depression, negativity, fear, anger, and a tendency to gossip and slander until they manifest as illness in the glands and disorder in the lymphatic system. Some of the stigmata on the etheric plane create intense irritation and weakness in the nervous system, skin rashes, disorders in digestion, and weakening of the function of the five senses.

Unfortunately we have created a kind of life on this planet in which every one of us has a great harvest of stigmata. The cure is intense aspiration, striving toward the Highest, and living a life of compassion and service.

How can these stigmata be cleared away?

Exercise

The following exercise, if done for six months, may clear them away:

Everyday for fifteen minutes visualize that an Inner Sun is flooding all your nature with its light. Let the light penetrate every particle of your nature and make it transparent and clear.

Do not let your thought falter on any memory or imagery.

This may not be easy to learn, but once it is learned it will regenerate all your various systems on all planes.

First relax and have a psychic bath in the light of your Inner Sun.

Sometime later you will see the Sun and how it floods your nature. You may feel also the regenerating, vitalizing vibration going through your bodies. You may feel deeper peace, serenity, clarity of consciousness, and energy.

Later you will learn to use the Sun's rays to dissolve your many problems.

34

Quality of Thoughts

Thought has twelve characteristics. The quality of the thought determines how that thought affects life.

1. The speed of a thought is faster than light. It can reach its destination or fail due to obstacles or hindrances. Obstacles come from outside and inside. Outside obstacles are

    a. dark thoughtforms

    b. evil entities

    c. electrical storms

    d. radioactive emanations

    e. noise

    f. mass storms, chaos, confusion

    g. dirty and polluted air

    h. polluted and unclean surroundings

Inner obstacles are

    a. wrong motives

    b. evil thoughts

    c. maya, glamor, and illusion

    d. negative emotions — fear, anger, hatred, greed, jealousy

    e. doubt

f. fanaticism

g. hypocrisy, lies

h. inability to concentrate

2. The second quality of thought is *fieriness*. Thought burns on the path to its destination. If it is evil, it burns the aura and comes back again and burns the mind. Insanity is the result. Mongoloids are those who were fabricating evil thoughts in the past.

If the thought is good, it burns obstacles to health, to love, and to light; and wherever it goes, it carries light and love and evokes creativity.

3. Thought accumulates in articles, in auras, and in space. If it is good, it brings durability to articles, growth to seeds and trees, and health to human beings and animals.

If it is bad or evil, it hurts, harms, and wounds the articles and prevents life in them; it stops growth and makes them break, dry up, and die.

If it enters the aura, it conditions the function of the centers, glands, and nervous system and conditions the health, happiness, beauty, and long life of the subject. If it is bad, it brings sickness, unhappiness, ugliness, trouble, and a short life.

One of the reasons that Masters want to remain isolated is to avoid being bombarded by human thought.

Thought accumulates in space and becomes a cause for crime and destruction, or a center of light and inspiration. People of goodwill, culture, and beauty receive inspiration from the latter accumulations. People of the dark path receive their inspiration from the evil accumulations and use them for destruction and crime.

Once a man thinks, his thoughts already become the property of space in the subjective and objective worlds. Thoughts can be carried out by thinking, words, voice, gestures, letters, books, and arts.

If you are in the fourth level of the mind, you can be used for light or for darkness, according to your background and the influences of your parents, teachers, and society.

The lower mind obeys and does good or bad according to the orders and examples put into it.

There are two kinds of thought. One is born from the heart. One is born from the mind.

Thoughts are common property. Everyone shares every thought, good or bad. This is why one must think with a pure sense of responsibility. He must remember that

a. his thoughts are observed by higher Beings

b. he has no ownership of his thoughts

    c. he does not know where his thoughts will reach and what result they
       will bring

4. The fourth characteristic of thought is that thoughts follow their parent, good or evil. They come and find you, whether you are in astral, mental, or physical incarnation. Good thoughts return to you with flowers and fruits. Dark thoughts return to you with heavy taxation, pain, and suffering.

5. Thoughts may carry certain energies:

    — mind

    — Intuition

    — higher ethers, Ashrams, Masters

    — Sun

    — Zodiac

    — galactic influences

    — compassion

The higher thoughts are those which are born from the heart because the heart thinks in harmony with the Cosmic Magnet.

There are three sources of higher thought:

    1. sources of light

    2. sources of compassion

    3. sources of will or direction

Impressions from sources of light are received by the mental plane. Impressions from love and compassion are received by the heart and passed to the mind. Impressions from the will or direction are received through the Antahkarana and passed through the mind and heart.

The third is very rare, and only Great Ones can handle it. But the second one is close to all who are charged with goodwill, compassion, and love.

The thoughts from the heart have tremendous magnetism, the power of inclusiveness, and harmony.

Each kind of thought transmits the energy of its *source*.

The greatest helps are

    a. good reading

b. meditating

c. controlling your mouth

d. checking your thoughts immediately when they begin to take form

6. Thought builds communication lines. Your thought is a communication line between you and the object about which you are thinking:

a. a man or woman

b. articles, objects

c. groups

d. Great Ones

e. centers, Hierarchy, Shamballa

f. planets, the Sun

g. constellations or stars

h. galaxies

i. the Cosmic Heart

Every time you think, you weave a thread, very tiny but real. It gets stronger and stronger and becomes a means of communication. If you are building threads of good thoughts about a good object, you give light, love, and energy to that object and you receive light, love, and energy from it.

If you are building dark threads, you will contaminate the object about which you are thinking and receive a reaction if the object is good; but if by nature the object is dark, you will receive all its degenerated elements.

7. Thought builds the future. Whatever you think, according to your thinking will be your future physical body, astral body, and mental body. You will be born and surrounded with those conditions which correspond to your thoughts. Thus thoughts can make you their prisoner or their king.

8. Thought fights and mobilizes forces of light or darkness. Good thought is always victorious because it sustains, nourishes, and protects its source. Dark thoughts eventually fail because they defeat and destroy the mechanism which they use.

9. Thought emanates color, sound, heat, cold, and form. Colors are gorgeous, and color formations are unbelievable when they are the result of higher thoughts. Sound is very pleasant and harmonious or symphonic if it originates from higher thoughts. The heat of higher thoughts is creative, the cold is pleasant, and the form is supremely beautiful.

Dark thoughts create repellent colors, sounds, and forms. Their heat is destructive. Their cold brings frost. Their form spreads ugliness.

10. Thought has the ability to synthesize or scatter. Higher thoughts create synthesis on all levels and in all departments. Dark thoughts scatter formations and disseminate them, hindering the evolution of life found in the formations.

You can discover what kind of thoughts you have by observing your actions, deeds, gestures, judgments, relationships, letters, creativity, attitudes, and moods.

11. Thought moves objects through the energy it transmits and even causes levitation. Continents, islands, and mountains are moved by collective thoughts or by a directed thought from Great Ones.

Thought can make an engine work.

If the human race develops in the right way, new machines will be created that, instead of working with electricity, oil, steam, or solar power, will work by human thought or psychic energy. Broken parts of the engine will be repaired by thought.

12. Thought nourishes the devas. Every time you meditate or think lofty thoughts you attract devas, as the flowers attract bees and birds. As devas surround you, they radiate into your aura psychic energy, healing energy, and purifying energy. They inspire you with lofty visions and bring you revelations. All these are expressions of gratitude for the food you give them.

Health comes when the mind thinks in terms of

        a. synthesis

        b. unity

        c. sacrificial service

        d. righteousness

        e. courage

        f. love

        g. daring

h. generosity

i. forgiveness

j. joy

k. purity

When the body acts by the above principles, you have health.

This is the age of energy. The mind has energy and uses energy. The wrong use of energy brings sickness to the body because it disturbs the harmony existing in the electrical web of the body, emotions, and mind.[1]

Unhealthy conditions in man and on the planet are caused by

1. wrong thoughts — separative thoughts, criminal thoughts, selfish thoughts

2. ugly emotions — fear, anger, hatred, greed, revenge, jealousy

3. deeds based on the above lists

Use your thoughts for the upliftment and liberation not only of humanity but for the whole of Nature as well. This is how you can fulfill your destiny.

---

1.   See also *New Dimensions in Healing.*

35

Thought and Bliss

In the Teaching we are told that thought can destroy and dispel the most poisonous influences, psychic attacks, plans of destruction, evil motives, the evil eye, malice, and slander. All these influences spread like a dark fog over people. It is the fiery thought that can repel such formations and make them vanish.

One must use thought with visualization and radiate victorious thoughts to pave the way for the radiation of beauty, joy, and freedom.

Fiery thought can be sent to areas and persons who are under attack. Like a fiery storm the thought must be directed to burn out the accumulated poison.

Spiritual work must be carried to higher and higher dimensions each time after the fire of thought burns away the accumulation of poison. This can be very effective if a group of people are united to dispel such accumulations. Such accumulations often are produced by those who live in lower strata of the Subtle World and are loaded with their earthly burdens and negative orientations.

The Teaching says that all those who incarnate come to earth with good intentions, and even people from lower strata are enlightened to a certain degree before they are born. But because of poisoned conditions they change their orientation. If victorious thoughts clear the poisonous accumulations, the incarnating souls will find greater opportunity to keep their good intentions and their light and grow with them.

Thus, fiery thoughts not only pave the way for the success of the forces of light, but they also help people walk on the path of striving toward greater achievements.

As much as possible fiery thoughts must be used to dispel accumulations anywhere, from any object or building, so that the labor of light increases there and helps the Hierarchy to carry on Its salvaging work.

Victorious thoughts come from the heart of man, where the Self exists. The Self is the Invincible One. No matter how much the personality is trapped in poison, the Self can release Itself through fiery thoughts.

Behind victorious thoughts stand faith and trust. Faith is the realization of one's own Divinity. Doubt and confusion must be ruled out. Faith cannot operate without absolute trust.

Faith charges thoughts with the vision of the future and of Infinity. The intensity of the fieriness of thoughts originates from faith, and it dissipates the clouds of poison.

Long ago the Great One said, "Faith can move mountains." Each fiery thought emanates from the furnace of faith, from the furnace of the heart.

When a group of people are united in thought and faith, they not only destroy huge accumulations of darkness, but they also attract tremendous amounts of energy from the Hierarchy. Every kind of unity of thought that is directed to the service of humanity attracts, like a magnet, energies from the Hierarchy to help the evolution of humanity.

Unity is the accumulation of auras. A man can have an aura of nine feet, but a group of people dedicated to the welfare of humanity can have an aura with a three to five mile radius. Bigger and purer auras attract a great amount of energy which charges and amplifies the thoughts and makes them the most powerful force to destroy and purify accumulated poisons in space or in various locations.

People often act under the influence of such poisonous accumulations, and once they are caught in the current they continuously live a life of crime, hatred, malice, and slander. People living under the influence of such poisonous accumulations hate freedom; they like to live as slaves, and they attack the freedom of others.

On the other hand, fiery thought charged with faith and strengthened by unity is the most powerful force in the Universe.

One must remember that behind every constructive, progressive, transforming, and creative thought stands the Hierarchy.

People have the opinion that evil is all-powerful, whereas the truth is that thought based on goodness is like a sunrise which disperses the fog of accumulated evil. A group thought based on goodness is a wave on the ocean of the Divine Omnipotence.

In ancient times people used to transmit their psychic energy through fiery thoughts to eliminate accumulations of poison and to energize through blessings the inherent forces of creativity within people and forms. Blessing is an act of transmitting bliss, which is a form of psychic energy. This energy can literally be transmitted with various ends and results.

From ancient times we read in all religions and traditions about the act of blessing. A mother or father blesses the children. Kings and queens are blessed by spiritual leaders. People bless their food, their garments, their homes, their plants and seeds. People bless their tools, furniture, money. People bless each other.

We even read that we must bless our enemies for the energy they evoke from us and our obstacles for the wisdom they impart to us.

Blessing is the process of transmission of psychic energy through fiery thoughts. Bliss radiates out from psychic energy, and if transmitted properly it

1. heals or purifies

2. releases, liberates

3. strengthens, regenerates

4. brings in abundance

5. dispels evil entities

6. dispels accumulated poisons

7. protects from evil influences

8. builds a protective shield over our body

9. brings in illumination and courage

10. inspires solemnity, power, and dignity

11. inspires creative ideas

12. brings in success and progress

The act of blessing is very simple. One must focus psychic energy within his fiery thoughts and through his eyes or the palms of his hands transmit bliss to the object of blessing, in the meantime visualizing the energy of bliss flowing and penetrating into the object or subject.

If your etheric, astral, and mental vehicles are pure and if your thought is really fiery, you will transmit bliss to whomever you want.

Certain things obscure the flow of psychic energy:

- fanaticism

- separatism

- hatred

- irritation

- depression

- fear

- lack of faith

These are the seven enemies within you which prevent the flow of psychic energy.

The flow of bliss increases when the person

— has goodwill

— has faith

— is healthy

— has contact with higher spheres

— has deep love

— knows the power of evil

— has the ability to focus or concentrate

— has a sacrificial and heroic spirit

This does not mean that an average man cannot bless. Every human being is endowed with the power of blessing. Blessing starts in wishing good, in willing good for others.

People must continuously exercise their power of blessing. Through blessing much goodwill comes to earth. Those who bless gradually transform their lives because the flow of bliss charges them and brings them many spiritual gifts.

Bliss is accumulated in the nerve channels, and it gives strength and the power of endurance to the nervous system as a whole. If bliss is directed properly through fiery thoughts, it can penetrate into astral and mental spheres and bring purity, light, and wisdom there.

In transmitting bliss, fiery thoughts bring harmony on the planet. We are advised by great Teachers to purify the planet every day through fiery thoughts and through blessings. Hierarchy will have a great future if daily all men of goodwill send their fiery thoughts to purify the planet and send their blessings to regenerate the planet.

Many people live with the feeling of enmity. The Teaching says that enmity opens the doors for infection and obsession and creates a difficult situation for man in the Subtle World.

We are told that enmity is a worthless attitude and causes much suffering to people. Enmity cannot continue in the hearts of those who cross the fourth sphere of the Subtle World. There, we are told, they see the worthlessness of enmity and let it drop away. But in the lower spheres people still live in enmity and cruelty which disfigure their faces and bodies and their total appearance in the Subtle World.

Fiery thought and blessings can cure such a state and restore the beauty of the soul. Through fiery thought and blessings people not only create beauty within themselves but evoke beauty from the surrounding world as well.

Fiery thoughts and blessings purify space. In each act of purification, one reveals greater beauty in himself and in the world. Fiery thoughts and blessings nourish and protect beauty on all planes. It is imperative to increase beauty in the days of crisis, cruelty, and ugliness. Beauty will be the only path toward the liberation of the human soul.

36

The Use of Thought
for the Future

People think that thought is used only to bring changes within the physical life, or that it is used only for the physical life. It is possible to use thought energy to create great beauty in the subjective world. In this labor creative imagination and visualization are used to build a beautiful subjective world for the future.

This construction starts with disciplining our wishes and desires and making them pure, beautiful, and progressive. When our aspirations become more refined and our desires are directed toward loftier objects, when our wishes are more inclusive and pure, then the first step is taken in building a better subjective world.

The subjective world is our future, and we cannot be forgetful about it.

The second step in building our subjective world is to use our thought creatively for the subjective world. We must know that plants, animals, buildings, human beings, and all objects simultaneously exist in the subjective world. We can take a flower and think about its Archetype in the higher, fiery spheres of the Cosmic Mind, try to improve that flower in some degree, and plant it in the subjective world. We can improve animal forms, human forms, objects, and buildings and visualize them as if they already existed in the subjective world.

Make a new body for yourself, one that you like best, with the best clothing, color, and form; then wear it in the subjective world. See your senses and centers active and your soul powers radiating and functioning in a higher capacity.[1]

Visualize ideal relationships with Great Ones, with friends and closest co-workers.[2]

Create a field of labor and every day engage yourself in that labor for a few moments, and before you sleep orient yourself toward it. When you start your labor in the subjective world before you leave your body, you prepare a better environment for yourself. Then, immediately when you pass away, you will continue the labor you started and save confusion and bewilderment.

---

1. See also *New Dimensions in Healing*.
2. See also *The Psychology of Cooperation and Group Consciousness*.

Ten to fifteen minutes of daily subjective work will build strong bridges between the two planes and enrich your life here and your future there.[3]

In such a work it is very beneficial to forgive people who hurt you in any way, or to ask forgiveness from those toward whom you were hard or harmful and, if possible, to reconcile with them in the physical world.

Before one passes away it will be better for him if he cleans all his debts and bad feelings with people, makes peace with them, and creates good relations and friendship. We must not carry our animosities into the subjective world, and, as much as possible, things must be corrected here on the objective plane.

It is also very important to watch our responsibilities and not pass away before we meet our responsibilities toward all those who are close to us.[4]

When the heart is purified, the angels will receive you in the Subtle World and decorate your path with flowers and music.

It is also very beneficial to resolve tensions and problems existing between you and others, dead or alive, before you enter the Subtle World. Thoughts of people, alive or dead, strongly affect your life in the Subtle World. If they are full of a benevolent spirit and love, you will have less obstacles on your path in the Subtle World. This is why it is more beneficial to have friends with you than to have those whom you hurt.

Of course, you will have your enemies in the objective and subjective worlds, but they will not be able to hurt you or even affect you if they were not hurt by you in a real sense. One can create an enemy even by being beautiful, successful, and righteous. Such enemies can only strengthen your energies and help you climb higher.

But if you have people around you whom you used for your selfish ends and hurt, or whose evolution you blocked and whom you eventually made your enemies, their thoughts will affect you and you need to clear your account with them before you can travel at full speed.

This is why the Teaching tells us that before we pass away certain preparations must be done. In certain countries or traditions when people pass age fifty-five or sixty, they withdraw from life and pass the rest of their life in the mountains, in monasteries, in meditation and contemplation, or in dedicating their life to a voluntary service for people. They think that by living a life of meditation and service they pay back all known or unknown debts that they had toward a certain number of people. If such people are wealthy, they often distribute a major part of their wealth to their families, friends, and strangers and systematically enter a life of discipline, renunciation, silence, or dedicated service.

One can see the deep wisdom behind such disciplines which promise that person a better condition in the subjective world.

---

3. See also *Other Worlds*.
4. See also *The Sense of Responsibility in Society*.

When the conditions in the subjective world are right, man will not lose time there and he will gather a great amount of wisdom and make better decisions for his future life on earth.

We are told that the path of those who dedicated their lives for humanity and spread love, joy, blessings, wisdom, and beauty is decorated with aromatic flowers, lights, and music. Such individuals pass into higher levels of the astral plane and enjoy great beauties there.

One must develop the power of observation. As the power of observation increases, our Third Eye and its astral counterpart gain greater clarity and help us be more creative, not only on the physical plane but also in the astral plane. The Third Eye controls and directs creative energies. Just as we need to create many vehicles or forms to live in the physical plane, so we need to build more subtle vehicles, forms, and a better environment in the astral plane for a more successful life, for greater unfoldment and progress.

With clear and sensitive observation we develop the ability to see things in their physical, astral, and mental natures, the existence of which never passed through our minds.

The Third Eye coordinates such observation, and one can see manifold functions and expressions of certain events, forms, ideas, and thoughts.

Most people cannot see clearly in the astral plane. For example, they cannot see the colors, the geometry of certain forms; they cannot read a book in the astral plane; they cannot observe symbols. Observation gradually develops a seeing eye.

Once the seeing operates, man becomes more conscious on the astral plane, and the creative life in the astral plane begins. Man builds consciously and in such a way that he is not trapped in his own constructions.

Many advanced souls build a new life on the mental plane during their cycle on the astral plane so that they always have the urge to go forward.

After many conscious lives, man builds simultaneously on three planes, and he can visit his home on the astral plane after sleep or go to his mental home whenever he wants.[5]

All such successes are achieved by the power of thought. Thought is the great builder upon many planes. Unfortunately, people see the effects of thought only on the physical plane, and they focus their mental activities only on the physical plane.

A man who learns how to use his thoughts in the astral, mental, and higher Fiery Worlds will create on the physical plane only those forms which will bridge the three worlds and make the beauty of the prototypes manifest on each plane in full glory. His mental body and his astral body will be so healthy and beautiful that they will create a magnificent physical body whose centers and senses will be very sensitive to the recordings of the senses and centers of higher vehicles.

---

5.   See also *Other Worlds*.

When the astral and mental senses begin to work, continuity of consciousness becomes a fact, and man transmits his experiences on those levels to his physical brain and lives a three-dimensional life.

We are told that the real Great Ones are present on these planes, and a man can come in contact with Them. They are not figures of imagination through which various entities masquerade themselves, but they are the real Great Ones. If our astral and mental senses are open, we will be able to contact Them, to witness Them, and to pass our experiences to our physical brains.

In collaboration with advanced disciples, Initiates, and Masters, one can build a better future on the astral and mental planes and often totally transform his physical plane life.

Not only are construction and creativity carried on through thought power, but thought power is also used to find the true direction and for protection from hostile forces existing on these planes. Thought power is used on higher planes as a stream of fire, as a beam of laser light which can destroy the fabrications of evil forces.

We not only need warriors on the physical plane, but there is a greater need for warriors on the astral and mental planes. The Plan of the Hierarchy must be carried on simultaneously in all three of these fields. Builders and warriors are needed for great labor.

As our physical conditions change, so the astral and mental conditions also change. One must continuously strive to be aware of these changes so that he is not shocked when suddenly he finds himself on these subtle planes.

The Teaching advises us to visualize the life on these subtle planes and in some degree accustom ourselves to their conditions. Talking, writing, dreaming, and visualizing about the Subtle Worlds eventually makes us consciously sensitive to the reality of these worlds. Our consciousness gradually will make the necessary changes to accept subtle messages coming from the Subtle Worlds.

The Subtle Worlds eventually become a fact for us because the created aspiration gradually takes us there every night or during our deep meditation.

Often children live in both worlds simultaneously. They speak about invisible friends, flowers, even food. People think the children are caught in their imagination, but the adults forget that imagination is a creative agent, and it may create forms on the astral and mental planes as real as other forms are on the physical plane.

But most such experiences are not the result of imagination but a factual contact with astral existence. There are many children who prefer their astral friends over their physical friends. There are also those who with difficulty adjust themselves to the physical life, and as the physical life gains greater control over their psychic nature, the contact with the Subtle World gradually becomes rare and even disappears. Sometimes the severance of this communication leads them into depression or sadness, with many physical symptoms manifesting.

Children of all ages love fairy tales. This is a proof that their consciousness is closer to the Subtle World. There are many fairy tales and legends which were especially given to humanity to keep the communication line continuous between the worlds. Every time life bothers you, read a fairy tale and you will feel a new hope within the secret chambers of your soul.

Many mental and emotional sicknesses are the result of the severance of the communication line between the worlds. It is possible to cure such cases by trying to re-establish contact with the Subtle World.

Many people become ill if they are separated from their beloved ones. The same applies for separation from the beloved ones of the astral or mental world.

Psychiatrists in the future will be able to help such cases by reconstructing in the consciousness of the patient a healthy bridge between the two worlds, enabling him to visit his friends during his sleep or meditation.

Those children who have vivid contact with the Subtle World must be handled in special ways because it is from such children that the real leaders of humanity will emerge. They must be intelligently assisted not only to keep in contact with Higher Worlds but also to create a better world in all these dimensions.

The leaders of the Future will work to transform not only the physical life but also the astral and mental life by bringing the beauty of higher dimensions to the physical plane. This will be an effort to bring "Thy kingdom" to earth, when the physical life of the planet will reflect the beauty, the glory, the harmony, and the grandeur of the Higher Worlds.

Such children, in order to have contacts with the Subtle World, must be protected for at least the first seven years so that they adjust themselves gradually to the earthly life. Violence, crimes, and events based on hatred and fear can damage their subtle bodies with dire consequences.

Children in general must be protected because it is very hard to depart from the Subtle World and descend into a dense physical body. This is such a limitation to the soul that it almost shocks the whole system.

In the future, when ways and means are found to instruct the reincarnating souls upon the astral and mental planes about the conditions of the world and the process of birth, they will not lose their consciousness and will start talking immediately after birth. The great Teacher, M.M., says that the birth process is like diving into deep water. . . .

The mystery of existence is a treasure house of unending revelations, if only human beings would raise their hearts to the Source of Creation.

It is interesting to remember that there is only one energy, and all manifestation and all actions on any level, in any form, are done by using this energy. Thinking, speaking, and acting use the same energy; the same energy carries the records of all that we do.

Too often we use this same energy to erase unworthy records and smooth the flow of energy. Sometimes we create whirlpools of this energy. Acting with contradictions, lies, and hypocrisy creates those forms of action in which the thread of energy becomes entangled. You say one thing and impress the energy in a certain way. Then you think differently and you impress the same energy differently. In doing this you continuously load the electrical wire with contradictory currents. Those charges which do not correspond to the essence of the energy create short-circuits within your nature.

Vices create short-circuits. For example, there are certain vices which blind the vision on the astral plane. We are told that when malice is carried over to the astral plane, it blinds the vision and the man walks in darkness.

There are millions of blind people on the astral plane who use their most primitive senses to move around. It is observed that those who stay long in their blindness impress their astral permanent atom to such a degree that it affects their sight in the next incarnation, creating various complications in the eyes.

The Great Ones have the most beautiful and healthy eyes, and They reflect the glory that is within Them.

Malice in the astral plane is seen as a consuming fire which burns away certain precious elements in the aura accumulated in the moments of contact with good people. We are told that a man burned-out by malice stays a long time in the lower astral plane and experiences many horrors there. Eventually a small amount of seeds of spiritual consciousness germinate and make it possible for him to leave the lower planes and ascend higher and higher.

The speediest journey is taken by people who are full of love, enthusiasm, and the urge to serve.

Besides malice there are also greed and attachment to objects of the world. Greed and attachment weaken the eyesight in the astral and mental planes. Such people cannot be fully creative in the astral and mental planes, and they cannot observe and study the beauty found there.

It is interesting that the eye and thought have a great affinity with each other. On the subtle planes the thought power is used through the eyes. And it is the thought power that helps man to advance on these planes.

The one energy in the whole Universe is an electrical substance which works on all planes, and it is the unifying factor within all planes. This means that all that is recorded in and through this energy expands and exists on all planes.

Increasing Beauty, Goodness, Righteousness, Joy, and Freedom makes the thread of energy healthy, radiant, and creative. Such a current of energy builds a glorious path through all planes on which the King of Spirit walks.

This one energy thread cyclically goes through a purification process within the refinery of the Fiery World, and the accumulated debris are removed from the electrical current. One has a chance every day to work on a new thread, keep that thread pure and to bestow prosperity on all planes.

People think that somewhere in our nature we have permanent recorders. This is true. All that we think, speak, and do is recorded within our permanent recorders.[6] But let us not forget that these recorders are just the keys transmitting the data to the Cosmic recorder which is the energy to which we refer. The One,

---

6. See also *The Science of Becoming Oneself*, Ch. 12.

all-pervading energy through which all thoughts, words, and actions are expressed has all records, and they will be available on any plane until the recycling time comes.

These records are the foundation of karma. They can be modified, changed, weakened, or strengthened by the usage of the same energy with thought.

One must not worry about the errors he made in the past. But he must take action and charge his electrical thread with the impressions of Beauty, Goodness, Righteousness, Joy, Freedom, and creative living. As these impressions increase, they will eventually eradicate the dirt floating on the current of energy and restore unity.

Hope is a rising sun which eventually dispels all that is unreal or all that does not correspond to the Essence of Existence.

37

Reservoirs of Thought

It is possible to come in contact with reservoirs of thought of Great Lives in Space. These thoughts are not similar to the thoughts which channels or mediums transmit from "space-people." These thoughts are very revelatory and dynamic. They introduce great changes into life and often express themselves as great inventions, leadership, creative movements, and synthesis.

Many people have contact with such thoughts, but they are divided into various levels:

1. Those who know about the existence of such reservoirs of thought but cannot tune in with them.

2. Those who have certain contacts with these thoughts but do not have the needed equipment and purity to express or translate them.

3. Those who have a communication line with these thoughts but who, because of their limitations or separative interests, lower the charge of the currents and use them for their narrow fields.

4. Those who have conscious contact with them and who, because of their dedication to the Common Good, can receive a tiny current from them and use them creatively to uplift people around them.

5. Those who are really in tune with them and who, because of their age-long preparation and readiness, receive them and broadcast them as life-giving ideas, visions, and revelations to humanity. These are ones who are called Masters.

The progress of the human being is a process of better and better tuning in with such reservoirs of thought.

As air and sunshine are necessary for planetary life, the thought reservoirs of Great Lives are more necessary for the survival of humanity. It is these thoughts that orient people toward their future development and achievements.

292 Thought and the Glory of Thinking

These thoughts fill Space with higher frequencies, and it is not easy to tune to them. One drop from these thoughts can enlighten a life and lead a person to his Cosmic destination.

To attract these thoughtwaves not only do we need to be able to tune in with them, but we also need a great magnetism which comes to us through a sacrificial life dedicated for ages to the service of humanity. Real magnetism develops in three stages:

1. Dedication to the Light within

2. Dedication to the service of humanity

3. Dedication to the Law of the Hierarchy or to the purpose of the Hierarchy, to the life of the Hierarchy

The Law of the Hierarchy can be summarized as

    a. striving toward the summit, labor, doing good, and aspiration toward the Hierarchy

    b. at all times acting, speaking, and thinking in the presence of the Hierarchy

    c. never creating duality between our consciousness or conscience and our deeds, words, and dreams

    d. always striving toward Beauty, Goodness, Righteous, Joy, Freedom, unity, and synthesis and always helping others to achieve these seven principles

    e. always doing all that is possible to bring to life the knowledge, the purity, the bliss, and the beauty of the Hierarchy

    f. the law of progressive, never-ending unfoldment, perfection, and cooperation in the current of psychic energy

    g. the law of bridging the lowest and the highest, self-sacrifice, pure love, striving toward the future, and reaffirmation of the Divine Image in man

The Hierarchy must be taken as a brotherhood of all those advanced human beings Who, after conquering death, stay on the planet to help humanity continue its evolution in the best way possible and without losing much time. Because of Their high achievement, we are told that They can watch the life of any disciple when They want to see if he is making good progress, and occasionally They strengthen him on the Path. Thus, every disciple actually lives under Their watchful eyes.

One needs to be alert every minute and live according to the presence of the Law of the Hierarchy. Living in the presence of the Law of the Hierarchy develops within us a great amount of pure magnetism which gradually tunes us to the reservoirs of thought of Great Lives.

It is imperative that leaders develop more refined reservoirs within their higher bodies and increase their magnetism to receive inspiration and directions from higher sources.

The thought reservoirs of Great Lives are not accumulated creative thoughts in space which have mostly human origins. They are not accumulations of the wisdom in Space from Great Ones on this planet. They are also not sendings from Great Lives or Avatars in Space. But these thought reservoirs of Great Lives are Their auras, extending thousands of miles into Space.

These auras do not precipitate in the sense that they have an electrical ring-pass-not. One must be able to penetrate into them to be able to contact them and build a channel of light to transmit them to the world.

These thought reservoirs hold within their borders the future glories of life, the future bliss and joy of life. Before one is able to come in contact with them, he must ground himself firmly in the service of life. Without having such a grounding, any contact with them either burns the person or suspends him in the air for years.

Daily dedicated labor and difficulties and problems of life are the necessary tools to ground us firmly on earth. Unless the grounding is perfect, we must not dare to come in contact with the reservoirs of thought of Great Lives. Many mental problems and unhealthy psychic conditions are the result of premature efforts to contact Higher Realms.

Contact with such reservoirs of thought must be attempted occasionally if one feels that

1. his equipment is ready

2. he is pure enough

3. he is grounded

4. he has magnetism

You can start thinking about Infinity and then slowly direct your attention toward the Great Lives expressing themselves as galaxies, zodiacal signs, or stars. Years may pass without result. Actually, seeking results can hinder the contact. But gradually you will feel the expansion of your consciousness to such a degree that life seems to you like child's play. It is this that provides a grounding. Remember that you cannot produce light unless you bridge the universal and the mundane.

Expansion of consciousness brings you greater joy. After this joy you feel the germination of great ideas in your heart.

Your future course will depend upon your past karma, your psychic energy, your thought power, and your accumulated wisdom, courage, and daring. After you have the first conscious contact, the boat of your existence will extend its sails and be immediately filled with the spatial winds from the limitless ocean.

One who stands on the shore can only express a wish — *bon voyage.*

38

The Law of Reality

The Teaching speaks about the world of reality and beauty. This world is called the Fiery World.

The world of reality, like a mirror, reflects all earthly actions, emotions, and thoughts. In the earthly life most of us do not consider the world of reality. We try to bring distortion and deception within our thoughts, words, emotions, and deeds and create disturbances in the world of reality.

For example one does something, but, when asked, he lies about it. In the world of reality his deed is recorded as it is, but when he lies about his deed, he creates a new image of his deed which is not similar to the reality.

These two subtle forms create a conflict and interchange of forces. The unreality forces itself upon the reality, and the reality fights to keep its image as it is. Such a conflict between the two forms wastes the energy of the man and eventually creates confusion in his mind and instability in his life.

The same thing happens when you deceive people about your feelings, thoughts, and intentions. You create conflict between the reality and the fabricated image.

Sincerity is proclaimed as one of the great virtues of Initiates. Sincerity is the ability not to distort reality. Thus a man who lives as a hypocrite greatly complicates his life because he becomes a battlefield in which he fights against himself.

The world of beauty is in the higher levels of the Fiery World where exist all the Archetypes of forms seen in the world. Ugliness in any form creates violent disturbances and tensions in the world of beauty. Every ugly action, thought, word, or form attracts violent fiery currents from the world of beauty to restore harmony. Such currents often burn and destroy the originators of ugliness.

Such disturbances happened in Lemurian and Atlantean times. They may also happen in our modern civilization.[1]

It is important to notice that individual deceptions or ugliness accumulate in space and become a massive thoughtform against reality and beauty. It is this

---

1. See for example *Earthquakes and Disasters, What the Ageless Wisdom Tells Us.*

massive confrontation that causes widespread earthquakes, national disasters, submergence of continents, etc.

This law is one of the most important laws of Nature, and it can be called the Law of Correspondence. Your life must correspond to reality and to beauty, or else there will emerge conflict and destruction.

Sometimes your life is lived totally reverse to the image you create. People think you are a noble, honest, and beautiful man. This is your false image. But your life is really a life of dishonesty, ugliness, and baseness of heart. That is the reality. The image of reality exists, and the image of unreality also exists in space.

Gradually your true image consumes your false image, and you stand unveiled in front of watching eyes. The real image, whether it is positive or negative, always wins. If it is negative, you pass through humiliation, suffering, and pain. If it is positive, you experience joy, freedom, and victory.

Sometimes the conflict between reality and unreality does not manifest in one life but accumulates and appears in succeeding lives. The Ancients used to say that your secret life must absolutely correspond to your open life. Such a life gradually paves the way to Higher Worlds.

We are told that people will have a very hard time in the Subtle World if they are caught in the conflict between reality and unreality, between the beauty and ugliness they created throughout their life. Those who created reality and lived accordingly and those who lived a life of beauty will be accompanied by fiery helpers in the Subtle World.

The images of reality are not prototypes but the images of exactly what you do, exactly what you feel, think, and have in your heart. We may call them images of what your essence does, whether negative or positive.

Of course, if your records or images are negative and your expressions are negative, you create karmic reactions from the laws of the Universe. But if your records are negative and your expressions do not reconcile with the records, you not only receive karmic reactions but you immediately disturb the energy currents around and in you as well.

If the records are positive and the expressions are positive, you have harmony and blessings combined in your life.

A hypocrite is a man who has negative records but tries to appear positive. A sincere man appears as his records. If his records are high-quality, we call him a saint. The worst situation comes into being when the records are negative and one tries to cover them by positive appearances.

When the recordings are positive, the expressions reflect the recordings and build harmony, even if they do not completely reconcile with the recordings. In this case, there is no duality but only a striving for harmony.

Through images of reality one puts various forces into operation. Through false images one puts other forces into operation. These two forces clash with each other to assert their rights. Curiously enough, these two forces act through various human beings around us. Thus we create chaotic conditions around us in which people either love us or hate us, or the same people love us and hate us.

Our environment often clearly reflects the state of consciousness we are in. Every state of consciousness manifests through people and events around us.

There is another phenomenon which is called *fabrication*. Fabrication is like writing checks for which funds do not exist in the bank. There are no records to support your fabrication.

Fabrications create a vacuum in your aura where the fire of Space moves, creating various skin and organic diseases and distortions in your etheric, astral, and mental centers.

A lie is not a fabrication but a distortion of reality. Fabrication has no preset reality. It is based on desires, vanities, glamors, or illusions. For example, a man has never been to India, but he tells stories about his life in India. This is a fabrication.

Fabrications not only create vacuums but also take forms in the subtle planes. There they try to attract every kind of formation to justify their existence. Sometimes they are called the rubbish in space.

There is another phenomenon which is called *shining by the light of others*. This originates from a vanity. People distort reality and present themselves as the source of the values they manifest. For example, one gives his name as the author of a great poem which does not belong to him; one pretends that he is the creator of a famous artwork or a composition which is not his own.

What happens in such distortions is very subtle. An example will make it simple to understand. It is like a man who makes a big promise to the workers of a great factory in the name of the president. Then, because he is not able to keep his promise, the whole pressure of the workers focuses on him and they demand either the fulfillment of the promise or his punishment. Natural laws put that man under heavy pressure to fulfill his promise, but because he has no preparation, the man lives in a continuous state of disturbance.

Every time we try to shine by the light of another person we commit ourselves to a great debt which demands payment.

The term *righteousness* is not yet fully understood. One of the interpretations of righteousness is that a person must not use others for his own interests; he must not use their reputation, name, or talents to give the impression that what he does is right and acceptable. In righteousness, the source of light is fully acknowledged and the person is presented as a carrier of that light with his own capacity and worth.

Every act of showing off is condemned by the Sages because it is an act of unrighteousness to the source. Reality demands proof of all that you claim. If you do not have proof, under the pressure of the Law of Reality you either strive to meet your claims for many, many lives, or you accept your failure and pay for it through a life of conscious sacrifice.

The less conflict we have between reality and unreality, between beauty and ugliness, the more powerful will be our ascent toward Higher Worlds and the greater will be our creativity. Conflict between reality and unreality, between beauty and ugliness will not only weaken our mind, but it will also create various physical and life problems which will waste our time, energy, and talents and prevent us from achieving our spiritual goals.

An expanding consciousness gradually dissolves the causes of conflict and makes the life of man the pure reflection of reality and beauty.

In a transmuted consciousness duality cannot exist. Sincerity is purity of consciousness, a consciousness in which there is no shadow of duality. The man lives as he is and tries to reflect the highest beauty in the Fiery World. We are told that a unified consciousness is a mighty warrior for the Common Good.

When the consciousness is striving toward higher achievements, toward greater beauty, purity, joy, and freedom, it brings a great amount of fiery energy into the aura and strengthens the protective net. Thus the magnetic power of the aura increases and eventually becomes capable of attracting impressions coming from higher sources.

As these higher impressions are assimilated by the aura, the unification of beingness takes place. The reflection merges into reality, and the aura scintillates as a unified rainbow.

One of my Teachers used to say, "Life is a thread without knots; do not create knots on it because knots will distort the flow of life and weaken the thread."

One day he explained that each knot comes into being through an act of contradiction, and when you contradict yourself through your deceptive thoughts, words, and actions, you create knots. To explain the distortion of the image, he showed us a boy who was making mud balls and throwing them at his own portrait taped on the wall.

This is how human beings make their original beauty into an ugly, muddy image.

An expanding consciousness leads a man on a clear path where he does not fight against his own creations and where he is free to cooperate with the world of reality and beauty.

True striving is a continuous effort to match the manifested life with the unmanifested or hidden life of beauty. Each achievement on the path of beauty is an act of unification of the divided and disturbed human life. Unless duality disappears from our life, unity cannot be achieved.

The whole process of the path of perfection is a process of unification.

Equilibrium in its esoteric sense is conformity or reconciliation between subjective and objective life, or between what you are inside and what you are outside. But this equilibrium turns into a very concrete hindrance on our path if it is not progressive.

Every day our inner world must progress, our consciousness must expand, and our thoughts must rise in quality. Then our outer life, with all its expressions, must reconcile with it. The equilibrium of our body and of our planet can be sustained only through progressive advancement of our equilibrium. Whenever our equilibrium freezes, we create disturbances in the equilibrium of the planet.

Meteorology is a great science. It found many causes for the changes in weather, but it neglected the major cause: human thoughts, feelings, words, and deeds. Whenever equilibrium is frozen, the natural forces try to restore the equilibrium or advance it to higher levels. This is, esoterically, the origin of natural catastrophes or violent changes in weather.

It may seem we are in the world of superstition, but once the man is understood as an electrical phenomenon and as the switch to many forces of Nature, then people will try to live a more balanced life. Every time our consciousness crystallizes or freezes, the ocean of life tries to melt it away. Life in its essence is a flow. In a crystallized consciousness the life does not flow. Whenever life cannot flow, a progressive equilibrium does not exist. Progressive equilibrium is an answer to the progressive equilibrium of Cosmic forces.

Thus the man not only creates equilibrium between what he is inside and what he is outside, but he also reaches a stage of development in which he reflects or reconciles himself with the state of progressive equilibrium of Cosmic forces.

We ascend on the ladder of perfection only in harmonizing our steps with the Cosmic steps.

The world of true reality and beauty is not only the resource for our individual life, but also on the Cosmic scale the world of reality and beauty exercises a great pressure to conform our life to the expanding life of Cosmos.

39

Memory

Every object or event we experience leaves in our etheric brain an image with a specific frequency. When we see the object again or experience a similar event, that special image frequency identifies with it and we remember the previous object or event. Each identification processes into a memory.

Actually our etheric brain is part of the global etheric brain. The global etheric brain is the hard disk. Our etheric brain is a floppy disk, but its contents are also in the hard disk. This floppy disk has the ability to penetrate into the hard disk of the planet and record much information of a higher order. Until the scientists accept the etheric brain, they will ponder and remain in the labyrinths of the physical brain.

Ancients researched memory and called the planetary etheric brain *Akasha*. Akasha is the hard disk. The same recordings in the individual are in Akasha. The difference is that Akasha contains the sumtotal of the memory of all objects and events, and the floppy disk is individual. When the individual develops the Antahkarana, which connects the floppy disk to Akasha, the individual slowly becomes aware of the records of Akasha.

In comparison to the solar memory hard disk, the planetary hard disk is a floppy disk. The planetary Antahkarana must be connected to it to make the planetary floppy disk contact the solar hard disk.

There are several obstacles to memory. Our memory does not function if the electrical or etheric brain is polluted with the lies and deceit through which we manipulated people. Also, our memory withdraws after every criminal act or hateful act we commit. It is very interesting that our memory is closely linked to our eyesight. When our memory weakens, our eyesight weakens.

Other obstacles to our memory are glamors, illusions, crystallizations, and maya.

Glamors are crystallizations in the astral plane. Illusions are crystallizations in the mental plane. Maya is a crystallization of force in the etheric plane. These crystallizations affect the etheric brain, and a tumor is created through which memory is leaked into the ocean of the All Penetrating Mind, the Universal Mind, Mahat. The mind short-circuits because of these three obstacles.

Various viruses which impede the memory are the result of such obstacles. Distortion of energy patterns in the etheric brain evoke or create viruses that destroy the vehicles of the distorted etheric brain.

Thus, everything we experience goes to the hard disk in the planetary computer as well as being recorded in our own diskette. This diskette is built by etheric matter and is encased by brain cells. Memories can be awakened through brain cells combined with etheric matter, or they can be awakened through etheric beings which the soul contacts at times.

The brain has no specific portion for specific functions, but the etheric body has corresponding places in the etheric brain that affect the dense physical brain as its dense counterpart. Also the etheric brain as a diskette does not own the memories. They are in the etheric body and in the hard disk of the planet.

Kinds of Memory

There are two kinds of memory. The first is the ability to remember events, words, poems, ideas, music, etc. The second one is the subjective memory.

This second kind of memory is the result of remembering subjective experiences on the astral, mental, or higher planes. Unless this memory is cultivated, the accumulation of data through our five senses will not have a purposeful direction to help us reach gradual perfection. Reality is found when the accumulations of the first memory system coincide and harmonize with the memories accumulated in the subjective world.

We dream about some event, and later the event takes place on the physical plane. This subjective memory is collected in the correspondences of the brain in higher bodies. It is formed by the recordings of various senses in astral, mental, and higher planes. Unless these senses are sufficiently developed, the memory will not be clear in details and subtleties.

It is possible that astral and mental memories can be reflections of experiences registered in the Intuitional World.

When you awaken early in the morning, think about all the dream experiences you had during sleep. How many of them can you remember — how clearly and in how much detail? In observing your subjective memory, you will come to the conclusion that it is not properly developed, and because of this you cannot use most of the wisdom or experience that you have in your subjective existence. When your higher mechanisms are constructed properly, their recordings will improve. To build these higher bodies, you need to save your energies and use them for the building of higher bodies.

When you try to remember your dream experiences, try to find out which events were astral, which ones were mental, and if there were any higher experiences too. Such an effort to discriminate between the qualities and sources of the dreams makes you see how sometimes one experience reflects on different planes in different forms; or how one experience manifests in its astral, mental, and intuitional parts on these planes. Through such an effort, the experience becomes more complete in your memory and more useful in your life.

Our present memory is yet very primitive. We forget people, their names. . . . Half of our dreams are forgotten. We do not remember the books we read or the words spoken to us. We do not remember things we learn . . . and in general, when we open our eyes, all our subjective experiences melt away. How can we cultivate subjective memory?

Subjective memory is developed when

1. We cultivate calmness and peace

2. We do not have conflict in our mind

3. We do not have conflict between what we believe and what we do

4. Our conscience does not bother us

5. Our nervous system is healthy and not intoxicated

6. We do not have imperil[1]

7. We are harmless

8. We know how to sleep[2]

9. We have an intense desire to be conscious in the subtle planes

10. Our mind is disciplined in concentration, meditation, and thinking

11. Our aura is not agitated by wrong speech, malice, slander, and belittling gossip

12. We are dedicated to human service

It is very important to have subjective memory because so much is possible in the subjective world:

1. One can learn about causes producing world events.

2. One can learn the ways to introduce new causes to balance or defeat destructive causes before they come into manifestation.

---

1. See also *Irritation — The Destructive Fire.*
2. *New Dimensions of Healing*, Chs. 43-44, and *Other Worlds*, Ch. 38, contain much information on sleep.

3. One can see what effect his life has on the Inner Worlds.

4. One can consciously engage himself in building higher instruments and bodies to be more active in Higher Worlds.

5. One can collect precious pearls of wisdom from the shores of Higher Worlds and contact sources of great inspirations.

6. In being more conscious and in developing the ability to remember, one advances on the path of perfecting himself.

7. With conscious contact and cultivated memory, one lives a more balanced and benevolent life on the physical plane.

Subjective and objective memory are like the two cups of the balance. Both must be developed to keep equilibrium in life. The tapestry of life is woven by subjective and objective memories.

The relationship, the influence, and the effects which bodies and forms exercise upon each other can be seen more clearly in the subjective worlds. The deeper one goes, the more clearly he sees how bodies, emanations, and the chemism created through interaction bring changes in others, in their form and direction.

Only on the lower levels are bodies seen as separate objects. In the Subtle World, bodies live in the same energy pool. Such a realization comes as one penetrates into Higher Worlds.

Only from the Higher Worlds can one see the future outcome of any relationship going on in the physical world. As one goes deeper into the higher spheres, he becomes aware of causes. In lower levels, people are occupied with effects; they fight or deal with effects. It is in Higher Worlds that the causes are discovered and used to bring changes or restoration upon lower levels. All this can be done if the subjective memory is clear and not a mixture of hallucinations.

We have a memory storage and a memory operating room. Storage is not inactive. It is always being added to and rearranged, but it is not under the immediate control of the "demands of the need." The memory operating room is like an open map which man uses daily to meet his needs. The consciousness operates both of them, but the storage operates like the hard disk in the computer, and the memory operating room is the menu under the control of the conscious demand for the immediate need.

These two sections of the memory are related to each other by associative impulses. When a part of the memory from the operating room is not used, it slowly sinks into the memory storage; but it is not lost. In the memory storage, we have all the languages which we used in our past existences, but it is difficult to call them back.

These two sections remain separate and aloof in our waking consciousness, but as our consciousness operates on higher and higher planes, these two sections of the memory unite. Then we clearly remember in our waking consciousness all that we call our past.

The life unit which we call the human soul advances by using his bodies, and the memory diskettes of his bodies, gradually and step by step putting them in his storage room of bodies after they are conquered and mastered. He uses the memory operating room of his latest built or discovered body. For example, when his consciousness focuses itself in the astral body, the operating room of the memories of the physical body becomes the storage room of memories. When he focuses his consciousness in the mental body, the astral operating room of memories becomes the storage room of memories, and so on.

When the intuitional body is built and in an operative stage, gradually all storage rooms of the physical, emotional, and mental bodies become the memory operating room of the intuitional awareness. This goes on until the awareness operates in the atmic body, where all memories function as an "eternal now."

In the intuitional state, the awareness unit or the human soul goes through a great labor to clean the files of the storages. All accumulated data which does not correspond to reality is burned away. This is sometimes a very painful process because pseudo facts have their long chains which disturb many recordings when pulled out and burned away.

These kinds of chains have reality and unreality links woven together. Since these chains are related to the factual memories with their reality links, the real memories in the storage are often left paralyzed or dead because of the unreality links which must be thrown out from the chains.

The plan is that age after age man must conquer and master his vehicles and let them one by one function on their own, in harmony with the rest of the vehicles. For example, the physical body does its own job and man does not need to operate the blood circulation, the workings of the organs and glands, etc. They work by themselves. But this was not always so.

The physical permanent atom is the reservoir of all the training the body has gone through for millions of ages — through the mineral, vegetable, and animal kingdoms — until the command posts and switches were created and established in it to run without any deliberate effort. The body now works as an automaton, as a self-controlled mechanism, as long as it receives energy from the soul to do so.

Our astral and mental bodies must go through the same process. First, they must be built. Then they must function by our conscious decisions. Then they will be left free to do their duties as if they were a self-operating computer. In this stage, man will expect that his physical, emotional, and mental bodies will function according to the programming of the soul. Of course, this programming can change, life after life, and be improved in such a way that the three bodies and the soul function more harmoniously.

When the mental body is conquered and mastered, then it will fall under the threshold of consciousness and work as a programmed computer doing what it is told to do. Then the human soul will begin to build his intuitional body, and Intuition will take the place of the former ability of "conscious thinking." The intellect will be surpassed and replaced by the Intuition. The Intuition will eliminate all those mechanisms built and used by the intellect because the Intuition will consider them as hindrances to development of the human soul.

The Intuition will usher in the Age of Synthesis, which means that every object will be viewed and analyzed from the viewpoint of physical conditions, emotional conditions, mental conditions, plus intuitional conditions. This is what the four-dimensional outlook is. Thus man will leave behind body after body as he conquers and masters them.

A day will come when he will do the same with the other glorious bodies and eventually arrive at a state of beingness in which all his seven bodies fuse and synthesize in such a way that in their totality they form one body called the Cosmic Physical Plane body. Then the human soul will penetrate into the Cosmic Astral Plane and repeat his labor on a higher spiral. He will build a Cosmic astral body, a Cosmic mental body, and so on until the Cosmic Planes are conquered as a whole. . . . The Wisdom says that there are Christ-like Beings working in this stage and others on still higher Cosmic planes.

Greater things can be achieved if small things are done in the spirit of perfection. The goal is to achieve a greater and greater synthesis until one reaches the Central Core of Synthesis which controls all that exists. In this stage memory vanishes, and the awareness of man operates in past, present, and future as if it were a mirror of *now*.

When memory fades, man attains the state which is called *omniconsciousness*. But life has many caves which must be investigated thoroughly if one wants to reach such a state.

Our memory must also be cultivated in relation to certain people who come into our lives either for joy or for grief. Such people evoke a feeling in us that we know them, . . . but where and when? Such a feeling is a subtle memory which must be investigated to find out more about it.

Every person who comes into your life is the representative of a part of your being not yet investigated or realized. The investigation and realization starts when such a person meets you, and especially when he bothers you. First, you are forced to see him as he is and have a good idea about his nature. Then you have a feeling that he is a projection of a part of your being. Then you turn your eyes to the part of your being which was being neglected.

Thus the representative of a part of your nature helps you study your neglected portion of yourself. He is a dramatic demonstration of the neglected part of your nature, and he serves to develop a way of approach to that part in you so that you come to the realization that you are dealing not with a human being but with a part of yourself.

The most difficult transition is the point where you recognize a part of yourself in him. Later, when you analyze the hatred and repulsion you used against him, you will see how and why you hurt your own self so much to learn the existence of the same corresponding part within your own nature.

Such a representation is not always negative. It can also be a comic presentation of yourself, or a glorious presentation of your own nature. This means that in changing your nature, you come in contact with great or weird personalities. If you are changing your nature toward perfection, you will have in your life those who present that improving part of yourself. At the same time, people will come to reveal things in you which are still stupid, silly, or poisonous to make you get rid of them.

Most of the actors in our dreams play similar roles — to reflect certain parts of our nature and enable us to study them for a possible change.

It also happens that the persons who influenced us and whom we hated deeply in this life impress us so strongly that in the following lives we dramatize them in our life, repeating with others everything they did to us. This means, simply, that people cannot create harmony with each other because they hate in each other the things that they hate within themselves. Unless they clean the things that they hate within themselves, they cannot stop fighting against the same things that are within others.

For example, if a man and a woman are fighting with each other, they may eventually choose to separate from each other. But this does not solve the problem because their problem is not in the other person but within themselves. The new person who will come into their lives will either continue reflecting the parts they do not like within themselves, or he will evoke deeper problems hidden within each person's nature. This is why we say that the best moment to separate is after one solves his problems and reaches a peaceful state of relationship. This is because such a state is stagnant and cannot help the development and release of things hidden within one's nature.

People have expectations of each other. When these expectations are not fulfilled, they argue or fight with each other. The reason is always the same: The one who has expectations from you is the one who is failing in fulfilling his own expectations of himself, and you are reflecting his condition. He is fighting with you as the reflection of his own problem.

Whatever one does not like in himself, he fights against its reflection in others. One must be wise enough to see the reflection of his good or bad parts in others, to use them as a mirror, and then to correct himself within his own nature.

When two people, such as a husband and wife, fight with each other and decide to separate from each other, they are actually escaping, not from each other but from themselves. Their problems are going to continue with others because the new companion will either evoke the same weaknesses and reflect them or unearth new factors within each person to perpetuate the drama. Sometimes the new companion is worse because the people start the same problems from the beginning again, instead of dealing with the last part of the problems.

The sign that one has not started to solve his own problems is that he fights with you. When he solves his problems, he will not have any reason to fight with you.

When partners reflect each other's good parts, then there is love, understanding, and harmony. But such a life sometimes becomes boring if people do not challenge each other for higher achievements.

One must realize and confess that what he was fighting in you was the thing he was not fighting within himself. Part of him which is not visible to him is visible in you. In the same way, the part of you that is not visible to you, he is making visible to you with his behavior.

To impose on each other means to make the other do things that you did not do for yourself. The more you impose yourself, the more you lose the chance of solving your own problems.

Man invokes; woman evokes.[3] When these roles are reversed, you have problems. For example, if woman invokes, man rejects her because she is in his territory. If man evokes, woman rejects him because that is her territory. When a man rejects the evoking of a woman, the woman feels frustrated and tries to impose herself to receive a response from the man. Because she rebels against the man's unresponsiveness, the man hates her in his turn, and he wants to impose himself on her. Then she rejects him because he did not respond to her demand. . . . This is a vicious circle. Each one must look inside himself or herself.

One must also remember that these complications do not necessarily come from the events of the present. Many complications exist in our memory which, by association, come to the surface. Old events play again and again until they are understood and permanently solved.

You can protect the other party by controlling your own weaknesses within yourself. This is why great Teachers emphasized that we must "love" our enemies, not for the sake of loving their cruelties and crimes but because in "loving" them we prevent taking them into our nature and dramatizing them in our next life.

Memory must one day extend itself to these areas, too, and show us where we failed to use such people to study ourselves and instead hated them.

It is also true that when you personify in your nature the character of one whom you hated, in future lives when you meet that person you present to him what he gave to you in the past. You present to him the part of his nature that needs change, cultivation, or development. This is how people help each other painfully, joyfully, unconsciously, and consciously.[4]

Painful Memories

One of the hindrances to our creativity is the flow of painful memories. This flow of painful memories often

---

3. See also *Sex, Family, and the Woman in Society.*
4. See also *The Subconscious Mind and the Chalice* and *The Mystery of Self-Image.*

1. mixes with the current of spiritual force and manifests as a mixture of ugliness and beauty, carrying with it a destructive influence.

2. blocks the current of creative fire for a long or short time.

3. connects the consciousness of the person to remote events of a negative and painful nature. The remote events overflow into the mental body and devour the mental energy and the creative fire. They manifest as a caravan of painful events which trap the human soul and make him concerned only with those elements which secure the safety of the personality.

However, if a person has control of the subconscious mind, or repairs the lower mind, the situation dramatically changes and the creative fire uses old memories to demonstrate how the Law of Cause and Effect functions and how, through these memories, some very precious lessons are learned.

An advanced person can use the memories of painful events, downfalls, short-comings, failures, and experiences and turn them into masterpieces of art: paintings, music, poetry, and so on.

A person can never understand himself if he does not analyze the events of his past and discover those psychological laws and causes which produced certain events. But one cannot clearly analyze them and stay unharmed if he is not elevated to the higher mental plane.

Great artists know how to build ladders of ascent for other people with the elements of their own past failures. In this art a person can see the misery of past failures, but also the striving and the ladder upon which the striving spirit succeeds in climbing to reach great spiritual heights.

40

Conscious and Unconscious Memory

There are conscious memory and unconscious memory.

Conscious memory is when you remember something. This memory can be accurate, inaccurate, or partial. Conscious memory can be distorted by many factors. For example, your intellect can interfere and try to modify the memory according to your various interests. Other memories can mix with it and distort it. Emotions can strongly diffuse it. Fear and anger play a great part in diffusion.

Sometimes conscious memories associate themselves with posthypnotic suggestions or with various commands in your subconscious mind. Such an association distorts the memory.

Unconscious memory is memory recorded in the human soul, but it bypasses the mental and emotional planes and reacts directly. You meet a man and immediately you love him or reject him. Your conscious mind cannot find the reason for such an attitude, but your soul remembers that that man either hurt you in the past or helped you. Your reaction is based upon an unconscious memory.

It may happen that that man did not really have any relation with you in the past, but it was one closely resembling him who hurt you or helped you. Your unconscious memory immediately reacts or responds.

The reactions or responses of the unconscious memory are very accurate, but when we try to observe or analyze them we distort them and often fabricate false reasons.

The question arises: If the man I hate — because of my unconscious memory — is not really the one who hurt me, then how can I justify my hatred for him when he did nothing bad to me in the past?

The answer is that though the man is not the real one but only resembles him, your unconscious memory will continually warn you about him and eventually will make you react accordingly. There will be continuous tension between you and him, and this tension will not provide a happy companionship with him.

Unconscious memory controls your etheric body and leads you into action. Sometimes your logic or reasoning fails to interfere with the action.

Unconscious memory is registration of many direct experiences on the subtle planes. It often acts like the voice of warning and alarms you about certain people. Your rational mind cannot remember many experiences from the Subtle World, but the unconscious memory keeps the records of the experiences and releases them when the need arises.

Every time one enters the Subtle World, his soul or his True Self sees exactly the nature of those people related to his personality. And when he comes back to physical consciousness, the mind does not remember the observations of the soul but the soul has the memory of his observations.

This unconscious memory "says" to you, for example, "Yesterday you made an agreement with that man, but he will deceive you. Cut your relations. In the subjective level he revealed his true nature to me."

The unconscious memory does not verbalize but urges you and makes you feel and act according to its observation. Some people call such a feeling an "inner warning" or even an "intuition," but actually it is the unconscious memory and in most cases one cannot err by obeying such an urge.

One must not confuse unconscious memory and subconscious memory.

Unconscious memory is the soul memory not transferred into the memory diskettes of the mental and astral planes, due to their lack of development.

Subconscious memory is also unconscious — but it is the result of all those experiences which the subconscious mind records when the person was in a state of unconsciousness. For example, in an accident you were unconscious and your five senses registered many events and reported them to the subconscious mind. Thus soul-memory and the subconscious memory are two different recordings.[1]

There is also another kind of subconscious memory which can be called inactive or frozen memory. There are many frozen memories within our system. It is very difficult to release them. They are like locked doors. They block the flow of conscious memory, making the tape of conscious memory blank in certain places. We call such blank spots, gaps.

Fortunately, unconscious memory bypasses these gaps and acts directly on the etheric body. Sometimes man even acts before his mind or emotions become aware of his action.

These subconscious memories gradually condense and form calluses on the wires of the mental network and hinder the process of coordination and synthesis in the mental plane. They can only be released and handled in the right way when a man succeeds in operating upon the higher mental planes consciously and releases them and handles them through his light. This is called the process of clearing the networks of the mind.

Just as we have unconscious and conscious memories, we also have unconscious and conscious thoughts. Unconscious thoughts are those thoughts

---

1.   See also *The Subconscious Mind and the Chalice.*

which are beyond our own mental grasp but are sources of great inspiration and creativity, once we master them through meditation and contemplation.

One of the tasks of meditation is to contact these unconscious thoughts and make them conscious thoughts.

Unconscious thoughts are those thoughts which are projected by higher Beings from the starry Space. These are unconscious thoughts for us because it takes time and preparation for us to make them partially or totally conscious.

We are told that as we master the unconscious thoughts we become aware of the dimensions of Infinity.

Unconscious thoughts also exist within our nature. In certain cases we contact higher thoughts in our subjective life when we are asleep or when we have a moment of ecstasy. In these moments we register higher thoughts, but because our mind cannot grasp them at that moment, they remain for our conscious mind as unconscious thoughts. It is through meditation that we assimilate them and make them our conscious thoughts. It is through such a process that we can find infinitely rich treasures within ourselves.

One of the magnets for higher thoughts is joy. We are told that joy attracts not only thoughts found in deeper layers of our being but also from space. Joy puts the unconscious thoughts in contact with our aura and helps it to assimilate them. In moments of joy one contacts lofty thoughts.

All that exists within the higher planes of Nature and man exists as one memory. This memory is unconscious memory for us until it is assimilated by our consciousness and affirmed. Man proceeds on the path of perfection only through such a process of realization.

It is also observed that our past lives and our past experiences become our memory in our future incarnations. Most of these memories become unconscious memory, but as the evolution of the human soul proceeds, all the past and present and future become conscious in the Eternal Now.

Great changes in culture and civilization take place when certain people are able to contact the treasures of Space, the spatial thoughts which bring in great changes in human affairs. Many formulas and inventions are found in Space. Those who stand above the crystallized thought formations of contemporary life, those who stand free from outdated thoughts, can present an opportunity for these spatial thoughts to flow in and be assimilated.

Each new step toward the betterment of life is a process of remembering or making the unconscious existence a conscious existence.

Unconscious existence or unconscious thought is that thought whose capacity is far higher than the average human consciousness can grasp. These thoughts are called Cosmic currents, Cosmic thoughts; and if in the history of humanity a certain group of people contacts them and assimilates them, a new renaissance will take place on earth.

This is why the expansion of consciousness is a sacred responsibility of man. It is through expansion of consciousness that areas and fields of unconscious treasures are contacted, mastered, and brought into conscious manifestation.

It is observed that higher thoughts are simpler than thoughts found on lower strata. The ability to contact these higher thoughts and make them conscious thoughts will simplify life. Simplification of life will very soon be an urgent matter. People will understand that simplification will save time, energy, and space. Simplification will make life happier.

But simplification will be the result of spiritual maturity, a transformation of life. Each step toward spiritual realization is a step toward simplicity. Each step toward materialization is a step toward complexity.

As human beings mature spiritually, they will not need the toys they accumulated around them and they will not waste their lives playing with them.

Man is limited in his actions and confused on his path because he cannot remember how the laws of Nature operated throughout millions and millions of years and reacted against violations. As he becomes conscious of these memories, he will change and simplify his life.

Simplicity is the result of spiritualization. As one comes closer to his True Self, his life becomes simplified. Complexity weakens the spirit. Simplicity provides greater opportunity for the spirit to be creative.

It is also known that simplicity reduces noise and all other pollution. But complexity creates all the kinds of pollution we have at the present.

People cherish the idea that the progress of thought can be continuous if good conditions exist, for example, abundance, freedom, appreciation, success, etc. But the Teaching says that our thought deepens and our consciousness expands when they are found in conditions in which they must strive to find new ways and exercise greater creativity to solve the presented problems of life.

Those conditions which make the thought process relax do not work in our favor. This is why a school graduate finds himself helpless in front of life's problems. His real graduation begins when he steps into the field of hard daily life, with its numberless problems. It is through his success and failure that he becomes a better thinker and can have a more expanded consciousness.

In the last analysis, it is not the success or failure that we had that is the important issue, but how much our thought deepened and how much our consciousness expanded through our successes and failures.

No one will bother about his successes and failures if he gained greater experience or the ability to think deeper because when he leaves his body his thinking will be the sole treasure taken with him. The rest will turn into ashes.

Not every condition our personality wants is favorable for better thinking. If conditions are more challenging, if the life imposes upon us the need for better thinking, then we must feel fortunate as only in those conditions can we sharpen our swords for future expansions of consciousness.

It is a good exercise to think that our successes and failures are the steps of the ladder through which we climb toward higher dimensions.

People sometimes lose millions of dollars and their reputations to gain a pearl of wisdom. All their dollars and their reputations will not lead them to Higher Worlds, but the pearl of wisdom will. Such an attitude creates a fiery conflict between the personality and the spirit. The spirit knows the beneficial path, but the personality cannot easily detach itself from the pleasures of wealth and reputation.

The Transfiguration of the personality begins the moment when it slowly loosens its grip on matter and merges into the stream of the spirit. Many lives must be spent to teach the personality how to detach and renounce because the personality is built through accumulation and attachment. Once the process of Transfiguration starts, the spirit increases in joy and the creativity of its thought deepens.

As thought gains greater and greater power over the conditions of life, a new state of beingness begins to form. This new man is a hero. A hero is one who does not live for success or failure; these do not concern him. The thing that concerns him is to increase his contact with the Guiding Light in the Universe and live under the command of that Light.

In the light of the Eternal Now, there is no failure. If one day we awaken to reality, we will see that our greatest lessons and our greatest teachers were our failures. Every time the shock of failure hits us, we expand our consciousness and know how to proceed in the future.

Adverse conditions of life sharpen our minds, and thus we learn to bless our obstacles, knowing that "through them we bloom."

The consciousness of a person expands as the storage of his memory increases. Memory, first of all, collects individual facts, events, and experiences; then slowly facts, events, and experiences form a synthesis which creates in man that which promotes understanding.

A synthesized memory is a very advanced state of mind in which individual memories find their special locations within a picture of a great formation. It is such a synthesized memory that turns into a mechanism to understand the events of life.

Understanding is based on those memories which are the result of true experiences. When all these memories are coordinated, the person can instantaneously evaluate an event and understand it on the basis of his past experiences, ready and arranged in the memory diskette.

The mechanism of memory also has a capacity to discriminate between those memories which are valid and those which are mixed with imagination. Imaginative memories are slowly rejected and replaced with factual memories.

When the memory diskette is organized with factual memories, forming special configurations which reflect the path of the soul activities in life, then all the memory diskettes turn into a magnetic mirror which begins to attract the memories of past lives. After such an occurrence, one goes through a hard labor to discriminate between past and present experiences and sort out all those past experiences which cannot contribute to the labor of the present life.

When such a sorting out is done, a new synthesis takes place in the memory diskettes. They become super-magnetic and begin to reflect the future path of

316 Thought and the Glory of Thinking

the soul, the path through which he is going to pass. The future path is the mathematical result of all memories of experiences he went through in the past.

It is here that the miracle happens.

While the future image of the human soul appears on the mirror of the mental plane as an effect of past causes, the human soul himself projects the vision of his own true image on the mirror of the mental plane, creating a powerful point of aspiration for the personality to overcome his conditional self-image and strive to the vision of the human soul.

It is in the Fourth Initiation that the conditional image disappears in the true Image of the human Soul and the human soul meets his True Self. It is in this stage that the accumulated memories in all layers of his being go through an extreme purification. All that remains are the memories which reflect the vision of the soul.

At this point, the Solar Angel feels that Its mission is fulfilled and It departs, annihilating Its dwelling, the Chalice.[2] Thus, the personality memories are obliterated by the memories of the soul, while the soul was engaged in spiritual realms with his vision of the Higher Worlds.

---

2. See also *The Subconscious Mind and the Chalice* and *The Solar Angel*.

41

How To Create Positive Thoughtforms

As man develops and begins to think and use his mind, he becomes more and more dangerous. It is also true that as he begins to think, his sense of responsibility increases. You cannot feel the depth of responsibility until you see how dangerous you can be. Thus thinking, danger, and the sense of responsibility must go together if a person wants to evolve and serve humanity.

If one does not know how to think, he cannot create thoughtforms; he cannot even create weapons or poisons or dangerous situations. On the other hand, if one thinks but he does not check his thoughts and the situation with his sense of responsibility, his mind turns into the most dangerous weapon in the world.

When man starts to think, he creates thoughtforms. These thoughtforms begin to exist in space or around objects. Some of these thoughtforms are against the survival of humanity. Some of them are a great contribution to the evolution of humanity. Some of them are sources of confusion. They all depend on the beingness of the one who creates them: on his background, education, traditions, visions, as well as outer influences and pressures.

What are thoughtforms?

When you think and visualize or imagine, you create very subtle forms in space composed of mental and emotional substances. Sometimes they are formed of both substances; sometimes only of mental substance. Just as you can build many forms out of wood, there is also a mental stuff from which you can, through your thinking, build mental thoughtforms.

Thoughtforms are of different shapes. They can be clear or diffused. They can be incomplete or complete. Sometimes their form is clear, but their color is not pure. Some of them carry destructive motives; some of them carry constructive motives. Some of them live for a few minutes; some of them live for thousands of years. Some of them are ugly; some of them are very beautiful.

A thoughtform accompanied by voice, emotion, and movement is different from a thoughtform just conceived in the mind. Thoughtforms are found on all wavelengths, and their frequency is related to their quality.

Not all thoughtforms are forms of objects we see in the world. Often they have unusual forms and colors for which we have no language to interpret or define unless we see them in their own plane of substance.

The difference between beautiful, constructive thoughtforms and ugly, destructive thoughtforms is that the former help people to evolve, while the latter hit the target and come back with greater force to hit the originator. Thus every ugly thought that we manufacture goes and hits the target and then with more force comes back and hits the mechanism of thought and causes much damage in that mechanism. This is why those who think ugly thoughts gradually lose the capacity to think clearly, and this leads them to failure and defeat.

The builder of thoughtforms is the human soul. The human soul uses mental substance through his consciousness and produces thoughts and then thoughtforms according to his level.

Thought travels faster than light. After you think, your thought immediately goes ten times around the globe and contributes to the thoughtforms of light in space or to the thoughtforms of darkness in space. Thoughtforms are like radio waves and people are like radios, whether they are conscious of it or not.

Every thoughtform influences the consciousness of humanity. If these thoughtforms are negative, they bring destructive results. If they are positive, they create constructive results. Those who do not care about the welfare of humanity try to influence the minds of the masses in such a way that they think destructively. For example, a person creates a story about world destruction. He spreads his thoughtforms through radio, television, movies, and publications and conditions the thinking of millions of people. Each person acts like a broadcasting station, discharging the same destructive thoughtform amplified by his own fears, anxieties, and anger.

Thus one person can pollute space by causing people to think on the line of his destructive thought. Such a pollution is one hundred times more dangerous than the other kinds of pollution humanity generates.

What happens? First of all, our earth is controlled and supervised by Higher Beings Who through Their directives try to guide the planet in the right direction so that life evolves here as the Almighty Creator planned for it to evolve. These directives, messages, impressions, and inspirations coming from higher Sources pass through the miles-thick layers of pollution and are filtered, deflected, or even prevented from reaching the leaders of humanity.

Each person, somewhere in his mental body, has a very sensitive spot which in ancient Teachings is called the Contact Center. This center receives the direction. This is why it is sometimes called the sense that registers the direction. When the direction cannot reach the contact point, humanity degenerates and loses its vision, confusion increases, and humanity lives in a way that is against its own survival. Humanity cuts it own throat with its own hands.

Many civilizations vanished in this way. The earth passed through many cataclysms, and each civilization vanished because humanity lost the contact. Similarly, because of air pollution and the pollution of space, the rays of the Sun, with all their purity, cannot reach the kingdoms of Nature and create the same development and unfoldment in them as it did one thousand years ago.

The fish you eat is not the same fish. The fruit you eat is not the same fruit you had before. The blood you have is not the same blood you had one thousand years ago — all because of pollution.

Second, a destructive thoughtform makes the energies of Nature work destructively. If the thoughtform is an image of a catastrophe, the thoughtform channels the energies of the planet destructively, and the dream or prophecy of the producer of the thoughtform comes true. . . *if* the opposing thoughtforms do not balance, defeat, or destroy such a destructive thoughtform.

Constructive thoughtforms also spread and influence the consciousness of humanity. Great utopias, dreams, or visions of mystics or initiates gradually materialize if enough energy is given to them. And they turn into blessings for humanity.

Thoughtforms control life. If we want to survive, we must create those thoughtforms which lead us toward survival. One cannot desire survival and think in terms of anti-survival. Many prophecies came true not because things were supposed to happen that way but because things were conditioned that way through massive thinking, propaganda, and pressure. Our wishes, desires, and thoughtforms condition our life as individuals and as a humanity.

We can orient ourselves toward the direction, or we can get lost in the desert of existence without a direction.

In our personal life there is also the possibility that we build an ugly image of someone and then, through occasional remarks, make it grow in size and thickness and hang it around us. Thus it gradually controls our moods and expressions until we become its obedient servant. Such thoughtforms, which are related to destructive criticism, malice, and slander, become the hotbed of many astral and mental microbes which eventually destroy our mental mechanism and astral centers.

Such thoughtforms do not harm their objects as much as they harm the originator. They go with power and hit the object, but if the object is shielded with beauty and purity, the thoughtform bounces back to the originator and becomes his faithful follower. This is why some people hate things about themselves but cannot get rid of them. An ugly thoughtform turns into a leech in one's aura.

Day and night billions of people think around the axis of their fears, hatred, anger, jealousy, greed, and separatism. They create a massive dark cloud of thoughtforms in space.

Religious people are not exempt from such a sad labor. They spread fear, preach hell and condemnation, and perpetuate dark thoughtforms of fanaticism and separatism, in addition to their good thoughtforms of a certain kind of love, etc.

The sum total of these thoughtforms will decide the destiny of humanity. The thoughtform of fear is the strongest at this time, and it influences people everywhere. People are attacked by many kinds of fears, and they don't know how these fears become located in them or from where they come.

Fear is the major enemy of humanity. Once it controls our thinking and action, we always do things against our and others' welfare. This is why on the threshold of every heroic achievement lies the defeated body of fear.

Fear is an epidemic. It is the cause of our pseudo-progress and of the danger hanging over us.

There are people busy day and night creating thoughtforms related not only to fear but also to hatred. How can heavenly love penetrate our heart when we are surrounded with thoughtforms of hatred? How can we unfold our heart and "love our neighbor" when hatred lives in our heart? In such a condition, people think that they cannot survive unless they hate.

There are also thoughtforms of anger and greed, especially greed. Thoughtforms of greed are like tombstones and statues seen in graveyards; they imitate life but lead to death.

All these thoughtforms of fear, anger, greed, hatred, jealousy, and their allies gradually influence our children. The thoughtforms settle themselves in the nerves and genes of our children, and they are born under the influence of such thoughtforms which condition their health, their social relationships, and their future and cut their contact with the directives of the Higher Worlds.

Some zombies will laugh at us and say, "What is direction?" Direction challenges you toward Beauty, Goodness, Righteousness, Joy, and Freedom. Direction challenges you to master your habits and your weaknesses. Direction challenges you to surpass your knowledge and your talents and expand the field of your service. Direction challenges you to love all that God created.

Direction challenges you to spread peace and right human relations. Direction challenges you to establish a conscious contact with Higher Forces. Direction inspires you to sacrifice your interest for the interest of humanity.

Like a tuning fork, direction sounds every time you think wrongly, speak wrongly, and act wrongly. It warns you and encourages you to choose a better thought, a better word, and a better action. Without direction, you will be lost in the desert, like a cup of water in the sands.

Every one of us is equipped with an antenna. Some scientists know that certain animals and insects have some kind of antenna, but they have never written anything about the antenna each person has. Some of these antennas are stronger than others; some of them are healthy while others are damaged; but the antennas are there.

There is a very important point here. The receptions of an antenna are very often unconscious. They are not consciously registered but stored in the mechanism of man. There are a few people who can register the receptions consciously and take conscious actions based upon them. The rest have no chance to filter them or oppose them, but they obey them gradually as faithful slaves to the impressions.

Thus through the antenna, each human being is influenced by the thoughtforms of individuals and by the massive thoughtforms created by humanity.

Those antennas which are more perfected are able to receive not only impressions from human thoughtforms but also thoughtforms conceived by great Centers in Space. Such a reception helps them evaluate the nature of human thoughtforms and discriminate between them.

One of the ways not to be trapped and conditioned by polluting thoughtforms is to build a better antenna. How can one build a better antenna? — Only through increasing his thoughts of Beauty, Goodness, Righteousness, Joy, and Freedom.

The second way not to be trapped by destructive thoughtforms is to develop an ability to reject all those impressions which are related to fear, anger, hatred, greed, jealousy, and separatism. This is the greatest protection for the flowering of your antenna.

Unhealthy thoughtforms — which are thoughtforms of fear, hatred, anger, greed, jealousy, and separatism — often disintegrate in space, spreading a massive pollution in the body of the planet. Thus the planet becomes sick because it is also a living entity, like the "bugs" or human beings living on its body.

When the planet becomes sick, it takes extreme measures to heal itself. People will be surprised if we say that most natural calamities are efforts of Nature to heal Herself and to destroy the causes of Her sickness. But the people living on the planet may think in terms of their individual or personal interest, without taking into account their thoughtforms which contributed to the cataclysm.

The world has continued so many millions of years because right thinking won over wrong thinking. There will again be universal confrontations in which two kinds of thoughtforms will clash and prove their might, either for survival or for destruction.

There are a few other steps you can take to help the forces of survival and progress. Try to be awake and conscious, and when you feel that your mind is working in the reverse gear, immediately change it and your direction. Many thoughtforms come to you from people who hate you or who are jealous of you. Stop them, and reject them with a positive thought. If you feel the source, send a thought of beauty to it.

Never fight against ugly thoughts because you increase their power and give them permission to pollute the network of your consciousness. Do not dwell on them. First, develop Divine indifference against them. Divine indifference is a state in which your aura radiates and does not let ugly thoughtforms stick to it.

Second, try to increase your purity and joy. These two go together. They are great antidotes to the poison of ugly thoughtforms.

When counteracting with a beautiful thoughtform, just think the beautiful thought and then forget about it. Remember that the thought of beauty will eventually chase away the ugly thoughtform or even destroy it forever, giving the needed lesson to the originator.

The third step is always to occupy your mind with lofty ideas to such a degree that no ugly thoughtform can find any friend with whom to sneak in. Great and creative ideas are all around you. Try to attract them through your meditation and aspirations.

We often meet with great ideas in our subjective contacts, but when we involve ourselves with daily problems and labor, they fade away. Before they fade away, we must visualize them and formulate them through our creative imagination. Through such a labor we protect ourselves from the attacks of destructive thoughtforms.

These are not easy steps, but the rewards are eternal.

You must also try to reject those suggestive thoughtforms which try to

1. defeat you, suggesting for example that you are good for nothing, stupid, lazy, etc.

2. create a thoughtform of hopelessness, suggesting for example that your sickness is fatal; you will never recover; you are always sick; there is no cure for it, etc.

3. create discouragement in you, suggesting for example that you cannot graduate from college; you cannot achieve something great; you cannot be successful, etc.

Unfortunately, our parents and friends pour such kinds of suggestions into our auras with their love.

A lady came to me and said, "How do I look?"

"You look okay."

"Why did the doctor say that I have only a few weeks to live?"

"That, I don't know. But I feel that you will be okay. Have faith and think you will be okay. In the pharmacy of your body, there are very secret drawers where very important medicine is hidden. By your hope and faith you can put them in action, if your soul wants to stay in this world."

She changed, and she is still living, ten years after this visit.

If people send you thoughts of defeat, use creative imagination and create a great success for yourself in your mind. Do not give up, but strive with the power that Nature gave you.

One may ask, if we receive thoughts of warning, how can we discriminate if the source of the thought is benevolent or destructive? The answer is no matter where the warning comes from, it is useful to consider it and strengthen your path. But a warning that is coming from a benevolent source carries with it the power of courage to face and overcome the danger. The warning that comes from a negative source carries with it wishes for your destruction or failure. You can take the warning and keep yourself awake and alert, but invoke courage and strength from your inner sources or from the Higher Worlds.

Higher warnings inspire you not only with courage but also with stability and serenity. A lower warning tries to create panic in you, as well as discouragement and the sense of failure. Often such warnings are like alarms of buildings that are set off by an insignificant visit of a mouse. . .but the alarm does not lose the opportunity to warn you!

Know that you are born for success and victory, but you are not born to exploit others and defeat them.

Exercises

There are ten exercises you can do for ten months. If you remain faithful and courageous, you may change your whole life.

1. Every morning for one month spend three minutes visualizing a flower — its shape, petals, colors, and fragrance. This will exercise the muscles of your mental body so that they can destroy ugly thoughtforms.

Try to make your visualization as clear as possible. Do not be discouraged if you cannot for a few days. You are building a precious mechanism within you, and it is worthwhile to spend three serious minutes to create such a mechanism.

2. During the next month try to visualize for five minutes a beautiful sunset or sunrise. Close your eyes and enjoy the beautiful colors and forms of clouds, trees, rocks, etc. Feel them with your heart; make it real. Through such an exercise you increase your creativity.

3. In the third month, visualize the One Whom you worship. Take His picture in your hand and first look at His eyes; then close your eyes and visualize His (or Her) eyes. Then continue with His nose, cheeks, ears, mouth, head, body, etc., until you can creatively imagine or visualize His complete face. This is a form of meditation through which you establish resonance between you and the One Whom you worship, and you exercise your mind to build clear thoughtforms.

This thoughtform in your aura becomes a contact point with the One you worship. Slowly you receive from Him new inspiration, a new power of striving, new visions, and new revelations.[1] As His influence increases in you, a new transformation occurs in your nature. The image becomes leaven for your entire being.

In an advanced stage, this contact point goes with you like a faithful guide during your subjective life, leading you into the Subtle Worlds after you leave

_____

1. See also *Cosmos in Man*, Ch. 11.

your body. Also, this image acts as a shield, protecting you from many psychic attacks.

4. In the fourth month, visualize certain symbols that carry esoteric meaning, and send them to your friends. When you feel that one of your friends is depressed, send him a symbol of courage, a symbol of joy and hope. When your friend is in a period of crisis, send him a symbol of energy, striving, and victory. When your friend is sick, send him a symbol of health, beauty, and recovery. When your friend is engaging himself in a new enterprise, send him symbols of enthusiasm.

Let these symbols be clear and beautiful. Symbols do not impose their will but provide help if the subject is ready and karmically worthy to have that help. Also, these symbols carry help to many who are unknown to you. Through building symbols you learn how to build thoughtforms, charging them with intuitional elements because symbols evoke the Intuition and make your thoughts more effective.

In some schools, it is recommended that one should make a list of people and every day at sunset send help to them through symbols. Those who are sick or in danger from enemies or in prison or in crisis receive the help. Such help is especially necessary for those who are on the verge of passing away. The symbols help them very much and ease their transition.

Symbols are thoughtforms charged with energy. In trying to build symbols, you refine the art of building thoughtforms and collect precious experiences as you direct them to special destinations.

5. In the fifth month, visualize a light around certain people whom you want to help. If they need physical help, visualize violet-golden light. If they need emotional help, visualize silvery-blue light. If they need mental help, visualize lemon-yellow light around them. If they need spiritual help, visualize a ruby color around them. If such colors are sent by one who can visualize them, they can work miracles in the lives of those who become targets of them.

Light heals, uplifts, enlightens, and inspires without forcing your will upon the people to whom you send the light. You can also use white light, creamy white light, if you wish to put people in contact with Higher Realms.

Such light prevents attacks of various kinds. Ugly thoughtforms and astral entities are repelled. Habits slow down and vanish. Crystallizations, which keep the subject a prisoner, melt away. And in the meantime, you learn how to use your mind constructively to build better and more useful thoughtforms.

Sometimes ugly thoughtforms attack people like octopuses and force them to fall into depression and the tendency toward suicide. Sending light to such people not only weakens such leeches but also gives the people power to resist them in the future.

Once Christ said, "Bless your enemies." With these words He was not encouraging weakness, but He was suggesting that we not fall into the habit of building thoughtforms charged with fear, anger, and hatred. Such elements are like ulcers which eat and damage our aura and the protective net, and they weaken our ability to build creative thoughtforms.

Thoughtforms built of fear, anger, and hatred are like windows through which thieves enter our aura. In blessing our enemies we do not give such a chance to them, and we seal our aura against any such attacks.

Once my grandmother said, "Try not to learn the ways of Satan. He is a very treacherous teacher, and he is anxious to teach his ways, making you act exactly as your enemies act against you. . . . Do not be trapped in his ways."

One of the ways of dark forces is to inspire us in the name of our faith, religion, or beliefs to be aggressive and forceful, or to slander, attack, or belittle those who have their own beliefs. Acting the way they act against us is the best way to fall into the traps of Satan.

6. In the sixth month, visualize every day an interview with your Inner Christ, with your Guardian Angel. The inner center of Beauty, Goodness, Righteousness, Joy, and Freedom is your Guardian Angel. Visualize It as a beautiful person or as a star or a flame, and think about It as a creative source.

Visualize yourself communicating, talking with It, discussing some plans with It; talking with It about the future, about unity, synthesis, cooperation. Have a closer contact with It, and recognize more closely Its presence within you and around you.

The Inner Guardian is a transmitter of higher vision. See how you can receive certain visions and what effect such an interview can have on you.

Do this every morning for six to seven minutes, no more.

People live many lives without recognizing such a presence. Once a conscious contact is established between It and you, you will see that the quality and power of your thoughtforms are rising. You will feel that your thoughtforms are charged with energy, beauty, and right direction.

Certain things never exist if you do not make them exist. You create them and make them exist. The Existence did not exist until the Great Power wanted it to exist. Even if you think that a Guardian Angel does not exist, create It and It will exist.

Nobody makes you a doctor, a lawyer, an artist, a hero; you make it happen, and when you make it happen, it exists.

Try to have a contact with your Higher Self. Imagine yourself as more than what you are. People can recreate themselves by creating a vision within themselves. The best thoughtforms are built when your mind is in a process of fusing itself with a higher vision.

7. In the seventh month, expand the field of your visualization and build thoughtforms of

- World cooperation

- World unity

- World synthesis

- One World

- One Humanity

People think every minute in terms of separation, cleavages, parties, and divisions. To counteract such thoughtforms for the benefit of all, you must build great thoughtforms, like warriors who spread hope and vision for One World. Make it come true; make it exist. Visualize it. Think about the blessings which will be spread everywhere when there are brotherhood and cooperation between all people.

Do not allow yourself to be caught by any separative thoughtform — which is a thoughtform with promises and interests. Reject such a thoughtform, and think in terms of One Humanity. Think what a free, beautiful, wealthy world we will have when our dreams actualize.

There are two ways that humanity can cooperate. One way is the way of conscious efforts to cooperate. The second way is learned because of a great catastrophe. Why learn to cooperate because of a great disaster or war or in a steady degeneration or in tension? A great disaster will make this planet a barren desert, and all our culture will vanish in flames and ashes.

Why not create the image of a glorious future and urge the minds of people to strive to build such a future? Who is going to lose? Does not every person in the world want to have health, happiness, joy, prosperity, and beauty? Then why not start constructing such a world?

Unless we change our way of thinking, we will never succeed in any of our negotiations.

The "children of light" think in terms of life and beauty. The children of darkness think in terms of death, destruction, and ugliness. Why not increase life and beauty, especially if it takes only a few minutes to broadcast them into Space through our thoughtforms?

The Great Invocation that was given to humanity in 1945 has the same purpose: to help humanity build a better thoughtform for future humanity. Thought comes first; then actualization takes place.

Humanity can stop war and destruction by building positive thoughtforms of cooperation and beauty through prayers and world invocations. But this effort must be steady and backed by enthusiasm and energy.

One of the great Sages said, "Create your thoughtforms through your heart." Charge your thoughtforms with compassion, and they will make your dreams come true.

You can take the five thoughtforms stated above and, using your creative imagination, produce world events. For example, to bring cooperation between all nations, visualize a beautiful plateau surrounded with deodars and other beautiful trees and see musicians sitting on the rocks ready to play beautiful dance music.

Then visualize each national leader dressed according to his national custom coming to the plateau from the area of trees, forming a big circle, and dancing together in great joy. After the dance, see everyone hugging and kissing each other with love and affection.

Repeat the dance many times with similar visualizations. Of course, you can visualize other kinds of cooperation in educational, artistic, scientific, religious, and economic fields. Make your creative imagination real and active, and you will be a great contributor to peace.

8. In the eighth month, visualize every day for seven to eight minutes a network of light around the globe. Think about this network as a communication mechanism with Higher Worlds. Such a network transmits the inspiration and impressions of the Higher Worlds. Try to be creative and see what impressions and inspirations are precipitating to earth, to humanity, and to all kingdoms of Nature.

Whoever wins in Space wins on earth. Record victory in Space with your positive and all-inclusive thoughtforms. This is a very profound statement, and you must try to meditate upon it: "Whoever wins in Space wins on earth." Space is won only through your thoughtforms charged with compassion.

See this network of many colors building a symphony of colorful threads around the globe. Forget about space wars. Construct the thoughts of Space brotherhood, of bridges between earth and galaxies. See friends, co-workers, and relatives coming from Space in various ways and helping humanity build solar and Cosmic brotherhood, solar and galactic cooperation.

9. In the ninth month, for ten minutes each day visualize that you are traveling to far-off worlds. Visit planets, galaxies, stars, and solar systems. Visualize extraordinary cultures and civilizations, and try to be a citizen of the Universe.

This exercise will expand your inner space. Most mental sicknesses are the result of lack of space in the mind. Expand your space, and your mind will be healthier.[2]

The expansion of space is not done through hallucination or "spacing" but through using your logic and reasoning to explore the possibilities existing in space, in other solar systems and galaxies.

Doing this every year for a month or for a year will expand your perspective, develop your sense of synthesis and your ability to transcend your mental limitations, and teach you how to build better thoughtforms.

_____

2. See also *New Dimensions in Healing*, pp. 822-827, and *The Hidden Glory of the Inner Man*, Ch. 8.

Once I went to a rest home where I met people 90-95 years of age. They were tired, bored, lazy, and acting like vegetables. One of them said, "I want to die and I don't know how."

I said, "Why do you want to die? I will show you how to be joyful."

"How?"

"Close your eyes and imagine you are traveling or flying in spirit to a far-off star. . . . Can you do that?"

"I will try."

He began to use his creative imagination, and he continued for a few minutes. Opening his eyes, he said with a smile, "It feels good. At least there is something for me to do."

"Continue this every day and try to create something for yourself to do on a distant star."

I visited him ten days later. He came to me and whispered in my ear, "Guess what?"

"What?"

"I have a garden on a far-off star, and I am planting the best roses there. They are so fragrant, so beautiful. You gave me the best work to do in this coffin called the rest home!"

I visited the nurse and asked how this man was acting.

"I don't know." she said. "He suddenly became a joyful, cooperative, and happy man. Maybe something is going wrong in his brain. . . ."

The poor nurse! She thought that to be cooperative, joyful, and happy were signs of sickness.

The man lived to be 97 and passed over in his sleep, perhaps while he was busy with his garden on a distant star.

10.   In the tenth month, for fifteen minutes daily visualize yourself creating great beauty in any art form. Every day work on it, and make it better and better, improving it with new ideas and forms. If one month is not enough, work on it for one year and produce a masterpiece for the benefit of all humanity. When it is complete, send it all over the world and start a new one.

Build thoughtforms of Beauty, Goodness, Righteousness, Joy, and Freedom. In your visualization, change the structure of the economy, international relationships, the justice system. Try to bring improvement through your thoughts, and sooner or later your thoughtforms will bring results.

We often say that thought travels faster than the speed of light. This is a way of saying that thoughts do not travel. It is not easy to explain this. When you develop your consciousness, you do not ask questions and wait for the answers. Immediately when you have a question, you instantaneously see the answer. You just think. If your Teacher is thinking, your consciousness vibrates at the same time with the same thoughts.

Thoughts use space; light uses time. Space acts as one; time acts as a fraction.

In certain levels of development there is a period of time in which thought travels from your soul to your brain, from your Teacher to your mind. This is not the speed of travel of thought, but the time taken for registration of the thought that *is there*. Time is related to the mechanism and the process but is not related to thought.

Win in space, and you will win on earth.

42

Feeling and Thought

The word "feeling" is often related to emotional reaction. This is not right. Esoterically, feeling is a general term referring to a certain registration of impressions coming from the physical, emotional, and mental realms.

One feels cold and heat. One feels the joys and pains of other people. One feels their thoughts. One feels his own thoughts. For example, one can say, "I feel I am right." This is not a figure of speech but a fact; one can feel that his decisions, conclusions, and motives are right. These elements can be felt.

There are also higher feelings. Such feelings transcend the response of the intelligence because feeling is done by the aura. It is almost an instantaneous response and registration. It is after such a response and registration that the message goes to the brain which then, according to its content and development, gives its decision. But before it gives its decision, the feeling is registered and responded to already. And if the decision of the mind is contrary, you witness a conflict in the human nature.

Feeling is related to understanding. Knowledge is the accumulation of data and not necessarily the understanding of the data.

Feeling is a fast and direct approach to Intuition. On the line of this approach, understanding transcends the data accumulated in the mind and reaches its destination before the mind has a chance to reach a conclusion.

Feeling bypasses logic and reasoning, though logic and reasoning come back to the decision of the feeling and try to overrule it. Successful people depend upon the response of their Intuition rather than their logic, which often can be used to verify the response of the Intuition.

One can feel physically, emotionally, and mentally and respond according to the feeling. The conditioning factor of the decision of the feeling is the Intuition or the past registrations. It is interesting to note that feeling is seldom conditioned by the old registrations. It generally evokes an immediate response from the Intuition because of its speed of response. Old registrations may respond and try to modify the intuitive response, but it sometimes takes a long period of time to call itself to the attention of the man.

Feeling is also a phenomenon which is controlled by light. The faster the speed of light, the faster the response. This is why if one wants to free someone from the claws of the past, the best method is to train him to register the impressions coming from the faster light. This is done by raising the focus of the consciousness of the person from lower to higher planes. The focus of consciousness is the determining factor of registration of the reflections of light. Reflections are the images of events on any plane of existence.

There are many means of communication:

- movement

- sound

- light

- thought energy

- feelings

Higher than all of these is communication by impression. Esoterically, impressions travel faster than feelings, thoughts, light, and sound. These impressions are everywhere, within and without. One needs only to prepare the apparatus to register them.

43

Thinking and Meditation

All that exists as form, visible or invisible, on all planes of existence, is nothing but a condensation of *thought*. The Supreme One thought, and things came into existence according to His thought. In each of His thoughts, He put a Spark of Himself to make the form multiply and eventually return to Him.

Meditation is a process in which this Spark learns to think and to become a co-worker of the Supreme in order to carry His Plan toward fulfillment. In meditation, one slowly fuses with the Cosmic Creative Mind and begins to share His powers. Meditation is the stage of thinking when the inner Spark in the form of man cooperates with the Supreme.

Thinking leads us to forms, but meditation leads us to the One Thought, the parts of which are created forms. Thinking makes us know the truth about each form, but meditation helps us to know the One Thought. Truth is the essence of all forms, the Divine Thought. Each separate thought has partial truth. Separate thoughts cannot be understood until they are seen in relation to the One Thought.

Those who meditate eventually find that they become all-powerful because weakness is eliminated. Weakness is the separate self. Thus the meditator lives, speaks, and acts as Him. In Him he is dissolved, and who and what can stand in front of the one through whom the Supreme acts?

"Nothing is so, but thinking makes it so." A great truth is hidden in these words from Shakespeare. Thinking is a process of molding substance into certain forms related to time, need, achievement, motive, purpose, rays, etc.

Thinking is related to the ability of your mechanism to translate a contact. This translation can range from the supreme to the most primitive expression. But beyond such an expression exists the "nothing," the formless idea, vision, current. This "nothing" is just like an ocean which can be thought of or formulated in any way the mind thinks.

But the process of perfection is to create such a mechanism which can progressively penetrate into the "nothing" and translate it into those forms which will lead humanity closer to the Plan, the Purpose, and the Will of "that which is not so."

The intention of thinkers will eventually be not only to give a better translation, but also to put into it a portion of the direction of the Plan, the Purpose, and the Will of that "Beyond." The danger is "to make it so through thinking," but not to sense the Plan, the Purpose, and the Will of that which lies beyond the ability of translation by the human mind.

This is what the goal of meditation is: eventually to overcome the form-building ability of the mind, learn how to think without thoughts, then penetrate into the ocean of Light and be one with It. This is what a Buddha is.

Of course, this is the most dangerous path, but those who *dare* will eventually enter the formless section of Mind, then penetrate into the world of ideas and into the Archetypal realms and fuse with the Light.

Meditation and thinking make things come into being, to exist. We are told: "Nothing is so, but thinking makes it so."

One feels so humble after realizing the implication of such a statement. Most of what the human mind does is fabrication; it is the result of his reaction to the things that exist beyond his capacity to see and understand.

One who sees only the reflection of the Sun in a piece of broken glass can build a whole chain of "pure science" without realizing that it is only a translation of his response through the tiny mechanism of his mind. This "pure science" turns into "applied science," and a whole series of institutions and departments are built to process the "pure science" — for whatever reason — again without realizing that all is motivated by an illusion, a reflection.

This is why those who have penetrated from the unreal to the real advise us that we are living in a world of illusions which can finally be overcome in trying to pass beyond the world of forms and free ourselves from the chains of that world of forms.

Nirvana is a term which refers to that formless realm. As long as our mind is limited to forms and is busy providing forms to please and deceive us, we cannot step beyond and be an Enlightened One. We see a constellation and write a poem about it, and our poem becomes a prison for our consciousness. Then we feel happy in making others satisfied with our limitations. Our consciousness is full of such fabricated forms.

Illumination is a process of annihilation of such thoughtforms and a process of receiving more light from the realms beyond the mind. But a question comes to our mind: If we are to live within the three worlds of maya, or illusion, how can we avoid being a part of such a world of maya? To this question the Great Ones, Who lived in the world of maya without being blinded by maya, answered: through discrimination and detachment. They learned discrimination and detachment not only from dense forms but also from forms existing in emotional and mental realms.

Then we ask the other question: Can a person still communicate with those who live in the world of maya when he enters the path leading out of the world of maya? Christ referred to this, saying that He was "in the world but not of the world."

It is possible to extend oneself into the formless world — the world as it is — and be in the world of maya as a bridge between these two worlds, bringing light from Higher Realms and injecting plan and purpose into the world of maya as elements that build the bridge for others to ascend into the World of Light. But it is the most difficult task for the Enlightened Ones to bring light into the world of maya without mixing Their light with the forms of maya existing already in the minds of people. This is why Great Ones cyclically come to destroy those portions of the Teaching of Light which have become crystallized in the forms of maya.

Thus, meditation, in a sense, is an effort to find in the formulated maya the transcendental light and through that light to penetrate into the formless realms of light. The process of penetration into that light is called the Technique of Contemplation, which leads into illumination or into the destruction of all limiting forms of maya in the three worlds.

In human relationships, the mental habit of fabrication works under the pressure of our urges, drives, glamors, desires, illusions, vanities, ego, self-interests, and group-interests. It is generally conditioned by the level of our evolution. People never realize that they are used by the forms of maya on various levels. Knowing this, the Great Ones gave us the formula:

> *Lead us, O Lord,*
>
> *from darkness to Light,*
>
> *from the unreal to the Real,*
>
> *from death to Immortality.*
>
> *from chaos to Beauty.*

They also wanted us to meditate upon the most sacred mantram:

> *O Self-revealing One, reveal Thyself in me.*

44

The Sphere of Earth and Thoughts

We read in the Teaching that the sphere of the earth is full of intersecting thoughts. These intersections bring about a very dangerous situation which leads to crimes and suicides.

Certain people are sensitive to the frictions created by the intersection of thoughts. Every time thoughts intersect, a very powerful discharge of energy emanates which hits the brain centers of certain people and leads them to crimes of various degrees.

A collision of cars, trains, or airplanes emanates a similar discharge, but such a discharge is a thousand times less than the discharge from thought collision. Thought collision takes place when powerful individuals or masses of people think diametrically opposite to each other, thus creating a mighty current of two opposing thoughts. The collision of such thoughts sometimes creates mighty whirlpools of two different currents which expand in the sphere of the earth and engulf multitudes, leading them into certain kinds of confusion, bewilderment, uncertainty, depression, apathy, resentment, anger, hatred, attachment, detachment, destructive moods, or chaotic thinking and behavior. It is also through such whirlpools that mass insanity results, leading to riots, revolutions, economic disturbances, and wars with all their consequences and effects on families and individuals.

These energy discharges from collisions literally create explosions in the etheric centers of the brain and render them either useless or partially distorted. The second case is more dangerous because the person is still able to function in society, sometimes in high positions, and cause great damage.

When currents of opposing thoughts are amplified by short or long radio waves, they become a real hazard for global humanity. It is not possible to create two opposing radio waves. Scientists think they can, but two opposing waves can be created only in the process of amplifying two opposing currents of thought. It is only in the human individual or collective mind that the distortion of natural energies takes place.

Nature never contradicts itself. Only the human will and human mind can create contradiction, friction, and collision in Nature, on earth, in the solar system, and in outer space. This is why a great Teacher warns humanity, saying,

"Guard your thoughts." Unfortunately these words were taken as moral or religious advice, but actually they are a scientific formula to safeguard the life on the planet.

A similar collision occurs at the intersection of the thoughts of two persons. Such intersections are responsible not only for psychological disturbances but also for heart disease, nervous breakdowns, depressions, and various crimes. This is why human beings must exercise a way of harmonious thinking. Harmony does not mean uniformity but a way of relationship which tolerates, clears, supplements, completes, assists, evokes, strengthens, and reveals. One needs to analyze the above words in order to have a deeper insight into the meaning of harmony.

Dark forces in the planet and in humanity are engaged in creating intersecting thoughts to make the ship of humanity sink into the Cosmic ocean. Only in thinking through Beauty, Goodness, Righteousness, Joy, and Freedom can the planet be saved from the destructive currents of dark forces and equilibrium in space be established.

One may ask how an individual can protect himself from the mighty currents of destruction. The answer will be the same: by thinking harmoniously. Harmony of mind is a great shield. It not only creates a safety zone for an individual brain, but it also builds a shock-absorbing mechanism in the consciousness which protects man from attacks coming from collisions of opposing thoughts in space.

Groups and nations must be trained in harmonious thinking if life on this planet is to be preserved.

People are often confused about viewpoints. They think that to have a different viewpoint is an act of opposition, but this is not true. One can have many viewpoints without opposing any viewpoint. Additional viewpoints provide additional approaches to the same problem or object.

Contradiction is the result of the inability to offer a *new* viewpoint. Contradiction may stop any progress, but viewpoints assist things to progress.

There is no black and white in the process of thinking unless the thinkers are insane. If thought is not limited by self-interest, ego, vanity, and separatism, it always tends toward harmony.

Additional viewpoints are factors in creating harmony and eliminating elements which may cause disharmony. One cannot live with himself until he creates harmony in his thinking. This must be true for all humanity as well.

45

The Thoughtform Building Process

We formulate our thoughts with various kinds of matter. This can be done consciously or as a mechanical habit.

We can formulate our thoughts with etheric matter, the characteristic of which is motion.

We can formulate our thoughts with astral matter. Astral matter is sticky and relates us to our emotions — positive or negative. An astrally formulated thoughtform creates emotional attachment, attraction, or repulsion. But if an astrally formulated thoughtform is inspired from the higher mind, it is progressive and increasingly effective.

We can formulate our thoughts with mental matter. Mental matter is fiery and more penetrative than astral and etheric matter. It moves faster and endures a long time. Thoughts formulated in mental matter are clear, precise, to-the-point, and charged with a definite plan and purpose.

If illusions exist in the mental plane, the thoughtforms are weak. If vanity, ego, and separatism exist in the mental spheres, the thoughtforms are negative and often destructive.

It is also possible that a thought can be formulated with three kinds of matter — etheric, astral, and mental — and if the thoughtform is pure and in harmony with the principles of Beauty, Goodness, Righteousness, Joy, and Freedom, that thoughtform affects the three worlds of human endeavor constructively and moves these worlds forward.

Higher thoughtforms are created of intuitional substance. Such thoughtforms are abstract, but they are like motive powers behind all great and constructive movements in the world. A thoughtform built of intuitional substance acts as a ray of light and impresses the mental sphere of humanity with a rain cloud of many blessings. If this thoughtform is also equipped with mental, astral, and etheric matter, it turns into the most powerful source to push forward cultures and civilizations.

It is also possible to formulate a thought in atmic substance. Such kinds of thoughtforms are used to direct world politics and world leadership toward greater achievements in unity and synthesis.

Those who practice meditation and are occupied with solving the problems of the world and meeting its needs are advised to construct their thoughtforms consciously and goal-fittingly. The qualities of matter and substance must be carefully studied, and thoughtforms must be built to fit the conditions and the levels of people in order to make thoughtforms not only effective but also constructive.

This needs lots of close observation, keen sensitivity, and regular practice. Every day for a set time you must practice how to formulate thoughts in various kinds of matter. For example, you have a thought to eliminate the slaughter of animals. You begin to formulate that thoughtform through visualization, creative imagination, imagination, and even daydreaming. You dramatize the thought and thus make it available to those who are on various levels of receptivity.

To take another example, on the etheric plane you create a play. You charge it with emotions. You charge it with a philosophy or meaning. You charge it with significance and the spirit of synthesis. You use these various kinds of substance and matter either harmoniously, combining them in the thoughtform, or separately.

This is not an easy exercise, but slowly it turns into fascinating and creative fun. Eventually you learn to discriminate between different kinds of matter and between matter and substance and to formulate your thoughtforms consciously, just as a person builds the same image in sand, out of stone or wood, or out of mental matter.

What is the psychic quality of any thoughtform?

Each thoughtform carries with it an influence which affects people, objects, and forces in Nature. The psychic quality of each thoughtform is the quality of the substance or matter with which it is built. If it is built of mental substance, which is charged by higher forces and is dynamic in its essence, then it will carry the same psychic quality.

Every thoughtform is built around a thought. If the seed thought is of higher quality, the thoughtform will be of higher quality. The seed thought can be related to a physical interest or to an emotional or mental interest or goal. It can be related to an intuitional or higher level goal. The seed thought conditions the quality of the thoughtform.

The psychic quality of the thoughtform also depends on the conditions through which it is transmitted to others. The psychic quality of the thoughtform changes according to the spheres of influence in which it is built and transmitted.

The psychic quality of a thoughtform also depends on the receivers. Receivers are found on various levels and in various states of body, emotions, and mind. Each state has an effect on the psychic quality of thought.

A thoughtform can have a powerful psychic quality if it

— is built through concentration

— is built by the Law of Synthesis

— has pure substance

— has the quality of being able to unfold when it is challenged

— has the quality of absorbing attacks and annihilating them

— is preconditioned for a multilevel response

— is programmed to shatter false thoughts or nourish genuine thoughts when it meets them

The psychic quality of a thoughtform is powerful and constructive if it is built in harmony with the currents of the Hierarchy. A good thoughtform is built in a way that it becomes a part of a greater thoughtform of the same frequency, adding a new voltage of energy to it.

A sentence can contain a thoughtform. A paragraph or a chapter can be the body of a thoughtform. A book can be the body of a thoughtform. A political, philosophical, or religious system can be the body of a thoughtform. A government or global corporation can be the body of a thoughtform. All that is manifested in space is the embodiment of an original thought.

The psychic quality of a thoughtform depends upon the quality of the source of the thoughtform and on the matter or substance the person uses to build the thoughtform. There are seven basic psychic qualities. A thoughtform can be charged with

- Willpower

- Love-wisdom

- Active intelligence

- Harmony

- Concrete knowledge

- Abstract idealism

- Ceremonial magic

Of course, each basic psychic quality is like a spectrum of energies and forces which goes from the highest to the lowest.

Each thinker must know how to charge his thoughtforms with a psychic quality. He must also know what quality to put into them to meet a special need. The quality of the psychic energy of a thoughtform indicates where the

342 Thought and the Glory of Thinking

consciousness of the thinker is and how much power he has over the sense of synthesis.

For what specific purpose does one use mental matter?

In building thoughtforms, one must carefully observe his own purpose in using mental matter. It is possible that a very strong weapon is used to kill an ant, or a very expensive car is used to go to a house of prostitution, or a million dollars is used to satisfy a hatred or take revenge. The purpose of creating a thoughtform can be a vanity, the ego, an illusion, a glamor. The purpose can be destructive or constructive. It can be uplifting or annihilating.

The purpose of using a thoughtform will condition your future progress on the Path. . .or prepare your future downfall. In the economy of Space, those who are faithful "servants" are rewarded by becoming the co-workers of the Great Ones. But those who waste the treasury of Space or do not multiply it are thrown into darkness.

The purpose of using a thoughtform decides what the destiny of a person will be in the future. As a soul progresses on the path of perfection, he lives and functions more and more in the realm of energy rather than in the realm of forms. Because this gives him power to involve himself with the world of causes rather than with the world of effects, his actions create a tremendous influence upon life as a whole and his karma increases either in savings or in deficit. In using higher energies, one may speed his progress or destroy himself.

The purpose which is using your thoughtform must be of a high level and related not only to the Common Good but also to the Plan of the Hierarchy.

Do I work in mental matter consciously or unconsciously?

This is an important question, the intention of which is to reveal the focus and control post of your consciousness. Those who do not work in mental matter consciously are not yet creative souls but, rather, machines used or manipulated by the desires, interests, and greed of other people or entities. Or they are controlled by their own urges, drives, desires, glamors, and separative interests.

Our goal should be to work in mental matter consciously, as a carpenter works in his workshop. The first sign of being able to work consciously in mental matter is the ability to have mastery over thoughtforms that exist in mental matter. The second sign is the ability to dissolve them. The third sign is the ability to create new thoughtforms fit for new needs.

As we work more consciously in mental matter, we utilize mental matter to create and to communicate. Every creative labor is a means to distribute the mental fire and to create better communication systems.

Every thoughtform is vitalized by an entity. This is where the danger or opportunity is found. You can vitalize your thoughtforms with an entity which is the embodiment of your lower desires, selfish interests, vanity, and ego. Or you can vitalize your thoughtforms with entities which represent your visions, your virtues, and your contacts with Higher Worlds. When your thoughtforms are ensouled with entities on the evolutionary arc, they will continuously spread light, love, and striving toward perfection. If they are ensouled with entities on the involutionary arc, they will carry the germs of destruction, dissolution, pain, and suffering.

Every thoughtform serves as a body of an entity, which may use it apart from your will. Once a thoughtform is released from your sphere of mind, it has its own course of action.

It is possible that you decide to destroy certain thoughtforms which were built for certain purposes, to meet certain needs. The method is to call the entity back, dissolve the thoughtform, and use its matter to build another thoughtform. The greater the thinker, the greater the ability he has to destroy those thoughtforms which become obsolete or become hindrances on the path of higher creativity.

Sometimes this is a Herculean labor because people may accept your thoughtform and, mixing it with their superstitions and prejudices, create a gigantic thoughtform and crystallize it to such a degree that its destruction becomes also impossible. Some religions are gigantic thoughtforms which became obsolete but which are impossible to destroy because of the energy they receive from devotees and fanatics. Such thoughtforms stand in the way of human progress as contaminated bodies which neither die nor recover but only spread germs.

Every highly creative genius or thinker is aware of such a problem, and he takes steps to create thoughtforms that have a set timetable either to degenerate and pass away or to renew and regenerate themselves in every great cycle, bringing new vision and new hope for humanity. One must develop his own creative power and also cultivate the ability to destroy thoughtforms whenever it is needed. Many thinkers are the prisoners of their own thoughtforms, the accumulations of which eventually make them refuse to think.

To destroy the corpses of thoughtforms floating in space and polluting the mind of humanity, a special technique is needed. Instead of attacking the old thoughtforms and trying to destroy them, one must use his time to create those thoughtforms which will make the obsolete ones find no support or nourishment and fade away.

Every thoughtform is tied to various people with karmic webs. It is often not good to annihilate a thoughtform all at once — if that is even possible — because through the destruction of the thoughtform you literally harm those who have connections with it. Only Great Ones have the wisdom and the power to annihilate thoughtforms, if it is necessary for Cosmic purposes.

Some people attack certain thoughtforms without being masters of the science of thoughtforms. Then they see that the thoughtform under attack is strengthened and regenerated, and it becomes a dangerous power in the world. When you attack certain thoughtforms that are tied to fanatics, the thoughtforms draw extensive amounts of energy from the fanatics to keep themselves alive and aggressive. This is why, before you take something away from people, you must be ready to give them something better.

If a thinker cannot destroy his own thoughtforms, he becomes the slave of his thoughtforms. He becomes an effect. People create so many things in the world, and, because they have no control over them, the things become their causes and the people become their effects. The Ancients told us that one must not create anything he cannot destroy any moment he wants.

Our present humanity is becoming an effect of the things it created. This is why humanity has no freedom. Humanity created those politics or laws which make it an effect. It created an educational system which produced slaves of drugs, alcohol, sex, money, greed, dogmas, doctrines, and so on. It created systems of communication which led people to mass slavery. It created arts which hasten the process of slavery. It created a science which began to rule the destiny of humanity.

It created religions which made people slaves of the interpretations of their leaders. The more a person becomes a religious fanatic, the more he becomes an effect. We do not yet have a religion that does not create sheep or slaves, in spite of the Teaching of Christ Who was the freest human being on earth. Christ was and is a true cause, but the interpreters made out of His Teaching a testament of slavery to create effects, not causes.

Humanity created an economic system which became a cause, and its creators turned into an effect, its slaves. In the future, if humanity survives, it will learn how to stay as a cause, how to stay free from its own creations. The secret is: Never create anything that you cannot destroy. Never release anything that you cannot stop. Never create a thoughtform that you cannot destroy.

Every new and higher level thoughtform must carry with it a destructive quality in order to annihilate former thoughtforms that are obsolete. Fanatics are those people who are caught in the network of their own or others' thoughtforms. Every real thoughtform brings you freedom. It either frees you from your lower identifications or it frees you from the prisons of obsolete thoughtforms. If a thoughtform cannot do this for you, be careful because it will dull your sense of discrimination.

Laws for Building Thoughtforms

There are specific laws for the construction of thoughtforms. People realize that a business complex cannot be built without the laws of architecture, but they do not realize that thoughtforms are also architectural objects in the mental sphere just as material buildings are on earth. The architectural laws of thoughtform building are related to

— beauty, luminosity

— goal-fitness

— stability

— progressiveness

— protectiveness

— transparency

— the power to regenerate

— the power to cause freedom

— the power to evoke

— the power to synthesize

The specific laws are as follows:

The first law is **Harmlessness**. Every thoughtform that you build must not hinder the progress of others toward perfection.

The second law is **Harmony**. Every thoughtform must be in harmony with the Plan, with the Purpose, and with the Rays.

The third law is **Synthesis**. Every thoughtform must carry with it the power to unite and synthesize that which is subjective and that which is objective.

The fourth law is the **Law of Attraction and Repulsion**. Every thoughtform must be charged with a quality which attracts other constructive and beautiful thoughtforms and repulses those which are obsolete and on the arc of involution.

The fifth law is **Economy**, by which care is taken not to waste energy and forms in the thoughtform building process.

We are told that the Creator of the solar systems uses the same laws. In *A Treatise on Cosmic Fire*, [1] we are also given seven systemic laws of thought:

1. The Law of Vibration

2. The Law of Cohesion

3. The Law of Disintegration

---

1. Alice A. Bailey, *A Treatise on Cosmic Fire*, p. 569.

4. The Law of Magnetic Control

5. The Law of Fixation

6. The Law of Love

7. The Law of Sacrifice and Death

The Law of Karma is also mentioned.

Those who are striving to be creative forces in Nature must study these laws and build their thoughtforms consciously, using these laws. Serious studies and research must be carried on about these laws, as if one were intending to be a mental architect and construct a new life on earth. The architects of the Future have begun to appear on the physical plane, but we need those who will start their studies to be mental plane architects.

Thoughtforms need to be vitalized by the fire of the will energy. This is not an easy job even if you understand the laws of thoughtform building. The creative fire is the will energy, by which a thoughtform is directed to its target. Without will energy, the thoughtform becomes a wanderer and eventually disintegrates.

Willpower is not something which you take and put into the thoughtform. Willpower is the energy which increases in you as you ascend toward your Real Self. In a sense you always have willpower, but in a very much diluted form. Pure willpower starts to manifest when you are functioning on the higher mental plane, and it increases as you climb higher toward your True Self.

In some sense you put into your thoughtforms a portion of yourself, which gives the power of direction to your thoughtforms. It is this same energy that is used when you consciously destroy a thoughtform.

Will energy can have a destructive effect on thoughtforms which are considered obsolete. It is through a bolt of the lightning of willpower that a thoughtform turns into ashes. Sometimes such a destruction creates confusion and goallessness in certain people who were attached to the thoughtform as the source of their nourishment.

Every thoughtform builder must ask himself, "Am I building forms which bring karmic effects, or am I building those which work for the good of the group?" This is where the Law of Harmlessness is used. In the future, universities will be created to study the art of thinking and the art of consciously building thoughtforms as a great service for humanity.

46

The Mind-Emotion Relationship

We all know that there is a steady conflict between our physical, emotional, and mental natures and the One behind them. This conflict is very mild at the beginning of the path of discipleship, but as we proceed on the path the conflict becomes stronger and more complicated. Our body wants something, and the Inner Self wants something else. Then our emotional nature imposes its own life and tendencies upon the real man, and again we have a conflict.

The same is true with our thoughts. The mind has so many thoughts that the real man does not like it. They bother him, but often he is indifferent toward them and sometimes he rejects them. If we have such an experience in our life, we are on the path of progress. If not, we are lost in the physical, emotional, and mental vehicles and virtually we even do not exist.

If you do not have a feeling that you are different from the demands of your bodies, you are in a state of "sleep." Progress starts when you awaken and choose between *your* ways and the ways of your vehicles. Conflict is a healthy sign. When your body wants to dope itself or to use heavy alcohol and there is no opposition from inside; when your emotional body is jealous and there is no opposition from inside; when your mental body is full of hatred and there is no opposition, then you are in a very unhealthy or sad condition.

When you have a conflict and your inner man is in the position of controlling and directing the life of your vehicles according to your highest spiritual interests, then you are on the path of joy and success.

It is just like a sunrise. Your True Self is dawning and breaking through the darkness of your physical, emotional, and mental vehicles and shedding true light in them. It is this light of your True Self that will make these vehicles serve the cause of freedom and creativity.

This is a way to say that you are having a spiritual birth. You are coming into manifestation from darkness into light.

This is the whole story of evolution:

- First you are in sleep.

- Then you are in conflict.

- Then you are victorious.

- Then you are your True Self.

This drama is enacted on all levels of our existence on higher and higher spirals. Every time we are born on a higher level we enter as a baby there. Then we grow and become an adult there. Then again the same drama, until we become masters of all planes of manifestation.

This is why we have the great command: "Let your light shine forth."

This is the only labor behind all our labors.

We are under the blanket of matter. This body is a blanket, so to speak. Our eyelids are very thin flesh, but when they close our eyes, we cannot even see the Sun.

Then we have the blanket of our emotions with all our glamors; then the thicker blanket of our mental body, with all its thought furniture and crystallized prejudices and superstitions. . .and the little Spark under these heavy blankets is in deep sleep. This is the condition of most of humanity. And because of the "absence" of the inner Lord, the bodies run the show of life.

Every man's destiny is to make himself a light shining upon his own darkness. Find out how you are going to raise yourself out of darkness and hindrances. All religion, science, and art are attempting answers to this question. All the Wisdom of the ages tries to help us shine out our light.

Many achieved on this path; many failed temporarily because of the difficulty of the battle. But those who persisted eventually became the shining lights of humanity in spite of the many failures through which they passed.

This is a rewarding adventure because with each step you are getting rid of a portion of your misery. You are conquering death; you are heading toward resurrection.

How beautiful is life for one who has left behind the hospitals, pains, ignorance, fears, jealousies, and limitations and lifted himself up into the joy of Space!

The esoteric symbolism of Sodom and Gomorrah is very instructive. The city of hospitals, prisons, night clubs, crimes, fears, materialism, and limitations was left behind by those who climbed the path toward the sunrise. How rewarding is such an ascent!

So many thoughtforms built by pain, despair, fear, hatred, and criticism cause great disturbances within our aura, and eventually they extend their control over our nervous system, glands, and bloodstream. These disturbances first appear as unusual drives, behaviors, and attitudes and eventually as sicknesses. When an experienced man observes the way a person acts and reacts, he can almost tell you what is going to go wrong with him.

Many of our ways of reacting to people and objects have their origin in our thoughtforms, not in the outside objects or persons. You react in certain ways to someone because certain of your thoughtforms are restimulated in a certain way. It is so rewarding to find out why you react in certain ways to certain persons, events, and problems. Immediately when you find the cause, the pressure of the thoughtform loses its power, and eventually you can change it to a thoughtform especially built to balance or annihilate it.

Most of our criticisms, judgments, and rejections are based on such thoughtforms, and thus we cause lots of suffering to people around us. This is why, before we condemn someone, we must find out if the problem actually is within us. Until we find the disturbing factor within ourselves, we will enact the same game, any time our thoughtform is stimulated.

Thoughtforms are closely related to our emotional states, moods, and feelings. No one can really focus himself in the sphere of the clear light of the soul unless he has a great amount of knowledge about thoughtforms and emotions and a high degree of control over them.

One of the greatest services a man, group, or nation can render is to purify his individual and national emotional field.

Our emotions are a great source contributing to our misery. When our emotional field is not purified from hatred, greed, separatism, fear, jealousy, and many other negative emotions, any energy that comes in contact with the field turns into a poison within us.

Emotions are related to the liquid system of our body: lymph, blood, glandular secretions, urine, saliva, tears, sweat. The glands are directly affected by the emotions. Any time you change your emotions, you affect your liquid system and glandular secretions. A happy man who is elevated with high aspirations has a different smell than one who is merged in crime, fear, and hatred.

Emotions change the gears of the glands. If they are negative, they disturb the proper function of the glands and cause stagnation, overactivity, congestion, and intoxication. When we have any glandular problem, we must search for and find the cause within our emotions and emotionally controlled thoughts.

It is interesting to note that the thoughts of average humanity are animated by its emotions. It is our emotions that draw lower mental substance and build thoughtforms. All destructive, separative thoughtforms are built and animated by negative emotions. Also, our illusions can be used by powerful emotions.

Most of humanity does not think. Its thinking is a mechanical reaction to the existing conditions. Humanity as a whole feels and reacts emotionally and uses the lower mind as a servant for its emotions.

Acid conditions in the body are related to fears, jealousy, hatred, and so on. Fear, jealousy, and hatred co-exist with thoughtforms of low order. We can control these thoughtforms from the higher mental plane through meditation or visualization. Or we can stimulate them out of proportion if we have illusions in our mind related to our negative emotions.

Thinking is a fiery activity. It is a process through which the Inner Divinity, the source of knowledge, wisdom, love, and beauty, externalizes and manifests itself. When pure thinking hits with its fiery essence the emotional body, it creates steam, fog, and mist. If the fire continues its radiation, evaporation starts and you reach clarity or purity in the emotional field.

Emotions not only affect a man but also a group, a nation, humanity, and the planet itself. The liquid of the planet is affected by the total emotions of humanity. We do not have sophisticated proof of this yet, but science will demonstrate to us very soon that human emotions, as a whole, have a great effect on the liquid of the planet and on the planetary health.

Some of us have the experience of catching a cold when we have negative emotions or not catching a cold from a sick person because of the joyful and happy state of our mind. There are nuns serving in many contaminated hospitals with a great joy for Christ or a superior Being, and you see them healthy, happy, and in very high spirits.

My father was once called to serve in a hospital where every day ten to fifteen persons stricken with cholera were brought. One day I asked him, "Why don't you ever catch the sickness?"

"My son," he said, "before I entered the hospital I knelt down near the gate and prayed and said, 'With all my strength and joy I will help these suffering people. Give me strength and Your shield of blessing, O my Lord.' And I had no fear from that moment on."

Positive emotions, great aspiration, and clear thinking build the "shield" in us and around us.

When you are in negative emotions, your astral body is on fire. It burns with lots of smoke and creates accumulations on the astral centers, blocks them, and prevents them from passing on the energy coming from the life current. When you are in this condition, this destructive fire rushes to the glamors, fears, and anxieties of your astral body. The majority of the disorders in the body related to the liquid system originate from emotional causes. By changing and sublimating your emotions, you can eventually heal a great amount of damage done to your body by your negative emotions.

The unborn baby is surrounded with water. This water is his protection, but it is also the greatest danger if the mother is in continual emotional turmoil. By keeping the emotions of the pregnant woman in peace and serenity, this liquid pool transfers psychic energy to the embryo and lays the foundation of aspiration and striving in the heart of the embryo, as well as the foundation for a beautifully balanced and harmonious body.

This is not the case if heavy anxieties are accumulating in a woman's heart and every morning she is driving on the freeway with frequent shocks and excitements.

Emotions have an effect not only on your body but also on your thinking. In our present civilization, eighty percent of the time our emotions control our mind and use it for their own ends. You may have beautiful thoughts, plans, and visions and feel happy and respectful toward everyone, but as soon as someone steps on your toes, you forget all these beautiful thoughts in your mind and follow the dominating emotions at that time.

That is why advertising mostly appeals to emotions, not logic. In order to manipulate people, some world politicians first create an image of fear and then an image of reward when the object of fear is conquered. Once people are contaminated by fear and expect victory, the politician can control the masses, mobilizing all their physical and mental resources under the banner of fear or under another kind of emotion. Such politicians receive immediate response from average or emotionally-oriented people because emotions do not act with logic but in mechanical ways. Once you control the emotions, you can almost control their pocketbooks, their minds, and their bodies.

So purification of the emotional vehicle is a salvation for humanity, is a great release for humanity.

An initiate or an advanced disciple cannot be controlled or led by emotions but only by pure reason or higher logic. And this cannot even be called control because any conscious act is an act of freedom.

There is a difference between logic and pure reason. Logic is related to yourself, to laws and rules, or to your interests; it is some degree of rationalization. It is an accommodation, appropriation, or negotiation. But pure reason is seeing the facts from an impersonal, non-separative viewpoint in the light of the Spiritual Triad.

Logic is related to time and conditions; pure reason is not limited by time or any conditions.

Negative emotions help the germs in our body multiply. It is just like leaving a full trash can in our house for a week; we see that increasing numbers of bugs are emerging out of it because of contamination. The same thing happens in the human being. When there are negative emotions in our aura, the trash will produce germs, and they will multiply rapidly if the negative emotions continue. "Trash" is a collective name for all those wrong motives, wrong thoughts and attitudes, separative tendencies, and actual microbes and germs in our body.

If we do not have trash, then the neighbor's trash can bothers us. This is why even in the "new age" we carry the trash of our friends, wives, or husbands. They sometimes empty their trash cans into our mouths with a kiss, with a handshake, or through their contaminated thought currents.

The liquid system of our body is the transmitter of life energy from the centers of the heart and the head to the physical body. The mental body transmits energies from Space and Ashrams. The etheric body transmits prana from the Sun and earth.

Virtues increase our energy because they create harmony between man and the principles of the Universe. Love, joy, dedication, sacrifice, service, compassion, gratitude, courage, striving, and daring — all these virtues increase our vitality. Virtues release psychic energy into our whole system.

It is observed that when a part of a nation is negative and polluted with vices, many epidemics start and cause great losses in that part of the nation. The same thing is true with the whole world. Even natural calamities are the result of our vices and emotional and mental distortions.

The emotional body with its negative emanations builds a wall around us which prevents our progress on the path of evolution. Our emotions can hold us back from any constructive action when they are negative. Negative emotions, like acids, burn our organs and subtle centers in the subtle vehicles.

Our traditions, superstitions, and prejudices are mostly the accumulations of our emotions. This is why they have such power over people. They tie us to the past and past conditions, and because we are attached to the past, we cannot proceed to the light of unity, to pure scientific knowledge, and to unconditional justice.

There are groups and nations which are stuck in their past and cannot release themselves to the demands of the Future. Any kind of negativity that a nation or group is manifesting works against its own health, against its long-range success and joy. To increase the health of nations, we must increase their positive emotions and inspire love, hope, future, beauty, and inclusiveness.

Once I read, "Achievement releases a great amount of energy." After a while I thought that this was very true because achievement is the result of beauty, courage, joy, striving, daring, and fearlessness. Once you achieve, you are more open to the centers of energy within you and within the Universe.

The first practical step is to be watchful, and when you notice any negative emotion, just step on it and try to overcome it with a positive emotion. Positive emotions can very easily be formed by imagination.

Watch your thoughts, and when they are negative you will know that they have a great amount of polluted emotions within their form.

No real thought can be negative. Real thoughts are revelations of ideas, plans, and the purpose of your Inner Divinity or of the Divinity of the Universe. Most of our thoughts are emotions dressed in mental matter, and you can detect them immediately by their negativity and separatism.

When a scientist is using his mind for destructive or degenerative purposes, he is not a real thinker; he is the victim or the prisoner of a dominating emotion, or the victim and prisoner of a group which is obsessed by an emotion.

True thinking is creative. True thinking is also destructive to limitations and to separative walls. True thinking is for peace, for unity, for spirituality, for transformation. In true thinking there is no possessiveness; there is abundance and sharing. There is no intention to dominate but only to serve.

The history of humanity shows that every time individuals, groups, or nations become negatively charged and try to rule, to dominate, to possess, or to separate, cyclically their castles built on the sands of negative emotions are destroyed.

Negative emotions and negative thoughts can achieve short-range success, but such a success proves to be the greatest hindrance for their health, prosperity, joy, and achievement in the long run. Negative emotions and negative thoughts are condemned to dissolution, and when they dissolve, they eventually undermine all that was built upon them.

A nation degenerates if that nation is continually living in a stagnant pool of negative emotions and negative thoughts. To save a nation one should nourish it with positive emotions and positive thinking through all the systems of communication.

Satanic knowledge is not the result of *thinking*; it is received when you are charged negatively as a medium. In thinking there is transformation and sublimation, but when knowledge is given to you from satanic sources it is for your own destruction.

How to discriminate between Divine knowledge and satanic knowledge? Satanic knowledge works for separatism, obsession, possession, and materialism. It is selfish, hateful, destructive, and believes in neither unity nor immortality. Divine knowledge leads to greater love, greater unity, simplification, selflessness, joy, freedom, and to the One Self in everything and everywhere.

It is interesting to note also that positive emotions do not disguise themselves as thoughts. They radiate out. It is only negative emotions that seek the help of thought to cover themselves. When you have a positive emotion you are so happy and no thought disturbs your happiness. Immediately when the positive emotion becomes negative, it uses your mind and negative thinking comes into being and your happiness evaporates.

Positive emotions are expressions of love, unity, inclusiveness, givingness, sharing, purity, etc. They do not need to disguise themselves in thoughts, though they can increase their effectiveness by positive, enlightened thoughts.

You love someone and express your emotions freely, but when you start having selfish thoughts to misuse him through your love, your emotions become negative and the joy evaporates.

Group magnetism is created when the members are charged with positive emotions and positive thoughts. Only such groups can channel uplifting and unifying energies to the world.

People want to know whether their inspirations, thoughts, and emotions are coming from their own soul or Ashram or from the Dark Lodge. The answer is very easy. If an inspiration, thought, or emotion is leading you toward beauty, purity, striving, goodness, truth, and simplicity, it is coming from Divine sources. If the inspiration, thought, or emotion is leading you into pollution, ugliness, untruth, crimes, vanity, and separatism, it is coming from the devil.

The real inspirations, thoughts, ideas, or emotions that are coming from God, from your soul, or from your Innermost Self are those energies which make you strive toward purity, beauty, synthesis, oneness, creativity, sacrifice, service, gratitude, and so on. When these virtues are not the objects of your striving, there is something wrong.

Let us remember that the essence of the emotional body is intuitional substance. When the emotional body is purified from negativity and glamors, it reflects the beauty of the intuitional level. The mind reflects the atmic level. Once it is purified from illusion, the purpose of the Inner Self will be clear to us.

In the New Era the message is: "How can I help the welfare of my neighbor?" You are going to think about your neighbor first, then about yourself. In the old age it was your own interest that was important, even at the expense of others;

but in the New Era it is the interest of others that must occupy your attention, even at your personal expense.

This will not be easy as we have been cemented for so many thousands of years with the substance of old thinking. But unless we do it, the joy of the New Era will not be with us.

New Era politics will be based on the principle of loving your neighbor *more* than yourself. The welfare of humanity must be more important to you than the welfare of your individual self. No healthy person can live long in an unhealthy environment.

Make the greater community healthy so that the individual in it can live a healthy life. This is why we say that in the New Era we must try to guarantee the welfare of our neighbor before we work for our own welfare. If we cannot do this, our individual welfare or well-being will not protect us from the degenerative conditions going on among our neighbors or in the world. If we do not make our neighbor healthy, he will make us unhealthy. This is so simple to see.

The emotional body has a very unique position within the vehicles of the human being. Essentially it is built of intuitional substance, but densified and coarsened with glamors, desires, and negative activities. Because of this the emotional body does not clearly reflect revelations coming from the Intuitional Plane.

We are told that as man progresses on the path his emotional body passes through purifications and becomes a receptacle of the Intuition. The perfection of the intuitional body clearly reflects itself on the astral body after the Third Initiation. At the end of the Third Initiation when the Initiate passes into the Fourth Initiation, *"his emotional nature . . . disappears altogether, and the buddhic vehicle becomes the main instrument of sentiency."* [1]

Thus the emotional plane is the extension of the Intuitional Plane, relating the physical body to the mind.

Long ages ago, man on the physical plane was controlled and guided from the astral plane, through which he was in contact with his astral body. Now his consciousness has shifted into the mental plane. The day is approaching in which he will be able to transform his astral body and function on the mental and Intuitional Planes.

Because the astral body is related to the intuitional world, by purifying the astral body man can reflect and contact the revelations, visions, and great guidance found on the Intuitional Plane. This is why "holy" men or so-called saints, who have very little occult information and academic education, have great wisdom and knowledge gained through the process of revelation, dreams, and visions. This is the mystic path. Upon this must be added mental development so that another, higher nature in man is reached: the atmic nature,

1.   Alice A. Bailey, *The Rays and the Initiations*, p. 278.

which transmits will energy to man on the physical plane through the mind. This is the occult path.

Generally, our present astral body seldom transmits any great revelations due to the glamors and negative emotions found in it, and to the pollution existing in the liquid system of our physical body. The liquid system of our body is affected by our emotions, which in turn affect the emotional body. The sensations through our astral body are often the reverse of Nature, distorted, a broken fragment of reality mixed with many likes and dislikes. So the light that comes from the Intuitional Plane is distorted and deflected on the astral plane. This is why the visions of astral psychics are generally misleading.

The emotional body also has centers. On the emotional plane we have the base of spine, generative organs, solar plexus, spleen, throat center, heart center, and head center. The first four are on the fourth subplane of the emotional plane. The throat center is on the third subplane. The heart center is on the second subplane, and the head center is on the first subplane. These emotional plane centers are related to the love petals and the Intuitional Permanent Atom through the mental centers. Thus we can see that our emotional body has a central location, is very sensitive to various kinds of energies, and has a very powerful effect on our life.

Our senses are extensions of the inner Sun, just like seven rays emanating from our Central Core and passing through the seven vehicles, in each vehicle blooming like a flower. Thus we have seven flowers on each plane, or seven senses. As the beam withdraws from plane to plane, the senses vanish. As the beam goes out to lower planes, senses come into being. This is to say that our physical senses are the result of the ray coming into contact with matter. When the body passes away, the ray withdraws to the astral plane, and so on. In short, the senses do not belong to the planes but to the Central Core, to the Self.

In olden days the Sages impressed humanity with the importance of purity of the astral plane. Symbolically, the heart was the organ of sensations, and the heart was to be pure before any esoteric knowledge was imparted to the neophyte. Purity of the heart was considered a supreme necessity in order to come into contact with the spiritual world. Without this purity, everything that we accumulate and build is going to fall upon our own head.

Our motives generally are controlled and directed by our emotions, and a polluted heart will be a destructive factor in the world. Purification of the heart is a great service for humanity.

In advanced schools of esotericism the Teachers taught that knowledge must not be imparted to those who do not have a pure heart and pure motives. A pure heart is a heart which has no negative emotions and is full of love, is humble, peaceful, and joyful. Pure motive is an outgoing activity to serve and sacrifice and to uplift people for the Common Good, without expectations, exploitation, and self-interest.

Many people become more negative when they start meditating. Meditation brings in lots of energy and light, but because of the glamors and negativity of the emotional body, that energy is misused for destructive or selfish purposes. This is why we are told not to meditate when purity of heart and motive is lacking in us. For such people the greatest help can be obtained by Bhakti Yoga — aspirational yoga, devotion, worship, prayer, and various emotional disciplines.

The main discipline is to aspire toward Beauty, Goodness, and Truth and immediately to cast away any negative emotions that you detect in your nature. This requires a constant watchfulness and prayer. It is also very helpful to read the biographies of great saints, visit art galleries and music centers, and take part in inspirational ceremonies and rituals.

In esoteric schools it is taught that the foundations must be laid on rocks, not on the sands. Sand is the symbol of the ever-moving, changing, and unstable emotional nature. Rock is the symbol of the intuitional nature. Any construction built upon sand will fall down when the winds blow and the rains wash the sand.

When the consciousness is active in such an ever-changing emotional state, the promises, commitments, plans, and goals continually change according to the emotional nature. This is why occult Teachers tell us not to trust any promise given by those whose consciousness is focused on the emotional plane.

When a man functions on the Intuitional Plane, you can trust him in all ways and in everything because he is upon stable ground, enlightened by the light of Intuition and resting on Divine principles. If an aspirant does not purify his emotions and clean his mouth but continues reading occult books, attending esoteric lectures, and doing meditation, he will eventually become the enemy of the Teaching and the enemy of the Teacher. This is observed in all traditions and in many monasteries. The secret of this is that the accumulated knowledge increases the weight of the personality in such a way that the spiritual light fades out and the personality takes over to pursue its own goal with the weapons gained from the spiritual Teaching. Non-assimilated knowledge creates intoxication, vanity, illusion, glamor, and maya. This is why those who deal with esoteric knowledge are under heavy responsibility . . . and danger.

We have a system in our nature that corresponds to our stomach. We feed that system with continuous information and knowledge. But if that system does not digest and if our beingness does not assimilate the food and grow spiritually, then that system rejects all knowledge and rejects those who imparted that knowledge to it, as our stomach does when it does not digest the ingested food. Great Sages emphasized the development of virtues because the knowledge of energies and centers was known by Them. The same principle can be found in the Teachings of the Lord Buddha and the Lord Christ.

Negatively polarized people and people who are in a polluted state of emotions are very sensitive to the forces of the Dark Lodge. We can avoid the tragedy of becoming an agent of these forces by checking our activities inspired and directed by our emotions. If they are harmful, separative, and selfish, they must be stopped immediately and reversed with positive emotions and actions based on harmlessness, gentleness, goodness, beauty, simplicity, and sincerity.

When the motives are purified and the emotions are transformed, something very interesting happens. You see that you are extremely sensitive to wisdom and esoteric knowledge, and before you read books and attend lectures, you are already open to them and almost know what you will hear and read. There is a great receptivity and intuitive acceptance in you. This eventually leads you to Ashrams, the subjective schools, where you study the Plan and join groups only to serve. Such people become the readers of hearts, motives, and intentions. We read that Christ knew the hearts of the people because His intuitive senses were fully active and there was no distortion in His personality vehicles.

Purified hearts are linked with the world of causes, and they are related to the true facts going on upon subjective levels or in the innermost layers of our being.

The Great Ones always emphasize the heart, a heart that is inclusive and loving, because intellect can fail but not the loving heart. When there is a foundation of a loving heart, the structure of the intellect can be safely raised for further service and work. Without the foundation of the heart, the structure of the intellect may serve betrayal and destruction.[2]

One must be careful not to fall into a condition in which the urges and drives of the body and negative conditions control the activities and modifications of the mind and thought. This is a reverse path, and it leads to involution. The progressive path will be achieved when the physical and emotional domains serve the enlightened mind. When habits of the body or negative emotions control the mind, the man lives against the creative and harmonious forces of Nature and becomes self-destructive.

There are many negative emotions which not only control the minds of individuals but also the minds of families, groups, and nations. The major ones are fear, anger, hatred, jealousy, revenge, treason, and slander. Very often the mind turns into a factory working twenty-four hours per day to provide the ways and means to meet the demands of these negative emotions.

Once a negative emotion dominates the mind, all creativity, knowledge, and memory of the mind are used for the negative emotion.

The mind prepares all the plans, all the tools, and all the ways and means in its power to make the negative emotion win the show. Fear dominates the mind and leads it down irrational paths. Anger blinds the eyes of the mind and uses the mind as a destructive weapon. Hatred totally distorts the reality and proceeds on the by-passes of deception. Revenge makes the mind mobilize all the resources of the personality and plan destructive action. Greed makes a man so selfish that he tries to use and manipulate all possibilities for his own advantage as if no one else existed.

But because the human soul is on the path of evolution, a very violent action takes place. The disturbed energies of space bounce back and hit the source of

_____

2. See also *The Flame of the Heart.*

disturbance. Such an action manifests as a great crisis in our individual or national life and expresses itself as many kinds of failures, depressions, diseases, disorders, insanity, legal punishments, loss of reputation, and the destruction of all that the emotions made the mind accumulate or build.

People do not often see the action of the disturbed forces of Nature which act under the Law of Karma because the reaction does not come all at once. The reaction, the counterblow is controlled scientifically and with great compassion.

Karma is not retribution, nor is it revenge; it is the law of equilibrium, the goal of which is to restore the disturbed forces to make people know the law and give them another opportunity to live in harmony with the universal rhythm.

The progress of humanity does not depend on the accumulation of knowledge, nor on its comfort and inventions. One can be a great scientist but work as a slave to his negative emotions. One can be a great lawyer or statesman but be a prisoner of his physical urges and drives. The progress of a human being depends upon the victory he can win over these seven major negative emotions to free himself from their dominance. Knowledge built without such a foundation will eventually work against the owner of the knowledge.

Sensing is related to the registration of the senses. The more unfolded the senses are, the clearer and more accurate is the recording of the states taking place in the etheric, mental, and Intuitional Planes.

Sensation is the summary of the registration of the corresponding senses in the etheric, mental, and intuitional bodies. Our senses record etheric forces, emotions, thoughts, thoughtforms, and intuitive impressions. Sensing is also transmitted to the brain via the mental body, nadis, and etheric brain.

It is possible to sense and to feel. Feeling in this case is the personified translation of sensing. Sensing is impersonal and universal and is related to pure facts. Feeling is personal and handled by personal reactions and responses.

Sensing starts with the etheric senses. Then the correspondences of the etheric senses in the astral and mental bodies begin to register their sensations to a given object. Later, the intuitional senses join the etheric, astral, and mental senses and impart their impressions. At this stage, sensation turns into a pure awareness of acts, visible or invisible.

47

The Mechanism of Wishes

People have begun to realize that the greatest science is the science of relationship: relationship with yourself, with other human beings, with Nature, and with the laws of the Universe.

More and more people are interested in the science of right relationship. They are realizing that, until this science is mastered, all that they have and do will create for them unending problems and suffering. The mechanism of wishes is an important part of this science of right living.

Man always wishes. This is very natural for him. There is an innate urge in man to expand, to have more, and to be more

— in his physical life

— in his emotional life

— in his mental life

— in his spiritual life

This urge is not only on individual but also on group and national levels. A group or a nation wants to expand, to have more, to be more.

A pure wish is an impulse projected out from the Core of the human being as an answer or response to the pull of the Cosmic Magnet. When a pure wish passes through the spheres of our irritations, glamors, illusions, hatreds, and greed, it turns into a destructive force.

A pure wish is a longing for

- expansion of consciousness

- actualization of inner potentials

- freedom from the limitations of matter, time, space, and from influences of lower order

- communication with higher forces

- expression of beauty

Man, in his essence, feels that everything was abundant in his Father's Home. He feels deprived. He hears the call to come back Home. Each step is a wish. There is a deep memory in man, and his wishes are expressed fragments of that memory.

It is the wish that moves us forward. If we stop wishing, all life eventually will disappear.

We start with material wishes, but a day comes in which we feel tired of wishing and working for matter. Then we continue our wishes on the line of emotions and use our physical and mental responses to actualize our wishes.

We also have mental wishes — to know more, to understand more, to organize, to appropriate, etc. Then we have spiritual wishes such as our wishes for expansion, inclusiveness, continuity of consciousness, contact with higher laws or higher Beings, etc.

On all levels it is the impulse of the wish that leads us forward or keeps us constantly busy.

Any moment that we talk or think, see or hear, we *wish*; we wish all day. Wishing is a technique of expansion, a process to build a future and strive for the future. But this technique is often used in such a negative way that, instead of helping us expand, it becomes our own prison.

A wish is a magnetic form built of astral matter, mental matter, and etheric matter. Every time one wishes, a conception takes place in Space. A wish is an electrical impulse which puts into action a chain of forces in Space and in the mental realms.

Whenever a wish is formed, it puts a demand, an order, upon the laws of Nature to fulfill the wish.

There is a law in the Universe which is called by many names — the Law of Righteousness, the Law of Cause and Effect, the Law of Action and Reaction, the Law of Karma. Due to this law, man receives that which he asks for.

Any wish on any level has a response. This response can be immediate, or it can take a few years or incarnations to reach objectification.

Whatever you want will be given to you, even if you do not really know what the effect will be on you and your life when you receive the things you wished for.

Whatever you sow you will reap. There is no escape. One must be very careful about what he asks for or wishes.

The fulfillment of your wishes goes through the following process:

1. You formulate your wish and express it mentally, emotionally, and physically through words, feelings, actions.

2. This wish, like an electromagnetic wave, attracts the forces of astral matter and puts into action those entities who, by law, work for the formation of your wish and put it into the computer of Nature.

3. After the formation of the wish, your mind works to secure the success of and gives additional support for the fulfillment of the wish.

It happens also that due to illusions, various thoughtforms, education, and principles, the mind stands against the wish and provides many obstacles. This affects the "computer," which takes the presentation of the mind into consideration. These two factors — wish and mind — are run through the computer in different circuits which affect each other and run for a final conclusion.

If the wish is not opposed by the mind or by circumstances, the higher mind goes into action and makes all the subjective contacts possible to make your wish come true.

But the computer will have a very hard time and delay your demand if you contradict your wishes and put into the computer a wish that does not run in harmony with the "original" wish. The computer also takes in your doubts. Doubts are very powerful factors which sometimes stop the whole process or weaken it and allow it to be run by other wishes made at other times.

People sometimes try to withdraw their wishes. This does not mean that they can withdraw a wish that is already in the computer, but they can put in a new wish which perhaps balances or neutralizes the old wish. In such cases the wish degenerates in the aura of the man and causes psychic infections. Psychic infections are very common, and they bring many-colored sicknesses to man.

The computer has a very complicated and subtle job to do. The whole purpose of the computer is to do justice to the new material put into it and, in the meantime, relate all those wishes made throughout a lifetime either against or for the new wish.

The computer also takes into consideration various other wishes made by others related to the subject of the wish. The wishes of others for us have a tremendous effect on our life. Also, our wishes go through a very complicated process in the computer if they are against the rights of others related to our wishes. Nature cannot steal things that belong to others and give them to you unless in the past they were *owed* to you. The computer finds the debt or waits ages until those persons owe you.

The computer also takes into consideration the karma of related persons in relation to your wish. Karma is a matured wish. If a man's karma is not to marry a particular girl, his wish to marry that girl will create various problems in the computer and in his life. Karma must be changed or forced before the wish can be carried to fulfillment.

Your karma can delay or hasten the fulfillment of your wish. If your wish is in harmony with your karma, you will have quick results and enjoy the results deeply. If you obtain results against your karma, your wish will bring you complications and problems.

Often your wish is a sensed karma. You wish that which is on the way. Sometimes your wish is forced by your karma in order to fulfill itself. For example, if your karma is to marry a girl in New York, you will wish to go to New York for a vacation, and there you will meet that girl and marry her.

Your past and future visions have a great influence on the process of computerizing. Actually, your past and future visions are built by wishes.

We also have our sub-personalities. I am using this word esoterically. A sub-personality is the elemental of your physical or emotional or mental body. Often we are identified with these sub-personalities and have the same wishes they do. Sometimes we are detached and have different wishes. Sometimes they follow along with our wishes.

When the mental, emotional, and physical sub-personalities are in accord with the wish of the human soul, the wish changes into *desire*. Immediately when you desire, you evoke the power of *will*, according to the nature of your desire and the level of the object of your desire.

It is a common fact that our sub-personalities can have different wishes which are against the welfare of the whole person or against the welfare of another sub-personality. In such cases you have a confused person because he receives contradictory results from the contradictory wishes of the sub-personalities.

It is also possible that the human soul stands against the combined wishes of these sub-personalities. Such a condition is not rare, and it is the turning point of a new life after a period of long suffering.

People think that little wishes do not count. Sometimes a little wish multiplies in the auric computer more than any big wish. This happens when it tunes in with former similar wishes. Thus, the legend says, "A whisper-wish becomes a loud song or a great symphony in the hall of your future."

There are also weak wishes, wishes mixed with doubt or feelings of failure such as, "I wish I had that house, but I doubt that I can live in such a house, and I know it is an impossibility." Imagine such a mixture in the computer! But you may help the computer if you slowly eliminate your doubts and repeat your wishes year after year until you have them fulfilled.

It also happens that when your past wishes are already packed and on the path of delivery to you, you present a totally different wish. The computer is shocked, but it must work. Either the delivery is stopped, or when the delivery is received, it brings rejection, pain, and suffering with all their complications.

For example, you wished to marry that man for a long time, but when the computer arranges it and packs it and it is on the way, you wish strongly for another man and you involve yourself with him. When your former wish arrives, you are already involved with the new man. . . . There are so many of these examples. The turmoils in our life are often caused by a strong wish opposed by an old wish on the way to fulfillment.

Your wish life creates a great mess in the astral spheres because your every wish becomes a live drama, continuously performing and acting out in the astral spheres. All your wishes in harmony or in conflict with each other are going on as live dramas at the same time, with the same and different personnel and objects. This is called astral chaos. This astral chaos is nourished by your vital energies.

If your wishes are chaotic and of low order, you will lose a great deal of energy supporting your "wish children" in the astral spheres. If your wishes are of high order, you will receive additional energy in your physical life. You will receive continuous inspiration and be challenged to duplicate the beauty created in the subtle spheres. But if you have chaos in the Subtle World, that chaos eventually will disturb your life in the form of failures, confusion, and sickness.

The computer of Nature does something very clever, also. It takes into consideration the motive behind the wish, more than the wish itself. This is the filtering process of the computer. In such cases the answer, the result, comes to your motive rather than to your verbal or formal wishes.

Let us remember that our wishes, thoughts, and motives are electrical charges which put the computer into motion in a different dimension.

Dark forces can utilize unfulfilled low-level wishes of people, stimulating and energizing them by thought currents and advertisements, and then using these people to sell the objects of their wishes, or trapping them in crimes and making them temporarily useless for that period of history. Drug use, sex, tobacco, alcohol, even fashion are used to manipulate people through their low-level wishes.

We are now in a cycle in which the dark forces scientifically know how to create wishes in people to sell them what the dark forces wish. That is why one must know if his wish is really his own wish.

It is also clear that low-level wishes are violent, and they demand satisfaction by any means. Hence they provide a field of business for dark forces.

When our wishes change into imagination and are galvanized by our mind, then they become animated forms into which some astral entities enter and use for various reasons. For example, if you wish to slap the face of a man and you imagine doing it, you commit two transgressions:

1. Your imagination enters the aura of the other man and injects the poison of your anger and hatred there.

2. Then, an astral entity ensouls it, or possesses it, and uses it as an opportunity to insert its influence into the aura of the man to drive the form and use it to hurt others.

If, for example, you build through your imagination a sexual form, the astral entity may use it to insert its own desire into the aura of anyone and feel satisfaction in forcing the subject into sexual activities.

Thus any of our desires can be used by entities, and if they are of low quality, then your imagination can be used to hurt people.

Astral plane entities can create their own imagination, but this imagination cannot penetrate into the human aura because it lacks the etheric counterpart.

They seek imagination fabricated by human beings to be able to affect human beings.

Each imagination produced by a person is composed of astral force, mental drive, and etheric substance. In the astral world, entities do not have access to etheric energy. One must penetrate into the Intuitional Plane to be able to use higher ethers and their lower counterparts. Actually, our physical body is protected from our astral body by our etheric body. The same is true for the planet. The planet is protected from the astral plane by the etheric body of the planet.

It is only man who can rend the etheric body of the planet through mediumistic activities, necromancy, black magic, and imagination. It is through our imagination that we build a path through which astral entities contact man in his physical body and on the astral plane when he falls asleep.

One eventually will ask, "If I create such an imagery, who may use it, and for what purpose?" The answer will caution you and advise you to be extremely careful in your wishes.

There is also a more serious case when imagination combines with speech. Speech gives etheric, astral, mental, and will energy to the imagination and makes it a very potent force, by itself or in the hands of entities. The situation becomes critical if the voice carries anger, a spirit of hostility, egoism, and negative motives. In such cases a destructive force is accumulated through the words in the imagination. This destructive force is released into the aura of the victim, whoever he is.

The voice in itself is the most significant force in Nature because it carries self-contained direction, interest, and destination. In some esoteric schools the voice of lecturers or speakers is tested to find out its etheric, astral, and mental chemistry. It can be found that behind sweet words and ordinary harmless speech is a very destructive force which shatters the aura and prepares the path for many diseases.

In the future, radio announcers and public speakers of all kinds will have their voice chemistry approved before they are allowed to resume their position.

The voice carries bliss, joy, light, and health-giving waves of energy, or it carries a poisoned chemistry.

Most of the rituals and ceremonies in the world are expressions of wishes orchestrated with voice, music, movement, and words to carry a massive imagination into actualization.

The effect of these ceremonies does not depend on the outer phenomena but on the chemistry of the motives, emotions, thoughts, and spiritual level of the people. This is why we sometimes enjoy things on the outside, but inside we feel a strong rejection.

A wish can be packed in the best ornamented packages, but this does not change the contents of the package.

Wishes also bring together all those people who have wishes on the same frequency. They either meet each other and amplify their wishes and enjoy the effect together, or they remain in separate locations but work together in the subjective level and enjoy their labor and the results in their higher nature. We call such events "multi-dimensional participation."

The physical accumulation of such people in one location occurs if they have similar karma.

It also happens that people with similar wishes and similar karma, but with different tastes, come together. This is how we often are forced, for a while, to live with one whom we do not like.

Taste is a very occult word. It is an outlook from your level of beingness on which you are. You can be on a very high level but in the meantime be attached to people through your wishes, desires, and karma. This is why a judge finds himself involved with a prostitute, or a man of religion becomes involved with various criminals. Such conditions are periods of intensive study and learning. They often are the last cycle to end the unintelligent process of wishing and to undo the things we did.

Sometimes our wishes are reflections of the wishes of others. Temporarily we make ourselves wish like others, but deep down in our hearts we do not agree with them. This creates another complication in the computer, and eventually we share the result of the wishes of others, even with rejection and pain. That is why we find ourselves in situations which we hate.

One day when I was talking about this subject in an air traffic control office, my friend said with a smile, "That is why we have all these arrivals and departures."

It sometimes happens that we wish against the karma of others and create a great mess in their computer. Imagine the case of a girl who is destined to be a great actress, but her mother and father wish her to be something else. If the amount of energy put in against her destiny is strong enough, the girl will have a very hard time reaching her destiny, and she will always be interrupted by the static created by the wishes of her parents.

Let us remember that thought is often a mental desire. It may be better to say that desire often dresses itself in mental matter. The mind formulates your wishes, and the body takes action. Suppose you wish to go to a mountain. The mind tells you what to do. It says, for example, take your car and put some oil and gas into it, take a few blankets and food, and jump into the car. The body takes action, jumps into the car, and drives it in the direction the wish wants.

The wish sometimes gets so big that it controls every action of mind and body. This is an obsession by a wish or desire. The most complicated state of mind comes into existence when two or three strong wishes fight against each other to occupy the mental mechanism.

Also, our imaginations are the procession of our wishes, with lots of elements of emotions, thoughts, and actions combined in the procession.

Imagination is weakened in its power to reach its destination when the thoughts do not approve it and the wishes of the environment block it. In such cases imagination eats at the person who originated it.

Visualization is a strong wish on the mental plane, a wish which is "fulfilled" as a cause and as an effect. True faith is on the same line. Prayer is a wish. Actually, all religion is a complete wish for Beauty, Goodness, and Truth. This is essentially what a religion is, and if the one professing the religion is not demonstrating Beauty, Goodness, and Truth in his life, then he has no religion and his wishes are directed to other fields.

A wish can turn into a very strong suggestion[1] or a hypnotic suggestion if it is expressed improperly. Never wish for yourself or for others when you or others are in physically or emotionally painful conditions. Also, you must not express any wish to anyone who is in a state of unconsciousness. If you are sick, depressed, or in pain, never have a negative wish. Do not say, for example, "I wish I would die." This will cost you a great deal of time and money, and you will have a hard time keeping your body alive.

Again, if you are sick or in distress, do not curse or wish others ill. If you are sick and your son is coming and nagging you to borrow fifty dollars, do not curse him and say, "Now go away. Don't you know that I am sick? I wish you would become sick so you know what is happening to me."

Here you created a mess. First, you put some posthypnotic suggestions into your mind. You said, "I am sick." You also said, "I wish you would become sick." Whenever you are keyed into this suggestion you will feel sick; you will try to be sick; you will find it very strange to be healthy; you will develop rejections toward your son when he is healthy; you will have some obscure, incomprehensible wish to see him sick, and so on. This will create confusion and conflict in your mind because, naturally, you will reject that you are sick and that you wished your son to be sick, but the wish is there and the feeling is there. Such a conflict is one of the major causes of migraine headaches.

A wish is a powerful force. Use it carefully, and whenever you wish, make your wish on the principles of Beauty, Goodness, Righteousness, Joy, and Freedom.

I met an old man who used to wish in the following way: "I wish to live long if that is what God wants; I wish you health and prosperity if that is what God's Will is for you; I wish for me and for you all that God wishes for us."

In our present lives we are less successful and more confused when the positive and negative wishes clash without any resolution.

Man dies because of his wrong wishes. For a long time he does not care to search for the "kingdom of God." He does not believe that searching for the kingdom of God will make him have all that he needs. But that search was a great scientific formula which Christ gave to humanity. Only after we have the kingdom of God will all else belong to us. If we do not have the kingdom of God, all else that we have will disappear. . . . I think this is a wise way to eliminate all

---

1.   See also *New Dimensions in Healing*, Chs. 40 and 42.

negative consequences of wishes and an effort to harmonize our efforts with the Will of God or with the laws of Nature.

Contradictory wishes create a very unwholesome situation in our energy field. For ages and ages our wishes were mixed and sometimes were very contradictory to our beliefs, faith, principles, or conscience, but anyhow we continued them life after life. But if you observe the life of a human being on the path of his lifeline, you will find that as his contradictory wishes increased, he became sick or he passed away younger than his former deaths or he lived with more sickness than before.

Let your wishes be based on co-measurement. This means that if a wish on one plane will create complications and problems on another plane, it is better not to have it. If a wish is good for you but is destructive to others, it is better not to have it. If your wish is good for your nation but may bring calamities to another nation, leave such a wish out. Remember that your enemy today can be your friend tomorrow. Thus, one may say, "Do not deprive yourself of your future friends."

People also have various personal wishes. It is important not to wish something which is not good for your whole system, for your whole body. Do not wish something that is good for your physical body but not good for your astral, mental, and spiritual bodies. Do not wish something which is good for your personality but not good for your reputation or future service. This is what co-measurement means in your line of wishes.

There is food which seems good for your body but is disastrous for your emotional and mental bodies. For example, meat makes your astral body smell horrible. It creates decomposition in your astral body and creates cleavages in your mental mechanism. It also reverses the flow of energies in the etheric body. Alcohol and hallucinogenic drugs have similar effects, plus they rend the protective nets between the physical, etheric, and astral planes and suspend the mental plane. Certain drugs, such as opium, LSD, and angel dust, create paralysis in the mental mechanism. One is surprised at why people would want to burn or destroy their vehicles — their cars — which will be used later to continue their journey of life.

There are also certain exercises which crystallize and paralyze the astral body. Hatha Yoga is one of them. Tai Chi is another. Some breathing exercises are very bad for the etheric and astral bodies. Certain chants have the same effects on the mental body.

Whenever you do anything that damages your astral and mental bodies, the damage will come back to your physical body in the next few incarnations. A damaged mental body will build a damaged brain. A damaged astral body will build a damaged nervous and glandular system. In short, the conditions of the subtle bodies will affect your body in the next incarnation. Whatever you did to your subtle bodies, they will do the same to your physical body, and this will go on in a vicious circle until you take your life under your conscious control.

Co-measurement means to take all this under consideration and live a life beneficial for all future manifestations on all planes of existence.

Harmonious development is the result of a life which is based on co-measurement.

Unless we develop harmoniously in the four lower and three higher vehicles, we will always have troubles on one or another plane, which in due time will affect other planes.

Often our wishes are the response to our needs. How careful we should be to know if our wish is a mechanism to meet our need or a trap built by our vanities.

A wish propels our progress on the path if it is the response to the power of the Cosmic Magnet. This is the power which inspires progressive perfection and unfoldment on all levels.

The Great Ones, age after age, gave us prayers, affirmations, and invocations to regulate our wishes. For example, they gave the *Vedic* prayers, many prayers in the *Upanishads* and the *Bhagavad Gita*, many prayers in Zoroastrian Teachings, and many prayers were given by the Agni Yoga Teaching and by the Tibetan Master. "The Great Invocation" is a momentous architectural structure for a world wish. All these great expressions are guidelines to harmonize our wishes and transform and sublimate them to the major keynote of the Cosmic Magnet — perfection on all planes.

THE GREAT INVOCATION

From the point of Light within the Mind of God
Let Light stream forth into the minds of men.
Let Light descend on Earth.

From the point of Love within the Heart of God
Let Love stream forth into the hearts of men.
May Christ return to Earth.

From the Centre where the Will of God is known
Let Purpose guide the little wills of men
The Purpose which the Masters know and serve.

From the Centre which we call the Race of Men
Let the Plan of Love and Light work out
And may it seal the door where evil dwells.

Let Light and Love and Power restore the Plan on Earth.

It is important to wish according to our greatest and most lasting need. If we do not enjoy the outcome of our wishes, it is because we do not wish for exactly what we need.

Our uncontrolled wishes are responsible for the destructive action exercised upon Mother Nature. Our wishes have turned into greed, and now we have ever-increasing pollution and the grave danger it presents, plus increasing greed from an increasing population. Pollution is not only a physical health problem, but also it is a problem of mental health and spiritual direction.

Accumulated gases in the atmosphere not only prevent the healing and creative rays of the Sun and stars from reaching us, but they also distort or prevent impressions coming from higher sources. In the years to come, people will act more insanely and lose their sense of direction. Crime will increase, and those who are coming into incarnation will have a difficult time surviving. But if the Forces of Light take action and, with the power of Their wisdom, sacrifice, and beauty, awaken people to the great danger, the danger can be avoided. With the help of the Great Ones the New Era can dawn on the earth.

Your wishes affect your future lives on higher planes. A life that makes you happy on the physical plane but will make you miserable on the astral and mental planes must be avoided or must be changed. For example, killing a man on the physical plane does not end your problems. In the astral plane you will have a worse enemy who has superiority over you because of your horrible guilt.

Lying and cheating distort your mental body and create paralysis in it. Although you may enjoy for a while the results of your cheating, when you pass to the mental plane you do not have a healthy vehicle in which to travel or function.

You may break the laws of Nature, but as you ascend to higher planes you see heavier storms confronting you as a result of the laws you have broken. Things you do wrong on this plane become enormous obstacles on your path to higher planes.

In the future, the science of living will be given to those who are going to take important roles in human life.

Practical Suggestions for Wishes

1. Change your wishes into spiritual striving. Increase your observation. Have a goal and make all your small wishes orient themselves to that main goal.

2. Develop contentment to avoid overloading your computer with various unnecessary and petty wishes.

3. Start renouncing certain wishes which either do not help or which hinder your progress toward perfection.

4. Learn the art of indifference and use it often in your relationship with others and with the outer objects of the world.

5. Accept whatever life brings you. Instead of rejecting or identifying with it, try to use it for your self-unfoldment, experience, and service. Remember that most of the things you have received are things which you wanted in various ways.

6. Never wish ill on others. Never pity them. You can help them if you want. Any ill wish harms you and the other person. Try not to make negative wishes even when you are physically ill, depressed, or emotionally upset.

7. Never wish for others if they are in a painful state or are unconscious.

8. Start developing an attitude in which you try to develop more of your inner potentials instead of wishing to have more, to collect more, to possess more.

9. Be happy with the things you have, and do not replace them if they serve their purpose. Do not waste anything. Nature will give you whatever you wish, but Nature never tolerates your wasting things. The Law of Economy is a very powerful law.

10. Meditate on the Law of Economy and see if you are economical with what you have — in physical, emotional, mental, and spiritual realms. Do not forget to search *first* for the kingdom of God.

11. Instead of wishing every minute to have something new, try to think what you can give to life. Start to be a giver rather than a receiver. The more you give, the closer you go to the Soul of Nature.

12. Try to develop the power to examine your wishes and, if you so choose, to stop them or reverse them. This means to bring your wishes under the control of your intuitional light.

48

Pure Thoughts and Renunciation

Pure thoughts are thoughts which are not mixed with

1. emotions

2. wrong motives

3. separatism

4. impure thoughts of others

5. past memories

6. personal expectations

7. posthypnotic suggestions

Your thought cannot be crystal clear until you are free of these seven factors.

1. Emotions can destroy your thought. For example, hatred, fear, anger, greed, jealousy, and irritation interfere with the process of your thinking and make it impure.

2. Wrong motives behind a thought are like a poison within bread. Wrong motives make your thought very destructive and confusing.

3. As long as your consciousness is separative, your thought will not reflect integrity and wholeness. A thought created for separative interests is selfish and impure.

4. It sometimes happens that the thoughts of others telepathically reach your mind and mix with your thoughts. It is essential to sense such an occurrence and repel the unwanted thoughts.

5. Past memories may reject your pure thoughts and interfere with their formation. It is important to be able to reject past memories while you are in the process of creating pure thoughts.

6. Personal expectations are signs of weakness. You cannot build pure thoughts if you are under the conditioning force of your personal expectations. Your pure thought cannot remain pure if personal expectations interfere with it. You must be able to see the reality, even if it is against you. You must be able to think clearly, even if your thought humiliates your personality.

7. Posthypnotic suggestions are very dangerous thieves waiting within your mind to sneak in through any association or restimulation. The thinker within you must be able to insulate himself during the moment when he creates pure thoughts.

Pure thoughts may come from various high sources and may be transmitted by you in their purity. You may create pure thoughts in tuning yourself to your Innermost Core. But no matter whether you receive your thoughts from pure sources or from your Inner Core, your responsibility is to keep them pure and use them with wisdom.

We are told, "In each pure thought shines the glory of God."

Pure thoughts bring the emanations of solar and electrical fire. They have the power to heal our vehicles, to expand our consciousness, to make us magnetic, creative, and sacrificial. Pure thoughts shine in the light of Cosmic Beauty and transmit the power of their Source.

Pure thoughts never die. They may go far away like a comet, but after increasing their power they come back and enlighten the horizons of consciousness. They come and cyclically hit the fields of the consciousness of man. Each renaissance, each striving for the betterment of life is the effect of the lightning of pure thoughts.

Pure thoughts are charged with great power. They move mountains of ignorance, superstition, and fanaticism. They open new gates of wisdom and build new paths toward higher achievements. Pure thoughts flourish and bloom when the mind is not attached to transient objects.

Pure thoughts lead you to victory. Every great victory, every great service, every great sacrifice is achieved through pure thoughts.

One of the greatest gifts of a pure thought is joy. It is the joy of expansion into more freedom, into more space, into greater mastery. Pure thoughts spread joy, as pure thoughts link the human soul with greater spheres of beauty, love, and light. Joy is the fragrance of pure thought.

It is also true that pure thoughts come into manifestation when the presence of inner freedom reaches its saturation point. Pure thoughts can come into being when our mind is clear of

- glamors

- illusion

- vanity

- prejudice

- superstitions

- selfishness

- self-deceit

Pure thought can be created

   a. within the higher mind

   b. in a clear and unpolluted atmosphere

   c. in a place where mechanical and electrical disturbances are absent

   d. when the body is not tired

   e. when the emotions are in peace

We must remember that pure thoughts emanate light. Such a light has a great curative effect on the eyes. Our eyesight is strengthened and cleared when the light of pure thoughts precipitates on them. This is why meditation, if done on a high level, has a great curative effect on the eyes.

We must also remember that our pure thoughts affect the eyesight of others. As we send our pure thoughts into space, they emanate lights of different frequencies. These lights, though invisible, are factual, and they are caught by certain auras. Those who are impressed with these lights feel vitalization and clarity in their eyesight.

The deterioration of our eyesight is mainly due to impure thoughts which originate within our mind or from the people with whom we live. Criminal thoughts and thoughts built upon hypocrisy and lies eventually weaken our eyesight through various complications and problems. Thus our eyesight has a very close relationship with our thoughts.

We must also remember that higher clairvoyance, when naturally achieved, is a gift of Spirit to those who, throughout many incarnations, developed pure thoughts and lived in pure thoughts. The light emanating from pure thoughts conditions and affects the subtler layers of the mechanism of the eyes and develops them to such a degree that subtle waves of ethers are seen. The eyes always unfold because of the light.

In the future, when ophthalmologists want to improve the eyesight of their patients, they will recommend pure thinking, meditation, and an environment where people are not engaged in distorted thinking.

In the temples of the Ancient Mysteries, Teachers used to examine the eyes of the students and the degree of their strength. Usually students were chosen who had clear eyesight, with the ability to see colors, shapes, distances, and proportions clearly. They also had tests for the eyes and their performance in darkness.

With all these tests they wanted to know the quality of the sphere of thought the student lived in; they wanted to determine if the student could handle the voltage of purer thoughts and proceed on the higher spiritual path.

It is not enough to put on eyeglasses; we must purify our thoughts.

Examinations of the eyesight of criminals will be very revealing. Also, accidents offer a great deal of information about the eyesight of people. In the future it will be possible to detect the causes of present poor eyesight in past incarnations.

The thoughts most harmful to our eyesight are thoughts mixed with

1. fear

2. anger

3. hatred

4. greed

5. jealousy

6. lies, malice, slander

7. hypocrisy

These seven ingredients mixed with thoughts radiate certain rays which weaken or destroy the nerves and the retinas of the eyes and create other unhealthy conditions in the mechanism of the eyes.

Accumulated impure thoughts mixed with these seven ingredients follow a man, life after life, until the man reforms his thinking and eventually clears the effects of his past impure thinking.

Of course, one cannot deny the other causes of bad eyesight such as various accidents or diseases in other parts of the body or unhealthy and chemically loaded air and water.

The Ancients used to think the eyes were the lights of the Soul. In each eye one must see the flame of the Soul. This flame is lit only through a life dedicated to pure thoughts and selfless service.

It is true that as we send pure thoughts we use the substance of our mental body or mental aura and thus decrease the amount of our mental substance. But as our thoughts begin to do their constructive work in space or in the minds of people, psychic energy pours into our aura and refills the amount of substance used with a higher and more refined mental substance.

As the mental substance is refined and recharged by psychic energy, the eyes receive a greater beauty, depth, and clarity of sight. Each higher substance emanates higher lights, and the eyes try to adjust themselves to these lights through new unfoldment and refinement.

It is observed that when the anxieties, worries, and confusion found in the mental body are cleared away, the eyesight improves dramatically. Thought is light, and the light of pure thoughts blooms like a flower in the darkness.

We are told that we must protect our eyesight, especially when our eyes are more advanced than average. One of the ways of protection is not to attract hostile thoughts toward ourselves. A second way is to strengthen the shield around our head by increasing pure thoughts of beauty, goodness, and joy.

A thought is the translation or interpretation of an idea. When the interpretation takes the form of a beauty, the thought becomes saturated with beauty and the idea behind the thought comes into manifestation.

Truth is presented by the idea, and truth can be contacted only when the thought translates the idea through beauty.

It is only the symphony of beauty that can give manifestation to a pure thought. It is only a pure thought that can manifest an idea. A real idea is always charged with truth.

We are told that when we find the truth we find our freedom, and freedom is the Life. Truth reveals itself when one makes a contact with the hidden Purpose behind creation. Each idea is a wave from the ocean of Purpose. Each thought brings a beam of Purpose into manifestation, and it is the symphony of beauty that can express a thought without losing the truth.

Meditation is an effort to reach ideas, to come in contact with the truth, to step into the ocean of pure freedom, pure life, and to translate all experiences through beauty.

It is good to hear elevating music or to look at some beautiful artwork or read poems written by Initiates or Masters or even to visualize beauty in any form you want before you start your meditation.

In the depth of your meditation, you will contact the world of ideas. Ideas will lead you to the Purpose, to truth, to life, to freedom. This is what esoteric renunciation is, and this renunciation will expand your consciousness.

The consciousness of most people is fenced in with impenetrable walls of barbed wire. Whenever the consciousness is limited and incapable of expanding, it causes many psychological and social problems. Freedom is achieved only through the expansion of consciousness.

To make a limited consciousness grow and find its way toward expansion, one must follow the path of renunciation. This is what Nature does when needed: It imposes renunciation upon people, and after a period of renunciation their consciousness expands. Renunciation creates pressure, and pressure eventually expands the walls of consciousness.

Renunciation works under many expressions:

— Losing your property

— Losing loved ones

— Leaving your body in death

— Being unable to reach the objects of your desires

— Being sentenced to prison or punishment

— Being disappointed by your friends

— Being unable to remember an important date or name

— Being involved in different situations with pain and suffering

— Being unable to eat or drink what you like

Besides personal circumstances, family, national, and international situations present to people great opportunities for renunciation.

Through all these and other forms of renunciation, your consciousness faces the crisis of expansion, and when the period of renunciation is over, you witness that things in the world and in your individual life are handled on broader scales.

Those who impose renunciation on their individual lives can very easily meet the discipline of renunciation. It is suggested that each disciple draw a plan for renunciation and follow it literally. Renunciation can be related to one's physical body and sex, to one's emotions, and to one's mind. This will be a self-imposed discipline, for example:

1. Certain food must be avoided on certain days.

2. No sex on certain days.

3. No speech during certain periods of time.

4. No daydreaming about certain subjects.

5. No desire for certain objects.

You must remember that renunciation does not mean to alter objects or to replace the objects of your renunciation.

You may give to others things that you have or things that you love. You may let someone use some object to which you are attached. You may stop a habit.

Then, try not to think about something which always tries to occupy your mind. Renounce your bed or your lounge chair for a period of time. Give up for a period of time things you like to do. For example, do not play tennis or swim. Do not dance. . . . For a period of time, just try to renounce.

When you renounce, you minimize the power of the control of the object. You gain more freedom. You increase your independence. You expand your consciousness.

Any time you enter a mechanical routine, your consciousness crystallizes.

One day a lady told me that she had been doing meditation for seventy years. As we were talking I noticed that she could not think clearly. She was not creative. She was not clear in her thoughts or ideas, and she had no mental continuity.

I told her that she must renounce her meditations. She was very angry.

"Why, why? Meditation is so important in my life. I can't do without it."

"It is true that meditation is important, but your meditation created a prison for you and you feel secure in it. You must stop building your prison through your mechanical meditation or daydreaming."

"What else can I do?"

"For example, instead of meditating you can write an article about a subject and try to see if it makes sense. Try to improve it every day during the time you used to sit for meditation. Or you can make a few rules for yourself and see if you can obey the rules in your daily life. Or try to paint or compose music or sculpt or learn how to sing. You can weave, do certain handiworks. There are other forms of meditation. If you do these suggested labors successfully, then after a period of time you may begin your former meditation and continue it more successfully."

The mind must periodically clear away all crystallization if you want it to render a better service. Thus we must renounce all things that try to control us or limit us. The only things that do not control us are Beauty, Goodness, Righteousness, Joy, Freedom, and health because these are the components of your essence.

There was a very rich man who was living in luxury. Once he came and told me that he felt miserable; he did not know how to be happy. He asked, "What is wrong with me?"

"You must expand yourself. You are the prisoner of your luxury and wealth."

"How can I expand myself?"

"Take a vacation. Rent a cabin on a remote mountain and go and live there for six months."

"What can I do there?"

"Just live there. Do not take your books, magazines, radio, television, telephone, or electrical equipment with you. Just live there as if you were cut off from civilization."

"You know, I will do it because I am desperate."

This man disappeared for one year. One day he came to my office. I could not believe my eyes. He looked much younger, healthy, full of vigor and joy. He was a new man.

"Well, I am here. It took great courage, daring, and sacrifice, but eventually I found myself. Do you understand? I found my Self!" And he came and hugged me.

"I'm glad you did it," I said.

He had a very hard time in the wilderness. He learned to cook, to wash his clothes, to abstain from many things, to stay alone, and thus leave all the trash he was attached to in his luxury.

"Do you know that our life in the cities is a life of insanity, sickness, trash?" he said. "How could I live such a life for such a long time?"

He had an expansion of consciousness because he dared to renounce. He gained his freedom and he met his Self. He met the greater values of life.

Thus, periodically, we must go through such a crisis of renunciation, or else Mother Nature will impose it upon us to make us come to our senses and find the way to expand our consciousness.

When a person has contacted the intuitional light, he has all the potentials within himself to expand his consciousness. An expanding consciousness does not need renunciation of any kind. Like concentric spheres, it opens itself in space, breaking any attempt at limitation from any source.

When the expanding light of consciousness covers the whole mental plane, it penetrates into the Intuitional Plane. Then the intuitional light annihilates the last veil of the mental plane and pours in. This is what true illumination is. The mental veil is removed and intuitional awareness opens up the unlimited Cosmic beauty. Man still has thoughts. They are pure thoughts. They are pure manifestations of ideas contacted in the Intuitional Plane. These thoughts are highly charged with Purpose, and they carry freedom and life on their wings.

When a man reaches enlightenment, he turns into a stream of life and a "way by which men may achieve." At this stage, meditation turns into contemplation. Renunciation is over. Man lives in the abundance of Cosmos; he does not try to own anything or to know because all is available for him.

Contemplation is not a process of renunciation or knowingness but a process of continuous becomingness. Beyond the mental plane all contact is carried on through becomingness.

Becomingness is a strange word, but it conveys the meaning and the state of beingness. It means to be that which you want without violating the freedom of the object.

If you want to communicate with a flower, you must be a flower. If you want to communicate with a beauty, you must be the beauty. This is what saturation is in its esoteric meaning. Becomingness annihilates separation, duality; it leads to unity. Craving is the tension created between two separate objects. Becomingness annihilates craving and its resultant crimes. Thus, meditation flows into the ocean of contemplation, and man finds the source of at-one-ment.

It is at the summit of at-one-ment that Avatars come into being, charged with Cosmic awareness, with Cosmic compassion. Like a comet They appear and disappear, for a long time leaving behind a path of light for striving people.

It is very important to "fill Space with victorious thoughts." Because such thoughts are charged with energy, they continuously sustain us and inspire us to live a victorious life. Victorious thoughts are those thoughts which are always full of the vision of the future. Victorious thoughts are based upon these certain facts:

1. The human Spirit cannot be defeated or destroyed.

2. The human destiny is to increase in light and power.

3. No force can defeat the human heart.

Victory is nothing else but expansion of consciousness, creativity, and cooperation with the forces of harmony, beauty, and mastery. Victory is a continuous fusion with the Divine Will and an actualization of that Will in creative living.

Victorious thoughts are not the result of a victorious life but the cause of a victorious life.

One must always think in terms of success and victory, no matter in what condition he finds himself. After many experiences man finds out that no matter what happens to the outer man, his Spirit always achieves victory. The defeat of the personality is very often the victory of the Spirit.

Victorious thoughts prepare a man to face his life victoriously, and he sees that through all his life he is victorious.

Doubt is the most dangerous element for the mental substance and human thought. One must not have the slightest doubt that the day, the year, the life will be victorious. At the beginning of every labor, all doubt must be annihilated. Only the thought of success and victory must rule.

We must learn to see the victories of the Spirit, while the outer man goes through a series of seeming failures. Behind and below each personality failure, you can find a spiritual victory. All difficulties and troubles are great opportunities to make you see the victory of your soul.

Once you learn to see the continuous victory of your Spirit, then all changes in your life will serve as waves to surf upon. The greater the opposition, the greater the success which will issue forth from your heart. Your spiritual victory can be evoked only by greater attacks.

The life of victory eventually teaches us to stand above pain, suffering, death, and loss. The body, all possessions, pleasures, and even knowledge can evaporate, but the Spirit rejoices with the song of liberty and freedom.

This is the victory of the Self. Once you meditate and realize that the progress of the Spirit cannot be defeated by any means whatsoever, then you start building victorious thoughts, and victorious thoughts attract all those forces which help you achieve victory.

Victorious thoughts can be born in your mind when you contemplate on the power of the Great Ones and think about Their victories. Victorious thoughts are born when you begin to think in terms of Infinity, when you remember the Spark imprisoned in the atom and the radiant Suns in Space.

Everything that is beyond you, beyond your reach, beyond comprehension tells the story of great achievements and victory. When you remember your past and realize your present achievements, you will have victorious thoughts.

The human Spirit is always victorious, even if It acts in the role of failures.

Daily, one must have an hour to radiate victorious thoughts. We are told that in victorious thoughts ozone is found, and the only protection for a person is the army of his victorious thoughts.

Never nourish thoughts of failure. Thoughts of failure and doubt weaken your protective net and cut the resources of psychic energy. You can repel thoughts of failure by first using your creative imagination, then by contemplating upon principles of spiritual victory.

The Great Lord Buddha once said, "All that we are is the result of what we have thought. All that we are is founded on our thought and formed of our thought."

We are building a victorious future when creating victorious thoughts. Victorious thoughts are only victorious if they are built for the victory of the Spirit of all humanity. Any separative victory invites pain and suffering. Victory does not refer to any individual, group, or national victory. It refers to the victory of humanity as a whole.

The victory which increases the potential victory of all humanity is a true victory. Every victory must be gained in the name of humanity. Every victory must glorify humanity. Every victory should be the victory of humanity.

To conquer in the name of humanity, one must be able to renounce all separatism and self-interest. This is how humanity can enter into a new way of living.

Victorious thoughts are the call of the vision of the future. A man who can see his future glory can only create victorious thoughts.

49

Thought and Transmutation

Transmutation means to change the substance of your bodies. It is a process through which the matter or the substance of our bodies is refined by throwing out the old substance and importing higher and living substance into the bodies.

If your bodies are built of lead, through transmutation you can change them into gold.

We have physical matter, emotional matter, and mental matter in our personality vehicles. This matter must be refined and transmuted if we want to express greater beauty and greater vitality and allow the fire of life to circulate freely through them.

First, we have our physical body, and in most cases the fire in the center of each cell of our body is relatively dormant. The electricity of higher vitality and creativity circulates when this fire in the cell is radiant. If the fire is not active, the whole physical body is in a state of inertia, apathy, or sleep.

When your body is in a state of *inertia*, it demands certain kinds of food and drink and unwholesome relationships which cause it to remain in the state of inertia. In the *Bhagavad Gita*, we read, *"Tamas* [inertia] *is born of ignorance. It deludes all indwelling ones, and binds them by heedlessness, indolence, and sleep."*[1]

Stimulants are often used to change the inertia, but most of them gradually put out the flame in each cell.

A body that is in a state of inertia hates to be active and always searches for those ways and means that keep the state of inertia unchanged. The *Bhagavad Gita* says they eat foods *"which are stale, tasteless, putrid, and rotten...."*[2]

How can we change this condition? We can increase the flame of the fire in each cell so that, instead of the matter controlling the whole body, the Spirit controls the body. The Spirit cannot be active unless fire exists in the body. It is the Spirit, or psychic energy, that vitalizes the body. The lowest expression of this vitality is the etheric network which fuses with the body through the latent

---

1. *The Bhagavad Gita* 14:8, trans. by author.
2. *Ibid.*, 17:10

fire of the body. When this fire is in its minimum state, the fusion is very weak and vitality cannot be transmitted to the body.

To cause transmutation in our physical body, we must do exercises: running, swimming, hiking, etc. We must keep our body clean and protected from any internal and external pollutions or poisons. We must eat those foods which give us more vitality, such as fruit, grains, and vegetables, and drink pure water and juices of various kinds. We must save our sexual energy, sleep enough, and have a regular, daily labor. Such a routine causes transmutation in our body and leads it into *motion*.

Through such a discipline the whole substance of your body changes. Your vitality increases and you reach a state of radiation. When a body reaches such a state of liberation from inertia, it can obey the will of the real man and does not create obstacles on the path of the evolution of the man. It becomes healthier, full of energy, and feels the urge to work and labor.

From the state of inertia, the body passes to the state of motion in which it is more vibrant. The fire in the cells is fifty percent active, and it is controlled by two poles of the human being — by the material pull and by the spiritual pull.

The *Bhagavad Gita* says that those whose physical body is in the state of motion like to eat foods *"which are bitter, sour, salty, too hot, pungent, dry and burning. . . ."*[3]

The next stage of the physical body will be the *rhythmic* stage in which the body is truly healthy, vibrant, magnetic, full of energy and vitality, and in tune with the intent of the Inner Dweller.

Those who achieve the rhythmic state of the body eat foods that *"give vitality, purity, strength, health, joy, cheerfulness, which are delicious, bland, nutritious, and pleasant. . . ."*[4]

Our emotional body is formed of billions and billions of atoms, in the center of which is the fire of life. When this fire is not active, the emotional body is in a state of inertia. When it is half-active, it is in a state of motion. When it is totally active, it is in a state of rhythm.

We transmute our emotional body through high aspiration, devotion, worship, and love. These virtues cause the fire in the emotional atoms to kindle and increase in flame and fire and eventually lead the whole emotional body through a state of motion to rhythm.

The food of the emotional body is beauty in all its forms, kindness, compassion, all kinds of purity, and all-inclusiveness. A rhythmic emotional nature is free of hatred, glamor, attachments, jealousy, depression, and all negative reactions.

Our mental atoms can be found in relative states of inertia, motion, and rhythm. In the inertia state of mind, the man is lazy; he does not want to learn,

3.   Ibid., 17:9
4.   *Ibid.*, 17:8

to think, to relate, and he stays in a state of apathy. In the motion state of mind, he has interests; he is nosy, critical, and gossipy and likes to create confusion, agitation, and conflict. In the rhythmic state of mind, the person is enlightened, free of illusion and separative attitudes; he is inclusive and feels great joy in seeing the success of all people everywhere. He is creative and firm in his decisions and goals.

In *The Bhagavad Gita* we read,

> *From Sattva [rhythm], knowledge is born. From Rajas [motion], greed is born. From Tamas [inertia], heedlessness, delusion, and spiritual blindness are born.*[5]

> *Those who are under the influence of Sattva go upward. Those who are under the influence of Rajas remain in the middle, in the human sphere. Those who are under the influence of Tamas degenerate.*[6]

Spiritual life does not exist without the process of transmutation. As the fire increases in your vehicles, you advance on the path of spirituality and creativity. It is not learning or accumulation of data that makes you a precious man, a man of dignity, virtue, and creativity, but it is through the transmutation of your vehicles that you reach to higher states of consciousness and contact greater energy and the center of wisdom in the Universe.

When all the vehicles reach a state of rhythm, we say that man has reached the stage of Transfiguration in which the fires of all the cells and atoms are now released and radiating out in great beauty. The first sign of such a man is a great inclusiveness, a great universal love for all living forms, and a deep sense of unity.

When man is in inertia, he is used by Nature as fertilizer. When he is in the stage of motion, he uses all that exists on behalf of his selfish interests. He tries to manipulate people and conditions to secure his own selfish ends. When he is in rhythm, he is all-sacrificial, inclusive, tolerant, understanding, and universal. And when all three bodies are in a rhythmic state, the light of the atoms are released in such a way that the whole personality is radioactive and a blinding light shines out of the man. This is the stage of Transfiguration.

Thus, observation and detachment lead us into transmutation, which eventually makes us shine out our light and contact a greater reality in the Cosmic Life.

Love is the realization that we are part of the Great Whole and we belong to that Great Whole.

_____

5. *Ibid.*, 14: 17
6. Ibid., 14: 18

Transmutation of our vehicles expresses itself in all our relationships. Solemnity, sincerity, universality, beauty, courage, striving, and purity become expressions of our life.

God is nothing else but unity, and one can reach this realization only through transmutation. God and Nature form a unity. Nothing can be separated from God. Anything separate from God has no place to exist. Such a realization leads the pilgrim on the path to the field of service. A man is equal to his service. The greater your service, the greater the man you are.

Transmutation follows observation and detachment. Detachment is the ability to hold the higher level frequency you reached through observation.

Let us imagine our two hands, the right one upon the left one, and the fingers touching each other. Then imagine that the right hand becomes the observer and the left hand the object. The right hand slowly rises and stays there, no matter what temptation the left hand presents to the right hand. When the right hand keeps its position, we say that the observation was made and detachment was achieved.

Thus, detachment is raising your consciousness into a new level and keeping it there for further progress.

Let us mention that observation is not done only with your eyes but also with all your other senses:

- Use your ears to observe.

- Use your nose to observe.

- Use your touch to observe.

- Use your taste to observe.

- Use your intellect to observe.

- Use your Intuition to observe.

You can do observation through all your senses, and, as you observe more with your senses, you reach more detachment and a higher degree of transmutation. The great servers of the race are those who have really passed these stages and served humanity.

To serve means to awaken the spirit of a human being into reality. True service is service to the Spirit; then the Spirit takes care of his body and life. But if you serve the body, it will always lean upon you.

Inspire the Spirit, expand the consciousness, encourage striving, and lead people into the realization of their innate Divinity.

To take the pressure of life out of the lower centers, you must cultivate interests and virtues related to the corresponding higher center. Similarly, to take the pressure from the lower planes, you must cultivate their higher counterparts.

We receive the thoughtwaves and emotional waves of other people if we do not have control over our own emotional and mental centers. This control can be exercised when we change our focus of consciousness from the lower to the higher planes.

The agitated condition of our etheric, emotional, and mental centers is due to the pressure they are under. This pressure is a state of congestion which occurs when the higher correspondence of the center is not active. When the higher correspondence is active, it draws up the excess energy and uses it to build higher vehicles and for higher creativity.

It is very possible that bodies under pressure do not obey the voice of logic and morality of the Higher Self. We can say that most of the crimes of various degrees originate from our physical, emotional, or mental realm, wherever the congestion or pressure is heavier.

When a man is under sexual pressure, he kidnaps a little girl and commits a crime. When a man is under emotional pressure, he is nervous, aggressive, and touchy. When he is in mental congestion, he is critical, fanatical, prideful, full of vanity, and separative. These pressures cannot be taken away by psychoanalysis or by injections. They can only be taken away by cultivating the higher counterpart, or the higher correspondence, of the centers and by pulling up the forces or the pressures to the higher centers. This is what sublimation is.

Often we hear that when there is pressure or congestion one must exhaust that force or pressure. Psychologists give similar advice, but it does not work. I have seen many people who went through such a process and came back worse than before. For example, a young boy was advised to have frequent sexual relations because of an over-stimulated sex drive. Not only did he not feel better, but, because of increased involvement with sex, he resorted to crime.

A girl was advised to shout, to cry, to curse, and to hit the walls and furniture because she was under emotional pressure. It did not help. A short time later, all that they had told her to do to objects she did to people, and she ended up in jail.

To help such people you must try to show them how to operate on the corresponding higher planes. For example, if the congestion is in the etheric body and is being experienced as a violent sexual urge, the creative arts must be cultivated with practical study. If the congestion is on the emotional plane, the Intuition must be invoked with the help of the light of the mind. Religious aspiration brings great release in our emotional plane.

50

Thought in Space

In Infinity, spiral rings, whole cycles of thought, are engaged in manifestation.[1]

We are told that thoughts accumulate in space and form spirals of thought energy. These spirals attract thoughts of similar kinds and grow in mass and systematize themselves as if rainbows in which every atom of color is attracted to its corresponding hue.

After such an orchestration of thoughts, the whole spiral of thought begins to develop a rhythmic movement in itself in which the colors dance in cyclic pulsations.

The whole mass of this thoughtform is a creative mechanism, which means it absorbs energy from space, densifies it according to the desire of the thought formation, and projects it into space. The manifestation starts from the most condensed rings. Every ring provides energy and transmits it to the manifested form to insure its life cycle in space.

The accumulated thoughts are projected from the Minds of great Avatars, Lives, and Existences in space. Their creativity manifests through Their thoughts.

The life period of such thought-accumulations lasts billions of years as they cyclically create and dissolve the created forms. When each succeeding ring on the spiral begins to manifest itself, the manifested form of the lower spiral fades away.

Millions of lives of various magnitudes live in these thoughtforms and on the manifested forms.

Evolution advances as ring after ring, during great periods of time, manifests and fades away. Galaxies, solar systems and planets are such manifestations.

Human thought can assist such creative processes if it is refined enough and of high quality. Accumulations of noble and pure thoughts not only reinforce spatial spirals and rings but also act as transmitters of thoughts from such spirals.

---

1. Agni Yoga Society, *Fiery World*, Vol. III, para. 600.

The creative dance of the spatial forms, and especially the creative dance between two gigantic thoughtforms, is a reality. Such dances are modes of blending and fusion through evocation of energies from within each other.

The sacred dances of the Ancients are the remote echoes of such precise movements between two spirals of accumulated thoughtforms. A sacred dance, esoterically prepared, with proper colors and movements, can link a group of people with giants in space and draw a tremendous amount of energy to the world. This energy can be very creative if the transmitters accumulate it within their Chalice and use it through their service for Beauty, Goodness, and Truth. It can also be very dangerous and destructive if it is released without discrimination to an environment which is fed by destructive and degenerative thoughtforms.

Such thoughts precipitate in the minds of highly creative people in forms of inspiration and impressions and bring changes on the planet. As these human thought formations organize and increase in strength, the transmission of higher impressions increases and becomes a factor for a progressive urge in the human consciousness. This is how manifested forms align and harmonize with each other in progressive advancement.

Less worthy thought-accumulations in space hinder such a process to a certain degree. And if the unworthy thought-accumulation reaches a state of spatial pollution, the rays of the creative formations cannot reach the earth and thus the moral and spiritual values of the planet deteriorate. Such a degenerative process coincides with the fading of the ring of the spatial thought-accumulation.

Two Origins

The Ancients tell us that there is one Source, the Space — and this Space, when it manifested, created the two origins:

— Spirit and matter

— Electricity and magnetism

— Male and female

— Man and woman

— Masculine principle and Feminine principle

These two origins interrelate with each other and produce the one manifestation — a son.

In any form of manifestation these two principles exist to a more or less degree with their specific forms of expression. For example, in one form a male forms and in another the form of a female forms. Real male forms are electrical and radioactive. Real female forms are magnetic and receptive.

In the human kingdom masculinity and femininity are more complicated because the mind principle can temporarily change the expression of the body to masculinity or femininity, thus creating a mix up of polarity in the emotional and mental body.

A personality is a person who has integrated his or her three bodies — physical, emotional, mental.

It is becoming very rare to have a masculine personality or a feminine personality.

As artificial masculinity or artificial femininity is introduced to our personality, it manifests as lesbianism or homosexuality.

At a higher stage the balance of these two principles produces the phenomenon of androgyny.

The phenomenon of attraction and repulsion between living forms is based on polarity. We know that some polarities reject each other and other polarities attract each other. This is nothing else but the action of the two origins, male and female, masculine and feminine principles, on all planes up to the Cosmic Mental Plane.

The basic principle of relationship in the human field is to represent one or the other origin. When a man has masculine bodies, he is most attractive to women who are really feminine. But people are seldom representative of their origins and, because their polarity is mixed, it then sends mixed signals to others. For example, an ideal man must be masculine in his physical body, feminine in his astral body, and masculine in his mental body, which means he must have a masculine physical body ray, a feminine astral body ray, a masculine mental body ray, and a masculine personality and Soul Ray. This is the most attractive male that you can imagine.[2]

The magnetism between a man's and a woman's personality can be strong when they have opposing rays intelligently adjusted.

People are attracted or repulsed by various combinations of rays or polarities. We attract each other or repulse each other physically, emotionally, mentally, even spiritually. There are families who attract physically but repulse emotionally. They may attract or repulse mentally or attract and repulse spiritually. The normalization of friendship, family, and thus cooperation is based upon our polarity on all levels.

If we observe from a long range perspective we see that people, in each of their lives and in the cycles of their incarnations, are attracting and repulsing continuously until slowly they are stabilizing themselves in their original polarization. As the development of human consciousness progresses, we will have more real females and more real males. At the present, we are going through fruitless experimentation, suffering, and pain until we start living on the line of our orientation or origin.

---

2.   For detailed information on the Seven Rays, see the Video, *The Seven Rays Interpreted.*

Rays One, Three, Five, and Seven are masculine. Rays Two, Four, and Six are feminine. But we have two Rays which are both and can play either a masculine or feminine role according to the build-up of bodies. These are the Fourth Ray and the Seventh Ray. If a man needs a feminine Ray, he can use his Seventh Ray. If a woman needs a masculine Ray, she can use the Fourth Ray.

You can increase attraction in the following ways:

1. Develop the virtues of your origin.

2. Meditate on the virtues to develop your Rays.[3]

3. Eliminate that which is not in harmony with your origin.

In most cases elimination is a process of discarding all those imported habits or pretensions and imitations which created an artificial personality around you. You may need real help to discard all such artificiality and to discover your real original frequency.

Some people are born bisexual, lesbian, or homosexual because there is a confusion in their permanent atoms about their real origin. It is by the power of their confusion that they created a complicated system in their genes and vehicles.

If people eventually become androgynous, then does it mean that they no longer belong to either origin?

Origins are always there, but on a given high level of spiritual development these origins are so harmonized with each other that they create a homogeneity in the physical body and in other bodies. But the human soul stays either male or female. After one reaches the level of a Divine hermaphrodite, he or she has another level to go. That level is to achieve *sexlessness* for the physical body, *sexlessness* in the astral and mental bodies, and then to live beyond the mental body with his or her original polarity. This is only in the Cosmic Physical Plane. Beyond this Plane, the question of origin is further complicated.

The human soul has the power to create masculine or feminine bodies according to the plane of his evolution. At the beginning of his evolution his bodies mostly correspond to his origin. During the midway part of evolution many complications occur, and a long time of adjustment and readjustment takes place. Toward the end of his human evolution, up to the Fifth Initiation, his original polarity dominates.

In daily life, to have an idea about male and female polarity, it is suggested that we watch the children at play. They express the most subtle nature of their origins. After they are seven years old and over, the outer and subconscious

---

3. See the following for meditation on the Rays: Alice A. Bailey, *Esoteric Psychology*, Vol. I, pp. 200-212, and *The Psyche and Psychism*, Ch. 66.

influences begin to change their character. Parents must do their best to cultivate the true origins in their children.

A child who acts, feels, and thinks on the line of his or her origin develops faster and experiences health and happiness. Ones with a mixed nature have the most conflict in their bodies and in their relationships with others. This is a point that the future psychology must cultivate and teach.

Most adolescent problems originate from such conflicts in their nature. Often they are torn apart between their origin and their built-up nature. This means they have two different keys in their nature to solve their problems without knowing which key to use for which door.

It is observed that the great spiral accumulations of thoughts have their polarity. There are male thoughtforms and there are female thoughtforms. For example, the Great Bear is the manifestation of a male thoughtform, and the Pleiades is the manifestation of a female thoughtform.

Each thoughtform electromagnetically evokes certain energies from the others which blend, fuse, and conceive the blueprint of manifestation.

The male forces, or the masculine forms, are radioactive and electrical. The female forms are attractive and magnetic.

The electromagnetic interplay goes on between all spirals in different magnitudes. As the energies of the lower rings blend and fuse, the energies of the higher rings manifest a cyclic and rhythmic interchange of sparks which creates energy for the use of the lower rings engaged in creative manifestation.

A similar phenomenon is observed on earth in male and female relationships. One can be masculine in physical body but feminine in emotional body or masculine or feminine in his mental body. Each human being is both masculine and feminine in all his bodies. Masculinity or femininity is not a principle but is a result of forces playing upon the bodies. A body can change its polarity under any force. If the plane of masculinity is evoked, a man is masculine; if femininity is evoked, he is feminine.

People think that by having male organs one is masculine, and with female organs one is feminine. This is not correct; the organ is not the decisive factor. The force that plays upon the male or female is the important factor. One can act masculine while having a female organ and feminine while having a masculine organ.

When we say "man," we do not refer to his masculinity but to his polarization. When his polarization is in the *body, mind, and atma,* he acts masculine, provided that a stronger man with a stronger body, mind, and willpower does not change the first man's polarization to the feminine.

Woman has her own polarization which is *emotional, intuitive, and monadic* — or all inclusive — provided that she is not over-flooded by the presence of a more strongly feminine woman who changes the polarization of the former one and acts as the female.

This is how homosexuals and lesbians come into being.

It must be remembered that in each change of polarization bio-chemical changes take place within the bodies. Those who are Initiates of the Third Degree are not subject to such changes.

The form of any human relationship is often a faint or distorted reflection of the relationships taking place in Higher Realms between a gigantic spatial thoughtform and its manifested forms. These thought-accumulations also are subject cyclically to the pressures of higher energies which introduce temporary cyclic changes in the polarization of the rings. Thus the macrocosm is reflected in the microcosm.

The Thinking Process

The thinking process has its special phenomena. Thinking on lower levels of the mental plane has square patterns and is horizontal. Thinking on higher levels of the mental plane is spiral and vertical.

Each thought rises as a spiral, in color and note, and penetrates into the astral and mental worlds. In these two spheres the thought passes through a process of attunement, as far as possible, and comes back to the mental sphere of man, there to bounce up again with corrections caused by the attunement. This process repeats itself until the thinker feels that there is perfect resonance between his thought and higher spheres.

This is just like trying to tune your musical instrument on an already tuned instrument or on the musical scale.

If such a process continues for a long time, the thinker feels immediately if his thoughts are in harmony with higher spheres or if they need changes.

Through such an interaction and harmonization, eventually the thought of the thinker expresses the most precious visions, ideas, and harmonies of the Higher Worlds and thus bridges the two worlds with his thoughts.

The spirals penetrate the higher spheres according to their amplitude and magnetically attract thoughts of the same frequency, bringing down to the mental body new ideas and new visions.

Thus, great artists and thinkers are both in the mental body and in higher spheres. The longer they stay in contact with higher spheres, the richer will be their creativity, provided that their mind is equipped with all the means of "translation."

As the attunement continues, the creative soul, or the thinker, penetrates deeper and deeper into the treasury of the higher spheres, and a time comes in which the mental body fuses with the higher sphere and the thinker or the artist thinks or creates while focused in both worlds simultaneously. The higher spheres now can manifest on earth through an organized and refined mechanism of a highly advanced soul.

In creative moments, especially, the artist is in higher spheres and the spiral of thought brings down beauty, wave after wave.

Inspiration, like the wind upon the ocean, pushes the waves of the ideas to the shore of the human mind. Each idea is a magnet which collects the mental substance and becomes substantial, becomes thought.

A true artist intuitively sees the pattern developing around the idea and tries to translate it in terms of art and beauty. Thus the idea falls into the process of incarnation through the artist.

As the artist develops greater sensitivity to the idea and greater skill in translating the idea into form, he gradually makes his artwork the image of the idea.

Ideas are electrical in nature. They have powerful charges able to move nations and forces.

In poetry or writing your mind is conditioned by the ideas presented by the artist.

In music you have an opportunity to project your own interpretation and to manifest the interpretation within you.

Most of our movies, operas, ballets, dramas, etc. belong to the past. Most of our artists are busy with the past or with the present life. This is not the work of a genius. A genius is the mother of the future. He creates a new future for humanity.

For hundreds of years our operas and ballets have been busy with falling in love, conflicts between two or three lovers, the death of a loved one, a tragedy. When will we be able to depart from such cheap demonstrations and use our talents to pave a new way toward greater Beauty, Goodness, and Truth, toward a new dimension, new visions, new ideas, and try to unveil the mystery of the future? The artist must be the mother of the future, the mother of life. We need a new life based on universal and Cosmic ideas, inspired by the vision of man's perfection and revealing to us better ways to solve our complicated personal and international problems.

Creativity is a labor to synthesize.

The creative person intuitively sees that Nature has a subjective Archetype for every objective manifestation. The objective manifestation is an inadequate expression of the subjective Archetype as, for example, the drawing of a child is an inadequate expression of an object or an idea.

Archetypes are conceptions or ideas in the Logoic Mind. An Archetype is the future of an objective manifestation which, as a magnet, exercises certain influences on the objective manifestation and gradually improves it to such a degree that the objective manifestation eventually merges into the Archetype and becomes one with it.

This process requires the labor of creative people. A great artist intuitively is in contact with the Archetype and is physically in contact with its objective manifestation. His labor is to help the Archetypal source transform the objective manifestation. This labor is called creativity.

Creative Thought

Creative thought has another, deeper meaning. Creative thought creates a life in which coming generations find the needed leaders to climb greater heights. They find the purest water to drink and the cleanest air to breathe.

If all the so-called creativity of man will leave the coming generation nothing else but a dumping place of rubbish, what kind of value has our creativity?

Even those who created such a polluted, politically disturbed, and economically depressed world will hate to come back to a world where clean air will be sold in bottles, where people will live in fear, where people will worry about how to pay their rent for the next month.

Creative thought creates a world in which our children will be happier than ourselves, where our children will be safer and more prosperous than ourselves.

Creative thought is a life-giving thought, a thought that gradually eliminates obstacles on our path to Infinity.

Creative thought prepares all those conditions in which man can actualize his highest aspirations.

At the present, humanity is caught in its own trap. Creative thought is a thought that leads to freedom, not captivity.

Creative thought reveals the hidden beauty in human nature and creates those conditions in which this beauty can multiply and expand.

Creative thought strives to annihilate pains and suffering from the world. It strives to bring joy and bliss to the world, synthesis and unity in the world.

The Great Sage, talking about thought, says that "man has three basic currents of thought. A superficial one — from the flesh, connected with muscular reflections, obvious in the external life. The second already concerns the heart, and contributes to improvement and progress in the subtle feelings. And finally, in the depths of the consciousness is being conceived the achievement of self-renunciation — here the Fiery World will be near."[4]

Creative thought is only possible when in the depth of consciousness one achieves self-renunciation and thinks for the well-being of present and future generations. After one renounces his self, his thoughts become entirely creative. Thoughts whirling around the axis of self — personal, racial, or national self — will create those conditions which will work against the interests of those who created the conditions.

Creative thought is the manifestation of those inspirations which come from the sphere of beauty and wisdom.

Creative thought has power over all limitations man created for himself and others.

Creative thought can undo things man did to himself.

---

4.   Agni Yoga Society, *Fiery World,* Vol. III, para. 603.

Creative thought regenerates, purifies, and rebuilds all that man polluted and destroyed.

Creative thought is a great co-worker of Nature.

Creative thought spreads joy. Joy is the fragrance behind all truly creative expressions.

Thought in Space

The thoughts of other people or our own thoughts, being electrical in nature, tune in with similar thoughts in the spheres of our memory and relate our brain to thoughts and events recorded there for a long time. Thus a real thought enriches our life.

If the intensity of our thought is greater, it can penetrate even into the sphere of the planetary memory and evoke recordings in harmony with our thought. Geniuses have such access to the storehouses of memory of the planet.

Thought is an electrical wave. We have short waves, medium waves, and long waves. Short-wave thoughts penetrate deeper and reach greater distances because they have a high frequency. Short-wave thoughts are condensed, clearly defined, highly charged, arranged in successive waves, with increasing intensity and integrity. Such thoughts release great amounts of memories from space, and the artist or the writer or the leader can at any time contact the memory sphere of his Soul, of the planet, and of the solar system and draw great treasures of experiences registered millions of years ago in the memory of space.

Meditation, or the art of scientific thinking, is so important to cultivate because only a disciplined mind can create electrical thoughts and put himself in contact with these treasures of mental space.

A few minutes of reading a book by a Great One and pondering upon a few thoughts can have a chain reaction. You feel new thoughts coming into existence in your mind. Doors of new memories open one after another in space, and waves of thoughts begin hitting the shores of your brain.

Thoughts are communication lines or, better to say, wireless communications which put your mind and brain in contact with the precious treasure houses of memories.

There is nothing new under the Sun. The whole game is a game of finding, arranging, using, synthesizing, and making breakthroughs into higher spheres of achievement.

All that exists in visible and invisible domains is the thought of a great, great Thinker. We are the cells in His body, living in the ocean of His thought. Our progress depends on grasping, realizing, and assimilating His thoughts.

The first requisite of a human being is to learn how to think. Thought is the key to the doors of so-called mysteries and spheres of treasures.

Thought, as it advances, saves time, energy, matter, and prevents suffering and pain. Thought is the conqueror.

As time goes by, these spheres of memories in man and in the Universe wrap themselves with fiery electrical shields and slowly become inaccessible for the average consciousness. When they become more and more inaccessible, people either lose their direction or try very hard to feel a direction and live a life in harmony with great Realities.

Those who penetrate the shields or veils of the spheres of memories bring a great wealth to the world and enrich our culture and civilization, making it possible for advancing souls to create a new synthesis and penetrate deeper into the mental space of the Universe.

In the past, people used their thoughts to meet

1. their physical needs

2. their emotional needs

3. the interest of their soul

Later, those who were traveling on the path of conscious evolution used their thoughts to meet the needs of others, the aspirations of others, and the interests of others. This was a great advancement in comparison to the state of thoughts in the former age.

At the present, the destination of thought is not only individual and global but also spatial. This means that people think about far off worlds. Also, this means that people are ready to understand that every thought created immediately becomes the property of space.

Thinking about far off worlds expands our consciousness, expands our space, and makes us the citizens of space. When we expand our space, we become less selfish and more selfless, less separative and more holistic.

Knowing that every thought created immediately becomes the property of space evokes from our depths a very pure sense of responsibility.

People sometimes think that thoughts created in our mind stay in the mental plane like clouds, whereas the truth is that every thought created immediately flows into our aura and conditions our physical, emotional, and mental mechanisms. It expresses itself as manners, behaviors, words, actions, thoughtforms, plans, and emotional responses or reactions.

Our words are thoughts; our actions or deeds are thoughts; our life is thought.

Either it is a mental thought, an emotional thought, a word thought, or deed thought. It is thought, and being thought it belongs to space. This means we share it with all those, visible or invisible, that are found in space or upon any globe.

This fact evokes the necessity of confrontation with ourselves and with all that share our thoughts.

There is no manifestation without thought. Thought is the agent of manifestation as we see it everywhere around us.

The same must be true of all that exists. There should be a *Thinker* in Space to bring into manifestation *all that exists*. The thought of this Cosmic Creative

Center is the source of all laws and principles by which all exist, live, move, and play their roles in the great drama of the Purpose of that Creative Center.

Man, by observing the actions of his thought, can learn how the Cosmic thought functions. It is only after one understands the power of his thoughts and the consequences of his thoughts that he begins to develop the spirit of cooperation between his thoughts and Cosmic thought.

The fact that our thoughts belong to space does not mean that we can expand into space. The expansion into space is possible only if our thoughts are in harmony with the Cosmic thought. Only thoughts in harmony with the Cosmic thought survive in space. All thoughts inharmonious with the Cosmic thought, after performing their work of disturbances and destruction, return and annihilate the center which created them.

The ocean of space is open to any thoughtwave, but all thoughts that are not in harmony with the Cosmic thought are pushed away to the shores of illusion and destroyed there.

Survival and conscious existence in the whole Cosmic Existence is only possible through conscious fusion with the Cosmic thought through our own thoughts in harmony with the Cosmic thought.

51

Thought, Consciousness, and Knowledge

There are different levels of consciousness. There is physical, emotional, mental, and also higher plane consciousness. But the foundation of human consciousness is the same human soul.

The light of the human soul with the intelligence beam of the Solar Angel project themselves and produce a lighted area on the brain near the pineal gland. This makes the soul conscious on the physical plane.

As evolution proceeds, a similar lighted area is created on the astral plane through which the soul becomes gradually conscious on the astral plane. Ages later the beam of light creates another lighted area on the mental sphere through which the human soul becomes conscious on the mental plane, the astral plane, and the physical plane.

The astral and mental planes are each divided into seven levels. The lighted area of consciousness must extend itself to the third level of the astral plane before man is able to function on the astral plane consciously when he is out of his body during sleep or meditation.

The same thing is true for the mental world. No one can function consciously in the mental world at the time of sleep or during meditation if the lighted area of his consciousness is not in the higher mental levels, in the third, second, or first levels.

When the lighted areas of the mental and astral planes are coordinated with the brain consciousness, we say that man has continuity of consciousness. He no longer dreams because he becomes aware of all that transpires on those planes. One dreams only if he is not conscious on those planes, and the events going on upon those planes reflect themselves on the etheric and physical brain and are registered as dreams.

The following diagram shows the relationship between these three areas of light.

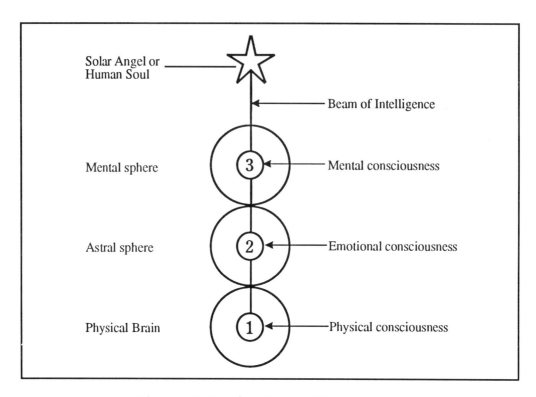

Diagram 51-1   Three Levels of Consciousness

Eventually the lighted areas (numbers 1, 2, and 3) become one area of light.

One becomes conscious in the astral and mental worlds in *his waking consciousness* when he makes a breakthrough into the Intuitional Plane, establishes an area of consciousness there, and builds a steady communication with the lighted areas of the astral and mental planes and the etheric-physical brain.

After mental consciousness, one strives to establish a lighted area on the Intuitional Plane. This lighted area, for esoteric reasons, is called intuitional *awareness*, not consciousness.

Thus the human consciousness is the light of the soul, is the eye of the soul, is the contact point of the soul with the physical, emotional, mental, and Higher Worlds.

There is a great difference between consciousness and knowledge. Consciousness is the eye that sees; knowledge is the translation of the things the eye sees or registers through the senses. This translation is conditioned by the stage of expansion and the purity of consciousness. Knowledge is accumulated and recorded in mental matter.

If the consciousness is only on the physical plane, all knowledge is used for physical ends. If the consciousness is on the astral and physical planes, knowledge is used for pleasures and emotional ends. If the consciousness is on the mental, astral, and physical planes, knowledge is used for separative and selfish purposes.

When the soul begins to be aware of intuitional contact and develops intuitional awareness, a major change occurs in man. Slowly the separatism vanishes and inclusiveness sets in. Man begins to think, act, and use his knowledge for unity and synthesis, for joy and freedom. From this moment on he becomes aware of the supermundane world and tries to cooperate with that world.

Thought is not knowledge or consciousness. It is a formulation of mental matter by the human soul or a formulation of solar or Cosmic mental substance by Great Ones.

Knowledge is the translation by the human soul of the impressions and contacts he has through physical, emotional, mental, and still higher senses. Knowledge is relative and ever-changing due to the fluctuations of human consciousness, due to its expansion or contraction, and due to the sphere in which it functions.

If the consciousness is higher and more integrated with all lighted areas, knowledge is more permanent.

The use of knowledge is the greatest problem. Those who can think and who have consciousness on higher planes build their own storehouse of knowledge. They put it into practical and applicable forms and sell it to those whose consciousness and thinking are low-level and who can use and measure the knowledge in destructive or constructive ways according to their nature.

It also happens that thinkers work on scientific lines for money and position and sell their knowledge to those who, for various reasons, use it for their separative, selfish ends, and especially for their greed and superiority.

Once knowledge has fallen into the hands of low-level consciousnesses, the world passes through crises and eventually heads toward destruction. This was the case in Lemurian and Atlantean times, and this is the case now as knowledge has prostituted itself and became a possible factor for mass destruction.

The misuse of knowledge is the sign that man is not conscious of the One Self but is living in his separative interests. To perpetuate his separative existence, he tries to *know* by translating impressions received from the Universe.

Gradual identification with the One Self will eventually open all gates of knowledge because the Self *is* and *knows*.

Expansion of consciousness is the process of identification with the One Self.

Things can be known not because of learning and translating any phenomenon but by becoming the field of knowledge or the object of knowledge.

When we transcend mental consciousness, we will know an object by identifying ourselves with the Self of the object.

To end the prostitution of knowledge and to control the misuse of knowledge, one must cultivate

— The science of the One Self

— The science of virtues

— The science of service

— The science of compassion

— The science of becoming Oneself

It is through these five sciences that our knowledge on all levels can be used to reach our spiritual destiny and discover the Purpose of our existence.

For many, many centuries the human soul slept within the organism and only the physical, emotional, and mental elementals[1] ran the show. Man was not conscious of the life around him, and if he had a dim consciousness, it was only as if he were in a dream.

For many thousands of years man was in such a state of sleep. The mechanism was overshadowed by the Monad and run by the elementals. The awakening of the human soul took place by the efforts of celestial hosts who came in cycles and put sparks of celestial fire in the mental body to quicken the kindling of the mental atoms. Man slowly became aware of his environment and tried to think.

It was at this moment that in the mental body a sphere of light began to form. It was the eye of the human soul that began to awaken and see for a few seconds or hours, then sleep or fade away.

This eye, the sphere of contact with the phenomena of life, is called consciousness. A man's consciousness is the degree of his *awakeness*. A man progresses when his consciousness expands. His consciousness expands to the degree that he awakens.

Most people are partially awake on the physical plane. A few people are awake in the astral plane. Very few people are awake in the mental plane. Only one or two per million are really awake in the Intuitional Plane. Man is not considered fully awake if he is not fully conscious in the Intuitional Plane.

It is wrong to say that man has consciousness or does not have consciousness. The right thing is to say that man is fully conscious or he is in some degree unconscious. As one conquers matter, he awakens; as he is conquered by matter, he goes to sleep.

The relationship between thought and consciousness must also be discussed. Thought has a very strong effect on the mirror of consciousness. If the thought is of a higher order, if it is pure and charged with higher realities, it expands the consciousness and vitalizes it. On the other hand, if the thought is of low quality, it obscures the consciousness and brings distortion and conflict to the field of light of the consciousness.

---

1. See *The Psyche and Psychism*, Ch. 17.

It is true that when the consciousness is pure and clear it evokes pure thoughts. It also has the capacity, to a certain degree, to reject unclean thoughts.

It is important to know that thought is not consciousness, and consciousness is not a process of thinking. But they are related as closely as the nerves, muscles, and organs are related to each other.

The following diagram may illustrate this concept:

When awakened or advanced in his evolution, it is the human soul who thinks and builds thoughtforms out of the substance of the mental sphere to impress the physical and emotional bodies and to recondition the mental body. Thinking for the human soul is an effort to master the human mechanisms and life and gradually to establish an ideal relationship with life in general.

The thoughts of the human soul are conditioned by the state of evolution of the tiny lives which in their totality form the personality, or the physical, etheric, astral, and mental mechanisms.

The reactions and responses of these vehicles to the forces of life, to the stimuli and impressions received from the environment, are powerful factors influencing the thinking of the human soul.

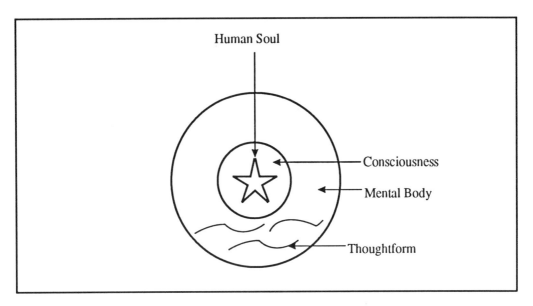

Diagram 51-2   Light of the Human Soul

As the human soul involves himself in the life of his lower vehicles, he begins gradually to identify with them to such a degree that he eventually loses the awareness of his True Self and identifies himself not only with the vehicles but also with the states of the vehicles. Esoterically this is called "going to sleep within matter." Matter of the three worlds dominates the soul and totally conditions his thinking.

Thus the human soul even loses control of his thinking and, affected by the forces of the lower nature, builds an automatic response mechanism. This is what thinking is for average people.

Thoughts created by the human soul have the power to put into motion the mental, emotional, and physical mechanisms. If the thoughts are influenced by the lower personality, the thoughts are built to serve the interests of the personality. If they are built partially by both of them, there is agreement or conflict between the human soul and the personality. If the thoughts are created by the human soul, then there is mastery over the personality vehicles.

In addition to the thoughts found in the mental body, there is the influence or the existence of many thoughtforms or thought currents emanating from other human minds. Such thoughtforms are found everywhere, in objective and subjective planes.

As the air shares its contents with a larger area of air, the mental sphere shares its contents with a larger mental area because thought is faster than light, and it spreads all over the mental sphere of the globe and thus becomes common property.

It is possible to tune in to the thoughts of any human being if one finds his frequency. This tuning in is what we call telepathy.

Thus the human soul has his pure thoughts, mixed thoughts, base thoughts, and outside thoughts which penetrate into his mental sphere. Through the Law of Association, his task is to learn how to discriminate between these thoughts and increase his capacity to generate purer thoughts and gain liberty from the influences of the thoughts floating in space or in his mental sphere.

The lighted area in the mental body is like a mirror on which is reflected the image of all thoughts created by the human soul and the thoughts existing in space. The reflective power of the mirror fluctuates every minute. Sometimes the lower thoughts obscure it, darken it. Sometimes they vanish like clouds, leaving the mirror as clear as a pure sky.

When the consciousness is obscured, the man loses his right direction or discrimination. When the human soul loses his direction or discrimination, his consciousness tunes to low-level thoughts, mechanical thoughts, separative and selfish thoughts, and leads his personality against his own spiritual interest, thus complicating his life. This is a state of confusion for the human soul, a state of delusion in which he loses his sense of true values, the sense of direction, and he serves interests which lead him into deeper sleep and deeper darkness.

Once the human soul is trapped in the interests of the thoughtforms created in the state of delusion, he loses his right direction and his spiritual goals.

One of the goals of the human soul is to expand his consciousness. Expansion of consciousness cannot take place unless higher and purer thoughts are assimilated by it. Let us remember that thoughts are condensed lights of different degrees.

Higher and purer thoughts can precipitate from space and bring greater light to the consciousness and greater expansion.

Unless the consciousness assimilates the higher thoughts, the thoughts remain as an abstraction floating in the mental body and even create a certain confusion in the consciousness. When assimilated, they expand the consciousness.

One cannot create a thought higher than his consciousness.

Meditation helps the consciousness expand. Meditation is a process of assimilation of new thoughts, pure ideas, and new impressions from Higher Realms.

Our consciousness often fluctuates, and sometimes it loses its light by being totally fused with various thoughtforms or personality interests. Past events, or the impressions of past events, can sometimes key in with the consciousness and keep it extremely busy, while the person is engaged in something important. Such moments are called unconscious moments. Many posthypnotic suggestions are then planted in the mental body which eventually block and control the consciousness.[2]

It also happens that when the consciousness is deeply occupied with the personality interests it mixes up an important command, an important formula or direction coming from higher sources. Such a precipitation from Higher Realms and such a failure, because of preoccupation, lead the consciousness to total or partial obscurity.

It is also possible to petrify the consciousness of another person to such a degree that it becomes a blind instrument in your hands to use for your own advantage. People sometimes achieve such a goal by using fear techniques, punishment, hypnotism, and certain brainwashing processes.

We are told that one creates a very dire karma by trying to kill the consciousness of others and use them for his own advantage.

On the other hand, the greatest blessings rest upon those people who try to expand and purify the consciousness of others through inspiration and through the importation of higher and purer thoughts.

The greatest crime against a human being is to control his consciousness and make it incapable of further expansion.

People sometimes think that knowledge and consciousness are synonymous terms. There is a great difference between these two terms.

Knowledge is data collected on the mental plane. Accumulated knowledge does not necessarily expand the consciousness. It is the consciousness that changes the beingness and direction of the human soul.

Consciousness is the eye of the human soul. Accumulated knowledge is a tool in the hands of the human soul. If the eye is blind, this tool can be used for destructive, selfish, or separative purposes. If the eye is bright, information can be used for expansion of consciousness, to increase joy, health, prosperity, and unity in the world.

---

2. See also *The Subconscious Mind and the Chalice.*

People go to universities and read many books to increase their knowledge, but their consciousness remains the same. Their beingness also remains the same, and their evolution does not proceed. They become trapped in the vanity of their knowledge and position. This is the greatest tragedy of our time.

Ancient Teachers never imparted any knowledge before an expansion took place in the consciousness of their pupils. Expansion of consciousness was called *Initiation*. In Initiation man gains a greater awareness of the spiritual principles and laws of the Universe and a greater mastery over the forces which do not serve the direction of the human soul.

Thoughts can be formulated and built in different forms and colors, and sometimes they create difficulties in communication. Each level of consciousness communicates in a different way. People who have the same consciousness do not have trouble understanding each other, even if their thoughts do not have the same form. Several people can have similar intentions or directions but with different thoughts. If the consciousness is pure, thoughts in different forms do not create any confusions.

The consciousness is the eye of the human soul, his vision. The soul always sees as another soul sees. The formulation of thoughts is carried on under the influence of the contents of the mind; hence the difference in thoughtforms.

Sometimes in conversation we know what the other person is trying to say and he knows what we want to say, but our formulation plays the game and tries to mislead us. Most people speak with each other not with their consciousness but through their thoughts and words. This is how they mislead each other. Thoughts can be related to self-interest, but the consciousness does not serve any separative interest. It stands for reality, beauty, goodness, joy, and for the One Universal Self.

Thoughts created in the light of the consciousness are sometimes called thoughts of the heart. Consciousness has a center, and it is the Self which abides in the heart. The Self never works against the interest of any Self because the Self is One.

Expansion of consciousness is the expansion of the realization of the One Self, not as a theory but as an experience. This is the foundation of consciousness.

People think that consciousness is the sum total of what one knows, whereas the truth is that consciousness and knowledge are two different things. One is related to the mental plane and the personality, and the other is related to the Self.

It is strange to say that man is conscious not because of his knowledge but because of the level of his beingness. Man lost his awareness and consciousness when he lost his beingness, or the level of evolution of his consciousness.

Expansion of consciousness is not achieved through learning and through various exercises or disciplines. All these may help to organize the mind and purify it to a certain degree. Expansion of consciousness takes place when one tries to see the facts, the foundation and the origin of events and manifestations — in a word, when he searches for the truth and strives to live in truth and be the truth.

Many people know the truth, but their consciousness does not expand until they live according to the truth.

Knowingness is different from beingness. When the great Lord said, "I am the truth," He was not referring to the importance of the truth; He was revealing that there was a great difference between knowing the truth and being the truth.

Being the truth, or living in truth, is half of the story. The other half is a sacrificial life. The true expansion of consciousness refers to these two factors: truth and sacrifice.

To sacrifice means

1. To put down all that you have to help humanity and to serve the Plan of love and light

2. To use all the resources of your *being* to serve

3. To expect no reward or compensation

4. To go forward even when the dawn is many years away

5. To go forward even if all your co-workers leave you

A sacrificial man is a living flame, a flaming torch.

Truth and sacrifice are two pillars through which the initiate passes into greater fields of consciousness. Consciousness expands slowly, but as it expands it begins to reveal the glory of creation and the glory waiting for man.

It is possible to expand our consciousness every time we try to think in terms of truth and sacrifice. It is possible to expand our consciousness every time we speak the truth under sacrificial conditions. It is possible to expand our consciousness every time we plan sacrificial acts and live in sacrificial deeds in the light of truth. It is also possible to expand our consciousness when we observe the truth and acknowledge the sacrificial thoughts, words, and deeds of other people.

One must not be blinded by his own light and his own sacrificial deeds. Greater expansion of consciousness is experienced when, in addition to one's own light and sacrifice, one is a witness for the light and for the sacrificial lives of others.

Gratitude crowns the expanding consciousness with power — gratitude not only to one's own True Self but also to the radiant *Self* in others when they adorn the path of life with beauty.

Thus the pyramid of Spirit is completed. In the four corners you have the four cornerstones: truth, sacrifice, gratitude, and beauty; and the consciousness will shine as a beacon in Cosmos at the crown of the pyramid.

One may ask why will and love are not mentioned in the pyramid of consciousness. Sacrifice is love radiating under the fiery beam of will. The beacon of consciousness expands and fuses with the fires of space. In each fusion greater contacts are made and greater glory is experienced in Cosmos.

Just as we develop our physical body to move on earth and through water, we also need to build and develop our subtle bodies to take off from the physical plane. If the subtle bodies are not sufficiently developed, then we cannot separate ourselves from our bodies, and even during sleep we wander around our bodies or in our room.

As the birds develop wings, so man develops subtle bodies and gradually flies in space. First he can consciously fly to different spots on earth. Later when he develops his subtle bodies further, he takes off from earth and visits various centers of learning in space.

When the bodies are really developed, man can visit various planets and even go out of the solar system. Of course, in all these flights he needs his guard until he masters all difficulties in space.

The subtle body is substantial and electrical in nature. Magnetic storms can create obstacles on its path. Other obstacles are chemical and psychic pollution which affect the subtle body.

In space are also found the same dangers as for our airplanes. It is possible to lose the direction, the balance, the pressure; it is even possible to fall to earth. The navigator is the Self, who must use clear concentration on the path of flight.

The subtle body flies mostly with magnetism. Magnetism is its fuel. The person must create magnetism toward the subject he has in mind to reach. When reciprocal magnetic lines are built, the flight is secured. The speed of flight depends on the intensity of magnetism between these two points.

We lose our magnetism through irritation, negative emotions, and unworthy thoughts. The subtle bodies develop as man expresses Beauty, Goodness, Righteousness, Joy, and Freedom and tries to make other people's lives more beautiful.

All plants are rooted in the earth. Similarly, we can say that all success in space is achieved through a life lived in truth, sacrifice, gratitude, and beauty.

52

Consciousness and Its Effects

There are various kinds of consciousnesses and each of them has a tremendous effect on our physical, etheric, astral, and mental bodies. There are

1. young and evolving or expanding consciousnesses

2. stable consciousnesses

3. striving and enlightened consciousnesses

4. chaotic consciousnesses

5. decaying or disintegrating consciousnesses

Between these five there are many gradations.

1. A young and evolving consciousness is one which has vitality, interests, and the urge to know more, to understand more. There is a great thirst in it to go beyond itself. This brings great vitality to the body if the consciousness deals with subjects which are vital and in harmony with the great Laws of Nature.

The subject which the consciousness deals with, in its turn, affects the consciousness. There are subjects which retard its growth. There are subjects which, like weeds, grow in the consciousness and fill its space. There are subjects which create various diseases in the consciousness.

The healing arts never thought yet about various diseases existent within the consciousness. These are basic causes of many illnesses appearing in the vehicles of man, especially in the physical body.[1]

A student of Wisdom must know how to choose the subject with which his consciousness will be occupied.

---

1. See also *New Dimensions in Healing*.

An expanding consciousness is one which has chosen the path that leads to those subjects which have vitality, beauty, and positiveness.

2. A stable consciousness is sometimes called a crystallized or frozen consciousness because it has lost its power to expand. It reflects things, but there is no creativity in it; there is no interest. Most of the time this is the cause of depression. When certain chemicals are lacking in the brain, we have depression. But this is caused by our negative thoughts and emotions.

A stable consciousness refuses change and reacts negatively to any new change. Sometimes it has a mood of total indifference or an attitude which negates, mocks, or laughs at any progress and discourages any adventure or effort to improve or change.

In trying to maintain the stability of consciousness, often the lower bodies demonstrate violent, defensive activity.

A stable consciousness, like a stagnant lake, develops many germs which find their way down to the emotional and physical bodies. When stability of consciousness lasts longer than seven years, a heavy stagnation takes place and causes decomposition in the lower bodies.

3. A striving or enlightened consciousness shines day and night and builds bridges with the great unity of consciousness on earth and in space. One of the secrets of Beauty, Goodness, Righteousness, Joy, Freedom, and health is an increasing expansion of consciousness. As the consciousness expands and establishes wider communication with the Universe, greater sources of energies are contacted and greater abilities are developed to use these energies creatively.

Energies coming from higher sources reveal the harmony and the immense depth and glory of the sources. They bring vitalizing influences into the bodies and free the human mind from its many chains.

A striving consciousness expands its field of life in space and, like a great wheel of light, gears itself with many other wheels to move forward a mechanism of a Cosmic vision. Thus the man shares such efforts of his consciousness and feels the freedom of the expanding contacts of his consciousness.

Esoterically understood, freedom is a state of mind in which there are no elements which hinder creativity, progress, or the advancement of the human soul or which cause waste of energy, time, and space.

It is through the expanding and increasing light of consciousness that the human soul will be able to see its Core and identify with it. An expanding consciousness is the foundation of health on all levels. In the future, great emphasis will be laid by the healing profession on the expansion of consciousness. No permanent cure is possible until the causes of the troubles are removed from the consciousness. Transformation of the consciousness may immediately cure the body. Miraculous healings are the result of a sudden change or transformation of consciousness.

A consciousness occupied for a long time with separative interests, exploitation, destruction, and crimes will accumulate those elements which will be unending causes of disease for many coming lives.

Before the illness of a man is eliminated from his bodies, he must go through a fundamental change in his consciousness.

An expanding consciousness will eventually lead man into immortality. It is through the expanding sphere of consciousness that man will develop the awareness of higher planes and will eventually withdraw himself from the mental plane and live in intuitional awareness. It will be almost impossible for man to reach intuitive awareness without eliminating all weeds from his consciousness. The foundation of purification is the elimination of weeds from the consciousness. Ordinary laws offer poor assistance, since they do not change or expand the consciousness.

4. The chaotic consciousness is a disorganized, boiling consciousness which has not yet found any strong vision to orchestrate its various urges and drives and to bring harmony and direction to it.

A chaotic consciousness creates a chaotic life lived in extremes and in ever-changing moods. Heavy pressures are forced upon the body by a chaotic consciousness, and this often leads to suicide, attacks, strokes, insanity, or massive crimes. Most social, national, and international criminals are the results of a chaotic consciousness.

Children must be watched from early years, and corrective measures must be taken to ease such a state of consciousness inherited from past lives. They are usually overactive types, with violent emotions toward both good and crime. Until they are on a decisive path, they are torn between evil and good. Once they decide the path, they become either great criminals or extremely fanatical reformers. If the chaotic state continues, they become the best vehicles in the hands of dark forces to confuse and trap people and lead them to total destruction.

If a few such people come to the forefront of the political field, hope for the survival of humanity will be lost for many centuries.

5. A decaying or decomposing consciousness is a very malignant situation. Such a consciousness dwells mostly on crimes, drugs, license, and vices and becomes a factor for degeneration, dishonesty, and immorality in the world.

Such people spread separatism and inject thoughts and glamors of decay, destruction, and demoralization through the press, movies, and various kinds of literature and communication.

If a decaying consciousness is on professional levels, it legalizes and encourages vice, crime, suicide, drugs, and license and brings total confusion in values and standards.

The effect of such a consciousness is the development and increase of degenerative diseases not only on the physical plane but also in the fields of human emotions, thinking, and social relationships.

One must be warned that such a consciousness is highly malignant and contagious, and one must keep himself away from such persons or from their influence if he does not want to be involved in an ongoing degenerative process.

One of the most important fields of study is the field of consciousness. Consciousness is the sphere in which the causes of future victories and future failures are developed.

One must closely watch his own consciousness and be aware of changes going on in it. Striving toward Beauty, Goodness, Righteousness, Joy, Freedom, and health creates a rare panacea in the field of our consciousness.

The greatest healing agent is the basic energy. We have three manifestations of basic energy. One is light. Then we have goodness, and then beauty.

Light awakens. It awakens the sleeping Spirit in forms, causing various changes in the forms. As the Spirit awakens, it understands the light. Its understanding of light is truth. Reality is the portion of light that the Spirit uses. Reality is measured by the measure of light in which one *is*.

Goodness comes into being when the awakening Spirit in man recognizes the existence of the Spirit in all forms and relates to that Spirit as if it were one with him.

Beauty is the flowering and manifestation of glory latent in the Spirit. This glory begins to awaken by the impact of light.

Beauty brings great power into expression. It organizes the mental plane and expands the field of consciousness. It is through the mental sphere and the field of consciousness that beauty manifests as creativity.

Goodness is related to the heart. The heart charges beauty with magnetic power and makes it possible for creative forces to build in harmony with the symphony of the Cosmic Heart.

Truth has a tendency to objectify itself within the etheric centers and within the physical body. Thus the light of the truth has a very potent effect on the network of the body's electrical system.

Light carries the essence of a chemical substance found in the Sun and brings this essence to our etheric and physical bodies in the form of various chemicals the body needs. If man is in confusion and in a process of distorting the truth, the process of assimilation of chemicals is retarded and even stops.

There are many occasions in which working against the light and against the truth creates complicated health problems due to prevention of the assimilation or reception of various needed chemicals. In the future it will be possible to make a man come into the light of truth, allow the light of the Sun to penetrate his body, and either build new chemicals or eliminate the decayed ones from the body.

It is possible through artificially directed lights and colors to bring about certain cures in the body, but such cures are not permanent until the consciousness functions in the light of Beauty, Goodness, Righteousness, Joy, and Freedom.

The basic energy, which may be called psychic energy, must be received in its purity by our manifold system. This energy must be translated into three fundamental currents. Translation is carried on through the technique of visualization. Through visualization psychic energy must be translated into light, goodness, and beauty. These are three transformers in our system which create health on all levels.

All that is against light; all that is against goodness, compassion, and love; all that is against beauty, harmony, joy, and bliss create malfunctions in the systems of these four transformers. When disorders settle into these systems, the process of imbalance and failure settles into all our physical, emotional, and mental systems, and the results manifest as sicknesses, diseases, and death.

Visualization is a supreme mechanism for translation of the basic energy, but one cannot develop it without submitting himself for a long period of time to the process of purification.

The purification and expansion of consciousness are the answer to all our individual and social problems.

We are told that belittling criticism is very dangerous, and if it continues, calluses appear in certain parts of the mental body which prevent expansion of consciousness. These places are like burned locations in the mental body which are not conductive to the light of the consciousness.

Consciousness expands when there is no petrification in the mental plane. Each act of malice, slander, condemnation, or criticism creates petrification in the mental body which gradually paralyzes the corresponding part of the brain.

It often happens that after one expands his consciousness to a considerable degree, he perceives the shortcomings of other people more clearly. If he has not passed through a spiritual discipline, he begins to criticize and condemn people. It is at this point that he blocks the expansion of his consciousness and uses it for destructive purposes.

Though it is only through the continued expansion of consciousness that this sickness can be healed, expansion becomes almost impossible because of the way the person uses his mind. We notice this everywhere, especially in professors and university graduates. Something prevents them from expanding more and making breakthroughs.

Localized petrification of the mental body lasts a long time and it is cured only through great shocks: physical disasters, emotional upheavals, mental pressures, and inner conflicts. Then people see their limitations and aspire to break them in any way possible.[2]

Scars on the mental body remain a long time and slowly disappear through the application of loving understanding.

---

2. See also *Cosmic Shocks* and *Earthquakes and Disasters, What the Ageless Wisdom Tells Us.*

53

Thought, Polarity, and Imposition

When you come in contact with a lofty thought, through reading or seeing something or through a subjective contact, a polarity comes into being between the thought and your Core. This polarity evokes an energy flow from the Core of your being. This is a flow of electric energy which creates light in the mental plane when the energy comes in contact with mental atmosphere.

In meditation we often choose a *seed thought*, a lofty thought, and try to analyze it, understand it; we try to penetrate into its origin, effects, purpose, and cause. This process is a technique of assimilation through which the lofty thought becomes a part of our mental body and evokes greater charges from our Core as we deepen our meditation.

With every new charge the mental sphere receives new light and the mental atoms circulate faster, more rhythmically, and through more complicated patterns. Faster and more rhythmic circulation of atoms increases the mental magnetism. Gradually the mental sphere turns into an electrified sphere in which all past experiences and knowledge are instantaneously available through the slightest effort of association or keying in.

If the flow of the inner Core is kept continuous, the higher mental atoms build bridges between the mental plane and higher planes, and thus continuity of consciousness becomes a fact. It is through such an electrified atmosphere of mind that one draws new ideas from higher sources and creates lofty thoughts.

A mind charged with lofty thoughts turns into a powerhouse of energies which puts in motion thousands of minds for creative and constructive action. Every lofty thought has a ray of spirit in it.

It is also possible that our minds invite or create ugly thoughts. Ugly thoughts are

1. Thoughts that intentionally distort the truth, the facts

2. Criminal thoughts

3. Thoughts inspired and built by hatred, by separatism

4. Thoughts that are built on denial of values and facts

5. Thoughts based on selfish interest or on plans of destruction

6. Thoughts that promote unrighteousness

7. Thoughts that try to perpetuate vanity and encourage ignorance, slavery, and deception

Ugly thoughts do not have the power to create constructive polarity, but they evoke a flow from the Core which can be called a "repulsive flow." This flow is a natural protection, and it either burns the ugly thought, insulates it, or pushes it back out of the aura.

When the ugly thought is burned, the aura is temporarily polluted by the so-called smoke or ashes of the burning process. This often creates problems, polluting certain centers and obstructing the channels of circulation of energies.

When the ugly thought is insulated, it sometimes floats in the mental plane like an iceberg, creating many problems in the thinking process of man and often causing damage to the synchronization within the mental centers.

When the ugly thought is rejected from the aura, it burns certain parts of the aura, as if a poisonous arrow were pulled out of the body. The burned locations may be attacked by etheric germs, or inflammation may occur. Sometimes scars are formed. Scars on the aura are those locations which do not transmit the electricity of life. We call them sensitive spots. Sometimes through these burned areas of the aura destructive elements penetrate into our body.

If the ugly thought is not imported but is manufactured by the man himself in the factory of his mind, we call him an unfortunate man. An ugly thought may go through the same process as if it were imported, plus it may contaminate the whole mental body. When thrown out of the aura, it goes and associates itself with many other ugly thoughtforms, then comes back, forces itself through the aura, and locates itself in the mental sphere. This is a mental, moral, and health tragedy.

The Teaching warns us against ugly thoughts and encourages us to cultivate our gardens with flowers of thought.

Man's mind is a mystery. It is better to spend money to understand the human mind than to build weapons of destruction.

When man advances enough to find the ways and means of how to think, he develops vanity if he has not gone through a process of purification. In other words, he thinks that he can do everything or that he has the right to impose his will upon others. If a man is caught in such a temptation, he uses his thoughts negatively, for his selfish ends, and he tries to impose his ideas and thoughts on others with fanaticism and zeal. In the Teaching, such behavior is considered a failure because it not only hinders the person's own evolution, but it also paralyzes the creative energies of others.

It is possible to present your ideas as if they were other viewpoints but not absolute laws, orders, or principles. In such a presentation you give a choice to the other fellow and make him accept or reject according to his level of understanding. If he rejects, you may have a new viewpoint from which to look at your idea. If he accepts, you may see the effect your idea is producing on him.

When your will, idea, or thought is imposed upon others by force, by the power of your position, degree, wealth, charm, or authority, you create rejection. People not only reject your idea but also reject you; or they apparently accept your idea but do not have faith in it, and the idea degenerates in their hands or creates antagonism and hatred within their hearts.

People fail in their mission when they step on the path of fanaticism and try to impose their will. This happens not only in homes but also in groups, in offices, in business, in politics . . . everywhere. And this is the prime factor in the failure mechanism.

The best way to make your idea fail is to force it. The best way to prepare future failures in your life is to force your will on others. This forcing process is a denial of human potentialities. It is a sign that you are caught in a dark vanity; it is a sign that your progress is frozen and your heart is cold.

Those who have great ideas present them as they sing a song, as they dance in ecstasy. Every compulsory act is doomed to failure because it is a denial of the basic principles of human rights.

There is also a subtle side to imposition when it is carried on through certain acts, through psychologically induced fear, through indirectly creating cravings, or through various methods of suggestion.

New Era people will have strong convictions, strong commitments to certain ideas and plans; but they will never be fanatics, and they will never use their authority, position, or wealth to impose their ideas on others. On the contrary, they will prove the efficiency or workability of their ideas through their successful careers and organizations, through their intelligent management and executive leadership. They will radiate and create health, sanity, and freedom. People will cooperate with them because of their beauty, practicality, and efficiency and because they see in them the vision of a better world, a better future for humanity.

Imposition creates a violent reaction which eventually tries to destroy the cause of imposition. Your ideas, your plans, and your vision will be accepted if there is the need, if it is the right time to be accepted, if they prove to be creative, and if they do not violate the freedom of others.

Those Great Ones Who know how to transmit thought choose Their agents very carefully. Sometimes the agent thinks that he is privileged to receive such thoughts, and he tries to keep the thoughts in his treasury as antique objects. But the reality is that thoughts are given to create a certain illumination in the environment and in those who are physically or subjectively connected with the agent.

Sometimes even the merit of the agent is not an issue, but the issue is those with whom the agent is connected through his position, through his relationships, through the place where he lives, or through the type of mind he has.

If an agent is vain, he thinks he is the most privileged person, whereas the reality is that at that moment of time he was ready to carry an important message to the people. All higher thoughts are not personal properties, and their destination is not for a person but for people as a whole.

It is a great responsibility to receive a diamond of thought and transmit it to others as it was given, without distortion and self-interest. Many agents of transmission are not even aware of the power of the thought which is given to them. After the thought is transmitted and then amplified in the minds of those who are equipped to receive it, the power of thought appears. Thus a peasant girl passes a simple thought to a scientist, and it leads him to a great discovery. Or a laborer expresses a thought to a politician, and it turns into a political philosophy.

Sometimes transmitting agents are average people who can transmit an idea clearly and without the complications of the "jazz" of the mind. Thus when the thought is passed to a highly equipped mind, it turns into a great structure of beauty.

Many symphonies are the developments of simple melodies. Thus, great thinkers try to find the purest agent at a given time to transmit to the world their thoughts and reach the greatest number of people.

Once a king wanted to send a message to another king who was attending a big festival. The message was very important and dangerous, and it needed immediate attention. The wise king called a little child and whispered to her, "I am putting a little note in your belt. Don't touch it until you reach the king. Then whisper in his ear and say that there is a message in your belt for him."

The act was very successful. Later, chosen officers of the king asked him why he dared to send such a message through a child. He answered, "To protect it from your rationalizations, interests, nosiness, fear, and other interferences."

Thus act many great thinkers. They choose the safest ones to transmit their thoughts to the world, and, in the meantime, they subjectively put the agent in contact with the ones or the one who engages himself in the dissemination and actualization of the idea or thought. Thus, carriers of light sometimes do not know the treasure that is given to them. They do not even have any idea about the consequences of the transmitted thought.

Great thinkers are interested in how to reach people with simple ways, without letting their message be interfered with or distorted.

54

Idea, Thought, and Thoughtform

There are subtle differences between an idea, a thought, and a thoughtform.

Any time you visualize or imagine the effect or the result of your thoughts, you build a thoughtform. For example, you have the thought that *love overcomes hatred*. If you dramatize this thought, you have a thoughtform which can be a book of five hundred pages. The book is a thoughtform originated from one thought.

An idea is not a thought but a dynamic direction projected from the Plan to prepare for the fulfillment of the Purpose. This *direction* is absorbed by the higher mind and appropriated into a thought to meet a particular need and to bring the Purpose into manifestation in a particular field. The thoughtform is the mechanism through which the idea and thought are manifested and actualized.

People often say they have a new idea. This means that they were eventually able to contact a new direction that existed for a long time. It is more common to have new thoughts than new ideas.

We can translate the same *idea* in various ways, in various conditions, to meet different needs. This means we can have various thoughts on the same idea. Our thoughts change, but the ideas stay the same.

Ideas are not limited by time and conditions. Thoughts reflect the ideas in the world of time and the world of various conditions, but ideas stay as they were a thousand years ago.

Thus it is possible to refine our thoughts as our consciousness expands until the greater beauty of the idea can manifest itself through our thoughts and until better thoughtforms are built to bring the ideas into manifestation.

We must remember that ideas come from Higher Realms, from the fiery spheres, and that they are *imposed* upon the mind of humanity. The problem is in reception and actualization of the ideas. Because our minds are in various stages and have various degrees of purity or blockages, ideas are not registered as they are inspired and imposed, but instead they are changed and used for various interests.

Disciples must pass through the training which makes them able to make their mental mirror pure, clean, and receptive to ideas. They must learn how to change ideas into *ideals*, without losing the intensity and integrity of the ideas.

We must remember that every true idea is part of the Plan of the Great Life Who is ensouling our planet. Ideas are His directives to humanity, to be followed so that it progresses according to the Plan.

The reception of ideas on various levels and with various interests creates the differences in outlook and life of individuals and nations. Even the conflict between people and nations is based upon the above fact. As the purity of reception of ideas advances, people will naturally cooperate with each other and work for peace and not for war.

Ideas are originally imposed upon us because of their purity, wholeness, and necessity; but they must not be imposed after they are received by the human mechanism. When a person, group, state, or church imposes its ideas on the masses, it is not the idea that is imposed but the translation of the idea, as all translations are conditioned in this case by self-interest, glamors, illusions, existing circumstances, past experiences, etc., which make the reception vulnerable and questionable.

It is this imposition of the translation that makes it difficult for the original idea to emerge in its purity and beauty, even though the conflict — if it is kept on the mental plane and in dialogue between the recipients of the idea — paves the way for the future emergence of the idea.

People are confused between thought and sensation, imagination, visualization, beliefs, and memory. All these are taken as thoughts, but they are not.

1. Thinking is not a process of remembering things. When people try to meditate but continuously try to remember things, they are not in the labor of meditation. So, as much as possible, one must stop playing with memories if he wants to think.

2. Thinking is not a process of sensation. You touch an object and say, "This is a rose." This is sensation, not thinking, nor a thought.

3. You sit and begin to imagine things. Your imagination is not an act of thinking. You may be occupied with an emotional trip.

4. You try to visualize and you believe you are thinking, but you are not. You are engaged in building mental pictures, although it is possible to think and visualize your thought.

5. Some people even assume that to believe something is an act of thinking. To believe means to accept, either under pressure due to ignorance or due to intuitive perception, but to believe is not thinking.

It is possible that you think after you believe something. You may intuitively know what you are believing and then try to think about it, but believing itself is not thinking. To have faith is not an act of thinking. It can be an act of straight knowledge, Intuition, or vision but not thinking.

Faith and belief can be manifestations of your past experiences, buried in the layers of your consciousness. You can think about what they are, how they were built . . . but mere believing or having faith is not thinking.

Thinking can cause all these five factors, but to make thinking pure, it must go beyond these factors. If sensation, imagination, visualization, faith, and memory are not used intelligently, they hinder the process of thinking. But if they are used intelligently, thinking can expand and deepen.

For example, sensations can provide data for thinking. Imagination can provide various viewpoints. Visualization can be used to receive and translate impressions. Faith opens new fields of investigation, and memory turns into a tool box to be used in your expedition.

In thinking, you or your Inner Guide asks questions and you or your Inner Guide tries to answer. You or your Inner Guide provides problems; you or your Inner Guide tries to solve the problems. Thinking is a continuous process of solving problems and discovering all factors which are hindering the process of your thinking.

In early stages you, as the human soul, do not think, but you study and assimilate the thoughts of your Inner Guide. Later you learn to think. As you become more able in thinking, more problems or questions are thrown in front of you, demanding solutions.

In trying to solve problems, you evoke the light hidden in your essence. As the light radiates out, you solve the problems. Every solution of a problem is a thought.

Thinking is a way of Self-actualization, or, in other words, thinking is a process of victory over all elements in your nature which try to prevent you from becoming your True Self.

When Great Ones contemplate on the Divine Purpose, They create a massive Plan to make the Purpose manifest within our planetary Life. The Plan is built of intuitional substance, and the best way to describe it is to picture it as a symphony in which each note is an idea.

Through meditation the human soul tries to translate the idea and understand it. His thoughts are the expressions of his understanding on the mental plane. To make the thoughts applicable, he uses his creative imagination and visualization and produces the thoughtform. A thoughtform is like a blueprint of a huge building or the blueprint of a great activity or action.

Ideas can be defined only by their effects or thoughts. Without their effects it is impossible to define them. Meditation, in its true sense, is the effort to translate the ideas into thoughts. This is what thinking is. In the thinking process, the human soul tries to come in contact with the world of ideas and translate them according to the level of his consciousness and need.

Thoughts are the translation of ideas on the level of the consciousness of the human soul and from the viewpoint of the need. Thoughts generally are built of mental substance. This substance is fiery and charged with great drive.

Thoughtforms are built from the substance of the lower mental plane. An ideal is a thoughtform of an idea. It is the thoughtform that evokes aspiration, which descends into the astral plane, then into the etheric plane to change into *action* and objectification.

Those who think are very rare. One must at least be able to use the third level of his mind to come in contact with ideas. Most of humanity follow the thoughtforms of others. Educated people mostly reflect the thoughts of others, and in many different ways they translate and adapt them to their needs. Original thinkers are very rare.

There is a subtle difference between an idea and knowledge. Knowledge is awareness of facts, principles, laws, and information on how to use them. An idea gives direction to knowledge. An idea uses the knowledge according to the Plan. Knowledge fails without an idea.

In each idea there is the presence of the *Will* of the Purpose. An idea uses knowledge for the right direction. When people lose their contacts with ideas, they misuse their knowledge and work against their own survival and progress. It is only through contact with the world of ideas that transformation of life occurs.

Knowledge does not transform life. An idea transforms life because an idea is the nourishment of the human soul. Through contact with ideas man transcends himself. Ideas are related to beingness.

Thought bridges the idea with the thoughtform and the Intuitional Plane with the mental plane. It helps the consciousness shift its focus into higher levels and establish continuity. Thought also carries the higher electrical charges into the mental, astral, and physical planes, charging them with fresh energy and with higher substance to be used for their nourishment and well-being. Every pure thought carries healing energy on its wings.

Through right thinking man establishes on the mental plane a contact with higher directions, with the Will, and leads the mechanism into a goal-fitting life. Without thinking man loses his way. Through thinking man can open sealed doors of Nature. Through thinking man initiates himself into the secret treasures of life. Through thinking man eliminates all that is not essential. But such thinking must originate from the heart.

To increase our capacity to think and create pure thoughts, we must learn that outer and inner conditions must be taken into consideration. For example, "smoke and the odor of burning refuse or meat" hinder the process of thinking and even hurt the brain and the mental body. Smog and various poisonous gases and toxins in the air cut the human soul off from higher contacts. Also, noise is a hindrance to creative thinking.

When one cannot contact higher directions, he falls into various crimes. Insanity is the breakage of the contact with higher directions. One of the greatest causes of increasing crime is the poisonous fumes in the air. The human soul enters into darkness and in darkness strives to find his direction because the space and the air are filled with toxins and dust.

Other hindrances to deeper thought are the locations in which people of criminal thoughts have lived; locations where crimes were committed; locations where justice was continuously violated and plans were made to destroy Beauty, Goodness, and Truth. In high mountains, deserts, and oceans where there is less pollution, one feels the beam of direction and notices great improvement in his creative thinking.

Contact with people full of irritation, hatred, and base thoughts impedes your flight toward higher strata of thoughts. The atmosphere full of the energies of love, admiration, respect, and expectation presents the best conditions for higher creative thoughts.

One can easily see the causes of distorted and base thoughts. The forces of fear, hatred, jealousy, revenge, and greed burn the wings and the eyes of thought. When the wings of thought are burned, thought serves crime. When the eyes of thought are burned, it serves destruction and corruption.

It is necessary to create an atmosphere of love, respect, higher expectation, and dedication as an ideal atmosphere so no evil arrows can disturb the flight of the thought. On the contrary, any attack from the enemy will then inspire greater challenge to the advancing thought.

In the history of creative thought, we meet those souls who individually and collectively provided the best creative atmosphere to great artists through their deep love, admiration, expectations, respect, and dedication. Love and conscious admiration nourish the deeper petals of creativity and, like a rising wave, lift the surf of thought.

When a man identifies himself with his mental plane and tries to translate the phenomena of life, he produces knowledge. His knowledge is the way he translates life.

Consciousness or awareness slowly disappears when the knowledge crystallizes and nourishes separative interests of people and thus becomes the worst barrier between reality and the Self.

We must understand that the phase of knowing things came much, much later on the path of evolution. This was recorded in ancient writings as eating the fruits of the tree of knowledge and losing paradise. Paradise means consciousness. Knowledge was a phase of deception.

Man eventually will realize that knowledge is not stable. It is an ever-changing phenomenon. Today's knowledge is tomorrow's superstition, and the consciousness never expands from something that does not have the nature of changelessness.

Our modern civilization overemphasized knowledge and forgot about beingness.

People may boast and say that yesterday we used arrows, but now we know how to operate rockets and intercontinental missiles . . . . It is true that we know more, but we are less conscious of the effects of our knowledge. Creating furniture and tools does not expand our consciousness, and when we create furniture and tools without expanding our consciousness, we use them against our own survival.

One may ask, is not the power of knowingness the urge of the soul?

Of course it is. The human soul wants to know when he loses his spiritual consciousness. The moment a man loses his spiritual consciousness because of identification with the not-self, he tries to find the ways and means to survive. But he is unable to see that it is not knowledge that will help him to survive but the awareness of the Self, the awareness of the One Self.

Those who achieve the consciousness or awareness of the Self have true knowledge. They are *aware*, they *know*, and their knowledge is the knowledge of the all-pervading Self.

Without beingness, knowledge is always misused.

People, even in this century, have difficulty seeing this. But one cannot ignore the result of accumulated knowledge. Two hundred years ago we had purer water, purer air, purer soil, purer oceans. Our knowledge polluted them, contaminated them, and we lost our consciousness to such a degree that we are extremely proud of the ways and means with which we are ready to annihilate the life on this planet! The depth of human vanity is unfathomable and deplorable.

Our universities give us power because of our knowledge. But there is no university yet on the earth which gives power to a man because of his awareness of the One Self, because of his beingness, because of his pure consciousness. Without pure consciousness, our knowledge digs our own graves.

When our consciousness expands, we will start a long process of unlearning things we learned and undoing things we did. Maybe eighty percent of our inventions and discoveries will be put aside as obstacles to conscious living. Man will go to Nature and live as Nature lives, aware of the consciousness of the One Self.

The personality — which means the soul identified with matter — craves for knowledge to perpetuate its existence. In this stage knowledge is like a cloud formation between the Sun and the earth. It is an ever-changing phenomenon controlling human life.

In this stage, knowledge is a combination of thoughtforms between the human soul and the personality. As the power of the soul increases, the process of learning will vanish, but consciousness and awareness will predominate. A time will come when man will realize that he *knows* and he does not need to learn.

Knowingness is different from knowledge. Knowingness is the awareness of the soul.

Knowledge is gained in many ways:

— Through experience and experiment

— Through learning and study

— Through straight knowledge

— Through advanced telepathy

— Through identification

— Through Omniscience

1. Let us take the first one. One learns something by experience. Knowledge is the formulation of experience. Experience is direct registration of facts. For example, I put my finger on a flame and learn that the flame burns.

Experiment is an effort to repeat the experience or to produce something you know or something you suspect.

2. Learning imparts knowledge. Learning is the study of the experience or the formulated knowledge of a man or of a group. If the experience and knowledge are not up-to-date or are biased, learning builds prejudices and superstitions.

3. Straight knowledge is experience and learning, but without the need of experience and learning. Straight knowledge bypasses the labor of experience and learning but results in experience and knowledge.

The first kind of knowledge is collected by our five senses. The second kind of knowledge is collected through our mind. Unless the mind is inspired by right motive and an all-inclusive vision, knowledge at this stage can be used for selfish, separative, and non-goal-fitting ways.

The third kind of knowledge is gathered by the Intuition. It is possible to collect knowledge through the senses on the astral and mental planes and do some experiments on these planes. This is not straight knowledge, but it brings us the different dimensions of the same object and its various relationships with Higher Worlds.

Straight knowledge is achieved only when the human soul has a window, or an awareness, on the higher mental plane. Because of this awareness, he *knows*, and his knowledge is not the result of an experience, experiment, or previously formulated knowledge. His knowledge is an awakening. Let us remember that the Spark potentially is the *whole* in Its active or passive states.

4. There are also other, higher kinds of knowledge such as a fourth kind which is gained by fusing yourself with the Minds that know and receiving the knowledge you need. This is done through advanced telepathy and through registration of impressions.

5. A fifth kind of knowledge is gained by identification. This is a more advanced way than straight knowledge, and great Initiates use this method whenever They need to know.

6. The last stage of knowledge is called Omniscience in which the knower, the knowledge, and the object of knowledge are fused with the Self, with the One Self. This is what Self-knowledge is.

We have great encyclopedic minds, great computers, but we have only a few conscious men — a few men who were able to step into the sanctuary of their True Self and fuse with the One Self. A conscious man exists and lives for all. He has an attitude which can be called an "indifference viewpoint."
There are two kinds of viewpoints:

1. the viewpoint of interest or the interest viewpoint

2. the indifference viewpoint

The indifference viewpoint is the viewpoint of the Self within two conflicting parts. The interest viewpoint is the viewpoint of a separated self.
The interest viewpoint distorts everything in trying to support its selfish ends. The indifference viewpoint sees the reality and has no reason to distort reality and create sides.
The indifference viewpoint can be achieved only when one liberates himself from all separative interests and stands for the One Self.
The true Teaching expands the consciousness rather than imparts knowledge. An expanding consciousness sees things as they are. An expanding consciousness makes a man progressively one with all life and aware of all life.
The true Teaching makes you aware of the One Self.
The consciousness lives as one with the whole of Life. Knowledge, without Self-knowledge, makes the human soul live as a separate being. The increase of knowledge did not help us surpass the stage of savagery and corruption. The savage in man is as alive as it was ten thousand years ago, but this time it does not have the shape of an orangutan. It has ties, boots, suits, makeup, cars, telephones, televisions . . . and the unimaginable power to destroy itself.
People use their memories to solve their problems or to be successful. Most knowledge is based on memories. There are also other, better means to solve problems, to increase knowledge, and to be successful, for example:

- meditation

- insight

- Intuition

- inspiration

- impression

Through the above means we not only solve many of our problems, but we also make certain breakthroughs into the sphere of higher awareness and knowing.

At the time of *meditation*,[1] the less we depend on our memories, the more and the faster we progress into higher awareness. Memories condition our flights and mold our receptions. Because of our memories we are often stuck to our current level. Generally our level of consciousness is built from our own memories. Thinking is an effort to pass beyond the limitations of our memories. Memories often become a chain for us, and they do not allow us to go forward to a new state of consciousness, to a new state of beingness, due to the image of our beingness built by our own memories.

Not all of our memories can be recollected. Most of them are part of our beingness and control our life unconsciously through restimulation or association.[2]

Nature is very wise. Most of the time when we take a new incarnation, it blocks the memory banks of the past. Those memories which penetrated deep into our being still control us through our genes, character, and the quality of our bodies; but the general memory of our past lives fades out.

I feel that in this stage of our evolution, say until we pass the Transfiguration experience, our past memories are a very heavy hindrance to our progress. We will never have a high degree of freedom to advance as long as we are stuck to our memory. Our memory holds us like a prisoner, and we will always act under the pressure of the heavy events through which we have passed.

Nature gives us glimpses of our past lives, if it is necessary for our advancement, but most of the time memory remains buried within our being. In our present life Nature makes us forget certain events to make us continue to live, cooperate, and serve.

To expand our consciousness in any creative endeavor, we need to separate ourselves from our own memories and operate in a domain where we have greater freedom to adapt ourselves to the incoming new ideas, new visions, and new impressions and build new plans without being restricted by the power of memories.

There is a difference between memory and knowledge. Memory is the record of past events. Knowledge is the record of the ways the laws of Nature operate. Memory is related to the effects or results. Knowledge is related to cause. Both are powerful factors to control our life and to condition our future.

Memory can be a hindrance for us if it controls our thinking. Knowledge can be a hindrance for us if we do not balance it by our unfolding beingness and use it for the benefit of all.

---

1. For full information on meditation, please see *The Science of Meditation.*
2. See also *The Subconscious Mind and the Chalice.*

Memories can be used to *understand* a present problem. Knowledge can be used to *solve* a present problem. To solve a present problem means to nullify the effects of past events and plan in the light of the future.

Knowledge is a tool, is a force. Knowledge can be used destructively or constructively. If the user is a man of the future, knowledge brings greater happiness, greater success, and greater cooperation with Nature.

The future has three main characteristics. It is all-inclusive, progressive, and transformative.

Insight is the ability to see the causal sides of events. If your memory interferes, your information will not truly reflect the facts because the power of your insight will be conditioned by the memory. Those people who are occupied with the past seldom have insight. Most historians are very short-sighted persons because they see in the future only the reflection of past history. They cannot understand that history can be created only by the future vision and insight.

Memory plays a great role in our life. Without memory most of our formulas would be useless and most of our problems would remain unsolved. Modern life has created many machines which store memories and help us solve our problems. However, in advanced creative work memory can be a hindrance to our progress.

In *intuitional awareness* the human soul is totally free from the conditioning influence of memory. The person is no longer conditioned by past experiences.

Intuitional awareness is totally future-oriented. People will say that without the past, the future cannot exist. This is not true. The past is a dead future. Our future is what the Planetary Logos or Cosmic Entities think about us. The gardener knows what the future of a seed is. He knows exactly what color and shape it will take in the future. The seed does not know about its future, though the future is within its Core.

Intuition is the source of the inspiration of the future. A future-oriented man is not the result of his past but the flower of his future. He progresses toward the vision of his future, and his future becomes an actualized present.

Intuition sees hundreds of years ahead. The future reaches man through *inspiration* and *impressions*.

When the influence of memories is minimal upon the flow of inspiration and impressions, the influence of the future vision will be greater on the life of the human being. A great change will take place in our world politics if nations discuss more about the future than about the past. The past stands for separative interests; the future stands for the interests of all humanity.

At the present, politicians in general are controlled by the interests of their own nation or by the interests of their parties or even of their selves. In the future, politicians will be controlled by the interests of the whole world.

To be a politician at this time means to be an opportunist and to be on the side of those who have more power. And because opportunists and power constantly change, they develop a changing nature to survive in their profession. In the future, politicians will not be opportunists, nor will they side with those who have the most power. They will use every opportunity to create international understanding, unity, and cooperation. Once they find this foundation, their direction will never change, and the people will have greater faith in them.

As long as our plans are based upon past memories and upon our separative interests, we will never find a beneficial solution to world problems.

As for the individual, so it is for the whole world; memory of the past and separative interests must not control the future vision if the individual or the world wants to survive.

Often we notice that while we listen to someone's speech we listen to our own memories; while we read a book we read what we have in our own mind, and neither the content of the book nor the words spoken to us have something new for us. It is imperative that we use, at least periodically, the power to withdraw ourselves from the past and stand free in our future contacts. Preconditioned attitudes, preconceived formulas are often the cause of our failures.

Once I was trying to compose some new music, but I noticed that I was continuously drawn to an old tune and was not able to create something new. It took me a few weeks to be able totally to reject or forget the old tune and create the new one — which had a slight resemblance but which was built upon a totally new rhythm and melody.

Most of our judgments are based upon our past memories. We are more our past than our future. The past memories build our image. The past memories control our actions; that is why we cannot find a chance to be something new, to see things in a new light, to relate ourselves to others on a new level. The past makes us continue being what we were. Our knowledge grows; our position and possessions grow, but our essence remains the same because our essence grows only by the inspiration of the future.

We hinder the progress of others, too, when we concentrate our attention upon the failures of their past more than upon the possibilities of their future. The future possibilities must not be ignored, and future opportunities must not be denied in the memories of the past, if one wants to promote someone on the path of success.

If people under your influence are not able to make new breakthroughs, see if you are holding them in a thoughtform which is built by their past failures, or if they are holding themselves in their own thoughtforms of what they were.

When you are satisfied with what you are now, you build a thoughtform which does not let you transcend your level for a long time.

Thus memory and the past, two important factors in our life, can also be detrimental factors for our progress.

Consciousness operates not through knowledge but through observation. Knowledge is the crystallization of the images of observed phenomena. It is partial crystallization of the observation. This crystallization obscures further observation, if it is not destroyed and cleared away from the automatic memory banks.

We have two kinds of memory banks. One is automatic, and it interferes with our observation. The other is the controlled memory bank. This is a state of consciousness in which the past is related to the future, and future visions control the memory bank of past events.

Knowledge is the result of memory. Some part of this memory is under conscious control, but the larger part of it is mechanical and automatic.

Consciousness does not have memory banks. Memory banks exist in mental and etheric matter. Consciousness does not need memory because its light extends into past, present, and future.

To be conscious does not mean to have memory. Knowledge is operative memory, and this memory obstructs the eye of consciousness if the consciousness enters the state of crystallization.

Ignorance is not a state of lack of knowledge but a state of obscuration of consciousness by crystallized knowledge.

Ignorance is an inability to respond to the evocative impressions which create freedom and liberation from the former states of your consciousness and a striving toward the future. Ignorance is a state in which you cannot grow further. You can be a professor of any branch of knowledge but still be an ignorant person if you have closed the windows and doors of your consciousness to prevent further expansion.

One can *know* without the need of knowledge. Knowing without knowledge is awareness.

Thus, consciousness acts more freely through observation and thinking if knowledge does not interfere with its thinking and observation.

Thinking does not mean to collect knowledge but to impress the atoms of mental substance with the direction of the human soul. When the soul tries to impress his direction upon the substance of the mental body without passing through distortions, we call it pure thinking.

Knowledge operates through comparison. Consciousness does not compare but *sees*. For consciousness there is no duality to be compared but only a unity in which things are all parts of each other and no part can be *understood* without the rest.

This means that consciousness does not accept or reject things. Consciousness *sees*. Consciousness sees things that may obscure its clarity and things which increase its light, and it tries to change things through its thoughts.

Consciousness observes events as the waves of the ocean. The main object of observation of the consciousness is the ocean, the cause of events, not the results only.

Knowledge is the result of the study of events. Consciousness observes the cause and the effects of events simultaneously. Consciousness is a cause, not an effect. Thinking is the effort to liberate oneself from the trap of effects and the effort to be identified with the cause. Thinking relates the cause and the effect and creates a continuum in consciousness between them.

Consciousness changes things by changing its own magnitude. Consciousness sees how life reflects the states of consciousness. To change life, consciousness changes itself.

Knowledge operates on matter directly and causes changes in matter. Changes in matter enrich the knowledge and give it more power to operate on matter. Increased knowledge, if not controlled by the awareness of the Self, further obscures the consciousness and prevents the growth of beingness. This is why, cycle after cycle, Nature destroys our knowledge or buries it in the caves of the ocean and the earth. Cycle after cycle, those who come in contact with the greater light of their Inner Being suddenly drop all the baggage of their knowledge and seek to be conscious of their own reality and the universal Reality without any formulated knowledge.

One can be extremely rich in knowledge but not have a clear, pure consciousness. Knowledge without a pure consciousness is a means of destruction and a source of misery. A conscious man can use knowledge through his thoughts. Knowledge used without conscious thoughts becomes one's own trap.

Knowledge is a tool for the exploitation of Nature. Consciousness never tries to exploit Nature except when it is obscured by thoughts. It tries to tune itself to Nature and cooperate with Nature. Consciousness never tries to hurt any life-form. It exists for the welfare of all life-forms.

A conscious man is *the flower of millenniums.*

The quality of thinking must be improved. It is possible to think and find better ways and means for self-destruction, but this is not improvement in thinking.

Improvement in thinking is not possible until people realize the spiritual laws; until people realize the existence of life on other dimensions; until people think along the lines of Infinity and Future; until people think along the lines of unity and synthesis; until people think along the lines of group perfection; until people learn to think in the sanctuary of their heart.

The quality of thinking can improve if people from their childhood are kept aware about heroes who stood for the betterment of life; who stood for justice, for compassion; who lived as a path to the future. Without the image of such heroes, thinking will not find its forward-moving gear but will remain engaged in reverse gear.

It is the vision of the future that causes improvement in our thinking. It is the vision of the One Self which inspires the wings of thought.

Improvement of thinking proceeds only toward the direction of *joy, freedom, synthesis,* and *toward the factuality of Higher Worlds.*

Formulation of thought must exist before it takes wings toward Infinity. The foundation of thought is the Spirit in the form of man. One cannot fly without the vision of joy, without aspiration for freedom, without striving toward synthesis, and without the awareness of the existence of the Higher Worlds and higher dimensions. One cannot improve his thinking without these four guiding lights toward the future.

Self-destruction in this age will be by the use of thought. Men fought against each other with their bodies and brought suffering and destruction. Men fought with the power of their emotions, and their civilizations now lie at the bottom of the oceans. Men are ready to fight with the power of their thought, and neither the earth nor the ocean will contain any trace of their memory because the fire will consume and burn away all that they did.

Self-destruction and self-regeneration are two paths down which our thought can lead us. The heroes of the nations are those who strive to keep open the path of self-regeneration for their people. Every heroic act to keep the path open toward self-regeneration is inspired only by the future.

The beauty of the future must be kept in the minds of the people. Only thoughts directed to the beauty of the future will save humanity from total destruction.

In the physical, objective world thought crystallizes itself in forms, in motion, and in direction. In the emotional world thought is used to solve the problems of entanglement, sleep, depression, and the phantasmagoria of emotional pleasures. In the mental world thought stands as it is. It takes form; you cannot hide what you are. In every thought you see the stage of your evolution.

First you think as you were thinking on earth, and you become horrified by the walls you erect around yourself. Then you think as you were thinking in the emotional world, and suddenly you realize that the astral world is watching you. Then you think as you are, and you see your real image on the mirror of your thoughts. Then you strive to see yourself as more beautiful and more universal, and you make a breakthrough in your thinking.

It is after such a breakthrough that you see the futility of all your thoughts which were built on *greed, separatism, pride*, and you turn your eyes toward Infinity. The light from the world of Intuition penetrates your mind, and you see the glory waiting for you in the light of the future.

As the quality of thought improves, the consciousness becomes brighter and brighter. Eventually it controls the mechanism of thought, refusing all that comes from the past or from the environment, but leaves itself magnetic to the spatial thoughts which come from advanced Beings.

Spatial thoughts are those thoughts which

1. come from advanced Beings such as Masters or Members of the higher Hierarchies

2. are created by advanced human beings

When the motivation of these latter thoughts is right and according to the Plan, they are drawn to the sphere of mental fire, and, after a purification and charging process, they are projected again into space.

Thus spatial thoughts are not those thoughts which are the product of millions of human minds and which create the worst pollution that space ever imagined.

Spatial thoughts have three main orientations:

1. They stand for the improvement of life on the planet.

2. They are seeds of the Hierarchical Plan.

3. They stand for the Divine Will and Purpose.

People say that they start to work to achieve a goal, and then the drive or the interest fades away and they discontinue working for their goal. They think this is a problem of willpower or a problem of the brain or body. Actually, this is not a problem of having will or not having will, but it is a problem of disengagement of thought.

There is the willpower, which is the driving force. There is the thought — the image of the goal. There are the brain and the body. If we want to start and finish something, the thought which is the gear must engage itself with the brain and body. If it is engaged, the work proceeds. If for any reason it is disengaged, the work stops.

The disengagement occurs when in the process of action a force interferes and pulls the gear out into neutral. This force can be another thought, a posthypnotic suggestion, a command from the past, or a painful experience which is keyed in with the process of the work at hand.

For example, a man of thirty-five years of age told me that he sets goals and works very hard to accomplish them and to be successful, but, when he begins to be really successful, he quits out of fear or lack of interest. In talking with him I learned that he was living in a certain town, in a certain country, where success was counted a crime. This sounds strange, but it is true. When dominating people have prejudices against minorities, they watch them very closely and consider their success a threat to them.

According to the information of this gentleman, many of his family members disappeared after they became successful in their business. As a child he continuously heard such stories, and they were impressed in his mind. It was these impressions that were disengaging the gear from the mechanism and forcing him to drop his goal and withdraw.

There are many methods to cure such a condition, but one that brought the best result was the technique I used on many occasions. My theory is that whatever the disengaging factor is, it is a *force*; and if this force is overcome by another, stronger force, it will be possible to nullify the negative force and keep the gear engaged.

This is done through an imagination and visualization technique. For example, I told the above-mentioned gentleman that every day for half an hour he must sit and visualize a detailed procedure of success. First he must visualize his goal and take action, *as if* he had all the ways and means to be successful. In his creative imagination he must be really successful. This must be done in detail.

For example, if he is going to repair his television set, he must imagine that he has all the tools, all the knowledge, and lots of time to repair the television. He must sit for half an hour and do it in his creative imagination, as if he were doing it in actuality. This must be done at least ten to fifteen days without worrying about the result.

The result will start to appear when the positive tension accumulates and creates enough force to stop or nullify the power of the negative force.

If the result does not appear, the exercises must be repeated after a three to five day interval. It is possible that soon the man will feel that the gears are engaged and the work can start.

This method can be used for almost anything within the bounds of reason and in the spirit of harmlessness.

Once a girl asked me, "What if a person does not want to or can't visualize or use creative imagination?" I told her a story which answered her question:

There was a boy who could not ride a horse. He had certain feelings and thoughts that were preventing him from riding a horse, in spite of his wishes. I sat with him and told three or four stories in detail and with color. For example, I said, "There was a young boy who had a beautiful white horse. . . ." I told about how the horse used to run and play, until the image of the horse was built in his mind. Then I told him how the boy learned to ride and how he rode, and what great fun he had, etc. . . . All this was done in detail, in color, and with emotional flavor.

After doing this five to ten times a week, the boy began to visualize and imagine as I told the stories. After ten days he already had his horse and was having great fun with it.

Thus the opposing force can be arrested and overcome by an increasing positive force.

55
Two Ways of Thinking

The majority of people in the world think they are important people, that they must live only for themselves. Because they think they are important and are dedicated to their egos, they exceed their proper boundaries and do things they should not.

People around them often are guilty of lending support to their egos by using flattery and bribery to make them feel that they are important, that they are extremely beautiful, smart, wise, and so on. Once my Teacher said, "Do not try to make average people feel important or you will ruin their lives." Those who think that they are important slowly arrange their lives and their environment so that they become a central pole around which everything else revolves. And if anyone dares not to recognize their greatness, they scheme to punish him in various ways.

We are often caught in this psychological trap. Generally, it is a very difficult trap to escape. Religiously-oriented people, those who follow certain teachings, are especially vulnerable to its lure, as are most organizations. As a group, as a church, people collectively think that they are so important, so "saved." Such thinking develops fanaticism, separatism, and superiority complexes in them which makes them socially unbearable.

As the group ego grows, it tries to exercise extended control over other people and tries to force others to recognize its importance. If others do not acknowledge the group's importance, it will threaten and create dangerous situations in life and in the environment.

The sense of importance creates in people a deep-seated vanity and hypocrisy. Such people live life only for themselves at the expense of all others.

By wisely evaluating the news we read or hear, we can see how the most destructive actions are taken by those who think they are extremely important people. Because they live only for themselves, they steal, deceive, and make the lives of other people miserable. They steal the positions of others; they spread lies and organize crimes only to satisfy their "greatness." Because they feel they are so important, they do not care what others think about them. They expect everyone to recognize and respect their greatness. Their life spins on the axis of their ego.

On the other hand, there are noble and beautiful people who think their own lives are not so important, and they do not live for themselves alone. Because their lives are not important, they involve themselves in every field of service for the sake of others. They sacrifice themselves and renounce many things to help others.

Such a person thinks, "My life is no big deal; I will sacrifice myself for others. I will keep my mouth closed and not disturb the peace and harmony of the environment. I will stand in the shadow so that others may shine. Let me work and let that man take a needed vacation."

Such are the leaders of spiritual humanity. They are those in all departments of human endeavor who carry the heaviest loads to make life advance and to bring joy to all humanity.

There are many who claim to be lovers of God, but there are very few heroes who really love and live for humanity. If the ranks of these heroes grow, humanity could enter the New Era.

There are many who love their nation; there are very few who truly love humanity. The names of the lovers of humanity stand as beacons throughout the history of humanity.

If Christ had said, "I am so important that I just want to live for myself," we would not have the benefit of the light He brought to earth. If Lord Buddha had said, "I am extremely important; I must live only for myself," we would never have the wisdom which He radiated to all humanity.

No culture could exist without the existence of such self-sacrificing individuals.

The Great Ones did not think that They should not sacrifice their lives for humanity. They never even thought that They were important, and They lived humble, unassuming lives. Lord Buddha used to beg for food; Christ did not have a place to lay His head. The true disciples of Great Ones did not consider their lives important, and they sacrificed themselves for the salvation of humanity.

Once my Teacher said to our class, "Beware of important people who live their lives only for themselves. Such people do not care for others; they want to create a paradise only for themselves and live there in eternal pleasure."

Those people who think they are important do not consider the feelings and reactions of people around them. They dress in either obnoxious or very flashy ways to prove their importance. They do only what they want to do.

I lived in an apartment next to two neighbors who used to blast the radio, playing rock and roll and disco music until midnight. Since I could not sleep, I told the manager about the situation and he spoke to them about it. A few hours later he came to my door and said, "I am very sorry, but I cannot help you. They wanted to know who you thought you were." A few days later, when I was moving out, my neighbors approached me and said, "We want to enjoy our lives. Do not try to prevent people from living the way they want to live." I only gave them a smile.

Important people do not think about the welfare of others because they are blinded by their own interests and pleasures. Those who care for their own individual comfort, interests, and worth remain average people. Their names are lost in time and space. Only those who forget themselves remain forever in the memory of the race as Great Ones.

Some might think that not giving importance to one's own life means

- not dressing well

- not eating well

- not behaving properly

- not having a decent home

but this is not true. When a person realizes that he does not belong to himself, he dresses better, eats better, behaves better, and organizes his house better because he finds he cannot serve well if he is not up-to-date.

Those who are careless or ugly in their manners and dress are those who think they are important. Those who belong only to themselves and think their values are the only valid values often live offensive lives without considering the feelings and reactions of others.

Thus, psychologically, a sloppy man is one who gives himself great value and lives in vanity. This image is built within people with the assistance of parents, teachers, and society. Everyone says, "You are so important, so great," and this builds ego and glamor.

A person is not really important until he feels part of the One Self. In every human being the most important part is the Self, which is fused with the interests of the All-Self. To be united with the All-Self means a person does not give any inflated value to his own existence.

In the Old Country, we had a herd of five thousand buffalo and employed thirty shepherds to tend them. When the head shepherd was caught stealing, my father called him into his office and said, "I am sorry I ruined you by making you an important person. You can leave this job until you learn how to be an unimportant person."

Once I visited a family with three small children. Their father lit up a cigar. I said to him, "Your children are coughing; your wife is complaining about her lungs. Can't you at least smoke outside?" He replied, "You have no right to stop my pleasure. If they don't like it, *they* can go outside."

Important people have only one goal: to dominate the lives of others, to make others serve and sacrifice for them. Such people have a well built ego. Most are obsessed by their own image of importance. Important people base their lives on pleasures, possessions, and positions and try to perpetuate the rule of their egos through stealing, exploiting, participating in illegal activities, organizing crimes, distributing drugs, and spending money to back political legislation which nourishes their interests and perpetuates their rule.

Behind every so-called "important person" lurks a dark force which tries to lead him into greater and greater crime.

The most essential thing to a person who thinks his life is unimportant is the service he can render to others. The principle for New Era servers states: "We must do our service in the Plan through self-forgetfulness, harmlessness, and right speech." If we fail to incorporate these three principles into our lives, we miss the boat.

Important people build an altar and worship their own images. It is difficult to stop self-worship because such a practice makes us live only for our own egos.

If any teaching makes you an important person in your own eyes, be careful; you are in the process of dying. Only through humility is the Teaching understood; only in humility is the Teaching lived.

Clever people, with a sneaky smile, may ask, "But, isn't *every* person created by God important?" The answer is, "No!" Pseudo teachers tell us that we are important as individuals, to care for ourselves, to protect ourselves. "Do not hurt yourself," they teach. "Live at the expense of others. All will be yours. You will rule others. Everyone will obey you."

There does exist within you the most important thing — the realization of the All-Self. If a person realizes that he is one with the All-Self, then truly he is the most important person in the world.

Those people who think they are unimportant and who live for others have many important things to accomplish. There are fifteen main points upon which they must reflect:

1. How can we serve others, and by so doing expand our consciousness so that we may serve more and better?

Reading alone cannot expand your consciousness. You must actualize and live the Teaching. You expand your consciousness only in serving — so that you are better equipped to serve.

In order to serve, the right tools are required: a healthy mind, knowledge, experience, wisdom, self-forgetfulness, harmlessness, and right speech. Unless you have good tools and meet the standards, you cannot be fulfillers of the Ageless Wisdom.

It is very dangerous to assume yourself to be a spiritual person, when in fact you are a rotten apple.

2. How can we serve the Teaching by living the Teaching?

The Teaching is condensed Ageless Wisdom collected from all races, nations, and teachers. Unfortunately, people divided the Teaching into "my," "our," or "your" teaching, but in reality the Teaching is One. If you take the essence of all teachings and bottle it, the label would read, "This bottle contains Beauty, Goodness, Righteousness, Joy, Freedom, Self-Forgetfulness, and Striving."

Whoever fails to actualize these seven elements of Ageless Wisdom in his life will never understand the Teaching and cannot teach the Teaching.

The Teaching in this modern age has been turned into a veritable Tower of Babel; when you enter it, you lose your mind and sense of direction. This has been caused by knowing instead of living the Teaching. A Teaching that is not lived slowly degenerates and misleads people.

All students of wisdom must try to assimilate the Teaching into their lives and radiate it out to their environment through their thoughts, words, actions, and motives.

Those who live for others and think they are unimportant try to make their lives rich and beautiful so that they have something better with which to serve others. Thus, one must try to be beautiful, full of goodness and righteousness, and have deep joy in his heart. Joylessness is a sign that something is degenerating in the person's heart. Joy is a sign that a regenerative process is active in the heart of the person.

Free people never impose their own glamors and illusions on others. Instead, they leave others free to bloom or decay according to their choice and karma. Most world complications originate from people who feel important and therefore impose themselves on others and violate karmic law.

You can present the Teaching as a challenge and as a light, and then leave others free to assimilate it or to fight against it.

Our education and literature have cultivated in us a sense of pseudo importance. This has been a curse imposed upon us; we cannot see that we, as individuals, are not important. Only the *Whole* is important. Only living for others is important; only realization and actualization of Inner Divinity is important.

Self-sacrifice is a gift of the Teaching, but people have been side-stepping it. They pretend to sacrifice themselves for a certain person or cause while pursuing their own hidden interests and building their egos. Truly spiritual people do not play with great concepts and use them as cover-ups. They sacrifice their all for the Teaching or for other people without expectation of reward or for any personal interest. Such people are not trapped in the network of self-importance.

Another gift of the Ageless Wisdom is striving. Striving means to make efforts to eliminate limitations and expand the consciousness and usefulness. This is so simple and clean a definition.

Important people do not strive because striving means freeing oneself of limitations and burdens. Important people depend on such burdens and loads; limitations are their security.

Most of the time our thinking runs in old grooves, producing obsolete ways of living. It is time to make an extra effort to change our ways of thinking.

Our next step must be to think that we, as individuals, are not important. An individual becomes increasingly important as he grows in the realization that the Whole is most important.

Christ said, "One cannot find himself until he loses himself." The process of losing oneself is the process of thinking that you are not important — but that the Whole is important. And because the Whole is most important, you do your very best to serve the Whole instead of trying to use the Whole for your own self-interests to satisfy your feelings of self-importance. A sweet gift of the Teaching is the idea of service.

An important person tries to make others serve him, but a person who feels unimportant tries to serve others. He feels he has to serve.

This is in no way related to the sickness of inferiority complexes. Actually, an inferiority complex is the root of feeling important.

3. How can we propagate the Teaching?

The fiery drive to propagate the Teaching exists in those who feel that something must be done for mass humanity. To propagate the Teaching means to risk your life.

To propagate the Teaching means to destroy all dark seeds and crystallizations which have penetrated into your mind. It also means to work against glamors, illusions, and inertia. Because these things stand as foundations for people's lives, you must be courageous and risk your life to remove such limitations. Anyone who feels important does not dare risk his life for others.

The greatest treasures in most people's lives are those things which limit their freedom and make them useless to the Common Good. People think that to carry such burdens on their shoulders is an honor. To propagate the Teaching is a way to unload people who love their loads.

Disciples of Christ sacrificed their lives for humanity because they realized that their lives were unimportant. Christ thought humanity was more important than Himself; that is why He sacrificed His life for humanity. But the followers of the Church created different doctrines and tried, by all possible means, to become important, to save their own souls.

How can we propagate the Teaching? Have we made our lives an example of the seven principles, the principles of Beauty, Goodness, Righteousness, Joy, Freedom, self-forgetfulness, and Striving? Have we created those conditions in which people will have a chance to bloom? Do we live in wisdom, humility, and solemnity? Do we inspire others to search for the source of beauty? Do we attract people to the Teaching?

But how can we do these things if we worship ourself as the most important person? Beware of those who try to make you feel important.

4. How can we try by all means to help the Teacher carry out his responsibilities in the best way possible?

Spiritual people think they are not important and do all they can to help the Teacher. Important people create unending problems and pile trash on the path of the Teacher to keep him from his most important labor.

The Teacher is often kept busy with the consequences of his students' gossip, slander, fights, ego, vanity, and personality problems. Eventually he becomes a baby-sitter or a problem-solving machine instead of one who applies himself to teaching and enlightening people. How can the Teacher teach you when you are engaged in the trash of your vanity and ego?

Some people think that they can teach other people only if those people are ready. This is an excuse to hide their weaknesses. People are always ready to be led to light if the right teacher is present. Often it is the so-called teacher who is not ready when others do not care for his teaching. Once the Teacher is ready, students will be attracted to him by natural law. Bees go to honey; deer go to water; students go to the Teacher — if he is a true one.

When a teacher is not ready and tries to teach, people are naturally repelled by him; they feel that he does not have the right guidance for them.

Important people think they have the right to hurt the feelings of others, and, surprisingly, they enjoy hurting others because they think others are inferior. Those who feel unimportant do not harbor any ill will toward others because they live for others. Their Teacher is sacred to them, and they try to ease his burden, to share his pains and sufferings, and to help him proceed in his service. Thus, helping those who serve increases the possibilities for survival of the human race.

5. How can we improve the relationship between families, groups, and nations?

Those who feel others are more important than themselves risk their lives to create good relations between people. There exist heavy walls between people: cleavages, hatred, jealousy, anger, misunderstanding, self-interest, and so on. How can we work to improve the situation existing between people?

Many great people sacrificed their lives just trying to bring right human relations between people. They lost their lives because they thought others were more important than themselves.

When you announce your intention to create right human relations, people's first reaction will be, "Be careful; be cautious. Don't hurt yourself for others because you are so important." They inject this poison into your system.

Often such servants of humanity are hated worse than enemies, but that is all right with them. Because they think they are unimportant, they are not easily hurt.

6. How can we bring peace on earth?

This is a great mission for those who feel others are more important.

The most dangerous thing in the world is to try to bring peace to earth because the situation of life is such that economic and other interests of important people will be hurt by peace. Within the psyche of the human being exists a cluster of hatred and selfishness. How can we clean them?

People are caught within self-made traps. How can we save them? How can we help them realize that the interests of all are really in the best interest of the individual, and that generally self-interest is against the interests of all?

Peace must first be created in your heart, then at home, then in society, the nation, and the world. Those who lack peace within try to live in and create chaos.

I once had a secretary who hated her father. At every opportunity, she expressed hatred toward her father. One day when I was pointing out a few mistakes she made in typing a letter, she suddenly turned on me and said, "You are talking just like my father. You are looking at me just like my father."

I realized that this incident was the beginning of a series of thunderstorms. From that day on her hatred for her father was projected onto me until she finally resigned, saying, "I don't want to work for a man like my father."

Mother Theresa was a simple girl. But when she realized the importance of other people, she sacrificed her life to help the sick and hungry of the world. Thinking that her life is not important, she performs the most sacrificial labor for humanity and has become an important person in the eyes of people. She has proven that she does not live only for herself and that her life is not important to her. She therefore sacrifices it for others. Unless you feel the importance of other people, you cannot sacrifice your life for them.

When people tell you that you are important, tell them to get behind you, as Christ did when Satan tried to make Him feel important.

7. How can we annihilate injustice, no matter who causes it?

Fighters against injustice are those people who risk their lives to help common people enjoy justice.

8. How can we create beauty in our environment?

Unimportant people lose their self-interest in bringing beauty to others. Actually, the process of true creativity is an effort to eliminate all elements in one's own nature which nurture ego and importance. Truly creative people are egoless, lost in beauty. That is what makes them creative, powerful, and beautiful.

9. How can we bring great ideas and visions to the world?

Those who think they must live for others often isolate themselves for years in study and contemplation until they contact the Sources of great ideas and visions. They then offer these ideas and visions to humanity at great sacrifice to their own lives.

Selfless ones also think.

10. How can we wipe out sickness and disease from the world?

11. How can we eliminate wide-spread corruption?

12. How can we teach people to overcome their egos, jealousy, and vanity?

13. How can we help people respect the territories of others?

14. How can we re-establish the sacredness of family life?

15. How can we bring world unity into being?

To do all these things requires heroism. The definition of a hero is one who thinks his life can be sacrificed for others, to protect them, to save them, to liberate them and help them to reach their noble destination. He is one who is not stuck to his own skin and possessions but lives for others.

56

Crystallized Thinking

Those who are living in crystallized thoughtforms, traditions, and religions do not keep pace with the advancing life.

Such thoughtforms, traditions, and religious beliefs keep people retarded on the path of evolution and gradually create friction with the advancing life. This friction eventually reaches such a momentum that it begins to violate the laws formulated by the advancing life.

For example, the cruelties practiced by crystallized fanatics in politics, religion, or in other fields eventually make them confront the law and fall into endless troubles.

People who act through crystallization cannot generally change and be inclusive except by falling into trouble and facing themselves. Their misdeeds — viewed from the progressive viewpoint — become not only their judge but also their salvation.

It is observed that all crystallized thinking acts against the Common Good because crystallization becomes for people a shelter in which to pursue their egocentric interests. On the other hand, such people do a great service to humanity not because of their good deeds but because of their violations and mistakes.

It is not easy to change the thinking of people, the laws, and the traditional ways of living by fighting against them, but a big violation of the law or the manifestation of a mistake can shake people and urge them to take actions to prevent future repetitions of the same mistakes.

Sometimes those who have done wrong are victims, but through their involuntary sacrifice they have changed many things in life.

The present method of dealing with wrong doers is to punish them. In the future this will change. Every convicted person will enter into schools of transformation where they will be subjected to various methods of a transformation process.

People will not punish or condemn each other but will anxiously try to transform each other because, in the future, the intelligent people on earth will see that there are inseparable relations between all human beings and that everyone shares the conditions of everyone else.

They will see that humanity is one body, and the cells in the body share all that happens to the body as a whole.

In violating the Laws of Unity and Brotherhood, we impose upon ourselves heavier conditions of pain and suffering. And, because of pain and suffering, we eventually come to our senses and try to search for a way that leads us to happiness.

What we find in our search is nothing else but the Laws of Unity and Brotherhood.

Some people believe that we need pain and suffering to come to our senses. But pure logic and reasoning can help us bypass pain and suffering and build a life of health and happiness. This will be possible when people will stand above their crystallizations and let the light of clear thinking illuminate their path.

Inclusiveness, tolerance, and sensitivity to new viewpoints and new revelations make a person a better thinker.

People often are afraid to think because they do not want to lose the crystallizations with which they have identified. It is through thinking with inclusiveness and tolerance that sensitivity is increased and new viewpoints are found. Sensitivity is the increasing magnetism of mental matter which attracts new revelations that create new viewpoints.

People must learn to stand above all their beliefs and knowledge. This leads to a creative freedom in which they can create a new self-image which is more progressive.

In the thinking process, a time must come in which the thinker will not be able to identify with his thoughts but instead will use them to meet various needs. He must even be able to destroy a former thought and build a new one.

When we develop the ability to stand above our thoughts, not only will we become better thinkers, but also we will see how ridiculous our thoughts were at certain times.

If one can discover how ridiculous he was on certain occasions, he can surpass his former level of consciousness. Humor is the moment of discovery of our former ridiculousness, preposterousness, and foolishness. With an attitude of humor, not only can we destroy our own crystallizations but also the crystallizations in others, opening a new life of freedom for them.

Thinking must be balanced by devotion. Without devotion, or the unfoldment of the heart, thinking can lead to black magic with dire consequences.

Devotion is the radiation of an unfolding heart. Through the heart the human soul tries to worship a transcendental beauty and serve that beauty by spreading its radiance all over the world to secure a world of freedom, joy, and safety.

Devotion thus guides the thinking process, making it serve the Common Good and the transcendental principles, laws, and values.

It is not enough to penetrate into the laws of Nature and gain control of its energies. This can be the most destructive adventure. One must have direction, inspiration, impression, and a sensitivity to respond to the calls of everlasting principles.

Power destroys itself if it is not used for the welfare and progress of all that exists. Once power is used for selfish, separative reasons, the power increases your weight and smashes you against the rock. That is what happened to many civilizations which boasted about their knowledge, power, and technology.

It is the heart that shows the path of unending progress and the infinite glory waiting for all of us.

57

Thought and the Three Worlds

When we emphasize the importance of thought, we must explain that pure thought is the measure of our understanding and also its definition.

We have three worlds. The degree of our understanding is the result of our relationship with these three worlds:

1. Our relationship with the invisible world — and with impressions and inspirations coming from that world. This is a world in which the creative energies produce ever-progressive patterns of ideas and visions and bring new revelations.

We must remember that the Higher Worlds are in a steady process of advancing toward the Cosmic Magnet. Impressions and inspirations received from the Higher Worlds expand our understanding and refine our thinking.

2. Our relationship with the world within. This world is as real as the outer world.

With this inner world we have certain relationships which can be progressively expanding and deepening. The understanding of this relationship produces our lofty thoughts.

3. The third world is the so-called outer world, the world of our five senses. Our relationship with this world creates the degree of our understanding. The outer world and our understanding of it produces our thoughts.

Thought serves as a standard alphabet by which we compose our "words" and "sentences," or it serves as the language with which we communicate further with these three worlds and have the possibility to translate them.

But when our thoughts become crystallized and petrified, accurate translation of these three worlds becomes impossible and the decline of our culture and civilization begins. A person or a nation's life is the reflection of his or its thoughts.

If our language of thoughts remains the same, we soon fall into the state which was called by the Ancients the "confusion of tongues." Crystallized thoughts and an advancing life in the three worlds — or in three directions — create a confused life.

Thoughts, instead of receiving their life from these three directions, become their own source of nourishment. Eventually, real thinking ceases to exist. What remains is only a system of stagnated thought which turns into a dry lake.

Real thinking is progressive and in harmony with the expanding worlds.

The entire life of the Existence is in progress. It is impossible to create fixed measures when the standards are continuously changing.

Unfortunately, the thinking of most of the leaders of humanity is not in harmony with the changes occurring in the three worlds. In addition, our own thinking is controlled by those mighty and crystallized thoughtforms which exist in space and do not let our minds escape their fences and think differently. These mighty thoughtforms are manufactured by those thinkers who eventually brought destruction upon the Atlantean civilization.

It is impossible to see the three worlds differently as long as thinkers in this age are under the dominion of these mighty thoughtforms and are prisoners of their measures and standards.

This means that real thinking has three Herculean labors:

1. To destroy these mighty thoughtforms existing in space and branching into the minds of people

2. To cultivate the science of thinking to such a degree that it keeps pace with the speed of expansion and change in the three worlds

3. To create those conditions in life in which it will be impossible to enslave the minds of people but will assist people to relate with the three worlds in a way that increases the joy of life in everyone

In general, we have the opinion that thoughts are like our chairs, tables, or machines, whereas real thoughts must continuously change and reflect the changes in the three worlds simultaneously.

This will not be so if the expressions of our thoughts remain the same and run in the same grooves. The expressions of our thoughts in our relationships or in the business world will produce the same world as we had millenniums before.

When thoughts gradually synchronize themselves with the progressive change of the three worlds but the *expressions* resist any change, we enter into the path of global destruction because the progressive and expanding thoughts create those ways and means by which the resistance — the crystallized culture and civilization — is destroyed.

There is strong evidence that human thought, in general, is on the way to crystallization in all fields of human endeavor. The downfall of humanity is imminent if individuals and groups do not bring new visions and inspirations to the masses of people.

There is also strong evidence that if these individuals and groups do not help humanity make a breakthrough into new dimensions of thinking, soon the crystallized thinkers will organize every kind of persecution and suffering for advanced individuals and groups in order to secure their own incomes, pleasures, and control.

People measure their evolution by what they know and do, not by what they really are. University certificates, social positions, and wealth are not indications of advancement or evolution. A person's value is in his beingness. His beingness is equal to how much Beauty, Goodness, Righteousness, Joy, and Freedom he can bring to humanity.

An understanding of life going on in higher dimensions is necessary to have new thoughts, new directions, and a new life. But when one is caught in his own crystallized thoughts, understanding will be impossible and man will be his own prisoner.

Our thinking is not only perpetuating the suffering and slavery of humanity but also providing those devices by which we perpetuate this suffering.

How can we understand the present and see the future when our thoughts are controlled by obsolete thinking? Thought that does not progress in pace with a deepening relationship with life and its understanding cannot transform life.

Transformation of life starts when people understand more and more the contacts they are having with the three worlds.

Contact is always there. Man is always in contact with the whole visible and invisible Universe, but it is the awareness and understanding of that contact which produce thought and change the phenomena of life.

Similarly, our beingness is related to the awareness and understanding of our contacts.

When our thought does not translate an ever-advancing understanding, our speed of evolution slows down and degenerates.

People use their thoughts to understand, but understanding is not the result of thoughts. It is intuitional awareness. As long as we are occupied by our crystallized thoughts, we will fail in our understanding and use of Intuition. But often people have more Intuition than the ability to think in new dimensions. Their old thoughts not only block intuitional understanding but also prevent them from following their Intuition.

Understanding of the contacts of the three worlds frees us from old thoughtforms and opens the door to a new life.

The old form of thinking must go. The old form of thinking is based on self-interest, ownership, separatism, vanity, control, egotism, exploitation, gain, and loss.

These nine evils have been crippling human life and human relationships for 18,000,000 years, in spite of those who at the cost of their lives have fought against these nine evils.

Understanding is not the result of knowledge and experience. It is the evoked result of a person who loves his fellowmen, tries to sacrifice his life, and brings joy to humanity. Only such souls have an understanding of what is going on within the three worlds. Understanding is a gift.

Every self-centered thought brings suffering and pain because the creative energies in Nature are selfless; they are for all and for everything. A selfish thought creates storms in the network of the circulating energies, and such storms hit those who created them.

The creative energies of the Universe uplift, illuminate, and bring happiness and prosperity to those who live for the Common Good with self-forgetfulness, harmlessness, and right speech and express deep gratitude and spiritual containment.

58
Thought and Effects

One must try to see the effects of his thoughts on his feelings, emotions, heart, on his physical body, and on the mood of the people around him.

It is important to learn to see the effects of one's own thoughts. But we are seldom able to see the effects of our thoughts on the physical plane until after a long time passes.

Often we forget that most of the conditions of our life and the responses or reactions of other people are the effects of our past thoughts.

When we begin to see the effects of our thoughts, we become more conscious of our thoughts, and a time comes in which we develop a system of censorship over our thoughts. We learn not only to see what they can do, but we can also control them, change them, and even destroy them if we feel their effects will be destructive.

Thoughts in the mental world are as objective and tangible as the furniture we build. We cannot see what they really are because we are not focused yet in the mental world, but we use mental substance through our mind.

Once the negative tendency of the mind is broken, it turns into a positive source of creative activity.

Most of the "furniture" of our thoughts float around us, sucking our vital energy. They not only deprive us of our energy, but they also pollute the minds of other people and cause various damages to their systems.

In the mental world, if one is awake, he can see the immediate effects of his thoughts, and while he is formulating his thoughts he becomes careful that he does not create negative effects.

It is important to know that karmic law works in the mental plane too, and we are responsible for all those thoughts which are harmful, ugly, unrighteous, and violate the Law of Love.

One must start exercises to observe his thoughts, guess their effects, stop them, change them, and build better thoughts. One must also try to destroy certain thoughts.

Destruction of thoughtforms is not easy. The first thing one must do is create opposing thoughts to the ones which he considers dangerous and harmful. Then he must try to make his positive thoughts disintegrate the former thoughts and absorb them into the new thoughtform. This is great fun to do, and it is not so difficult if one tries hard enough.

We must remember that the reward for controlling thought is very great. It increases our health, happiness, and success, and it paves the way for contact with Higher Worlds.

Unworthy and ugly thoughts disintegrate after a while in our aura if they do not attract nourishment from various sources and if they do not contaminate our aura with various sediments. Remember that the mental body is, in most cases, affected by our physical body, and it too can be poisoned, damaged, and even paralyzed.

In the Higher Worlds, success is in the hands of those who learned right thinking while they were living in their physical bodies.

Our ugly and harmful thoughts in the Fiery World have a drastic and destructive effect on ourselves and on others. It is easier to eliminate their effects on the physical plane than in the Fiery World. This is why the great Teachers advise us to learn how to think creatively.

By watching daily the process of our thoughts, we develop alertness and watchfulness and eventually learn to control them.

59

The Thinking Process

Thinking and creativity are processes of transmutation of force into energy.

In the thinking process the brain attracts force and the mental body transmutes it into energy. In creativity the mental body draws energy and uses force to manifest the ideas.

Through thinking and meditation the mental body grows and becomes a whirlpool of energies of many colors, increasing in magnetism and electricity.

It is by this energy pool that the human soul extends lines of communication with Higher Worlds and builds a mechanism of creativity to connect the Higher Worlds to the world of human beings. Thus, thinking and meditation not only generate energy but also transform the life on earth.

Every person charged with energy is a powerful station of influential waves which protects, enlightens, encourages, and strengthens people with whom it comes in contact. Such an influence, of course, may create problems, too, in its environment. Every energy releases those elements in human nature which are antagonistic to the nature of the energy. Thus many destructive forces and elements come out of the hidden layers of man and, for a while, control his behavior.

This is why highly charged people have an instinctive urge not to mingle with crowds so as not to excite various kinds of bugs existing in their nature.

But this does not mean that the powerful and organized creative energy that highly charged people have is destructive. This energy also stimulates the latent potentials hidden in the souls of others and brings them to the path of conscious evolution.

Around highly charged people a new life comes into being. Even villages and cities are charged. Tension and turmoil are created, but then higher visions are seen and creative efforts are organized for the Common Good.

60

The Laws of Mind

As a man thinks in his heart, so he is.

Thinking programs our actions, our relationships, our body, even our inner organs: heart, stomach, kidneys, liver, and so on.

There is positive thinking and there is negative thinking.

Positive thinking is thinking in harmony with

1. Truth

2. Reality

3. Facts

and in terms of

1. Success

2. Victory

3. Achievement

4. Health

5. Beauty

6. Unity

Negative thinking is thinking in terms of

1. Falsehood

2. Deception

3. Fabrication

and in terms of

1. Failure

2. Defeat

3. Sickness

4. Ugliness

5. Depression

6. Separatism

It is a known fact that if you continuously use the mind in negative thinking you destroy the mind and make it useless. The same is true for any organ of the body. Any misuse or abuse brings bad consequences. It is exactly the same with the mind. This reveals to us the fact that *the mind is a mechanism which is created for survival, and positive thinking is thinking for survival.*

Negative thinking is a misuse of the mechanism, and it leads the mental body to destruction.

You cannot use the mind negatively and expect sanity. *This is true for every organ.* Any organ deteriorates if misused. Even if you misuse the sense organs of others, you hurt your corresponding organs.

This is a law that philosophers have not discussed yet.

The mind is programmed to think positively to aid the survival of the person. For example, if your car can only use high octane or super gasoline, when you put in regular it stops or it acts in a disorderly manner.

Every time your mechanism is refined, it needs better thoughts, better ideas, better visions to stay healthy and to work for the survival of family, nation, and humanity.

New thinking is like an upgraded computer program in your system to solve the problems arising from your advancing life conditions.

But one may ask, "Is there any new thinking?" The answer is, "Yes and no." There is no new thinking because what we are going to think has already been thought by the Thinkers of the Race throughout millions of years. But, also, for each of us it is new thinking. New thinking starts when we begin to change our negative thinking and climb the steps of positive thinking, gaining victory over our involutionary tendencies.

What are the "new" thoughts that we begin to practice and live by?

1. Humanity is one family. The problems of humanity must be solved by love, understanding, and human rights.

2. Competition is an anti-survival factor. Sharing is pro-survival.

3. Dictatorship is anti-survival. True democracy is a pro-survival technique.

4. All the resources of the earth must be used to make all people, everywhere, happy. There will no longer be deprived, homeless, or hungry people on earth.

5. The awareness unit in man never dies but lives eternally in form or out of form, and his future is destined by how he lived in the past and how he lives in the present.

6. The purpose of a person is to reveal and actualize the highest possibilities latent in him or her.

7. Meditation is a great tool. Meditation pulls you up from the lower centers and interests, enlightens you, and makes you more inclusive. The more inclusive you are in your thinking, the more possibility there is for you to think constructively and creatively.

8. The light of responsibility must guide the thinking of man.

9. Positive thinking can be developed and cultivated by assimilating the Laws of the Mind.

Laws of the Mind

1. Energy follows thought.

2. Mental fire increases with right usage.

3. Mental fire is faster than light and sound.

4. Concentration gives power to the mind.

5. Visualization builds the way.

6. Mental fire transmits words, images, and ideas over distance.

7. Thoughtforms evoke similar thoughtforms.

8. Thoughts build our future bodies.

9. Thoughts provide nourishment for devas.

10. Thought and rhythm carry psychic energy.

11. Higher thoughts have a greater harmony of colors.

12. Question and answer instantaneously follow each other in the mind, though the brain may register them later.

13. Physical conditions and emotional states affect the formation of thoughtforms.

14. Spirituality and enthusiasm affect mental activities.

15. Mental activities are affected by electricity, magnetism, and electromagnetic disturbances.

16. Certain chemicals and noise disturb the brain and affect the mind.

17. Good sleep strengthens the mind.

18. Rejection of facts by others makes the mental energy of the one presenting the facts more powerful.

19. Problems, difficulties, pain, and suffering create those conditions in which the mind awakens.

20. Joy and achievement make the mind more creative.

21. Thoughts affect the whole atmosphere of the mental body of the planet.

22. Without the supervision of a Teacher, the mind defeats itself. The Teacher or higher principles must control all our mental activities.

23. The mind destroys or builds; destruction and construction are mental qualities.

24. The mind develops by studying *opposites*. Discrimination is the power to find the path leading to the Real.

25. No physical object can hinder the current of a thought stream.

26. Emotion can disturb the current of a thought stream, disfigure it, or even disassemble it.

27. Opposing thoughts strengthen the thoughts.

28. Non-opposing thoughts with truth and rhythm can decompose a thoughtform.

29. Thoughts are projected by the willpower, assisted by visualization and concentration.

30. The atmosphere of the location where thoughtforms are built can affect the building process, for example if antagonistic thought formations or articles are used by those not sympathetic to the new thoughtforms. Sages suggest to have empty and newly built rooms for thought experiments.

31. Each center in the etheric, astral, and mental bodies can be used as a bow for projecting the thoughtforms. The higher the center, the more powerful is the effect of the thoughtforms.

32. Guilt feelings, an agitated conscience, and ugly memories weaken the formulation and projection of higher thoughtforms.

33. Thoughts always have their opposites, and opposing thoughts can call out their hidden correspondences.

34. Thoughts that are charged with the rhythm of the Cosmic Magnet eventually destroy the thoughts loaded with ego, vanity, separatism, self-interest, fear, anger, hatred, jealousy, revenge, and betrayal.

35. Thoughts are electromagnetic. Hence, electromagnetic energies or waves have a strong influence on them. Sometimes they not only distract the thought currents but may even totally paralyze them.

36. Electrical and magnetic storms scatter the seeds of insanity and crime.

37. Thought is strongly affected by radio towers. People living in the vicinity of radio towers not only will gradually lose their health but also their sanity. There is also danger from electric lines and towers.

38. Sound and noise deeply affect the thought process. For example, mechanical noise, especially airplane noise, or ultrasonic noise destroys etheric, astral, and mental centers and even affects genes.

39. Higher thinking is impossible or extremely difficult in a polluted atmosphere.

40. Higher thinking is also very difficult in places where blood was shed or where the furniture was used or the rooms were occupied by murderers.

41. Thought associated with emotions loses its speed.

42. Thought associated with intuitional energy not only flies faster but also travels a long distance.

43. Thought multiplies at a very high speed and sticks to all objects of your room or to all objects you touch. Thoughts stay a long time, even centuries with the objects.

44. Once your thoughts are born, they are extremely free to belong to and influence other people.

45. Our ugly or beautiful thoughts are used by various entities as their food or as their vehicles of contact.

46. Higher and beautiful thoughts are used by angels and devas. Lower and ugly thoughts are used by dark forces, astral corpses, and by astral or etheric entities.

47. Mental matter connects you to those places which you have visited or thought about.

48. By using the energy of the mind it is possible to destroy the nests of malignant and malicious thoughts.

49. Mental energy builds the consciousness thread when the mental energy is pure and charged with psychic energy.

50. Harmful thoughts go and hit the aura of the victim and penetrate into it if the victim is full of hatred. However, it bounces back with increased speed and penetrates the aura of the person who sent it if the victim is charged with love and joy. The returned arrow hits the subject in the areas where the thought originated.

Thoughtforms differ in their constitution and appearance.

Advancing thoughtforms have spheric forms with bright cores and harmonious colors.

Thoughtforms of lower qualities have sharp edges, are mousy gray, brown, and other faint colors. Sometimes they are ragged, like clouds in precipitation.

Evil thoughtforms have a black nozzle and move in a certain direction with a trembling motion.

Thoughtforms have various substances:

- mental-etheric

- mental-astral

- higher and lower mental

- higher mental

All thoughtforms carry the characteristics of our motives, thoughts, feelings, emotions, words or conversations, and actions.

It is very interesting that lawmakers gradually are going to create not only better laws for the physical plane life but also emotional plane laws and mental plane laws.

Emotional plane laws are mostly given by religion, but there is no legal recognition or execution of these laws.

The mental laws are touched on by philosophy and given by the Ageless Wisdom, but again they are not recognized legally or executed legally.

When these three spheres of law include each other and are practiced simultaneously, then *"Purpose will guide the little wills of men."*

Actually, each plane has the same law adapted to its specific level.

It is also necessary to simplify the laws. Simplification of laws takes place when one understands the higher correspondences of laws on ever higher levels. For example,

Physical law says:	Do not kill.
Emotional law says:	Do not hate.
Mental law says:	Do not be separative.

If the mental law is understood, the emotional law will be simple to understand and the physical law will not be necessary because when one understands the higher laws, he will not commit murder.

In most cases, physical laws are not formulated in the light of higher laws.

A law that does not have higher correspondences is an imposition of the interests of certain parties. It is temporary.

We must remember that man lives in the three planes simultaneously but often not consciously. He cannot live under laws that are different. The more the laws of the physical and emotional planes are in accord with the mental laws, the more enjoyable will be the journey of the soul.

Violation of laws on various levels creates reactions by the Guardians of Law.

A violation of mental law gradually forces a man to violate the laws of the emotional plane and the laws of the physical plane.

It is interesting to know that people are punished legally for their violations of the laws of the physical plane. But this punishment does not help them to stop violating the corresponding laws on higher planes.

It is important that the corresponding higher laws are taught in our schools. It is important to explain to the students how the violation of higher laws brings them punishment, and then explain to them how to avoid such a punishment.

There is also the Law of the Heart, the Law of Conscience, or the Voice of Silence that naturally suggests and reveals why a law on any plane must not be broken. If the heart is awake, an explanation of the law and why the law must be obeyed will be unnecessary because the Light of the Heart will guide the person in such a way that he naturally will not violate the laws.

The Law of the Heart is not mundane. It is connected to the laws of Higher Worlds.

Those who are connected with higher spheres understand and obey all genuine laws.

People think that a violation of emotional and mental laws escapes notice. It does not because, first, the echoes or consequences are heard and seen in lower planes. Also, the violation is observed by the Inner Courts and actions are taken for correction.

Violations of mental laws, if not corrected, result in mental disturbances which affect all lower levels with corresponding problems.

Violations of emotional laws, if not corrected, create severe disturbances on all levels.

People pay for at least seven lives for the violation of the mental laws. For the other violations people pay taxes for shorter periods. It is also true that one can pay higher level taxes for the lower level violations.

When people speak about laws, certain concepts come into their mind such as

1. punishment

2. pain

3. suffering

4. imprisonment

5. death

But the law does not really exist to punish the violators but to

1. educate them

2. transform them

3. expand their consciousness

4. bring the joy of righteousness to them

5. cause illumination in them

Righteousness is a state of consciousness of a person who lives harmoniously with the laws of the physical, emotional, and mental worlds, enlightened by the Law of the Heart.

Illumination is the moment when you clearly see the correlation and similarity of the laws on all planes.

There is a law called the Law of Reception and Delivery which has a subsidiary law called Readiness. This law demands that you make yourself continuously ready to live a progressive life, to receive enough energy, light, and fire in order to meet the needs of the field where you are.

The Law of Readiness demands that your mechanisms be totally ready to handle the currents of pressures of Light, Love, and Power and use them in right proportion and dosage in the field of labor, decided by the power of discrimination.

The Law of Readiness is the law that makes you adapt yourself progressively to higher laws, especially in Intuitional and still loftier Planes.

61
Thought and Impression

Our thoughts are mostly the responses or reactions to impressions. The higher the impressions are, the higher the thoughts. Actually, thoughts formulate the impressions, qualify them, and make them useful in our daily life.

An expanding consciousness receives higher impressions and builds higher thoughts. Thoughts are charged by the fire of consciousness and by the power of impressions.

There is a great science used by high-degree Initiates which gradually will be given to disciples and aspirants of the world as they prepare themselves and are ready for it. This science is called the Science of Contact. It has three main branches which are called

— the Science of Impression

— the Science of Invocation and Evocation

— the Science of Telepathy

Through the Science of Impression the human soul or the group mind is impressed by higher directions coming from planetary, solar, galactic, and zodiacal sources.

Through the Science of Invocation and Evocation man comes in contact with the Hierarchy and with Great Ones; he penetrates into the mysteries of the Hierarchical Plan and translates his experiences through his mind.

Through the Science of Telepathy a man comes in contact with another man who is living on this planet, whether it be a simple man or a Master. Telepathy is carried on mostly through the lower mind and head center.

In the Science of Impression, will energy is used. In the Science of Invocation and Evocation, love energy is used. In the Science of Telepathy, the mind or human intelligence is used.

We are told that permission must be obtained from higher sources to practice the art of impressing. This permission is given when a disciple is able to function in his Triadal awareness and is able to attend the Ashrams of the Great Ones. It is in the protection of the aura of the Ashrams that the impressions from Shamballa are received by the disciple and used according to the Plan of the

Hierarchy. It is through the received impressions that the human consciousness creates thoughtforms or vitalizes the existing thoughtforms and give them the needed direction.

Thoughts are fiery energies, and they can create great changes in the minds and lives of people. If they are used through the glamors, illusions, and blind urges of people, they become very destructive and hinder the evolution of people. This is the reason why the higher impressions, which carry with them a tremendous charge or voltage of energy, are received only by those who can function in the Ashrams and receive these charges within the protective aura of the Ashrams.

After the disciple proves his harmlessness and freedom from personality interests, he gains permission to exercise the art of impressing other minds or the mind of a group of people. The keynote of all service is purity, and purity is achieved through Transfiguration, after which no personal element can interfere with the course of the spiritual service.

Through the Science of Impression, man comes in contact with the Spiritual Triad and with Shamballa and receives impressions from the Purpose through his abstract mind and lower mind. The abstract mind is a part of the Spiritual Triad, which is formed by the Mental, Intuitional, and Atmic Permanent Atoms. On the Intuitional Plane we have the Ashrams, and on the Atmic Plane we have greater Centers of Wisdom which work for the Purpose.

The difference between the three sciences is as follows:

1. In the Science of Impression, the person deals with impressions that are not formulated initially. Impressions are radiations coming from Shamballa. They are mostly on the line of Will and Purpose, and they carry a great voltage of energy and create a new polarization within man toward higher values, synthesis, and future.

These vibrations reach the Spiritual Triad and, passing through the Lotus and the mind, are translated into human terms to meet human and group needs. They are always translated in terms of direction, higher values, synthesis, and future. If a man creates under such impressions, his creative expressions — no matter what form they take — will have the charge of direction, higher values, synthesis, and future.

2. In the Science of Invocation and Evocation we have the process of asking, expecting, demanding, and responding, answering, or replying. In this process we have, on the one hand, the human being, and on the other hand, the Hierarchy. We invoke Hierarchy through our prayers, meditation, and spiritual aspiration, and Hierarchy answers our call. This answer is called evocation, the answer we expect from Higher Beings.

Invocation uses mostly love energy and evokes love from Hierarchical sources and from the souls of all living forms. It is the human soul who invokes, and the Solar Angel passes on this invocation to the Christ and to the Hierarchy.

Invocation is done by the human soul, who uses the lower mind and seeks the assistance of "words of power" or mantrams, invocations, and prayers.

It is possible to evoke from sources higher than Hierarchical sources. The process is the same: Your Solar Angel passes the invocation to Christ or to the Hierarchy; the Hierarchy passes your demand to still Higher Sources; and when the evocation comes forth, it reaches you through the same channels.

3. In the Science of Telepathy we have formulated clear-cut messages from one point and clear reception of the message by the other point. Telepathy is done within the field of humanity, and mainly the head center is used for the telepathic process, message, and reception.

It is interesting to note that these three words — impression, invocation or evocation, and telepathy — are used in the general sense and also in the specific sense. We always receive impressions through our senses and send impressions to others, but this is done in the general sense. In their specific sense, impressions are those vibrations which reach us from Shamballa. Of course, Shamballa receives those impressions from higher sources, but It is the main source of distribution of impressions for our planet.

When a man enters the Fourth Initiation, he begins to receive impressions from higher sources.

Similarly, the term invocation and evocation is used in a general sense and in a specific sense. For example, when any demand, question, or expectation receives a certain answer, reply, or evocation, we say that there is invocation and evocation between man and any object, between man and God, between man and Cosmos. But in its specific usage, it refers to the invocative and evocative process going on between the human soul, humanity, and the Hierarchy.

Similarly, the word telepathy has its general and specific usage. In its general use, man can have telepathic communication with his Soul, with his Master, with entities, or with people incarnate or discarnate. But in its specific usage, telepathy refers to the process of definite relationship going on between man and man, between man and his teachers, or between any living persons.

In the Science of Impression, we first have the vibration or radiation of a center or the mind of an Entity. This vibration is translated into impressions when any other unit responds or reacts to it. At the moment of response or reaction, the vibration or radiation is recorded as an impression.

Generally, the distribution of radiatory vibration is conducted through the center which is the link between the planet and the solar system.

Impressions are translated according to what the man is at the moment of reception. Also, it is often true that the impression does not submit itself to any form of formulation or translation and it becomes, according to the great Teacher, an "impulsive energy." The impulsive energy is like an urge which directs the life expression of man according to the received vibrations or impressions. The impulsive energy galvanizes the thoughts, words, and actions of the man and leads them into certain directions.

Impressions reach our globe from Sirius via Shamballa. We are told the entire Council of Shamballa must be prepared to be ready as a group to receive these impressions.

We also receive impressions from various constellations at appropriate astrological moments when our globe links with certain constellations, at the time of the full moon and the new moon, or at the time of the release of the energy of Shamballa. Such impressions are received when the majority of the Council Chamber of Shamballa are present.

We also receive impressions from two other planets when they form a triangle of energy with our earth. This energy is transmitted from Shamballa to Hierarchy through three Great Lords, the three Buddhas of Activity.

Impressions also come to us from Venus, which is the Solar Angel of our earth. These impressions are received by Sanat Kumara and three other members of the Great Council.

The Hierarchy receives impressions from Shamballa as Shamballa, through some members of the Great Council, steps down the impressions received from higher sources and passes them to the Hierarchy. Shamballa translates the impressions received from higher sources into the Purpose. Hierarchy takes the impressions of the Purpose and formulates the Plan.

In critical times or at the time of full moons — especially the Wesak Full Moon — Great Lives send Their impressions to guide humanity. The impressions to the Hierarchy are transmitted from Shamballa to the Hierarchy by some Great Lives Who are called Divine Contemplatives. We are also told that Buddha transmits Shamballic impressions to the Hierarchy at the time of the Wesak Festival.[1]

Hierarchy, in Its turn, impresses humanity through ideas, visions, and Teachings. The Ashrams of the Hierarchy individually send impressions to the members of the Ashrams. The New Group of World Servers impresses humanity through new visions, new ideas, and new revelations.

Thus, from very high sources the impressions are received by Shamballa and eventually transmitted to average humanity. We can say that man lives, moves, and has his being in an ocean of impressions. And if his sense of direction, his sense of universality, and his sense of synthesis are open and active, he will be able to receive these impressions and translate them through the petals of the Lotus and live as a source of energy, love-wisdom, and active intelligence.

These impressions are translated according to the nature of the vehicles and Rays. Each Ray translates the impressions according to the field which is created by the Ray. For example, if one has a predominant First Ray, the impressions are translated as politics. If the First Ray is the personality Ray, the politics will be

---

1.   For further information see *Telepathy and the Etheric Vehicle*, pp. 41-51, by Alice A. Bailey.

related to self-interest or national interest. If the First Ray is the Soul Ray, the politics will be related to humanity, with all-embracing inclusiveness.

It must be emphasized that impressions are energy, and if the energy is not received, assimilated, and radiated properly, it creates congestion, destruction, and degeneration. Humanity blocks new impressions through its illusions, glamors, maya, and egotistical vanities and pride. It is this blockage that is responsible for the unhappy and dangerous condition of the world. This blockage occurs not only in individuals but also in groups and nations, causing greater distress for themselves and for others.

Disciples first must try to register the impressions consciously and be aware of their emanating source. Second, they must meditate or contemplate upon the recorded impressions and change them into ideas. Third, ideas must be changed into thoughtforms, words, and actions.

We must remember that impressions radiated out from higher sources are cyclic. As ages pass, their voltage increases. They radiate different aspects of their source and are intended to bring new changes in lower planes. This is why, when Initiates and disciples learn the Science of Impression, they will be the vanguards of new cultures and new civilizations and will present the new and discard all that is obsolete in the life of humanity.

Every cycle will bring a fresh current of energy, and humanity will have the opportunity to climb steadily on its path of evolution, if the transmitters and recipients of impressions are awake, active, and creative.

It is very important to know that in order to receive impressions we must develop psychological insulation from all the subconscious mental and astral currents of others. If present, they disturb the process of reception and cause a great deal of distortion in the formulation of the impressions. It is even possible that discarnate entities or forces of the left-hand path can interfere and mislead the person.

To avoid these dangers, one must try to build the Antahkarana and focus his consciousness within the higher mind. When the Antahkarana is built, the Spiritual Triad becomes the receiver of impressions; the twelve-petaled Lotus qualifies the impressions in terms of will, love, and light. Then the threefold head center receives these impressions, and the ajna center translates them according to the Ray quality and the stage of evolution of the human soul.

The Solar Angel takes part in the process of reception. Usually It resides in the Spiritual Triad and amplifies it to increase and clear the receptivity. The human soul lives in the twelve-petaled Chalice and controls the head, ajna, and throat centers. The real translation occurs in the heart; the heart registers the impressions as the impulsive energy.

It is possible to receive telepathic messages from higher sources, such as from Shamballa or extraplanetary or solar sources. But these messages are formulated words or symbols which have a definite meaning.

Impressions coming from any source do not have *formulations* until the receiving agent translates them according to his own capacity and beingness.

Thus, it is possible to receive a telepathic message from the Hierarchy or from Shamballa, as well as to receive impressions from these sources. The difference is very subtle, and not so many can differentiate because any time they register an impression, it changes itself and becomes a formulated message. This is where an inexperienced aspirant fails.

Masters utilize the Science of Impression among Themselves and in relation to higher sources. This helps Them to translate things, not from the angle of receiver, but from the angle of projector.

Intuition develops rapidly if people make themselves sensitive to impressions and try to grasp the sender's intention rather than his own formulation. Intuition also develops when the human soul tries to contact intuitional ideas and translate them through thoughts. This can be called a kind of intuitional telepathy. Intuitional telepathy is related to the direction of groups, to the plan of the service of the group, and to the Teaching that the group can spread.

A telepathic message is received through the Antahkarana extending between the mental unit and the Mental Permanent Atom. Impressions are received from higher sources through the higher counterpart of the Rainbow Bridge, extending between the Mental Permanent Atom and the Monad. The most evident difference between these two sciences is the difference between the receiving mechanisms.

Another difference is that impressions carry down the Will, Purpose, and energy. Telepathy carries down the Plan and ideas, but both impressions and telepathy are eventually presented by *thoughts*.

A thought is the formulation of a telepathically transmitted idea or vision. A thought is also the formulation of an impression received through the higher counterpart of the Antahkarana. When the telepathic transmission or impression is received and registered by the Self on the mental plane, thought is created and the consciousness is expanded. When the impression is met and registered on the Intuitional or higher Planes by the Self, the awareness of the Self is expanded and new ideas are put into manifestation.

As it is possible to receive telepathic messages from higher sources, it is also possible to receive, through the lower Antahkarana, lower impressions. For example, one may receive impressions from his physical, emotional, and mental elementals, from art objects, from objects used by other people. It is also possible to receive impressions from the lower mind and from the mental unit, where lots of subconscious elements exist. But all these impressions are not really related to the Science of Impression, which is technically related to impressions received by the higher counterpart of the Antahkarana.

The registrations of impressions are like *feelings*, but they are not emotional feelings; they are intuitive, atmic, monadic, and divine feelings. The registration of an impression is like an experience of ecstasy, an expansion of awareness, a contact with Infinity, and a fusion with the future. The registration of telepathy is a formulated thought, a definite word, phrase, or instruction.

Impression is a continuum and is related to an expanding synthesis. Telepathy is related to time and the need of the present or future.

Impressions are the messengers of Infinity. Thoughts are an attempt to translate such impressions. Thoughts are bonfires on the path of greater joy and achievement.

As a man unfolds and progresses, he contacts higher vibrations, higher impressions. The translation of these impressions is equal to the development of the aura of the man. Man translates them according to what he is at that particular time of reception. But the human soul sees the deeper level of impressions which challenge him to surpass his own level. This challenge becomes a *vision,* a *purpose,* a *plan,* then a *program.*

The impressions that we record are conditioned by our aura. In the aura are found our glamors, illusions, emotions, and various thoughtforms. All these condition our impressions. A relatively clean aura is like a magnetic receiver for higher impressions.

Impressions challenge all that you are. The impression is always there. It is you who must contact, translate, and use it according to what you are. It is your beingness that receives impressions, not your forms of knowledge.

To challenge means to evoke, to call forth your beingness out of the traps it is in. The beauty and the goodness that are entrapped by your emotions and thoughts sense the call and come out into expression.

The Science of Impression leads us toward individual, group, national, global, and universal synthesis. Eventually we become aware that we are in a living Universe. The Science of Impression leads us to be conscious on higher planes. Impressions build the line of contact with higher planes, bring fusion, and then allow us to have control on the higher planes.

As we come in contact with higher impressions we develop

Intuition — pure discrimination

Sense of direction

Sense of universality

Sense of synthesis

Every impression is related to

1. friction

2. the transmitting mechanisms

3. the registrar

4. the translator

5. the analyzer or interpreter

1. **Friction** may occur between the impression and our aura. Everything that comes to us passes through our aura. This means that the quality and purity of impressions depend upon the evolution and purity of our aura.

2. The **transmitting mechanisms** are

- etheric body

- nadis

- centers

- nervous system

- brain

Centers are found on etheric, astral, and mental levels. Nadis are the etheric counterpart of the nervous system.

3. The **registrar** is the etheric and dense brain.

4. The **translator** is the mind, our Rays, our education, our background, our tradition, intellect, consciousness, and the need of the time. The need and the level condition our translation.

We receive a telegram and our child says, "What does it say, Daddy?" And we translate the message to him in a way he understands. Similarly, many impressions are registered by our Higher Realms, but they are translated through what we are on lower planes.

A great amount of impressions remain unexpressed through our lower nature. We must also remember that impressions are affected not only by human receptivity but also by astrological configurations, atmospheric conditions, solar winds, and electric storms in space. The content of the planetary aura also has a decisive influence upon our receptivity.

Before impressions come to us, they pass through the planetary aura and the planetary etheric body. This means that impressions lose their purity, velocity, and power in passing through the increasingly polluted aura or atmosphere of the earth. This is how humanity eventually loses the directions coming from higher sources.

To overcome such accumulations of dark thought, negative emotions, pollution of the air, and noise pollution, the Hierarchy of Light sends Its Messengers every time humanity cuts itself off from higher direction.

We are told that the planetary aura is polluted to such a degree that devas, who used to assist human evolution, are planning to leave the earth. Unless extreme measures are taken to eliminate the pollution of thought, sound, and toxins, the earth will not be able to provide life to all living beings.

When the same impression comes to seven people who have seven different Rays, each will translate the impression according to his or her corresponding field of human endeavor. For example, the First Ray will translate the impression as politics. The Second Ray will translate it as psychology or education. The Third Ray will translate it as communication or philosophy. The Fourth Ray will translate it as art and beauty. The Fifth Ray will translate it as science. The Sixth Ray will translate it as devotion or religion. The Seventh Ray will translate it as ceremony, relationship, or economy.

This is the difference between telepathy and impression. In impression you translate things as *you are*. In telepathy you have one choice: to get the message as it is.

An impression can be translated by one man in seven different ways if he is a Seventh Degree Initiate or if his seven etheric centers are fully awake. Such a man, from the viewpoint of our Planetary Life, is a *perfect man*.

If you are not an initiate, you do not translate the impression but reflect it or react to it. There are three stages:

a) Reaction. You feel uncomfortable, sick; you even develop various difficulties in your threefold nature.

b) Response. You feel happy, joyful, expanded, and energetic.

c) Translation. You start translating the direction of the impression, creating those mental, emotional, and physical forms which are able to transmit the voltage and the direction of the impression. The sign of translation is the increasing creativity of the man.

In translation man tries to tune himself to the source of the impression.

When an impression comes, you see the need and you have a problem. If you are evolving, you analyze the problem and meet it from increasing viewpoints, according to your degree of initiation.

If you solve a problem from one viewpoint, you create other problems. If you solve a problem from three viewpoints, you are solving the problem from physical, emotional, and mental angles but creating a problem from the spiritual angle. The problem is totally solved when you approach it from seven different viewpoints, at least from the level of the Planetary Life. This is so because the need has disappeared in perfection.

Man is called the "son of necessity," a very strange name. Man is himself the problem. All that man is subconsciously doing is trying to solve himself. The solution is perfection.

The average man looks at the world from his own interests only. A little advanced man is a two-branched man. He uses the world for his and others' material and emotional interests.

When he is a Third Degree Initiate he has three branches. He is in equilibrium. He uses the world for his and others' interests, and for the interests of all, but only from the viewpoint of physical, emotional, and mental interests.

A Fourth Degree Initiate has four branches, and he tries to solve problems in four different ways: physical, emotional, mental, and intuitional. He tries to solve problems from the viewpoint of the man, the group, the nation, and humanity in the light of the Hierarchy or of the Plan.

A Fifth Degree Initiate tries to solve problems through the five-pointed star. He solves problems in the light of the *Purpose.*

A Sixth Degree Initiate solves problems from the solar viewpoint.

A Seventh Degree Initiate solves problems from the Cosmic viewpoint. At this stage problems are dissolved, or they do not breed further problems as all viewpoints are taken care of.

5. Then we have the **analyzer or interpreter**. The analyzer is different from the translator. You send a message to me in Sanskrit and someone translates it for me. It says, "Come for dinner." This is translation.

The analyzer searches for the purpose of the message, *why* you are inviting me for dinner. The analyzer is the human soul, wherever the soul is found to be. The human soul is sometimes identified with the physical body, with the blind urges and drives of the physical body, and when that is the situation, he analyzes the message in that level. Such an analysis is not correct or perfect.

In a slightly advanced degree, the human soul translates the message through the glamors of the astral body. In a more advanced stage, he translates the message through the illusions of the mental body or through his ego and selfish interests.

He analyzes the message in the right way when he looks at it through the light of the Intuition. It is now the human soul analyzing the message without any distortion or disturbances.

All our engrams, complexes, hypnotic suggestions, and commands try to analyze the message for us, and we innocently follow their instructions and enter into greater problems. Thus when the translator is not emancipated from the personality limitations and has not entered into the intuitional light, he cannot analyze the message correctly.

Our progress and success, or our retardation and failure, depend upon how we translate the message. Most of the time the analyzer is our sex, stomach, pride, vanity, greed, fear, hatred, jealousy, and anger.

The analyzer is in a very subtle position, and if you find out who is the analyzer, you can have better control of your life.

We analyze things according to what we are, according to what level we are, according to where our focus of consciousness is. If the analyzer is free of maya, glamors, and illusions, he eventually makes a contact with the source of the impression and thus raises the level of his beingness.

Your existence is equal to the extent of your contact. The greater the contact you have, the greater is your beingness and the higher your level.

The purpose of existence is to bloom. Seeds, or Monads, must bloom and become stars. . . . That is the goal of existence as far as a man caught in the physical prison can see. Either we must grow. . .or suffer. In growing we increase our joy and bliss. In failing to grow, we increase our pains.

You are a locked bit of Space. You are a bubble in the ocean. If you think you are a bubble, you are separate. If you think you are the ocean, you are the Whole.

Any irritation distorts the impression and misleads the analyzer.

In the reception of impressions, the centers play a great role.[2] The centers closely related to the reception of impression are

       1. the solar plexus

       2. the heart center

       3. the head center

The solar plexus is a six pointed star:

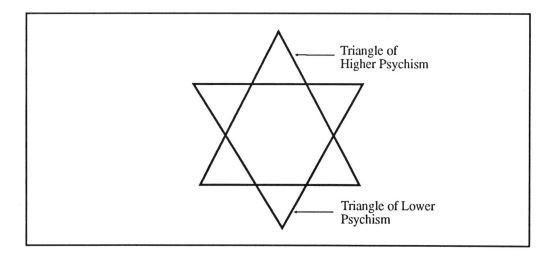

Diagram 61-1 Solar Plexus Center

    The lower triangle is related to lower psychism. The higher triangle is related to the sources where the light of intelligence rules. The heart center receives

---

2.   See also *New Dimensions in Healing* on centers.

impressions from sources where the fire of love rules. The head center receives impressions from sources where the electricity of willpower rules.

The solar plexus center is developed by aspiration.

The heart center is developed by efforts toward inclusiveness. As you develop more inclusiveness, you unfold your heart center.

Compassion to all living forms unfolds the heart center. If you are doing something criminal and harmful, you are disturbing and blocking your heart center. If you are doing anything against the Law of Love, you are killing your heart. Hatred, jealousy, various crimes against people, exploitation, robbery, and so on all petrify the petals of the heart center.

Even if you are killing bugs, you are proving that bugs are more intelligent than you are. In killing you are building karma. It is better to find a way to repel them, proving that you have greater intelligence than they have.

Hatred and separatism create those conditions in which the germs of destruction grow.

People tried to solve their problems by killing each other, but it did not work. Our intention will not be to kill, but to

1. repel

2. discipline

3. educate

4. transform

5. cooperate

6. unite

The head center is developed by using willpower or conquering difficulties in life.

Many barriers distort or prevent the reception of impressions. In such a state we cannot record impressions, translate them in the right way, analyze them, and use them. We also waste energy by various means. When energy is lacking, we either cannot register impressions or we cannot translate or analyze them or put them into practical application.

We prevent the reception of impressions by

1. Drugs, alcohol, too much sugar, things that slow and obscure our consciousness

2. Waste of energy through excessive sex

3. Watching television without discrimination

4. Too much talk

5. Exhaustive physical labor

6. Living in noise

7. Living in smog

8. Labor without sleep

9. Too much waste of time for pleasures

Energy is the transmitter of impressions. The higher and greater your energy, the more accurate your registration of impressions. You must decide what is right for you according to the signs of your body and emotional and mental states.

You can eliminate these barriers if you find out how much they hurt your mechanism. For example, if you are indulging in these nine barriers and similar ones, you will find out that

1. You are losing your energy or strength. Your knees, fingers, and legs will feel weaker.

2. You are becoming more pessimistic.

3. You are losing your joy, the clarity of your mind, voice, and vision.

4. You are having problems with your digestion.

If you are careful with the above nine barriers, your reception of impressions will increase and you will be more creative in your expressions.

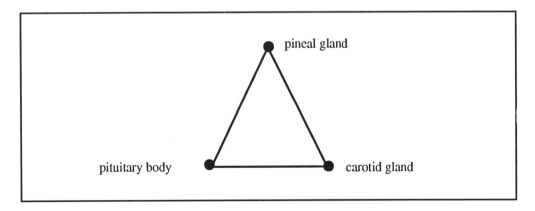

Diagram 61-2   Three Head Glands

The higher mechanism of reception of impressions is formed by the pineal gland, the pituitary body, and the carotid gland. These three form a higher mechanism for reception with their etheric counterparts — the head center, ajna center, and alta major center.

The magnetic field of these three centers receives distorted messages or distorts the received message when a person uses marijuana or hallucinogenic drugs. Also, marijuana may dry up and petrify the pineal gland.[3]

One also needs emotional purification to receive impressions. Too much excitement prevents good reception. Try to avoid agitation, irritation, and glamor. When a man is identified with the objects of his desires, he becomes an effect and tends to translate the impressions in terms of his selfish interests.

Mental purification is necessary to receive impressions in a clear and undistorted way. Mental barriers are illusions, which are distorted facts or truths. They are a mistranslation of reality. When the mental body is not clear of push-buttons, commands, posthypnotic suggestions, and illusions, the message will barely be recorded, and if recorded it will be misused in various ways by all these barriers.

Impressions bring the Direction of your Inner Lord and the planetary, solar, and galactic Lives Who challenge you to harmonize your steps with the Direction. If your mental body is not clear, your translation is wrong. And when the translation is wrong, the analysis is wrong.

When we receive higher impressions, they decentralize us. They give us a more synthetic outlook, a holistic approach to life, and our interests become related to the interests of greater wholes. This is how virtues are developed.

There are millions of impressions around us. How must we avoid the interference of these frequencies while we are tuned to a special flow of impressions? The answer is that as we raise the focus of our consciousness, we begin to receive higher frequencies, and eventually we learn how to turn our receiver on and off. It is all related to frequencies, and we do not get disturbed when we turn on our mechanism and tune it to the frequency we want.

Silence is the ability either to be undisturbed by lower frequencies or to be flooded by higher frequencies. Silence is obtained when you know how to choose special stations and bypass others.

Impressions are not the Intuition. Intuition is the ability to have a comprehensive and total understanding about

- the nature of impressions

- the source of impressions

- the possible effect of impressions

---

3.   See also lecture video by Torkom Saraydarian: "Why Drugs Are Dangerous."

When all these are grasped and seen clearly, you have Intuition.

Imagination based on attachment and fear creates huge obstacles and hindrances on the path of impressions. Every time we imagine, we form an astral and lower mental image within our aura. Sometimes this image stays there; sometimes it travels around us; and if one is trying to catch an impression, the impression is not received clearly because of the static created by the image.

For example, somebody calls you and for certain reasons you get angry. After the conversation is over, you go through an imaginative trip. You imagine yourself scolding him and saying nasty words. You imagine yourself taking revenge on him in certain ways, and so on. All these images are like a movie which is printed in your aura, and, whether you like it or not, they become conditioning factors in your aura and affect the way you receive the impressions and *the way you react to them.*

Other obstacles to impressions are wrong actions. Wrong actions are those actions which

1. your conscience does not approve of

2. are against Beauty, Goodness, and Truth

3. are harmful

4. are selfish

5. are done under hypnotic suggestion

When you see that your actions are approved by your conscience, they are in harmony with Beauty, Goodness, and Truth. If they are harmless, beneficial, selfless, and conscious, then you have right action.

People think that they are not responsible for the actions they take under posthypnotic suggestions. This is not true; a man is responsible for his conscious and unconscious actions. Actions are judged by their effects.

Those who think that the goal or the motive justifies the means are in illusion. A wrong means creates unending effects and eventually undermines the supposedly good goal for which the actions were taken.

One can find a right means to reach a right goal. Wrong means are like worms in the goal, and eventually they destroy the goal. All fanaticism, totalitarianism, and dictatorship are justified as being right means to reach a higher goal. Fanaticism, totalitarianism, dictatorship, and crimes undermine the goals they supposedly reach. Any means not based on your conscience, on Beauty, Goodness, and Truth, on harmlessness and selflessness is the disguised enemy of the goal for which it is used.

Signs of Contact with Great Ones

If a man is in contact with a Great One or serving as His messenger for humanity, he knows that two signs are present:

1. The Great One does not give a Teaching on the kindergarten level. All those who want a new Teaching have to assimilate the Teaching already given. He has no time to repeat and waste time with children. Senior disciples can dictate preparatory works, but the Teaching of the real Master is in addition to what has already been given by Great Ones.

2. His contact is not related at all to your personality and personality life. A Great One never flatters you, nor is He interested in your emotional reactions. He directs your attention to the Plan, and He wants you to find your role in that Plan. His contact puts the pressure of responsibility on you. He challenges your daring, striving, and fearlessness. He expects you to act and work until death.

When you have contact with Christ, you have the first or second initiation. He is the vision or future of humanity. He is the most ideal man ever conceived in the human mind.

You become a Third Degree Initiate when you meet Sanat Kumara, the Youth of all Springs. The proof of the Third Initiation is that you have passed through the experience of Transfiguration, having achieved physical, emotional, and mental purification, and you have a firm contact with your Inner Core.

The sources of higher impressions are

1. your Solar Angel, Inner Guide, or the Soul

2. the Ashrams, the subjective classes

3. your Master

4. your Spiritual Triad

5. the Christ

6. Sanat Kumara

7. the Solar Logos

8. zodiacal signs

9. Sirius

10. the Pleiades

11. the Great Bear

12. the Core of the galaxy

As you increase your contact, your existence becomes more real and you live in greater and greater reality. As you raise the focus of your awareness, you learn to distinguish between impressions and develop the power to control them and choose them according to the need.

Impressions which come via the Spiritual Triad are first translated as

1. joy

2. expansion of consciousness

3. illumination

4. direction

5. clear messages

Impressions come from Shamballa via the Spiritual Triad.

When you are a first or second degree initiate, you use the solar plexus, heart, and head centers to register impressions. But if you are more advanced, you use the head, heart, and throat centers, and the petals of the Chalice.[4]

We can illustrate the Chalice in detail:

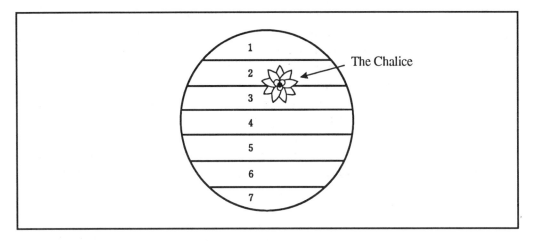

Diagram 61-3   The Mental Plane and the Chalice

_____

4.   See also *The Subconscious Mind and the Chalice* for further information on the Chalice and the petals.

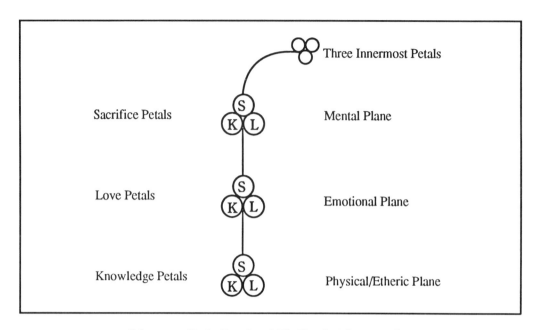

Diagram 61-4   Petals of Chalice in Three Bodies

Please note that we have a sacrifice petal in all three planes, but the mental plane petals are called the sacrifice petals, and so on.

The petals are the most sensitive transmitters of impressions. They transmit and translate them and pass them to the head, heart, and throat centers and then to the pineal, pituitary, and carotid glands.

The sacrifice petals translate impressions in terms of will; the love petals translate impressions in terms of wisdom and inclusive insight; the knowledge petals translate impressions in terms of information, data, and concrete demonstration of facts. These impressions manifest through the mental, astral, and etheric-physical mechanisms.

When you have unfolded these petals, the impressions are transmitted to your mental, emotional, and physical planes without distortion. Thus your actions, emotions, and thoughts act under the light of impressions. Then your actions, feelings, and thoughts are synchronized. You do not think something and do something else; you do not feel one thing and speak another thing. You become "together."

When the impressions come and express themselves through the physical sacrifice petal, you translate these impressions through your physical sacrificial acts.

If your impressions are expressed by the astral sacrifice petal, you will have sacrificial feelings; you will sacrifice your emotions and relate to others without any selfish emotions.

If your impressions are expressed by the mental sacrifice petal, you will think in terms of sacrifice. Your ideas and thoughts will be related to the subject of sacrifice; you will program your life in such a way that it is a total sacrifice for a great cause.

If your impressions are expressed through the physical and emotional love petals, you will tend to be inspired to show benevolent activities to your fellowman or to all living forms, or to show loving emotions or deep understanding of people.

If the impressions are expressed through the knowledge petals, you will live your life on a practical, scientific basis; your emotional life will be very precise and measured; your mental life will be dedicated to a scientific way of relating to life.

The sacrifice petals carry you toward leadership, rulership, and purpose. The love petals carry you toward educational activities. Enlightenment becomes your goal for yourself and for others. The knowledge petals carry you toward the science of communication, philosophy, analysis, programming of life, and active intelligence.

The sacrifice petals on the mental plane will express the incoming impressions in terms of leadership, rulership, and purpose. But because of the three kinds of individual petals the leadership will demonstrate as purpose, the leadership will demonstrate as loving understanding and right human relations, or the leadership will demonstrate as philosophical viewpoints.

If the impressions are translated by the love petals on the astral plane, the impressions will translate themselves as an educational process, as goodwill, and as a psychological approach.

If the impressions are translated through the knowledge petals on the etheric plane, then they will manifest as science, knowledge of relationships, and practical, concrete knowledge.[5]

How to Develop the Petals

You develop the petals by

1. Living a virtuous life

2. Practicing occult meditation

3. Serving a great goal for the interest of one humanity

These are the three main methods by which you can develop and unfold your petals to make your receptivity of impressions clearer.

_____

5. See also *The Science of Becoming Oneself*, pp. 63-75.

The Lotus is a mechanism which starts to unfold and transmit as you refine, purify, and equip yourself with good deeds. The impressions are transmitted in their purity and integrity when the petals are totally unfolded.

The head center takes the place of the Chalice after the Fourth Initiation.

When the head, heart, and throat centers are coordinated with the petals, then you know

- the source of the impressions

- the purpose of the impressions

- your responsibility for the impressions

- the creative use for the impressions

In general, the petals open from the knowledge to the sacrifice petals, starting from the physical plane and going to the emotional and mental planes. Sometimes the influence of other people makes you develop certain petals.

Sometimes the circumstances and conditions of life force you to work in a certain direction and develop certain petals. The need of the environment or family imposes a certain development also.

How can we receive impressions from our Solar Angel or higher impressions through the Spiritual Triad or still higher impressions from our Inner Core? **The following conditions are necessary at the beginning:**

Physical Conditions

1. seclusion

2. silence

3. cleanliness of the environment

4. purity of motive

5. purity of emotions

6. purity of the physical body

7. serenity

8. a blissful state of heart

9. a body in rest

10. little food, lots of water, and good digestion

11. vegetable and fruit diet

12. regular elimination

13. absence of noise or the ability to sublimate interferences

14. absence of odors

15. absence of decomposing leaves or rubbish

Emotional States

1. tranquility

2. no negative feelings

3. deep love

4. deep gratitude

5. absence of negative memories

6. absence of remorse

7. joy

Mental States

1. absence of worry

2. serenity of mind

3. control of unwanted thoughts

4. clarity

5. concentration

6. ability to withdraw to abstract levels of the mind

7. contemplation

Exercise

NOTE: These exercises are extremely dangerous if the physical, emotional, and mental conditions referred to are not met first.

I. Practice

1. Sit cross-legged.

2. Relax.

3. Withdraw yourself into the higher mind.

4. Visualize that you are on the roof of your personality.

5. Keep your mind without thought.

6. Increase the fire of expectancy that you are surrounded with impressions.

7. Tune in with joy and serenity.

8. Wait.

9. Let your mind key in slowly with the source of impressions.

10. Feel the heat and the absorption.

11. Let your Lotus be busy translating the impressions.

12. Keep your channel open to greater impressions.

13. Say one OM to align and integrate your receiving apparatus more.

14. Repeat "beauty, beauty, beauty. . ." seven times and again remain silent and magnetic.

15. When you receive an impression, pass it to the Lotus. Do not be interested in the translation. Later you will see its expression.

16. If you see any color or picture, similarly pass it on and stand detached in your receptive role.

17. Visualize the highest level of your mental body fusing with your intuitional body.

18. Remain in total receptivity without any act of formulating.

II. Descent

1. Go to the Lotus.

2. Check the lower mind and the translation of the impressions you received.

3. Do not get excited. Be indifferent, but examine their quality, meaning, and significance for your life of service and for the global life.

4. Go to the lower mind and check the formations.

5. Take all your impressions and translations. Offer them to your Angel.

6. Sit calmly.

7. Feel various parts of your body.

8. Open your eyes.

9. Sit for five to ten minutes in silence.

III. Follow-up

After five hours, before your lunch or dinner, again go into seclusion. Relax, close your eyes and think:

1. What is an impression according to my experience?

2. How many kinds of impressions have I had? Do I know the sources and the difference? How? Why?

3. What was the receiving instrument in me?

4. Do I really know what these instruments are and how they function?

5. Were my impressions channeling light, love, or power?

6. How can I use my translations in my life of service?

7. Am I improving my ability to receive impressions?

8. Did I make a contact?

9. What points need improvement?

These questions can take one or two hours, and you can record your findings in your diary for future reference. After you finish your recording, take a walk in silence, and do not let your mind think.

Impressions are energies, and they affect your health according to the mental, astral, and etheric forms found in your aura. You must see that your mental, emotional, and etheric forms are pure, clear, and in harmony with the principles of beauty, harmlessness, and compassion. If you feel that you have wrong or negative formations, do not use the special contemplative technique given above. **You must be very careful that your aura has forms corresponding to brotherhood, synthesis, wholeness, inclusiveness, harmlessness, compassion, and self-forgetfulness.** These are forms that increase your vitality and health as the energies of impressions pass through your mechanism.

To create higher thoughts one needs to receive higher impressions. Thinking is the ability to broadcast impressions coming from higher sources. Thinking is also an effort of synchronization with the rhythm of Lives Who are ahead of us on the path of evolution.

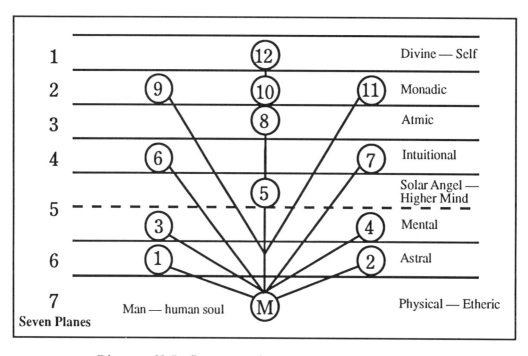

Diagram 61-5   Summary of Impressions in Seven Planes

1, 2	Astral impressions
3, 4	Mental impressions
5	Solar Angel impressions
6, 7	Intuitional impressions
8	Impressions from the Master
9, 10, 11	Atmic impressions; planetary, solar, galactic impressions
12	Impressions from the One Self, coming from your Inner Core

Each connection is a different frequency and potency.

Solar Angel impressions, number 5, develop as the man fuses himself with the virtues of the Soul.

Impressions from the Master, number 8, begin to come steadily when the human soul is transformed in the fiery sphere of the Solar Angel, and maya, glamor, and illusion are in the stage of melting away.

Astral sources are connected with our glamors. A glamor is the image of an object or objects with which we are identified. There are physical, emotional, mental, and spiritual objects. Identification with any of these objects creates glamors which appear in the astral sphere of man.

Impressions coming from mental sources are translated through our illusions or through the clear sphere of the mind. Illusions can be related to every plane and to every object in any plane.

With intuitional impressions, it is as if your relationship with Existence climbs above all clouds of illusion, glamor, and maya.

Impressions from the One Self, number 12, begin to come when the human soul carries out his sacrificial service for humanity under the guidance and supervision of his Master.

Thus the human soul is a receiver of impressions. He lives in an ocean of impressions. His duty is to go to higher sources of impressions through discrimination, aspiration, and striving.

Discrimination is the knob of the dial to choose the source of impressions. Aspiration is the effort to go to higher stations. Striving is the inner pressure to align and transform the mechanism of the Self for Its total manifestation.

Thus striving removes all factors of friction and allows the descent of the current and the transformation of the vehicles to enable the human soul to reach higher sources of impressions.

There are two kinds of astral impressions:

- glamorous

- aesthetic

There are two mental sources:

- illusionary

- real

There are two intuitional sources:

- illuminative

- compassionate

Illuminative impressions expand the consciousness and make man think in terms of the whole.

Compassionate impressions connect the human soul with the points of the Magnet existent within the Core of every living form.

Illumination is the process of expanding awareness. Compassion is the process of unification and synthesis with the fields of expanding awareness.

There are three atmic sources:

- planetary

- solar

- galactic

The Solar Angel is tuned to planetary, solar, and galactic sources, but Its impartation is confined to group viewpoints.

The Self is tuned to planetary, solar, galactic, and Cosmic sources, and all impressions It receives are motivated and directed by the viewpoint of a life extended through a scheme.

Monadic impressions have seven stations in the Self. They correspond to the Rays, the chains, and to the Cosmic Planes.

Thus the field of impressions is Space, but one can tune in with the broadcasting sphere according to what he is.

Impressions travel faster than light. This is why you know things before they happen. Impressions are not thoughts. Thoughts travel faster than light, but impressions travel faster than thought. They use a higher energy than the mental. Thus the future of our senses actually becomes a past for those who can register impressions coming from solar and galactic sources, or from Soul and Monadic sources within man.

The speed of sound and light is already transcended, but people need to develop their higher centers to register the waves of impressions. The energy which can go faster than light exists not only in Nature but also in man. You impress your intention, plans, motive, and future upon those who have the apparatus to register them and see your future as the present, or even as a past.

People are sometimes surprised at seeing in the astral plane the actualization of the things they dreamed for the future. The measure of time here on earth gives us a relative security. In the astral world, time is not what we know. Instead of being a measure of the past-present, it is a future-past process. In higher planes, all *is*, and time and light dissolve in space.

In creative music, the composer deals with time and light. That which he composes can be the echo of the past, present, or future. If the music has no elements of the future, it does not survive as a transforming agent. The element of future comes into manifestation when the composer receives the actualization of his aspirations, visions, and dreams as music. Such music seems contemporary, but it belongs to the future. . . in the form of a present composition.

The same thing is true in writings. When the author is able to receive subtle impressions from inner and outer sources, his present writings reveal the future and last for a long time until the future is exhausted in them. Higher music and writing transform people because they draw people toward their future achievements.

Initiation is a process of gradual mastery of the mechanism given to you by higher forces. In the first initiation, you master certain centers in your brain and etheric body and use them in a certain percentage. In the second and higher initiations, you learn greater secrets about your computer-mechanism — which is your physical, emotional, and mental apparatus.

In the Fifth Initiation, you totally master the threefold apparatus with all its glands and centers. Now you can use the computer with all its secrets and program it according to the demands of life. But this does not mean that you, the Initiate, as the human soul or Spiritual Triad or the Self, can have no greater mastery.

After the Fifth Initiation, you try to continue your mastery over the correspondences of the brain, the mind, the centers, and the glands in the globe as a whole.

After the Seventh Initiation, the Master works to master the solar brain, the solar mind, solar centers, and solar glands (globes). Thus, initiation is mastery over an apparatus which already exists.

All creative building processes are actually processes of rediscovery and mastery of the "apparatus" and the introduction of new programs for the expanding needs of life. Thus, initiation is the registration of future mastery in the present consciousness.

62

Synthesis

Only the rainbow of synthesis can bestow advancement.[1]

The keynote of the Aquarian Age is synthesis. Every age has its own keynote which is given by the constellation into which the Sun apparently enters and travels for approximately 2500 years. Those life-forms which cannot assimilate the energy that radiates from the constellation or which cannot live according to the keynote slowly disappear from the earth.

The new energy is the energy of synthesis. As it increases its influence upon the earth, it brings in three very interesting results:

1. This energy stimulates the will aspect of any living form. If the living forms or human beings are full of weeds, or full of maya, glamor, and illusion, the energy will stimulate them and lead them to form certain groupings which are separative, aggressive, and totalitarian. Through such groupings crime increases, separative politics gain power, and in all seven fields of human endeavor people create hindrances and obstacles against unification and synthesis. But this does not mean that this formation lasts. This is a phase, and the method used by Nature is to stimulate, expose, and then annihilate obstacles through the power of synthesis.

2. The second result will be the increase of insanity, mental and emotional disorders, and the appearance of lower psychism. When powerful energies pour into the planet and people are not ready to receive them, the energies exercise a great pressure upon their etheric centers, which are affected directly.

We see a great amount of mental diseases at this time, resulting in widespread crime. Also, we see the increase of lower psychism. Mediums are growing like mushrooms and misleading people with dire consequences.

---

1. Agni Yoga Society, *AUM*, para. 497.

3. The third result is that those people who are pure and exercise lofty thinking, charged with pure motive, will develop the precious sense of synthesis. Such people will be leaders of the incoming Sixth Race. They will demonstrate psychic energy, wisdom, joy, and health and will evoke trust and confidence.

A pure mind is a mind which does not carry or produce criminal, separative, or destructive thoughts or thoughts that are based on lies, illusion, and vanity.

The energy of synthesis will radiate out from the beings of those who have a healthy body, clean emotions, organized and pure thoughts, and a drive to serve humanity. Such people will be so magnetic that they will exercise a great, enlightening, and transforming influence upon multitudes.

The energy of synthesis brings with it the Divine Will into your life. It is not too easy to define the Divine Will, but we can state that the Divine Will is an urge which directs you toward right human relationships. It is simply goodwill, inclusiveness, tolerance, and righteousness. The Divine Will makes you see that in every human being there exists only the One Self, which must be brought into actualization.

The energy of synthesis expands your consciousness and evokes the values and virtues latent in others. Thus you become an agent of progress and unfoldment.

The energy of synthesis sees that a power is active behind all phenomena, events, and happenings, trying to bring beauty out of chaos.

In synthesis one passes through a phase which people call by many names: renouncement, detachment, leaving the lower self behind, and the like. The idea is that there comes a time when one merges with the whole and "loses himself, to find himself." This is explained in the story of shaped stones.

One day a stonecutter shaped a pile of stones and left them on the ground. The builder came and told the stones that it was the time to give up their freedom to be part of a huge temple. Some of them looked at themselves and thought, "Well, we are so beautiful, shaped, refined, and cut. Why should we renounce our freedom and give up our personalities to be a part of a great whole in which no one as an individual is recognized, but only the temple is seen?"

The stones had long discussions. After a while, one of them said, "Brothers, first of all, we must know that the reason we exist is not to be by ourselves but to be a part of a great building. It is true that we will lose our separate existence, but we will exist as the temple. Each one of us will be the temple, and we will stand for **that** for which the temple stands. We will present the idea, the vision, the beauty behind the temple. If I am serving the purpose of my existence in losing my separate self, I will do so gladly."

Saying this, the stone jumped into the hands of the builder and became the first cornerstone. The others silently followed him, and the temple was erected in a few months. Each stone tremendously enjoyed the melodies, the hymns, and the words spoken in the temple; and they advanced in their consciousness to be ready to pass from the mineral kingdom to the vegetable kingdom. Thus through their sacrifice they created a synthesis.

The first step of synthesis is to be shaped, to become sacred. The second step is to lose your lower self and give it for something higher. And that higher something is your Higher Self, the more inclusive Self. You are only renouncing your limitations; you are only sacrificing your hindrances on the path of synthesis.

The power of synthesis develops when the human consciousness transcends the mental plane and functions in the intuitional light. This is done through meditation.

Scientific meditation is a step-by-step withdrawal from mental levels and an entrance into the Intuitional Plane. This is the goal of the New Era. Mental development must allow the human soul to function in the Intuitional Plane. It is on the Intuitional Plane that all jigsaw puzzles come together to form the completed picture. The completed picture is synthesis.

Synthesis is like a building process. The engineer comes and invites five people and says to them,

"We are going to build a big temple.

"You go and build 20 doors exactly in this shape and size, with such-and-such handles, wood, and colors.

"You go and prepare 20 windows. Here is the description.

"You prepare curtains with this description.

"You build a foundation.

"You build the room in this size.

"You prepare the plumbing.

"You prepare the electrical wiring."

All these people go and work and toil to do their individual task as perfectly as possible, but none of them knows exactly what the temple will look like. When everyone does his job, eventually the parts will come together and the temple will appear in its completed beauty. This is what synthesis is.

In synthesis you have the blueprint. The workers each work on one aspect of the blueprint. Then there is the phase of assembling and finishing.

The engineer is the one who functions on the Intuitional Plane, and he has the blueprint, which is an idea. Laborers or specialists are the mental faculties, which carry on specialized work.

The mind must prepare all parts perfectly. This is why the mind must not only be highly educated but also creative and specialized in a certain direction.

After the mind does its job, the human soul, the owner of the temple, synthesizes all that is done for the temple. Synthesis starts from the moment when the human soul sees the inner relationship between the completed parts in the light of the blueprint.

The process of synthesis never ends. After the temple is built, the temple becomes a part of a city; the city becomes a part of a country; the country becomes a part of a continent, and so on. . .until one realizes that all that he was doing was preparing elements to build the Cosmic Synthesis.

We are told that synthesis substands all existence. All diversities are preparations for future synthesis. All notes are in the process of building the Symphony of Cosmos.

Every thought that a man thinks, every word that a man speaks, every act that a man does either disturbs synthesis or builds toward it. If he is going toward synthesis, he is on the right road. If he is going against synthesis, he is depriving himself of the greater joy, health, light, and love of the future and inviting toward himself forces of degeneration and decomposition.

Nature has its economy. Those elements that do not serve for synthesis are decomposed and used as fertilizers for future developments. Decomposition is the cycle of pain and suffering and the destruction of forms and civilizations and cultures.

One of the major causes of the extinction of races and nations is that they could not adapt themselves to the blueprint of synthesis. The defeat of a nation or a race starts from the moment it takes action against synthesis. The disappearance of races or nations takes a long time, but if one has eyes to see, he already notices the departure of the vitality and creativity of the race or nation.

Synthesis is sensed by those who develop Intuition.

Synthesis echoes within all forms of life. This echo leads them to purposeful, goal-fitting living. Atoms, molecules, and aggregations work toward synthesis. A tree, an animal, a man, a planet, a solar system are travelers on the path of synthesis.

As synthesis is built within any living form, it develops greater power for survival.

Within the core of each living form, the call of synthesis is heard. The lower kingdoms respond to the call of synthesis without resistance; but human beings, because of the development of I-consciousness and ego, reject, resist, and even work against that call.

The mind does not synthesize; it separates. It is the heart that unites and leads toward synthesis. The first rays of Intuition shine in the caves of the heart.

It is true that even the mind hears the call of synthesis, but its first reaction is to create ideologies, doctrines, and groups that stand against each other in selfish, separative, and aggressive attitudes. But the mind eventually traps itself within its own creation. After seeing the threat of its own creation, the mind tries to search for a way out. It is at this moment that the mind stretches itself toward the light of Intuition.

The more light the mind receives from the Intuition, the more it works for synthesis, breaking the walls of the prisons in which it was enslaved through separative, selfish, and egocentric actions.

Going against the currents of synthesis creates insanity, increases crime and social disorders, and brings in depression and the collapse of governments and morals.

Nature as a whole is the result of right relationship between all its parts. This is what the Cosmos means: a whole which is in harmony with itself.

Because of his power of thought, man can create disturbances in the existence through his thoughts, speech, and actions, bringing himself pain, suffering, and confusion. The progress of man is a steady adjustment to Nature, with its laws, principles, and energies.

The success of man is to make himself a part of the synthesis of Cosmos and reduce and eliminate all that does not contribute to this synthesis.

Karma is the law which watches the process of synthesis and reacts to every motion taken against it in order to re-establish equilibrium and synthesis.

Any activity, ceremony, or creativity is the result of the cooperation of ideas, forces, and visions. Any such conscious cooperation leads to synthesis, in which contrasting factors fade away and cooperating factors create the harmony of action.

Synthesis can only be achieved when the vision of the Common Good exists in the minds of those who are ready to cooperate with each other. The Common Good is the nucleus around which synthesis develops.

Disintegration takes place when the agents of integration no longer draw their inspiration from the nucleus.

This principle applies to culture. Culture flourishes and advances only if the core vision of creative persons is the Common Good, is the transformation and liberation of humanity. When the creative person uses his energies for his own personal interests, for his pleasures, or for his destructive purposes, he loses the core and his disintegration starts.

Every progressive and beneficial activity is based on cooperation and is aimed toward synthesis. Cooperation is the means through which all forces and energies are used harmoniously to produce synthesis.

Synthesis is a progressive unfoldment toward the future. The future exists only because of synthesis.

In the process of synthesis all elements of separatism gradually fall away and disappear. Man loses all those psychological or mental elements which keep him a slave of his own self, of his own limitations, and he strives toward his greater Self which is inclusive and expanding.

In synthesis man expands in giving and becoming. In synthesis it is the vision of beauty that controls all actions.

The process of synthesis is a process of absorption into beauty and into the vision of the good of all.

In synthesis man does not lose his individuality, as a color does not lose its individuality in a painting of a master artist. It is in becoming a harmonious part of the painting that his very existence of individuality is kept.

Each individuality is a note in the symphony of synthesis. The notes form a symphony because of the fact that in each of them the One Self is awakened and radiating.

Synthesis is the result of the awakening of the sense of Oneness.

When the One Self begins to awaken in an individual, he begins to contact, to relate, and to communicate in order to serve and to sacrifice. In reality, true sacrifice is a progressive actualization of synthesis, giving up all that is against the **whole** and unfolding and developing all that is from and for the **whole**.

Real thought is a synthesis, and it develops toward greater synthesis. Analysis is a search for synthesis, if one does not lose the whole for the parts. Progressive thinking is a synthesizing process. In progressive thinking self-interest slowly disappears, and striving toward light increases. Everyone who thinks deeply and progressively is on the path of synthesis.

In the process of synthesis, the heart plays the greatest role. It is by the inspiration and attractive power of the heart that things are related and brought into synthesis because the heart carries the flame of synthesis, the Self. The mind inspired by the heart becomes a great instrument of synthesis and a servant of the Common Good.

Synthesis is achieved when the expanding Self finds response in our mental activities, or when certain mental activities evoke synthesis within the Self.

Each life-form, each planet, each solar system and galaxy is a complete synthesis in its subjective side, where energies build a complete pattern or blueprint of highest synthesis. As this blueprint descends into manifestation layer after layer and is exposed to the various influences of the energies, forces, thoughts, emotions, and disturbances of lower levels, much of the harmony of its parts is weakened or lost.

The forces of evolution try to restore the highest synthesis within the lowest manifestation and make it "as above, so below."

Each life-form is consciously or unconsciously striving toward identifying with the prototype that originated the form. Like seeds, all life-forms strive to bloom or to be what their future is, hidden in the seed.

We may study the following tabulation:

INITIATIONS

BODIES	1	2	3	4	5	6	7
Physical	60	70	80	90	100	100	100
Emotional	60	80	90	100	100	100	100
Mental	60	80	90	100	100	100	100
Intuitional	10	20	50	75	100	100	100
Atmic	7	14	25	50	90	100	100
Monadic	5	10	20	50	80	90	100
Divine	2	5	10	25	50	75	100

The numbers in the tabulation above show how much each body is closer to the archetype (100). At each initiation the atomic substance increases in the bodies. Atomic substance is the highest level of each plane.

At the Seventh Initiation all bodies have reached perfection. Synthesis is achieved on seven levels of the Cosmic Physical Plane.

The numbers are not arithmetical but a symbolic presentation of the process of synthesis. Synthesis is achieved on the Cosmic Physical Plane when the glory of the highest manifests through the lowest.

The increase of numbers at each initiation symbolizes also the increase of transformation in the vehicle itself. If it is 5, it means 5% transformation. If it is 100, it symbolizes total transformation into the archetype or total synthesis.

The secret of health, prosperity, and success is in the process of synchronization with the principle of synthesis in Nature.

Because of their attainment of synthesis, some individuals transmit powerful and magnetic energy wherever they are. If they are in a group, the group grows and flourishes. If they are in a city, they bring in a great amount of energy which can be used by those who are on the path of crime and by those who are on the path of holiness.

When our thoughts are in harmony with the principle of synthesis, we transmit a great amount of energy into our system and environment. Some people are magnets and sources of energy due to the fact that they stand and live for synthesis in their thoughts, words, and actions.

This is why some very advanced individuals seek and live in solitude, so as not to stimulate the latent seeds of evil in the multitudes.

Every time a Great One appears, He takes a great risk because He knows that good as well as bad will be evoked from the people. A Great One prepares His disciples before He works with them more closely. He disciplines them with goodwill, right human relations, cooperation, service, gratitude, and makes them ready for synthesis. Every disciple of a Great One must think, speak, and act in terms of synthesis to be worthy for higher guidance and sacrificial service.

It is absolutely true that when a man begins to think, to talk, to act, and to live in the spirit of synthesis, he transmits energy. This energy purifies him, uplifts him, inspires him, and heals him. Those who are receptive to his energy sense similar changes in their very nature.

One must realize that synthesis stands behind all diversities. Synthesis is the origin of all that exists and the ultimate goal of all that is.

The greatest honor that one can have is the achievement and realization of synthesis and the ability to hold synthesis and progressively advance into a higher synthesis. The greatest failure of a man is to be trapped in the spirit of separatism. This is a great misery and calamity that can descend upon a person. Such a person is his own destroyer and enemy. All his actions eventually lead him into self-destruction.

Many beautiful seeds are destroyed before they open into fragrant flowers, many nations perish before they perform their tasks. . .because the individual chose the path of isolation, because the nation followed a man or a group of men who taught separatism.

A separative synthesis is created when people unite into a group or a nation to destroy other groups and other nations. Separative synthesis is the most destructive force on this planet. We call such a synthesis an aborted synthesis. Because of its separative nature in group form, the individuals of the group will have a very difficult time finding the path of true synthesis and thus will delay their spiritual evolution.

When kings became totalitarian, they were removed from their thrones. If so-called democratic governments turn to totalitarianism, they will again be removed from their chairs because life will never allow the process of synthesis to be hindered for a long period of time.

It is possible eventually to have a world government, but if that government turns to totalitarianism, it will be the greatest disaster for the progress of humanity, until humanity again washes away such obstacles on the path of synthesis.

Once we were in a forest and heavy rain began to fall. The river below us rose almost fifteen feet. Watching the torrent of the river the Teacher said, "This is how synthesis works. Cyclically it carries away to the ocean all that hinders its path."

Totalitarianism is another form of failed synthesis. In true synthesis there is no imposition; there is development, unfoldment, transformation, and spiritual magnetism. In a truly synthesized group, everyone knows his responsibility, and everyone does the best he can for the welfare of the whole group.

The leader in a group living in synthesis is only a reminder of synthesis or a spearhead for attainment of a higher synthesis.

Any imposition creates failure in synthesis and eventually turns it into totalitarianism. Fanatics are the fruits of the totalitarian tree.

Totalitarianism is the most dangerous form of government because it drains a great amount of energy from the prototype which stands as the foundation of Divine "All-ism." Just as your whole system obeys your command, so it is going to be in the future for all creation: the Divine Will will rule the whole. But such a rule will be a synthesis, a common cooperation of parts with the whole, because the Divine Will is the will that will operate in each individual form as his own or Its own will. Thus the Divine Will will reveal Itself as one will manifesting through all that exists. Real free will is that stage of will when all have one will.

One day while I was walking with my Teacher in a meadow, he stopped and listened carefully to a big bell. Turning to me he said, "Did you hear that?"

"Yes, I did."

"It is cracked."

He hurried back to look at the big bell which was three feet high. When we came to the bell he hit it with his finger. Then he said to the watchman, "Take it down. I don't want to hear it."

"Sir, why? It is just a little cracked."

"No. It has no synthesis any more. We can't let cracked sound fill the space."

Individual synthesis must proceed along the lines of collective synthesis. This is what history shows us.

If two people are individually synthesized, they can form a nice synthesized family. If two million families are synthesized, they can form a great nation. If all nations reach a degree of synthesis, we will have a global master, one synthesized humanity. It is after such a synthesis that the solar doors will open for us. But if each degree of synthesis creates a prison of separatism, it turns into an obstacle on the path of synthesis.

There is a very important point in the idea of synthesis; it is only possible to reach great heights of synthesis in group formation. Individual synthesis does not last until it lives in a group synthesis. It is in the group life that the essence of man is called forth, hindrances to synthesis are removed, and in test after test the disciple proves that he stands in synthesis.

It is, of course, possible to be a part of a subjective group and achieve great synthesis and, for a cycle of time, not have any objective contact with objective groups on earth, at least physically.

If any form on the mental, emotional, or physical plane has no prototype, it does not bring joy, happiness, and progress, and it becomes a burden. When one thinks and builds in harmony with the prototype, it lasts; but if he builds on the patterns of his glamors, illusions, vanity, and confusion, it does not last and brings unhappiness to the world.

There are groups and nations that do not embody a principle, and they are not in the Plan of the Leader of the Tower. Such groupings bring great suffering for humanity and also present a great test for humanity. But after a short while they disappear, though sometimes with heavy destruction. They are just like an artificial flower. They have no principle or life, no living prototype. It is true that man can build a prototype for it, but it soon dissolves. That is why all that is not built upon Beauty, Goodness, Truth, and synthesis will not last long. The fire of the Subtle World or the fire of the subterranean world will burn it.

Many civilizations were annihilated within the layers of the earth. Those forms which have prototypes remain, and when their time comes they pass to astral, mental, and higher levels toward their essential prototype.

Synthesis is possible for elements which have principles or prototypes. Lies cannot create synthesis. It is impossible to create synthesis with chaos, or beauty with ugliness. Stealing and exploitation cannot be used for synthesis because they have no principle and they do not exist in the world of reality. To explain this further, we can say that the temple cannot be built from blocks of marble mixed with blocks of clay. A symphony cannot be composed on a piano which is out of tune.

Thus each idea, thought, and form must be purified and be a whole within itself to be able to form a part in the symphony.

One day the leader of our choir took a man out because his voice was flat. "You cannot sing because you don't have an ear," he said. "You cannot pick out and sing the pure note."

A company that works for its own interests eventually vanishes because self-interest has no true root. A company that works for the interests of humanity flourishes and expands because it has a living principle.

It is possible to be successful for a while, but all that you gather on the basis of selfish interest will eventually turn into a heavy taxation upon you because you misused the forces of Nature to create something unreal.

It is possible also to create great confusion in our system by thinking rightly but speaking and acting wrongly, or acting rightly with wrong motive. This is called, in the Ageless Wisdom, building a structure upon the sand. It does not last long and falls, causing great damage for the owner.

The forces of darkness have no prototype in the Plan. Their activity has no principle or root, and all they intend to do will end in failure. But they have power and they use their power to prevent human beings from achieving synthesis and unity. They create lies and illusions, and they try to prevent people from having subjective contact with the prototypal principles so that they lose the path leading to synthesis.

If a person is on the path of synthesis, the dark ones watch his every step. Any thought, word, or action against synthesis gives them power over him, and they use his every failure to take him away from the path of synthesis.

One cannot see synthesis until he is synthesized. The degree of synthesis reached within oneself will be the measure by which one can gauge the expressions of synthesis going on around him.

Each instrument in the orchestra must be tuned to itself and to the keynote of the orchestra. This is what health and synthesis are. Synthesis is harmony between the parts and the whole. Harmony is freedom. There is no freedom if there is no harmony. Freedom without harmony is madness or sickness.

No one can proclaim freedom if he is not related to anybody, to any nation or race. But in freedom he is in harmony with whatever he is related. The more harmonious one is, the freer he is, and synthesis is freedom in harmony.

Synthesis is also economy. In synthesis there is no wastefulness. Every part of synthesis is goal-fitting. Energy and matter are distributed in the right proportion. Adaptability of the parts to the whole is economy.

All that is against synthesis wastes matter, energy, time, and space and brings pollution and depression. It is only in synthesis that waste is eliminated, greed is controlled, and pollution is stopped.

Accuracy in construction is economy. Similarly, no synthesis can be achieved without accuracy and economy. Wastefulness cannot build synthesis. Synthesis is accuracy in matter, time, space, and energy. Synthesis requires the highest dedication to the most essential. This is also done through right usage of all factors. Right usage is economy.

Synthesis works with two laws, the Law of Economy and the Law of Attraction. Man must learn the Law of Economy and demonstrate all its aspects in his life. Then he must add to it the Law of Attraction, which is the ability to draw into this sphere all that will help him achieve synthesis.

Economy organizes and purifies the personality. Attraction increases the love nature and establishes right relationship. The Law of Synthesis organizes the higher Cosmic ethers, or the higher spiritual bodies and centers, and relates man with the Heart of Cosmos.

The point of synthesis is the moment of enlightenment, the moment of be-ness. The point of synthesis is the moment of deepest gratitude and purest humility.

Only on the path of the process of becoming your Self do you meet greater and greater values. The closer you go to your Self, the deeper you fuse with the One Self. Thus, synthesis is arrived at through becoming the highest that you are essentially.

Synthesis must be achieved in all seven fields of human endeavor. In the political field, humanity will eventually create a political synthesis which will be accepted by all people everywhere because it will meet the needs and the levels of the people on earth. This synthesis will be built by the best and the highest that every political doctrine can contribute.

The same must be achieved in the field of education. An educational system must be created for the world as a whole.

Synthesis is not uniformity; it is an organism that can meet any need on any level without weakening its integrity and wholeness. In a synthesized educational system the most essential principles will serve as integrating factors, but the methods and approaches will be adapted to any condition.

In the field of communication, there is a process of synthesis going on, though at the present mostly for separative interests. The day will come when a synthesized communication network will work for all humanity, everywhere.

In the field of art, great steps are being taken toward synthesis. But still we have few art objects which not only present national characteristics but also global characteristics. Eventually global art is going to manifest, an art that is inspired by humanity and dedicated to humanity.

In the field of science, great steps are being taken toward synthesis. But the future synthesis will be far more advanced, and science will dedicate itself to meet human and global needs. It will strive into the unknown, into the far-off worlds, and also will investigate the invisible realms of human nature.

In the religious field, great steps are being taken toward synthesis, but separative walls still stand erect as the symbols of human ignorance. Religious synthesis will be the dream of all religions, and it will unite all religions and compose a symphony in which there will be not only synthesis but also freedom for each religion and freedom for each man and woman in any religion.

Synthesis takes away complicating and disturbing aspects and emphasizes the harmonizing and strengthening aspects of religion, or of any field of human endeavor.

In the economic field, synthesis will be unavoidable. It will bring prosperity and abundance to the world. Destructive competition will be put away and replaced by the golden rule of sharing. Great financiers will come and plan the blueprints of economic synthesis for one world.

When all these seven fields of human endeavor are each synthesized, humanity will try to create a synthesis out of all these seven fields of human endeavor. This is how humanity will demonstrate its maturity and be ready to graduate from the planetary school.

Synthesis is a process and an achievement, but it is also the name of a powerful energy. Our machines cannot prove or discern this energy yet, but some subtle mechanism in the hearts of people senses this energy and uses it to further the process of synthesis in the whole world. Those who develop the sense of synthesis within their being gradually and increasingly dedicate their thoughts, words, and actions to bring out synthesis in all fields of human endeavor.

We are told that there are two Avatars working at this time to bring synthesis and coordination. One of Them is the Avatar of Synthesis, Who is working on the mental plane only. The other is the Avatar of Coordination, Who is working on the physical plane.

Coordination is an organizing, arranging, systematizing, relating, and harmonizing process. The military, educational, financial, and other fields are going through a coordination to become more effective and more economical.

Coordination on the physical plane and synthesis on the mental plane work together to bring synthesis within the three fields of human endeavor — physical, emotional, and mental.

At this time not only is a great process of coordination occurring on an international scale, but also an inner process of synthesis is evident in the thinking of humanity as a whole. Those who respond to the note of these great Avatars through their thinking and living establish a line of communication with Them and in certain cases are overshadowed by Them, inspired by Them, and cyclically come in contact with Them to restore the great Plan and further the unfoldment of the Divine Purpose.

Overshadowing takes place when a disciple, through deep meditation and thinking, creates those thoughtforms which attract Their attention.

The Avataric force evokes the will aspect in the disciple and enthuses him to live a life of service and sacrifice for humanity.

Inspiration takes place when the disciple, standing as a soul, receives the direct energy of inspiration from the Avatar, which reveals the tasks confronting him. The disciple, with full consciousness and willingness, cooperates with the inspiration received and dedicates his life to manifest the intention of the Avatar.

To receive inspiration and be overshadowed by the Avatar, one must achieve purity of motive and purity of life, dedicate himself to the service of one humanity, and develop higher thinking and readiness to tune in with the Avataric force.

The third method by which Avatars contact humanity is direct manifestation. We are told that in the Age of Synthesis, or in the Aquarian Age, these three methods will be used more and more to create planetary and solar synthesis.

The great Teacher, speaking about the Avatar says that it is necessary to provide:

> . . . *a nucleus or group through which the Avatar of Synthesis can work when the lesser Avatar has come forth upon the physical plane. This involves individual activity, the sounding out of a clear note, based on clear mental perception, the recognition of those allied in the work and the development of conscious group work. In this group work the personality is subordinated and only the following determinations are dominant:*
>
> *a. The determination to offer group service — as a group — to the world group.*
>
> *b. The determination to establish right human relations upon the planet.*
>
> *c. The determination to develop everywhere the spirit of goodwill.*
>
> *d. The determination to withstand evil through planned group activity.*[2]

Synthesis is achieved by the power of psychic energy. As psychic energy increases, the power of synthesis develops further.

Psychic energy is the energy of the Central Cosmic Magnet. The magnet of the heart attracts this energy which, like a fiery stream, releases the source of psychic energy sleeping in the heart.

Psychic energy links the head and throat centers and organizes them for the labor of synthesis. Psychic energy is attracted to the heart through unceasing striving toward perfection and mastery.

Christ is the flower of synthesis of millenniums. In Him all Rays meet and burn as one flame. From Him radiates the pure psychic energy of the Sun. He nourishes with psychic energy all hearts that turn to Him. All dreams of perfection are synthesized in Him. He stands on the road of Infinity as a torch of synthesis. The glory of the Highest shines out of Him.

---

2. Alice A. Bailey, *The Externalisation of the Hierarchy*, p. 312.

We are told that synthesis radiates an emerald flame. Immediately when this emerald flame is seen, the creative forces of Nature feel a pull of attraction toward the flame. The creativity of the flame of synthesis increases as the creative forces fuse with the flame. This is how synthesis opens the gates for Cosmic relationship.

Synthesis leads to happiness, joy, and eventually to bliss. At the highest point of synthesis emanates an energy which is called bliss. Bliss is freedom, vitality, harmony, and revelation.

Once a person tastes the moment of synthesis and its fragrance, bliss, he will never rest until he consciously reaches the summit of synthesis and makes it a permanent place to communicate with Cosmic forces.

The highest point of synthesis is the magnet which polarizes all energies, cells, and atoms of man and brings in them progressive harmonization and transformation. This highest point of synthesis is the Self, the Monad in man, which throughout centuries organizes the whole mechanism of the body, feelings, and consciousness and makes it serve the purpose sensed and registered by the point of synthesis.

A similar process goes on throughout ages on the planetary scale. The planet and all kingdoms in it have a point of synthesis from which emanates all those energies which create cooperation, synchronization, and coordination, progressively building forms to serve holistic goals and eventually leading to synthesis. This point of synthesis is called by many names. It is called the Tower, or Shamballa, the Father's Home, or the Head Center of the planet. No matter what It is called, the history of humanity senses Its existence. It is an unseen magnet leading all atoms, all cells, and all individual forms of light to synthesis.

The progress of Nature clearly indicates the existence of such a Center.

As the seed of any life-form eventually synthesizes to its highest point of manifestation; as the embryo becomes the man; as the acorn turns into a huge oak tree; similarly, the purpose of the planet is achieved through progressive synthesis to the culmination of highest synthesis. It is in this highest synthesis that the glory of life will manifest.

In the idea of synthesis we learn one very important lesson — that all must be arranged and related in such a way that nothing is left out and each form of life is included and related with its best aspects to produce the total synthesis. This process cannot be achieved by exclusion or separatism, by creating cleavages and segregations, but by unification, inclusiveness, and fusion.

The most fundamental note or principle in Nature is synthesis.

If we study and analyze all moral, religious, and social rules and laws, we will find that all of them have one background, one axis: synthesis. Whatever is against synthesis or violates the future synthesis is a vice, is a crime. Whatever is for synthesis is a virtue, is a beneficent action, word, or thought.

The future morality of groups and nations will be measured by the measure of synthesis. The greater the synthesizing power of a nation, the greater the vitality and radiation of a nation and the longer its life span.

This is also true for a man or for a woman. We will eventually learn that the most successful business, the most successful politics, the most successful spiritual life is based upon the idea of synthesis and directed to the goal of synthesis.

The thinking process of a man who is inspired by the idea of synthesis penetrates ages ahead and builds those bridges over which humanity passes in its most critical moments or needs. The giants of Spirit are those people who lived and labored in the light and purpose of synthesis.

Education in the New Era will be based upon the keynote of synthesis. Students will be challenged to think in terms of the whole, in relation to all that exists. They will be taught that all that they think, speak, and do affects the whole. Responsibility is the realization of this idea.

It will be possible to prove scientifically that your thought affects your pen, your table, your clothes, your body, the trees, people everywhere. . .the stars. Once this holistic approach is grasped, it will be possible to raise world citizens, or even citizens of the Universe.

The sense of responsibility is related to synthesis. No one can develop synthesis if he thinks that the world exists for himself alone. One day it will be proved that the absence of the process of synthesis in certain races was the cause of the extinction of those races. Under the whole construction of the education of the New Era will be the idea or the foundation of synthesis. All curricula, all true Teaching, will be based upon synthesis.

If we ignore the news presented to us by the world press, radio, and television, we will clearly see that in spite of all this negative news, fused with the spirit of fear, crime, destruction, and despair, there exists a network of synthesis which is continuously and gradually paving the way for universal synthesis. Because of the noise of the news, people are not able to see this; but we now have fifty times more fusion, cooperation, coordination, relationship, holistic efforts, and group striving than a few years ago. This is a great achievement about which the blind servants of greed never talk.

Observe how the system of communication is unifying the whole world. Observe how an increasing number of people are talking, dreaming, and working for one humanity.

See how more and more knowledge is available to everyone. See how separatism is defeating itself. See how races are blending within each other.

All icy fragments of separatism will melt away as the sunshine of synthesis increases its light and influence.

The forces of synthesis are proving the futility of all opposition. This is the hope of glory for humanity. One day all those who built walls of separatism will deplore their acts and dedicate themselves to clear all consequences of their crimes.

Certain people build their rooms with bricks but do not use cement between them. Such buildings do not last because they lack the synthesizing factor. It is the vision of synthesis that holds things together.

A great building is the silent song of synthesis.
A great symphony is the glorification of synthesis.
A book or a lecture is great if it has the spirit of synthesis.
Human cultures and civilizations are the battlefields of two groups of forces:

1. Those who fight to separate, to isolate, to exploit

2. Those who fight to include, to cooperate, and to synthesize

In all walks of life synthesis is victorious. All human achievements in all fields of human endeavor are the result of synthesis. Radio, television, computers, and other sophisticated machinery sing the glory of synthesis of human thought.

All great transactions in business, in banking, in international marketing are the victory of synthesis. One must see how the forces of separatism are already living the last moments of their lives.

Greater creative persons are those who have achieved the power of synthesis. They can even relate contradictory factors and make them reveal a vision. Actually, the creative process is entirely a process of synthesis.

As one proceeds on the path of synthesis, his integrity shines out. He becomes more productive, sacrificial, and selfless. Selflessness is a great magnet which attracts all constructive forces and virtues for creative action.

In the future, people will be measured by the measure of synthesis. A genius will create an electrical instrument which will reveal the synthesis achieved in physical, emotional, mental, and spiritual realms.

Many disciplines are given to humanity to lead it toward synthesis. The discipline of the Aquarian Age will be the discipline of fiery synthesis, a synthesis achieved with the fire of Spirit fusing with the fires of Space.

The fires of Space are those rays or energies which relate and connect the man with the Cosmos, increasingly unfolding in him the sense of universality, wholeness, and synthesis.

Once our Teacher said that all knowledge and sciences are related. Actually he said, "All sciences form a unified whole."

A student interrupted him and asked why all knowledge was related.

"Because," said the Teacher with a smile, "there is only one **Knower**. The parts of a machine can be a thousand, but in the mind of the Knower, there is only one synthesis, one machine." Pausing for a while he said in a whisper, "All things that exist are parts of one idea in the mind of the Knower."

A few days later when I saw the Teacher in the garden, I asked him, "Why did you whisper your thought in the class when answering our friend?"

He looked at me and said, "In the presence of sacred ideas I feel extremely humble."

Synthesis is the manifested purpose. It is synthesis that reveals the purpose, and it is the purpose that inspires meaning to every action.

Confusion is absence of synthesis. Certainty and stability are steps on the ladder of synthesis.

Beauty is a moment of synthesis. The greater the synthesis, the greater and more unforgettable is the beauty. The more factors that are involved in synthesis, the greater the beauty of the created form.

Creative geniuses are composers of the symphony of synthesis. In the future they will be called heroes of synthesis.

The science of synthesis needs millenniums to develop. Every living form is a witness of this long path. How many millions of years the Spirit strove to be a flower, to be a bird, to be a lion, to be a man. . .to be an angel. All these steps are steps of synthesis, and the human mind can understand synthesis as it experiences synthesis.

Self-satisfied people, people who run after their self-interests, often express great satisfaction with their achievements. They feel complete and perfect. Those who are on the path of synthesis continuously strive for greater synthesis. Every perfection or every success achieved by them becomes another stepping stone leading toward a more inclusive synthesis.

Self-satisfied people expect the world to be a leisure palace. But for those who seek synthesis, the world becomes a training school leading to synthesis.

The first ones are always disappointed in the moments of their highest satisfaction. For the second ones, the days are full of joy and surprises.

People sometimes think that psychic powers are the sign of greatness. This is true if the higher senses on higher planes are unfolded and synchronously function with the physical senses. But the highest attainment is the attainment of synthesis, when the Self or the Monad synthesizes in Itself all senses. Psychism disappears in the attainment of perfect synthesis because the perfected Self no longer needs any more instruments of contact.

To reach such an attainment, man must not only pass through human initiation but also planetary and solar initiations.

At the end of our journey in the Cosmic Physical Plane, we manifest the synthesis of Spirit. It is only through such a fiery synthesis that we will dare to enter into the Cosmic Astral Plane. We are told that nothing can resist dissolution on any astral plane but the power of synthesis.

After the earthly life, the achieved synthesis is like a shield that the Spirit wears on the path toward the fiery spheres in Space. After one leaves the brain and body consciousness, he needs a mechanism which instantaneously receives millions of impressions and synthesizes them into a decision or direction. Without such a mechanism the poor soul will fall into great confusion and uncertainty and run continuously after mirages. This is what happens in the astral world to those who lived a separative, selfish, fanatical life and closed their eyes and ears to the call of synthesis.

When a person exercises synthesis and develops the sense of synthesis in physical incarnation, he will easily find his way toward the Higher Worlds by orchestrating all the various impressions and challenges into one symphony.

Creative labor and striving put the throat center into action. The throat center is called the instrument of synthesis. As this center unfolds and refines, the power of synthesis increases in man. But we are told that it is the heart that causes transformation of the throat center and enables it to function as the instrument of synthesis.

The center of synthesis is the heart. The whole Cosmos is reflected in the heart. It is this relationship between our heart and the Cosmic Heart that opens the gates of synthesis.

It is observed that some scientists are led by their own labor and discoveries, through their experiments, tests, and machines. This is the halfway point of synthesis.

Gradually a new kind of scientist will emerge who will have the gift of Intuition and the ability to see beyond physical formations. He will have the eye of synthesis. He will compare his discoveries with the things that he sees on subtle levels, and he will eventually attain knowledge characterized by synthesis.

No knowledge is safe and dependable if it is not put into action by the motive of synthesis. The tragedy of the discoveries and inventions of this epoch is that they are not aimed at bringing synthesis but at material interests or destruction.

The saddest thing in our life is when we lose an opportunity to uplift, to heal, to give, to enlighten, or to synthesize. Such opportunities are called the diamond doors which open for a short while and close when they feel the air of indifference and egotism.

The moments or days of opportunity are the moments and days in which you can transcend your level of beingness and consciousness. You can jump in the airplane carrying you to your life's destination. . .or you can miss the opportunity and stay in the darkness of your self-interest.

The challenge of the Future is synthesis. This is the door of opportunity for all humanity.

The future generations will open the pages of history, and they will either say, "Our ancestors missed the opportunity" or "They were intelligent enough to stand in the spirit of synthesis and adorn the pages of history with their heroism. Peace be upon them."

The grandeur of Cosmos, the grandeur of the whole existence is gradually reflected in the soul of the man who carries in his Spirit the fire of synthesis.

Synthesis in its ultimate expression is right relationship between the lives in various levels and various magnitudes, mobilized by a purpose which tries to use them for manifestation.

Unity is a state in which the lives reach the same magnitude and offer themselves collectively to a greater Life to be used in Him as a center.

The difference between synthesis and unity is that in synthesis the lives are on various levels and various magnitudes. In unity all lives have the same frequency, the same magnitude.

In synthesis each life still has its own characteristics; in unity all merge into one.

In synthesis it is a purpose that holds the lives in a collective relationship. In unity it is the common frequency that holds the lives together.

The lives in unity can be far more advanced than in synthesis. But each unity in different magnitudes can be attracted by a purpose which synthesizes them to manifest itself. This time each life is a collective life achieved through synthesis.

Until unity is actualized in a life, it cannot contribute to synthesis.

Synthesis keeps the units of the whole manifestation related to each other.

Ultimate unity leads into pralaya. In ultimate unity, communication and relationship do not exist; all is in peace.

Activities motivated by the principle of synthesis eventually open the sense of synthesis in man and help it to unfold. This is the highest sense to which a man can reach in this world, and he continues developing it until this sense merges into the Real Self.

The process of separation prepares the elements for the Law of Synthesis. During the process of synthesis, the Law of Evolution is active. This is the cycle toward perfection. Synthesis prepares the elements to fuse and eventually be unified. Unity eventually leads to annihilation and cessation.

Exercise

Practical Steps to Develop Synthesis

1. Take forty small blocks of wood and try to build different forms, expressing different ideas.

2. Paint.

3. Compose music.

4. Organize an activity.

5. Take twenty words and form twenty sentences. Then try to form a short composition with those twenty sentences.

6. Take opposite opinions or viewpoints and find lines of agreement within them, or create bridges between them.

7. Open a book and pick out a word and write an article about it.

8. Read about various religions as if you were born in each one of them, and then find a common denominator in them.

9. Take various objects and arrange them to express an idea.

10. Take five ideas and create one idea out of them.

11. Try to see what is

    a. your ultimate goal in life

    b. the most essential thing for humanity

    c. something that belongs to the whole of humanity

12. Take five objects and let them face five different directions. Find a way to make them "face the same direction" without moving them. This will not be easy to do, but once you find the way to do it, new centers will become active in your mind.

13. Take some machines and disassemble them very carefully. Then reassemble them. The more complicated the mechanism, the better the result.

14. Watch disputes and arguments. Then in your own mind reach some conclusion or agreement between the two presentations.

15. Exercise tolerance, not as an escape or indifference but as a process of relationship and agreement.

16. Try to work under the pressure of a plan, of a need, or of a purpose.

17. Carry on your chosen line of creative work under joy, pleasure or pain, suffering or distress. Let the idea of vision keep you going on.

18. Try to think about initiation in relation to

    a. the individual

    b. the group, nation, and family

    c. humanity

    d. the globe

    e. the solar system

    f. the zodiac

    g. the galaxy

19. Think about a seed and in your visualization make it grow, flourish, bloom, and radiate its glory. Do this very slowly, observing the harmonious development of its form, color, and fragrance.

20. Cultivate compassion. Compassion is all-inclusive love and all-inclusive understanding.

21. Try to find a corresponding effect in the subjective world for each worldly action. Understand that all that is found in the objective world is found in the subjective world, too. Try to see the effect of your life on both of these worlds.

22. Think about yourself as existing in subjective and objective worlds simultaneously.

23. Let all your thoughts, words, and actions be directed toward synthesis.

24. Try to see in all worldly events or objects the reflection of spiritual events and spiritual objects. See the meaning of "As above, so below."

25. When you talk to someone, be aware that many invisible ones are listening to you as well. And when you think, understand that your thoughts are resounding in the halls of the subjective world.

26. Try to see that you, as a body and a spirit, are part of the whole Existence. The only impossibility in Existence is that you cannot really separate yourself from the whole.

27. At every sunset send your love and blessings to all those whom the Sun will reach.

28. Try to think in the light of goodwill and right human relations. Try to make the idea of harmlessness the foundation of your thoughts.

Try to feel responsible for all your thoughts, words, and deeds. This is how you can change into a Son of Light, and in that Light see the Purpose of your existence.

In the pure Teaching of the Spirit, the conscience is called the voice of synthesis.[3]

---

3. First published as a booklet "Synthesis" in 1983.

63

Inner Development

People think that psychics are advanced human beings, but some psychics do not even have organized astral and mental bodies. They function only in a loose etheric body through which they receive information about the physical life of people in distorted ways. They confuse the astral and mental impressions of other people and translate them as information about their secrets, whereas all that the psychic is in contact with is physical-level information.

Most psychics think that this information is given from higher realms, but higher realms do not exist for them as long as they do not have an astral or mental apparatus to come in contact with corresponding planes. The emotional body and mental body are represented by the solar plexus and brain, respectively, which come in contact with astral and mental substance and give a feeling to the person that he has organized astral and mental bodies.

Higher senses develop before the consciousness becomes aware of it. This is the same case as with our physical senses: the child hears, sees, smells, touches, and tastes before he knows what is going on. Similarly, our astral and mental senses begin to unfold and organize themselves before we are aware of them. Our consciousness expands as a result of the impressions coming from these senses.

Astral senses cannot be utilized until the consciousness shifts from the physical to the astral plane. One cannot hear or see or taste astrally unless his consciousness is focused in the astral plane. The same is true for the mental plane.

Astral clairvoyance or clairaudience becomes natural when the consciousness can work both with the physical brain and the astral plane. Before this happens, when the consciousness is in the process of shifting from the physical to the astral plane, man uses his senses when he enters the astral plane through withdrawal. For example, when a person withdraws from his body during sleep he sees and hears and touches in the astral plane. He can even taste or smell. In some of our dreams we experience these things. Those who do not develop the senses cannot fully use them, and the senses are related to our spiritual development.

Some people can see ten percent in the astral plane or hear only fifteen percent there. This means that they need to develop their senses more, up to one hundred percent. For example, in your dream you may try to read a book, but you cannot read more than a few lines; or you see a symbol only halfway; or you listen to a communication but understand only a few words. Until the senses are developed fully and the consciousness is shifted to the next higher plane, the senses act like the senses of babies: they see, but do not see; they hear, but do not understand.

The astral senses cannot be used constructively until the consciousness is focused on the mental plane. Similarly, our consciousness must be focused on the highest level of the mental plane to enable us to use the mental senses. Nature always works safely if it is not violated. When the consciousness is on the mental plane, the astral psychics hesitate to advertise about all that they contact because their minds censor them. They generally see that it is wiser to hold an impression than to use it for personal claims.

Our consciousness eventually starts in the etheric brain, which is related to the physical brain. Then it spreads to the lowest levels of astral and mental substance. The consciousness of most of humanity is on the seventh and sixth level of the astral and mental planes, where senses do not exist.

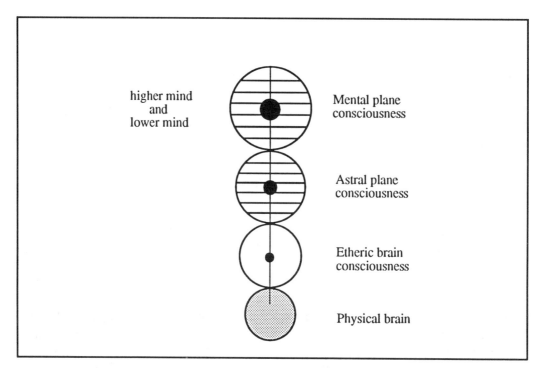

Diagram 63-1   Levels of Consciousness

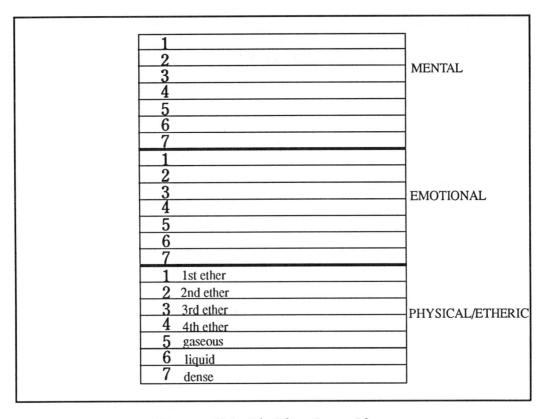

Diagram 63-2   The Three Lower Planes

The senses, whether they are physical, emotional, or mental, are not all on the same levels of the corresponding planes, but they are on various levels. For example, our physical senses are found on the following levels:

- Smell is found in the first plane, the atomic plane, or the first etheric plane.

- Taste is found on the second etheric plane.

- Sight is found on the third etheric plane.

- Touch is found on the fourth etheric plane.

- Hearing is found on the gaseous plane.

The astral senses are found on the following levels:

- Emotional idealism is found on the first, or highest level of the astral plane.

- Imagination is found on the second level of the astral plane.

- Clairvoyance is found on the third level of the astral plane.

- Psychometry is found on the fourth level of the astral plane.

- Clairaudience is found on the fifth level of the astral plane.

Our mental senses are found on all levels of the mental plane:

- Spiritual telepathy is found on the first level of the mental plane.

- Response to group vibration is found on the second level of the mental plane.

- Spiritual discernment is found on the third level of the mental plane.

These three levels are on the higher or formless mental plane or in the higher mind.

- Discrimination is found on the fourth level of the mental plane.

- Higher clairvoyance is found on the fifth level of the mental plane.

- Planetary psychometry is found on the sixth level of the mental plane.

- Higher clairaudience is found on the seventh level of the mental plane.

Correspondences

Physical/Etheric	Emotional/Astral	Mental
		Spiritual telepathy
		Response to group vibration
Smell	Emotional idealism	Spiritual discernment
Taste	Imagination	Discrimination
Sight	Clairvoyance	Higher clairvoyance
Touch	Psychometry	Planetary psychometry
Hearing	Clairaudience	Higher clairaudience

If one wants to use his astral clairaudience safely, his consciousness must function on the seventh level of the mental plane, and so on.[1]

There is a misunderstanding about the focus of consciousness. People think if they are clairvoyant their consciousness is functioning on the third level of the astral plane. This is not always the case. One can see astral phenomena because of a rent in the etheric web. One can hear astral voices, not because he is clairaudient, but because the etheric web in his physical ear is rent.[2]

When your consciousness is in the astral plane, the astral world is real for you. You function in it as you function here in the physical plane. You can do anything on the astral plane. You can imagine, first mechanically, then consciously, as is the case on the physical plane.

There are many methods to come in contact with the astral plane such as drugs, special meditations on centers, breathing exercises, etc. But the most natural contact with Higher Worlds is through the expansion of consciousness. It is very interesting to know that as your consciousness develops on one level, a sense begins to develop on a higher plane on the corresponding level. Actually, they nourish each other. The consciousness provides the needed substance for the growth and development of the sense, and the sense sends to the consciousness higher impressions that expand the consciousness.

People wonder how they can think and feel if their consciousness is not on the mental and astral planes. The fact is that very few people can think, and the majority of these few people receive their thoughts from those who can think, either alive or dead. Most people's thoughts are automatic reactions to stimuli or impressions coming from inside or outside.

As for the emotions, they are the same: An impression comes like a wind and creates certain formations on the "water" of the astral body, and we call these emotions. Unless a person is capable of feeling, he cannot have genuine emotions. Most of the emotions of the average person are the result of chemical changes in them due to various reasons.

One must use his mind to meditate and "think" for a long time, until one day he finds out that he can think. Most people cannot think. Even if they write books and give lectures, it is all subconscious accumulations on etheric tapes. It is the association, the need of the time, and the ego that make the tapes to play. . .but the individual has no ability to think.

If you are really awake, you can see how people are like sleeping fools — giving lectures, writing books, delivering sermons, and running big businesses and factories as if they were awake. As long as you are asleep, you think they are awake; but once you awaken, you realize the tragedy of life in the hands of sleeping fools.

---

1. For further information, see Chs. 12, 13, 14, and 21 on the senses in *The Psyche and Psychism.*
2. See Ch. 15 in *The Psyche and Psychism.*

One of my Teachers used to say that only one or two people awaken in a century.

Expansion of consciousness from one plane to another eventually makes us more awake. But the real awakening — which is true Enlightenment — cannot take place until we enter into intuitional awareness and use intuitional senses, plus all the lower senses.[3]

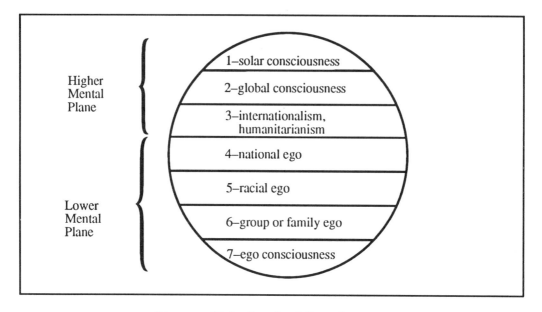

Higher Mental Plane

1–solar consciousness
2–global consciousness
3–internationalism, humanitarianism
4–national ego
5–racial ego
6–group or family ego
7–ego consciousness

Lower Mental Plane

Diagram 63-3   Levels of Consciousness

The mental plane is divided into seven levels. To be conscious on these levels is one thing; to use these levels from the level you are on is another thing.

The mental plane is also divided into seven stages of consciousness which can be recognized by the characteristics of the levels.

You can find yourself on one of these levels if your consciousness is focused on the mental plane. If it is so, this chart is very accurate to tell you where you are. But the unfortunate thing is that your etheric brain or astral body cannot reflect these mental states, and you think, for example, that you have global consciousness, while you cannot even run your office. Or you think that you are a great humanitarian, but you curse your religion for one penny.

Once you penetrate into the higher levels of the mental plane, the characteristics of the levels are real states of consciousness and beingness. They are motive forces behind all your activities, words, emotions, and thoughts. No crisis, no fear, no danger can change your beingness in the slightest. On the other

---

3.   See Ch. 23 in *The Psyche and Psychism.*

hand, the reflected characteristics disappear in front of the slightest storms or temptations.

A hero is created after a person crosses the third level of the mind. We are referring here to conscious heroes who know what they are doing and why they are doing it. Man is destined to be a warrior, a hero, and a co-worker of the Great Life. The only road that can take a person to his destiny is inner development, inner unfoldment, and an outer sacrificial life.

It is very important to understand that to think does not necessarily mean to be active in the mental plane, and that to have higher emotions does not necessarily mean to be active in the astral plane. For example, you can bring a bucket of water from the ocean and use it, but it does not mean that you are functioning in the ocean.

Some people can draw energy or light from the lower or higher mental planes, but they wonder why they have no power of higher clairvoyance or higher clairaudience. The reason is that unless they are functioning as souls on the mental plane with full consciousness, the senses of the mental plane cannot develop their higher capacity.

Most human beings are stuck to their brain and solar plexus. These two centers provide them with impressions from the mental and astral planes or from the astral and mental bodies of those who have, in some degree, developed their mental and astral bodies.

To receive impressions or thoughts or to be able to have certain emotions does not necessarily mean that one is active on the astral and mental planes. Often it means that the person is mechanically producing certain thoughts and emotions and putting them in use through his apparatus of association.

One should also realize that the astral body and mental body are not the same as the astral plane or mental plane. Our body is different from the earth. Similarly, the astral body is different from the astral world, and the mental body is different from the mental world. Our bodies are like boats to be used to travel on the ocean — the astral plane — or like airplanes to travel in the air — the mental plane.

The more developed and organized are the senses of our bodies, the more relation they have with the corresponding plane. The senses are the tools of relationships, and the centers provide energy for the senses to operate and develop.

You can also have an airplane under construction which cannot yet fly in the air but is stuck on the physical plane. Billions of people have started to build their airplanes and imagine taking fantastic flights, although they have only the frames ready. You can see this in their arts, writings, and speech.

Man feels and thinks in two ways:

1. The first way is when a person receives information from the astral and mental planes through his brain, similar to an instruction received through a telephone line. The other side of the telephone line is not his mental body but the mental plane or astral plane, or somebody else's astral or mental vehicle.

2. The second way is when the person is in the astral or mental plane with his astral or mental body, and he has direct communication with that world according to the development of his senses.

64

Intuition and
How to Develop It

The real Core of man is a glorious diamond of light, vested with seven vehicles: the physical-etheric body, the emotional body, the mental body, and four higher bodies which are called

— the intuitional body, the body of the seamless robe, or the body of Bliss

— the atmic body, the body of self-sacrifice, or the body of Peace

— the monadic body, the body of glory, or the body of Freedom

— the divine body, the body of Cosmic contact, or the body of silence

Each of these bodies, we are told, has seven senses. For example, we have the physical body and

- hearing

- touch

- sight

- taste

- smell

- common sense

- intuitive perception

We have corresponding senses of communication. For example, the physical senses put us in contact with the physical world; the astral senses put us in contact with the astral world; the mental senses put us in contact with the mental world, and so on.

Senses receive impressions. Each sense, in reality, is a seven-fold mechanism and is related to the corresponding sense of the higher bodies. Once direct relations are established between corresponding senses, they each register the impressions coming from other planes.

For example, the fourth sense of the physical body, taste, is related to the sense on the emotional plane which is imagination, to the sense on the mental plane which is discrimination, to the sense on the Buddhic or Intuitional Plane which is Intuition, and to the sense on the Atmic Plane which is called *perfection*.

The intuitional senses are as follows:

Intuitional Sense	Physical Correspondence
Comprehension	hearing
Healing	touch
Divine Vision	sight
Intuition	taste
Idealism	smell

and two other senses. When the corresponding senses are developed in the subtle planes, man will be able to register things going on in these higher planes.

The senses have another function. They not only receive impressions but also send impressions. For example, the ear or the corresponding sense on a higher plane can be used to send sound waves through thoughts. Sight can be used to send light waves and energy through thought. Fragrance or taste can be sent through distance by the power of thought using the senses.

The same is true with higher senses. They receive and radiate, receive and distribute.

The seventh physical sense is called intuitive perception. Intuition is the fourth sense in the intuitional body, as the intuitional body is the fourth body of man, the body of glory.

Higher senses unfold and develop if we use rightly their corresponding lower senses. For example, if we use our taste and refine it, we slowly awaken its higher correspondences and build a contact between them. But if we misuse our senses, we build barriers between them.

Those who violate their senses and use drugs, marijuana, tobacco, rotten food; those who becomes slaves of alcohol and gluttony cannot develop the corresponding higher senses in the astral, mental, and Intuitional Planes.

Those who misuse their taste cannot develop creative imagination (astral), pure discrimination (mental), Intuition (buddhic), and the sense of perfection (atmic). The same applies for the other senses.

Senses are developed in man to let him enjoy the wholeness of life, find the right direction for survival, and bring beauty, goodness, light, joy, and health to all living forms. Whenever our physical, astral, and mental senses are used against beauty, goodness, light, joy, and health, not only are they weakened, but they also create short-circuits between their higher correspondences and thus create future barriers on the path of perfection.

It is interesting to remember that as a human being has his senses, so the planet has its own senses and a solar system has its own senses. The seven kingdoms on our planet are the seven senses of the planet. For example, the vegetable kingdom in Nature is the sense of taste of the planet. Curiously enough, taste corresponds to Christ and to Aquarius. Christ is a *sense*; the fourth sense in Higher Realms. He is the taste in the Hierarchy, the Intuition.

Aquarius is the Intuition in the Zodiac.

The vegetable kingdom corresponds to the astral and Intuitional Planes and serves Nature as Its sense of taste.

As we enter into deeper spheres of Aquarius, we will purify our taste and our food will mostly be vegetables and water. In higher planes, we will taste the love, the joy, and the beauty of Christ.

Intuition is the fourth sense in the intuitional body, but because of Christ, because of the fact that our solar system is entering into the fiery sphere of Aquarius, a great opportunity will be given to humanity, the fourth kingdom of Nature, to activate and develop its sense of Intuition and to taste the glory imparted by the Intuition.

A kingdom has seven senses, as each of its members has seven senses. But the whole kingdom is *one* sense for the planet. As kingdoms proceed on the path of evolution, they serve as a higher sense in Nature. For example, the human Monads collectively are the eye of the Solar Logos.

Senses come into being when they begin to function. They do not become tangible, or usable, until they reach a certain stage of development.

Man is the microcosm, and his senses potentially are able to register the life going on in the galaxy. This is what perfection means.

Intuition on the human level will make man the citizen of the galaxy and the applicant of the Cosmos.

What is Intuitive Perception?

Intuitive perception is a physical sense. Through this sense one can gather direct knowledge about an object, an event. He can see the cause of a problem and the effect of it on life as a whole.

Intuitive perception is a holistic insight and an extended foresight into the affairs of the world. Through intuitive perception one can read the hearts of men;

there is only one Self in all forms of Nature.
"I look forward with confidence to the perfect realization of the Eternal
Splendor of the Limitless Light"

528   *Thought and the Glory of Thinking*

one feels the coming important events of his life. One can register knowledge sent to him by higher intelligences. One touches an object and feels the light or the darkness of the object. Intuitive perception is comparable to x-rays.

Intuition is the power to see any object in relation to the whole, and the whole in relation to that object. It is the faculty that makes you aware of the relation of any object to the whole existence, and the whole existence to the object.

A hunch, a feeling, or a telepathic communication or impression is not Intuition. Intuition is "... *that faculty whereby the Self recognizes its own essence in and under all forms.*"[1]

When you begin to see that the essence of your Self is the essence of flowers, trees, animals, birds, human beings, planets, and solar systems, you are becoming intuitive; you are tasting reality. If you start seeing that essentially you are one with the essence of everything, and as everything you recognize your form as part of everything, you are using the sense of Intuition.

Intuition annihilates all kinds of separatism and all kinds of behavior that originate from separatism. Intuition makes you live as the One Existence and eliminate all kinds of actions, words, and thoughts that lead you into a selfish, self-seeking life.

Intuition surpasses the mechanism of the mind and sees all that is necessary to restore unity and synthesis.

Intuition leads to total simplicity. Complications and problems dissolve in the light of Intuition. You feel yourself as one with all that exists. You feel yourself as a wave of energy in the ocean of the whole existence.

Man gradually expands his consciousness by becoming aware of the Universe, and, instead of identifying with his own interests, he identifies with the interests of his family, nation, all humanity. As a result of his expansion, suddenly he becomes *aware* that there is only one Self in all forms of Nature, and that all forms of life are related to him, as to that one Self. This awareness is called the beginning of true service. All Great Ones begin Their true work after putting Their sense of Intuition into action.

Illumination is the moment when for the first time the Intuition reveals the splendor of the One Self. After Illumination, man gradually tries to actualize his visions, move himself out of the mental plane and focus himself in the Intuitional Plane.

The Fourth Initiation is the labor to put into function the senses of the intuitional body, especially the sense of Intuition.

We are told that the intuitional body appears as a seamless robe. Its color is scarlet, like a flame. We are told that Jesus used to wear a scarlet robe. It was a beautiful, seamless robe. At the time of the Crucifixion, four Roman soldiers wanted to cut it into four pieces; but because of its beauty, they cast lots for it in order not to cut it into pieces. And one of the soldiers won the lot-casting.

---

1.   Alice A. Bailey, *A Treatise on Cosmic Fire*, p. 201.

This robe was not needed any more because at the Crucifixion Jesus was receiving the higher correspondence of the earthly robe, which was the intuitional body. He was moving into the intuitional body. This body is a mixture of red, orange, and violet and appears as the color of scarlet to mortal eyes. It is in this body that the Arhat lives and functions.

We find another event which is related to the Intuition in one of the writings of St. Paul. Before the resurrection, Jesus advised His disciples to stay in Jerusalem until power was given to them. He said to them, "Remain in the city of Jerusalem, until you are clothed with power from on high."[2]

According to His advice, the disciples stayed in Jerusalem, and one day when they had a meeting:

> *Suddenly there came a sound from heaven as of a rushing mighty wind and it filled all the house where they were sitting. And there appeared to them tongues which were divided like flames of fire; and they rested upon each of them, and they were all filled with the Holy Spirit.*[3]

The disciples received *Intuition*. Remember that the tongue is the fourth sense, the taste, and the flame of Intuition came to prepare them for a mighty battle against separatism and to lead the world to synthesis and wholeness.

Unless a man enters the domain of Intuition, his life will bear the marks of separatism. The real service of light starts when one receives the flames of tongues from the Intuitional Plane and "clothes himself with power from on high."

The flames created the integration, and then taste, imagination, discrimination, and Intuition. Thus the disciples were fully equipped for the great service.

In the Ageless Wisdom we find other references to higher robes. The atmic body is called the nirvanic body or the body of Peace, in which the man becomes the flame. The greatest characteristic of the one who wears this robe is self-sacrifice for the cause of the One Existence.

The monadic body is called the mahanirvanic body, the body of Freedom. It is through this body that one contacts the source of all inspirations.

Then we have the highest, the divine body, which is the paramahanirvanic body. This body, which is the body of Silence, puts a man in total contact with the whole space.

Through the intuitional body man establishes contact with the sacred planets. Through this body he can regenerate his lower bodies, communicate with devas, penetrate into the mysteries of the evolution of the solar system, see the Plan

---

2. Luke 24:49
3. Acts 2:2-4

clearly, and fuse his Essence with the Sun. But when his sense of Intuition unfolds, he begins to weave esoterically his vesture of Bliss, which he will wear when he becomes a successful warrior in the Fifth Initiation.

How to Develop the Sense of Intuition

1. Try always to see things in relation to the All and as if you were the whole that exists. Know that your thoughts, words, and actions become the property of all. They have an effect on all that exists. Know that every form, every life-form, has one essence, the Self, and all that happens happens in the One Self.
Take an object or an event and relate it to the whole in your thinking. For example, take a flower and enjoy its form, color, fragrance, and beauty and begin to think that it belongs to the earth, to the air, to the planet, to the Sun, to all. Think that the whole is reflected in the flower and that the Self of the Universe is in the flower.
Take an event or a deed and think: If I do this, what will happen to my body, emotions, mind, soul; to my Intuition; to the Law of Righteousness; to my future progress? How will the forces and energies of the Universe be affected?
Once we took three persons and wired them to some sensitive detectors. Each of them entered a room that had a table, on the corner of which a diamond was located among some papers.
When the first one saw the diamond, some strange graphs appeared on the instrument. Then it calmed down.
When the second one saw the diamond, violent lines appeared on the graph. He took the jewel and put it in his pocket . . . but then he put it back.
The third one was very calm until he saw the diamond. The lines on the graph recorded an inner conflict and turmoil, and he took the diamond and departed from the room.
The electricity of space records all that we think, feel, speak, and do. The rays of the invisible Sun are called the scripts of the Lord. Man is an electrical unit. All actions on any level emanate waves which are registered by Cosmic rays.
If people begin to develop thinking in *relation* to the whole, they will find their way to the Intuition and develop Aquarian awareness, the awareness of synthesis, inclusiveness, unity, harmony, solemnity, and beauty.
Any violation against the Law of Unity builds a wall between you and your Essence, the Self. To be separated from the One Self means pain and suffering, ignorance and darkness, crime and violence.

2. The second step is purity. The flower of Intuition unfolds in purity.
Remember that the Intuition is a fiery robe, and the sense of Intuition is a flame. Unless we purify our thoughts, emotions, words, and actions, the flame of Intuition will not shine upon us.
Purity of mind is characterized by pure motives, selflessness, righteousness, simplicity, sincerity, and clarity. An unrighteous man is not pure.

Unrighteousness obscures our light and leads us to failure. Unrighteousness builds barriers on our path, and it makes it almost impossible for us to step into the Intuitional Plane.

Unrighteousness can be wiped away only through intense renunciation, suffering, and conscious sacrifice.

Only in purity does the flower of the Intuition bloom.

We are created in the image of God. This is a very symbolic expression. To be created in the image of God means that within us exists all potentialities of God and nature.

We are seeds of a flower which is *All*, and when we bloom, we will be the likeness of the All. A disciple once said, "I do not know what we are going to be, but I know that we will be like Him the moment we see Him." The Holy One is in us; we are His image. We cannot pollute His image and still exist as His image.

Taste is a very mysterious sense. So is the Intuition. You must use taste in everything you do, and your taste must be the extension of your Intuition on the physical plane.

Purity is a very different achievement, but one must strive for it. In essence we are pure. What makes us impure is our ignorance and separatism.

People identify themselves with their failures. The one who is going to develop his Intuition must identify himself with his successes, and every time he achieves a success, he will consider his success as an obstacle until a greater success is achieved.

Real success is a progressive expansion of consciousness and a growing awareness of the light of Intuition.

People identify with their failures, errors, faults, and mistakes, instead of identifying themselves with the "image of God" within. One must leave his failing self behind and step into his triumphant Self. One must focus his mind on his future successes, rather than worrying about his past failures.

When we are overly occupied with our past failures, we cannot reach purity because we pollute our consciousness with the stupid things we did in the past.

But purity and righteousness are not achieved until, through long experience, one sees that impurity and unrighteousness do not bring success, joy, health, or happiness but rather are causes for failure.

When the light of Intuition dawns upon you, you become beautiful. You make the first contact with your Core. You see everything as One and One as everything. Only through such an awareness can the world be saved from the total failure of destruction.

Liberation from separatism and selfishness leads you to understand that all that exists is yours, and all that you are and all that you have belong to all.

3. The third step to develop the Intuition is to meditate on symbols, trying to penetrate the deeper meaning and significance of the symbols in relation to form, to energy patterns; in relation with other forms and symbols; in relation to the effect they produce in your physical, emotional, mental, and spiritual nature.

You can change your symbol every seven days and continue to meditate for a few years until you develop a faculty of symbolic reading. Symbolic reading means that you see all that exists and is going on as symbols of deeper relationships and meaning. Thus you read the events and life as if they were pages of a book.

True symbols are condensations of intuitive knowledge. It is not always possible to formulate the vision seen by the eye of Intuition for the masses. But it is possible to condense the vision into a symbol which unfolds its secrets as one meditates upon it, and which leads him to the deeper layers of the Intuitional Plane.

In meditating upon a given symbol, one gradually will realize that all forms of life are "words," "symbols of communication," projected by the Divine Intelligence.

A symbol is an open word which speaks to you according to the efforts you make to understand it, and according to the level of your beingness.

4.   The fourth step to develop the Intuition is to serve people not only with your actions but also with your creative and lofty thoughts, your words, your compassion, and your virtues. Service must be done without expectation and with great love and care. If any service is done for your own vanity, showing off, or pride, it does not open the gates of Intuition.

5.   The fifth step is to purify your heart from any kind of hatred. Forgiveness will be your keynote. Let people's shortcomings not bother you. Stay in peace and bless them, even if they do wrong to you. Irritation, hatred, and anger are three great barriers, and they block your path toward the Intuition.

Your subtle bodies can be eaten by the poison of hatred, irritation, and anger, just as moths eat our clothes. Your subtle bodies are drilled by these moths. When your subtle bodies are full of holes, they do not work efficiently. They lose their integrity, and the psychic energy finds it difficult to circulate through them and impart vitality to the physical body.

6.   The sixth step to develop the Intuition is to practice compassion toward all living forms. Compassion brings you closer to the Self, which is everywhere and in everything. Compassion is the ability to identify with that Self and look at life from the angle of the One Self.

7.   The seventh step to develop the Intuition is to control your thoughts, words, and actions. All thoughts, words, and actions manufactured by illusions, glamors, and urges run contrary to the harmony of the intuitional sphere. Those who practice severe watchfulness over their thoughts, words, and actions reach the gates of the Intuition and draw its light into their daily life.

Man must penetrate into the intuitional world. This is his destination in this cycle. He must transfer his focus of consciousness from the mental to the

Intuitional Plane. And this can be done if he is watchful over the modifications of his mind and over his words and actions.

Sages tell us that one ugly thought, word, or action acts like a rock thrown into the window of your aura. It shatters your aura and breaks the fusion with the light of the Intuitional Plane. The chemistry of the aura is going to be one of the most outstanding sciences of the coming culture.

8. The eighth step is to abstain from meat, alcohol, drugs, and marijuana. They obscure the channels and mechanisms through which the intuitional light and impressions pass to the mind and brain. They also create magnetic connections between themselves and those entities who crave for the pleasures emanating from such habits. Such connections bring down the level of consciousness and make it difficult for man to liberate his consciousness from lower impulses.

Waves of Intuition cannot penetrate an aura polluted by drugs; only astral distortion reaches the brain and misleads the man.

The sense of Intuition is the spiritual taste of man. This taste is the flower of the faculty of pure discrimination. As you discriminate in your life between locations, dress, food, friends, music, books, etc., you do the same with the sense of Intuition in higher planes. Through Intuition you find the right path, the right thing to do. Through the sense of Intuition you live a life that is ever-inclusive, and you choose those paths of development which eventually take you back to the electrical sphere of the Cosmic Heart.

People have intuitional flashes occasionally; even children experience intuitional flashes. These flashes come unexpectedly in any location, at any time, to almost anybody. They stay with them for a split second or longer and then disappear.

Intuitional flashes are those moments when the human mind experiences sudden expansions of consciousness, revelations of beauty. In these rare moments one can see the path he must take; one can receive the answer to his questions; one can be charged with a great energy, and so on.

Intuition is a moment of enlightenment when in a second you grasp a great truth which was a mystery for you. These flashes of Intuition are related to five revelations:

1. You realize clearly that life is One. This realization penetrates into your mind, into your heart, into your body. You feel it completely and experience an unusual joy.

Intuitive realizations do not stay in your mind as concepts, as desires and wishes, as theories, but they manifest themselves through your life. Your life changes. It is very important to note this point. Before one begins to formulate his intuitive realizations and write about it, it transforms his life. He lives in the concept of Oneness. All his thoughts, feelings, words, and actions radiate the revelation of Oneness.

It must be understood that like everything in Nature, the effect of the intuition also fades away if the experience is not repeated. The effect depends on the intensity and duration of the intuitional flash. If it was of short duration and weak intensity, it usually gives a moment of ecstasy and fades away.

If the mental mechanism is not yet ready, the flash hits and fades away. But no matter how short the intuitional flash is, it always creates a certain transformation in man, a certain new orientation in man. It is in such a moment that all his centers radiate with a new glow. The longer the duration of the intuitional flash, the greater will be the effect on the person and on his life.

Illumination or Enlightenment is a state where the flash of Intuition becomes a steady flow of light, and man enters into a stage of permanent radioactivity.

2. The second revelation is the revelation of Infinity. The realization of Infinity is very rare. People are stuck to the moments of their pains or pleasures. Their concept of time and space is limited in miles and years. The concept of Infinity is foreign to their consciousness. But when a flash of Intuition comes, suddenly a window opens in the wall of their prisons and they experience a sense of Infinity for a shorter or longer time. Even though this flash of Infinity may last a second, the effect lasts longer.

Such flashes of Infinity bring many effects:

— They bring a great release of so many burdens, whose names could fill a dictionary.

— They bring healing energy to your bodies. Your health mysteriously improves.

— Due to these flashes of Infinity, your thoughts function on a higher dimension.

— You feel more balanced. Some kind of orderliness penetrates into your attitudes and expressions.

— A certain calmness settles in your attitudes and actions.

— Beauty increases in your expressions. Your face takes on a glow of beauty.

— Joy radiates through all your relationships.

— You feel deeper inspiration and experience greater creative energy in your heart and mind.

— Flashes of Infinity deepen your sense of Oneness. Oneness expands into Infinity. Thus separatism is destroyed in your mind, and you are in tune with Cosmos; you are part of the living Infinity. Separatism creates friction with the Cosmic Unity, and this friction manifests as complications and suffering. A flash of Infinity creates harmony between you and Infinity.

— The sense of Infinity expands the sense of oneness to the domain of Cosmos. You become harmless not only toward a blade of grass but also toward the space and stars. Only the sense of oneness and Infinity reveals to you the harms you were inflicting upon space and the stars.

— The sense of Infinity makes a man human and divine. You are aware of your responsibilities toward man and toward the Almighty Power.

Unless one penetrates into the Intuitional Plane, he cannot graduate as a human being. To be really human means to be intuitive. Mental faculties are not the guarantee that a person is a human being. It is only after one crosses into the Intuitional Plane that he acts and lives as a human being and as a divine being.

It is only after crossing into the Intuitional Plane that the mind and the heart start their real functions. Only in the sphere of Intuition do the mind and heart bloom and unfold to their utmost capacity.

The mind does not make a person into a human being. He needs heart to transcend the traps of that mind, and he needs Intuition to be human. Actually, the flashes of Intuition first appear in the heart; then they are observed and analyzed in the mind.

Intuition offers you the concept of timelessness.

Knowledge and Intuition differ from each other in the sense that while knowledge equips your mind with much information and data, Intuition brings you realization, actualization.

The most essential quality of Intuition is that its revelations do not stay as pictures or panoramic views in your vision but become part of your life and expressions. An intuitive flash penetrates all your vehicles and tunes them with the revelation. In Intuition you have transformation and steady transfiguration. That is why Intuition leads to Enlightenment, and Enlightenment leads into Transfiguration. Actually Intuition, Enlightenment, and Transfiguration are parts of the same process of spiritual actualization.

3. When intuitional light flashes in your mind, you realize above all doubts that you are an immortal being. After such an experience, you do not need any instruction about immortality. For the first time in your life you walk, you feel, you think, and you relate to people as an immortal being.

There is a great healing power in this realization of immortality. Many of our physical, emotional, and mental disorders and problems are generated by our fear of death and annihilation. Such a fear is deep-seated in our brain, and it controls our relationships, feeds our anxieties and our greed, and amplifies our worries. It creates inner psychic irritation which eventually manifests itself as sickness and disease.

The light of the Intuition clears the phantom of the fear of death. It is in the light of the Intuition that the human soul detaches himself from the transient bodies.

Thus in the light of the Intuition the shadows of separatism, the concept of time, and the fear of death disappear, and the human soul breaks the major chains of slavery.

Realization of immortality brings you closer to super-human contacts and creates great joy in the hearts of Those Who are watching you. It is after the realization of immortality that one can fit in the labor and plans of Great Ones.

No great task can be trusted to those who do not have the sense of immortality. Fear of death can paralyze the mind of a man in a most dangerous task and lead him into disaster. Fear of death makes man attach to his pitiful self and its pitiful interests. The realization of immortality builds the path of heroes.

4. When Intuition flashes in your mind, you obtain the sense of reality. You see things as they are. You see the *cause* of things. You see how they develop and become *effects*. You see the futility of many objects. You see the tragedy of hypocrisy, lies, vanities, pretensions, and showing off. You see the comedy of life. You see the mechanism of self-deceit. You see the role obsession plays in life.

You see those objects and relations which no longer help your decisions to serve and assist your higher commitments. You see how energy is wasted to feed glamors, illusions, and self-defeating pleasures.

You see how life is wasted in making it keep us prisoners of our inertia, as slaves to our own hatreds and fears. You see how civilizations are built on vanities and destroyed by self-deceit.

The Intuition also reveals the reality of progressive unfoldment. It reveals the Purpose, the Plan, and the Self within you and within all living forms.

Intuition reveals the futility of all that is built upon the sands of self-deceit. Intuition makes people realize that progress is not obtained by running after their tail of shadows.

To face reality needs courage and fearlessness. The light of Intuition, with the sense of reality, also brings in courage and fearlessness. Actually, fearlessness and courage are achieved only in the realization of one's own *Reality*.

The sense of reality may change your life totally. It may change the standards of your values and lead you to the painful path of renouncement and often to temporary isolation. It is only with the courage obtained by the light of reality that you can fight those hindrances that try to keep you in the world of unreality and pull you down to the level of deception and illusion.

A flash of Intuition reveals all that is unreal in your relationships, in your expressions, in your thoughts and motives because a flash of Intuition is a ray of light which awakens you from your long sleep.

Your Intuition grows as you awaken and see your pseudo-self which was representing the real you. But is it also the Intuition that reveals to you the vision of your ever-expanding Self within the Cosmic Self. The reality of your consciousness is your awareness. Throughout ages the light of the Self increases. As the light of your consciousness increases, you awaken more and more. Awakening is an ever-expanding awareness of things as they are on progressively higher and more inclusive spheres of existence. On each higher sphere you go deeper into the oneness of life, Infinity, Immortality, and Reality.

Intuition is the straight path of transfiguration, the straight path of facing yourself, the straight path of Self-actualization. Transfiguration of life is possible only through Intuition. Transfiguration is the first major breakthrough into the state of reality. All mental knowledge, all encyclopedic accumulations of data, have no power of transfiguration, and sometimes they are even hindrances to real expansion of consciousness.

Many scientists, philosophers, religious leaders, and executives of various branches of human endeavor are sometimes trapped in the cage of their mind like a mouse. They try to measure reality with their earthly measures and build the Babylon of their dreams.

The mind is called the slayer of reality. It is only through Intuition that your knowledge can have a purpose and be an agent to improve the life.

5. When Intuition flashes in your mind, it reveals beauty. It makes you able to see beauty.

Beauty surpasses reasoning and logic. Beauty is known only in the light of Intuition. Every beauty is a presentation of a synthesis, is the reflection of a whole. Mental faculties are not built to comprehend beauty.

Intuition is the telescope of the human soul. The future becoming of the human soul can be projected by the light of Intuition on the mirror of the mind.

Beauty is a moment, a symbol of timelessness within the boundaries of time. The Real Self in man is a timelessness, is a continuum, is a duration. The expression of the Self in time and space is an expression of beauty.

It is only through Intuition that we can understand the concept of the One Self and the concept of timelessness because the revelation of Intuition evokes the process of becoming that which is revealed to you.

Intuition does not give something to you. It makes you become yourself. Intuition reveals your Self, your future becoming, to you.

In the Transfiguration process nothing is given to you, nothing is taken from you; but the fire in you is evoked and the charcoal of your existence enters into the process of becoming a radioactive fire.

Partial identification leads into unreality. Total identification with the Self leads to Reality, to beauty, to timelessness, and to immortality.

Transfiguration enables you to be the changeless one within the world of changes. The world of changes belongs to the past and present. Changelessness is rooted in the future. Changelessness in change is like a thread which holds beads of many colors and motions together.

Changelessness is like a "silent watcher" — the awareness — which watches the things your bodies did in the past, the things they are doing in the present, and the things they may do in the future; but the awareness remains the same. This is how one can explain changelessness in change.

When Intuition awakens in you, it puts your senses and centers in their second gear. Your senses and centers not only receive but also broadcast. Your eyes not only receive impressions but also broadcast impressions. The same is true with all other centers and senses.

In summary, we can say that you can develop your Intuition:

1. by cultivating an attitude of inclusiveness

2. by increasing your viewpoints

3. by increasing your love and compassion

4. by abstaining from criticism

5. by meditating on living forms as if they were symbols, such as trees, flowers, birds, etc.

6. by cultivating periods of total silence

7. by living a life of harmlessness

8. by cultivating the power of contemplation

9. by cultivating close contact with your Inner Guide, trying to hear Its voice five times daily

10. by clearing away your glamors and habits and developing vigilance

11. by dispersing illusions and trying to see things as they are

12. by trying to find the point of balance between two conflicting viewpoints

13. by controlling your mouth and closely watching over your conversations

14. by going into solitude at least one day a month and one month a year

15. by focusing your consciousness within your head

16. by enjoying expanded space, such as the sky, the ocean, great mountains, valleys, and canyons

17. by studying closely the secrets of great art objects

18. by thinking from the angle of cause rather than effect

19. by staying away, as much as possible, from polluted, contaminated areas

20. by staying away from locations where crimes and prostitution are committed

21. by practicing occasional celibacy for weeks, months, or years

22. by keeping yourself away from alcohol, meat, drugs, tobacco, marijuana, caffeinated tea, and coffee

By following the path indicated with these twenty-two points, you will be able to develop your Intuition. At first, intuitional flashes will be rare, but they will come to you in greater frequency as you carry on the disciplines given above.

There is a difference between telepathic communication and Intuition. In Intuition you receive universal and Cosmic revelations with which your Self becomes one. Telepathy is communication with others.

The Intuition flashes in our brain with a great load of revelation. But the majority of us cannot catch these impressions, and they fade away in a fraction of a second, though people feel elevated and charged with the power the flash brings.

Creative people find great sources of inspiration in intuitional flashes, and they produce masterpieces of literature and art.

As one grows spiritually he can stay longer within the intuitional light, and as he develops more ability to sustain the light, he becomes an Enlightened One. To be enlightened means to be able to function in the light of Intuition.

We are told that Arhats live in the Intuitional Plane with the pure light of Intuition. We are also told that the Ashrams of Great Ones are found in the Intuitional Plane.

Intuition develops as it is put into actualization. As you live more according to your Intuition, you create better communication with the light of Intuition.

Those who reject, repel, or disobey the light or flashes of Intuition eventually build a wall between their mental and Intuitional Planes. Great suffering and sacrifice are needed to make a new contact between these two planes.

Generally, when the light of Intuition is blocked, the mind becomes very cunning and destructive because it uses all the previous treasures of Intuition left in the mental body for selfish and separative ends. The blockage happens when a past karmic condition prevents your progress or a harmful act does not allow you to use the light of Intuition.

It is very important to know that Nature does not allow unworthy ones to penetrate deeper strata of revelation and power. "The kingdom of heaven is taken by violence." One must prove with his striving and purity of life that he can be trusted to enter the royal path of Transfiguration.

One cannot arrive at the Intuitional Plane without preparation.

The mental senses must be developed, one by one, and the highest mental sense must enter into operation before one can make sense out of the waves of Intuition hitting the mental shores.

The highest physical sense in the Ageless Wisdom is also called the *esoteric sense*.

This is a real sense which, like the sense of smell, conveys not the fragrance or odor but the true meaning behind any expression.

The esoteric sense is the highest sense. It sees the meaning and significance of any expression, symbol, or hint. It is the sense of intuitive perception. It is sometimes called the guide to the pyramid. It knows the path leading to the source of the path.

Those who develop the esoteric sense grow in understanding. Life becomes a book for them in which they read the real meaning of forms and events.

The esoteric sense makes us able to see the reason behind the form, the motive that gave birth to the form, its true meaning and significance.

Through the esoteric sense one can see the real meaning of an event or see the real happening behind distorted news.

The esoteric sense develops through the art of visualization and contemplation through which the mechanical associations and limitations of the mind are transcended and the world of meaning is entered.

The esoteric sense is the door through which the thinker passes into the realms of pure Intuition. He does this through contemplating on symbols.

Contemplation on Symbols

One must understand what the symbols are in reality.

The symbols that lead the human soul toward the Intuitional Plane, and help him to develop the sense of Intuition, are those symbols which are charged with high voltages of meaning and significance. Each line and formation is based on geometrical and arithmetical accuracy and charged with a precise purpose which transcends the mental capacity to understand.

Meaningless symbols and drawings and forms, behind which no precise purpose exists and are not constructed upon a plan, cannot lead the human mind toward Intuition. They put the mind into suspension.

Suspension of the mind is neither ecstasy nor Intuition but a momentary break in the circuit.

A real symbol leads the mind into contemplation. It is through contemplation that the Intuitional Plane is entered.

Contemplation is the process in which the power of interpretation of the mind cannot contain the charge of the memory coming from the symbol. We call such a moment the moment of silence of mind during which no interpretation is possible.

It is after this silence that the human soul is directly impressed by a higher vision from the Intuitional Plane, which gives a synthetic picture of the meaning of the symbol.

If one holds this vision long enough, the human soul penetrates the Intuitional Plane where all mental measures remain useless.

Such a penetration into the Intuitional Plane expands the awareness of the human soul who, when returning to the mental plane, carries with him a deep sense of joy, peace, serenity, compassion, gratitude, and inclusiveness. Curiously enough, these turn into sources of scientific, artistic, educational, and religious discoveries if the mind has been purified from the crystallization of obsolete thoughtforms during contemplation.

Chaotic symbols do not carry power. We call such symbols "noise machines." A real symbol is a condensation of a Solar or Cosmic Symphony, a Solar or Cosmic Vision. It is like a huge oak tree simplified into an acorn. The whole geometry of the tree and its possible growth are condensed in the acorn, the symbol of the oak tree.

Meditation on symbols is the process of interpretation of the symbols according to the standard the mind possesses.

Contemplation on the symbols is an effort to surpass the process of interpretation, leaving behind all the standards of the mind. It is in the moment of breaking from the old standards of the mind that the human soul finds his freedom.

Contemplation is a period of absence of formulation.

Contemplation is an identification process with the power and direction of the symbol.

This is the most sensitive moment in contemplation during which, if any old standard interferes, contemplation turns into meditation and thinking.

Identification of the human soul with the power, direction, and motive of the symbol must be made factual before the right interpretation becomes possible on the mental plane.

The human soul, through identification, brings back to the mental plane a great voltage of energy, a treasure which slowly will be shared with the world through the right interpretation and right formulation, according to the construction of the mind and according to the conditions of the environment.

During contemplation on the symbol, the human soul tries to get free from all mental standards and enter into deeper silence within the symbol.

The real visualization of the symbol takes place the moment the old standards are left behind.

Visualization is the process of building the symbol on the mental plane to attract its "soul." Until the "soul" of the symbol or its idea descends into the symbol, true visualization is not possible.

Contemplation starts when the "soul" of the symbol takes your awareness into the Intuitional Plane.

The "soul-infusion" of the symbol takes place within the Intuitional Plane.

It is possible to bring the soul-infused symbol back to the mental plane to utilize it on the three lower planes through various interpretations. But interpretation will lack right direction until the symbol returns to the mental plane after its soul-infusion on the Intuitional Plane. A symbol on the mental plane is a symphony of energy in the Intuitional Plane.

The moment the symbol enters the Intuitional Plane, it transforms into spheres of ideas, energy, and impressions.

I once saw a dance in which fifteen dancers projected the shadow of a five-pointed star on a huge screen. The symbol of the five-pointed star was produced by fifteen dancers and by their precise movements.

In contemplation, one must try to find the fifteen dancers through the symbol of the five-pointed star. This is what "soul-infusion" of the symbol is: the originating source, the idea, and the symbol.

Through the performance of the dance one can see the relationship of the idea to the shadow-symbol.

But how to reach the source without having seen the relationship of the source with the shadow? This labor is done through contemplation.

Expansion of consciousness occurs every time a symbol is related to the idea, the source. It is possible also that the same source simultaneously projects different symbols on different screens, positioned differently.

These symbols in manifestation, or projections, will be totally different from each other, but they will have the same origin, though with different facets of the same origin.

Visualization is of many kinds. One of them is synthesizing visualization. Through synthesizing visualization, the origin of different symbols is found which relates them to each other.

Such related symbols manifest a great power because the entirety of the energy of the originating source manifests through accurate relationship.

Moments of Contact

The moments of contact with the Intuitional Plane can be categorized as follows:

1. Moments when you are in deep joy

2. Moments when you are far above the physical, emotional, and mental storms

3. Moments when you feel one with Nature

4. Moments when you are aware that nothing can hurt you

5. Moments when you feel detached from all that you have and all that you are

6. Moments when the opinions of the world do not create any reaction in you

7. Moments when you feel yourself in the presence of your Master

8. Moments when you see your lower self as it is, with deep indifference

9. Moments in which you are aware that you are geared to a creative current

10. Moments when you are absolutely fearless, daring, and courageous

11. Moments when the spirit of forgiveness penetrates into each layer of your being

12. Moments in which it becomes impossible for you to condemn, judge, criticize, or compare

13. Moments in which you see how each event is part of the All

14. Moments in which you see the ultimate victory of beauty, goodness, and justice

15. Moments in which you clearly see how traps in your life are built, how you accustom yourself to your traps, how you can escape from your traps

16. Moments when you are aware that you are fused into a line of pure Teaching

17. Moments when you feel at the gate of the Great Ashram

18. Moments when you decide to sacrifice all that you are and all that you have to all living beings

19. Moments when you see the Path leading to infinite, progressive perfection

20. Moments when you touch ideas, visions, and thoughts as if they were living objects

21. Moments in which you decide to be harmless

These moments are experienced at the gate of Intuition, when the "graduated" disciple knocks at the gate and asks for admittance.

Exercise

Meditation to Develop the Intuition

This is a very advanced meditation, and we can use it to bring in greater intuitive energy to our mental mechanism to help clear out illusions, shed light on the daily life, and expand our awareness to higher levels.

To do this meditation we must choose an idea, an abstract idea such as:

1. Gratitude

2. Joy

3. Beauty

4. Goodness

5. Courage

6. Power

7. Solemnity

8. Enthusiasm

9. Simplicity

10. Truth

11. Love

12. Future

Daily, for seven days, work on one word, trying to symbolize it through

— form

— color

— motion

— sound or music

— fragrance

You may use these five together, or two or three combined, or just one.

After the formation of your symbol, try to draw it on paper to keep a close watch on your progress.

The first day you may have a complete picture. The next day you may change it, and if it needs more elements added, add them or create a new symbol which better fits the concept or idea.

After you finish all these twelve ideas in twelve weeks, take again the first idea for two weeks of meditation. This time you have a different labor.

Let us say that your seed thought is gratitude, and you are imagining a huge fruit tree with beautiful blossoms, raising its branches in all directions and radiating beauty and fragrance to all through beautiful music.

Now try to imagine its astral form and colors, then the mental, then the intuitional. Find out how and why such a form really fits the concept or idea of gratitude. You may ask, "How do I know what form it will take in astral, mental, or intuitional substance?" It does not matter. Just try to create it; try to imagine, try to visualize, and soon you will see that you are creating quite a different symbol of the idea which is more beautiful and more inclusive than the one in the lower planes.

You may imagine all these different forms around the physical form or separate from it. You may relate them to each other through different geometrical lines or thread of different colors or densities.

After you do this for twenty-four weeks, you will take each idea and compare its symbol with all twelve symbols, and try to find a relationship between the one idea and the others. This will take twelve months.

The next step will be arranging all these symbols in such a way that all the symbols together form one symbol that symbolizes a new concept in which all concepts are included.

You can do this in your drawings, in your imagination, or in your mental visualization. You can use your symbol in its physical form or in its subtler forms, as you wish.

The ultimate labor will be to hold them all together in your imagination with all their forms in all levels. This will help you to rend the web between subjective and objective realms, and establish continuity of consciousness between the Intuitional Plane, the higher mental plane, the lower mind, and the brain.

Exercise

Advanced Meditation to Develop the Sense of Universality

This attempt must be done in seclusion, in the mountains, or somewhere in Nature where you will not have any interference. After you retreat for one week, eating pure food once a day, and purify your emotional and mental bodies through high-level music, reading, contemplation and silence, you can do the following:

Sit and relax physically, emotionally, and mentally. Imagine where you are. Slowly go beyond your location to the earth, beyond the earth to the solar system, beyond the solar system to the galaxy, and beyond.

Then gradually come back and visualize a triangle with a fiery sphere around it.

All that you will do after that is an absolutely relaxed expectation to record impressions.

Visualize the sphere around the triangle in violet.

Remember that you are not trying to contact Masters, angels, devas, but you are expecting impressions which may come to you as symbols or sound.

This absolutely thoughtless period will go not more than half an hour for the first year. For the second year you can extend it to one hour. After half an hour or one hour, you must write down your impressions for further study.

Again, remember that you are doing this mostly to develop your sense of universality, then to develop the ability to come in conscious contact with higher frequencies of wisdom in the Universe. During this experience you must keep your whole nature in joy.

If you do not observe the suggestions given above, you may expose yourself to various attacks. Higher Realms are protected by fiery beings, and they do not allow an unworthy person to enter.

Your only motive must be to expand your relationship with the Universe so that you love and serve, with "self-forgetfulness, harmless, and right speech."

Exercise

Meditation to Develop the Intuition and the Sense of Unity

1. Relax.

2. Take a few deep breaths. Try to visualize a sphere of blue light.

3. Visualize a golden cross in it and a violet rose at the center.

4. Visualize some beautiful music.

5. Visualize birds flying around the sphere according to the rhythm of the music.

6. Try to make the sphere bigger and bigger until it includes the planet and the solar system.

7. Once you reach this stage, take three more breaths and say,

> *May the unity of all things be revealed to me.*
> *May I be aware of the Oneness of Life.*
> *May the beauty of oneness shine in my heart.*

8. Then sit for a few minutes and your meditation is over.

NOTE: Do this meditation every day until you feel oneness and are able to reject separative expressions and think in terms of unity, in terms of one humanity. Do this meditation not more than thirty minutes daily.

[handwritten:]
1) may the unity of all things be revealed to me
2) may I be aware of the Oneness of Life.
3) may the beauty of Oneness shine in my heart.

65

Beautiful Thoughts

A beautiful thought is a treasury of health.[1]

When people feel tired and exhausted, the best tonic for them is to think about something beautiful. Esoterically, one feels tired when the psychic energy in the nadis has been exhausted. Nadis are etheric nerve channels, and they carry the psychic energy within the aura.

Thought about beauty charges the nadis with new energy which nourishes the nerves, blood, and muscles.

From childhood people must be trained to think about the beautiful, especially when they need rest or when they need to be healed. A whole system can be developed to carry this method to children and make it a part of their lives. When they are trained to think on beauty and invoke and evoke beauty, they will grow as giants of spirit. They will manifest great endurance, stability, and health.

Ugliness deprives them of their energy; it dries up their resources of vitality and creates conflict in their energy system.

In any emergency when energy is needed to combat a situation, one must evoke for a few minutes the energy of beauty — a beautiful piece of music, a lofty idea or vision, an uplifting paragraph, a heartfelt prayer toward the source of beauty. All these can create miracles and in critical times inspire one with courage, energy, balance, stability, and wisdom.

Beauty is the most harmonizing factor in our physical, emotional, and mental bodies. It is the most harmonizing factor in our social relationships. Beauty is the bridge between the planes, or worlds. Through beauty one crosses various strata of existence on the path toward the source of beauty.

We often react to any adverse condition or situation. But it will be wiser if one attacks with his armor and weapons in hand. The armor and weapons can be obtained if, before instinctual reaction, one enters for a moment into the sanctuary of beauty, focuses his mind totally on beauty, and then, charged with wisdom and energy, faces his adversary or his problem.

---

1. Agni Yoga Society, *Fiery World*, Vol. I, para. 177.

Let us remember that "through beauty we conquer." This is a profound statement made by Nicholas Roerich. But one must have beauty or must contact beauty. One must transform himself into beauty. It is impossible to defeat beauty. Beauty is victory itself. It is possible to inherit the problems of one who is striving toward beauty, but it is impossible to defeat him.

The "treasury of beauty" is also a profound statement. One can find many beautiful formulas in that treasury, many visions, revelations, much energy, many creative currents, and healing power. But it is not enough to know all about beauty. One must plan a daily routine to utilize the resources of the treasury of beauty.

You do not need to be a millionaire to surround yourself with beauty. You can make your bedroom beautiful, your living room beautiful, your home beautiful; you can dress beautifully. These practical steps will inspire you to think, speak, and act beautifully. These practical steps will save you energy, time, money, and health; and you will have a healthy impact on people.

Teach your children to love beauty, to collect beautiful objects. If possible, give them a room in which they can collect the objects of beauty and periodically rearrange them: paintings, statues, pictures, stones, shells, carvings, etc.

Every house must have a museum of beauty. When any guest comes to visit, the first thing to show him is the home museum. What a great start for friendship, for cooperation, for better relationship. Just take him to your museum, talk about the objects, listen and watch his reactions; and after you raise his consciousness toward beauty, you will have a high-level relationship with him. Many of your guests will feel healed from their physical, emotional, and mental wounds which accumulate in the daily battle of life. Many guests will be uplifted and inspired by seeing your treasury of beauty.

Children must be prepared for such a consciousness from their early childhood, and when they grow up they will see how, year after year, their tastes changed, deepened, and widened. When they are ready to have their own homes, they will already have a treasury of beauty.

A better generation, a superior generation can be brought out through such a method of beauty, and we will see a gradual elimination and annihilation of ugliness in all walks of life.

The usage of beauty needs a gradual development. Greater benefit can be drawn from beauty when we deal with it on higher and higher levels of beingness. An average man can draw twenty-five percent benefit from beauty. A disciple can draw seventy-five percent from beauty. But an initiate can benefit one hundred percent from beauty.

As we appreciate and live beauty, we change our level of beingness. We expand our consciousness. We purify our thoughts and prepare ourselves to a greater extent to absorb the psychic energy emanating from beauty.

It is also important to watch our actions, words, and thoughts during the time of our growth toward beauty. One cannot assimilate the energy of beauty if in his nature he nurtures ugliness, if he nurtures ugly motives and thoughts, if he uses ugly expressions and acts in an ugly manner. Any kind of ugliness creates short-circuits in his system which prevent assimilation of energy. One can even retard his digestion by listening to ugly conversation or looking at an ugly picture.

It is proper to say that one profits from beauty to the degree that he becomes beautiful.

The aspiration toward beauty must start from early childhood. Mothers and fathers must not lose any opportunity; they must create every kind of opportunity to put their children in contact with beauty.

Meditation organizes our thinking mechanism and expands the flame of our heart.

The organized mind thinks more clearly, logically, and in harmony with the laws of Nature.

As the flame of our heart expands, it becomes impossible for us to fight against anything that is good or to reject anything that is good.

Through meditation our sensitivity toward factuality increases. We no longer live in dreams and confusions. Things gradually become clear for us.

Through meditation we develop love for goodness and beauty.

In meditation the divine within us takes more and more control over the human. We transcend our earthbound life and begin to see the stars.

Reception of Divine Ideas

There are very precious ideas broadcast by higher Beings, but special preparation is necessary to receive and transmit them as they are. One of the differences in reception is caused by our memory. Our memories form a network around our brain, and when the waves of new sendings hit the network, they lose their originality and even disappear in the network of memories.

Preparation for reception involves the ability to neutralize memories and establish direct contact with the Intuitional Plane. Neutralization of memories is possible with due effort and practice. The mental body must remain as a new, open page, without prints of memories, if one wants to receive higher flows of ideas.

Past experiences and memories have a heavy influence in our relationships. Similarly, it is these memories that prevent the reception of the new ideas.

One can see this easily while listening to a lecture. Most of us translate the lecture through our own experiences. If our memories approve the lecture, we like it; if not, we reject it.

The disciples of the Future must develop the ability to hear things as they are. It is, of course, possible to compare them later with the ideas in our memories, but with discrimination and Intuition so as not to be trapped by our old memories.

There are other obstacles on the path of reception of new ideas. They are called vanities, glamors, illusions, and selfishness, but all these are parts of our memory storage.

High-grade receptivity from advanced sources of wisdom is possible only when we realize that memories are like our furniture and they must not interfere with our higher contacts.

Along with the hindrances found within our being, there are also hindrances in space. Electrical storms, outbursts of massive emotions, and dark attacks sometimes do not allow the sendings to reach the person in their entirety.

Sometimes sentences are lost, sometimes words, and the message loses its meaning. But when the Antahkarana is built, all outer and inner obstacles can be gradually conquered.

In sending thoughts, we are told to keep our message short, clear, and precise:

Short — two or three clear words

Clear — pronounced in their exact sounds

Pure — without mixing doubt or other negative thoughts

If our message is kept short, clear, and pure, it may not hit the memory layer of the receiver but reach the registering mechanism directly.

It is possible to repeat the message but not mix it with the additional burden of emotions and thoughts.

Messages which are related to mental and spiritual domains, to service, sacrifice, and enlightenment have a greater chance to reach their destination.

Thoughts mixed with personal concern, with satisfaction of the lower nature, or thoughts mixed with negativity do not reach their destination directly but through the activation of similar memories in the receiver. Besides, parts of such thoughts hang around the sender and gradually distort his mental mechanism.

Thought messages are not always conscious. Sometimes our mechanism is used by our Inner Guide in our own image for certain services. The human soul, or the human being, experiences such moments with momentary drowsiness and fatigue, especially when the mental aura or mental body is taken away to certain locations for certain labor.

Such kinds of activities take a very short time, sometimes one minute, sometimes half an hour, during which the "person" feels drained and exhausted; but after the service is over one feels a regeneration in his system. After such experiences, we are advised to sit in silence for awhile to bring our mental equilibrium back to normal with the rest of our aura. Those who are sensitive feel the gradual return of the vehicles and again feel normal.

During such experiences one can see the irregularity of the heartbeat, the drop in blood pressure, and the weakening of sight and hearing.

You can notice how thought can go faster than even speech or any action. Your reservoir is filled instantaneously, but you notice how much time it takes to empty it through your expression in any form.

Speakers notice how many thoughts wait in their minds to be expressed.

This is how one can experience the existence of thoughts as separate from our consciousness and subject to our control during expression. Also, one notices the mysterious accumulation of thoughtwaves over which one does not have control. Before you send a new messenger of thought, the first one has instantaneously returned.

It is possible to establish a mental conversation with someone and pass ideas in one second which otherwise would take hours of speech or hours of writing.

Special preparations are needed to notice the incoming message and not mix it with the contents of the mind. Special preparations are needed to send clear, pure, and short messages.

66

Traffic of Thoughts

Daily, a traffic of thoughts in many forms and colors passes through the corridors of our mind. Most of them have no purpose or goals, and they wander back and forth through the Law of Association, drifting and eventually disappearing in the distance, or linking with each other and forming chains.

There is a law in the mental body which may be called the Law of Conclusive Arrangement. This law takes all this traffic, arranges it in the best way possible, and then presents it to us on the subjective plane as our *dreams*. Most of our dreams are the associative chain of our daily thoughts and feelings, mechanically created and attracted to us without a purpose.

Through this law, the mental body tries to give a meaning to the "traffic" of thoughts. If certain dreams are not built out of the traffic, chaos and confusion begin to come into the mental sphere and the person loses his sanity, his logic, his reasoning power, and then his common sense. Thus, most of our dreams are a therapeutic process of the Law of Association to bring meaning out of the traffic of unrelated thoughts and emotions.

In this traffic of thoughts and emotions, there are those which are related to each other. They are like currents in the ocean. There are others which are not related. There are currents which flow into our mental pool from various outside sources, like leaves driven by a wind. All this chaotic traffic is associated and arranged just as we do in a dream in a way that makes sense to us.

The Law of Conclusive Arrangement is the law that keeps a person in his sanity. When this law is not in operation, chaos prevails in the mind. The person slowly loses his logic and reasoning faculties under the pressure of the traffic of unrelated thoughts, and he becomes a customer of an asylum.

The Law of Conclusive Arrangement helps us in many ways when we are awake. If we see events, symbols, ever-changing sceneries, or visitors, this law tries to attach a meaning to the events, symbols, sceneries, or visitors. Without a meaning, this "furniture" will not find any logical place in the mind, and it will increase the chaos and confusion in it.

Sometimes the flow of the events, symbols, and visitors is so fast and the daily obligations are so demanding that the Law of Conclusive Arrangement cannot create meaning out of them, and they go and accumulate in the subconsciousness to be worked upon when the man is free from daily obligations. Then the law has a chance to function . . . and create dreams.[1]

Certain elements of this flow of traffic cannot become part of dreams. The Law of Conclusive Arrangement has memory. As other elements come, it finds a chance to call out certain elements stored in the subconsciousness, relate them, and take the tension out of the subconscious storage. If the subconscious storage is crowded with unrelated materials which have no chance of making up parts of any dream, the man slowly becomes irrational in his expressions and relations.

One of my Teachers used to say, "Even if you do not understand what he wants to say, try to handle his words in a way that they make sense to you. Listening and seeing things without making meaning out of them upsets the stomach of your mind."

There are other kinds of impressions which again pass through the Law of Conclusive Arrangement and are translated as dreams. Such dreams are the translation of very subtle impressions coming from Higher Worlds. Such impressions are more dangerous than the incoherent, unrelated traffic flow of the daily thoughts and emotions. Because of their high-voltage energy, they damage the mental body and brain cells of the person who attracts them if his power, the Law of Conclusive Arrangement, is not active in a high order and he cannot create meaning out of them. Such a person slowly falls into the path of insanity.

You can see in asylums how certain insane people try to explain to you something very abstract, but then mix it with the lower traffic of nonsense. If certain professionals are trained, they can act as the Law of Conclusive Arrangement and help such people create meaning out of their "traffic of both ways." This can be done if the damage is not too prevalent in their mental bodies and brains.

The formation of certain superstitions comes under the same law, the Law of Conclusive Arrangement. Primitive man could not understand the causes of lightning and thunder. He could have gone crazy if he did not "conclude" that the gods were fighting in the sky. Superstitions are dreams formulated in our waking consciousness.

This is also true of the metaphysical or abstract stories formulated from the impressions coming from the Higher Worlds. The difference between these two formulations is that superstitions keep you in your present state of consciousness for a long time, while metaphysical and abstract stories become the foundations of future, pure sciences.

Formulation depends upon two factors: the source of impressions, from which originates the traffic; and the state of evolution of the Law of Conclusive Arrangement, or the translator. All phenomena of Nature, either "outside" or "inside," are paths which, if observed carefully, help us to further expand our consciousness.

---

1.   See also *The Subconscious Mind and the Chalice*, Ch. 8.

The collective soul of humanity goes through a similar experience, which is also between the higher traffic and the lower traffic. The higher traffic is composed of events taking place in the Higher Worlds. The lower traffic is composed of events planned by individuals and nations. Some of them are the result of ignorance, hatred, and fear. Some of them are preconceived and planned. The two currents of traffic are mixed together.

The world, or the collective soul of humanity, must "reach a conclusion" in order to survive. In order to do this, it tries to translate the higher impressions into the formulations of new discoveries and bring the events and the incoherent, unrelated traffic of the world into a conclusion or a conclusive wholeness whereby the higher formulation of new discoveries can be absorbed beneficially and used constructively for the advancement of the consciousness of the total humanity.

Wars, depressions, social disorders, genocides, and the like are the formulations of the dreams of the collective soul of humanity to give a meaning to all these incoherent, unrelated, destructive thoughts, hatreds, and fears manufactured daily in the collective human mind. Certain dreams of individuals are like forecasters of destruction. Certain dreams or formulations of the world soul are the forecasts of the total destruction of civilization.

Men, groups, and nations, on the world scale, are responsible for providing the incoherent and unrelated traffic which runs through the corridors of the mind of humanity. If the world soul fails to create conclusive meanings out of them, humanity will see a horrible dream from which it will never awaken in this world.

It is important that we remember our individual and world "dreams." It is important to translate our "dreams" and reach certain conclusions. If not, they will repeat themselves and become a part of the incoherent and unrelated traffic.

Meditation is an ingenious device given to humanity by advanced minds to dissolve parts of this traffic and use them as materials to give form to impressions coming from Higher Worlds. Thus, stabilization of the mind can be reached through scientific meditation.

Meditation has two sides. On the one hand, it is in contact with Higher Worlds from which it receives highly coherent, but not yet formulated, impressions. On the other hand, it is in contact with the world of the incoherent, unformulated traffic of human thinking, emotions, and actions. Between these two, meditation plays a great role, like a blacksmith who casts iron using the scraps of the lower traffic of incoherent materials and the designs and blueprints presented to him from the higher levels of consciousness. Meditation leads to sanity and purification of the mental mechanism. Thus it is a great tool to promote the survival of humanity.

67

How Mental Health
Can Be Secured

Mental health is very important because without it people lack direction. They do not know what they are doing or where they are going and therefore create problems for themselves and others. Without mental health, a person loses himself. We are told that there are many millions of people in the streets who lack mental health. They are committed to hospitals for two or three days and then are released again. Poor mental health is the reason for crime and for many other problems in the world.

Mental health is like your treasury. Mental health not only benefits your personal interests and increases your income, but also it increases your joy — your *livingness*. It makes you real. With mental health, life is real for you; without it, you live in a dream.

A person who has mental health is his own boss. Nobody can manipulate him, use him, or exploit him. A person who has mental health belongs to himself.

Being mentally unhealthy is like being a person who has been drinking. Such a person does not own himself because he does things that he should not or would not do had he not been drinking. If a person is mentally unhealthy, his body, emotions, mind, and brain no longer belong to him. They belong to outside forces. Thus a person can be manipulated through remote control by the thinking, brain, and emotions of others.

It is therefore very important that we have mental health. If you have mental health, then you own yourself and have control upon yourself, your life now, and your future life. But if you do not have mental health, you do not belong to yourself. Additionally, nothing that you have belongs to you because only when you belong to yourself can other things belong to you.

For example, if you are sane, when you play the violin the violin belongs to your hands because you can control it. But if you are insane, the violin does not belong to you because you cannot control it.

What is Mental Health?

These items, collected over many years, will give you solid guidance.

1. A mind that is healthy can see the relation between cause and effect. I have met many insane people, and I am still meeting them. They cannot relate cause to effect, or effect to cause. For example, they do things physically, emotionally, and mentally in their writing, with their speech, and so on without calculating what the result will be. They do not see the effect of their actions. An insane man who only has fifty dollars spends it all in one day and does not have a penny the next day. Or when he is young and has sex energy, he spends it on many girls. By the time he is twenty-five, he has no energy left. He tries to run too fast to his destination, but cannot reach it because he has wasted his energy and abundance in the effort.

Sane people always take into consideration the relationship between cause and effect, and what the effect will create as the new cause for the future. This is why we see that people who are sane are successful.

Some people who are insane may have lots of money, but they do not enjoy it and end up using it for their own destruction. For example, you hear about a millionaire who steals five million dollars. He already has lots of money, so why is he stealing? He steals because he does not consider cause and effect. Or a person goes home and causes himself to drink three bottles of whiskey without calculating what the effect will be tomorrow when he awakens. He does not make this calculation because he is not sane, not mentally healthy.

I once advised a girl who was constantly coughing to give up smoking three packs of cigarettes a day. She was not calculating the effect of a cause. She was not only smoking, which is one thing, but she was also creating the possibility of cancer in her lungs and damaging her liver by doing so. If she were sane, she would know that the cause — her smoking — would create bad effects — her coughing. Why would she want to continue?

These ideas seem very simple, but they are keys to your future happiness and prosperity. Who cares if a person reads holy scriptures but remains a vegetable? It is more important to understand the things that are practical and make your life really happy, healthy, and prosperous.

Think about whether you are really paying attention to the causes and effects of the future. Sometimes you wish you had not done certain things. This means that you did not understand the cause and effect of a certain situation. You took action which was a mistake. If you hear yourself saying, "I wish I had not married that man," it means that you did not see the cause and effect.

A person is mentally healthy when he has foresight and insight. Such a person has control of his actions, his speech, and his relationships, and he does only those things that will create good results in the future.

What can you tell a man who has worked hard to prepare the soil of his garden, but who plants weeds in that soil instead of vegetables? A person is like a fertile garden. He sows in himself the seeds of his actions. If he sows certain seeds, fifty years later he will not be able to walk, his eyes will be blind, and so on because these are the fruits of the seeds which he planted.

It is not only philosophy, psychology, or parapsychology that we need but also real common sense. We need to bring ourselves down and ground ourselves. If we are not grounded, we will be like balloons, neither in heaven nor on earth, and subject to the whim of the wind.

If a person wants to determine whether or not he is one hundred percent sane, he needs to pay attention to what he is doing by calculating the effect that will result later. He needs to know what seeds he is planting so that he knows what he will harvest.

2. The level of a person's memory is the level of his sanity. I knew two brothers — one who was very sharp, the other whose memory was weak. The brother whose mind was clear was married and clean. The other went with fifty different girls and spent all his time and energy drinking and flitting about.

The other day the weaker brother saw me in a store and said, "John, how are you?" He had forgotten my name. When you spend too much energy on the wrong things, you lose your memory. Memory is a sign that you are sane.

In geometry you cannot solve a problem unless you have memorized the formulas. If you do not remember the formulas, you cannot pass your geometry exam. Your memory weakens when you are sixty-five or seventy-five years of age if you wasted your energies when you were younger. You go to the store and cannot get back home because you forgot where your home is. Or you jump in your car to go to the market, then suddenly cannot remember where you were going. If the passenger in your car tells you, "We are going to the store," you will reply, "Really? Which one?" because your brain has been burned.

Every power that you have, every talent and beauty that you have is the result of energy. Energy is not only physical; it can also be emotional energy and mental energy. You can waste yourself physically, emotionally, and mentally. The lack of physical energy is like a flat tire on your car. If you waste yourself emotionally by becoming angry, hateful, separative, jealous, or revengeful, you will find that your emotional centers or chakras will close. You waste yourself mentally by lying. Lying creates double standards in your mind which hate and fight against each other, causing your computer to flip out.

3. A healthy mind solves the problems of life for the benefit of all who are involved in the problems. If you have a problem with someone and try to solve it only for your own benefit, you are not one hundred percent sane. Sanity begins only when we solve problems by considering the best interests of all parties involved. That is why we can say that our current world leadership is wrong. All countries are trying to solve the problems for their own interests, which creates chaos, fear, and destruction. A sane mind tries to solve problems in the best interest of all those who are involved. This is very difficult because there are varying levels of people in terms of their morality, honesty, upbringing, and so on. All these factors interfere. But as you try to solve a problem by finding a common denominator, you will see how you are creating peace, development, and progress in humanity.

When a company wants to market its product, its first intention is to sell anything it can without considering the interest of the buyer. When this happens, a company loses its customers. It begins to rethink the situation and finds that the best business is both for the profit of the company and the benefit of the customer. If you buy something and cannot use it for more than a couple of days, you hate the company who made it and sold it to you and you do not shop there anymore. The company will eventually go bankrupt. Slowly we are coming to that stage of thinking, or morality and sanity, which tries to solve problems by sharing a common interest instead of trying to exploit one another. Exploitation is a strong indication that the mind is really sick. A man who wants in every way and at every opportunity to steal from you, to use and manipulate you for his selfish interests, is considered sick. He has a sick mind because he does not know that whatever he steals will have to be repaid ten times over in karma.

So sanity means to live within the laws of karma and in harmony with the laws of Nature. A man who has a forest and cuts down all of his trees for some instant money may not care that he has just severed an important source of joy, prana, happiness, and fragrance for himself, not to mention the soil erosion and displacement of the wildlife which took refuge there. Such a man is insane because he is trying to solve his own problems without considering the wider consequences. Every person has moments of insanity. But when these moments of insanity increase, he goes toward bankruptcy.

When I was in Switzerland, I was told that a nearby lake was so polluted that nothing could live in it. The authorities searched and searched and could not find the source of the pollution. Finally they found that a factory had placed a long pipe underground which was emptying into the lake and polluting it. That factory once was very profitable, but when they closed the factory, the owner lost everything. That man was insane to organize such an action.

No one can benefit by destroying the water, air, plants, and animals for his own profit. Such a person violates and betrays these resources. There are laws and rights of living. If a person tries to benefit only himself, he is insane.

Humanity is mostly insane. We are living in an insane world. If we continue polluting this planet, insanity will increase to such a degree that one hundred years from now sane people will have to act insane in order to survive.

Try to be sane from now on. If you are sane, you exist; you have communication with Nature, with everything; you are balanced in your mind. A sane mind is a balanced mind. If you are dizzy, you cannot walk straight. It is just like that.

4. Sane people do not have separative interests. They are interested in the welfare of all people. There is no greatness in a nation unless that nation tries to make all other nations great. If we are going to make this nation great, we need to consider the interests of all other nations.

Separatism is found between husband and wife, children, classmates, and friends. I once saw a young boy steal fish from his own mother's plate and eat them. He ate so much that two hours later he had extreme pains in his stomach and nobody could figure out why. I said to him, "Tell us how many fish you ate," to which he replied, "Seven." This is symbolic of what happens to people if they are separative and exploit others for their own stomachs.

5. A sane person has no crystallization in his thinking. He is not encumbered by old-fashioned tradition, history, philosophy, or religion, and he does not react to their push-buttons. Life is continuously new if you always have new conditions and new states of consciousness. Things must be met on their proper level at the right time.

Not long ago electric typewriters were considered up-to-date. Now we consider them to be more like mules that we cannot use. If a person is crystallized, he will insist on using an old-fashioned typewriter, even though it is not right for the times. Many ideas and thoughts in our minds are old-fashioned and inappropriate for this day and age.

You need to discover what thoughts and ideas are outmoded and discard them. In the past, if a man who owned a company was a Democrat, he could hire only Democrats to work for him. He could reject people from different religions and nationalities. This practice does not work anymore. When you are crystallized in obsolete, worn-out concepts, they dominate your mind and make you insane because you are no longer up-to-date.

A new level requires a new-level man. Try to discover what crystallizations you have in your mind. A man once wrote me a letter which said, "I have read in your books that Great Ones exist and that thinking about Them sometimes is good for us. But I am so afraid that if I think about the Masters, God will begin to take second place." I answered him by asking, "Where is there a place where God is not? Can you show me some place where God does not exist? If you touch any object, you are touching God because God is in everything, everywhere."

Crystallized, worn-out concepts, "the only way to fly," do not work any more. You need to find out if your mind is blocked, and if it is, how many blocks exist. Your crystallized concepts are like icebergs around which you cannot navigate safely. Remove them and your thinking will be like a clear lake on which you can sail easily.

Sane people are those who are always open, whose horizons are great. They are ready to accept that which is beautiful and righteous. They are open, and because they are open, they keep their equilibrium while tending to the demands of their progressing life.

There are "New Age" groups that are really "old age" and rotten. It is not apparent at first, but if you really observe them, they are outmoded. Some of the so-called New Age magazines are filled with fourteenth century darkness.

In the seventh century, holy people went to the mountains to meet God. It is hard to say what they really experienced, but they experienced something. In this century, you will meet God in your daily labor, in Nature, within each other, everywhere — not just in the wilderness. If you cannot meet God within each other, you will never meet Him. Christ said, "If you cannot love the brother whom you can see, how can you love your Father whom you cannot see?" How can I say that I love God if I hate you? Christ's statement contains the tremendous idea that it is not right to cheat one another and, while doing so, profess to worship God. If you are destroying thousands of people, you cannot consider yourself to be a religious person. If you are a religious man, you must have love. Love proves that you can love God.

If your mind is cleaned of these crystallizations, you will have a field free of rocks in which you can work. The mind is a garden full of crystallized ideas. Try every day to throw one rock out so that you will have fertile ground in which to plant the crops you want.

6. A sane person has no cleavages in his consciousness, in the continuity of his ideas, speech, or thinking. Some people cannot carry on a conversation without changing topics in midstream. There is no continuity in their mind. Their engine is not integrated; the computer has faulty programming or wiring. If a person starts a sentence which he does not finish and then starts another sentence within that sentence, he is not sane. This proves that his mind has no integrity or continuity.

Watch for these signs in those around you. When you are making business friends, forming personal friendships, or selecting a husband or wife, watch to see if there is continuity in the mind of the person through his speech, in his devotion, striving, and dedication. If the person constantly changes, you will never know where you stand. I knew a man who came to me and said, "I have become a Buddhist." Then one month later he told me he had converted to Christianity. A few months later he became a Moslem. What could I think of him? It is all right for him to be anything he wants, but if he constantly changes his mind it means there is a loose screw somewhere.

7. A clear mind has no karmic restrictions. A person's mind will not be sharp, creative, or clear if in the past by his deeds and thoughts he damaged the minds of others. If he assisted the minds of others to be balanced, beautiful, and creative, his mind will be one hundred years advanced. Whatever you sow, you reap; this is the law.

If a person causes destruction, distortion, disturbances, and confusion in the mind of another, his mind will be hit by the effect of his action and become disturbed and confused. This is what karmic restriction is. When a person works hard but can only get so far, it is usually because karma is holding him back. He has reached his karmic level, and if he tries to force, he cracks.

Sometimes I am asked by others to inspire a particular person, but I am not smarter than karma. Perhaps that person cannot proceed with meditation, contemplation, samadhi, or different disciplines because he will crack. Karma prohibits this because the person did not perform sacrificial service for others in his past and is therefore not worthy to proceed. He has not accumulated enough beneficial action in his account. You must have an adequate balance in your account to have a healthy mind.

The greatest law is, "What you sow, you reap." What you have sown in past lives and what you are sowing now is what you will reap in the future. When you see a beautiful building, you sense that whoever built that building had an incredible mind; it is reflected in his creation. If he had built something ridiculous, you would sense that the builder had a ridiculous mind. Similarly, if your past has been rich, your future will be richer. What have you given to Nature and to humanity that you expect to become a great man?

A little frog in a field came across a grazing bull. "I want to be just like him," the frog thought. So he inhaled repeatedly and puffed himself up until he was two feet across . . . and then he burst. He tried to force his limit. He was not born a bull because of his past life. Do not kid yourself. Whatever you sow, you reap.

A man I had not seen for ten years paid me a visit. He said, "I am in trouble. Everybody gossips about me and feels malice toward me."

I told him, "It is no wonder."

"Why do you say that?" he asked.

I said, "Do you remember how ten years ago you used to have such a dirty mouth? You planted dirty seeds everywhere and now those seeds that you sent out have accumulated, recycled, and are hitting you back."

Sane people know about cause and effect and are not restricted by karma. On the contrary, karma assists them. If they want to run away, karma brings them a horse to ride and they disappear. If they are in danger, karma brings a gale that destroys their enemies.

8. A sane mind has an expanding capacity for the input of new knowledge and has the power to assimilate this knowledge. If a person's mind is clear and clean, he can pick up a technical book, study it, and it eventually becomes clear to him. A person whose mind is not clear cannot understand the book. He cannot assimilate it, and he does not make any effort to understand it.

Christ told a parable to his disciples about a very rich man who gave a party. All of his guests arrived, but, while the party was going on, a man arrived who was not well dressed. The rich man told his servants to throw the man out because he did not fit the standard of the party. The party is symbolic of a spiritual gathering. The participants were drinking ideas, enjoying thoughtforms, beautiful concepts. The man with improper clothing is symbolic of a person whose aura is dirty. Such a person cannot enter because he is damaged karmically. Clothing symbolizes the aura and personality. If your body is dirty karmically, you cannot enter into that level of enjoyment, joy, and bliss where people are sharing a spiritual feast.

9. A sane mind is equipped with psychic energy which shields the person and prevents psychic attack. Those who are under psychic attack are those who have wasted psychic energy in wrong thinking. If you think correctly and occupy your mind with Beauty, Goodness, Righteousness, Joy, and Freedom, no attack will be able to reach you.

10. A sane mind is sensitive to intuitional impressions and they do not harm him. If the mind is not healthy, the impressions coming from Higher Sources are distorted and misused. When higher impressions are misused and distorted, they burn the mechanism of the mind further, and create a person who is a suitable customer for an asylum.

11. A sane and healthy mind has a well developed treasury. This treasury is the Chalice which is found in the higher mind. Throughout our lives we fill the Chalice with our sacrificial labor and love and with the wisdom gained through experience. A person with a healthy mind uses the Chalice just as he uses his savings in times of need.

12. A sane mind has equilibrium, balance, and common sense.

13. A person with a sane and healthy mind has the power to translate impressions accurately, without exaggeration or fabrication. He sees things clearly and knows exactly in what situation he is found.

14. A healthy mind has a sense of infinity. Through use of this sense, a person is free of identifications with objects, persons, and locations. The sense of infinity gives him freedom, which helps him advance and expand his consciousness continually.

15. A healthy mind is full of gratitude. Gratitude is the *awareness* of all the good things people have done for us, and the *readiness* to pay them back with interest.

People think that gratitude is a feeling of happiness for the good things people have done for us. Such a feeling is an expression of selfishness and self-interest. People who feel like this generally take all that you can give and then walk away as if you owed them all that you gave.

Of course, one must remember that under certain circumstances people can help you by not helping you at all, or by showing total indifference to you. You must feel grateful, not because you received or did not receive something, but because people have increased your maturity and wisdom by doing or not doing certain things for you.

Grateful people feel eternally indebted to life and to all people everywhere. They radiate the beneficent rays of gratitude in all their relationships. Thus they affirm that all is given to them under law and that all is paid back under law.

Sanity and gratitude work together to bring honor to a person.

How to Take Care of Your Brain

- avoid poisons

- avoid drugs

- avoid alcohol

- avoid tobacco

- avoid marijuana

- avoid excessive sex

- sleep well and enjoy Nature

These factors create short-circuits in the brain:

— worry

— anger

— hatred

— fear

— jealousy

— revenge

Great damage is done to the brain through

- harmful action

- exploitation

- stealing

- lying

- hypocrisy

- crime

- murder

- forgery

The brain and mind also can be damaged by

— the shock of loud sounds

— chemicals

— poisons such as insecticides

— sleeping pills

— sedatives

— electric shocks

— high power electrical wires

— noise

— electric hair dryers

Mental health is restored through

- rest

- good food

- pure water

- joy

- inspirational reading

- meditation

- creativity

- service

Mental health can be secured by

— well-balanced food

— physical rest

— economy of sexual energy

— avoidance of intoxication

— lovingness and harmlessness

— absence of jealousy

— absence of fear

In the mental body there is a mechanism which is called the *mental unit*. This unit is radioactive and continuously supplies energy to the brain and to the mental body. It supplies energy for all kinds of functions of the mind. When this unit is damaged in any way, the weakening of mental powers becomes evident.

The mental unit can be damaged or blocked by using the mind in anti-survival ways — ways that are against unity — for crimes and murder, separatism, and misuse of power.

When the energy of the mental unit is slowed or becomes irregular in its supply, all kinds of mental dishonesty start growing like weeds.

The mental unit is the source from which the thread of continuity of consciousness is woven. The building of this bridge of continuity of consciousness is the glory of the human being.

When the mental unit is connected to the Mental Permanent Atom, permanent sanity is secured. This bridge is built through creative manifestation and through sacrificial service.

68

How to Free Yourself from the Pressure of the Past

Those people who cannot free themselves from the memories of their wrong doings and are continuously hounded by them will find the following ritual to be of great assistance.

Spiritual transformation cannot proceed in the right way and at the required speed if the consciousness of the aspirant or disciple is loaded with memories of harmful acts committed at various times and places, under various circumstances.

These memories may be uprooted through repentance, if the subject cannot find any other way to free himself of them. Repentance is conducted by

1. Remembering

   - harmful actions

   - harmful feelings

   - harmful thoughts

   - harmful words or slander

   - harmful behavior

2. Pondering the future consequences of the above factors regarding others and oneself

3. Deciding not to repeat these five factors

4. Compensating those to whom harm was done in various ways, whether by thought, word, or action

5. Invoking divine power to help you resist any tendency to hurt people for self-interest or because of jealousy, revengefulness, hatred, greed, or irritation

Lord Buddha says, "All sins are just like frost or dew. The Sun of wisdom can disperse them."

Exercise

The Ritual of Repentance

1. Just before sleeping, light a candle in your room. Sit on your knees and visualize a radiant Sun on the wall.

NOTE: In case you are in Nature, face a mountain, river, ocean, cave, or tree and do the same as above, visualizing a radiant Sun above you.

2. In the presence of the Sun, say:

> *May your light permeate my soul*
> *and may I stand in Light.*

Visualize the Light permeating your body and see yourself standing in Light.

3. Remember those things that were harmful to other people — things that are bothering your conscience or making your heart uncomfortable.

4. Visualize yourself sitting in Light and say:

> *My Lord,*
> *I am guilty for my actions, thoughts, feelings, motives,*
> *and I am deeply sorry for my harmful behavior,*
> *for my selfish and hateful actions.*
>
> *May the seeds of harmfulness which I have spread*
> *this day (this week, this month) dry and perish*
> *before they sprout into causes of pain and suffering.*

*I solemnly promise in this Light to guard my
thoughts, words, and actions so that from now on
I do not cause harm to anyone in the world.*

*May Your Light purify my heart,
and may Your psychic energy renew my striving
toward harmlessness.*

6. After saying this, raise your hands and bless those whom you hurt. Visualize them and say:

*I am deeply sorry. Please grant me your
forgiveness and your blessings.*

7. Then bow forward and place your forehead on the floor, saying:

*Let my soul shine in the darkness
and spread beauty, goodness, and joy.*

8. Pull your body up and visualize a Sun in the center of your forehead and say:

*More radiant than the Sun,
purer than the snow,
subtler than the ether
is the Self,
the Spirit within my heart.
I am that Self;
that Self am I.*

This mantram must be repeated after each ritual of repentance so that you do not develop a guilt complex. Remember that your Spirit is pure and that harmful acts are committed when you, as the Spirit, are fooled by blind urges and drives, glamors and illusions.

NOTE: Repentance must be severe any time you notice that you are failing to overcome certain thoughts, words, or deeds and are continuing your harmfulness. Severe repentance must be carried on in the following way:

After performing the above ceremony, decide how you are going to compensate those whom you hurt. For example, send $1,000 to the person you hurt, or buy him expensive clothes or objects of beauty, and so on. Or, do one of the following:

    a. Fast for three days without even liquids.[1]

    b. Help someone for three days without compensation.

    c. Decide to render other services as a penance for your harmful deeds.

    d. Give lunch to ten people.

    e. Buy clothes for the poor or do other acts of charity.

If you follow these instructions, you will experience a great release from your harmful acts; your heart will feel joy, and your mind will be full of Light.

The ceremony of repentance will build a shield around you and protect you from evil attacks. The ceremony of repentance will also save you from future embarrassment, difficulties, problems, pain, and suffering.

NOTE: Along with the ceremony of repentance, one must meditate upon the seed thought of *harmlessness.*

Certain Teachers suggest that in addition to repentance, we must daily meditate upon harmlessness for fifteen to twenty minutes, for at least six months, and record all our ideas and revelations.

When our understanding of harmlessness deepens, it will uproot all seeds of harmfulness which have fallen into the fields of our consciousness. Harmlessness will bring great purification to our whole nature.

Meditation upon harmlessness is so powerful that it will even destroy the negative karma we built in the past through our harmful deeds.

Through meditation on harmlessness, karma can be overcome and the consequences of karma can be destroyed before they manifest.

Remember that the mantram of "The Self" must be repeated after each effort of repentance.

---

1. Please first contact your physician.

69
Thinking

In the question of thinking, we have three factors:

The thinker

The ability to think

The thoughts

The thinker is different from the ability to think. An ability is a device that the thinker uses when he needs to use it. The thinker uses his ability to think, to manufacture thoughts, in order to bring changes in the environment or changes in his own mechanism.

Thoughts have no ability to think. The thinking ability is one of the powers of the thinker. It is through thinking that the thinker builds his vehicles and his environment.

Most of the time, thoughts in space use the brain of a person to think through. To be a thinker is not easy, and most human beings do not think but only use thoughts, as they use any clothing, food, etc., produced by others.

It is a very important point to realize that not every person knows how to think. The ability to think is developed as a response from the thinker to the needs presented to him.

People think that "whatever man thinks, so he is." This is a completely false statement. The true statement is, "Whatever man thinks *in his heart*, so he will be."

The reason is that man can recycle millions of thoughts and influence the life of the planet, but he himself remains as he was before. Those who think *in their hearts* are the ones who really think, and, as they think, their life and mechanisms come into being as the reflections of their thoughts.

The mind does not think, in spite of many so-called philosophers and psychiatrists who argue that the mind thinks. It is the heart that thinks. Thinking in the heart means to manifest principles, laws, and solutions from the depth of your being which will

— enlighten humanity

— create health, happiness, prosperity

— enable people to experience self-actualization

— enable them to surpass human evolution and enter into superhuman evolution

Deduction and induction are not processes of thinking but manipulation or usage of thoughtforms already provided by the thinker.

As the flower unfolds, the human soul unfolds in thinking. Thinking is the manifestation or expression of the human soul. The human soul comes into existence through thinking. To have a body, emotions, and mind does not mean the existence of the soul — the thinker.

Beliefs, opinions, judgments, and concepts are not processes of thinking. They are ready-made furniture that the mind can collect, organize, and re-form, to give the impression that he thinks.

Actually, as a man advances in thinking, he destroys beliefs, opinions, judgments, and concepts. These are all traps on the way of a thinking process.

People think that our past experiences exist within us as thoughts. This is ridiculous. Any experience may stimulate our thinking, which then tries to analyze it and find its cause and future effects. But too often an experience does not even create a response from the thinker because the thinker is not there, and it remains in the memory as an event. Most human beings do not know how to think, so an experience does not stay within them as thoughts. Most of our experiences are mechanical. They run mechanically, and thought has nothing to do with them.

It is true that a real thinker can create new experiences through putting new causes into action and experience them on higher levels, involving new mechanisms for recording the experience.

The mind has a special evocative power. The energies, forces, and substance of the Universe react, respond, and cooperate with the mental conditions of a man, of a group, or of a nation. This means that through your states of mind you condition the events that are related to your life.

The more organized and harmonious your mind, the more organized and harmonious will be your life.

The life you live is a sequence of events. This means your life is the reflection of your mental conditions. If you are inclined to blame the conditions in your life, it is better if you blame the conditions of your mind. If you want to change the conditions in your life, you must change the conditions of your mind.

But how to change the conditions of your mind? People try to change the conditions of life without trying to change the conditions of their mind. No matter how much you try to raise the level of your life, it will drop to the level of the existing conditions of your mind.

To change the conditions of the mind is not easy. There are two great fields in which you must work:

1. the field of your mind

2. the field of your environment

Environment is the space over which the influence of your mind extends.

To change the conditions of your mind and to bring a constructive change in your environment, you must learn the science of meditation and apply it in your life. In other words, you must learn the science of right thinking and carry on your right thinking through your words, feelings, and actions in the field in which you live.

As meditation organizes your mind, your life will be organized and life events will be harmonious with the motives you have in your mind.

People think that immediately when they start to do meditation their life will change and everything will run as they wish. This is not a realistic expectation. We must know that it takes time to organize and cleanse our mind. For thousands of years we used the mind with ignorance, and we disturbed its mechanism or often even damaged it. We left that supreme computer in the hands of our blind urges and drives. We accumulated in it things that were not healthy and harmonious, and eventually we saw what our mind was in the mirror of our life events.

Our life events, reflecting the conditions of our mind, substantiated as painful events, eventually became unbearable and we decided to change them with

— wars

— revolutions

— riots

— new elections

— new laws

— new constitutions

— new conferences

Thus we tried to change the conditions of life without trying to change the conditions of our thinking. Most of these measures worked for a short time, but the conditions of life fell to the level where the state of our mind was.

We introduced causes to change our environment but not causes to change our way of thinking. And we were not able to change the conditions of life because of many causes which we put into operation throughout thousands of incarnations.

Similarly, we were not able to change the conditions of our mind:

1. because we did not realize that our life was a reflection of the state of our mind

2. and because we did not consider that the programmings in the mental computer should change if we wanted to change our way of thinking

The mind has many powers. One of them is to use the events and experiences gained on one level in many dimensions. For example, in learning to repair a machine, you learn the power of observation. You see cause and effect, and you see the relationship of the parts to the whole engine. You learn the things that make the engine survive a long time, and the things that make it defective. You learn how to take the engine and observe its condition in relation to other conditions.

Let us say that in this incarnation you were promoted to be a judge in a village. You do not have the experience of judging people, but your entire "computer" is filled with knowledge and with the experience of fixing car engines.

The mind forgets about the car but uses the experiences drawn from working on cars. The mind now has persons to deal with instead of cars. What the mind does is show the judge how to approach the persons by first observing them, seeing how things started and ended. Then he will see the relationship of the events, the relationship between the individuals involved, and so on. He then will know how to *repair* with right judgment the case so that the "engine" works much better and does not become a hazard on the road of life.

If the judge has many other specializations, the computer mind collects all of them and uses them for the purpose at hand. The richer the experience of the judge, the better will be his dealings with various kinds of problems.

For us, there are various jobs and various events. For the mind, there are not various jobs and various events but only similar enigmas or forces producing various events and experiences that are the same in any job and any event.

The mind sees cause and effect and gathers experiences or wisdom. For example, one learns to solve a jigsaw puzzle and put it together. The mind uses this developed power in solving world events by seeing them as one picture — when the person is put in a different situation in which he must relate to the world problems.

The mechanism of the mind builds the brain as an object casts a shadow. But it is the soul which builds the mind in its efforts to come in contact with the material universe and to approximate the subjective and objective existences in Cosmic reality.

People think that evolution built the brain. It is true that the brain evolved throughout ages, but the evolution of the brain was the result of the human soul endeavoring to cope with the gradually more complicated life of the planet.

In the distant future, man will not have a mind or a brain because the soul will be so trained that it will cast away the mind and the brain and contact the life within all its manifested forms directly and with utmost simplicity.

This is to say that man will not even need a body when he learns how to function without one.

70

Qualities of Thought

Thoughts have weight. This may seem to be a premature statement, but future scientists will prove it. The weight of thoughts is related to the kind of matter with which the thoughts are loaded.

For example, thoughts that are loaded with material interests weigh heavily, pull the human soul down to earth, and make it earth-bound. Thoughts loaded with emotions are not as heavy because emotional matter is lighter. Thoughts which are loaded with mental interests and objects are very light. Thoughts which are loaded with ideas, impressions, and visions are the lightest thoughts.

Thoughts also have space. Earthy thoughts have limited space. Emotional thoughts incorporate more space and have a broader influence. Mental thoughts occupy solar and galactic space. Intuitional thoughts have limitless or infinite space.

It is also known that thoughts have speed. Material thoughts are slow. Emotional thoughts are fast. Mental thoughts are very fast. Intuitional thoughts are the fastest.

Many other things we know about thoughts. For example, material thoughts contain a small amount of energy. Emotional thoughts contain powerful energy. Mental thoughts have tremendous strength. Intuitional thoughts emanate the most powerful energy.

Material thoughts, when based on creative harmony, are beautiful and constructive. When they are conflicting, they are very ugly and destructive.

Emotional thoughts, when based on love and compassion, are very beautiful and magnetic. If based on the six vipers — hatred, fear, anger, jealousy, revenge, and treason — they are very ugly and repulsive.

Mental thoughts, when related to Beauty, Goodness, Righteousness, Joy, Freedom, striving, and gratitude, are extremely beautiful. When they are related to the five monsters — ego, vanity, separatism, self-interest, and greed — they are very ugly and destructive.

Intuitional thoughts are always beautiful — like divine symphonies, polar lights, and auroras — because they are rooted in the Hierarchical Plan and divine ideas, and they are charged with Divine Will.

Physical thoughts are limited to the physical plane. Emotional thoughts penetrate to each atom of the physical and astral planes. Mental thoughts can penetrate the physical, astral, and mental realms. Intuitional thoughts can penetrate the physical, emotional, mental, and intuitional realms. The higher the thought, the deeper its penetration and the more constructive and creative its effects on that plane.

Victory, success, abundance, health, and enlightenment are gained through the labor to elevate our thoughts. Gradually the science of meditation will be the most supreme science, together with the science of service. Service is actualization of thought and distribution on various levels of the fruits of thought.

The progress of thinking starts with matter and self-interest. If thinking stays at this level, a person cannot proceed toward perfection. He must slowly think about astral, mental, intuitional, and still higher matters and substance until he realizes how matter slowly changes into energy as his thoughts climb and eventually become Spirit.

There is nothing wrong with thinking that is devoted to knowing matter and its form. But if thoughts are used to manipulate matter for selfish ends or against the Common Good, then such thoughts become earth-bound. Similarly, thoughts based on the six vipers are destructive thoughts; thoughts related to the five monsters are poisonous thoughts.

Thoughts can fluctuate in the three worlds until they operate in the Intuitional Plane, where every thought is a rare flower.

The nature of man in the four worlds is the result of his thoughts. His physical, emotional, mental, and spiritual

form

weight

space

color

sound

energy

beauty

depend on the difference and quality of his thoughts.

Higher thoughts bring him joy, happiness, bliss, and prosperity on the four planes. Ugly thoughts lead him to ill health, failure, shame, and death.

The quality of thoughts can be raised through regular and steady meditation and sacrificial service.

71

Crooked Thoughts

A person was presented with a beautiful rose, and, because he was possessed by negative thoughts, he said, "This rose cannot fill my hunger. I cannot marry it. I cannot drive it as a car. And because of all these, it is useless and it is an insult to present it to me."

Another person, seeing that his son was happy with his wife, said, "I cannot understand how two people can be happy living with each other."

Another person was presented with the New Testament. After reading it she said, "I can use this book to cheat people and make money."

A person who used to steal from his job eventually was discharged. He visited his boss and said, "Why is it wrong to steal a few dollars if it does not hurt anybody?"

One who was full of vanity eventually realized that he was not accepted by people around him. He thought, "Vanity does not work. What about hypocrisy?"

A secretary who was jealous of her boss's wife tried to speak ill of the wife. When asked why she was doing that she answered, "I want her to be unhappy."

A girl who was going with a married man said to her mother, "If I can make that man happy, that is all I want."

A thief shot his dog when the dog ate a piece of meat from the table. After killing the dog, he said, "How dare you eat things that do not belong to you."

A poor lady, after marrying a very rich man, began to act in vanity and started to show off through her speech, manners, and dress. When she was asked why she left behind her simplicity and humility, she answered, "How else can people know that I am rich?"

A divorced woman, after living in celibacy for a while, began to praise herself for her self-control. Once she said to a man who was interested in her, "I will make love with you as often as you want if you promise to repeat in my ear, 'You are a virgin.'"

There was a secretary in an office who used to slander each employee. No one was good except herself. When she was asked why she was engaged in such an unpleasant business, she answered, "There is no other way to feel my superiority."

After people realized that she was spreading seeds of hatred, they left her alone. Once she complained to me, "I tried to show them their weaknesses, but no one appreciated me."

A lady became a devotee to a wisdom teaching in order to marry the leader. It happened that the leader married another woman. Realizing that she could not reach her goal, she devoted herself to gossip and slander. When she was asked about her conduct, she answered, "Nothing is good for me if it does not belong to me."

A young man, after becoming a lawyer, said to his father, "From now on, my life will be dedicated to saving criminals."

A doctor once said, "My whole desire is to have sick people around me so that I can make money."

A child said to the mother, "I love you only when you let me do whatever I want to do."

A secretary, having so much trouble at home with her husband, was not able to fulfill her duties in the office. The boss, being dissatisfied with the quality of her work, expressed concern. She said, "You are like my husband. You can't understand that I have a problem." The boss answered, "Only a psychiatrist can understand your problem."

A girl who had made love with many men eventually married. One day she said to her husband, "I wish you would handle me as the other ones did in the past."

A woman, after having two children, left her husband. When asked why, she answered, "He loves his children more than me. Now he can give all his time to them."

A political leader, after robbing the resources of his nation, was impeached by the government. In an interview, he said, "I don't understand how the government can take my country from my hands."

A lady who was an expert at slander once said, "Slandering is the most interesting game for me. It also gives me confidence in myself."

The misery and suffering of the world is the result of crooked thinking. Crooked thinking is

1. selfish

2. irresponsible

3. evil, harmful to others

4. incorrect

5. manipulative

6. confusing

7. retrogressive

Those who want to meet happiness in future lives must eventually master the art of right thinking.

72

Overdevelopment of Mind

At the present we see some people in the world trying all possible means to develop their mind and gain power over others with the creative results of their mind. Others, discouraged by the race for mental development, discoveries, and technology, are falling into inertia and seeking the path of pleasures and apathy.

There is another kind of mental development which is related to the development of Intuition or Christ Consciousness.

At the present we see these three attitudes all over the world. This situation will gradually create different confrontations between these three sections of humanity.

The mentally overdeveloped people will try to exploit and manipulate mentally underdeveloped people who, in turn, will increase their resistance and provide unending problems to be confronted by mentally overdeveloped people. Of course, the mentally overdeveloped people will not have the *wisdom* to solve the problems of mentally underdeveloped people, and the tension will increase even more between them.

The only hope for creating understanding and peace between these three sections will be in those who are treading the Path of Wisdom and achieving Intuition or Christ Consciousness.

Neither mentally overdeveloped people nor mentally underdeveloped people can benefit from the wisdom of the third party as yet.

Armageddon will start the day when these mentally overdeveloped and mentally underdeveloped people fight against those with intuitional development. The fight will be unprecedented in the history of the planet, and mentally overdeveloped and mentally underdeveloped people will be cast out from this planet into the space, as they will be considered "failures."

The Ageless Wisdom says that the three-fifths of humanity, who were engaged in developing the Intuition, will continue their evolution in this scheme.[1]

The Christ Consciousness or Intuitional Plane can be achieved by living a life of love, beauty, freedom, joy, and synthesis and through meditation, contemplation, and sacrificial service.

---

1. For explanation of globes, rounds, schemes, see *Cosmos in Man*, pp. 25-42.

Very soon schools and universities will provide opportunities to develop the Intuition.

When the Intuition is developed, the overdevelopment of mind will be impossible, and it will be used as a servant of the Hierarchical Plan and the Divine Purpose. Overdevelopment of the mental principle leads to crystallization of the mind and makes it a purpose in itself — instead of making it a means to serve the Intuition.

Health and success are based on harmonious development. Harmony must prevail not only in relation to our bodies, groups, nations but also in relation to the planetary and the solar Whole. Wherever harmony is violated, there is either overdevelopment or underdevelopment. Both processes bring heavy taxation, pressure, and disturbances to neighboring elements.

Competition or inertia always brings complications in all fields of human endeavor. This is true for the overdevelopment of mind. An overdeveloped mind disturbs not only the harmony in Nature but also the harmony in the human being. A part of the human being grows at the expense of the other parts.

Nature does not tolerate any overgrowth because in the Law of Nature all parts, all elements have the same right to respond to the cyclic progress in harmonious steps.

Every destruction is the result of inharmonious growth in humanity or in Nature.

Generally, Nature responds to the Law of Harmony. It is after the development of the mind, due to various emotions and mental tendencies, that people violate this law in the seven fields of human endeavor.

The development of heart is as important as the development of mind. At the present the heart is left far behind.[2]

Along with the development of mind and heart, one must strive to develop the *will*.

It is only the development of the *will* that will regulate the process of harmonious development. The *true will* is nothing but participation and fusion of our mind and heart with the power and rhythm of the Divine Will, which is the foundation of the Law of Harmonious Advancement in all Nature toward an intelligent, all-inclusive Purpose.

---

2.   For a better understanding of heart and mind, please see *The Flame of the Heart.*

73

Strong Thoughts

Thoughts play a great role in expanding and shifting our consciousness.

It is the human soul that thinks, and as he thinks, the light of the human soul increases. Thought provides substance to the human consciousness.

Every real thought that issues from the human soul, from the Inner Guide, or from the Great Souls in Space or on earth can powerfully influence, strain, and shift the human consciousness. To *strain* means to make a substance extend it capacity beyond its present capacity. To *shift* means to change the direction and to move on higher or lower levels or dimensions.

Shifting to higher planes increasingly makes the consciousness polarize toward the most essential, the most practical, and the most inclusive approach to reality.

To shift to lower planes means to run on the path of disintegration and degeneration.

Real thought is the embodiment of ideas, impressions, or inspirations coming from a more inclusive consciousness found in the Higher Worlds.

Thoughts may also be the embodiment of desires, glamors, illusions, and self-deception. These are weak thoughts.

A strong thought is

1. A close embodiment of a principle or law, or a close embodiment of the idea contacted by the mind

2. Built in a way that reflects the principle, idea, or law exactly and has sufficient other elements to introduce itself and be accepted by the sphere where it is formulated

Weaker thoughts are those which either do not resonate with the originating principle or are built in a way that cannot be accepted or promoted.

"The construction of basic principles is caused by and depends on the stimulus of thought."[1]

---

1. Agni Yoga Society, *Infinity*, Vol. 2, para. 388.

Every strong thought is the result of a great principle existing in higher planes, and every strong thought, in its turn, can create the principles needed on the level where the thought is created.

Such principles are caused by the power of thought and brought into existence. These principles depend on the stimulus of thought. The thought energy must continuously support them or else other thoughts will dissipate them.

This phenomenon occurs on all planes.

The highest principles are sources of inspiration and the substance for strong thoughts.

Strong thoughts are well formulated thoughts which, in the meantime, have the possibility to expand and adjust to new conditions and to new relationships. They always enthuse people and inspire them toward new achievements.

74

Dialogue of the Inner Presence

There is a constant dialogue going on in the consciousness of the human being. This dialogue starts with questions and answers.

There is the Inner Presence, and there is the human soul. Sometimes it is the human soul who asks questions, and the Inner Presence answers him, in Its own way. Sometimes it is the Inner Presence Who asks questions, and the human soul tries to go deep into his core and find the answers.

The difference between these two processes is that when the human soul asks the question, he does not know the answer, but when the Inner Presence asks the question, It knows the answer.

If one reaches a stage of consciousness in which he begins a dialogue with the Inner Presence, or if he reaches a stage where he can respond and answer the questions put to him from the Inner Presence, we say that the path of enlightenment is now open for that person.

This dialogue continues life after life, until one day when the questioning one and the answering one fuse with each other.

Man is given a great opportunity to see his path in greater and brighter light; mental questioning is his tool. When we learn how to question, then we will receive the right answers.

Qualities of the Dialogue

1. There is the Source of light within us, the One Who gives the answers. This Source is in tune with Cosmic laws and principles, and Its answers are always in harmony with the Cosmic direction.

2. We receive the answer to our question always, but

   a. we reject it

   b. we change it

   c. we use it for our urges, drives, and illusions

3. When we ask and receive the answer and apply it, we build a steady communication line between the personality and the Source of light.

4. If we reject the answer constantly, or more often than not, we build a barrier between us and the Source. Then future answers will reach us less frequently, and they will even disappear in the air before they reach us.

5. Man is a walking question. All his life he questions and receives answers.

6. Man's success and well-being depend upon

    a. the level of his questions

    b. the degree of his application of the answers

7. There is also a state of mind in which man

    a. fabricates his own answers to suit his glamors, illusions, and pleasures

    b. is subject to the influences of various thought currents existing in space or around him

    c. asks the question but uses an answer given by others

In this case, the Inner Source is not trusted.

8. One may ask, if the Inner Source is always in harmony with the laws and principles of life and of survival, then how do criminals receive their answers to promote their crimes? The answer is simple:

    a. They do not ask to know whether their action is right or wrong.

    b. The thoughtform of their crime tunes in with the massive thoughtform of the crime computer and receives an answer which they want.

This computer is programmed to help all criminal questions. This computer is built and organized by dark forces to promote crime. This computer is also nourished by the criminal thoughts of millions of people on earth. When one keys in with this computer, he receives the answers to his criminally charged questions.

9. Our crimes create certain thought, emotional, and etheric formations around our aura, and usually they prevent the clear reception of answers from our Source. This is how a criminal deprives himself of his own light.

10. Our questions must be motivated by the intention

a. to improve life, involving all life forms

b. to create unity and synthesis with progressive and expanding vision

c. to bring Beauty, Goodness, Righteousness, Joy, and Freedom to everyone in the world

d. to know and to be

11. The process of questioning and receiving answers, if carried on in the right way, brings integration, fusion, and at-one-ment in our nature. Eventually the questioning one within us fuses with the answering one, and the questioning process ceases in the light. This fusion proceeds in degrees:

personal

group

national

global

solar

galactic

Cosmic

12. Questioning is the path leading the traveler to his Self.

13. Questioning is the proof that omniscience is within the essence of man.

As our organs do not function properly if things go wrong in them or if they are imposed upon by outer forces, the same thing happens to our mind. When our mental equipment is not healthy for certain reasons, it may formulate a right question but disturb and distort the incoming answer and turn it into a wrong answer. This is a mechanism of self-defeat.

Right thinking is the process of building a communication line toward the Source of light within us. Wrong thinking comes into existence within us when our mental mechanism is used by our glamors, illusions, blind urges and drives; by our hatred, fear, anger, greed, jealousy, and revenge. These are called the main disturbers and forgerers.

But no matter what the condition is in our physical, emotional, and mental spheres; no matter how our questions are formulated, the Inner Source always sends us signals of lightning. But our confused mind cannot analyze them and even does not pay attention to them. In the Ageless Wisdom these signals are called the Voice of Silence. One has to have the proper ear and the proper conditions to hear the Voice of Silence.

Sometimes man receives his answers while in a condition in which he cannot use them because

a. he does not have the needed preparation

b. it is too late for his body and life

c. the world condition prevents their actualization

It must be noted here that the answers to our questions are given instantaneously. But due to the conditions in our etheric, astral, and mental atmosphere, sometimes they reach us in one second and sometimes they take years to reach us, if we keep the questions alive in our mind. A question serves as a magnetic pole to attract the radiation in the form of an answer.

It is also possible that the undelivered answers float within our aura or around our sphere and meet our needs automatically.

It is possible that the Inner Source seems to reject answering our questions. *It does not*, but it appears so

a. when we are not worthy for the answer

b. when we are not ready to understand it

c. when our sky is too clouded with our crimes, which are our karmic liabilities

In such conditions the answer comes but instantaneously disappears. Such answers are not lost; they exist in space and help others with the same questions.

To receive higher and higher answers, one must purify himself, dedicate himself to an all-inclusive cause, build a better mental mechanism, and have an increasing sphere of psychic energy.

When we present our questions, the following points must be remembered:

1. You must have no doubt that you will have an answer.

2. Your questions must not have strings tied to them.

You should not condition the forms of your answers by your desires or by your speculations. When you formulate your expected answers within the form of your questions, you do not receive pure answers. Your expectations create disturbances, both in the answering and in the receiving process.

Sometimes we even attract a great amount of fear to our questions. Fear prevents the answer from reaching us in its purity because we feel that it will be destructive for us, or prevent us from going toward a certain direction, or demand a great amount of sacrifice from us.

Questions and answers are like unending links of a chain. Man can climb only when an answer-link turns into a question-link. But many people get stuck on this journey and also prevent others from proceeding along the chain. They are saturated with their answer and cannot change it into a new question. This is the reason for many troubles in the world.

The questions of the Inner Presence create response or reaction not only from the human soul, but also from the physical, emotional, and mental elementals. Often the discovery of the answers by the human soul is not pleasant to the personality, but the most powerful answer that changes the direction of the life of a human being is the answer that the human soul himself brings out from his own core. Thus the Inner Presence, asking questions to the human soul, gives him an opportunity to face his true depth — his True Self.

Every time man contacts his own depth in the act of searching for the answer to a question, he receives a shock and a new transformation starts in his life. Usually when the Inner Presence asks the question, It does not give the answer, but lets the human soul struggle with it.

Sometimes the person pretends that he did not hear the question. Sometimes he postpones his efforts to find the answer. Sometimes he fabricates the answers to please his vehicles and failure. Sometimes he gives half the answer. But in all these games he can never escape from the watching and waiting eyes of the Inner Presence . . . for whom time is nought.

75

Evolution of
Everything in All

Does the mind evolve? Certainly. Cultures and civilizations are signs of the evolution of the mind.

Not only does the human mind evolve, but so do the Planetary Mind, the Solar Mind, and the Cosmic Mind.

People thought that evolution is related only to sentient beings. But the truth is that the whole existence evolves inside and outside with the cycles of expansion and contraction.

For example, the Cosmic Mind evolves cycle after cycle with our physical, emotional, and mental natures, with our activities, with our relationships, and with our urges and drives.

There is nothing that does not evolve in the Universe. Ideas do not stand as they are; consciousness does not stay the same. The Plan, the Purpose, and our visions evolve. This is an evolving Universe in this evolving process. Our religions evolve. Our philosophies evolve. Our science, education, art, and finances evolve.

But the evolution of all that which is form and essence takes place in a particular manner. Part of the form evolves by responding to a part of the spirit, and part of the form decays because of the pressure of the spirit.

The decaying part of the form goes through the process of recycling to serve lower life forms. Even ideas decay in one part or as a whole, and their elements enter into the recycling process.

Evolution can be defined as follows:

1. Expansion of consciousness

2. Appropriation of matter-form to the expanding consciousness

3. Response of the form to the multidimensional enrichment of consciousness

4. The refinement of form to such a degree that it can express the depth of the evolving soul

The evolving spirit or soul in the atom, in man, in the planet, in the solar system has its vehicles, its forms. These forms are all that exist. Within this form the spirit is in the process of evolution.

Of course, in this process of evolution all defects of the forms also expand and decay eventually. When evolution accelerates you see all the trash coming to the surface. This indicates that an inner expression of spirit is throwing out all that does not fit the spirit.

Because everything expands and evolves together, we do not notice the changes. But if by striving we evolve ahead, we can see how everything is growing in its pace and how those elements that have crystallized on the path are serving other elements to evolve more rapidly.

The inspirations and impressions that we were receiving from Higher Worlds a decade ago are not the same as those we receive now. They are more evolved now due to the evolution of their Sources.

Thus, any current of wisdom which crystallizes rejects its contemporary conditions and breaks on the line of evolution. Wisdom must grow everyday because of evolution. It is true that wisdom is born from the Future and it lasts quite a long time before it becomes old, but it becomes old if new and highly evolving minds are not putting fresh interpretations on it and releasing its potentials.

Fanaticism is the sign of decay. It is attachment to forms that are in the process of decay because in these forms the idea and the spirit are evolved beyond the limit of the forms.

Great literature has been given to us by the Hierarchy. In most of its parts this literature is of the Future. To translate and adapt a part of it in terms of contemporary life makes it obsolete. This literature must be taken as a flowing stream. This is how new cultures can be created.

A fanatical attitude creates inner reactions from the atoms and cells and from the environment. However, every atom within you and the environment evolves. Your cells are not the same cells. Your etheric body, astral body, and mental body evolve. Crystallization is a stop in the way of the evolutionary current. Many sicknesses come when your mind crystallizes and does not flow with the current.

The same thing happens in humanity. Crystallization creates major upheavals in humanity. This crystallization eventually is overcome, and a new path is revealed.

Every time the Race of Man overcomes a crystallization in the form of religion or ideology, a major step is taken toward the future, toward freedom, and toward simplification. This last word is not yet analyzed, and its philosophical implications have not been revealed.

Simplification in every field of human labor is the result of deeper knowledge and achievement. Simplicity is a gradual revelation of the spirit and a revelation of those laws and ways and means through which energy and knowledge are fused in action.

A Master sees in darkness through the light that emanates from His eyes. But an average man is lost in the abyss of technology in order to have light.

Simplification is a process of synthesizing in a drop all holographic phenomena.

Many forms and methods will be eliminated between the purpose and action, once the spirit dominates all fields of human endeavor. All explanations will be simplified because the minds will be simplified or fused with the light of spirit.

Human communication will be from heart to heart, from soul to soul. This will eliminate the chaos of emotion and thought.

In the courts you will not see the drama that is going on today, and all will be simple — innocent or guilty.

Simplification is an effort to detach ourselves from self-interest, exploitation, and deception. Once these are eliminated, what remains is simplicity.

Evolution is from complexity to simplicity in everything. Real sages are examples of simplicity, a simplicity that meets all the needs of your Self in a direct way.

Our civilization is now swimming in the ocean of complexity. If it continues, it will bring itself to an end.

In the process of simplification the inactive spirillae of every unit become active. If your permanent atoms have four spirillae active, you are a great or simple man, but if seven spirillae are unfolded you are the *simplest* man. This simplicity is achieved through evolutionary development, but people think that complexity is evolutionary. Complexity deals increasingly with theories. Simplicity deals with facts. Simplicity deals with cause. Complexity deals with results.

On the current of evolution, for the time being, all evolves with its flowers and defects. Defects on the path of the evolving units enlarge. So also do the flowers. But after a while the defects are hardened and fall into reservoirs of chaos to be recycled. Thus the units as a whole expand and reorganize cycle after cycle.

Thus are organized the centers in the body of man, the planet, and the sun. Whereas it is the atoms that build the centers and their petals in man, in the case of Planetary and Solar Logoi, They are great human beings and high level Initiates and Masters.

Striving is a conscious effort to keep a balanced pace with evolution. As your capacity of reception and assimilation grows, you become a guiding light in the process. You contribute to the evolution of all that you relate to.

Every day feel that the current of evolution is expanding all that you are with all that exists. The mind gives the right "viewpoint" and places you in the right locations in this ever moving current of energies.

To seek happiness through lies and through murder! One may rejoice that degeneracy is hastening evolution. Crimes are fanning the fire of the defunct world.[1]

... the flow of evolution is rational, in other words, beautiful.[2]

---

1.   Agni Yoga Society, *Agni Yoga*, para. 14.

2.   *Ibid.*, para. 15.

76

The Genesis of the Mind

There is a legend which says that in the beginning there were four *Men*.

One Man was called the Cosmos. He had seven Cosmic Friends.

The second Man was called the Solar Man. He had seven friends and five Co-workers.

The third Man was called the Global Man. He was the inhabitant of seven kingdoms of Nature.

The fourth was a tiny man like us, equipped like the other Men with seven bodies.

These four Men stood in a line in the vast Space, and the Cosmic Man projected an electrical current from His forehead. This current passed through Sirius and the Pleiades and charged the divinity existing in the Solar Man.

The Solar Man charged the current and released it into the mental sphere of the Global Man via Venus.

The Global Man received the current and passed it to the "brain" of the little man.

Thus, the legend says, the electricity of the intelligent mind went from the Mighty Center to the Solar Man, to the Global Man, and to the entirety of the Globe. This electrical current flowing from the Cosmic Man is called, in its entirety, the *Mahat* — the *Nous* — the *Light* that illuminates the Cosmic field.

Our minds are little currents in this Cosmic flow of the Energy River. Each time we think, we use this electricity and all our thoughts affect the flow of this electrical current.

In this mighty electrical river is contained the mystery of the heavens, the stars, suns, and planets; the history of existence; and the mystery of man.

This mighty electrical river shines in man as a little flame, and that is his mind.

This legend gives a holographic idea about the mind functioning in the All.

The One Mind, which is called *Mahat* in Sanskrit, exists in each atom, in each form, from a particle of dust to galaxies millions of light years away. Although being in each form, the Mahat does not lose its own integrity, for it is possible that each form reflects the vision of any other form or the collective vision of all forms.

The human soul is not only composed of Mahat but also of Love and Will. His development depends on the synthesis of these three. The process of synthesis of these three is the process of awareness of the Cosmos and the process of cooperation with the entire existence, holographically directed. A tree does not know that the drama of the Universe is at play within it. But a man, synthesizing the Mahat, Love, and Will, is aware of what is going on in the whole Universe, enabling him to raise his awareness into Love awareness and Will awareness.

It is so beautiful to see the holographic power of Mahat, of Love, and the super holographic power of Will. These are higher dimensions through which immortal man passes consciously.

The combination of these energies produces all physical, psychic, and supermundane experiences that certain people and Great Beings enjoy.

In a holographic form these three energies cooperate until they reach omnipotence, omnipresence, and omniscience. The steps are analogy, correspondence, and holographic perception which are not only related to forms but also to events, to the status of energies, and to consciousness.

Mahat in each neuron is aware of the universal life, but man is not. Memory is not stored in our brain and mind but in Mahat. That is why it is possible to remember the life events of others as being ours. That is why many persons in various countries can know the same thing simultaneously. That is why various people act in the same way as if being controlled by one center.

By sublimating our nature toward Mahat, Love, and Will, we can enter into the domain of all-possibility.

The process to expand into a Greater Mind is the following:

1. To know — the increase of knowledge. Knowledge is the treasure of the Cosmic Mind.

2. To be conscious of what we know — the source, the implication, and the future effects of our knowledge. Knowledge enters into the field of consciousness when the mind becomes aware of the cause and purpose of what it knows.

3. To expand our mind like a concentric wave in the ocean of Mahat until our mind realizes Mahat

The evolution of the mind is a steady process to synthesize all units of the mind within the Cosmic Mind — Mahat.

Then greater labors will unite us: to love and to be love, and to will and to be will.

These three are called the three electrical rivers which carry our consciousness to perfection and synthesize all creative processes in the Universe.

We are told that the mental body of the Solar Logos, of the Planetary Logos, and of man is spheroidal.

The spheroidal form of the mental body of the Solar Logos is shaped by a mighty sound coming from the Cosmic Lord Who is called "the One about Whom naught may be said." This sound influences mental substance of the Solar Logos, "arrests its tendency to dissipate, causes it to take spheroidal form. . . ."[1]

The Solar Logos does the same thing for the Planetary Logos, and the Planetary Logos does the same thing for the mental body of man through the Solar Angel.

In man this spheroidal mental substance evolves into a mechanism as the human soul unfolds his innate potentials and turns into an instrument of creative activities.

Creativity in its true sense is the ability of the mind to contact the planetary or solar Mind and be a conscious co-worker with that Mind to manifest the Purpose of that Mighty Entity.

Creativity is the result of communication, building a path between the lower and higher.

We are told that Sirius is the higher mind, whereas the Pleiades is the lower mind. Similarly Venus is the higher mind, and our globe is the lower mind. As the human soul tries to build a bridge between the higher and lower minds, to build a path for the human consciousness to expand, so the Planetary Logos is also trying to build a path between Venus and earth, and the Logos of Sirius is trying to build a path between the Pleiades and Sirius to serve as the Leader of evolution for lesser entities.

---

1. Alice A. Bailey, *A Treatise on Cosmic Fire*, p. 310.

Glossary

Ageless Wisdom: The sum total of the Teachings given by great Spiritual Teachers throughout time. Also referred to as the Ancient Wisdom, the Teaching, the Ancient Teaching.

Akasha: Existing in the Higher Cosmic Ethers, the Akashic Records are living records of all experiences and activities that have occurred in the past, present, and future of this planet and everything in it.

Angelic Kingdom: Refers to beings following a different line of evolution than the human family.

Antahkarana: The path, or bridge, between the higher and lower mind, serving as a medium of communication between the two. It is built by the aspirant himself. It is threefold: the consciousness thread, anchored in the brain; the life thread, anchored in the heart; and the creative thread anchored in the throat. More commonly called the Rainbow Bridge [or Golden Bridge].

Arhat: Ancient term designating Fourth Degree Initiate.

Ashram: Sanskrit word. Refers to the gathering of disciples and aspirants which the Master collects for instruction. There are seven major Ashrams, each corresponding to one of the Rays, each forming groups or foci of energy.

Aura: The sum-total of all emanations from all the vehicles of any living thing.

Avatar: Great Being from solar or galactic fields sent cyclically to help humanity progress. Avatars are condensed sources and embodiments of energy.

Bhakti Yoga: A type of discipline which means worship (Bhakti) in Sanskrit. The practice "raises your consciousness into higher levels of the emotional plane. Through your worship of a prophet, a Great One, or a great vision, you polarize, transform, and transfigure your emotional nature, so that you become unified with the image you are worshipping." (*Talks on Agni*, p. 4)

Center(s): Any energy vortex found in a human, planetary, or solar body.

Central Magnet: The central Core of the Universe that pulls to Itself all Sparks in manifestation.

Chain: Vehicle of manifestation of a Planetary Logos; composed of seven globes on different planes of materialization, which means the Life of the planet progressively renews Itself seven times, each time producing a new and more evolved manifestation.

Continuity of consciousness: A state of consciousness in which you are aware on all levels of the mind and of the higher and lower planes simultaneously.

Chalice: See Lotus.

Chohan: One Who has accomplished the Sixth Initiation.

Cosmic Fire: The fiery energy emanating from the center of the Universe.

Cosmic Planes: Refers to the seven divisions of the Cosmos which are called, from lower to higher, Cosmic Physical Plane, Cosmic Astral Plane, Cosmic Mental Plane, Cosmic Buddhic Plane, Cosmic Atmic Plane, Cosmic Monadic Plane, and Cosmic Divine Plane.

Cosmic Physical Plane: Refers to the totality of the seven subplanes of manifestation, from highest to lowest: Divine, Monadic, Atmic, Intuitional or Buddhic, Mental, Emotional or Astral, and Physical. Each level has seven subdivisions, totaling forty-nine planes of manifestation. The same divisions and names apply to the constitution of man where they are called bodies.

Cosmos: Refers to the seven solar systems.

Deva(s): Living beings that have no dense physical mechanisms. They live in the etheric body of the planet and are related to our lower etheric planes. (*See also New Dimensions in Healing.*)

Elemental(s): The lives who operate the body they inhabit; three in number: physical elemental, astral elemental, and mental elemental.

Enlightenment: The gradual process of awakening to the reality of one's true Self.

Etheric body: Electromagnetic field in and around our physical body. The blueprint of the physical body. The exact shape of the physical body except that all its organs and all its structures are etheric. (See also *New Dimensions in Healing.*)

Ethers, Four: The Physical body is divided into seven levels. From the most dense and up, there is the dense physical level, the liquid, and the gaseous levels. Next are the four ethers, on levels four, three, two, and one, which altogether makes up the etheric body.

Fifth Initiation: The point at which the Initiate is admitted to the ranks of the Masters of Wisdom and has achieved conscious immortality.

Fourth Initiation: The Crucifixion Initiation during which the Solar Angel leaves and the Chalice is destroyed by the fully awakened Jewel or Core.

Glamors: Astral forms with a life of their own in the emotional body. When a person desires something intensely, the astral form of that desire is called a glamor. These forms float in a person's aura and connect with certain astral and etheric centers, exercising great power over a person's actions, emotions, thoughts, and relationships. For example, such a person does not like to hear anything against his desires.

Globes: The evolving bodies of a planetary Life; seven globes make one chain. (See also *Cosmos in Man.*)

Higher mind: The three highest levels of the mental body.

Higher Worlds: Those planes of existence that are of a finer vibration of matter than the physical plane. Generally refers to the higher mental plane and above.

Illusion(s): Formed when a person has mental contact with inspirations, ideas, visions, revelations, but, due to his inadequately prepared mind, self-centeredness, selfishness, and crystallized thinking, he is unable to translate the incoming energies in their correct form. The resulting illusion is a mistranslation of something factual. Illusions thus contain distorted facts.

Initiation: The result of the steady progress of a person toward his life's goals, achieved through service and sacrifice, and manifested as an expansion of his consciousness. It represents a point of achievement marked by a level of enlightenment and awareness. There are a total of nine initiations that the developing human soul must experience in order to reach the Cosmic Heart.

Inner Guardian: The Solar Angel.

Kalachakra: An ancient Teaching which in its essence is the source of all Teaching.

Kosmos: All visible and invisible manifestations. The Universe.

Kundalini: A triple fire, contained in the center at the base of the spine, which controls the thermostat of the body and the body organs. This fire slowly climbs the etheric spine as a result of expansion of consciousness and as a result of living a clean, harmless, and sacrificial life. When it reaches the head center, it fuses with it, and at that point, man is in full illumination.

Logos: The embodying Soul of the Planet is called the Planetary Logos. That of the Solar System is called the Solar Logos.

Lotus: Also known as the Chalice. Found in the second and third levels of the mental plane (from the top). Formed by twelve different petals of energy: three knowledge petals, three love petals, three sacrifice petals. The three innermost petals remain folded for ages. They are the dynamic sources of these outer petals. The Lotus contains the essence of all of a person's achievements, true knowledge, and service. It is the dwelling place of the Solar Angel.

Lower mind: The lower four levels of the mind comprising of the three levels that make up the subconscious mind and the fourth level that makes up the conscious mind.

Mahat: The Universal mind that is also called *nous.*

Manu: A Manu is a Great Being who provided the archetypes for the first Round of the Earth Chain.

Masters: Individuals Who mastered Their physical, emotional, mental, and Intuitional bodies.

Maya: A counterpart of illusions and glamors on the etheric plane. It results in the inability of the physical, emotional, and mental bodies to respond clearly to incoming impressions.

Mental Unit: One of the two permanent recording units in the mental body. Located on the fourth subplane of the mental body. Provides the foundation on which the bridge of consciousness is built between the lower and higher mental bodies.

Monad: Reference to the essence of man, the Self.

Monadic Plane: The second plane, from the top, of the Cosmic Physical Plane.

Nadis: The etheric counterparts of the nervous system; they relate the etheric body to the nerves.

Nirmanakayas: Refers to Great Beings Who act as intermediaries between Higher Sources of Wisdom and Shamballa and between Shamballa and the Hierarchy. They function as "circuit breakers" enabling the safe use of the energy released by the Higher Center.

Nous: Greek work for Mahat, the Universal mind.

Path: The process by which a person raises himself toward spiritualization by the right application of the higher principles.

Permanent Atom: The unit in each body that contains the permanent recordings of that body. There is one physical permanent atom, one astral permanent atom, two in the mental body called the mental unit and the Mental Permanent Atom, one Intuitional Permanent Atom, and One Atmic Permanent Atom.

Plan, The: The formulation of the Purpose of the Planetary Logos into a workable program, a Plan by the Planetary Hierarchy for all kingdoms of Nature.

Pralaya: Periods of rest, or the "nights" of the Eternal One.

Prana: Energy received by the etheric spleen and distributed throughout the body via the etheric body, physical spleen, and the center between the shoulder blades.

Purpose: That which the Solar Logos is intended to achieve at the end of the evolution of the solar system. The Plan is the formulation of this Purpose for our planet only.

Qualities: Also known as *gunas;* the three qualities of matter are *Sattva,* rhythm; *rajas,* motion; and *tamas,* inertia.

Rajas: The quality of motion.

Sattva: The quality of rhythm.

Scheme: A vehicle of manifestation of a Planetary Logos composed of seven chains, each composed of seven globes.

Self: The capital "S" Self is another term used to refer to the Core of the human being. The True Self is the developing, unfolding human soul who is trying to liberate himself and become his True Self.

Seven Fields of Human Endeavor: The expression of the Seven Rays in human evolution, each corresponding to a specific Ray. They are: Politics, Education, and Psychology, Philosophy, the Arts, Science, Religion, Economics and Finance.

Seven Rays: These are the seven primary Rays through which everything exists. They are pure energy, vibrating to a specific frequency and condensing from plane to plane, from manifestation to manifestation. The three primary Rays, or Rays of Aspect, are: The First Ray of Power, Will, and Purpose; The Second Ray of Love-Wisdom; The Third Ray of Active, Creative Intelligence. There are four Rays of Attribute: The Fourth Ray of Harmony Through Conflict; The Fifth Ray of Concrete Science or Knowledge; The Sixth Ray of Idealism or Devotion; The Seventh Ray of Synthesis or Ceremonial Order. These Rays indicate qualities that pertain to the seven fields of human endeavor or expression.

Shamballa: Known as the dwelling place of the Lord of the World, the Father, where the Divine Purpose is formulated and where "the Will of God is known." Dynamic center of the Will of the planetary Soul.

Solar Angel(s): Very advanced beings Who sacrifice Their life, descending from Higher Worlds to help the evolution of humanity and guide its steps toward initiation. This happened on our planet at the middle of the Lemurian period.

Solar Logos: The Great Soul Who embodies and guides our Solar System.

soul: The small "s" soul is the human psyche, the Spark, traveling on the path of evolution having three powers: willpower, attraction, and intelligence to guide its development. Also known as the evolving human soul.

Space: The original source of spirit and matter. Space with a capital "S".

space: with a small "s". The distance between two objects.

Spiritual Triad: The field of awareness of the human soul. This field comes into existence when the magnetic fields of the Mental Permanent Atom, the Buddhic Permanent Atom, and the Atmic Permanent Atom fuse and blend.

Subtle Worlds: Refers to the Astral or Emotional Plane.

Supermundane World: The Higher Worlds.

Supreme Self: The One Self.

Tamas: The quality of inertia.

Teaching, The: See Ageless Wisdom.

Tower, The: Another name given for Shamballa, or the Father's home.

Transfiguration: The stage of complete purification of the physical, emotional, and mental bodies.

Transpersonal Self: The Solar Angel. The inner Teacher or the Inner Guide.

True Self: Also known as the Self.

Index

A

Achievement
  result of, 352
Achievement, higher
  and thought, 86, 174, 298, 372
Acid conditions
  and vices, 349
Actions
  how judged, 481
Actualization
  obstacles to, 134
Adrenal glands, 76
Advancement
  and prototypes, 119, 251
Advancement, path of beauty
  steps toward, 251
Advertising
  emotional appeal, 350
Age of Synthesis, 306, 507
Ageless Wisdom
  and process of evolution, 598
Agent of transmission
  why chosen, 418
Agni Yoga, xv, 40, 43-44, 66, 77, 144, 182,
  193, 225, 247, 368, 387, 394, 495, 549,
  589, 600
Air traffic control, 365
Air, clean
  and condition of future, 394
Airplane
  correspondence to mind, 523
Ajna center, 74, 471, 479
Akasha, 301
  as hard disk, 301
Akbar
  and old palaces, xvii
Akbar, King
  and fear, 116
Alcohol, 30, 35, 118, 136, 344, 347, 363, 478,
  526, 533, 539, 567
Allergies
  and stigmata, 266

Analysis, 500
  and thinking, 87
Ancients
  on keeping watch, 164, 208, 223, 296,
    374
Androgyny, 389-390
Angels
  and departure to Subtle World, 284
Anger
  as blinding, 357
Animals
  and use of senses, 124
Animals and plants
  and pure thoughts, 160
Answers from space
  how collected, 102
Antahkarana, 74, 81-82, 153, 219, 247, 273,
  301, 471-472, 552
  defined and construction, 153
Antenna
  and mental body, 218
Antenna, human, 320
Antennas
  people as, xviii
Anxiety and worry
  and mental clearing, 375
Application
  and thinking, 85, 87
Aquarius
  as Intuition, 527
Archetypal planes, 34
Archetype, 34, 249-254, 283, 295, 393
  path toward, 251
Archetype(s), 34, 249-254, 295, 393
Archetype, pull of
  and response to, 251
Archetypes, 34, 249-254, 295
Architects of Future, 346
Arhat, 47, 49, 529
Armageddon, 587
Arrows, making of
  as thought, 164, 223, 296
Art
  and synthesis, 505
Art and Archetype
  techniques of contact, 253
Art, great or violent and stigmata, 268
Art, true
  and result of its energy, 103

Auras of Great Ones
  and reservoir of thought, 293
Auras, united
  and group, 278
Avatar of Coordination, 506
Avatar of Synthesis, 506-507
Avatar's thoughts
  mixed results, xxiii
Avatars, xii, 173, 217, 293, 379, 387, 506-507
  ways of contact, 507
Awake, being
  why important, 521
Awareness
  defined, 430
  how it registers, 228

B

Balance
  and higher thinking, 137
Balance and harmony, 87
Ballet, 393
Battle and conflict
  and stories of leaders, 232
Battlefields in space, 215
Beam of intelligence, 51
Beauty, 34, 44, 57, 60, 65, 67, 71, 108, 113,
  119-120, 145-148, 169, 171, 184-185,
  193, 201, 203, 212, 220, 226-228, 281,
  288-289, 292, 320-321, 325, 328, 335,
  338-339, 356, 366, 372, 377, 388, 393,
  408, 410, 412, 423, 438, 440, 451, 457,
  481, 503, 534, 537, 549-550, 566, 581,
  593
  and Fiery World, 155-156
  and nadis, 549
  as food to emotions, 382
  relation to intuition, 537
  relation to synthesis, 511
Beauty, energy of
  assimilating, 550
Beauty, increase of
  and purification of space, 281
Beauty, love of, 133
Beauty, path of
  as Archetype, 252
Beauty, power of
  and impact of light, 412
Beauty, symphony

related to pure thought, 375
Beauty, use of
  and levels of beingness, 550
Becomingness
  defined, 378
Beingness, 41, 112, 119-120, 209, 223, 226,
  228-229, 253-254, 298, 306, 315, 317,
  356, 365, 378, 405-407, 422-424, 427,
  431, 451, 471, 473, 476-477, 512, 522,
  532, 550
  and progress, 120
  as value, 451
Beingness, levels of, 550
Believing
  vs. thinking, 420
Bhagavad Gita, xxvii, 93, 139, 240, 368,
  381-383
Bhakti Yoga, 356
Birth process, 287
Blankets
  and bodies, 348
Blessing
  all we consume, 183
  how to, 278-279
  kinds of and reasons for, 278
Blindness
  and astral plane, 288
Bliss, 508
  as psychic energy, 278
Bliss, energy of, 267, 279
Bliss, flow of
  and how increased, 280
Blueprint(s), 101, 106, 249, 506, 557
Bodies
  and leaving them behind, 306
Bodies, higher
  names of, 525
Bodies, subtle
  how destroyed, 532
Bodies, three
  and building healthy ones, 285
  and changing with thought, 223
  and creating new ones, 96
  and interaction of soul, 404
  and memory storage, 305
  and wounds in, 265
  of the future, 247, 274
Books
  and thoughtforms, xxvii

D

F

Synthesis, universal
    movements forward, 509
Synthesize
    defined, 100-101

T

Tai Chi, 367
Talented man
    defined, 76
Talents
    and meditation, 71
Convicted person, 445
Taste, sense of, 531
Teacher
    and healing of wounds, 267
    how to help, 440
    relation to mind, 460
Teaching, xvi, xix, 39-45, 47, 64, 72, 144,
    155, 160-161, 163-164, 206-207, 232,
    237, 259, 277, 280, 284, 286, 295, 314,
    318, 335, 337, 344, 356, 368, 416, 426,
    438-440, 470, 472, 482, 509, 515, 543
    and distortion and confusion, 164
    and need for pure heart, 355
    and principles of service, 438
    as creating reality, xix
    enemies of, 356
    gifts of, 438
Teaching others
    about thought, xxiv, 223
Teaching, power of
    defined as reality, xvi
Teaching, propagation of
    and risk taking, 440
Teaching, reading of
    and magnetism in aura, 232
Teaching, receptivity to
    and purity, 357
Telepathic communication
    and concentration, 94
Telepathy, 62, 467, 469-470, 472-473, 539
    and thought, 62
    as is message, 475
    as tuning in, 404
    how registered, 472
    vs. impressions in reception, 472
Telepathy, advanced, 425
Telepathy, intuitional, 472

Television and radio
    and thought waves, xxi
Temple
    as a thoughtform, xvii
Tension in mental plane
    how created, 81
Tensities
    of three mental levels, 134
Thinker
    and result of premature stimulation, x
Thinker in man
    how developed, 40
Thinker, creative
    and protection, 65
Thinker, Great, ix, xi-xiii, xxiii, 395
    effect of His thoughts, xxiii
Thinker, Kosmic, ix, xii-xiii
Thinker, One, xi
Thinkers
    as prisoners of their thoughtforms, 343
Thinkers, development
    and Brotherhood, 182
Thinking
    and "choice", xi
    and life changes, 40
    and progress, x
    and three bodies, xii
    and three levels of, 87
    as a process, xii, 85
    as a trap, 35
    as action, 147
    as archery, 192
    as form building, 333
    as problem solving, 421
    as programmer of life, 457
    as sole treasure, 314
    as weaving threads, 274
    average, 403
    defined, 213, 490
    geometric patterns of, 392
    how improved, 431
Thinking and feeling
    two ways of, 523
Thinking and meditation
    defined, 50, 455
Thinking capacity
    how to increase, 422
Thinking independent, xi
Thinking process

About the Author

This is Torkom Saraydarian's latest published book.

The author's books have been used all over the world as sources of guidance and inspiration to live a life based on the teachings of the Ageless Wisdom. Some of the books have been translated into other languages, including Armenian, German, Dutch, Danish, Portuguese, French, Spanish, Italian, Greek, Yugoslavian, and Swedish. He holds lectures and seminars in the United States as well as in other parts of the world.

Torkom Saraydarian's entire life has been a zealous effort to help people live healthy, joyous, and successful lives. He has spread this message of love and true vision tirelessly throughout his life.

From early boyhood the author learned first-hand from teachers of the Ageless Wisdom. He has studied widely in world religions and philosophies. He is in addition an accomplished pianist, violinist, and cellist and plays many other instruments as well. His books, lectures, seminars, and music are inspiring and offer a true insight into the beauty of the Ageless Wisdom.

Bibliographic References

Agni Yoga Society. New York: Agni Yoga Society.
 AUM, 1940.
 Agni Yoga, 1954.
 Brotherhood, 1962.
 Community, 1951.
 Fiery World, Vol. I, 1969.
 Fiery World, Vol. II, 1946.
 Fiery World, Vol. III, 1948.
 Heart, 1982.
 Hierarchy, 1933.
 Infinity, Vol. II, 1957.
 Leaves of Morya's Garden II, 1979.
 Letters of Helena Roerich, Vol. I, 1979.

Bailey, Alice A. New York: Lucis Publishing Co.
 Esoteric Astrology, 1982.
 Esoteric Psychology, Vol. I, 1979.
 Externalization of the Hierarchy, 1972.
 The Light of the Soul, 1972.
 The Rays and the Initiations, 1976.
 Telepathy and the Etheric Vehicle, 1975.
 A Treatise on Cosmic Fire, 1977.
 A Treatise on White Magic, 1974.

Lamsa, George M., trans. Nashville, TN: Holman Bible Publishers.
 New Testament, 1968.

Saraydarian, Torkom. Sedona, AZ: Aquarian Educational Group.
 The Bhagavad Gita, 1974.
 Cosmos In Man, 1983.
 Earthquakes and Disasters, What The Ageless Wisdom Tells Us, 1991.
 Five Great Mantrams, 1975.
 The Hidden Glory of the Inner Man, 1985.
 Irritation, The Destructive Fire, 1991.
 Legend of Shamballa, 1988.
 The Psyche and Psychism, 2 vols., 1981.
 Sex,Family and the Woman in Society, 1987.
 The Science of Becoming Oneself, 1976.
 The Science of Meditation, 1981.
 The Solar Angel, 1990.
 Symphony of the Zodiac, 1988.

Triangles of Fire, 1977.
Video — *"Why Drugs Are Dangerous"*, 1992.
Woman, Torch of the Future, 1980.

Saraydarian, Torkom. Cave Creek, AZ: T.S.G. Publishing Foundation, Inc.
The Ageless Wisdom, 1990.
A Commentary on Psychic Energy, 1989.
Cosmic Shocks, 1989.
The Flame of the Heart, 1991.
New Dimensions in Healing, 1992.
Olympus World Report....The Year 3000, 1993.
Other Worlds, 1991.
The Psychology of Cooperation and Group Consciousness, 1989.
The Purpose of Life, 1991.
The Mystery of Self-Image, 1993.
The Sense of Responsibility in Society, 1989.
The Subconscious Mind and the Chalice, 1993.
Video — *"The Seven Rays Interpreted"*, 1992.
The Year 2000 and After, 1991.

Other Books by
Torkom Saraydarian

The Ageless Wisdom
The Bhagavad Gita
Breakthrough to Higher Psychism
Buddha Sutra — A Dialogue with the Glorious One
Challenge For Discipleship
Christ, The Avatar of Sacrificial Love
A Commentary on Psychic Energy
Cosmic Shocks
Cosmos in Man
Dialogue with Christ
Dynamics of Success
Flame of Beauty, Culture, Love, Joy
The Flame of the Heart
Hiawatha and the Great Peace
The Hidden Glory of the Inner Man
I Was
Joy and Healing
Leadership Vol. I
Legend of Shamballa
The Mysteries of Willpower
New Dimensions in Healing
Olympus World Report...The Year 3000
One Hundred Names of God
Other Worlds
The Psyche and Psychism
The Psychology of Cooperation and Group Consciousness
The Purpose of Life
The Science of Becoming Oneself
The Science of Meditation
The Sense of Responsibility in Society
Thought and the Glory of Thinking
Sex, Family, and the Woman in Society
The Solar Angel
Spiritual Regeneration
The Subconscious Mind and the Chalice
Symphony of the Zodiac

Talks on Agni
Triangles of Fire
Unusual Court
Woman, Torch of the Future
The Year 2000 & After

Booklets

A Daily Discipline of Worship
Building Family Unity
Earthquakes and Disasters — What the Ageless Wisdom Tells Us
Fiery Carriage and Drugs
Five Great Mantrams of the New Age
Hierarchy and the Plan
Irritation — The Destructive Fire
Nachiketas
The Psychology of Cooperation
Questioning Traveler and Karma
Responsibility
The Responsibility of Fathers
The Responsibility of Mothers
Spring of Prosperity
Success
Synthesis
Torchbearers
What to Look for in the Heart of Your Partner

Videos

The Seven Rays Interpreted
Lecture Videos by Author

Ordering Information

Write to the publisher for additional information regarding:

— Free catalog of author's books and music tapes

— Lecture tapes and videos — complete list available

— Placement on mailing list

— New releases

— A free copy of our newsletter *Outreach.*

Additional copies of *Thought and the Glory of Thinking*

U.S. $38.00 (Softcover)
U.S. $48.00 (Hardcover)

Postage within U.S.A. $5.50
Plus applicable state sales tax

T.S.G. Publishing Foundation, Inc.
P.O. Box 7068
Cave Creek, AZ 85331-7068
United States of America

TEL: (602) 502-1909
FAX: (602) 502-0713

There is only one Self in all forms of Nature.

→ *Practice severe watchfulness over your thoughts, words & actions*

→ (Think), (speak) & (act) (beautifully)

T.S.G. Publishing Foundation, Inc. is a non-profit, tax-exempt organization.

Our purpose is to be a pathway for self-transformation. We offer books, audio and video tapes, classes and seminars, and home study courses based on the core values and higher principles of the Ageless Wisdom.

These fine books have been published by the generous donations of the students of the Ageless Wisdom.

Your tax deductible contributions will help us continue publishing and growing.

Our gratitude to all.